Can Art History be Made Global?

Monica Juneja

CAN ART HISTORY BE MADE GLOBAL?

Meditations from the Periphery

DE GRUYTER

ISBN 978-3-11-071629-0
eISBN (PDF) 978-3-11-121706-2

Library of Congress Control Number: 2023930665

Bibliographic information published by the Deutsche Nationalbibliothek
The Deutsche Nationalbibliothek lists this publication in the Deutsche Nationalbibliografie;
detailed bibliographic data are available on the Internet at http://dnb.dnb.de.

© 2023 Walter de Gruyter GmbH, Berlin/Boston

Copyediting: Aaron Bogart
Cover design: Katja Peters, Berlin
Cover image: Atul Dodiya, *Meditation (with Open Eyes)*, installation. Photo: Tate Modern, London
Typesetting: SatzBild GbR, Sabine Taube, Kieve
Printing and binding: Beltz Grafische Betriebe GmbH, Bad Langensalza

www.degruyter.com

CONTENTS

ACKNOWLEDGEMENTS

When a book has had such an extended gestation period as this one, the trail of accumulated debts is long. In 2009, I took up a position at the University of Heidelberg, ambitiously designated Global Art History. As this was the first and is still the only professorial Chair of this denomination in the German-speaking countries, it was imperative for me to position my work in relation to a fashionable epithet, as well as to outline the possibilities of how such a field of study could be meaningfully delineated. This book represents a fruition and distillation of a theoretical perspective within the disciplinary landscape of art history; it is the result of more than a decade of research, teaching and intellectual exchanges, often across disciplinary divisions.

The outline of the book took shape in 2014, when I was invited by the University of Zurich to deliver the freshly instituted Heinrich Wölfflin Lectures. I am deeply grateful to Tristan Weddigen for inviting me to open the series, thereby providing me with an opportunity to place my initial ideas on the globality of art history for discussion with a lively audience of students, colleagues and museum experts. My thanks also to the Max Kohler Foundation, whose generosity made this possible. A fellowship of the Getty Research Institute, Los Angeles, in the following year enabled me to continue developing the structure of the work and flesh out arguments following enriching exchanges with colleagues at the Institute. My sincere gratitude to Thomas Gaehtgens, Alexa Sekyra and the wonderful staff at the Getty for helping to make my term there so productive. A further opportunity to continue researching and writing came with a fellowship of the Forum Transregionale Studien in Berlin for which I am grateful to Gerhard Wolf and Hannah Baader, who ran the Art Histories and Aesthetic Practices programme of the Forum with exemplary imagination and commitment. Not least, I am greatly indebted to the Volkswagen Foundation for honouring me with an Opus Magnum award that allowed me to take a year off from routine professional obligations and complete the book manuscript. A special word of thanks to Vera Szöllösi-Brenig and Silvia Birck for their support and flexibility through difficult pandemic times.

During the past years, as the initial lectures grew into more extensively researched and theoretically fine-tuned chapters, I have benefited from vital exchanges with innumerable colleagues, as well as the support of various institutions. Interlocutors whose insights and own work sustained the project, helping it refine its arguments, are numerous. A partial list includes (in alphabetical order) Naman Ahuja, Hans Belting, Susanna Burghartz, Manuela Ciotti, Sebastian Conrad, Annie Coombes, Burcu Dogramaci, Eva Ehninger, Larissa Förster, Atreyee Gupta, Kajri Jain, Christian Kravagna, Susanne Leeb, Saloni Mathur, Birgit Meyer, Parul Dave Mukherji, Ruth Phillips, Dhruv Raina, Sugata Ray, Chaitanya Sambrani, Indra Sengupta, Kavita Singh, Sujit Sivasundaram, Tristan Weddigen, Roland Wenzlhuemer, Gerhard Wolf and Karin Zitzewitz. My collaboration of many years with Sumathi Ramaswamy has been enriching and an enormous pleasure. I owe a special debt of gratitude to Claire Farago for inspiring my work through her own incisive writing; to her and Donald Preziosi my heartfelt thanks for stimulating conversations, encouraging feedback on the manuscript, and not least steady friendship.

Research initiatives and collaborative projects with museums have been an important plank of my practice as an art historian. I am particularly grateful to the members of our transatlantic research initiative 'Worlding Public Cultures. The Arts and Social Innovation' (WPC) funded by the German Ministry of Education and Research (BMBF) for intellectual solidarity during apocalyptic times. A special word of thanks to the Heidelberg WPC team – Eva Bentcheva, Franziska Kaun, Seung Hee Kim, Franziska Koch, Costina Mocanu, Miriam Oesterreich and Moritz Schwörer – as well as to Paul Goodwin, Birgit Hopfener, Wayne Modest and Ming Tiampo for lively, often controversial, exchanges. It has been a privilege and a learning experience to work with museums on exhibition projects and new practices of curation that seek to bridge the gap between the university and the museum. My gratitude goes to the dedicated team of curators at the Kunstsammlung Nordrhein Westfalen in Düsseldorf with whom I collaborated on the exhibition project 'Museum global. Mikrogeschichten einer ex-zentrischen Moderne' funded by the Kulturstiftung des Bundes. My association of many years with the Staatliche Kunstsammlungen Dresden (State Art Collections of Dresden, in short SKD) in the context of the projects 'Europa-Welt', the exhibition 'Miniatur Geschichten', as well as the institution of a Transcultural Academy has shaped much of my thinking on the mutually fructifying relationship between a theory of transculturation and creative practices of curating. A special word of gratitude here to Hartwig Fischer, whose idealistic vision was seminal to the start of my collaboration with the SKD. I am also extremely grateful to Marion Ackermann, Stephanie Buck, Noura Dirani, Petra Kuhlmann-Hodick, Léontine Meijer van Mensch, Friedrich von Bose, and Anne Vieth for our exciting work together. Artists and their work have been vital to many of the ideas developed in this book, interacting with them on a personal level has been a unique experience. My warm thanks to Atul Bhalla, Sheba Chhachhi and Pushpamala N., as well as to Atul Dodiya, for generously allowing me to use their work. The latter's memorable installation *Meditation (with Open Eyes)* that features on the cover of this book captures much of its spirit. All along the process of its making, different chapters of the book were presented in innumerable public lectures and keynote addresses in Germany and across the world. Though too numerous to list individually, I am grateful to every one of my hosts for their hospitality and to the audiences whose questions often remained with me for long and helped sharpen the critical edges of the book.

The University of Heidelberg – in the particular the Cluster of Excellence Asia and Europe in a Global Context and its successor the Heidelberg Centre of Transcultural Studies (HCTS), where I continue to be located – could not have provided a more congenial milieu for research, writing and teaching. For their commitment to scholarly excellence, for collegiality and friendship I am grateful to Christiane Brosius, Birgit Kellner, Joachim Kurtz, David Mervart, Axel Michaels, Michael Radich and the late Rudolf Wagner. Colleagues from neighbouring institutes – Johannes Becke, Sarah Fraser, Stefanie Gänger, Nikolas Jaspert, Hans Harder, Henry Keazor, Kama Maclean, Joseph Maran, Diamantis Panagiotopoulos, Lieselotte Saurma, William Sax and Melanie Trede – all exemplary scholars in their own fields, have also been enthusiastic interlocutors at all times. A special thanks to Joachim Kurtz and Michael Radich, with whom co-teaching was as inspiring as it was fun, and for intensive, stimulating discussions from which I never ceased to learn. I am also grateful to Michael for his helpful feedback on a chapter of this book. Sincere thanks are due to the staff of the HCTS, especially Oliver Lamers and Petra Kourschil, who unfailingly and cheerfully ensured the administrative support on which all scholarship depends. To Matthias Kirchner and his staff, a big thank you for the excellent IT-infrastructure as well as the invaluable help with computer crises that invariably felt like the end of the world. It would be very remiss of me not to thank the members of my department – Franziska Koch, Jennifer Pochodzalla, Jo Ziebritzki – for their unfailing and loyal support over many years. Madeleine Rettig and Constance Jame provided valuable assistance in building up my image bank; Abhay Bhalla was extremely helpful in chasing copyright issues in Delhi; thanks also to my student assistants Jens Doerr and Costina Mocanu for dependable support at all times. A special thank you to Mikeeh for helping out with the proofs, most of all for arbitrating in my perennial struggle with Oxford commas. To Jo Ziebritzki I owe an enormous debt of gratitude for going through the entire manuscript and doing much more than attending to matters of formatting or securing image rights. Her perceptive observations helped me read the book with the eyes and minds of young scholars, who are meant to be a crucial group of its readers. My debt to generations of students I have taught and mentored over long years is difficult to put in a summary sentence, except for saying that the book would not be the same without the enthusiasm and critical spirit they brought to the classroom.

My thanks go to Katja Richter of De Gruyter publications, whose faith in this project remained unshakeable, and of whose professionalism tempered with empathy I remain deeply appreciative. David Fesser and Aaron Bogart have been careful and painstaking editors; to them as well as to Sabine Taube and Sabine Ufer I am indebted for the final product. I am immensely obliged to the staff of the Universitäts Bibliothek Heidelberg, the Staatsbibliothek Berlin, the Bayerisches Staatsbibliothek Munich, the Göttfried Wilhelm Leibniz Landesbibliothek Hannover, for making valuable resources digitally available during the lockdown. My thanks to all the institutions and copyright holders of the images published here, who I have made every effort to acknowledge. A special word of gratitude to Atreyee Gupta for sharing some of her photographs with me.

The manuscript of this book was completed under the shadow of a pandemic that brutally drove home the dark side of accelerated global connectivity. In this time of incertitude, anxiety, and painful losses, I cannot thank enough those who provided the affective sustenance that is the lifeline of intellectual labour. My two families, in New Delhi and Neckargemünd, with the next generation spread across Berlin, London, Stuttgart and Canberra, were a pillar of strength, even from afar, in days when the media were full of accounts about people dying alone in hospitals and those unable to take leave of their loved ones. To Friedrich I owe more than I can say. Thank you for our shared journey that began with a fortuitous meeting in a Paris library, for three decades of intellectual partnership, for love and laughter, and for not failing to remind me of the world beyond my desk.

INTRODUCTION
CAN ART HISTORY BE MADE GLOBAL?

'[G]rounded theory … is a reflexive theory, a theory of how "history" is humanly produced not as an essence, but as openness-to-contingency.' – Achille Mbembe[1]

The Elusive 'Global'

Three words are most frequently used to designate the habitation of humanity: globe, world, planet. Though they often appear interchangeably, each has a distinct conceptual valence. The first two have a longer history within scholarly parlance in the humanities, notably since the early phases of modern globalisation. The conception of the Earth as planet, on the other hand, has gained ground more recently, with a mounting consciousness of the climate crisis, wherein humanity counts as but one member of a composite species encompassing all elements of the biosphere – animals, plants, minerals.[2] While scholars have only just begun to chart the spatiotemporal terrain of 'planetary humanities',[3] the 'global turn' in several disciplines was announced some three decades ago, as a response to the challenges of an increasingly networked world. The term 'global' derives its significance from an abstraction that serves to describe a space on which globalisation plays itself out, imagined as a surface, a sphere, a zone of networks and mobility, whose potential could unfold anywhere. In contrast, the 'world' stands for an inhabited place, spells situatedness, is marked by lived features, memories, relationships that provide a context, while they undergo change, prompt mobility or restrict it, and even produce exile. Worlds are plural – we are born into one, may engage it, retreat from it or move to another one; worlds may collide, collaborate, or collapse. The

1   Achille Mbembe, 'Theory from the Antipodes: Notes on Jean & John Comaroffs' TFS', Society for Cultural Anthropology, Fieldsights, 25 February 2012, https://culanth.org/fieldsights/theory-from-the-antipodes-notes-on-jean-john-comaroffs-tfs.

2   Dipesh Chakrabarty, *The Climate of History in a Planetary Age*, Chicago: University of Chicago Press, 2021; Eva Horn and Hannes Bergthaller, *Anthropozän zur Einführung*, Hamburg: Junius, 2019.

3   Chakrabarty, ibid; Hannes Bergthaller and Peter Mortensen (eds), *Framing the Environmental Humanities*, Leiden: Brill, 2019. A discussion of how the term 'planet' informed art history and exhibition practice at the onset of the 'global turn' follows in Chapter Five. The Postscript signals to its potential for carrying the discussion further.

imagination of a world imparts agency, for humans can create life-worlds, worlds of signification, they can engage in world-making as a reflexive exercise to produce knowledge, to conceptualise and shape praxis, not least its unfolding within scholarly disciplines.[4]

To address the question posed in the title of this book, we need to begin by attending to the etymological and iconic underpinnings that have fashioned popular and scholarly imaginations of the global. Cultural articulations of a 'globalised' Earth have touched the depths of individual and social consciousness and thereby informed the explanatory power of the term in shifting, often contradictory ways. Global (and its cognate globalism) draws its valence from globe – at once an abstract form and an iconic object – to generate a distinct set of associations. The abstraction of spherical geometry renders the globe overwhelmingly visual and graphic, even poetic, in view of its mathematical perfection, qualities that have unfailingly lent their charge to euphoric images of globalisation. The Earth as spherical orb, photographed for the first time from outer space by astronauts who had set out to study the moon, became the key visual to transmit the ideals of unity and de-territorialised spatiality. Photographs of the terraqueous globe, labelled 'whole earth' or 'blue planet', effectively replaced the mushroom cloud as circulating icon par excellence of a post-Cold War, globally connected world.[5] Though a product of the Apollo space mission of the National Aeronautics and Space Administration (NASA) during the 1960s and early 1970s, images of planet Earth acquired their highest popularity a quarter of a century later, through ubiquitous reproduction and circulation as an affectively charged visualisation of globalisation after 1989. The elated responses to such pictures were no doubt inspired by the persuasive mimetic power of modern photography; yet as a reassuring image of universal holism, the earthly disk draws upon and extends ideas of human territoriality that have deep historical roots in imaginations of several world cultures.[6]

Our access to the 'global' therefore has been enabled by its representation as abstract form. Its lack of cartographic specificity coupled with the absence of human presence frees the representation of contingency; its untrammelled rotational dynamism makes it a useful metaphor for a contemporary imperium of financial networks and communication lines drawn

---

4   Writings on the subject are extensive and come from different disciplinary positions, see for example, 'The World and World-Making in Art', theme issue, ed. Caroline Turner and Michelle Antoinette, *Humanities Research*, vol. XIX (2), 2013; Pheng Cheah, *What Is a World? On Postcolonial Literature as World Literature*, Durham, NC: Duke University Press, 2016; Nelson Goodman, *Ways of Worldmaking*, Indianapolis: Hackett, 1978; Arno Schubbach, 'Das Bilden der Bilder: Zur Theorie der Welterzeugung und ihrer bildtheoretischen Verpflichtung', *Soziale Systeme*, vol. 18 (1–2), 2012: 69–93. See also my discussion in Monica Juneja, '"A Very Civil Idea" … Art History, Transculturation, and World-Making – With and Beyond the Nation', *Zeitschrift für Kunstgeschichte*, vol. 81 (4), 2018: 461–85, here 463–64.

5   Of these, the photograph christened *Marble Earth*, alternatively *The Blue Marble* (Plate 1.0), is among the most frequently reproduced; very recently, it featured on the cover of Hildegund Amanshauser and Kimberly Bradley (eds), *Navigating the Planetary*, Vienna: Verlag für moderne Kunst, 2020.

6   A study of the globe within the cosmography of Western civilizations is Denis Cosgrove, *Apollo's Eye: A Cartographic Genealogy of the Earth in the Western Imagination*, Baltimore: Johns Hopkins University Press, 2001; for an investigation of the journeys of this iconic image and object in South Asia, Sumathi Ramaswamy, *Terrestrial Lessons: The Conquest of the World as Globe*, Chicago: University of Chicago Press, 2017.

across an unbounded spherical unit. And yet, the inherent iconic power of a global icon was not without ambiguity, for it could as well be re-appropriated to contest the illusion it was meant to transport, that of unrestrained harmony in a globally networked world. The globe itself, as form and object, recurs in the work of contemporary artists to draw attention to the darker side of its universalising language. The artist Mona Hatoum (b. 1952), for instance, deploys it in her work *Hot Spot* (2009): a spherical steel-cage, made to tilt at the same angle as the Earth, with burning red neon lights forming the outlines of the continents across its surface. Conflict, to paraphrase the artist, is no longer contained within borders of individual states, but has set the whole world 'ablaze'. The cage, at the same time a legible cartographic representation, here evokes the opposite of heady freedom invoked by enthusiasts of globalisation, to speak instead of global conflict as a mode of incarceration.[7] Denis Cosgrove, in turn, cites the photomontages of the artist Peter Kennard (b. 1949), which dramatically blend the NASA photograph of the 'whole Earth' with objects such as nuclear missiles, living trees, or a human foetus, harnessing the image to pressing global issues of militant nationalisms, war and environmental degradation.[8] And finally, an anecdote that signals the easy slippage from a global to a national imaginary: in 1984, when Rakesh Sharma, the first Indian citizen to travel into space on a Soviet Soyuz T spacecraft, was asked by the then Prime Minister, Indira Gandhi, about how it felt to look at India from outer space, he quipped 'Saare jahan se achcha' (The best nation of the world), the title of a popular patriotic song based on a poem by Muhammad Iqbal (1877–1938), and composed under colonial rule.[9] This handful of examples gives us a sense of the plural imaginaries of the 'global'; it also serves as a set of signposts, which mark the field of art history, aptly described by Donald Preziosi as a panoptic project, now confronting the challenges of the 'global turn' in the humanities and social sciences.[10] Contestations over a globalised art and art history unfold along two discursive axes: the emancipatory rhetoric of globalisation that eulogises a borderless world and its networks of cosmopolitanism, and the heavy footprint of the nation-state whose adherence to retrospectively invented and imposed tradition continues to frame the production and organisation of knowledge, conceptually as well as institutionally.

This monograph enters a field already densely populated with investigations and positions about what it means to write a globally framed art history and seeks thereby to make belatedness productive by refiguring the discourse from a fresh perspective.[11] It takes as its

---

7   See 'Mona Hatoum – Hot Spot' [video], YouTube (uploaded 4 October 2016), www.youtube.com/watch?v= bVyT8_0woj0, accessed 20 Aug. 2021.

8   Cosgrove, *Apollo's Eye*, 261–62; see also the website of Peter Kennard, https://www.peterkennard.com/ photomontage, accessed 20 Aug. 2021.

9   'Rakesh Sharma', Wikipedia (last modified 8 May 2022), https://en.wikipedia.org/wiki/Rakesh_Sharma, accessed 20 Aug. 2021.

10   Donald Preziosi, *Rethinking Art History: Meditations on a Coy Science*, New Haven: Yale University Press, 1989.

11   The numerous interventions till now consist mainly of articles and anthologies, with relatively few monographs. They map an amorphous field, extraordinarily difficult to demarcate or define. An issue with edited volumes that saps the coherence of their overall scholarly impact is that editors are not necessarily able to carry contributing authors with them along the same path, though this in turn depends

on the degree of conceptual clarity with which the project was defined to start with. An overwhelmingly large number of writings that engage with the global turn in art history focuses exclusively on the twentieth and twenty-first centuries. The following list, though not exhaustive, provides a general orientation: James Elkins (ed.), *Is Art History Global?* New York: Routledge, 2007; James Elkins, Zhivka Valiavicharska and Alice Kim (eds), *Art and Globalization*, University Park: Pennsylvania State University Press, 2010; Hans Belting, Andrea Buddensieg and Peter Weibel (eds), *Contemporary Art and the Museum: A Global Perspective*, Ostfildern: Hatje Cantz, 2007; Hans Belting and Andrea Buddensieg (eds), *The Global Art World: Audiences, Markets and Museums*, Ostfildern: Hatje Cantz, 2009; Hans Belting, Jacob Birken, Andrea Buddensieg and Peter Weibel (eds), *Global Studies: Mapping Contemporary Art and Culture*, Ostfildern: Hatje Cantz, 2011; Kitty Zijlmans and Wilfried van Damme (eds), *World Art Studies: Exploring Concepts and Approaches*, Amsterdam: Valiz, 2008; David Carrier, *A World Art History and its Objects*, University Park: Pennsylvania State University Press, 2008; Jonathan Harris (ed.), *Globalization and Contemporary Art*, Malden, MA: Wiley-Blackwell, 2011; Marsha Meskimmon, *Contemporary Art and the Cosmopolitan Imagination*, London: Routledge, 2011; Jill H. Casid and Aruna D'Souza (eds), *Art History in the Wake of the Global Turn*, New Haven: Yale University Press, 2014; Marcus Verhagen. *Flows and Counterflows: Globalisation in Contemporary Art*, Berlin: Sternberg Press, 2017; Sara Dornhof, Nanne Buurman, Birgit Hopfener and Barbara Lutz (eds), *Situating Global Art: Topologies – Temporalities – Trajectories*, Bielefeld: Transcript, 2018; Julia Allerstorfer and Monika Leisch-Kiesl (eds), *'Global Art History': Transkulturelle Verortungen von Kunst und Kunstwissenschaft*, Bielefeld: Transcript, 2017; 'Art History and the Global Challenge', theme issue, *Artl@as Bulletin*, vol. 6 (1), 2017. The recent questionnaire created by George Baker and David Joselit, editors of *October*, frames its questions in relation to 'global modernisms and global contemporary art' and invites scholars located exclusively in the Anglo-American academy, see 'Questionnaire on Global Methods', *October*, 180 (1), 2022: 3–80.
A few welcome departures from the presentist framing of the studies cited above are: Daniel Savoy (ed.), *The Globalization of Renaissance Art: A Critical Review*, Leiden: Brill, 2017; Thomas DaCosta Kaufmann, Catherine Dossin and Beatrice Joyeux-Prunel (eds), *Circulations in the Global History of Art*, Farnham: Ashgate Publishers, 2015; Mary D. Sheriff (ed.), *Cultural Contact and the Making of European Art since the Age of Exploration*, Chapel Hill: University of North Carolina Press, 2012; Dana Leibsohn and Jeanette F. Peterson (eds), *Seeing Across Cultures in the Early Modern World*, Farnham: Ashgate Publishers, 2012; Christine Göttler and Mia Mochizuki (eds), *The Nomadic Object: The Challenge of World for Early Modern Religious Art*, Leiden: E.J. Brill, 2018.
An exemplary collection, path-breaking for its time, is Claire J. Farago (ed.), *Reframing the Renaissance: Visual Culture in Europe and Latin America, 1450–1650*, New Haven: Yale University Press, 1995. See also Farago's critique of the 'global turn's' exclusive focus on the contemporary, 'The "Global Turn" in Art History: Why, When, and How Does it Matter?', in: Savoy (ed.), *The Globalization of Renaissance Art*, pp. 299–313.
A useful view from Eastern Europe, a region treated as marginal in accounts that speak from a North-Atlantic axis, is Piotr Piotrowski, 'Towards a Horizontal History of the European Avant-Garde', in: Sascha Bru and Peter Nicholls (eds), *European Avant-Garde and Modernism Studies*, Berlin: De Gruyter, 2019, pp. 49–58.
Among positions from a non-European perspective are Parul D. Mukherji, 'Whither Art History in a Globalizing World', *The Art Bulletin*, vol. 96 (2), 2014: 151–55; Cheng-hua Wang, 'A Global Perspective on Eighteenth-Century Chinese Art and Visual Culture', *The Art Bulletin*, vol. 96 (4), 2014: 379–94; Atreyee Gupta, 'Art History and the Global Challenge: A Critical Perspective', *Artl@as Bulletin*, vol. 6 (1), 2017: 20–25; Sugata Ray, 'Introduction: Translation as Art History', *Ars Orientalis*, vol. 48, 2018: 1–19; Alessandra Russo, 'Light on the Antipodes: Francisco de Holanda and an Art History of the Universal', *The Art Bulletin*, vol. 102 (4), 2020: 37–65; Melanie Trede, Mio Wakita and Christine Guth (eds), *Japanese Art – Transcultural Perspectives*, Leiden: Brill (forthcoming 2023).
While this book was in the making, I published some articles exploring the challenges and possibilities of a global approach – conceptualised as transcultural – to art history. These served as a sounding board of sorts for several ideas that have been developed more extensively and grounded empirically in this book. See Monica Juneja, 'Global Art History and the 'Burden of Representation', in: Belting, Birken et al. (eds), *Global Studies*, pp. 274–97; Monica Juneja, 'Kunstgeschichte und kulturelle Differenz: eine Einleitung', theme issue, 'Universalität in der Kunstgeschichte', Matthias Bruhn, Monica Juneja and Elke A. Werner (eds), *Kritische Berichte*, vol. 40 (2), 2012: 5–12; Monica Juneja, '"A Very Civil Idea" …'. Some of the key

starting point the paradox expressed pithily by Stephen Greenblatt: 'one of the characteristic powers of a culture is its ability to hide the mobility that is its enabling condition'.[12] While Greenblatt was writing a manifesto for a scholarly field now known as mobility studies, his insightful observation directs our attention to rethinking the processuality of culture. The theory of transculturation that vitally informs my understanding of the global develops this idea by attending to how the 'cultural' is radically made and remade: in processes of interaction with other units, not by necessity contained within the territorial fixtures of the nation-state. Transculturation as a process designates those long-term transformative relationships between cultural entities that follow from encounters and are constitutive for the actors, practices and epistemic configurations implicated. When distilled to furnish a set of explanatory principles, it partakes of those attributes of a 'grounded theory', described by Achille Mbembe in the opening epigraph to this chapter. This distinct ontology of culture, I will show in the following sub-section of this chapter, is equipped with a critical potential that enables us to dismantle the core of a discipline – art history in this case – rather than dealing with examples on its fringes. The theoretical force of the transcultural allows us to circumvent the conceptual traps of a facile globalism, whose trajectories and limits I will first elucidate in the following paragraphs.

The tension between the idea of the global and the nation-state referred to above is particularly palpable in the domain of culture. When framed within the space of the nation, culture is invariably conscripted to attributes such as stability, linguistic homogeneity and authenticity; belonging to the nation rests on valorising containment and consensus, and ends up concealing the turbulences that are constitutive of all culture. While the subjects investigated by art historians – artists, objects, pictorial/artisanal practices and canons on the one hand, museal displays and exhibitions, curators, patrons and collectors on the other – have all had mobile histories across the centuries, the disciplinary frameworks and institutional settings of art history have been constituted according to fixed and stable units such as the nation-state or civilisational entities dating to the nineteenth century. In what today has the appearance of a single world that has discarded its former tripartite division, the intimate connection between art and national identity retains its hold over imaginations in varying, though mutually constitutive ways. Art history as a modern scholarly field cannot plausibly be viewed as a purely 'Western' discipline, for it no longer retains an exclusively 'originary' attachment to its parochial beginnings in Europe; during its global journeys to other regions of the world it has acquired new roots and undergone adaptations and reconfigurations responding to local and regional contingencies.[13] Many of the young postcolonial nations of Asia and Africa, joined today by the younger post-Cold War nations of Eastern Europe

questions and arguments developed in this last, most recent article, have been recapitulated in this Introduction.

12   Stephen Greenblatt, 'A Mobility Studies Manifesto', in: Stephen Greenblatt, Ines Zupanov et al. (eds), *Cultural Mobility: A Manifesto*, Cambridge: Cambridge University Press, 2010, pp. 250–53, here p. 252.

13   The assumption that art history is a quintessentially 'Western' discipline that sits uneasily in contexts beyond the realm of Europe and North America underlies much of the writing on global/world art history.

and Central Asia, all seek to define national identity through notions of unique civilisational achievement. The practice of disciplines in the humanities is closely tied to identity formations around the nation: this has meant that the nation is the unit of analysis; a narrative of its unique achievements, past and present, explained almost entirely from within, is transmitted through its institutions – the university, the museum, the archive and the heritage industry. For those 'latecomers' in the race for nationhood, art bearing national labels remains an effective way of catching up with the present.

A central concern of this book is to examine the challenges posed by ongoing discussions of the tangled relationship between nations and cultures to art history and its institutional practices, as these debates urge us to develop new frameworks for scholarship. More specifically, how does art history negotiate the tension between national identity and such relationships that break out of national frames and inform memories and visions of so much of artistic production? When art is made to stand for or express allegiance to the nation, what does the art historical life of that entity embody at any given moment in the past and the present? Have art and artists been able to outline different modes of engaging with the idea of the nation? This book takes an approach that deviates from such endeavours of global studies, which by virtue of their very definition and self-positioning seek to transcend and transgress national space and scale as an analytical category. Instead, it aims to use the uneven and at times seemingly divergent regional valences and histories of the 'national' as a wedge to break open the idea of the nation. Conventionally characterised as a juridical, geopolitical entity, can the nation instead be conceived of as an imagined conceptual realm? In other words, can art history recuperate a vision of the nation as a domain not territorially bounded, but one that in the imagination of artists and scholars could both be local and transgress boundaries? The case studies investigated here explore the more complex dynamic between a critique of the national as a constricting ideological frame and the artistic uses of its past role as a ground of emancipation, especially in the histories of postcolonial nations. At the same time, emergent right-wing nationalisms at a global level have drawn attention to the congruence of globalisation and nationalism, to the persistence of the nation-state in politically and economically uneven globalisations of the present. The need for theorising the ambivalent relationship between globalisation and nationalism has assumed an urgency, also in view of contemporary populism of different shades across the political spectrum having become highly culturalised.

The years following the dramatic events of 1989 saw the formation of a domain of contemporary art as a system incarnating the cultural logic of globalisation together with its values of internationalism and multiculturalism.[14] The proliferation of biennials, art fairs,

---

See most recently, James Elkins, *The End of Diversity in Art Historical Writing: North Atlantic Art History and its Alternatives*, Berlin: De Gruyter, 2021.

14 Like all chronological signposts, 1989 has not met with consensus. Some diverging positions are: Ruth Simbao, 'What "Global Art" and Current (Re)turns Fail to See: A Modest Counter-narrative of "Not-another-Biennial"', *Image and Text*, vol. 25 (1), 2015: 261–86; Maria Hlavajova and Simon Sheikh (eds), *Former West: Art and the Contemporary after 1989*, Cambridge, MA: MIT Press, 2017; Michaela Ott, 'Die

and mega-exhibitions, accompanied by an expanding art viewing public, artists' residencies and itinerant curators in and beyond Euro-America, brought forth a characterisation of the 'global contemporary' as a freely circulating, ahistorical, non-situated and economically exploitable mass.[15] Since then, however, it has become necessary to shift the discussion of the 'contemporary' from the issue of visibility gained by art produced in distant corners of the world within the exhibition circuits and scholarly accounts of the 'mainstream' North-Atlantic West, to querying the conditions that make such visibility possible.[16] The new geo-aesthetic maps of globally networked 'artworlds'[17] that figured prominently in the Karlsruhe exhibition curated by Hans Belting and Andrea Buddensieg cannot be read as an unproblematic dissolution of hierarchies without examining the nature of relationalities that connect the luminous nodal points distributed across the surface of cartographic representation. The euphoria over the forces of globalisation expressed in the writings of the early 1990s that celebrated an effortless, even naturalised 'flow' of materials, goods, capital and human resources together with dissolving national and cultural boundaries, has given way in the new millennium to critiques of neoliberal economics and politics, the disregard of human sovereignty and evasion of environmental responsibility. The present conjuncture has generated a call for critical epistemologies within the humanities to empower a rethinking of the global in the domain of art, and its theorisation as a new 'cosmopolitics of resistance', as a resource for countering the logic of neoliberal capital and neo-nationalist cultural politics.[18] Some key questions for art historians might be: Must a global art history follow the logic of economic globalisation, or does it call for an alternative conception of globality to be able to effectively theorise relationships of connectivity that encompass disparities as well as contradictions and negotiate multiple subjectivities of the actors involved? What are the choices available to artistic producers to negotiate between complicity with or dependence on global capital and critical initiatives that foster transcultural modes of co-production and

kleine ästhetische Differenz', *Texte zur Kunst*, vol. 23, 2013: 101–9. A detailed discussion of this issue follows in Chapter Four below.

15   Hans Belting, 'Contemporary Art as Global Art: A Critical Estimate', in: Belting and Buddensieg (eds), *The Global Art World*, 38–73. See also the catalogue of the exhibition curated by Belting and Buddensieg at the ZKM Karlsruhe from September 17, 2011 to February 19, 2012, *The Global Contemporary and the Rise of New Art Worlds*, Hans Belting, Andrea Buddensieg and Peter Weibel (eds), Cambridge, MA: MIT Press, 2013.

16   Discussed in Juneja, 'Global Art History and the "Burden of Representation"'.

17   The term comes from Arthur Danto, 'The Artworld', *Journal of Philosophy*, vol. 61 (19), 1964: 571–84.

18   The expression is Athena Athanasiou's, see 'Formations of Political-Aesthetic Criticality: Decolonizing the Global in Times of Humanitarian Viewership: Athena Athanasiou in Conversation with Simon Sheikh', in: Paul O'Neill, Simon Sheikh, Lucy Steeds and Mick Wilson (eds), *Curating After the Global: Roadmaps for the Present*, Cambridge, MA: MIT Press, 2017, pp. 71–94, here p. 76. Boaventura de Sousa Santos argues for a faultline within globalisation(s) and urges that we distinguish between 'hegemonic … and counter-hegemonic globalization'. He uses the term 'insurgent cosmopolitanism' to designate a 'transnationally organized resistance' against inequalities and unevenness within processes of globalization that result in ecological damage and the destruction of livelihoods, see Boaventura de Sousa Santos, 'Globalizations', *Theory, Culture & Society*, theme issue, Problematizing Global Knowledge, vol. 23 (2–3), 2006: 393–99.

sustainability? How can art history enable us to view the historical present as a simultaneity of clashing and conjoining temporalities constituted by their pre-histories?[19] How does it handle issues of commensurability or its absence among cultures? How can it translate intellectual resources and insights of regional experiences beyond Euro-America into globally intelligible analyses?

One of the challenges facing these unresolved questions is the extreme slipperiness of the label 'global' itself, an attribute that derives from the term's etymological and iconic roots; notoriously over-used, it remains as contested as it can be vacuous. Signifying an encompassing quality, the global is beset by the problem of any totalising concept: the claim to an easy universalism that threatens to foreclose more nuanced explorations of the cultural field. Within art history the epithet 'global' has been used in multiple, often inconsistent, ways, as for instance to characterise art history as a discipline to be practised uniformly across the globe, one that would subsume 'local' art. Alternatively, it signals towards an inclusive discipline – also labelled world art history – that would encompass different world cultures and their canons, or one that searches for the lowest common denominator to hold together humans across time and space who have been making art for millennia 'because our biological nature has led us to do so'.[20] The term is equated at times with conceptual imperialism, at others with multicultural eclecticism.[21] Hans Belting's definition of 'global art' to characterise those contemporary artistic productions emanating from the non-Western world, which become publicly accessible through exhibitions and mega-shows, continues to inform most discussions on what could define the contours of a global art history, namely a focus on art worlds post 1989.[22] And yet the popularity of this definition overlooks not only its presentism, but also its Eurocentric premises: for art from 'elsewhere' to be recognised as global it must depend on the exclusive agency of Western curators, exhibition sites and publics, who accord (or deny) it this status. The dependence, in turn, becomes a drive towards producing a kind of art that might then be considered global. Globality in this understanding, an attribute to be constituted within and transmitted by a work through an interlinked set of agencies, con-

19 The discussion of alternate temporalities as resources for resisting and subverting Western teleological time goes back to Dipesh Chakrabarty, *Provincializing Europe: Postcolonial Thought and Historical Difference*, New Delhi: Oxford University Press, 2000. Bruno Latour refers to a temporality in which the contemporary is located 'along a spiral rather than a line … the future takes the form of a circle expanding in all directions, and the past is not surpassed, but revisited, repeated, surrounded, protected, recombined, reinterpreted and reshuffled. … Such a temporality does not oblige us to use the labels "archaic" or "advanced", since every cohort of contemporary elements may bring together elements from all times.' Bruno Latour, *We Have Never Been Modern*, New York: Harvester Wheatsheaf, 1993, p. 75.

20 John Onians, Introduction', in: John Onians (ed.), *Atlas of World Art*, London: King, 2004, pp. 10–13, here p. 11. For a more extensive discussion of these positions, see Juneja, 'Global Art History', pp. 278–80.

21 A recent survey of the field undertaken by Béatrice Joyeux-Prunel attempts to bring together innumerable strands under a single label, and in the process reveals the unwieldy, hold-all quality of the domain now designated as 'Global Art History'. The problem is partly due to indiscriminate selection by the author who pays little attention to frameworks of enquiry. See Béatrice Joyeux-Prunel, 'Art History and the Global: Deconstructing the Latest Canonical Narrative', *Journal of Global History*, vol. 14 (3), 2019: 413–35.

22 Belting, 'Contemporary Art as Global Art'.

tributes to cementing a hierarchical division of the world between what Gerardo Mosquera aptly calls 'cultures that curate' and those which 'get curated'.[23] The challenge therefore is to formulate a paradigm of the global that does not collapse into hegemonic localisms, but remains plural and multi-sited.

Taking a cue from the more extensive developments in the adjoining fields of global and world histories (again, terms frequently used interchangeably),[24] art historians too have begun to identify new paradigms to be able to adequately deal with multiple, dynamic and at the same time uneven transactions across space. Their aim is 'to provide an interface that is truly relational, connecting interlocked, even if potentially disparate, points in the globe'.[25] Mobility and migration studies, geo-histories of art, as well as network analysis are among the approaches informing studies whose focus has shifted from the 'stasis of nations and civilizations'[26] to the investigation of multidirectional networks, of encounter and exchange, migration and mobile materiality, to name some of the thematic categories of recent art histories.[27] Circulation, flow, transfer, translation, network, connectivity, cultural brokers, are

---

23　Gerardo Mosquera, 'Some Problems in Transcultural Curating', in: Jean Fisher (ed.), *Global Visions: Towards a New Internationalism in the Visual Arts*, London: Kala Press, 1994, pp. 133–39, here p. 133.

24　Writings of historians from Germany, however, broadly distinguish between the two, as Jürgen Osterhammel points out: while global history is conceived of as an investigation of connectivity, practitioners of world history continue to work in an earlier 'history of civilisations' framework. As a broad field, global history accommodates different approaches and 'types'; what they share in common 'is an approach to the past that is non-Eurocentric and focussed on long-distance connectivity across national and cultural boundaries'. See Jürgen Osterhammel, 'Global History and Historical Sociology', in: James Belich, John Darwin, Margret Frenz and Chris Wickham (eds), *The Prospect of Global History*, Oxford: Oxford University Press, 2016, pp. 23–43, here p. 31.
　　Some recent publications that define the field from a range of positions are, Sebastian Conrad, *What Is Global History?*, Princeton: Princeton University Press, 2017; Maxine Berg (ed.), *Writing the History of the Global: Challenges for the 21st Century*, Oxford: Oxford University Press, 2013; Margrit Pernau, *Transnationale Geschichte*, Göttingen: Vandenhoeck und Ruprecht, 2011; Lynn A. Hunt, *Writing History in a Global Era*, New York: Norton, 2014; Jürgen Osterhammel, *Die Flughöhe der Adler: Historische Essays zur globalen Gegenwart*, Munich: C. H. Beck, 2017. A seminal early work on pre-modern globalisation is Janet L. Abu-Lughod, *Beyond European Hegemony: The World System A.D. 1250–1350*, New York: Oxford University Press, 1989.

25　Diana Sorensen, 'Editor's Introduction: Alternative Geographic Mappings for the Twenty-First Century', in: Diana Sorensen (ed.), *Territories and Trajectories: Cultures in Circulation*, Durham, NC: Duke University Press, 2018, pp. 13–31, here p. 24.

26　Sorensen, ibid, p. 21.

27　See for instance DaCosta Kaufmann et al. (eds), *Circulations in the Global History of Art*; Thomas DaCosta Kaufmann and Elizabeth Pilliod (eds), *Time and Place: The Geohistory of Art*, Aldershot: Ashgate, 2005; Sheriff (ed.), *Cultural Contact and the Making of European Art since the Age of Exploration*; Béatrice Joyeux-Prunel, *Les avant-gardes artistiques 1918–1945: Une histoire transnationale*, Paris: Gallimard, 2017; Anne Gerritsen and Giorgio Riello (eds), *The Global Lives of Things: The Material Culture of Connections in the Early Modern World*, London: Routledge, 2017; Stacey Sloboda and Michael Yonan (eds), *Eighteenth Century Art Worlds: Global and Local Geographies of Art*, London: Bloomsbury, 2019. On migration, see Burcu Dogramaci and Birgit Mersmann (eds), *Handbook of Art and Global Migration: Theories, Practices, and Challenges*, Berlin: De Gruyter, 2019; Anne R. Petersen, *Migration into Art: Transcultural Identities and Art-Making in a Globalised World*, Manchester: Manchester University Press, 2017. The list is far from exhaustive. For a critical survey of the field of mobile materiality, see Monica Juneja and Anna Grasskamp, 'EurAsian Matters: An Introduction', in Anna Grasskamp and Monica Juneja

identifiably some of the most prolifically deployed notions within recent writing by historians of different domains – art, ideas, societies, and economies. The terms are at once metaphors and methodological tools, a circumstance which has a bearing on their explanatory potential. From among these, mobility and connectivity have emerged as signature concepts informing investigations that claim the epithet global; their use is marked by varying degrees of rigour, ranging from casual descriptions of displacement from point A to B, to more in-depth investigations of processes that use mobility to uncover the constitutive nature of relationships that unfold in its wake. The precision and discernment with which connections and transfers have been analysed is, however, contingent on the efficacy of concepts deployed for this purpose: terms such as 'entanglement', 'braiding', 'flow', 'circulation', 'hybridity', *'métissage'*, 'creolisation', to cite some of the most recurring examples, all invoke metaphors of natural, biological, or artisanal phenomena that condition their explanatory power. Metaphors of fluidity, be they riverine or physiological – for instance 'flows' or 'circulation' – are among the most widely used terms across disciplines, which end up eliding as much as they explain. The term 'flow', harnessed by globalisation anthropology of the 1990s to describe – rather than explain – macro-phenomena such as the movement of capital, or population, or commodities, ideas or events, invokes the natural law of gravity.[28] Its application to such domains where the laws of nature do not prevail, suppresses the role of human agency and the working of interests behind what is couched as a 'natural' process. Such interests, as Stuart Rockefeller reminds us, privilege the large-scale, 'a managerial perspective' over individuals and small-scale phenomena.[29] Using the term 'flow', or its companion 'circulation', places emphasis on movement per se, smooth, continuous and unimpeded, rather than processuality and transformation.[30] I will return to the issue of terms, which have become catchwords that elide rather than throw light on processes, in the following section that engages with the concept of transculturation. Another concept used to elaborate, quantify, and graphically represent global mobility is the 'network': it serves as a tool to encompass, once more, the transcontinental scale of empires, technologies, migration systems or art movements. Explaining the utility of the network, Bruno Latour invokes the poetic vision of 'Ariadne's thread' of interwoven stories 'that would allow us to pass with continuity from the local to the global, from the human to the nonhuman'.[31] While for Latour the network offered a corrective to the

(eds), *EurAsian Matters: China, Europe, and the Transcultural Object, 1600–1800*, Heidelberg: Springer, 2018, pp. 3–33.

28 The term 'flow' came into widespread usage following the writings of leading anthropologists. See Manuel Castells, *The Informational City: Information Technology, Economic Restructuring and the Urban-Regional Process*, Oxford: Blackwell, 1989; Ulf Hannerz, 'Notes on the Global Ecumene', *Public Culture*, vol. 1 (2), 1989: 66–75; Arjun Appadurai, *Modernity at Large: Cultural Dimensions of Globalization*, Minneapolis: University of Minnesota Press, 1996.

29 Stuart A. Rockefeller, 'Flow', *Current Anthropology*, vol. 52 (4), 2011: 557–78, here 565ff.

30 On circulation, in particular its evocation of the passage of liquids in human anatomy, see Stefanie Gänger, 'Circulation: Reflections on Circularity, Entity, and Liquidity in the Language of Global History', *Journal of Global History*, vol. 12 (3), 2017: 303–18; also Monika Dommann, 'Alles fließt: soll die Geschichte nomadischer werden?', *Geschichte und Gesellschaft*, vol. 42 (3), 2016: 516–34.

31 Latour, *We Have Never Been Modern*, 121.

modernist privileging of segregation and purity, its use, as for instance in art history, as a tool to destabilise myths of centres and peripheries together with the hierarchies they transport, begs more questions than it answers.[32] Providing a two-dimensional visualisation of a global spread, the nodal points and connecting lines of a network when, for example, used as a tool to study modernism, are not in a position to shed light on the third dimension that encompasses differences, unevenness and asymmetries of power, so constitutive of global modernist art movements. How do we measure varying intensities within the spread, the differential levels of entanglement? How do we identify the beneficiaries and losers within these relationships, the play of scales across the global to the regional, national, and local?[33]

Global histories – be they of art or culture, of economics or politics – mostly struggle methodologically with the problem of aspiring to be at once inclusive and 'synthetic'.[34] The historian Jürgen Osterhammel locates a deficit of global history within a 'lack of discursive autarchy and a shallow rootedness in mainstream historiography', which has made it of necessity dependent on 'conceptual inputs from outside its own purview'.[35] Several art historical forays in the field, having drawn on impulses from history, globalisation anthropology, mobility studies, postcolonial and, more recently, decolonial studies, tend to suffer from an overdose of eclecticism and empty buzzwords: the global is both 'transnational' and 'translocal', it could 'open up peripheries of all kinds', as well as highlight 'postcolonial problematics'.[36] Though initially concentrated within universities and cultural institutions of the North-Atlantic world, the 'global' as an epithet for art and art history has more recently acquired a footing in regions of the so-called Global South, more often than not driven by the feverish activity of exhibition and market circuits. Being global has rapidly become a

---

32 Joyeux-Prunel's use of the network to decentre canonical narratives of modernism is an object lesson in the limitations of this mode, which in the final analysis leaves existing Eurocentric hierarchies and explanatory devices in place. See Béatrice Joyeux-Prunel, 'Provincializing Paris: The Center-Periphery Narrative of Modern Art in Light of Quantitative and Transnational Approaches', *Artl@s Bulletin*, vol. 4 (1), 2015: Article 4.
    Also by the same author, 'Provincializing New York: In and Out of the Geopolitics of Art After 1945', *Artl@s Bulletin*, vol. 10 (1), 2021: Article 12.
    A more insightful use of the method can be found in Avinoam Shalem, '"What a Small World": Interpreting Works of Art in the Age of Global Art History', *Getty Research Journal*, vol. 13, 2021: 121–42.
33 A detailed engagement with these issues follows in Chapter Three.
34 The term has been used by Béatrice Joyeux-Prunel while introducing a special issue of the *Art@tlas Bulletin* titled 'Art History and the Global Challenge: A Range of Critical Perspectives'. She defines a 'truly global narrative' as one 'that would do justice to art from all countries' and at the same time produce 'convincing narratives with which to challenge the canon', Béatrice Joyeux-Prunel, 'The Global History of Art and the Challenge of the Grand Narrative', *Art@tlas Bulletin*, vol. 6 (1), 2017: 3–5, here 4.
35 Osterhammel, 'Global History and Historical Sociology': 24. Sanjay Subrahmanyam, another historian, who had coined the term 'connected histories' long before the so-designated global turn gained in prominence, continues to distance himself from the latter's current articulations: much of global history, according to him, suffers from a lack of clarity about its contours; additionally from chronological myopia and an inability to distinguish between 'global' and the 'universal'. See Sanjay Subrahmanyam, 'Global Intellectual History Beyond Hegel and Marx', *History and Theory*, vol. 54 (1): 126–37. On 'connected histories', Sanjay Subrahmanyam, 'Connected Histories: Notes Towards a Reconfiguration of Early Modern Eurasia', *Modern Asian Studies*, vol. 31 (3), 1997: 735–62.
36 Joyeux-Prunel, 'The Global History of Art': 3.

sign of being with the times. At the same time, the epithet resolutely connotes distance: it refers to the 'elsewhere', both cartographically as well as conceptually. Doing a global art history therefore becomes a gesture of inclusion, of accommodating the 'other', while the 'local' stands for where the author of that history is positioned. Viewed in this perspective, the call to 'challenge the canon'[37] turns out to be less an attempt to dismantle it than rather a plea to make it more inclusive. Inclusion or expansion are the catchwords of both contemporary art institutions as well as a popular brand of global/world art history. While the former strive to co-opt artists from across the world into a late-capitalist art system where even the most radical art positions can be commodified for the consumption of a public with an insatiable thirst for novelty, the latter is expansively charted to bring 'art from all countries' into its fold, though the underpinnings of its framing concepts remain unquestioned. Anchored within the undergraduate syllabi of universities in North America and parts of Western Europe, such world/global art histories locate themselves within a genealogy that goes back to the early formation of the discipline, when it undertook similar moves to produce authoritative knowledge about nations, cultures and the world.[38] Yet expansion or inclusion per se, this book argues, are methodological and pedagogical procedures that do not by their analytical intent undermine the frameworks they seek to transgress, or at best do so only tangentially.

The contestations surrounding the idea of the global coupled with its extensive ambitions, have given the term an amorphous, elusive quality that often begs more questions than it explains. When deployed as a perspective for art history, it has shown a proclivity to eclecticism that blunts its critical potential. Most practitioners of global art history have tended to conflate its subjects of investigation with the phenomenon of globalisation, rather than

---

37 Ibid: 4.

38 *Weltkunstgeschichte*, a genre of art historical writing that proliferated mainly in German-language texts of the late nineteenth and early twentieth centuries, was described as 'a history of art of all times and people', as the title of a six-volume work by the art historian and director of the Dresden Art Gallery proclaimed. See Karl Woermann, *Geschichte der Kunst aller Zeiten und Völkern*, 6 vols., Leipzig: Bibliographisches Institut, 1900–1922. This historiographical perspective is being upheld today as an example of a cosmopolitan movement in art history, one that prefigured the present global turn. Tracing a genealogical link while eschewing a genealogical critique serves as a mode of legitimation for a current of global/world art history today. Both, I argue in a detailed unpacking of this historiographical trend in Chapter One below, end up in producing merely one more variant of a master narrative.
Among efforts to connect *Weltkunstgeschichte* to the present are Zijlmans and Van Damme (eds), *World Art Studies*; Wilfried Van Damme, '"Good to Think": The Historiography of World Art Studies', *World Art*, vol. 1 (1), 2011: 43–57; Thomas DaCosta Kaufmann, 'Reflections on World Art History', in: DaCosta Kaufmann et al. (eds), *Circulations in the Global History of Art*, pp. 23–46; Joyeux-Prunel, 'Art History and the Global'; Ingeborg Reichle, '*The Origin of Species* and the Rise of World Art History: Ernst Grosse's Encounter with the Beginnings of Art', in: Trede, Wakita and Guth (eds), *Japanese Art – Transcultural Perspectives*; see also my 'Comment' to the Section 'Methodologies, Texts, and Discourses' in the same volume.
An exception to this framing of world art history that integrates nations and localities in 'regional networks of interaction' is Claire J. Farago, 'Imagining Art History Otherwise', in: Jane C. Davidson and Sandra Esslinger (eds), *Global Art and World Art in the Practice of University and Museum*, London/ New York: Routledge, 2018, pp. 115–30; Farago develops an alternative approach in her book in progress titled *Cultural Memory in the Era of Climate Crisis: Writing Borderless Histories of Art*, Routledge (forthcoming 2023). Further references can be found in Chapter One below.

attend to developing globality as a stringent, reflexive mode of interrogation. A more robust theoretical scaffolding is required in order to be able to shake up those epistemic foundations of the discipline that continue to shape our scholarly practice. The concept of transculture/transculturation – as the following section will elaborate – can form the keystone of a critical globality, which would enable art history to transcend parochialism of different shades – from that of Eurocentrism to the insularity of individual area studies.

Transculturation as Critical Globality

Thinking the global as a critical perspective rather than a spatial or temporal quality requires a separation of globality from the fact of globalisation. While the latter constitutes a set of economic, political, and technological phenomena, the former can be described as a conceptual matrix governed by a logic not informed by a neoliberal globalism that then morphs into right-wing nationalism. A critical globality that views art history neither as an all-encompassing, super-sized subject, nor as a narrative of contemporary globalisation, might instead begin by posing the question of culture in its conflictual genealogies and its concatenation with our disciplines and institutions. When applied to societies of the past and present, the discursive category of 'culture' has invariably existed in tension with the unruly and contradictory trends generated by mobility and extended contacts that have characterised regions and social collectives across the globe since the earliest historical epochs. The terms 'transculture'/'transculturation'/'transculturality' are an explicit critique of the notion, as it emerged in the humanities and social sciences in tandem with the idea of the modern nation. The nationally framed understanding of culture was premised on the postulate that life-worlds of identifiable groups were ethnically bound, internally cohesive and linguistically homogenous spheres. Coined by the Cuban anthropologist Fernando Ortiz (1881–1969), the concept of transculturation undermines the stable nexus between culture and the territorial container of the nation-state by drawing our attention to the processuality of cultural formations. To grasp the concept's relevance to the crises of the present as well as to the methodological challenge of rehabilitating the global, it would be helpful to pay attention to its genealogy.

The genealogy of transculturation goes back to the world-historical context of the mid-twentieth century. Politically, this was a time when fascism and militarism had engulfed much of Europe and drew the world into its destructive fold, while in the colonised peripheries anti-colonial movements – that saw the building of national cultures together with the fashioning of self-determining political structures – were already a source of ferment. More concretely, the year 1940 saw the publication of Ortiz's book, *Contrapunteo Cubano del tabaco y el azúcar*, where the term was coined.[39] In his study of sugar and tobacco cultures

---

39　Fernando Ortiz, *Cuban Counterpoint: Tobacco and Sugar*, trans. by Harriet Onís, New York: Knopf, 1947; reprinted with an Introduction by Fernando Coronil, Durham, NC: Duke University Press, 1995. All references here are to the edition of 1995.

in postcolonial Cuba, Ortiz saw transculturation as a process with an explanatory potential that went beyond the existing term 'acculturation', in that it helped reconceptualise processes of adaptation as transformation, as long-term processes that unfolded through extended contacts and relationships between cultures.[40] The context in which this investigation was undertaken – one marked by the changing geo-politics of empires, the emergence and subsequent fall of fascist regimes in Europe that coincided with the defeat of progressive forces in Cuba, together with the emergence of assertive voices in locations affected by colonialism – endowed the notion of transculturation from the start with a critical potential.

Oritz's historical analysis of the creation of national identity in Cuba unfolds as a critique of the cultural representations of colonialism and its strategies of rule, as a dismantling of the superior claims of Western modernity while at the same time consciously eschewing an idea of the nation as a site of 'authenticity' or a haven of purity. The anti-imperialist stance of the work has been developed within the framework of an emerging nation, a factor that accounts for the particularities of the book's structure and its literary qualities that to a reader today might come across as an idiosyncratic use of allegory in a work of history. Yet, the author remained very much in tune with his times when consciously deploying the literary modes that characterised writings on the nation in the mid-twentieth century.[41] A tension familiar to us today runs through the work that, on the one hand, sets out to recover the voices and agency of those who remain unheard; and on the other, to uncover dynamic processes of transculturation that followed from migration, multilingualism and ethnic plurality and were constitutive of the identities of those inhabiting the 'imagined community'.[42] Ortiz confronts these processes with such attempts to stabilize their unruliness that sought recourse to representations of an integrated cultural unit, cast as the bounded space of the nation and the ideological basis for all fixed identities. The invention of a past considered uncontaminated by cultural contact is analysed by him in terms that point to the workings of power within groups that cut across the coloniser-colonised divide, a perspective that avoids the trap of thinking in binaries that has characterised nationalist positions as well as much of postcolonial and, more recently, decolonial analysis.[43] By treating cultural forms as fluid

40 Ibid, pp. 97–98.
41 Fernando Coronil, 'Introduction', in: Ibid: xx. A more extensive study of the nexus between literary forms and nascent political formations is Pascale Casanova, *The World Republic of Letters*, Cambridge, MA: Harvard University Press, 2004.
42 Benedict R. Anderson, *Imagined Communities: Reflections on the Origin and Spread of Nationalism*, London: Verso, 1991.
43 A theory of transculturation owes a formative impulse to postcolonial critique that, at the time it was formulated, sensitised us to border crossings and cultural mixing. In addition postcolonial analyses challenged the claims to universalism built into historiographical narratives, especially of modernity, situated in Europe. Yet its matrix – in spite of the powerful expositions of theoreticians such Édouard Glissant, Gilberto Freire, Frantz Fanon or Paul Gilroy, to mention a handful – remains the coloniser-colony binary. A transcultural perspective allows us to locate these processes in a context that transcends this binary and views cultural phenomena as multi-sited interactions among units and places that are already a product of transculturation. I have discussed these questions at some length in a conversation with Christian Kravagna, see Monica Juneja and Christian Kravagna, 'Understanding Transculturalism',

and unstable, Ortiz's study directs our attention in two directions: the work is imbued with a political rationale to challenge national frameworks, while at the same time apprehending at once the destructive and constructive moments in histories shaped by colonialism and imperialism. Through its critical valorisation of popular creativity, the study of sugar and tobacco shows how the social spaces of those who lived under coercive conditions were made habitable by them. The underlying ambivalence of conditions of oppression as well as the double-edged quality of movements of emancipation are insights that have been generally overlooked by those who have studied transculturation in modern contexts.[44]

In his preface to the 1995 edition of Ortiz's book, Fernando Coronil draws our attention to conditions in which the book circulated and that determined its reception – a world divided into capitalist and socialist blocs; to these a third group of 'developing' nations was appended, who negotiated either of the two paths to arrive at modernity.[45] Ortiz's book, Coronil writes, 'did not quite fit the terms of this polarized debate. It was unconventional in form and content … and it proposed neither unambiguous solutions nor a blueprint for the

in: Model House Research Group (ed.), *Transcultural Modernisms*, Berlin/Vienna: Sternberg Press, 2013, pp. 22–33.

More recently, theories of decoloniality have staked a claim to a 'radical rethinking' of postcolonial positions, which, in the words of one of its advocates, continue to work with 'essentially Western instruments and assumptions' to 'inadvertently reproduce coloniality of knowledge'. See, for example, Madina Tlostanova, 'The Postcolonial Condition, the Decolonial Option, and the Post-socialist Intervention', in Monika Albrecht (ed.), *Postcolonialism Cross-Examined: Multidirectional Perspectives on Imperial and Colonial Pasts and the Neocolonial Present*, London: Routledge, 2020, pp. 165–78, here pp. 166–68. While an extensive critical engagement with decolonial perspectives is beyond the scope of this study, it needs to be pointed out that the notion of decolonisation and its various cognates are used in a wide range of contexts and in an eclectic manner, both as noun and verb: they could refer to a process of liberation from the colonial yoke, or designate an epochal condition and an epistemological frame, or serve as a call to action, to dismantle existing power constellations in domains such as museums, pedagogies, curricula, memory cultures … the list goes on. As a result, decolonial approaches mean different things, even as they all partake of a common polemical thrust. While the founding texts of decolonial theory critique what they conceive of as an all-encompassing totalitarian idea of modernity, the project of liberation that seeks to delink coloniality from modernity replicates the same totalising, binary structure between the so-called West – that is, Europe and the North Atlantic – and those it has excluded, by reducing a world of heterogeneous, unstable, transversal, and dynamic processes to a single, encompassing logic of coloniality. The totalising opposition between 'Western' epistemologies and 'Indigenous' languages ascribes a homogeneity or purity to each side, assuming that non-European epistemologies are innately egalitarian by virtue of being not from the West and by overlooking the hierarchies and modes of discrimination that structure the latter as well. A critical transcultural analysis over a long durée would instead sensitise us to the ways in which each of these allegedly hermetic categories was constituted through interactive relationships within the framework of colonialism as well as through pre- and early modern histories of connection.

See Walter D. Mignolo and Catherine Walsh (eds), *On Decoloniality: Concepts, Analytics Praxis*, Durham, NC: Duke University Press, 2018; Annibal Quijano, 'Coloniality of Power, Knowledge and Latin America', *Nepantla: Views from the South*, vol. 1, 2000: 533–80.

44　An exception that effectively combines postcolonial critique with a transcultural perspective is Christian Kravagna, *Transmoderne: Eine Kunstgeschichte des Kontakts*, Berlin: b_books, 2017. It has been recently published in English: *Transmodern: An Art History of Contact, 1920–60*, transl. Jennifer Taylor, Manchester: Manchester University Press, 2022.

45　Coronil, 'Introduction', pp. xi–xii.

future.'[46] The world today presents us with new conditions for an engagement with the core concepts developed by Ortiz: the dissolution of older polarities cemented during the Cold War, coupled with fresh tensions within national formations following globalisation, intensified migration and a backlash of xenophobic nationalism and transnational fundamentalisms. Ceaselessly debated questions surrounding citizenship, belonging, the fabrication of cultural pasts and visions of the future, all impart an urgency to the making of art and to writing about it, both forming a domain of symbolic action. A transcultural understanding of cultural belonging that from its outset functioned as a lens and an analytical frame has, as it enters the space of present, the potential of being adjusted, expanded and fine-tuned. In the recent years, the transcultural has become a buzzword of sorts, adopted by a range of scholars in different, at times loose and not always consistent ways, and framed by different disciplinary contexts. Not all of them respond to or even acknowledge the ground-breaking relevance of the reflections proffered by Ortiz.[47]

46 Ibid. Coronil further explains the marginal presence of Oritz's work in mainstream anthropological writings of the twentieth century as a consequence of an asymmetry between scholars and theoretical perspectives emanating from the periphery and those that form the mainstream. Even the work of Eric R. Wolf, *Europe and the People Without History*, Berkeley: University of California Press, 1982, that deals with very similar and related questions, does not consider Ortiz. Ten years later, Mary Louise Pratt drew on Ortiz to develop the notion of transculturation in relation to travel literature. See Mary Louise Pratt, *Imperial Eyes: Travel Writing and Transculturation*, Routledge: London, 1992.

47 Among the more recent theorisations of the idea of transculturation/transculturality is the work of the philosopher Wolfgang Welsch, 'Transkulturalität: Zur veränderten Verfassung heutiger Kulturen', in: Irmela Schneider and Christian W. Thomsen (eds), *Hybridkultur: Medien, Netze, Künste*, Cologne: Wienand, 1997, pp. 67–90. For a critical take on Welsch, see Juneja and Kravagna, 'Understanding Transculturalism', pp. 24–25.
Transculturation as a theoretical tool borrowed from Ortiz has been productively used by Finbarr Barry Flood in his valuable study of the interactive relationships between north Indian political elites and Islamic polities during the early medieval period. The concept enables him to destabilise essentialist constructions of identities ascribed to Hindus and Muslims in the wake of present-day politics, and serves instead as a paradigm to grasp dynamic patterns of mutual engagement, which worked to generate mutable and contingent identities. The book's somewhat excessive dependence on analytical concepts and tools drawn from a wide range of theoretical currents – from French post-structuralist philosophy and sociological theory, to globalisation anthropology, postcolonial theory, radical materialism and post-humanism – does not allow it to systematically investigate or develop the full potential of a theory of transculturation for the discipline of art history; that indeed is not the objective of this otherwise path-breaking work. The notion of transculturation provides the author a perspective and useful corrective to the projection of modern notions of ethno-religious identities within a 'clash of civilisations' model onto the past. The flip side however is an over-emphasis on the question of identity and its practices, which runs through the book and brings back the very problem the study seeks to eschew. See Finbarr Barry Flood, *Objects of Translation: Material Culture and the Medieval 'Hindu-Muslim' Encounter*, Princeton: Princeton University Press, 2009.
The term 'transcultural' has also been frequently invoked, though without reference to its sources or an attempt to flesh out its theoretical stakes, in contemporary art critical writing to propose a normative mode of cross-cultural pollination and artistic collaboration transcending national frames. See Nancy Adajania and Ranjit Hoskote, 'Notes Towards a Lexicon of Urgencies', in *Journal of Independent Curators International Research*, 1 October 2010, https://curatorsintl.org/research/notes-towards-a-lexicon-of-urgencies, accessed Dec. 2021.

Building on the insights extracted from Ortiz's allegory of Cuba, a potential theory of transculturation might be characterized as follows: the concept of transculturation provides both an episteme and a tool-box. By referring to a process of transformation that unfolds through extended contacts and relationships between cultures, it works to emancipate culture from the qualities of boundedness and essentialism ascribed to it when harnessed to a national framework. While transculturation presupposes for a large part spatial mobility, it is neither synonymous with nor reducible to it. Rather its focus on processes through which forms emerge within circuits of exchange make it a field constituted relationally. The new ontology of culture forms the kernel of a theoretical perspective that is distinct for its process-oriented dynamism and its concreteness. Its dynamic quality comes from opposing the presumption of static entities with pre-theorised transactions. In other words, the ostensible 'cultural' that a theory of transculturation takes as its object is not only fundamentally made through processes of transculturation in the first place, but continuously remade through all subsequent phases of its existence. Processual and continually morphing, such an ontology of culture is also concrete in that it is made from the ground up, precisely through its interaction between units that are constituted through these very processes. It partakes of what Achille Mbembe, in the epigraph to this chapter, terms a 'grounded theory' that is premised on reflexivity and is sensitive to the contingent. A theory of transculturation is concrete, also because it importantly attends to the numerous potential kinds of interaction that travel in the name of transculturation, and to the ways they shift in relation to particular contextual configurations in different historical and cultural settings. As I will discuss below, such a theory endeavours to bring forth a precise terminological apparatus to describe the kinds of interaction that constitute its core, rather than subsuming them all under blanket concepts, for instance hybridity or circulation.

A theory of transculturation can productively build on the groundwork of analytical approaches of the past decades – the linguistic-cum-cultural turn, postcolonial and gender studies – whose insights it has the potential to refine and take into more nuanced directions. As a critical perspective for art history, its reconceptualization of culture shows the way to rethinking the terms of the global away from its condition as a naturalised given or as an ensemble of institutional demands, towards a set of relations between units in a continual state of transformation. A transculturally framed history of art goes beyond the principle of additive extension and looks instead at the transformative processes that constitute art practice through cultural encounters and long-term relationships, whose traces can be followed back to the beginnings of history. Studying these multi-scalar relationalities across regional and local nodes urges us, in turn, to engage with various modes of defining globality, depending on place, time, and context. Casting art history in a critically global/transcultural frame involves questioning the taxonomies and values that have been built into the discipline since its inception, complicit with the formation of nations and empires, and have been taken as universal. These include the anchoring of style within single regions, the taxonomies of genres that are also hierarchies of value, and not least necessitate bringing back excluded materials, texts and questions centre-stage. Systems of value innate to art history classify its objects as fine or decorative art, ethnological object, craft, curiosities, or articles of mass consumption. Following these taxonomies, the objects of art historical investigation are relegated to different sites of display and storage, according to the often not very consistent logic of genres and regional labels. Is Delft chinaware art or an object of everyday use? Does a Fatimid rock crystal, mounted and transformed into a Venetian reliquary, qualify as Islamic or Christian art? Why is a painting by Cézanne a more privileged subject of analysis, considered to possess a greater iconological and semantic complexity, than an ivory box? Today, institutions that house and display these objects are confronted with the challenge of how to translate the transcultural lives of things into a curatorial and pedagogical practice that can effectively make a polyphonous object narrate its many stories, or how to find ways of naming and locating that avoid freezing its identity within a myth of origins. An important plank of an emergent transculturally reflexive art history is to use connected material cultures to unsettle many narratives of civilisational uniqueness, in scholarship as well as in the expanding world of curation and display. The instability introduced by the transcultural object within the ordered world of museum labels that once sought to allow a visitor, for instance, to read a 'culture' off a thing in a glass case, has already begun to suggest pathways for scholarship and curating, with a view to tackling the question of how matter shapes aesthetics and culture.[48]

Separating individual objects by organising them according to genres and plotting their lives in neat chronological sequences has brought forth the category of style to serve as a convenient tool for stabilising the endless mobility and metamorphoses of objects and forms. Shaped primarily, though not exclusively, by the development of artistic form, style functions as a key anchor of art history. It constitutes a vital premise of the temporal notion of an art historical 'period' or 'school' marked by similarities of form, thematic preoccupation, or technical approaches to formal construction or composition.[49] Critical globality as viewed through a transcultural lens questions the idea of stylistic development that is artificially maintained by attending to a single geographical location considered self-contained. More importantly, by undermining longstanding interpretations of cultural identity that served as an epistemic premise of the discipline of art history, a transcultural perspective allows you to rethink the notion of stylistic development that replicates a biological evolutionary model and thereby suppresses human agency as well as the transformative effects of the circulation of objects and practices. A global art history, conceived as transcultural process, intensifies the discipline's focus on objects and practices by reading them not as discrete phenomena, but themselves as a bundle of multiple interlinked processes that unfold at varying speeds

---

48 These and related issues have been discussed in Juneja and Grasskamp, 'EurAsian Matters – An Introduction'.

49 Jaś Elsner has traced the genealogy of style to the sixteenth century and ascribes its refinement and extraordinary subtlety to Heinrich Wölfflin's *Kunstgeschichtliche Grundbegriffe* (1915). Elsner refers to style as a 'crucial reminder of our discipline's depths', as its 'lineage', without however drawing attention to the elisions built into that lineage. Jaś Elsner, 'Style', in Robert S. Nelson and Richard Shiff (eds), *Critical Terms for Art History*, Chicago: University of Chicago Press, 2003, pp. 98–109, quote p. 108.

and intensities. It demands that the art historian tease out and describe the strands of this mutable assemblage. This approach can preclude the art historical impasse between a formalism that engages objects in a closed semantic circle of the present and a contextualism that privileges the singular moment, location and human agent of a work's production, all circumscribed within a fixed spatial and temporal unit.

Transculturation has inherited a prolific vocabulary brought forth by scholarship of the recent decades, which highlights 'porous boundaries', 'mobility', 'fuzziness', 'flows', 'entanglement', 'hybridity', *métissage*, 'creolisation', 'in-between-ness', and the like, all intended as critical tools to prise open units of investigation structured around stable entities. The much-used notion of hybridity, for example, once viewed with reservations owing to its biologistic overtones and associations with racial obsessions surrounding purity and miscegenation, was re-signified in postcolonial writings as a critical tool to undermine a conception of closed cultures.[50] Yet, today, these terms too have undergone a dilution of their one-time explanatory power owing partly to inflationary usage, but also to the fact that they end up as theoretical straightjackets into which a host of diverse experiences come to be accommodated. Their explanatory potential stops short of coming to grips with greater precision about the different kinds of relational possibilities built into processes of transculturation, involving agents, practices and temporalities in historically specific settings. As a perspective for the humanities in general, and art history in particular, a theory of transculturation seeks to develop a more differentiated vocabulary to capture the morphology of the processes through which difference is negotiated within encounters: through selective appropriation, mediation, translation, reconfiguration, re-historicising, and rereading of signs, alternatively through non-communication, friction, disconnection, rejection, or resistance – or through a succession or coexistence of any of these. Exploring the possible range of transactions built into these dynamics works as a safeguard against polar conceptions of identity and alterity, equally against dichotomies between complete absorption and resistance that have characterised recent studies, even as they admirably seek to write a connected art history across Europe and Asia.[51] Paying greater attention to multiple relationalities that unfold in any context, including overtly asymmetrical constellations as in the coloniser–colony divide, involves finding ways of remapping experiences and experiments of the art world. This in turn means attending to scale and to multiple sites of knowledge and to shifting perspectives within a generative agonism between power and resistance. The latter, for example, came to be an important driving force for modernist art within a colonial context.[52] Not least, the genealogical trajectory of transculturation has shown it to be an effective tool to deal

---

50   However, by privileging 'mixing', the notion of hybridity presupposes, if not produces, 'pure' original
      cultures. A critical take on the uses of hybridity as an analytical tool is Carolyn Dean and Dana Leibsohn,
      'Hybridity and its Discontents: Considering Visual Culture in Colonial Spanish America', *Colonial Latin
      American Review*, vol. 12 (1), 2003: 5–35.

51   One such example is Hans Belting, *Florenz und Bagdad: Eine westöstliche Geschichte des Blicks*, Munich:
      C. H. Beck, 2008.

52   Extensively discussed in Chapter Three below.

with issues such as racism as well as more recent forms of ethnocentrism that have permeated art worlds through the modern and contemporary periods.[53] The agenda of writing a transcultural history of art in the twenty-first century has grown in complexity as it faces constellations of the present: this has brought forth its set of routine orthodoxies in thinking about cultural difference, following the logic of economic globalisation and multicultural inclusiveness. Today, we experience multiculturalism as a progressive political imperative in liberal democracies, one that is characterised by an affirmation of cultural diversity as value per se. It celebrates cultural difference as a form of plenitude in which diversity exists side by side, with little interaction or dynamism among the diverse elements. Multicultural inclusion frequently results in an extended horizontal breadth that tends to de-historicise and flatten out contradictory relationships amongst those brought together in the name of tolerance and inclusiveness. The discussions in this book problematise the question of multiculturalism and its implications for art production and curation, and propose that we distinguish the multicultural from the transcultural.

A transculturally framed art history underlines the importance of studying concepts as migrant notions. It questions the assumptions, based on observations from the contemporary art world, that a global circulation of key terms – art, image, vision, to name a few – used ubiquitously also stand for a shared universe of meaning across the globe. It also takes a more nuanced view of the phenomenon of epistemic violence, held to be inflicted by imposing 'Western' analytical frames on 'non-Western' cultures. Instead, it argues that when concepts migrate – as for example they did from the Western world to Asian contexts – they disconnect from their original moorings while taking roots in new cultural settings. This is a process of transculturation where conceptual categories – like the notion of art itself – absorb other subterranean concepts, or become entangled with different practices and understandings, sometimes also producing conflicting positions within a single region. Recognising this, in turn, calls for taking apart meta-geographic designations such as Western or non-Western that become meaningless, as they ascribe stable attributes to concepts.[54] A transcultural study of artistic concepts requires, first, taking a close look at the negotiation between different linguistic sources and, secondly, it needs to extend the formation of the concept beyond purely lexical definitions to investigate the interaction between text and visual practice that is crucial to meaning-making and the production of a society's conceptual knowledge. In my previous research as well as in the case studies investigated in this book, I have drawn on this method to study a lexicon of art historical terms – including art, artisan, image, ornament, landscape, portrait, copy, to name a few – by accommodating a plurality of textual sources

---

53 This dimension has been examined at length by Christian Kravagna is his investigation of the Harlem Renaissance and African American modernism, see Kravagna, *Transmoderne: Eine Kunstgeschichte des Kontakts;* also Cornelia Kogoj and Christian Kravagna, *Das amerikanische Museum: Sklaverei, schwarze Geschichte und der Kampf um Gerechtigkeit in Museen der Südstaaten*, Berlin: Mandelbaum Verlag, 2017.
54 On metageography as a classificatory mode, see Martin E. Lewis and Kären Wigen, *The Myth of Continents: A Critique of Metageography*, Berkeley: University of California Press, 1997.

and pictorial media while charting the migrant trajectories of some of the key concepts of art history.[55]

Arguing against an established dictum by which 'Western' particularity is transformed into a model of universality, Ortiz's study of Cuba calls attention to the play of globally interconnected particularities. If the self-fashioning of sovereign centres, his book demonstrates, entails the making of dependent peripheries, it at the same time tells the story of actors on the margins who turn these into centres and fashion fluid identities through dynamic processes of interaction. Binary oppositions – West/non-West, centre/peripheries, dominant/dominated, white/dark – are treated not as fixed, but as mutable and productive owing to their transcultural formation. Thinking within this frame and carrying the analysis further allows us to recast a widely prevalent conception of polar oppositions in dynamic terms: notions of centres and peripheries, or mainstream and margins, global and local, are understood as constituted through imagined geographies, as part of world-making practices that unfold in specific regional or national or international contexts. We are thus required to view these categories as mutable and relational, and to pay attention to how they come into being and the adjustments they undergo in changing contexts on different scales. Art histories that take as their starting point projects emanating from global 'off-centres'[56] potentially work towards loosening the rigid linearity of canonical narratives; in addition a transcultural understanding of transregionally connected particularities can realign our perceptions of centres and peripheries through the study of comparisons, interactions and resonances. The recognition that even as actors and institutions in different localities are anchored within specific pedagogies and practices of art and continue to grapple with legacies that belong to particular pasts – such as colonisation – no locality, however specific its dynamics, is sealed off from others, is crucial to a revitalised global art historical approach.

By situating the struggle against Eurocentrism within the political and cultural confines of the nation and of reformist national thought, *Cuban Counterpoint* anticipates the predicament of many anti-colonial national movements across the globe. In other words, the nation offered the ground on which a politics of emancipation could be staged, while at the same time it partook of the production of notions such as separate, pure cultures, the authentic native, bounded identities, all to serve as artifices of power. Viewed in this light, the explanatory potential of the transcultural as an analytical tool exceeds that of the 'transnational', frequently used in global studies to transcend the boundaries of individual nation-states,

---

55 See for instance, Monica Juneja, 'Tracking the Routes of Vision in Early Modern Eurasia', in: Karin Gludovatz, Juliane Noth and Joachim Rees (eds), *The Itineraries of Art: Topographies of Artistic Mobility in Europe and Asia*, Paderborn: Fink Verlag, 2015, pp. 57–85; Monica Juneja, 'Likeness as a Migrating Concept – Artfully Portraying the Universal Ruler in Early Modern South Asia', *Histoire de l'Art*, vol. 82 (1), 2018: 55–70; Monica Juneja, 'From the Religious to the Aesthetic Image – or the Struggle over Art that Offends', in: Christiane Kruse, Birgit Meyer and Anne-Marie Korte (eds), *Taking Offense. Religion, Art and Visual Culture in Plural Confgurations*, Munich: Fink Verlag, 2018, pp. 161–189.

56 The term has been coined by Okwui Enwezor, to designate a location 'structured by the simultaneous existence of multiple centers', see Okwui Enwezor, 'Modernity and Postcolonial Ambivalence', *South Atlantic Quarterly*, vol. 109 (3), 2010: 595–620, here 601–2.

without however disrupting the nexus between the entities 'nation' and 'culture' through unpacking the former and delineating its internal faultlines. These are engendered when nations manufacture their version of the past through privileging certain strands of culture as authentically national, while others are relegated to categories that are also hierarchies, such as folk traditions or minority cultures. A transcultural position also sets itself apart from recent decolonial approaches whose analytical frame incarcerates nation and colonising power as uncompromising, undifferentiated oppositional forces.[57] Neither is the national, as I argue, entirely incommensurable with the global – this being an underlying premise of much of global history. The relationship between the two explored in this book is more complex and contradictory in view of the nation's role in resisting the violence of conquest and colonisation on the one hand, conjoined, on the other, to its need to stabilise its self-representation through a play of power, dispossession and everyday violence. The latter, in turn, is sustained by ideologies and technologies of power, imbricated in global/transcultural attachments. In the domain of art history, a transcultural perspective refuses the choice of the nation as a unit of investigation and characterising principle of the enterprise of art-making, even while acknowledging its potential as an imagined realm for artistic positions, a life-giving force in the face of colonialism and neo-colonialism. When adopted as an automatic gesture to frame surveys and units of art historical investigations, the analytical category of the nation

---

57   Mignolo and Walsh (eds), *On Decoloniality: Concepts, Analytics Praxis*; Rolando Vázquez, *Vistas of Modernity: Decolonial Aesthesis and the End of the Contemporary*, Amsterdam: Mondriaan Fund, 2020. The latter's reductive conflation of modernity and coloniality, a founding premise of decolonial theory, overlooks the long history of the former's migrations, mutations, reenactments on sites across the globe, where subjects, not least the colonised, have redefined and reenacted what it means to be modern. Since theorisations of decoloniality are primarily anchored in the experience of settler colonialism on the American continent, a context where the colonising power continues to occupy the territory of the colonised, such theoretical expositions tend to essentialise colonialism as a historical phenomenon. No doubt all colonialisms are exploitative by nature, marked by civilising missions and varying degrees of brutality; at the same time, processes of producing knowledge and art in different colonial contexts across the world play out in ways more complex and less reductive than those posited by the advocates of decolonial theory. A more nuanced view, though one equally based on the example of settler colonialism is Charlene V. Black and Tim Barringer, 'Decolonizing Art and Empire', *The Art Bulletin*, vol. 104 (1), 2022: 6–20. See Chapter Three below for a different understanding of modernity and modernism.

Another term that has appeared in recent scholarship – often conjoined to a decolonial approach – is the 'transversal'. It has been used, for example, by Ming Tiampo, more as a metaphor: 'connecting lines that in Euclidean geometry create equal angles at their point of intersection'. Tiampo then invokes transversality as a tool to study the connections of artists who came from different regions of the world to the Slade School of Art in London and are said to have built 'shared conceptual structures', without however unravelling the explanatory potential of the term itself. Moreover the author's use of the term 'decolonial' to characterize the modernism of artists from erstwhile colonies implicitly replicates the distinction once made between an unmarked (Euro-American) modernism, regarded as mainstream, and peripheral, alternative variants emanating from elsewhere. See Ming Tiampo, 'Transversal Articulations: Decolonial Modernism and the Slade School of Fine Art', in Okwui Enwezor and Atreyee Gupta (eds), *Postwar – A Global Art History, 1945–1965*, Durham, NC: Duke University Press (forthcoming). I am grateful to the author for sharing her unpublished draft with me. Marsha Meskimmon on the other hand develops the notion of transversality to analyse the workings of multiple, dialogical coalitions forged across social divisions and hierarchies and allied to radical practice. See Marsha Meskimmon, *Transnational Feminisms, Transversal Politics and Art: Entanglements and Intersections*, London: Routledge, 2020.

is bound to lapse into the ethnographic reflexes that underpin such a choice. And yet, as the themes discussed in this book will show, the category of the nation can equally function as a point of critical interrogation, built around questions rather than answers. It can as well serve as an opportunity to redraw the matrix of references within which concepts of culture might be recast.

A Potential Art History

Following Ariella Aïsha Azoulay, I conceive of a 'potential' art history as a way of bringing unasked questions about the past, suppressed or elided possibilities to the forefront of art historical narratives.[58] The potentiality of a reflexive, transculturally oriented globality works in two directions. It enables recovering those constitutive forms of encounter and relationships that unfolded at any historical juncture without being shaped exclusively or exhausted by projections of national thinking. In addition, it makes for a change of register to allow theory-building from beyond the unmarked Euro-American centre of dominant narratives. Exploring modalities of theorising experiences from a 'periphery', now opened up for a transcultural enquiry, is a step towards breaking the inertia of long-standing conceptual and institutional divisions by which 'regions' whose trajectories were positioned outside of an assumed 'mainstream' were then relegated to segregated pockets termed area studies. This means investigating the dynamics of art-making and theorising from these regions to ask how the insights they bring forth could in turn unsettle what has become a default mode of art historical practice. Reconfiguring key conceptual categories from the perspective of the so-called periphery without excluding its historical connections to multiple sites, both in as well as outside of Euro-America, can help create a more plausible theoretical scaffolding for the discipline to then respond to the challenge of cultural plurality. These broad concerns have translated into the more specific research located in South Asia that this book brings together in a move to supplement macro-perspectives by descending into the thicket of individual sites, thereby negotiating multiple scales beyond the global – nation, region, locality – and conjoining these to individual subject positions. It aims to unravel the dynamics of those interactive processes that make for a globally connected art history, one which breaks out of both national frameworks as well as well-worn paradigms of 'centres and peripheries' or 'the West and the rest'.

The term 'periphery' that features in the book's title, paradoxical as it may sound at first, connotes both a situation and a scholarly position. Though identified with marginality and obscurity, a so-designated periphery has the capacity to challenge foundational ideas of exclusivity and universality, and to offer alternative positions to sedimented intellectual claims. In other words, mining the peripheries to rebound on the centre, can effectively dismantle the Manichean dualism of centre and periphery. Such a proposition cannot, however,

---

58   Ariella A. Azoulay, 'Potential History: Thinking Through Violence', *Critical Inquiry*, vol. 39 (3), 2013: 548–74.

be carried out by simply reversing an established hierarchy, while leaving its teleology intact. Writing from the periphery, in the approach followed in this book, is premised on viewing both centres and peripheries through a transcultural lens, to argue that each site is a hotbed of transculturation and cannot be studied in exclusive pockets. For example, artistic production classified as Buddhist, whose origins lay in present-day India, grew into a full-blown visual and sculptural language in the wake of transcultural processes that covered the expanse of the Indian subcontinent and beyond, to encompass Afghanistan, Bactria, Greece, Central and East Asia. Similarly, the trajectories of modernist art in the twentieth century were constituted through the experimental energies of sites across the globe – from Paris, Berlin, Ljubljana, Cairo, Zaria, São Paolo, Bombay, Mexico City, Tokyo … the list goes on. Scholarship produced in regions, which since the twentieth century have been parcelled into national units or isolated area studies, does not feature in the contemporary canon of the global. Not only has it not found a place in a global repository of intellectual resources and narratives, its potential to exert analytical pressure on that repository, to recalibrate, even unsettle the certitudes of that canon, has yet to be fully realised. We might usefully imagine the periphery less as a place, instead conceive of it as a critical modality rather than a pristine locality.

The investigations in this book take as their starting point a region long regarded a periphery of Euro-America, to then open it to a transcultural analysis that would overcome the limitations of both a national framework as well as the provincialism of a single, sealed 'area'. They address the challenge of finding explanatory paradigms for dealing with processes which, following mobility and encounter, are formed through a tension between cultural difference and historical connectivity. Such processes might appear paradoxical in that they combine accommodation, partial absorption, refusal or engagement at different levels with cultural difference, without necessarily producing synchronicity. The agenda to look for cultural commensurability across distances has frequently led to exclusion or repression of aspects of distinctiveness or the non-commensurable. What are the analytical tools that would help us come to grips with the tension between the commensurable and the incommensurable? And what constitutes the 'commensurable'? Is that a category that depends on the intellectual and philosophical positions of modern scholarship? As we negotiate the tension or the shifting relationships between the culturally commensurable and the non-assimilable, we would then be able to recuperate practices fundamental to art historical investigation – such as vision, materiality, and canonical values – which have undergone erasure or flattening due to the diffusion of modern disciplinary taxonomies across the globe. Does the investigation of art history from a perspective outside of the West, though shaped through interaction with travelling Western concepts, challenge us to rethink some of the discipline's premises in a way as to grow beyond both claims of universality as well as radical cultural relativism, and instead privilege an approach that historicises difference and locates it in a field of forces?

Each of the chapters of this book is informed by the concern to link the 'region' to the 'mainstream' discipline so as to reflect on the latter's underlying assumptions and point the way to a non-hierarchical, critical, and capacious art history that can serve as a potential tool for unravelling connections, differences and frictions among regions across the globe. The notion of a meditation informing each case study draws its inspiration from two sources, distinct and yet perhaps linked by an invisible thread of affinity.[59] Meditation here might be understood as an assemblage of micro-stories, questions, arguments and tools of transcultural research which incessantly interrogates established frames. Through a process of methodological doubt, it seeks to rebuild knowledge from the ground up, to arrive at a mode of self-knowledge. The themes handled in the book are inevitably selective, often addressed to art history syllabi, both current as well as those aspiring to a global orientation. At the same time, it has been a conscious decision to move away from some of the prominent subjects – such as biennials and nomadic curators, exhibition circuits, the art market – with which a global art history continues to be largely identified, and which are fast acquiring the status of a new canon. These do not feature centrally, or do so at best tangentially, within the themes discussed in the following chapters. More importantly, my approach eschews a presentist view of global entanglements to investigate processes of transculturation long before the advent of finance capital and the digital revolution, to engage with the specific dynamics and tensions of pre- and early modern forms of encounter, circulation, and reception. While recognising the revolutionary import of digitality for the production and circulation of knowledge, the subject has not been tackled frontally in my discussion of the contemporary art world, owing to the continuing unevenness in the intensity and scale of digitisation across the world, which has created its own forms of 'locational hierarchies' that shape the production of both art and the writing of its histories.[60] The aim of the book is not to bring forth one more meta-narrative, but to focus on a selection of themes from one particular region that together signal to a possible path towards revitalising the global with a criticality whose shape is contingent at once on its situatedness as on its transcultural dynamics.

The book begins by investigating the genealogies of world-making within the practice of art history to query its legacies for the present global turn within the discipline. The first chapter, 'The World in a Grain of Sand: A Genealogy of World Art Studies', looks at a formative conjuncture during the late nineteenth and early twentieth centuries, when scholarship on art assumed a world-configuring function while seeking to produce authoritative knowledge about nations, cultures and the world. Investigating this trajectory of the discipline is important, not least because it has been recently hailed as prefiguring present attempts to make the discipline global.[61] The chapter focuses primarily, though not exclusively, on German language texts that came under the label of *Weltkunstgeschichte* and analyses the

---

59   I am indebted, first to Donald Preziosi, whose book (see note 10) carries the subtitle: *Meditations on a Coy Science*. The artist Atul Dodiya's memorable installation of 2011, *Meditation (with Open Eyes)* that features on the cover of this book provides another source: the work translates through an assemblage of photographs, objects and ephemera some of the transcultural thinking that runs through the pages of this book.

60   Gupta, 'Art History and the Global Challenge': 22.

61   See note 38.

premises and argumentative structures that characterised the efforts of art history to revitalise itself by bringing the world into its purview. I ask why the cosmopolitan potential ascribed to this current of art historiography remained unrealised during a moment of intense global exchange and challenges, not dissimilar to those of the present. What are the methodological implications of these initiatives for similar positions today? This genealogy of world-making in art history directs our attention to those epistemic foundations that continue to shape our scholarly practice, both in the North-Atlantic West as well as in those regions of the world where the modern discipline has journeyed and acquired roots, even as it responds to local contingencies. The exercise in unpacking the foundations of an art history that strove to be inclusive is an urgent one in contemporary times as the discipline endeavours once more to become 'global'.

Chapter two, 'Making and Seeing Images: Tracking the Routes of Vision in Early Modern Eurasia', takes as its starting point theoretical stances in the field of world art studies that have tended to alternate between two poles: between the view which considers seeing/vision as constituting a human universal, a common anthropological denominator that holds humans together across time and space[62] and the extreme relativist position which advocates the use of each cultural tradition's core concepts of visuality and the image, whose incommensurability and fixity are assumed.[63] As distinct from these positions, I propose that vision itself needs to be a subject of historical investigation. The case study discussed in this chapter focuses on image-making and circulation in early modern court cultures in South Asia framed in a Eurasian context. It examines the ways in which translating the 'seen' onto a two-dimensional surface of the image was a process shaped by the dynamic between cultural mobility across sites in Europe and Asia and new forms of self-reflection induced by itinerant images and objects, producing thereby different grades of commensurability and incommensurability. An important dimension in the transculturation of image worlds was the self-conscious use of art historical referencing in the practice of image-making – citation, repetition, copying, pastiche – as modes of cultural communication and articulations of worldly awareness. Intrinsic to a transregional and transhistorical circulation of objects and attitudes towards the image, the chapter argues, are cosmologies and questions of hermeneutics that account for the degree of their assimilability through translation as well as its refusal. This study, in addition, allows us to disaggregate a singular conception of vision into historically variable ways of seeing in which the materiality of image making equally informs vision to make it a synaesthetic experience.

Chapter three, 'Traversing Scale(s): Transcultural Modernism with and beyond the Nation', engages with the conceptual category of modernism, long viewed as a quintessential European phenomenon which then was said to have 'spread' to the rest of the world. My account participates in the critical scrutiny that such a position has undergone in the recent

---

62 Onians, *Atlas of World Art.*
63 James Elkins, 'Different Horizons for the Concept of the Image', in: *On Pictures and Words that Fail Them*, Cambridge: Cambridge University Press, 1998, pp. 188–209.

years in the wake of prolific research from a range of regional positions and the translation of these findings through the medium of the art exhibition. Studies of modernism 'from the peripheries' have questioned its monolithic nature and argued for an expanded definition that would include the artistic experiments of modernist artists in Asia, Africa, Eastern Europe, and Latin America. The challenge, however, remains that of avoiding the pitfalls of recounting exclusively local histories, or the trap of treating regional or national cultures as closed units. This chapter seeks to bring regions and nations into a more dynamic, non-hierarchical and, importantly, non-homogenising relationship with each other, arguing that this cannot be adequately handled without simultaneously delving into localities and negotiating multiple scales – the local, regional, national, and global. The story of modernism recounted here takes South Asia as its focal point to argue against both a diffusionist view as well as one which proposes 'multiple' or 'alternative' or 'regional' modernisms. Rather, it looks at connected processes of translation and reconfiguration, at encounters of persons and narratives, as well as at endeavours inspired by idealist internationalism that in the end faltered in the face of cultural difference. Differences that unfolded in local or regional settings, frequently cut across the coloniser-colony divide, to reach out to both shared global horizons as well as individual micro-histories. The final section of the chapter explores the migratory fortunes of the category of the 'primitive', designated the alter ego of artistic modernism. It does so by plotting aspects of its conceptual history from different locations across Europe and Asia onto a single matrix, to then uncover the ambivalent nature of its appropriation by modernist artists on the Indian subcontinent, working in the interstices of anti-colonial nationalism and worldly cosmopolitanism.

Chapter four, 'Beyond Backwater Arcadias – Globalised Locality and Contemporary Art Practice', continues the 'periphery-in' approach by drawing attention to those sites of cultural action crucial to contemporary art that loosen the rigid linearity of narratives segregating contemporaneity from the modern. Such vibrant peripheries – the chapter shows – produce both novel art as well as a critical discourse and therefore demand a fresh optic to theorise the context within which artistic projects as well as conceptual insights are born. They serve as a locus of the transculturation of the avant-garde as it becomes global. The quest for artistic selfhood in postcolonial contexts – here too the focus is on South Asia – has involved a staggering transformation of codes and media initiatives in which globalised locality constitutes a space to rethink tradition beyond the predicament of being always 'somebody's other'.[64] Drawing on the work of a handful of artists, the chapter fleshes out how a more politicised engagement with the dilemmas of the contemporary – induced by the crisis of liberal democracies, mass migration, and the spectacular regimes of global capitalism – has made contemporary art practice in a postcolonial nation-state a domain to explore forms of identity beyond the nation. Singling out the work of individual artists here – and in other sections of the book – is not to signal towards a return to a biographical, more often than

---

64 Rustom Bharucha, 'Somebody's Other: Disorientations in the Cultural Politics of Our Times', *Economic and Political Weekly*, vol. 29 (3), 1994: 105–10.

not celebratory mode of art history that treats the work of the single artist as the pinnacle of a creative process. Rather, facets of an artist's work are brought into relationship with other works and concepts in vectors that invite further exploration. The international spirit of global exchange has on the one hand encouraged transcultural affiliations and forms of co-production as ways to resist complicity with global capital. At the same time, such affiliations and the circulation of ideas remain to a lesser or greater degree dependent on big capital that sustains enterprises such as biennials and a globalised network of exhibitions, galleries, and art publishing.

Chapter five, 'When Art Embraces the Planet: The Contemporary Exhibition Form and the Challenge of Connected Histories', revisits the famous – also controversial – Paris exhibition of 1989, *Magiciens de la Terre*, conceptualised as the first planetary show of contemporary art, which at the same time sought to challenge the conventions of exhibition-making within the narrow confines of the art world and its modernist taxonomic frames. The analysis asks whether incorporating art from beyond the West within contemporary exhibition circuits can engender a discursive space to remap cultural geographies and theorise the dystopian/disjunctive condition of contemporaneity, or does it merely answer global capitalism's need for new commodities? Do new boundaries come into being in the wake of the connectivity that dissolves older ones? My investigation moves from the centre back to the periphery: it follows the bold topography of *Magiciens* across continents to those sites where the works that had travelled to Paris were produced and anchored, and to examine their post-*Magiciens* lives. My urge is to read objects, their producers and curators coevally, while restoring to different sites their particular historicity. The example of South Asia and its archives has been used to draw out the complex histories of cultures that live in a permanent and fluctuating relationality with one another, and whose dynamics get lost when we exclusively attend to dismantling the centrality of the so-called West, even if to castigate its cultural biases. These multi-scalar stories sensitise us to new faultlines within the domain of the contemporary, and to the complexity of inclusion as a curatorial strategy. Tracing a connected history of the first 'whole earth show'[65] in turn draws our attention to the emergence of another transcultural category, that of the 'global Indigenous' that has come to serve as an umbrella term for Indigenous art practices from across the divide of North and South, of settler-colonies and postcolonial nations.

Finally, the Postscript looks ahead to a fresh transition already under way – from the global to the planetary. Anthropogenic climate change, also described as a 'crisis of culture', has propelled the humanities towards the sciences, now brought under the rubric of 'planetary humanities'.[66] The implications of this radical turn ask us to recalibrate our understanding of culture by breaking out of Enlightenment ontologies that separate nature from culture. Could the transcultural, in turn, be re-envisioned to incorporate an all-embracing matrix

---

65   Benjamin Buchloh, 'The Whole Earth Show: An Interview with Jean-Hubert Martin', *Art in America*, vol. 77 (5), 1989, pp. 150–59, 211, 213.

66   See note 2.

of relationships wherein forms arise in a conjoint activity between human and non-human actors? And what would this imply for doing art history in a planetary, non-anthropocentric mode? These are some preliminary reflections that point in the direction of a new project to think the future of art history under the aegis of a new planetary consciousness.

CHAPTER ONE
THE WORLD IN A GRAIN OF SAND
A Genealogy of World Art Studies

'To see a world in a grain of sand and eternity in a flower.' – William Blake, *Songs of Innocence*

Kalo Bari, or Black House is a students' hostel created in 1934 on the campus of Kala Bhawan, the art school of Visva Bharati University at Santiniketan in eastern India. Its outer walls feature a series of asphalt coated mud reliefs showing copies of different styles of art from ancient cultures of the world – a seal from Mohenjo Daro, standing figures adapted from ancient Egyptian frescoes, an Assyrian lion copied from one of the reliefs in the Ashurbanipal series of the British Museum (Plates 1.1 and 1.1a). To complete the spectrum of styles selected from world cultures, a frieze shows birds in flight, one of them approaching the viewer in frontal foreshortening characteristic of the Italian Renaissance, which here unmistakably evokes the Holy Spirit of Piero della Francesca's *The Baptism of Christ*.[1] Conceived by the artists Nandalal Bose (1882–1966) and Binode Behari Mukherjee (1904–1980), this expansive art historical gesture was at the same time a pedagogical move to bring world traditions of art-making from early civilisations of humanity, remounting to pre-Christian antiquity, to this site of learning. Instituted by Rabindranath Tagore in 1919 as an anti-industrial refuge and intellectual retreat that would provide an alternative to colonial art education in British India, Kala Bhawan stood for the aesthetic ideals of an embryonic nation as envisioned through its art, which at the same time sought its place within a genealogy transcending the national space.

The intent to bring the world into the domain of art-making was not new for its times; within literary and artistic practices of modernism such an act of 'world-making' represented a mode of rethinking a relationship to the lived world.[2] Conceived as both normative praxis

---

1 On the Black House and its mural reliefs that were completed in 1938, see R. Siva Kumar, 'The Black House: In the Context of the Santiniketan Murals', in Sanjoy K. Mallik (ed.), *Black House*, Kolkata: Vishva-Bharati, 2016, pp. 29–58, and illustration, here 51, juxtaposing the birds in flight with Piero della Francesca's painting.
2 The term was coined by Nelson Goodman, *Ways of Worldmaking*, Indianapolis: Hackett, 1978. While the notion of 'world-making' has been coined in relation to modernity, the practice of referring to the 'world' within the work of art goes back to pre- or early modern societies, an aspect that will be discussed in the following chapter.

as well as analytical tool, world-making can be described as an act of looking outwards and beyond, towards other worlds to come.[3] A cosmopolitan gesture par excellence, it is at the same time imbricated in the materials and the structures through which it is created.[4] World making therefore cannot be separated from a constellation of institutions, practices, and relationships that can be contested, made, and remade through new figurations, stories, and narratives. These in turn mediate our apprehension of the world, even as we look beyond it to other worlds to come. Within a modernist setting, world-making inhabits a field of antagonistic pulls between the national and the cosmopolitan; by telling us that we can belong in many ways, it must negotiate the tension between the two.

Writing about art, both a narrative of its 'story' as well as a proposition for its pedagogy, has been from its inception one such act of world-making. Art history and museography, two faces of a single coin, are, to cite Donald Preziosi, rooted in 'an ideology of representational adequacy', one that presupposes a 'real history', which it imagines through the act of representing the world.[5] Producing this 'real history' in the nineteenth and twentieth centuries, when emergent nationalism and a connected world formed two nodes of a single matrix, required a constant movement between home/nation and world – to grasp the world so as to be able to make sense of one's own place and time. Art history emerges in this context as both a practice and a product of its discursive transactions. This chapter delves into one such site and juncture of making art history, one which experimented with ways of bringing the world into the purview of the story of art and offensively projected this disciplinary turn as a key to revitalising its practice. The following account explores the tensions and negotiations this form of world-making had to navigate during the course of the nineteenth and early twentieth centuries. Today, this historiographic current is being upheld as an example of a cosmopolitan moment that prefigured the present global turn in the discipline and its institutions. It is therefore worth taking a closer, more critical look at its workings in order to understand the founding premises of the discipline that continue to be largely unquestioned, even as it seeks, once more, to expand its range of vision.[6]

---

3   According to the literary theorist, Pheng Cheah, 'world' stands for more than a 'spatial-geographical entity'; it is a normative category and 'a dynamic process of becoming'. Pheng Cheah, 'What Is a World? On World Literature as World-making Activity', *Daedalus*, vol. 137 (3), 2008: 26–38, here 30–31. Also, Pheng Cheah, *What Is a World? On Postcolonial Literature as World Literature*, Durham, NC: Duke University Press, 2016.

4   Arno Schubbach, 'Das Bilden der Bilder: Zur Theorie der Welterzeugung und ihrer bildtheoretischen Verpflichtung', *Soziale Systeme*, 18 (1–2), 2012: 69–93.

5   Donald Preziosi, *The Art of Art History: A Critical Anthology*, Oxford: Oxford University Press, 2009 (2nd revised edition), p. 488.

6   For arguments that read certain currents of early art historical writing as a precursor of the modern global turn, see Ulrich Pfisterer, 'Origins and Principles of World Art History: 1900 (and 2000)', in: Kitty Zijlmans and Wilfried van Damme (eds.), *World Art Studies: Exploring Concepts and Approaches*, Amsterdam: Valiz, 2008, pp. 69–89; Wilfried van Damme, '"Good to Think": The Historiography of Intercultural Art Studies', *World Art*, vol. 1 (1), 2011: 43–57; Henrik Karge, 'Projecting the Future in German Art Historiography of the Nineteenth Century: Franz Kugler, Karl Schnaase and Gottfried Semper', *Journal of Art Historiography*, vol. 9, 2013: 1–26. See also more generally, in relation to anthropology that had a bearing on art history, Matti Bunzl and H. Glenn Penny, 'Introduction: Rethinking German Anthropology, Colonialism

After taking a site in Santiniketan as its entry point, the remaining content of this chapter shifts the focus to another continent and a different context: it will engage with a corpus of texts – largely untranslated – from the German-speaking regions of Europe that strove to include the world's art within a narrative of a young discipline in ways that have been constitutive for its practice since then. Yet, the two – Tagore's School of Arts and German-language World Art History – are not as unrelated as the continental distance that separates them might suggest: to locate the conceptual lens through which the prevailing canon of art history today looks at – or bypasses – an object such as the Black House, we need to recapitulate that canon's formative processes and epistemic underpinnings, if we are to rethink the discipline beyond its inbuilt hierarchies and claims.

All the World's Art

The long span of the nineteenth century saw a sharpening of the contours of art history: its construction as a unified field of knowledge, a *Wissenschaft* in German, as an institutionalised academic discipline, and not least a modernist enterprise in contexts of nationalism and colonialism that helped construct and embody the historical memories of nation-states. Even though Europe was three centuries into the expansion of its interests across the globe at this time, it was only now that art history sought to address the issue of globality: in other words, to respond to the challenge of finding a key to grappling with the world as a category. The urge to discover the meaning of one's own time through connections with the whole of humanity was a driving force for historians and art historians alike in the European empires through the nineteenth century. It provided the context within which *Weltkunstgeschichte* – an art historical survey of world cultures across time and geography and in accordance with principles of linearity – emerged as an important stream of German-language writing on art. The genre of *Weltkunstgeschichte* registered certain shifts during the period spanning the first half of the nineteenth to the early twentieth century, when it responded to a number of turns within the intellectual culture of these decades. An equally important factor shaping its course was the presence of objects from different regions of the world that came in increasingly large quantities to Europe and drew a range of actors and institutions into the web of their transactions. The following account of this historiographic current within art history will unfold less as an exhaustive survey of the textual production it brought forth; instead, it will deal in an exemplary fashion with a range of expositions within the field, to highlight the formative power of the genre for the future of art history – a power that in the longer term was more far-reaching than differences among individual iterations.

The textual practice of *Weltkunstgeschichte* emanated from the intellectual milieu of post-Hegelian Germany, identified with the consolidation of historicism: the nineteenth-century vision of history according to which a coherent narrative of the past embodied

and Race', in: Matti Bunzl and H. Glenn Penny (eds.), *Worldly Provincialism: German Anthropology in the Age of Empire*, Ann Arbor: University of Michigan Press, 2003, pp. 2–30, esp. p. 11ff.

relevant lessons for the present. The discipline of history, institutionalised in the 1820s by scholars such as Leopold von Ranke (1795–1886) and Barthold Georg Niebuhr (1776–1831), rested on a rejection of philosophy as a key to historical inquiry, to instead privilege empirical research. It was this empirical turn within historical writing that informed the texts of *Welkunstgeschichte* till the second half of the century, following which art history turned instead to the social sciences for inspiration.[7] The earliest survey texts encompassing art of the 'world', though produced at a time soon after art history was institutionalised as an academic discipline in Prussia, were not written exclusively for an academic readership; they were addressed instead to a broader educated public comprising scholars, artists, and art and cultural administrators, with the objective of refining the aesthetic sensibilities of an art-viewing public.[8] Most of their authors did not, at the time of writing, hold a university position. Franz Kugler (1808–1858), for instance, who authored the earliest of world art surveys, after having studied at the University of Berlin and the Berliner Bauakademie (School of Architects), held an administrative position in the Prussian cultural establishment. His colleague Carl Schnaase (1798–1875), who produced a similar multi-volume work almost at the same time as Kugler's textbook, was advisor for the arts in Düsseldorf – first at the Kunstverein für die Rheinlande und Westfalen and then the Kunstakademie – for almost two decades, before he returned to Berlin in 1849 to take up a state position. In 1898, at the end of a century that had seen both the proliferation of surveys of world art as well as a progressive weakening of the historicist paradigm, Alois Riegl (1858–1905) characterised the development of art history as one that had evolved from the universalising narrative of the survey handbook to the specialised monograph. In doing so, he posited a distinction that was also a clearly hierarchical relationship between two modes of historical writing: the magisterial overview, in his view superficial by nature and based frequently on an easy acceptance of second-hand accounts rather than a critical use of primary sources, as opposed to the rigorous, in-depth investigation of a single subject.[9] Riegl's description of the process as one where the work of the amateur gave way to that of the professional has had a long and tenacious

---

7   For an exhaustive account, Regine Prange, *Die Geburt der Kunstgeschichte: philosophische Ästhetik und empirische Wissenschaft*, Cologne: Deubner Verlag, 2004, p. 95ff. Heinrich Dilly, *Kunstgeschichte als Institution: Studien zur Geschichte einer Disziplin*, Frankfurt/M: Suhrkamp Verlag, 1979, pp. 123–32.

8   Franz Kugler, whose survey handbook on art history was among the earlier texts to encompass 'world art', identifies in its preface the groups it was addressed to as follows: 'friends' (*Freunde*), that would refer to readers of an educated middle class; 'young people' (*Junger*) to include students; and finally 'us' (*für uns*), that is, scholars working on art. He further explicitly states that his intention was not to produce a work exclusively dedicated to specialised scholarship. Franz Kugler, *Handbuch der Kunstgeschichte*, Stuttgart: Ebner & Seubert, 1842, pp. X–XI; see also Hubert Locher, 'Das "Handbuch der Kunstgeschichte": Die Vermittlung kunsthistorischen Wissens als Anleitung zum ästhetischen Urteil', in: Wessel Reinink and Jeroen Stumpel (eds), *Memory and Oblivion: Proceedings of the XXIXth International Congress of the History of Art held in Amsterdam, 1–7 September 1996*, Dordrecht: Kluwer Academic Publishers, 1999, pp. 69–87.

9   Describing the methods of authors of art historical survey texts, he wrote: 'sie nahmen das Überlieferte meist kritiklos hin, weil es ihnen eben an Zeit und Gelegenheit, und wohl auch an methodischer Schulung für Kritik mangelte'. Alois Riegl, 'Kunstgeschichte und Universalgeschichte', in: *Festgaben zu Ehren Max Budinger's von seinen Freunden und Schülern*, Innsbruck: Wagner, 1898, pp. 449–57, here p. 453.

afterlife:[10] among other things it resulted in survey texts being denied a place within the discipline.[11] The pedagogical uses of the genre in the domain of art education may well have been acknowledged, but the survey text was nonetheless rated as being intellectually inferior to the monograph.[12] The tendency to separate the study of art history's 'classics' – such as Jacob Burckhardt, Heinrich Wölfflin, Alois Riegl, Aby Warburg – from the works of the relatively lesser known (and till date largely untranslated) surveys of 'world art' continues into our times despite their connections with each other. An important example is Burckhardt, whose writings partook of the same discursive formation as those of Kugler and Schnaase that he drew upon for insights.[13] The conviction that one form of art historical narrative was ultimately superseded by a more modern and sophisticated form of scholarly practice can make us overlook the extent to which seemingly different approaches and varying content rested on a common ground of shared assumptions that continue to underpin much of art history. Today, *Weltkunstgeschichte* has either been relegated to a realm of academic historiography, or is being now revisited, idealised as a distinct cosmopolitan vision prefiguring that of our multicultural present.

The enterprise of writing a history of all the world's art responded to several impulses and challenges, not least those that followed from the prolific presence of objects from lands beyond Europe that for a long time had resisted modes of ordering. At one level, *Weltkunstgeschichte*, or 'the history of art of all times and peoples', as one practitioner titled his art historical survey text,[14] was meant to equip art history with a series of aesthetic categories and explanatory methods that would be able to encompass a new and ever-increasing diversity of objects the discipline was confronted with. The physical presence and continuous flow of archaeological finds, but also of miscellaneous *orientalia*[15] that made their way into European contexts through channels of trade and private collecting, had brought forth a fresh challenge – to museums, curators, publics – and not least to a discipline fixated aesthetically on Classical Antiquity. From the second half of the nineteenth century, museums of different kinds functioned as a primary site where viewers in the West could encounter non-European objects of art, and from where persuasive narratives of sameness and difference could be

10 'An Stelle der früheren universalen Darstellung trat die Specialuntersuchung, an Stelle der Dilettanten traten die Berufshistoriker', Riegl, ibid.

11 For example, Wilhelm Lübke, *Grundriss der Kunstgeschichte*, Stuttgart: Ebner & Seubert, 1860; Anton H. Springer, *Handbuch der Kunstgeschichte: Zum Gebrauche für Künstler und Studirende*, Stuttgart: Rieger'sche Verlagsbuchhandlung, 1855 (1st edition); further editions followed till 1928.

12 Dan Karlholm, *Art of Illusion: The Representation of Art History in Nineteenth-Century Germany and Beyond*, Bern: Peter Lang, 2004, p. 30.

13 A discussion of Jacob Burckhardt follows in the next section of this chapter. See also Monica Juneja, 'Reading Culture through Art – Jacob Burckhardt in the Twenty-first Century', in: Andreas Beyer, Susanna Burghartz and Lukas Burkart (eds), *Burckhardt.Renaissance: Erkundungen und Relektüren eines Klassikers*, Göttingen: Wallstein Verlag, 2021, pp. 174–90.

14 Karl Woermann, *Geschichte der Kunst aller Zeiten und Völkern*, 6 vols, Leipzig: Bibliographisches Institut, 1900–1922.

15 The term has been borrowed from Suzanne L. Marchand, *German Orientalism in the Age of Empire: Religion, Race and Scholarship*, Cambridge: Cambridge University Press, 2009, esp. chapter 9.

constructed and disseminated. Prior to the high noon of archaeological activities in West Asia led by German-speaking scholars, as well as the proliferation of museums, access to knowledge of cultures of the world beyond Europe was gained primarily through illustrated travel accounts or historical writings. One such example was the oeuvre of the Austrian scholar Joseph von Hammer-Purgstall (1774–1856) who wrote prolifically on the Ottoman regions and whose descriptions of history and geography were equally accompanied by accounts of Islamic art objects. His journal *Fundgrube des Orients*, published between 1809 and 1818, was a veritable trove of articles on myriad aspects of 'oriental culture'.[16] A large number of objects, labelled 'oriental' or 'Islamic' – carpets, ceramics, textiles, furniture, glass – inhabited the interstices of dealing, collecting, and scholarship. Especially in the case of Islamic art, mercantile and personal concerns dominated the field wherein scholarship came mainly under the rubric of 'applied' or 'decorative' arts.[17] This was in contrast to the art of East Asia, for which a tradition of learning grew alongside of a thriving art market or had developed independently of it. Indeed, a contentious question among experts was what kinds of objects really counted as 'art' in the sense that European, in particular German, elites understood the term, that is, a balanced synthesis of the ideal and the natural. Conversely, what kinds of craftsmanship – carpet weaving, glass-blowing, furniture design – were 'ornamental' or 'decorative'?[18] What kinds of taste and connoisseurship were required to distinguish a public fascinated with the consumption of lacquer boxes, porcelain, and other department store japonaiserie from an elite with a discerning eye for the 'real' art of the East? Decades before the Wilhelmine world joined the race for museums and spectacular collections, collectors and institutions struggled with ways of fitting 'oriental art' into the emerging system of museums. Curators of 'classical' antiquities were resistant to including artefacts from non-European cultures within their collections. The earliest ethnological museums date to the 1830s and the jumbled nature of their collections, often without labels, remained opaque to members of the public.[19] One challenge to art histories, therefore, was to

16   On Joseph von Hammer-Purgstall's multi-volume *Geschichte des Osmanischen Reichs*, see Klaus Kreiser, 'Clio's Poor Relation: Betrachtungen zur Osmanischen Historiographie von Hammer-Purgstall bis Stanford Shaw', in: Gernot Stein and Grete Klingenstein (eds), *Das Osmanische Reich und Europa 1683 bis 1789: Konflikt, Entspannung und Austausch*, Munich: R. Oldenbourg Verlag, 1983, pp. 24–43, here p. 24; see also Annette Hagedorn, 'The Development of Islamic Art History in Germany in the Late Nineteenth and Early Twentieth Centuries', in Stephen Vernoit (ed.), *Discovering Islamic Art: Scholars, Collectors and Collections 1850–1950*, London: I.B. Tauris, 2000, pp. 117–27, here p. 117.

17   Oleg Grabar, 'The Implications of Collecting Islamic Art', in: Vernoit (ed.), *Discovering Islamic Art*, pp. 194–200.

18   Marchand, *German Orientalism*, p. 392.

19   On the history of ethnographic collections and museums in German-speaking Europe, see Michael Hog, *Ziele und Konzeptionen der Völkerkundemuseen in ihrer historischen Entwicklung*, Frankfurt/M.: R.G. Fischer Verlag, 1981; on the ethnographic museum in Munich, that was founded in 1862 as the Königliche Ethnographische Sammlung (renamed first as Museum für Völkerkunde, then in 2014 as Museum Fünf Kontinente), see Sigrid Gareis, *Exotik in München: Museumsethnologische Konzeptionen im historischen Wandel am Beispiel des Staatlichen Museums für Völkerkunde München*, Münich: Anacon-Verlag, 1990, for a summary of debates about the nature of the collection and observations about its relationship to the public, pp. 149–55.

unravel and define the fuzzy category of the 'Orient' in relation to art of Classical Antiquity and modern Europe. Scholars in the historicist tradition were convinced of the need to have things grouped in clear lines of development, while connoisseurs of Asian arts were anxious to accord their objects an aesthetic status at par with European forms.

Franz Kugler, whose *Handbuch der Kunstgeschichte* was published in 1841–42, declared the function of his scholarly enterprise to be that of bringing order to 'a large mass of particularities', an ambition whose double play signalled to both facts and objects.[20] That 'order' here is meant simply as a corrective to disorder, without elucidating the principles that defined the process of ordering as such, is an aspect I will return to later. The same preface proclaimed the objective of the *Handbuch* as that of narrating the 'totality of art history'[21] from the origins to the present. It presented the history of world art as a linear narrative culminating in the art historical debates of Kugler's time; the account concentrated on works and objects, while eschewing philosophical questions. In its temporal and geographical scope, the *Handbuch* was more comprehensive than any other survey account before this. Kugler divided art history into four major epochs: 1) Prehistoric (including ancient Northern European Monuments, Oceanic, Pre-Columbian, Egyptian, Nubian, Asian art); 2) Classical (Greece and Rome); 3) Romantic (what we name the Middle Ages, including Byzantine and Islamic Art); and 4) Modern (European Art from the Renaissance to the nineteenth century). The first two editions, each comprising some 920 pages, had no illustrations. Only in 1851 was a visual supplement, a folio volume of 154 copperplate and wood engravings, published to accompany the *Handbuch*.[22]

The work approached the subject of world art from the position of the present, prompted by an attempt to understand contemporary art by establishing its origins.[23] The notion of origins had a dual connotation: it encompassed both the beginnings of civilisation as well as the idea of art that functioned as a kind of 'spiritual glue'[24] to bind the enormous mass of objects and facts into a 'whole'.[25] Kugler insisted on the importance of such a notion in order to elevate his enterprise into a higher unity, into something more than a sum of individual chapters. He admonished his readers never to forget 'that the particular receives its primary

20 '[E]ine so grosse Masse von Einzelheiten', Kugler, *Handbuch*, p. X. All translations, unless otherwise cited, are the author's.
21 '[D]as Ganze der Kunstgeschichte', Kugler, *Handbuch*, p. IX
22 Ernst Guhl and Wilhelm Lübke, *Denkmäler der Kunst zur Übersicht ihres Entwickelungs-Ganges von den ersten künstlerischen Versuchen bis zu den Standpunkten der Gegenwart*, Stuttgart: Ebner & Seubert, 4 vols, 1851–1856.
23 Kugler's Handbook opens with a prefatory dedication by the author of his work to King Friedrich Wilhelm IV of Prussia. This section explains the relevance of his work wherein the past serves to understand the present. The latter is, in his words, a time so rich in developments and lofty aspirations in the world of the arts, which appear to be on the threshold of a still higher development. Kugler, *Handbuch*, pp. I–II.
24 Franz Kugler, *Kleine Schriften und Studien zur Kunstgeschichte*, 3 vols, Stuttgart: Ebner & Seubert, 1853, vol. 1, p. 245, cited in Karlholm, *Art of Illusion*, p. 45.
25 The work begins with a discussion of the origins of art in raw, material needs, as: 'jene rohen Denkzeichen … der wirkliche und unmittelbare Ausdruck, wenn zunächst nur des einfachsten Gedankens', Kugler, *Handbuch*, p. 4.

meaning only as part of the whole'.[26] This unity was held to be anchored within a normative essence that forms a myth of origins of culture, whose function it was to ground subsequent cultural achievements, and against which the rest of the world could be measured and located on a developmental ladder.[27] Kugler's contemporary, Schnaase, who also produced a global survey of art in eight volumes, formulated the historicist investment in 'origins' as follows: 'History of our time depends for its formation on that which preceded it and so on until the very dark origins of mankind; an uninterrupted chain of tradition connects us with the first creation.'[28]

Following this model, accounts of world art characterised the so-called pre-classical cultures that made up the first section of their survey through that which they lacked or had not yet achieved, following a mode of argument that Dipesh Chakrabarty has identified as a characteristic of so much of modernist history.[29] In other words, art that is pre-Greek allegedly endeavoured to become 'classical' but did not quite get there. Chapter VII of Kugler's *Handbuch* turns to a discussion of ancient Greece, where art, in the author's words, 'achieved a self-contained perfection', becoming a 'general expression of European culture' whose accomplishments spread to regions of Asia and Africa, a sentiment also echoed by Schnaase.[30] Classicism, as elucidated in these accounts, furnished what Karlholm describes as a 'transhistorical concept of beauty' in tune with the historicism of the narrative.[31] Moreover, Greek civilisation featured in writings on *Weltkunstgeschichte* not as an irretrievably lost ideal, in the way we encounter it in Winckelmann's writings, but as a living expression of modern European culture. Its memories were kept alive by younger monuments such as Leo von Klenze's Walhalla, modelled on the Parthenon, which was inaugurated as a monument to national heroes the same year Kugler's *Handbuch* was published.[32]

The sections and chapters of Kugler's *Handbuch* oscillate between and combine two logics: that of defining the 'general character' (*Gesamtcharakter*) of each period and region or

26 '[D]ass das Einzelne seine vornehmste Bedeutung eben nur als ein Glied des Ganzen hat', Kugler, *Handbuch*, p. XI.

27 Culture was not necessarily regarded as an account of unequivocal progress, but dependent on the 'stage' (*Stufe*) or the scale of civilisation on which a given people found itself. 'Indem wir aber in der allgemeinen Geschichte keineswegs ein gleichmässiges Fortschreiten der Cultur wahrnehmen, indem wir stets neben Völkern, die bereits auf einer höhern Stufe stehen, auch solche erblicken, die sich von niedrigeren, ja von den untersten Stufen noch nicht erhoben haben', Kugler, *Handbuch*, p. 5.

28 'Die Geschichte der heutigen Zeiten verdankt ihre Gestalt der vorhergegangenen und so fort bis in den dunkeln Ursprung des Menschengeschlechtes zurück; eine ununterbrochene Kette der Ueberlieferung verbindet uns mit der ersten Schöpfung.' Carl Schnaase, *Geschichte der bildenden Künste*, 8 vols, Düsseldorf: Verlag Julius Buddeus, p. 1843ff., vol. 1, p. 80.

29 Dipesh Chakrabarty, *Provincializing Europe: Postcolonial Thought and Historical Difference*, Princeton: Princeton University Press, 2000.

30 'Die griechische Kunst gedieh zu einer in sich geschlossenen Vollendung; sie ward – wenn auch wiederum nicht frei von mancher Umwandlung – der allgemeine Ausdruck europäischer Cultur, und soweit im Alterthum diese Cultur in Asien und Afrika ausgebreitet wird, soweit fanden auch ihre Formen Eingang.' Kugler, *Handbuch*, p. 131. Also Schnaase, *Geschichte*, vol. 2, p. 526.

31 Karlholm, *Art of Illusion*, p. 47.

32 Karlholm, ibid., pp. 46–47.

civilisational unit, and of creating a larger unity through an evolutionist scheme that is animated by universal principles. The story of the world's art begins with Celtic grave monuments, proceeds then to Egypt and the Indian subcontinent. Each forms an individual unit and was treated as just that – a separate entity standing for a people and culture through which art could be read; objects have been grouped selectively, often with little regard for location, context, or chronology, with the intention of identifying family resemblances – a common denominator, then identified as specific to culture or cultural temperament. Each group of objects whose function was to testify to a cultural essence would also find its place in the unified domain of art history, whereas agents are missing throughout the account: the survey of world art described its objects rarely as produced by artists, rather by the conditions created for art by a 'cultural situation'.[33] This philosophy has a circularity: art is both an effect and a cause, a product of a culture that makes that culture readable and at the same time a means to improve and 'cultivate'[34] a culture. For instance, the section on the art of the Indian subcontinent in chapter six of the first edition of the *Handbuch* reads it as a product of excessive fantasy emanating from the 'richly populated' realm of religious belief, producing in turn a profusion of forms whose chaotic luxuriance left its stamp on a national character marked by a deficiency in dealing with abstraction.[35] (See also figs. 1, 2)

An opening statement in Kugler's preface to his survey, invariably cited by scholars who have engaged with his work, referred to art history as a 'young' discipline and his book as a map, imagining the world of art to be a kind of natural terrain that could be 'acquired' or 'conquered', and then surveyed, 'cultivated', and taxonomised by art historians.[36] The choice of metaphors, clearly drawn from concepts of territorial sovereignty deployed by modern nation-states, is unmistakably suggestive. Even as Kugler described art history as an uncultivated terrain whose rich resources needed to be exploited, it is also implicit that his book did not survey an already existing field; it rather constituted the field as an object of knowledge to be investigated. While scholars in the past, he asserted, had not been able to create a global account of art history, his work, coming at a particular historical juncture, would be able to respond to a need for a global sense of order, against which to plot the individual nation.[37] In

---

33 '[K]ulturgeschichtliches Moment', Kugler, *Kleine Schriften*, vol. 2, p. 438.

34 Kugler, *Handbuch*, p. X.

35 'Im Charakter des indischen Volkes ist eine grosse Weichheit des Gefühls, eine lebhafte Glut der Phantasie vorherrschend, eine reichgestaltige Götterlehre ... In dieser Einseitigkeit bildet der Charakter des Inders den grössten Gegensatz gegen den des Ägypters, bei dem ebenso entschieden die Thätigkeit des Verstandes vorherrscht. [...]Auf gleiche Weise verhält es sich mit der indischen Kunst, ... die fessellose Phantasie gestattet dem Gefühle nicht die Ruhe, die allein zu einer harmonischen Durchbildung führt; sie häuft Formen auf Formen und endet zuletzt mit dem Eindrucke einer fast chaotischen Verwirrung.' Kugler, *Handbuch*, p. 97.

36 '[D]as Ganze unsrer Wissenschaft ist noch gar jung, es ist ein Reich, mit dessen Eroberung wir noch eben erst beschäftigt sind, dessen Thäler und Wälder wir noch erst zu lichten, dessen wüste Steppen wir noch urbar zu machen haben; da wird noch die mannigfaltigste Thätigkeit für das Einzelne erfordert, da ist es schwer, oft fast unausführbar, ein behagliches geographisches Netz darüber zu legen und Provinzen, Bezirke, Kreise und Weichbilder mit saubern Farbenlinien von einander zu sondern.' Kugler, *Handbuch*, p. X.

37 Kugler, *Handbuch*, pp. IX–XI.

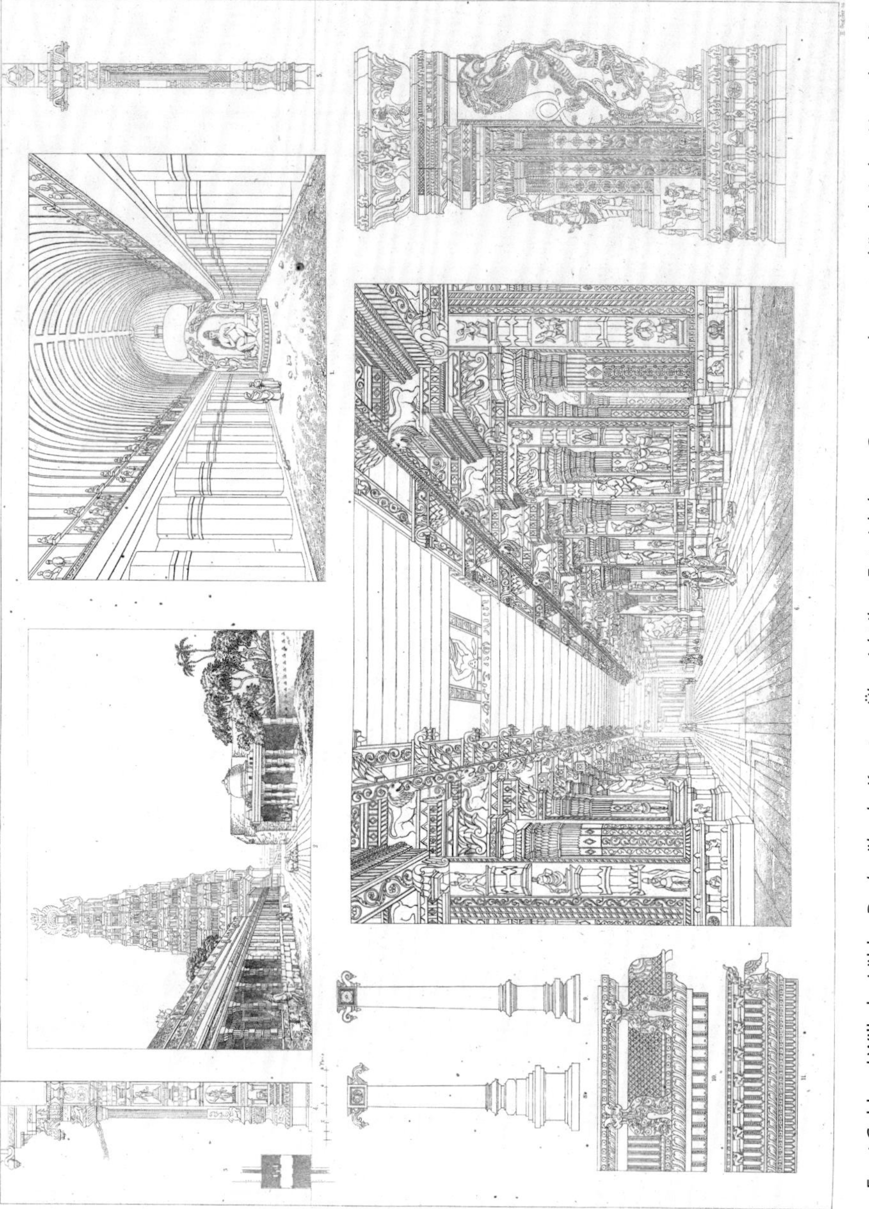

1   Ernst Guhl and Wilhelm Lübke, *Denkmäler der Kunst zur Übersicht ihres Entwickelungs-Ganges von den ersten künstlerischen Versuchen bis zu den Standpunkten der Gegenwart*, Stuttgart: Ebner & Seubert, 1851. Supplement to Franz Kugler, Handbuch der Kunstgeschichte, 1851: Tafel X

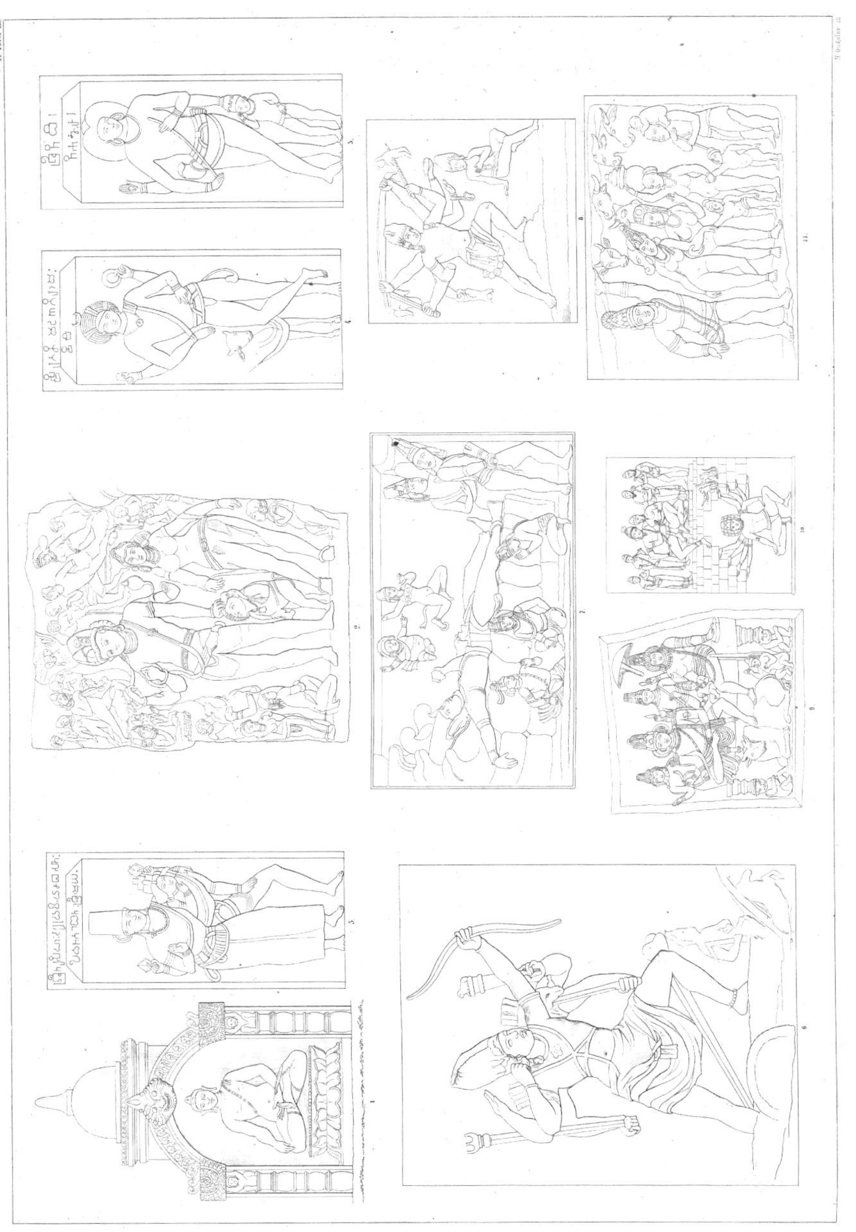

2   Ernst Guhl and Wilhelm Lübke, *Denkmäler der Kunst zur Übersicht ihres Entwickelungs-Ganges von den ersten künstlerischen Versuchen bis zu den Standpunkten der Gegenwart*, Stuttgart: Ebner & Seubert, 1851. Supplement to Franz Kugler, Handbuch der Kunstgeschichte, 1851: Tafel XI

fact, the subordination of individual elements to a 'whole' was as much a cultural-cum-aesthetic attribute as it was a moral and political category, applicable to the subordination of subjects to the nation. Conversely, the growth of a feeling of national coherence in a community, a development he had observed in Germany over the recent decades, would foster an art expressive of national character. Elaborating on the connection between 'universal' art history and nation building, Christine Tauber argues that Kugler's work was animated by the spirit of German national unification; it was carried more by national feeling than any theoretical reflection on the nation as a political entity. Responding to problems surrounding the unification of German states in the 1840s, Kugler launched a polemic against the 'unwholesome inclination of the German mind towards sectionalism/particularism'.[38] At the same time, he argued, to create the desirable close relationship between national character and art, the latter needed to be purged of its 'aristocratic element' and make place for the 'democratic'.[39] The art of the world, also classified as nations, could serve as a foil for German art, the cultural glue binding the nation.

While Kugler narrated his story of world art as partaking of an evolutionary scheme articulated through a society's monuments, his contemporary Schnaase conceptualised his equally ambitious *Geschichte der bildenden Künste* as an account of the mentality of the human race. His enterprise was motivated by a search for a philosophical-cum-aesthetic, synoptic vision for art and culture. This, he hoped, would lead to a far-reaching understanding of national traditions of art and the styles each brought forth. Schnaase's survey ended up being more selective than Kugler's of the peoples and cultures he chose to study, delving instead into the 'deeper historical and philosophical underpinnings of styles'.[40] To this end he took recourse to the Hegelian notion of a 'people's spirit' (*Volksgeist*) as a lens through which to grasp the unity he envisioned between people and religion, culture and nation, art and history.[41] His generalisations about a culture's art were frequently drawn from preconceived

38   '[U]nguten Hang des deutschen Geistes zum Partikularismus', Christine Tauber, '"Das Ganze der Kunstgeschichte": Franz Kuglers universalhistorische Handbücher', in Wolfgang Hardtwig and Philipp Müller (eds), *Die Vergangenheit der Weltgeschichte: universalhistorisches Denken in Berlin 1800–1933*, Göttingen: Vandenhoek & Ruprecht, 2010, pp. 90–121, here pp. 115. Addition by the author.

39   Kugler, *Kleine Schriften*, vol. 3, p. 406.

40   Schnaase introduces his eight-volume survey of world art with an extensive discussion of the sources of 'beauty' and aesthetics: Schnaase, *Geschichte der bildenden Künste.*, vol. 1, pp. 1–96.
     In his article 'Kunstgeschichte' for volume 8 of the *Brockhaus-Konversations-Lexikon* (9th edition, 1845), Jacob Burckhardt wrote: 'Erst in der allerneuesten Zeit haben wir eine allgemeine Kunstgeschichte erhalten in Kugler's "Handbuch der Kunstgeschichte" (Stuttg. 1842 fg.), welches das ungeheure Material in einer großen Übersichtlichkeit zusammenfaßt und den weltgeschichtlichen Epochen unterordnet. Eine Ergänzung derselben bildet Schnaase's "Geschichte der bildenden Kunst bei den Alten" (Bd. 1–3, Düsseld. 1843–44), welche weniger auf vollständige Aufzählung, als auf tiefsinnige geschichts-philosophische Begründung der Stile und Übergänge gerichtet ist.' Cited in: Henrik Karge, 'Die Kunst ist nicht das Maaß der Geschichte: Karl Schnaases Einfluß auf Jacob Burckhardt', *Archiv für Kulturgeschichte*, 78, 1996: 393–431, here 412.

41   Gregor Stemmrich, 'C. Schnaase: Rezeption und Transformation Berlinischen Geistes in der kunsthistorischen Forschung', in Otto Pöggeler and Annemarie Gethmann-Siefert (eds), *Kunsterfahrung und Kulturpolitik in Berlin Hegels*, Bonn: Bouvier, 1983, pp. 263–84, here p. 268.

understandings of religious and mythological texts that were then transferred to the arts, as for instance his claim that Islamic art's combination of exuberant ornament and despotic form reflected the Qur'an's juxtaposition of severe monotheism and excessive sensuousness.[42] At the same time, he considered a study of Islamic, Byzantine, Carolingian, and early Christian art to be interesting and relevant, as such an investigation would enable a better understanding of 'epochs of more mature artistic accomplishment'.[43]

Together with textual expositions, a selection of which have been presented above, the historicist paradigm of a cultural history of world art depended equally on visual media to co-produce a pedagogy to study world art. While the first two editions of Kugler's *Handbuch* – recast in 1860 into a more comprehensive version, the *Grundriss der Kunstgeschichte* authored by Wilhelm Lübke (1826–1893) – were unillustrated, the Stuttgart publishing company Ebner and Seuber set out in 1845 to produce a visual supplement to both the surveys. In 1851, the first section of *Denkmäler der Kunst* appeared – an immense compendium in four volumes of engraved images to accompany, visualise, and reinforce the textual narrative of Kugler's *Handbuch*.[44] Each plate of the *Denkmäler* reproduced not single works, but some fifteen, juxtaposed in rows on a single page. They were all line engravings that ended up reducing forms to outlines, largely suppressing nuances through their linearity. Above all, they make it difficult for the viewer to ascertain the medium – whether drawing, painting, sculpture, mosaic, or architectural fragment – of the object, nor did the editors of the compendium provide any information about the size or material of the numerous objects reproduced on each page. Though the textual narratives that the 'atlas of images', as it was also designated, was meant to supplement were devoted to showing a developmental sequence within the world's art, the predominant mode of visual display rendered this difficult to grasp. Yet, it would be useful to ask what such an arrangement of 'monuments' of art might contribute to the art historical argument of the survey text, instead of dismissing its visualisations as a deficient mimetic exercise. Making a pertinent distinction between 'reproduction' and 'illustration' – between 'producing a duplicate' and 'bringing something else to light' –, Dan Karlholm has argued that such a systematic arrangement of objects on the white pages of the collection could offer the viewer 'an art-historical argument', something the physical objects could not. Art, evacuated of its historical context, could then be 're-historicized' within the discursive space of art history to show those family resemblances and underline the common denominator, that is 'art', that cements the unified 'whole'.[45] This said, however, it remains that the main argument of the art historical narrative of world art that regarded each work as

42 Schnaase, *Geschichte der bildenden Künste*, vol. 3, pp. 325–26.

43 Cited by Marchand, *German Orientalism*, p. 392.

44 Ernst Guhl and Wilhelm Lübke, *Denkmäler der Kunst zur Übersicht ihres Entwickelungs-Ganges von den ersten künstlerischen Versuchen bis zu den Standpunkten der Gegenwart*, Stuttgart: Ebner & Seubert, 1851. An English translation appeared – according to Karlholm – around 1880, as *Monuments of Art: Showing its Development and Progress from the Earliest Attempts to the Present Period*, 2 vols, New York: E. Seitz (n.d.). For details, Karlholm, *Art of Illusion*, pp. 66–68.

45 Dan Karlhom, 'Reading the Virtual Museum of General Art History', *Art History*, vol. 24 (4), 2001: 552–77, here 561–63.

a lens to read a particular stage of cultural development could not have been made without the work of the text for the vital connection between art and culture to be decipherable.

Art, Nation, Culture

Though largely underestimated, the formative power of surveys of world art made itself felt in writings of the time, including those that cannot, strictly speaking, be subsumed under the genre of an encompassing art historical overview. One example of such a study – that occupies a transitional position between the earlier and later iterations of *Weltkunstgeschichte* – is Jacob Burckhardt's *Die Kultur der Renaissance in Italien* of 1860 that has now acquired the status of a classic for scholars in the humanities studying the Renaissance.[46] Burckhardt's conviction that studying a particular cultural period called for an understanding of the 'world' drew explicitly on writings on world art that strove to expand the scope of a still young discipline beyond the study of a few canonized themes and places.[47] Kugler's treatment of different world cultures as representing intermediate stages between the 'childhood' of humanity and 'true art' has direct historical links with Burckhardt's treatment of the Italian Renaissance.[48] The *Handbuch der Kunstgeschichte* evolved in collaboration with Burckhardt, who provided additional text and illustrations for the second edition of 1848. This edition divides world art into early art, classical art, medieval and modern art, and was illustrated under Burckhardt's supervision. In 1867, Burckhardt's observations on Italian architecture appeared in the fourth volume of Kugler's general history of architecture. The extensive collaboration between the two scholars, extending over many years, allows us to get an insight

46   The bicentennial celebrations of Burckhardt in 2018 have brought forth fresh reappraisals of his oeuvre. In addition to Beyer, Burghartz and Burkart (eds), *Burckhardt.Renaissance*, see Stefan Bauer and Simon Ditchfield (eds), *A Renaissance Reclaimed. Jacob Burckhardt's Civilisation of the Renaissance in Italy Reconsidered*, Oxford: Oxford University Press, 2022.

47   In the course of recent discussions about the relevance of Burckhardt's writings to the global turn in the humanities, the historian Jürgen Osterhammel – on the basis of Burckhardt's lectures 'Über das Studium der Geschichte', later published as 'Weltgeschichtliche Betrachtungen' – makes a case for the methodological lessons – 'eine in Bewegung gehaltene Morphologie von Mikroprozessen' – this work holds for practitioners of global/world history. He, however, qualifies his insights by the caveat that though Burckhardt can neither be considered a precursor of a modern generation of scholars of global history nor did he possess an in-depth knowledge of any region of the world beyond Europe, his thinking as a historian was shaped by an awareness of the global entanglements of his time. See Jürgen Osterhammel, *Jacob Burckhardts 'Über das Studium der Geschichte' und die Weltgeschichtsschreibung der Gegenwart*, Basel: Schwabe Verlag, 2019, p. 71.
Burckhardt's own views on the value of bringing the 'world' to bear on the study of art and culture were emphatically expressed in his article 'Kunstgeschichte' written for the 1845 edition of the *Brockhaus Konversations-Lexikon*, in which he juxtaposed Kugler's *Handbuch* to Schnaase's *Geschichte*, declaring them both to be pioneering studies, at the same time examples of two different approaches to the challenging task of organizing the extraordinary volume of world art into a clearly structured survey. Jacob Burckhardt, 'Kunstgeschichte', in *Allgemeine deutsche Real-Enzyklopädie für die gebildeten Stände: Conversations-Lexikon*, 15 vols, 9th edition, Leipzig: Brockhaus, 1843–1848, vol. 8, pp. 435–36.

48   '[D]er Mensch in Zeiten seiner Kindheit', 'Kunst in der höheren und eigentlichen Bedeutung des Wortes', Kugler, *Handbuch*, pp. 3–4.

into the formation of art historical taxonomies and modes of reading the nexus of art, nation, and culture that emerged from this joint work and has informed the discipline through its subsequent trajectories.

Yet, to avoid a short-circuited, reductionist reading, we need to first look at the apparent differences in the approaches of the two. While Kugler's *Handbuch* was animated by the spirit of an emerging, unified German nation, Burckhardt, whose writings on the Renaissance partly grew out of Kugler's work that he edited and supplemented, took a clear stance against the bureaucratic apparatus of the nation-state as embodied in Bismarckian state-craft.[49] It is therefore equally necessary that his study of Italian culture in the fifteenth century be re-contextualised in the setting of nineteenth-century nationalist politics. As has been often observed, Burckhardt's *Die Kultur der Renaissance* appeared only a year before Italy was unified as a monarchy and eleven years before the establishment of the unified German *Kaiserreich*. His book attacked the papacy for its weak attempts to impose unity through institutional control, while praising the existence of local communities.[50] To Burck-hardt the national community was ideally held together not by a bureaucratic structure but a common spirit and a set of common interests. He developed this stance by harking back to early modern times and arguing that the Italian nation had been in the process of formation since early Humanism: we are offered an eloquent paean to the achievements of civic com-munities like Florence, where Burckhardt discerned the germinating ground of true nations.[51] The final chapter of the first section, 'Das Italien der Patrioten', contains an impassioned plea that the nation be defined by a few highly instructed men.[52]

The first section of *Die Kultur der Renaissance* is intriguingly entitled 'Der Staat als Kunstwerk', 'The State as a Work of Art'. The choice of such a metaphor articulates a particu-lar understanding of a work of art; in doing so, it cements the nexus between a political and an aesthetic concept that is not without implications for the scholarly and institutional practice of art history. While delineating the genealogy of the notion of art across several centuries, Claire Farago has traced the modes of separating artistic genres; she connects what Leonardo da Vinci and others following him classified as the 'liberal arts' and inextricably associated with the notion of public virtue.[53] Burckhardt's description of Humanism too connected public taste with public virtue. His use of a political metaphor transmits this meaning to the state which he describes as an outcome of reflection and calculation – 'der Staat als berechnete,

---

49 Wolfgang Hardtwig, *Geschichtsschreibung zwischen Alteuropa und moderner Welt: Jacob Burckhardt in seiner Zeit*, Göttingen: Vandenhoeck & Ruprecht, 1974, p. 290ff.

50 Jacob Burckhardt, *Die Kultur der Renaissance in Italien*, (1860), Stuttgart: A. Kröner Verlag, 2009, pp. 2–3.

51 Burckhardt, *Die Kultur*, p. 158ff.

52 Burckhardt, ibid, pp. 105–6.

53 Claire J. Farago, *Leonardo da Vinci's Paragone. A Critical Interpretation with a New Edition of the Text in the Codex Urbinas*, Leiden: Brill, 1992, p. 373ff.; also Claire J. Farago, '"Vision Itself Has Its History": "Race", Nation and Renaissance Art', in Claire J. Farago (ed.), *Reframing the Renaissance: Visual Cul-ture in Europe and Latin America 1450–1650*, New Haven: Yale University Press, 1995, pp. 67–88, here pp. 72–74.

bewußte Schöpfung, als Kunstwerk'.[54] Thus, the arts of painting and sculpture are both contingent on as well as constitutive of an idea of the public that he perceived to be in danger of being lost in his age. Art would then serve as a foundation of the nation, given its potential to reveal citizenship to those freed from mechanical labours to practice public virtue. In this decisive domain, Burckhardt's conception carried forward the clear separation of the 'crafts' from the 'fine arts' that informs Kugler's survey of world art. A later work by Burckhardt, the *Weltgeschichtliche Betrachtungen* (1868), locates art as an entity within culture representing a distillation of the creative, edifying, and eternal that separates the extraordinary from the mediocre, 'the most elevated level of the reflective spirit' from the 'lowest technical activity'.[55]

Art historical experiments in placing art of the world within a structured developmental scheme were one important component within other strands of aesthetic thought which, when brought together with a concept of the nation that Burckhardt projected backwards on the Italian states of the fifteenth century, shaped the formation of his idea of a cultural Renaissance. Equally important was his dependence on the nexus between culture and the nation expressed in the writings of Johann Gottfried Herder (1744–1803) on comparative national literatures: the latter postulate that each culture, each language, remains discreet, bounded and incommensurable with any other. The assumption that cultural differences between individual, contained units were also an expression of hierarchies formed the underpinnings of all surveys of world art during Burckhardt's time. The nation or national character that in turn accounted for a cultural outlook was an organising principle for comprehensive art historical accounts of the mid-nineteenth century though – in the case of Europe – these units did not correspond to the political map of the time. Such an approach came to be cemented, even as Europe was well into three centuries of lived entanglement with large areas of the world that had brought forth innumerable encounters and migrations, most often within a context of the expansion of European interests. Studies of the Florentine art world, for instance, point to a complex mix of cultural forces at work there since the fifteenth century, when the work of Florentine painters was viewed and received alongside that of Netherlandish and Burgundian artists. Further, extensive cultural exchange between the Italian states and the Ottoman Empire is a significant aspect that recent research has not failed to highlight.[56] Confronted with the paradox between entangled worlds and a hermeti-

---

54 Burckhardt, *Die Kultur*, p. 6.
55 '[D]ie Weckung der höchsten Kräfte … vom höchsten geistigen', 'geringsten technischen Treiben', see discussion on art in Jacob Burckhardt, *Weltgeschichtliche Betrachtungen*, (1868), Munich: Beck Verlag, 2018, pp. 68–72, here p. 72.
56 Matthew Rampley, 'Construction of National Art Histories and "New" Europe', in: Matthew Rampley, Thierry Lenain, Hubert Locher et al. (eds), *Art and Visual Studies in Europe: Transnational Discourses and National Frameworks*, Leiden: Brill, 2012, p. 238; also Daniel Savoy (ed.), *The Globalization of Renaissance Art: A Critical Review*, Leiden: Brill, 2017; Jerry Brotton, *The Renaissance Bazaar: From the Silk Road to Michelangelo*, Oxford: Oxford University Press, 2003; Lisa Jardine and Jerry Brotton, *Global Interests: Renaissance Art between East and West*, London: Reaktion Books, 2000; Anna Contadini and Claire Norton (eds), *The Renaissance and the Ottoman World*, Farnham, Surrey: Ashgate Publishing, 2013.

cally sealed conception of culture, art historical scholarship of the subsequent decades had to look to a revitalised discipline through which to access the art of the world.

Art History as 'Exact Science'

Faced with a growing anxiety about the status of their discipline, often perceived as being overly dependent on history, leading art historians of the second half of the nineteenth century set out to redefine art history as a 'science' – as *Kunstwissenschaft* rather than *Kunstgeschichte*. The term *Kunstwissenschaft* carries a connotation of not only 'science', but also scholarship, as a path to exactitude rather than a 'purely literary pursuit', to cite Moritz Thausing (1838–1884), the first occupant of the chair in the history of art instituted at the University of Vienna in 1873.[57] Like Kugler before him, Thausing too defined art history as a 'young' discipline, but at the same time an 'exact science' that in his view was more closely related to classical archaeology than to aesthetics. Its new scientific profile, enhanced through practices such as archaeological documentation, formal and technical analysis as well as iconological methods, would secure art history from the charge of dilettantism, from being a mere pursuit of 'subjective' preferences when writing about art.[58] In 1891, the ethnologist and philosopher at the University of Freiburg, Ernst Grosse (1862–1927), carried the discussion further, making a powerful programmatic argument that ethnology, defined broadly as 'the science of peoples and nations', would foster a scientific approach to the study of aesthetic matters. In an article entitled 'Ethnologie und Ästhetik', he argued that art theory, by drawing on ethnology, would be able to transcend its Eurocentric bias, abandon its speculative character and come closer to the spirit of the natural sciences; this would in fact lead up to a revitalisation of the humanities.[59] Three years later, Grosse published *Die Anfänge der Kunst*, a landmark text that articulated the new methodological framing of *Weltkunstgeschichte*.[60]

Within a reinvigorated art history that looked more towards the social sciences for its methodological impulses, *Weltkunstgeschichte* acquired a fresh momentum in the works of a second generation of scholars. The remarkable expansion of archaeological activity – that often accompanied infrastructural projects such as the building of railroads – together with growing trade in artefacts after the 1870s posed a fresh challenge to those involved in exhibiting, classifying and interpreting art from sites beyond Europe. The following decades saw the efflorescence of museums whose budgets expanded enormously – the urge to acquire and display was not only propelled by a competition among nations, it coincided with

<hr>

57   Moritz Thausing, 'Die Stellung der Kunstgeschichte als Wissenschaft: Aus der Antrittsvorlesung an der Wiener Universität im Oktober 1873', *Wiener Jahrbuch für Kunstgeschichte*, 36, 1983: 140–50. For an English translation by Karl Johns: Moritz Thausing, 'The Status of Art History as an Academic Discipline', *Journal of Art Historiography*, vol. 1, 2009: 5–22.
58   Thausing, 'Die Stellung der Kunstgeschichte'.
59   Ernst Grosse, 'Ethnologie und Ästhetik', *Vierteljahrsschrift für wissenschaftliche Philosophie*, 15, 1891: 392–417.
60   Ernst Grosse, *Die Anfänge der Kunst*, Freiburg: J. C. B. Mohr, 1894. English translation by F. Starr, *The Beginnings of Art*, New York: Appleton, 1987.

the historicist desire to possess one of every possible type of object, to be able to document every step in a developmental process. At the same time, museums and collectors, seized by the anxiety that the so-designated primitive cultures of the world were on the way to being irretrievably transformed by modernisation, embarked on a race to acquire whatever was possible and to build up collections that would feed into scholarship.[61] This phase in museum-building saw the foundation of new ethnographic museums, most importantly the Berlin museum of ethnography (*Königliches Museum für Völkerkunde*), conceived in 1873, officially opened in 1886. Its possessions, which had been building up for years before the museum was officially instituted, offered an indiscriminating mix: they included collections such as those of Leo Frobenius from Africa that rubbed shoulders with Benin bronzes, Inca mummies, large quantities of metalwork from West Asia, and Heinrich Schliemann's Troy treasure. In addition to museums in metropolises such as Hamburg, Leipzig, and Munich, the decades following the 1870s saw the founding of ethnological museums in smaller or middle-size cities of the newly established Deutsches Kaiserreich, such as Bremen, Lübeck, Kassel, Darmstadt, Karlsruhe, Freiburg, Stuttgart, Dresden, Cologne, and Frankfurt.[62] Energetic competition to acquire the material culture of peoples from distant corners of the world soon led to overfilled rooms and basements; most visitors experienced a visit to a museum as an odyssey through halls that were jumbled and confused. Lamenting the state of Berlin's museum in 1901, an observer queried: 'Should these scientific collections from throughout the world be permitted to be mixed together like cabbage and turnips?'[63] For the world of scholarship, however, these collections enjoyed a singular value. Ethnologists were an important group who now claimed ethnographic museums as places exclusively to conserve the artefacts of the *Naturvölker*, arguing that their collections would serve as a laboratory for studying the world's most primeval cultures through their objects. It is therefore not surprising that art historians – notably the proponents of *Weltkunstgeschichte* – looked to archaeology and ethnology as key disciplines that would aid art history in its ambition to place the study of the relationship between art and culture on a systematic, scientific footing.[64] While Adolf Bastian, who was named the Directorial Assistant of the Royal Ethnographic Collection in 1869 and subsequently Director of the Berlin Museum of Ethnography, took steps to separate the collection of 'ethnographic' objects from those classified as 'antiquities' or 'art', now housed on the Museum Island in Berlin, historians of 'world art', such as Grosse or the Austrian scholar and artist, Alois Hein, as well as scholars such as Frobenius, all sought to reclaim the status of 'art' for those artefacts that they chose as their objects of investigation.

---

61 Ethnographers used the term 'Europeanisation' to refer to the radical cultural effects of colonisation and expanding international trade on regions of the world that till recently had remained in a pristine stage of civilisation, see Glenn Penny, 'Municipal Displays. Civic Self-Promotion and the Development of German Ethnographic Museums, 1870–14', *Social Anthropology*, vol. 6 (2), 1998: 157–68, here 160.

62 See Hog, *Ziele und Konzeptionen*, pp. 8–19.

63 Cited in Penny, 'Municipal Displays': 165.

64 Ernst Grosse designated the relationship between 'art and culture' as the prime subject matter of *Kunstwissenschaft*: 'Die wesentliche Aufgabe der Kunstwissenschaft besteht in der Erforschung der gesetzmässigen Beziehung zwischen Kunst und Cultur', Grosse, 'Ethnologie und Ästhetik': 416.

An important consideration animating the concern to write an inclusive art history incorporating all regions and peoples of the world and going back in time to the beginnings of humanity – that is, far beyond Classical Antiquity or even the age of the Pyramids[65] – was related to evolution. One pressing concern was to find a way in which art could serve as a criterion to register the humanity of its creator, to be able to locate human beings on the evolutionary ladder higher than animals. The search for the origins of art was equally linked to the question whether the earliest forms of art were a biological or a cultural phenomenon. These issues informed the study of art's origins, *Die Anfänge der Kunst*, authored by Grosse, Professor at the University of Freiburg as well as the Curator of the ethnological collection there. The prime subject matter of *Kunstwissenschaft* was, in Grosse's view, to study the systematic relationship between 'art and culture' crucial to the understanding of any art form; this in turn necessitated comparative studies of all cultures of the world in order to avoid the trap of theorising on the basis of a few selected examples from Western Europe. Only ethnology, he argued, could provide this methodological orientation, as it was an intrinsically comparative science that investigated the world's various 'peoples' or 'nations' in the totality of their environmental and socio-cultural settings.[66]

Proponents of a methodologically revamped *Weltkunstgeschichte* during the late nineteenth century argued that all cultures or peoples produce 'art': objects earlier designated as curios, trophies, idols, or cave drawings were now all subsumed under the category of art and seen as scientific data requiring documentation according to taxonomic principles. In *Die Anfänge der Kunst* Grosse recognised art or aesthetic sensibility as a human universal, a criterion to distinguish humans from animals. Though the discussion on art as a characteristic of the human species emerged as a lively one in the wake of Darwinian thought, it had a prehistory dating to the eighteenth century. In his *Abhandlung über den Ursprung der Sprache* (Treatise on the Origin of Language) Herder posited a clear distinction between the capacities of humans and animals along the division between reason and sense, between the capacity for abstraction and sensual perception. The idea of a 'humanist teleology', that is, the belief in the necessity of human development, also meant a hierarchy within humanity, among its diverse peoples who each strove towards 'constantly increasing perfection'; the notion continued to enjoy a reception through the following century, even as art history shifted its affiliation from aesthetics to the social and natural sciences.[67] For Grosse, building on Herder, universalism did not preclude cultural relativism: while aesthetic sensibility was

---

65 Evidently referring to the writings of earlier exponents of *Weltkunstgeschichte* such as Kugler and Schnaase who took the monuments of Egypt as the starting point of their enquiry into world art, Grosse cautioned against conflating the beginnings of art with its entry into history: 'wenn man meint, in dem griechischen Epos oder in der altegyptischen Architektur eine ausreichende Basis für Theorien über die Anfänge der Kunst gefunden zu haben, so vergisst man, dass die Anfänge der Kunst in der Geschichte keineswegs identisch sind mit den Anfängen der Kunst überhaupt.' Grosse, 'Ethnologie und Ästhetik': 413.

66 Grosse, 'Ethnologie und Ästhetik': 402; Grosse, *Die Anfänge der Kunst*, pp. 19–20.

67 Herder cited in Susanne Leeb, 'Primitivism and Humanist Teleology in Art History around 1900', *Journal of Art Historiography*, vol. 12, 2015: n.p.

acknowledged as a human universal, it was held to go hand in hand with differences in taste, in development and aesthetic feeling, which necessitated methods of explanation.

Die Anfänge der Kunst adopted a two-pronged approach: an empirical approach, coming from ethnology, rather than a speculative one alleged as a dimension of aesthetics; this was at the same time a bottom-up ('von unten') approach that took as its starting point and focus the object itself.[68] A close scrutiny of the object rather than texts bespoke an anti-humanist position that sought to revolt against classical philology that had long dominated art historical studies. The emphasis of Grosse, and following him Josef Strzygowski (see below), on objects as a clue to the development of a particular group of people or society was fully in keeping with archaeological findings and the collecting practices of the time. Based primarily in the new ethnological museums, the examination of objects was considered by an ethnographically informed art history to show the 'objective' route to the study of humanity. The examination of objects was undertaken to uncover the 'aesthetic feeling' (*ästhetische Gefühle*). 'Aesthetic products' (*ästhetische Objekte*) are objects that embody and evoke aesthetic feelings they expressed; this was inferred from their visual properties and not through an examination of either the underlying aesthetic principles or their method of production.[69]

Here, factors of geography, climate, and customs came into play; they were meant to help make sense of the choices people exercised and lead from there to the formulation of laws of artistic development, including form, taste, and talent. To do so principles of evolution were harnessed to provide the explanatory framework for cultural difference. Grosse claimed an intellectual genealogy for his methods that comprised of the writings of scholars such as the French historians and philosophers Hippolyte Taine and Jean-Baptiste Dubos and the English biologist Grant Allen (the author of *Physiological Aesthetics*, 1877).[70] Drawing on these sources, his argument was as follows: while art is a primordial biological urge ('*Spieltrieb*', a 'ludic drive'), it undergoes cultural differentiation according to stages of development and becomes a 'mimetic urge' ('*Nachahmungstrieb*').[71] Appropriating Taine's application of the Darwinian theory of natural selection to art history was a further way to anchor art history's authority firmly as a science.

The terms used in the discussion of cultural differences, of attributes of different people across the world are instructive: '*Völker*' (peoples) is the most frequently used, the term subsumes both physical and cultural characteristics and is used interchangeably with 'race' and 'nation'. Together they add up to a concept of culture – enclosed within the territorial formation of the nation that subsumes race under cultural difference and ethnicity. Having to grapple with the complexity of humanity, the idea of race went in this context beyond skin

68 Grosse, 'Ethnologie und Ästhetik': 399–400.
69 Grosse, 'Ethnologie und Ästhetik': 398–400; Wilfried van Damme, 'Ernst Grosse and the Birth of the Anthropology of Aesthetics', *Anthropos: International Review of Anthropology and Linguistics*, vol. 107 (2), 2012: 497–509.
70 Grosse, *Anfänge der Kunst*, p. 12ff.; Wilfried van Damme, 'Ernst Grosse and the "Ethnological Method" in Art History', *Philosophy and Literature*, vol. 34 (2), 2010: 302–12, here 308.
71 Grosse, *Anfänge der Kunst*, p. 294.

colour and blood ties, to be conflated with climate, beliefs, habits, morals – and aesthetics. The nexus of race-nation-culture of which art, the aesthetic domain, is an articulation and a marker becomes one of the main planks of modern art history. The writings on world art investigated here abound with observations about '*nationaler Geschmack*' (national taste) or '*nationale Geschmacksdifferenzen*': about Germans who are fonder of music while the French love form and colour, hence painting and sculpture, or that the drawings of the Aborigines of Australia owed their high artistic quality to the developed, sharp visual sense and finely tuned motoric capacities of peoples who lived by hunting and gathering.[72] In the discussion of such differences as well as the shifts within fields of artistic endeavour – literature, art, music, architecture – across time, that is, the study of national taste that undergoes transformation, it became important to find an explanatory paradigm adequate to comprehending stylistic change. Here, 'the developmental history of art' ('*die Entwicklungsgeschichte der Kunst*')[73] comes into play, corresponding to evolutionary classificatory schemes that typologized the world's cultures ranging from 'savage to 'civilised'.

The distinction between 'peoples of nature' and 'peoples of culture' ('*Naturvölker u. Culturvölker*') was a key conceptual category underpinning the thinking about 'culture' in scholarly discourses of the late nineteenth and twentieth centuries. Woodruff Smith draws attention to its early appearance in German-language writing with the entry 'culture' (*Cultur*) in the third edition of the *Staats-Lexikon* (1860), authored by the prominent liberal journalist and politician Karl Biedermann. It was only in the third edition of the *Staats-Lexikon* that the rubric *Cultur* was treated as a distinct subject, for earlier editions assimilated it to *Bildung*. Positing a binary opposition between culture and nature, Biedermann defined 'nature' as the 'physical universe' governed by forces beyond human control while culture encompassed those dimensions of existence 'created by the higher spiritual/mental powers of humans'. 'History', in turn, 'is the transference of steady cultural progress from race to race'.[74] According to Smith, Biedermann sought to bring together different approaches of mid-century cultural scientists within his definition. He tried, for instance, to integrate the idea that the power to tame nature was a key aspect of culture with the claim that culture was universal to humans, progressed continuously, and was passed from one people to another, anticipating thereby elements of evolution as well as diffusionist thought.[75] Within the domain of culture, now used in an anthropological sense, humanity's progressive achievements lent

72 Grosse, 'Ethnologie und Ästhetik': 405–10.
73 Grosse, ibid: 413.
74 'Unter dem Worte Cultur begreift man alles dasjenige, was durch die höhern geistgen Kräfte des Menschen geschaffen wird. Die Cultur bildet daher zu der Natur – dieses letztere Wort in dem engern Sinne verstanden, wonach es nur die mit blinder Nothwendigkeit wirkende Kräfte unter Ausschluß eben jener freischaffenden geistigen bezeichnet – einen Gegensatz oder, richtiger gesagt, eine Ergänzung und Fortsetzung … die Geschichte ist die Überlieferung des stetigen Culturfortschritts von Geschlecht zu Geschlecht.' Karl Biedermann, 'Cultur', in: Karl von Rotteck and Karl Welcker (eds.), *Das Staats-Lexikon: Encyklopädie der sämmtlichen Staatswissenschaften für alle Stände*, 14 vols, Leipzig: Brockhaus, 1860, vol. 4, pp. 227–39, here pp. 227–28. Also Woodruff D. Smith, *Politics and the Sciences of Culture in Germany*, New York: Oxford University Press, 1991, pp. 69–71.
75 Smith, *Politics and the Sciences*, p. 70.

themselves to a hierarchical ordering from the 'highest' to the 'lowest', the latter the domain of the 'people of nature'.[76] Such a position constituted a break from historicist thinking of the nineteenth century that had insisted on a clear separation between the realms of the non-historical – i.e. the domain of nature, that of necessity – from that of history – the realm of culture, of freedom. *Naturvölker*, 'peoples without history' were denied individual agency and memory.[77] An anthropological understanding of culture, informed by evolutionist thinking, eschewed such a cleavage between civilisation and its absence, positing instead the spiritual unity of humanity, while making allowance for different levels of the capacity to reason within the human conglomeration. Ethnological theory in Germany grafted onto this understanding the related concept of diffusionism, which postulated that cultural elements and material innovations were created only once and then could spread through processes of transformation, which in turn could be documented even in the absence of written records.[78] Such a spread however did not converge in an overall linear pattern of human development.

Such distinctions and definitions continued to be further cemented and refined over the course of the century and left their impact on art historical thinking. In *Stilfragen*, published in 1893, the art historian Riegl distinguished two sets of 'peoples of nature' – those no longer surviving and those of the 'present', whose existence belonged to a much earlier stage of civilisation.[79] An important landmark was the book *Naturvölker und Kulturvölker* authored by the philosopher Alfred Vierkandt (1867–1953) and published in 1896. Here, Vierkandt begins with an enumeration – that builds on other contemporary writings – of the polar opposites that define the two: predilection for sensual enjoyment versus capacity for abstract reasoning, passive versus active, blind submission to forces of nature versus rationality, acts of will and control that enabled a subjection of the planet to human rule; rigidity versus dynamism; instability versus stability.[80] Vierkandt further subdivided the *Kulturvölker* into those who could be classified as 'full cultures' and those as 'half cultures' ('*Halbkulturvölker*' and '*Vollkulturvölker*').[81] It is against this background that Grosse deployed the concept of the 'primitive', to designate the *Naturvölker* of the present, that is, those who still were living through a stage of the past in the full light of the present and could serve as an available model to understand humanity's phased cultural development. These included the Aborigines of Australia, or peoples of Africa and Oceania, or the Americas, living societies of the present, colonised by Western powers, yet said to be frozen

76 Biedermann, 'Cultur', p. 230.

77 Jürgen Osterhammel, '"Peoples Without History" in British and German Historical Thought', in: Benedikt Stuchtey and Peter Wende (eds.), *British and German Historiography 1750–1950: Traditions, Perceptions, and Transfers*, Oxford: Oxford University Press, 2000, pp. 265–87, here 272–74.

78 Karl-Heinz Kohl, *Ethnologie: Die Wissenschaft vom kulturell Fremden: Eine Einführung*, Munich: C. H. Beck, 1993, cited in Osterhammel, '"Peoples Without History"', p. 281.

79 Alois Riegl, *Stilfragen: Grundlegungen zu einer Geschichte der Ornamentik*, Berlin: Siemens, 1893, p. 17, cited in Leeb, 'Primitivism and Humanist Teleology': note 7.

80 Alfred Vierkandt, *Naturvölker und Kulturvölker: ein Beitrag zur Sozialpsychologie*, Leipzig: Duncker und Humblot, 1896, pp. 1–2.

81 Vierkandt, *Naturvölker und Kulturvölker*, p. 11.

in an immemorial past: 'living fossils' was how they were described in *Die Anfänge der Kunst* that devoted an entire chapter to this group.[82]

The dissolution of the opposition between art and ethnology that had decisively oriented the direction of *Weltkunstgeschichte* during the last quarter of the nineteenth century took a fresh turn during the early years of the twentieth. A growing intellectual critique of the pernicious effects of German colonialism in South West Africa as well as Oceania brought in its wake the advocacy of a 'scientific colonisation', wherein colonisers came to see their role as that of developing the potentialities of native inhabitants 'out of nature' to become 'productive contributors to the German *Kulturstaat*'.[83] One concrete dimension of the revision of colonial methods was a castigation of ethnological collecting *en masse* accompanied by endeavours to revalorise the artistic capabilities of the colonised. Art historians and critics now spoke for counteracting anthropology by taking recourse to an 'evaluative aesthetics', as the art historian and ethnologist, Eckart von Sydow (1885–1942), wrote in 1923.[84] Such a revaluation meant singling out individual objects from the mass to frame them aesthetically, as the art critic Carl Einstein (1885–1940) did when he photographed these from ethnological collections to reprint in his book *Negerplastik*.[85] This trend in turn triggered a debate on the naming and classification of objects followed among museums, bringing forth suggestions such as that to rename the Berlin Museum für Völkerkunde as Museum für Weltkunst, anticipating thereby a widespread tendency among ethnological museums of the present.[86] The aesthetic critique of anthropology meant that the notion of the 'primitive' soon became a key concept of modernist culture at the turn of the century: it emerged as artistic modernism's alter ego as Kobena Mercer put it. Further, it proved resilient enough to travel to those sites of the world cast by European ethnologists and artists as the realm of the 'primitive', where it was in turn appropriated and recast by fresh actors.[87]

---

82 Van Damme, 'Ernst Grosse and the "Ethnological Method"': 506; Grosse, *Die Anfänge der Kunst*, chapter 3, pp. 31–44.

83 Andrew Zimmerman, 'From Natural Science to Primitive Art: German New Guinea in Emil Nolde', in Cordula Grewe (ed.), *Die Schau des Fremden: Ausstellungskonzepte zwischen Kunst, Kommerz und Wissenschaft*, Stuttgart: Franz Steiner Verlag, 2006, pp. 279–300, here pp. 290, 294.

84 '[W]ertende Ästhetik'. He describes the intention of his work as the 'Bestreben, die bedeutendsten Kunstbezirke aus dem Gewimmel der belangloseren herauszuheben.' Eckart von Sydow, *Die Kunst der Naturvölker und der Vorzeit*, Berlin: Propylaen Verlag, 1923, Foreword.

85 Carl Einstein, *Negerplastik*, Munich: Wolff, 1915. Also Wendy A. Grossman, 'From Ethnographic Object to Modernist Icon: Photographs of African and Oceanic Sculpture and the Rhetoric of the Image', *Visual Resources*, vol. 23 (4), 2007: 291–336.

86 The art critic Paul Schmidt (1978–1955) castigated the ethnological museum as a 'monstrous' (*ungeheuren*) place where objects from the South Seas or the African continent were devalued for the sake of self-glorification by the Europeans: 'zur Ergötzung der lieben Europäer, die sich vor diesen Sachen lächelnd bewußt werden, wie erhaben sie über den kindlichen "Wilden" stehen', proposing that it be renamed as 'Museum für Weltkunst'. Paul F. Schmidt, 'Weltkunst oder Völkerkunde?', *Vorwärts: Berliner Volksblatt*, 30 July 1926.

87 As modernist art and modern art history inhabited a shared historical space, the notion of the 'primitive', I will argue, served as a link connecting the two. This aspect will be handled in Chapter Three.

The Primacy of the Object

The turn taken by *Weltkunstgeschichte* during the late nineteenth century – even as it reinforced evolutionist thinking – worked through its particular dynamics to undermine the classicist paradigm of cultural history by reclaiming an anthropological definition of culture, that is, one that was non-humanist and whose origins reached back into prehistoric times. The turn of the century saw yet another revolt against an art history framed by humanist principles, this time from a position rooted in the study of material culture, one that forcefully argued for the primacy of the object against the textual bias of the historian. It was spearheaded by Josef Strzygowski (1862–1941), an entrant to Austro-Germanic academic life from the outside, who had over the years acquired an extraordinarily first-hand knowledge of artefacts from across Asia.[88] Having published prolifically, he was appointed in 1909 to the Chair of 'Non-European Art History' (*Außereuropäische Kunstgeschichte*) at the University of Vienna, the first chair in Europe to bear such a denomination. What qualified Strzygowski, we may ask, as a 'non-Europeanist'? To start with, his attack on traditional historiography was made possible by the vast amounts of archaeological, ethnographic, and art historical material that had made its way into Europe during the second half of the nineteenth century and had revealed territories of human history unaccounted for in classical accounts. Strzygowski was among the earliest scholars to insist on the importance of material artefacts from West and Central Asia as well as from Germanic prehistoric sites to the understanding of European history, particularly to grasping the origins of late antique and medieval art. These origins he located ultimately in Iran and linked them to 'Aryan' and Nordic tendencies, while repudiating the role of the Mediterranean. Strzygowski developed several of his arguments in two important books, *Orient oder Rom* (1901) and *Kleinasien: Ein Neuland der Kunstgeschichte* (1903) (*Asia Minor: A New Territory for Art History*). Both these polemical texts berated scholars who emphasised the dependence of the 'Orient' on Greek forms, as well as those who linked Byzantine and early medieval art to late Roman developments. In the work *Asia Minor*, Strzygowski further argued that Greek and Roman culture had a negligible impact on Asia, where local traditions had prevailed – an argument that his contemporaries charged of being formed on the basis of sparse and rather dubious

---

88 Josef Strzygowski came from a family of German-speaking textile manufacturers in Austrian Silesia. Having decided to pursue a scholarly career, he studied in Berlin, Vienna and Munich, later travelled to Rome and Egypt. A useful account of Strzygowski's career and writings is Susanne L. Marchand, 'The Rhetoric of Artifacts and the Decline of Classical Humanism: The Case of Josef Strzygowski', *History and Theory*, vol. 33 (4), 1994: 106–30; also Marchand, *German Orientalism*, pp. 403–10. See also Matthew Rampley, *The Vienna School of Art History: Empire and the Politics of Scholarship, 1847–1918*, University Park: Penn State University Press, 2013, pp. 171–78; Piotr Otto Scholz (ed.), *Von Biala nach Wien: Josef Strzygowski und die Kunstwissenschaft*, Vienna: European University Press Verlagsgesellschaft, 2015; Eva Frodl-Kraft, 'Eine Aporie und der Versuch ihrer Deutung: Josef Strzygowski-Julius von Schlosser', *Wiener Jahrbuch für Kunstgeschichte*, 42 (1), 1989: 7–52; Georg Vasold, 'Riegl, Strzygowski und die Entwicklung der Kunst', *Ars*, vol. 41 (1), 2008: 95–109.

material.[89] One of his bolder claims was that the origins of the Christian basilica, for which no convincing prototypes were to be found in Rome, could be traced to models in central Anatolia.[90] In Strzygowski's overall explanatory scheme, Rome remained a mere province in a wider circuit of artistic production centred on western Asia. Over the years, his investigations in Asia came to encompass a territory extending from the Caucasus to the Himalayas, occasionally reaching beyond into China.

At the University of Vienna Strzygowski opened up several new areas for study and research in his department – Islamic, East Asian, Indian, and Central Asian art histories – all as part of his mission to undermine the existing humanistic, Eurocentric framing of art history and investigate reciprocal exchanges across Europe and Asia.[91] His own writings on each of these different regions appeared at a time when there were relatively few experts in the field, especially as his research was based on monuments and artefacts not easily accessible to every scholar in Europe. Islamic Art was one of the domains that opened up – thanks to Strzygowski's extensive writings and polemical positions – to contentious debates. Well-known among these is the long-standing battle of interpretations between him and Ernst Herzfeld (1879–1948) on the origins of Islamic art triggered by the discovery in the Syrian desert, and subsequent transfer to Berlin, of the monumental remains of Qasr Mushatta. Strzygowski was among those responsible for their acquisition and one of the first to publish a detailed study of the structure.[92] In an ambitious exercise in comparison that rejected the use of a philological approach, he set out to establish the similarities between Mushatta, which he deemed to be a palace, with similar structures in Sassanid Persia. He did so mainly on the basis of a typological comparison of ornamentation, making a case thereby for locating the origins of Islamic forms in the Seleucid site of Ctesiphon on the Tigris. Indeed, he carried his

---

89 Marchand, 'The Rhetoric of Artifacts': 121. See also, Jaś Elsner, 'The Birth of Late Antiquity: Riegl and Strzygowski in 1901', *Art History*, vol. 25 (3), 2002: 358–79.

90 Rampley, *The Vienna School*, p. 174.

91 For an account of the institutional apparatus built by Strzygowski at the University of Vienna, including reorganising the physical layout of the Institute of Art History and its library to give equal space to the world regions researched under his direction, see Georg Vasold, 'The Revaluation of Art History: An Unfinished Project by Josef Strzygowski and His School', in: Pauline Bachmann, Melanie Klein et al. (eds), *Art/Histories in Transcultural Dynamics: Narratives, Concepts and Practices at Work, 20th and 21st Centuries*, Paderborn: Wilhelm Fink, 2017, pp. 119–38, here pp. 121–23. During his professorial career at the University of Vienna from 1909 to 1932, Strzygowski supervised some ninety students who completed doctoral dissertations on an impressive range of themes spanning world regions, including the art of Gandhara, murals in Turkestan, mosaics of San Vitale in Ravenna, early Christian stone architecture in Sweden, Chinese elements in Persian miniature painting, the Taj Mahal, and the so on. For a complete list of doctoral theses supervised by Strzygowski, see Karl Johns, 'Josef Strzygowski (1862–1941)', *Journal of Art Historiography*, vol. 17, 2017: 1–46, here 39–46. Strzygowski's students, who included a large number of women, travelled far and wide, were shaped by his ideas and methods, but also grew beyond them. Among his students was Stella Kramrisch, whose career as a scholar of Indian art took her to England, India and then Philadelphia. On Kramrisch, see Chapter Three below, and more extensively, Jo Ziebritzki, *Stella Kramrisch: Kunsthistorikerin zwischen Europa und Indien: Ein Beitrag zur Depatriarchalisierung der Kunstgeschichte*, Marburg: Buchner-Verlag, 2021.

92 Josef Strzygowski, 'Mschatta. Kunstwissenschaftliche Untersuchung', *Jahrbuch der Königlich Preussischen Kunstsammlungen*, vol. 25 (4), 1904, pp. 225–373.

argumentative fervour further to claim that Persia was the most important source of cultural forms, both for late Hellenism as well as for cultural currents in India, Syria, Mesopotamia, and Armenia. A debate on the gate's origins that were inseparable from an examination of the foundations of Islamic art continued to rage for over a decade, bringing Islamic art to the centre of art historical discussions during the early twentieth century.[93]

Strzygowski's reactionary political attitudes, articulated by way of a strong anti-Semitism and the recourse to a pan-German nationalist-cum-racist rhetoric, are now well acknowledged and account for his having been ostracised from the world of liberal scholarship for several decades.[94] The recent years, however, have seen a revival of interest in the work of this controversial scholar, now being reclaimed as a precursor of a world/global art history.[95] Such a revisionist assessment rests on seemingly plausible considerations: Strzygowski's prolific oeuvre, more than that of any of his contemporaries, was animated by a searing critique of an art history centred on the achievements of European humanism, which in turn spurred him to propose a reoriented geography of art encompassing Europe and Asia within a single, shared frame. Methodological considerations have further sustained this appreciation of a scholar, whose life-long engagement with artistic currents beyond the European canon introduced fresh approaches to the investigation of art: an expansion of the canon rested on privileging comparative approaches together with shifting the paradigm of art historical research from the largely dominant diachronic approach of his contemporaries to a synchronic one.[96] Equally important to Strzygowski's agenda was making the study of materiality a foundation of art history, paying attention to the migration of forms and things as well as to those modes of expression much older than the art of writing.[97] Yet, it might be worthwhile to query the assumptions underpinning this commitment to art 'from beyond the West', and to examine the modes of argumentation deployed to create a more inclusive art history. While Strzygowski's indefatigable mission to harness incredible amounts of material artefacts as

93 See Eva-Maria Troelenberg, *Mschatta in Berlin: Keystones of Islamic Art*, Dortmund: Verlag Kettler, 2017, pp. 105–21.
94 Georg Vasold reports on a discussion at the University of Vienna's Institute of Art History 'some years back' (not further specified) about dealing with Strzygowski's legacy. This came in the wake of a proposal by the university's library to make his writings inaccessible for readership, especially among students. Vasold, 'Riegl, Strzygowski': 95, note 2.
95 See Pfisterer, 'Origins and Principles': 81; Thomas DaCosta Kaufmann, 'Reflections on World Art History', in: Thomas DaCosta Kaufmann, Catherine Dossin and Beatrice Joyeux-Prunel (eds), *Circulations in the Global History of Art, Farnham, Surrey: Ashgate*, 2015, pp. 25–45, here p. 33; Frodl-Kraft, 'Eine Aporie''. Matthew Rampley refers to the enabling role played by Strzygowski's writings on the historiography of art in regions that were once part of the Austro-Hungarian empire, for recent scholarship on Central and Eastern Europe, *The Vienna School*, pp. 177–78.
96 Joseph Strzygowski, *Die Krisis der Geisteswissenschaften*, Vienna: Kunstverlag Anton Schroll, 1923, with a dedication to Rabindranath Tagore, is a collection of eight lectures that contain a programmatic exposition of his methods.
97 An uncompromising critique of art history's dependence on philology runs through Strzygowski's entire oeuvre, it finds programmatic expression in three articles on art history and material culture in *Krisis der Geisteswissenschaften*, pp. 38–260. See also Marchand, 'The Rhetoric of Artifacts' for a perspicacious account.

vital sources to re-envision art history remains unsurpassed, how did he read the evidentiary value of material objects? Which methods did he take recourse to when setting out to establish origins, intentions, or transfers? What were the conclusions about the cultural meaning of art that his work chose to draw from the study of migrant objects? Addressing these questions could help introduce a note of caution as well as provide a clearer methodological orientation to the more recent enterprise of world art studies, if it is to avoid the pitfalls of bringing ethnocentric approaches in through the back door, even as it strives towards a temporal and spatial expansion of its field of investigation.

While Strzygowski's critique of the canonical assumptions underpinning the art histories of his times seems at first glance to resonate with present-day calls to provincialise the 'West', the terms of that critique were often reductive and trapped in binaries of 'East' and 'West'. The 'Orient or Rome' debate is organised around such an opposition that prevented the discussion, for instance, from taking into account long-term processes of transculturation shaping the cultural fabric of Rome, where classical and Eastern elements had been present over a long period. Despite the vast amounts of material that Strzygowski was able to marshal for his writings, their tenor frequently gets trapped within a similar opposition, where terms such as 'East' and 'West' or 'North' and 'South' that structure his central arguments, remain loosely defined. A particularly strident work in this respect is *Die bildende Kunst des Ostens* (*The Fine Arts of the East*), the pages of which repeatedly refer to a deep affinity between the 'Aryan East', that is, Iran, and the Germanic North, coining thereby the term 'Nordic East'. The author further advanced the idea that an art history of the world would emerge out of a creative opposition between 'northern and southern races'.[98] Such weaknesses – and the fact that his enormous oeuvre demands more specialised, closely attentive research – make it difficult to ascertain the extent to which Strzygowski's critique of Eurocentrism was founded on a firm empirical bedrock, or whether it was simply a product of ideological considerations. His mode of argumentation invariably followed a recurring pattern: from a painstaking, positivist engagement with minute detail using a morphological method of stylistic decoding, though not entirely free from intuition, the narrative would make a sudden leap to larger questions about cultural origins and the diffusion of cultures. It would then become a sweeping ethno-historical account that encompassed a seemingly boundless geographical space cutting across continental divides and reached deep into the recesses of prehistoric time. The objects he studied served primarily as data, as evidence for overarching theses about long-term and long-distance patterns of development, with seemingly little attention accorded to plausibly negotiating a sudden jump in scale. Among the large number of examples that run through Strzygowski's oeuvre and follow such a mode of argumentation, his account of the miniature paintings from Northern India in the Habsburg Collection, collages that till recently featured as part of the rococo panelling of the Millionenzimmer at the Schönbrunn

---

98   Josef Strzygowski, *Die bildende Kunst des Ostens*, Leipzig: Verlag Werner Klinkhardt, 1916.

castle, might be used here as an illustration.[99] The first part (Sections I and II) of the article Strzygowki published in *Rupam*, accompanied by illustrations, is devoted to a richly detailed description of the albums and their content: the individual fragments and their methods of re-composition within the rococo cartouches, choice of themes, rendering of figures, postures, gestures, physiognomies, landscapes, objects, attempts to ascertain through stylistic traits the provenance of different groups of paintings – in short, a close description based on observation that barely leaves any detail unreferenced (Plate 1.2).[100] In Section III, the account abruptly shifts register to a meta-narrative that addresses the question of the 'origin of Indian art'.[101] It begins by situating 'pre-Aryan' Indian art within an equatorial belt 'which must have had its centre in [prehistoric] Africa and which passed into Egypt in historical times', evidence of which, according to the author, could still be found in caves and rock buildings. With the 'immigration of the Aryans', so the narrative proceeds, India became detached from this southern belt and was brought in 'closer unity with [Central] Asia, which in its essence is Northern'. While migrating 'Iranians' adopted a mode of rendering the human figure, a characteristic feature of the 'South', the typology of 'geometrical landscape' could be found across vast spheres, 'in ancient Christian mosaics in Italy and in Chinese antiquities'.[102] Such a largely speculative concept of 'zones' of art that transcend continental divides runs through much of Strzygowski's ordering of Asian art.[103] In connection with India, it was further developed in an article that sought to position India within the 'art of Asia'. Here,

99 The *Millionenzimmer* in the Schönbrunn castle served as a reception room for diplomatic audiences during the reign of the Habsburg empress Maria Theresia. Its interiors are fitted out with a rosewood wainscoting within which some sixty rococo cartouches, each containing collaged compositions of fragments cut out of Mughal miniature paintings, have been embedded. The paintings were originally part of albums produced in a Golconda workshop and from there had travelled via merchants of the Dutch East India Company to the Netherlands and thence to Vienna. Strzygowski was among the earliest scholars who, together with his student, Emmy Wellesz, catalogued and classified the cartouches and recorded the patterns they follow.
See Josef Strzygowski, *Die indische Miniaturen im Schlosse Schönbrunn*, 2 vols, Vienna: Wiener Drucke, 1923. Also Josef Strzygowski, 'The Indian Room of the Empress Maria Theresia', *Rupam*, nos. 15–16, 1923: 59–66; Josef Strzygowski, 'Die Miniaturenschätze der Großmoguln in Wien im Rahmen der indischen Kunst', *Belvedere*, vol. 11 (1–2), 1932: 35–42; Josef Strzygowski (in collaboration with Heinrich Glück, Stella Kramrisch and Egon Wellesz), *Asiatische Miniaturmalerei im Anschluß an Wesen und Werden der Mogulmalerei, Im Anschluß an die Bestände in Wien*, Klagenfurt: A. Kollitisch-Verlag: 1932. On the Millionenzimmer, Dorothea Duda, 'Die Kaiserin und der Großmogul: Untersuchungen zu den Miniaturen des Millionenzimmers im Schloß Schönbrunn', in: Karin K. Troschke (ed.), *Malerei auf Papier und Pergament in den Prunkräumen des Schlosses Schönbrunn*, Vienna: Schloss Schönbrunn, 1997, pp. 33–55; Ebba Koch, 'The "Moghuleries" of the Millionenzimmer, Schönbrunn Palace, Vienna', in: Rosemary Crill, Susan Stronge and Andrew Topsfield (eds), *Arts of Mughal India: Studies in Honour of Robert Skelton*, Ahmedabad: Mapin Publishing, 2004, pp. 152–67.
100 Strzygowski, 'The Indian Room': 59–64.
101 Ibid.: 64.
102 Ibid.: 64. On the subject of landscape, Josef Strzygowski, *Perso-Indian Landscape in Northern Art*, London: India Society, 1922.
103 Josef Strzygowski, 'Three Northern Currents in the Art of the Chinese People', *Journal of the Indian Society of Oriental Art*, vol. 5, 1937: 42–57; Josef Strzygowski, 'Ein besonders beachtenswertes Stück ostasiatischer Frauenkunst', in: Bimala C. Law (ed.), *D. R. Bhandarkar Volume*, Calcutta: India Research Institute, 1940, pp. 205–211.

the 'northern zone' has been described as 'stretching across Europe and Asia' and as characterised by building materials used: 'wood, sun-dried bricks and such as go to make tents', speculating that 'prior to the stupas there must, no doubt, have existed wooden structures in India'.[104]

Strzygowski's interest in studying migration – of ethnic groups, forms, objects – so appealing to today's proponents of world art histories, followed from his tenacious search for origins and essences, while concrete processes of interaction, reception, and transformation that followed in the wake of mobility, escaped his analyses or were dismissed as detracting from an object's integrity and purity: an 'influx of elements' merely disturbed 'artistic effect'.[105] His description of North Indian miniature painting in the Habsburg Collection as 'a strange mixture of the Despotism of Westeren [sic] Asia and the contemplative wisdom of India'[106] is but an echo of Carl Schnaase's summary dismissal of 'Islamic Art' during an earlier generation of writings on *Weltkunstgeschichte* (see above). Indeed, Strzygowski's particular use of evidence indicates that the life-long endeavour to free art historical enquiry from the stranglehold of historicism and recuperate local traditions was grounded in a belief in the homogeneity of ethnic groups. Over the years of his career, the search for origins, be it of late Christian, Byzantine, Islamic, or Indian art, led him to Persia, which increasingly came to stand for the 'East'.[107] By highlighting originality and deep antiquity, he was able to locate in ancient Iran a pure source, an 'Ur-culture'. In *Die bildende Kunst des Ostens* he proposed a close affinity between the 'Aryan East' and the putative Germanic North for which he coined the term 'Nordic East'.[108] Matthew Rampley has drawn our attention to the enabling impact of Strzygowski's work on art histories in regions of Central and Eastern Europe – Croatia, Romania, Poland, the Czech Republic, Armenia, Turkey. Yet this positive reception could easily bypass his ardent commitment to a more capacious art history and draw on his legacy to produce nationalist narratives instead.[109] It is indeed telling that Strzygowski's efforts to challenge dominant art historical discourses of his time that led him to champion

104 Josef Strzygowski, 'India's Position in the Art of Asia', *Journal of the Indian Society of Oriental Art*, vol. 1, 1933: 7–17, here 8.

105 For instance, his statement that his 'main aim' was to 'understand European art by searching for its Indian roots', Strzygowski, 'India's Position': 8. See Vasold, 'Riegl, Strzygowski': 105.

106 Strzygowski, 'The Indian Room': 66.

107 The terms *Ursprünge* (origins) and *Wesen* (essence) recur obsessively through Strzygowski's entire oeuvre and can be encountered with clockwork regularity in the titles of books and articles – this was a concern that informed his work from the start. Art history, according to him, was best described as a '*Wesenswissenschaft*', a science of essences, see Strzygowski, *Krisis*, p. 37.

108 Strzygowski, *Die bildende Kunst des Ostens*, where the term of the Nordic East (*Nordischer Osten*) runs through the entire book.

109 Rampley, *The Vienna School*, pp. 177–78. On the nationalist appropriation of Strzygowski's work, Erno Marosi, 'Josef Strzygowski als Entwerfer von nationalen Kunstgeschichten', and Burcu Dogramaci, 'Kunstgeschichte in Istanbul: Die Begründung der Disziplin durch den Wiener Kunsthistoriker Ernst Diez', both in: Ruth Heftrig, Olaf Peters and Barbara Schellewald (eds), *Kunstgeschichte im 'Dritten Reich': Theorien, Methoden, Praktiken*, Berlin: Akademie Verlag, 2008, pp. 103–13; 114–33. See also, Matthew Rampley, 'The Construction of National Art Histories and the "New" Europe', in: Rampley et al. (eds), *Art History and Visual Studies*, pp. 231–46.

the autonomy of these regions from both Byzantine and Roman developments have now seamlessly lent themselves to nationalist appropriations.

Weltkunstgeschichte's Present-day Avatars

In the lecture 'Kunstgeschichte', subsequently printed in the *Krisis der Geisteswissenschaften*, Josef Strzygowski acknowledged the vital contribution of an earlier generation of art historians – Kugler, Schnaase, Burckhardt, and Springer – to the field. Their work, he claimed, 'had the courage to contemplate the entirety of the world', even as he was characteristically quick to point to their shortcomings that, for Strzygowski, were a result of their remaining trapped in humanist dogmas.[110] His own 'method of essential comparisons' (*Methode des Wesensvergleichs*), he continued, was ultimately instrumental in pointing to 'a new direction in scholarship'.[111] And yet, in spite of apparent differences of approach among the practitioners of *Weltkunstgeschichte* through the course of the nineteenth century, their commitment to a spatial and temporal expansion of art historical enquiry had shared underpinnings, whose legacy has continued into the present. The resurgence of interest among today's advocates of 'world art' in the writings of their 'forerunners' is therefore not surprising. Wilfried van Damme, a prominent spokesperson of the new World Art Studies, has underlined the importance of engaging with the neglected 'intellectual genealogies' of this field, whose roots he traces even further back, into the early modern period when European scholarship 'from an intercultural and … worldwide perspective' had already brought forth a diverse range of writings – from the comparative study of world architecture undertaken by the Jesuit scholar Athanasius Kircher to costume books of the Renaissance. For van Damme, each of these earlier works was informed by 'a broad anthropological conception of art' that can 'heuristically guide' scholars of world art today in their search for a 'culturally wide-ranging' approach.[112]

In view of the long history of European connections with other continents through trade, travel, and missionary activities, centuries before the high noon of imperialism during the nineteenth century, a scholarly interest in the world beyond the geopolitical horizon of Europe should hardly come as a surprise.[113] When evoking 'precursors' of an inclusive art history, it is crucial instead to query the terms of that inclusion, the discursive framework within which it operated, the assumptions, methods, conceptual understandings that made up the epistemic foundations of scholarship, which we have inherited and are keen to build on today. What are the implications of this inheritance for the profile of the 'World Art

---

110 Strzygowski, *Krisis*, p. 44.

111 Ibid., 57–58.

112 Van Damme, '"Good to Think"': 50–52.

113 A large body of writing on themes such as travel literature, missionary enterprises, or political governance exists in several European languages. For a systematic survey see Jürgen Osterhammel, *Die Entzauberung Asiens: Europa und die asiatischen Reiche im 18. Jahrhundert*, Munich: C. H. Beck, 1998; Eng. trans. *Unfabling the East: The Enlightenment's Encounter with Asia*, trans. Robert Savage, Princeton: Princeton University Press, 2018.

Studies movement', as one of its proponents loftily describes it,[114] and the directions that have emerged within this rather amorphous field?

The foregoing account of the development of *Weltkunstgeschichte* shows that it worked in an interdisciplinary discursive field; while art history during the first half of the nineteenth century remained indebted to an empiricist historicism, the subsequent decades witnessed a turn to the social sciences, especially ethnology, geography, and archaeology. A driving force throughout the century, however, was a 'national imagination',[115] a quality that predated the formal institution of a modern nation-state, yet retained its resilience beyond that moment and fostered the co-construction of categories of art and culture. The mission of *Weltkunstgeschichte* was inextricably intertwined with a broader discourse on the nature of human civilisation that in turn provided the backdrop against which the meaning of one's own time, a national culture to bind the nation as an enduring collective, could be fabricated. The early surveys of world art of the 1840s and 1850s – termed 'Überblick' (lit. overview), an ocular metaphor that presupposes the act of viewing the whole from a position of command[116] – sought to decipher the truths of humanity through its art with the ultimate aim of crafting a modern national identity. Art histories of the later period, instead, were increasingly dominated by anthropological questions that accepted the idea of cultural plurality. Yet, all variants of *Weltkunstgeschichte* partook of a belief in evolutionist thinking. While subscribing to a notion of culture that was not denied even to the earliest civilisations – or earliest human beings – this belief in the essential unity of humanity went hand in hand with a relativism that fell back on differences, which were at the same time hierarchies and were framed nationally. The account of all the world's art was not one of unequivocal progress; its evolution was fraught with setbacks and standstills, a product of the development of the peoples in question. Art – whether it was conceived selectively, as with Kugler and Burckhardt, or in its expanded definition, as with Grosse – always served as a key to access a culture. From the material surface of any of its objects, be it an archaeological fragment, a carpet, a bronze deity, a cave drawing, or a painted scroll, the state of development of a group of people could be read off. If a particular art is deemed raw or ugly, the same must be inferred about its makers. Such a procedure, it has been argued by Claire Farago, retained, in spite of the assumption that every human collectivity was capable of producing art, the formalist orientation of racial theories of cultural evolution.[117] The location of culture – and within it, art – came to be firmly bounded within territorial national formations. Such a founding premise elides any discussion of the role of dominant cultural groups who refuse to acknowledge the porosity of

114 David Hulks, 'World Art Studies: A Radical Proposition?', *World Art*, vol. 3 (2), 2013: 189–200, here 189.
115 Benedict Anderson, *Imagined Communities: Reflections in the Origins and Spread of Nationalism* (1983), London: Verso 2016 (revised ed.), p. 30.
116 Considered a technology of modernity, see Donald Preziosi, *Brain of the Earth's Body: Art, Museums and the Phantasms of Modernity*, Minneapolis: University of Minnesota Press, 2003, pp. 63ff.
117 Farago, '"Vision itself has its History"'; also Claire Farago, 'Imagining Art History Otherwise', in: Jane C. Davidson and Sandra Esslinger (eds), *Global and World Art in the Practice of the University Museum*, Routledge: London and New York: 2017, pp. 115–30.

cultural boundaries within national formations, or of the mechanisms of exclusion built into the nation-building process. Even the model of expansive spatial and temporal zones, as proposed by Josef Strzygowski, was made up of units: ethnic groups he believed to be culturally homogenous. His ostensibly recast geography of the world's art does not provide a fine-tuned analytical framework or the methodological tools to unravel the dynamics of the migratory movements he postulated throughout his oeuvre – rather these were framed by loosely defined, yet pre-constituted categories such as East and West, North and South, whose existence in turn was reaffirmed by the migrations he set out to trace. That his model could be conscripted to a nationalist-cum-racist ideology is less a paradox requiring explanation; it is more plausible to view its trajectory as a logical outcome of the assumptions underpinning it. The enterprise of *Weltkunstgeschichte* partook of an understanding of culture, hermetically sealed within a national container that worked to homogenise it in the service of national belonging. Such a model appeared in a variety of articulations through the nineteenth and twentieth centuries: these ranged from the liberal to the ethnocentric and the totalitarian, yet each one cemented the role of art as complicit with national identity.

An evolutionary model of culture where differences could be explained in terms of the degrees of cultural progress through which every society passes came to be replicated in the procedures and methods of art history as it was professionalised in emerging nation-states. The concept of style, a central category of the discipline, based on typological analysis, developed into a convenient tool to coordinate and stabilise mobility and metamorphoses of forms. The idea of stylistic development, now firmly anchored within art history, implies a scheme that is artificially maintained by attending to a geographic location as self-contained, and by suppressing the plurality of agency and the circulation of objects, forms and practices. Explanations of why the 'cosmopolitan' potential of *Weltkunstgeschichte* remained unrealised in the twentieth century are manifold – no doubt, the geo-politics of contemporary world history, marked by escalating nationalisms, wars, fascism, and their aftermath, were responsible at one level.[118] The mid-twentieth century saw the expunging of the recent past in many national narratives of a war-ravaged Europe; at the same time, it witnessed the emergence of young, postcolonial nation-states in Asia and Africa. Art history had already been on the way to becoming a global discipline with the spread of colonial modernity; for postcolonial nations the foundational values of the discipline, when appropriated, reconfigured and reaffirmed, served as an asset, as each of these assiduously cultivated its own narrative of cultural uniqueness. Thus, the most globally prevalent form of art historical writing we have inherited is a narrative framed within discrete cultural units – be they national or civilisational – and one that subsumes experiences of cultural braidedness under the taxonomic categories of 'influence', 'borrowing', or 'transfer'.

The legacy of *Weltkunstgeschichte* for investigations of world art today has moved in different directions, not least because the field that has constituted itself as World Art Studies still lacks a stringent definition or clear conceptual focus. Attempts to delineate its objects of

118 Pfisterer, 'Origins and Principles': 83.

investigation and methodological tools invariably end up in a haze of overarching generalisations.[119] The extreme difficulty in identifying a theoretical-cum-methodological frame that holds the different aspects of the field together – beyond a loose acknowledgement of 'art as a panhuman phenomenon'[120] – makes any systematic engagement with it difficult. My concern here is limited to identifying those directions within World Art Studies that consciously take their cue from *Weltkunstgeschichte* of the nineteenth and early twentieth centuries and strive to build on its approaches.

To start with, exponents of World Art Studies have revived the discussion initiated by art historians of the late nineteenth century about the relative value to the discipline of different forms of scholarly texts – the general survey as opposed to a monographic case study.[121] An initial response to such a call for an expansive art history came in the form of a curricular development within undergraduate art history programs, mainly at universities in the United States, though also in certain centres in Europe, for example at the University of East Anglia: the introduction of a survey course of world art that depended on single volume texts offering such an overview.[122] These frequently replicated the model of their nineteenth-century

119　The problem begins with the label itself, where both 'world' and 'art' remain undefined. Though today the terms 'world' and 'global' are interchangeably and often indiscriminately used to designate an art history that is not confined to one particular region or area, one of the main institutional locations of World Art Studies is the University of East Anglia, where John Onians gave it a significant impetus. Since then, the approaches of its practitioners have branched off in divergent directions. An anthology that reflects this eclectic composition of the field is Zijlmans and van Damme (eds), *World Art Studies*. The journal *World Art* initiated in 2011 has emerged as a forum for publication and discussion; yet a survey of the articles published shows it to be more of a container for any study not anchored in an established field of European art history. Many of the articles included under the banner of World Art could as easily qualify for publication in an area studies journal, so that the reader fails to get a sense of the methodological development of the field. What belongs to World Art Studies, what is left out, what gives it a critical edge over other approaches, are questions that remain largely unasked, or at best only partially addressed.

120　Zijlmans and van Damme (eds), *World Art Studies*, p. 7, a declaration that only begs the question.

121　In doing so, it picks up issues of hierarchy between different forms of art historical texts – between those who address the whole and others who delve into single parts, between amateur and professional scholarship. In a conference publication John Onians has argued for pushing the pendulum back to the universal/whole, and addressing world art 'in totality', by 'compressing' it into a book. See John Onians (ed.), *Compression vs. Expression: Containing and Explaining the World's Art*, New Haven: Yale University Press, 2006.

122　A number of these texts date to the early twentieth century and continue to be reprinted – for instance Horst W. Janson, *History of Art*, London: Thames and Hudson, 8th edition, 2016; Helen Gardner, *Art through the Ages*, 2 vols, Washington DC: Harcourt Brace, 1926, now in the 13th edition; E. H. Gombrich, *The Story of Art*, London: Phaidon, 1st edition 1950; Hugh Honour and John Fleming, *A World History of Art*, London: Laurence King, 1st edition 1982, now in the 7th edition; Marilyn Stokstad, *Art History*, New York: H. Abrams, 1st edition 1995. A recent survey and more ambitious text is Julian Bell, *Mirror of the World: A New History of Art*, London: Thames and Hudson, 2007. Bell, like his predecessors, follows a chronological approach. His engaging account ventures into cross-cultural connections, though these are unsystematic, based on personal observation rather than scholarly investigation. On the whole, juxtaposing, even comparing art from outside of the Western hemisphere to the prevailing canon ends up reaffirming that canon when the 'other' is merely included for the sake of diversity. A different approach is John Onians, *The Art Atlas*, London: Lawrence King, 2008.
　　In 2020, a move by Yale University to revamp its introductory survey course in order to make it more 'global' generated a heated discussion, revealing the stakes involved, even as the simple inclusion of a

precursors, in that they organised their narratives according to inherited categories such as nations, continents or civilisations, rather than questioning the hierarchies of knowledge that shaped the constitution of such units in the first place.[123] They presupposed their subject of study by accepting a narrow definition of art, assuming that it required no historical framing. Popular modern surveys of world art that take us from dingy caves to the light-filled white cubes of modern times inevitably echo the developmental paradigm they have taken over from forerunners of the past, even as they strive to eschew the hierarchical values built into historicist narratives. The conviction that a close analysis of objects can seamlessly lead to large-scale cultural understandings of a non-trivial kind is a pitfall that studies striving to 'place the world in a book' have not always been able to avoid.[124]

The lead article of the opening issue of *World Art* described World Art Studies as 'advancing not only a global perspective but a multi-disciplinary approach' – a statement of intent invoked throughout the article, though its methodological implications have not been fleshed out.[125] Another programmatic article published in the same journal two years later proclaimed World Art Studies as a long-needed corrective to 'a discipline that has become fragmented and surprisingly unambitious'. According to the author, David Hulks, the 'improvement' would be ushered by means of a 'macrohistorical point of view' that would facilitate the task of 'mapping the global distribution of artistic phenomena', since one denominator common to all practitioners of World Art Studies was the agreement that 'there is a thing called art … wherever there are humans'.[126] In addition to an insistence on the necessity of global mapping, the article posits a considerably broader temporal frame for the study of world art, to enable it to uncover patterns and the dynamics of human art-making across time and space. Such a programmatic assertion is closely reminiscent of the spatial-cum-temporal enlargement of scale attempted by art historians of the late nineteenth century, such as Grosse and, more importantly, Strzygowski, yet without signalling an awareness of the deeply problematic assumptions and methods that these positions transport. In fact, the voluble declaration of the aims of World Art Studies leaves the reader clueless about the methods through which 'mapping' is sought to be undertaken and, more importantly, the questions to be asked of such mapping, the criteria according to which its value as 'evidence' will be read. What does the project propose to investigate beyond documenting the location and distribution of art

selection of themes from outside of the European canon would be little more than cosmetic. See Dushko Petrovich Córdova, 'Where Should Art History Go in the Future? As Survey Courses Change, the Past Evolves', Artnews.com, 28 July 2020, https://www.artnews.com/art-news/news/art-history-survey-courses-yale-university-1202695484/ (last accessed Dec. 2021). A brief but helpful study of the history of survey texts in art history is Mitchell Schwarzer, 'Rethinking the Introductory Art History Survey', *Art Journal*, vol. 54 (3), 1995: 24–29.

123 For a critical view, Martin W. Lewis and Kären E. Wigen, *The Myth of Continents: A Critique of Metageography,* Berkeley: University of California Press, 1997.

124 A fresh and critically conceptualised approach to the study of world art is Farago, 'Imagining Art History Otherwise', as well as her book in the making, *Cultural Memory in the Era of Climate Crisis: Writing Borderless Histories of Art,* (forthcoming Routledge 2023).

125 Van Damme, '"Good to Think"': 45.

126 Hulks, 'World Art Studies': 190, 194–95.

across the globe? How helpful is a macrohistorical perspective when treated in isolation of processes that unfold on different scales and what are the criteria by which units of investigation will be constituted? How does a macro-level approach negotiate scale, if it is to engage with the objects of art history? If an important aim of the project to study world art is to 'avoid categories that depend on assumptions that are cultural',[127] what are the alternative categories that World Art studies privileges, and to ask what questions? Further, what are the histories of such categories, beginning with art itself, that remains remarkably under-theorised within World Art Studies? How do proponents of 'art as a panhuman phenomenon' intend to read the objects they identify as art without falling into inherited explanatory modes that read a mentality or culture off an object?

The abiding interest in matters of evolution shown by art history of the nineteenth century has bequeathed a legacy to one particular stream of present-day World Art Studies, which seeks to apply insights from biology and neurosciences to the study of art. Such an embrace of the natural sciences, moreover, is reminiscent of the strivings of art historians of the past to elevate their discipline to the status of a *Wissenschaft*. Neuroarthistory, a current associated with scholars such as John Onians, is today a subject of contentious debate.[128] Following from the conviction shared within World Art Studies that art constitutes a universal phenomenon across the globe, some of its proponents have been led to draw on evolutionary theory, according to which the capacity to produce and appreciate art is the outcome of a significant evolutionary leap in human cognition and neurological structure, a stage temporally located around the origins of Palaeolithic societies.[129] Artistic production, neuroarthistory claims, is explicable through certain patterns of neural development that are the source of what we understand as creativity. Conversely, the power of art to move and affect derives from its ability to stimulate certain neurological processes, likewise a product of evolution. Arguing that the human mind and the artefacts it produces are biologically determined – that is, the outcome of the anatomical and electrochemical workings of the brain – and that all humans therefore have similar emotional and motivational structures, a neuroarthistorical approach considers it 'obsolete and limiting to treat human behaviour as being *only*

---

127 John Onians, cited in Hulks, 'World Art Studies': 195.

128 John Onians, *Art, Culture and Nature: From Art History to World Art Studies*, London: Pindar Press, 2006; John Onians, *Neuroarthistory: From Aristotle and Pliny to Baxandall and Zeki*, New Haven: Yale University Press, 2007; John Onians, *European Art: A Neuroarthistory*, New Haven: Yale University Press, 2016; also Lauren Golden (ed.), *Raising the Eyebrow: John Onians and World Art Studies: An Album Amicorum in his Honour*, Oxford: Archaeopress, 2001. A systematic and far-reaching critique of neuroarthistory is Matthew Rampley, *The Seductions of Darwin: Art, Evolution, Neuroscience*, University Park: Penn State University Press, 2017: in particular Chapter 3; also Farago, *Cultural Memory in an Era of Climate Crisis*, (forthcoming).

129 An exhibition at the British Museum in 2013 entitled *Ice Age Art* featured objects that sought to put forward an argument that prehistoric art could be read as an index of human neurological and cognitive evolution. See Jill Cook (ed.), *Ice Age Art: The Arrival of the Modern Mind*, London: The British Museum Press, 2013; also discussed in Rampley, *The Seductions*, p. 74ff.

culturally or individually constructed'.[130] Art-making, therefore, being intrinsic to culture, is allegedly a biological phenomenon inherent to all societies and individuals; studying it from this perspective, the claim goes, offers a common ground for inclusion of entire humanity and therefore a corrective to the Eurocentrism of Western art history.[131] And yet, like other domains of World Art Studies, neuroarthistory does not come up with plausible methods to deal with seminal issues of cultural difference and a plurality of artistic practices, once the enquiry shifts to another scale. Does the search for universals rest on an elision of the modes of negotiating difference through semantic, conceptual, and formal practices, which form the bedrock of art historical enquiry? How useful, Matthew Rampley pertinently asks, is the assertion that art emerged as evolutionarily adaptive behaviour, as a statement about art and behaviour? Does it bring fresh insights to the concerns of art historians? Or does neuroart-history simply use art as 'data' to illustrate certain operations of the brain?[132] As with certain articulations of *Weltkunstgeschichte*, neuroarthistory too is chiefly preoccupied with locating the origins of art – this time within human biological conditions; it does not proceed to ask why, how, when, and under what conditions art took shape, migrated to other sites, was configured and reconfigured and, above all, came to be consecrated as art. Is providing a 'theory of causes',[133] we may well ask, sufficient justification for neuroarthistory's claims to being a new paradigm for thinking through cultural history and 'making more sense of art'?[134]

A distinctive attempt to make art history's investigation more capacious by drawing on phenomenological categories, while avoiding the trap of reading art through its putative universal biologically rooted traits, is David Summers's ambitious opus *Real Spaces: World Art History and the Rise of Modernism*.[135] Organised around the principle that art constitutes a mode of articulation of being-in-the world, Summers takes recourse to a set of concepts anchored in 'the conditions of human presence', conditions that are experiential, in other words, defined by the 'body's finite spatiotemporality, its typical structure, capacities and relations', which cut across cultural differences.[136] The latter to him are negotiable, translatable rather than incommensurable. In fact, he describes his book as 'an essay toward the negotiation, not only of differences between the modern West and other cultures, but between the modern West and its own foundational institutions'.[137] By the latter, Summers means the concepts through which visual arts from around the world are written about and understood. His search for non-essentialising categories to replace those of formalist art

130 Ellen Dissanayake, 'The Arts after Darwin: Does Art have an Origin and Adaptive Function?', in: Zijlmans and van Damme (eds), *World Art Studies*, pp. 241–63, here pp. 258–59 (italics in original).
131 Dissanayake, 'The Arts after Darwin'.
132 Rampley, *The Seductions*, pp. 42–43, 90–92.
133 Ibid., p. 93.
134 John Onians, 'Neuroarthistory: Making More Sense of Art', in: Zijlmans and Van Damme (eds), *World Art Studies*, pp. 265–86.
135 David Summers, *Real Spaces: World Art History and the Rise of Western Modernism*, London. Phaidon, 2003.
136 Ibid., p. 36.
137 Ibid., p. 25.

history led him to terms such as facture, place, image, planarity, virtuality, and space, that in his view could be deployed to grasp art produced anywhere in the world. His central methodological purpose, he asserts, is to replace 'the lingering formalist notion of the "visual arts" by what I call the *spatial arts*'.[138] Summers' book can be read as a response to the challenge of organising an expanse of material by redefining the concepts of art history, rather than by a mere act of inclusion of objects from the rest of the world into a discipline wherein its foundational principles together with 'its sense of itself' would remain intact.[139] Equally important is the author's approach which, even while searching for common denominators, underlines the potential of art to transform biologically acquired capacities by providing 'enabling conditions' for imagining and articulating shifts of experience.[140] Unsurprisingly though, Summers' work has been critiqued for using a concept of space that is as deeply imbued with the values of Western thought as the vocabulary it sought to replace.[141] While it can hardly be ruled out that an ambitious enterprise of this kind and scale undertaken by a scholar trained in the Western academy would remain entirely free of Eurocentrism, Summers' work shows up to be nonetheless sensitive to culturally specific ways of making art, even as he believes in its universality.[142] He is not unaware of the problematic dimensions of 'imposing presumptive categories of art, culture, and history itself on the lives and accomplishments of others', therefore considers his attempt a risk of sorts to be able to address 'a great array of specific cultural choices, patterns and traditions'.[143] Though Summers cannot be described as a practitioner of a transcultural approach, his work signals in that direction, as it refuses to exclude the possibility of translation as negotiation between cultures, a possibility that does not subscribe to the fundamental incommensurability of concepts, each sealed within the hermetic containers of individual cultures.[144] That his own investigation inevitably falls back from time to time into Eurocentric positions only underlines the impossibility of carrying through a project of this scale within the format of a single-authored work. Transcultural enterprises, which by the nature of their imperatives require a range of linguistic and cultural competences, cannot be conceived of without a transformed, collaborative research praxis.

The frequently heralded objective of an inclusive art history 'to put the world in a book' has over the years acquired a certain notoriety, for it has both been invoked as a promise of 'what [a future] art history might look like'[145] as well as branded as 'anachronistic',

---

138 Ibid., p. 41 (italics in original).
139 James Elkins, 'Review of *Real Spaces*', *The Art Bulletin*, vol. 86 (2), 2004: 373–381, here 377.
140 Rampley, *The Seductions*: 37.
141 Elkins, 'Review'; Susanne Leeb, 'Weltkunstgeschichte und Universalismusbegriffe', *Kritische Berichte*, vol. 40 (2), 2012: 13–25, here 17–18; Aruna D'Souza, 'Introduction', in Jill H. Casid and Aruna D'Souza (eds.), *Art History in the Wake of the Global Turn*, New Haven: Yale University Press, 2014: viii–ix; Parul D. Mukherji, 'Whither Art History in a Globalizing World', *The Art Bulletin*, vol. 96 (2), 2014: 151–155, here 153.
142 Summers, *Real Spaces*: 38.
143 Summers, *ibid*: 12, cited in Elkins 'Review': 377.
144 A discussion of this issue follows in Chapter Two.
145 Elkins, 'Review': 378.

threatening a return to 'foundationalism, be it biological or cultural'.[146] The perils of such an approach have been variously described as a trend towards re-inscribing the authority of the 'Western' as well as consecrating 'nativism and indigenisation'.[147] An expansion per se, either as a methodological or a pedagogical move, does not by its analytical intent undermine those frameworks it seeks to transgress, or at best does so only tangentially. An art history that strives to be non-hierarchical requires that we begin by unravelling the knowledge-making processes that enabled the discipline to tell its story in the first place. The precedents of a century ago, when art history nurtured the ambition to produce authoritative knowledge about nations, cultures and the world, direct our attention to those epistemic foundations that continue to shape our scholarly practice in contemporary times as the discipline strives once more to become 'global'.

146 Parul D. Mukherji, 'The Possibility of a World Art History'. Round Table with John Clark, Parul D. Mukherji, Omuka Toshiharu, Patrick Flores and Woo Jung-Ah, *Australian and New Zealand Journal of Art*, vol. 9 (1–2), 2008: 42–47, here 43, 45–46.
147 Patrick Flores, 'The Possibility of a World Art History'. Round Table with John Clark, Parul D. Mukherji, Omuka Toshiharu, Patrick Flores and Woo Jung-Ah, *Australian and New Zealand Journal of Art*, vol. 9 (1–2), 2008: 42–47, here 44–45.

CHAPTER TWO
MAKING AND SEEING IMAGES
Tracking the Routes of Vision in Early Modern Eurasia

'To ponder mimesis is to become sooner or later caught … in sticky webs of copy *and* contact, image *and* bodily involvement of the perceiver in the image, a complexity we too easily elide as nonmysterious.' – Michael Taussig[1]

Mass cultures of modernity have accustomed us to modes of perception that are predicated upon, as well as stimulate, acts of copying in which the sensuous and the intellectual exist in reciprocity. Technological possibilities opened up by the camera and film – such as enlargement and motion – have provided, in the words of Susan Buck-Morss 'a new schooling for our mimetic powers'.[2] Yet, the reliance of art history and visual studies on a Benjaminian understanding that considers a resurgence of the mimetic urge – that compulsive drive to 'become the Other' by emulation – to be a 'direct result of modernity', has produced erasures, making an engagement with visual practices of societies and regions beyond Euro-America, and during historical phases that lie between the ancient and the modern, an urgent task.[3] Such an engagement needs to begin by querying the conventional terminologies of art history – copy, imitation, derivation, representation, identification, and, not least, the concept of the image itself – and the values they transport. What do these terminologies depend on, what is the potential of mimetic engagement that they at the same time efface? Shaped in conjunction with the emergence of modernist art forms, much of art history continues to partake of modernism's anxieties about the nature of originality, thereby relegating acts of 'copying' to the realm of temporal and artistic backwardness. The chrono-politics of the discipline have depended largely on placing the so-called non-Western within the West's past, as perpetually striving to 'catch up' with novel 'scientific' modes of representation, more often than not fated to contend with being derivative. While postcolonial scholarship has sought to reverse the

---

1   Michael Taussig, *Mimesis and Alterity: A Particular History of the Senses*, New York: Routledge, 1993, p. 21.
2   Susan Buck-Morss, *The Dialectics of Seeing: Walter Benjamin and the Arcades Project*, Cambridge MA: MIT Press, 1989, p. 267. Buck-Morss draws on Benjamin's notion of the camera as the machine to open up the 'optical unconscious'. Cited in Michael Taussig, *Mimesis and Alterity: A Particular History of the Senses*, London/New York: Routledge, 1993, p. 20.
3   Taussig, *Mimesis and Alterity*, p. 19ff.

argument by signalling towards the potential of the 'copy' to destabilise the authority of the 'original',[4] the account below uses a theory of transculturation to highlight the diversity of transactions built into mimetic acts, as they unfold in dynamic relation to a range of migratory processes, social constellations, and agencies. It therefore looks at pictorial practice as a whole to uncover the different types of knowledge it both embodies and produces, and what this spelt for the makers and viewers of images. Investigating these dimensions in turn requires taking account of materialities, histories, and memories in their relation to a living consciousness about the ontological status of the image-object. In the discussion that follows, pictorial practice is conceived of not only as an outcome of transcultural connections, but equally as a ground on which encounters unfold and transcultural relationships are formed. The chapter sets out to demonstrate the ability of images to mediate between worlds and philosophical-cum-symbolic systems, to serve as a basis of knowledge about cultural difference. At a meta-level, the reciprocal relationship between making and seeing images is read as forming, as Kajri Jain drawing on Jacques Rancière puts it, the 'sensible infrastructures'[5] of the politics of early modern empires.

Let us enter the subject by looking at a work that dates to the early seventeenth century and problematises many of these issues in a subtle, yet self-conscious way. A single folio painting from the Jahangir album in Berlin's State Collection simulates the idea of a collage by placing four figures next to each other, above and below, on the flat picture plane (Plate 2.1).[6] Three of the figures are clearly artists: the one on the right is shown painting a landscape with agile figures that suggest a hunting scene, while the other paints what seems like a picture of the Virgin Mary. The artist on the left sits in front of a window that looks like a picture – invoking the overlap between the window and the painted view as in the Albertian formula, examples of which are to be found in several works of the time, copied from European prints that had travelled to South Asia from the mid-sixteenth century onwards.[7] As in other examples where artists have picked up the motif of the window/niche/painting, this image plays on different significations of the window in a new context of the North Indian

4   In the words of Homi Bhabha, 'The *menace* of mimicry is its *double vision* which in disclosing the ambivalence of the colonial discourse also disrupts its authority.' Homi Bhabha, 'Of Mimicry and Man: The Ambivalence of Colonial Discourse', *October*, vol. 28 (Spring), 1984: 125–33, here 129 (italics in original).

5   Kajri Jain, *Gods in the Time of Democracy*, Durham, NC: Duke University Press, 2021, p. 6.

6   Referred to in Gregory Minissale, *Images of Thought: Visuality in Islamic India 1550–1750*, Newcastle: Cambridge Scholars Publishing, 2006, p. 207. It has also been reproduced and discussed in Monica Juneja, 'Tracking the Routes of Vision in Early Modern Eurasia', in: Karin Gludovatz, Juliane Noth, Joachim Rees (eds), *The Itineraries of Art: Topographies of Artistic Mobility in Europe and Asia*, Paderborn: Wilhelm Fink Verlag, 2015, pp. 57–84, here pp. 77–79; see also Friederike Weis, ‚Blicke in die Welt indischer Malerei‘, in: Monica Juneja and Petra Kuhlman-Hodick (eds), *Miniatur Geschichten: Die Sammlung indischer Malerei im Dresdner Kupferstich-Kabinett*, Dresden: Sandstein Verlag, 2017, pp. 136–37.

7   See for instance the double-page painting *Zafar Khan and His Brother in the Company of Poets and Scholars* (c. 1640), ascribed to Bishandas, London, British Library; or the page from the Kevorkian Album, *Jahangir embracing Nur Jahan* (c. 1620), ascribed to Govardhan, Los Angeles, County Museum of Art, both reproduced in Amina Okada, *Indian Miniatures of the Mughal Court*, New York: Harry N. Abrams, 1992, pp. 161 and 192. See also fig. 1 below.

courts where it was received and re-appropriated. For instance, within the Islamicate tradition, the window was held to designate an opening into the inside world, an internal mirror through which to filter the outside world and see the immanence of God, an analogy that is frequently used in Sufi mystical texts.[8] And yet, the act of juxtaposing the window/image to other planes within this Mughal image works in the Derridean sense of a *parergon*:[9] it brings into the representation the realities of multiple positions and emphasises the lack of stability in a story that can shift ground and even move across time and scale. On the top left of the collage-like composition, an artist is shown offering a picture, in a posture of humility characteristic of court etiquette, to someone outside of the picture frame. A closer look at the details of the object he offers reveals it to be a self-portrait, which is proffered to a person who occupies the space of the viewer. Following the frequently used Indo-Persian literary device of placing stories within stories, this fragment features a picture within a picture that can multiply infinitely. The simultaneity of artists and their work, the co-presence of different temporalities within a pastiche-like composition problematises multiple, conflicting modes of organising pictorial space. The individual components – with several references to a diversity of themes and modes of representation – work here as notations that unseat certainties in order to show the complexity of pictorial practice when confronted with plurality. This single page from the album compiled for the Mughal emperor Jahangir can be read as a condensation of several issues that will be discussed in this chapter on producing and viewing images in early modern court cultures. We have a dense, enigmatic representation – a painting that paints painters painting – of three artists at work that is at the same time a (self-)reflection of artistic practice.[10] Such a practice involves a reflection of artists on the transactions built into image-making as well as the relationships such a practice engenders between making and seeing. By collapsing the distance between the two, the painting directs our attention to the multiple forms of value and efficacy available to images, and which have been ascribed to them by their makers and viewers alike. Mimetic practice, described here as engagement with difference, as infinite repetition, turns into a resource that goes beyond a mechanical act of emulation. Image-making involves mediation, allowing painting to reclaim authority as a form of knowledge.

Much has been said and written about images in recent years: debates have proliferated over their agency within a field of cultural production, as opposed to their function as a space of aesthetic contemplation, over their capacity to represent rather than express. Images are

8   The prolific references in philosophical and literary texts to veils, mirrors and windows are discussed below.

9   Jacques Derrida, *La verité en peinture*, Paris: Flammarion, 1978, pp. 44ff.

10   This form of 'self-awareness' has been discussed by Victor Stoichita with reference to oil painting, while W. J. T. Mitchell speaks of a 'metapicture' as one that stages the 'self-knowledge' of pictures. See Victor I. Stoichita, *The Self-Aware Image: An Insight into Early Modern Meta-painting*, New York: Cambridge University Press, 1997; W. J. T. Mitchell, *Picture Theory*, Chicago: Chicago University Press, 1994, p. 57. Mitchell's concept of a metapicture has been productively applied by Wu Hung to study Chinese painting, see Wu Hung, *The Double Screen: Medium and Representation in Chinese Painting*, Chicago: Chicago University Press, 1996, p. 237ff.

increasingly being read as an arena for enacting emotions; we ascribe to their materiality the power to mediate sacrality.[11] In the wake of the global turn in the humanities, the image has come to stand above all for mobility and cosmopolitan exchange. Within art history, trans-regional connections – configurations that disallow conflation with nation-states or other predetermined units – serve as productive criteria when constituting one's objects of investigation. Such an approach, however, brings with it the challenge of handling the tension that ensues when the existing taxonomies and canons of the discipline, which also determine its intellectual and institutional boundaries, are confronted with the wealth of evidence and questions brought forth by enquiry that is framed to follow the logic of complex circuits of exchange. The tension is a productive one that holds a promise of art history's potential to contribute towards theorising transcultural processes.

The exponential growth of trade, exchange, and collection in the wake of European expansion during the early modern period is said to have brought with it a privileging of 'optical authority' as a way of registering and controlling an unprecedented gamut of new experiences, desires, and knowledge.[12] Yet the visual, the act of seeing as a participant in innumerable transactions across the divide of the familiar and the alien, acquired multiple valences as it resonated on new sites and was translated and reconfigured in new contexts. Material objects were both the media and the agents in processes of transculturation, making their 'thingness' a formative component of that encounter. At the same time, reading an image as both a pictorial representation as well as a material product can work towards breaking down some of the hierarchies of art history that continue to privilege a 'dematerialised' notion of vision.[13] Addressing these dynamics works to expand and complicate our conceptions of the visual, which both relates to and further constitutes synaesthetic notions of sight in cultural settings beyond Europe.[14] Indeed, studying the itineraries of images-as-things across spaces and cultural sites leads to a questioning of the taxonomic dichotomy between 'image' and 'object' as both are drawn into a complex of multi-sensorial transactions that make vision a profoundly transcultured concept.

The art historical problem of conceptualising vision, which forms the core of this chapter, goes beyond the investigation of simple mobility and adoption of motifs or iconographies or even pictorial formulae, though these are also part of a circulatory regime and are constituent elements of a work of art. The latter becomes a site for a reflection on the cultural and philosophical underpinnings of its own practices as well as those which it encounters – these

11   See for instance the contributions that discuss visual media in Kishwar Rizvi (ed.), *Affect, Emotion and Subjectivity in Early Modern Muslim Empires: New Studies in Ottoman, Safavid, and Mughal Art and Culture*, Leiden/Boston: E. J. Brill, 2018.

12   Dana Leibsohn, 'Introduction: Geographies of Sight', in: Dana Leibsohn and Jeanette F. Peterson (eds), *Seeing across Cultures in the Early Modern World*, Surrey: Ashgate, 2012, p. 1.

13   Michael Yonan, 'Toward a Fusion of Art History and Material Culture Studies', *West 86th*, vol. 18 (2), 2011: 232–48, here 239.

14   A richly informative reading of texts from early Islamic societies to extract multiple registers – the aesthetic, cognitive and mystical – of the act of seeing is Gülru Necipoğlu, 'The Scrutinizing Gaze in the Aesthetics of Islamic Visual Cultures: Sight, Insight, and Desire', *Muqarnas*, vol. 32, 2015: 23–61.

dimensions will be empirically fleshed out in the following sections. This study of the ways in which vision is configured and reconfigured in the specific regional context of South Asia can be located in a small but articulate research field that brings together studies of visuality with encounters between Europeans and cultures in South America, Asia, and Africa.[15] While my work has responded to many of the impulses that have emanated from this field, it positions itself at the same time in relation to recent moves in art history towards incorporating different regions of the world within a single framework of shared questions. Within the field of World Art Studies, discussed at length in the preceding chapter, theoretical stances have tended to alternate between two poles: between the position which considers ways of seeing as constituting a human universal – a common anthropological denominator that holds humans together across time and space 'as they have been making art for millennia'[16] – and the extreme relativist stance, which advocates the use of each cultural tradition's core concepts of visuality and the image, whose incommensurability and fixity are assumed.[17] As distinct from these positions, I propose that rather than assuming it to be a factor common to human societies, vision itself needs to be a subject of historical investigation. This includes studying both the distinctive cultural possibilities that are built into the act of seeing as well as the formative shifts within its practices as new relationalities are negotiated in the wake of cultural encounters. Historicising vision means arguing that seeing and the representation of the 'seen' onto a two-dimensional surface of a painted page are culturally and socially constituted processes that need to be unpacked beyond simple cultural relativism. This in turn implies a deconstruction of those systems of representation that art history has canonised as modern and scientific in a universalist sense; in other words, it calls for a reflexive

15 Claire J. Farago, 'Vision Itself Has a History: "Race", Nation and Renaissance Art History', in: Claire J. Farago (ed.), *Reframing the Renaissance: Art and Visual Culture in Europe and Latin America 1450–1650*, New Haven: Yale University Press, 1995, pp. 67–88; Robert S. Nelson (ed.), *Visuality Before and Beyond the Renaissance: Seeing as Others Saw*, Cambridge, UK: Cambridge University Press, 2000; Christopher Pinney, 'Creole Europe: A Reflection of a Reflection', *Journal of New Zealand Literature*, vol. 20, 2002: 125–61; Hans Belting, *Florenz und Bagdad: Eine westöstliche Geschichte des Blicks*, Munich: Beck Verlag, 2008; Mary D. Sheriff (ed.), *Cultural Contact and the Making of European Art since the Age of Exploration*, Chapel Hill: University of North Carolina Press, 2012; Leibsohn and Peterson, *Seeing Across Cultures*; Monica Juneja, 'Braided Histories? Visuelle Praktiken des indischen Moghulreichs zwischen Mimesis und Alterität', *Historische Anthropologie*, vol. 16 (2), 2008: 187–204; Juneja, 'Tracking the Routes'; Natasha Eaton, *Mimesis across Empires: Artworks and Networks in India*, Durham, NC: Duke University Press, 2013.

16 John Onians, *The Art Atlas*, London: Lawrence King, 2008, p. 11.

17 James Elkins speaks of 'indigenous terms', see James Elkins, 'Different Horizons for a Concept of the Image', in: *On Pictures and Words that Fail Them*, Cambridge, UK: Cambridge University Press, 1998, pp. 188–209. For a critical take on Elkins, Parul D. Mukherji, 'Putting the World in a Book: How Global Art Can be Today', in: Jaynie Anderson (ed.), *Crossing Cultures: Conflict, Migration and Convergence*, Carlton: Miegunyah Press, 2009, pp. 109–15; Monica Juneja, 'Global Art History and the "Burden of Representation"', in Hans Belting et al. (eds), *Global Studies: Mapping Contemporary Art and Culture*, Stuttgart: Hatje Cantz, 2011, 274–97, here pp. 279–80. See also Elkins' subsequently more nuanced position, James Elkins, 'Afterword', in Thomas DaCosta Kaufmann, Catherine Dossin and Béatrice Joyeux-Prunel (eds), *Circulations in the Global History of Art*, Farnham, Surrey: Ashgate, 2015, pp. 203–29, here pp. 218–20.

engagement with the ways in which the disciplines, interpretive moulds, and languages that have evolved to explain and theorise these practices, are themselves a product of modern concerns.

A few words about the framing of this study: while the geographical focus of my research is South Asia, I place this unit of investigation within a transcultural frame. In other words, this chapter examines the history of visual representation and practices as formed through migration and the interrelationships between material objects, images, and actors spread across a vast Eurasian zone during the early modern period[18] and connected through conquest, diplomacy, evangelisation, and economic transactions, as well as through ritual, gifting, and kinship networks. The Mongol conquest of the eastern Islamic regions, often mythologised as a cataclysmic upheaval, was at the same time generative of a political geography that fostered an unprecedented dynamism enabled by the migration of artists, rulers, objects, and forms.[19] Early modern empires such as the Ottomans, the Safavids, and the Mughals, all looked back upon the post-Mongolian context as a genealogical source and formative period of many developments in the arts, especially manuscript painting. Within South Asia too, prevalent classifications of pictorial production into 'schools' such as the Mughal, the Rajput, and the Deccan, often further subdivided into regional styles, easily give way to a recognition of porous boundaries, once we trace the paths of migrant artists and uncover a spirit of experimentation within court cultures with circulating aesthetic idioms.[20] Such experiments frequently involved transcending the dividing lines separating domains that

18   The concept of a Eurasian zone was presented in Sanjay Subrahmanyam, 'Connected Histories: Notes towards a Reconfiguration of Early Modern Eurasia', *Modern Asian Studies*, vol. 31 (3), 1997: 735–62. It has proved to be a useful and influential unit of framing since then. For more recent interventions on early modernity, see the contributions to David Porter (ed.), *Comparative Early Modernities 1100–1800*, New York: Palgrave Macmillan, 2012; on the issue of periodization, Monica Juneja, '"Pre-colonial" oder "Early Modern"? Das Problem der Zeitzäsuren in der indischen Geschichte', *Historische Zeitschrift*, vol. 47, 2009: 449–68.

19   Linda Komaroff and Stefano Carboni (eds), *The Legacy of Genghis Khan: Courtly Art and Culture in Western Asia, 1256–1353*, New Haven: Yale University Press, 2002; Thomas Lentz, Glenn D. Lowry and Jonathan Rabinovitz (eds), *Timur and the Princely Vision: Persian Art and Culture in the Fifteenth Century*, Washington DC: Smithsonian Institution Press, 1989; Linda Komaroff (ed.), *Beyond the Legacy of Genghis Khan*, Leiden: E. J. Brill, 2006.

20   The origins of such classification go back to the mid-twentieth century, see Basil Gray, 'The Art of India and Pakistan with Special Reference to the Exhibition at the Royal Academy', *Journal of the Royal Society of Arts*, vol. 94 (4758), 1947: 75–81, 69–72 (plates); Douglas E. Barrett and Basil Gray, *Painting of India*, Lausanne: Skira, 1963; Douglas E. Barrett, *Studies in Indian Sculpture and Painting*, London: Pindar Press, 1990; J. V. S. Wilkinson, 'Indian Painting', in: Richard Winstedt (ed.), *Indian Art*, London: Faber & Faber, 1947, pp. 103–50.

The separation of the 'Mughal' and 'Rajput' schools of painting was proposed by Ananda K. Coomaraswamy in his two-volume study, *Rajput Painting: Being an Account of Hindu Paintings of Rajasthan and the Punjab Himalayas from the Sixteenth to the Nineteenth Century Described in Their Relation to Contemporary Thought*, Delhi: Motilal Banarsidass, 1976 (1916). For a revisionist position, see Molly E. Aitken (ed.), *A Magic World: New Visions of Indian Painting*, Mumbai: Marg Publications, 2016. On the fluidity between production centres of painting located in courts and the bazaars, or between the imperial centre and the provinces, see Stuart C. Welch et al. (eds), *The Emperor's Album: Images of Mughal India*, New York: Harry N. Abrams, 1987, p. 18.

modern scholarship has labelled as 'religious' and 'secular'. To what extent was the encounter with the world beyond the locality mediated through and constituted by the painted image? And following from this, how does the image, through its processes of production and enactment of multiple regimes of sight and time, become a metonym for mobility and communication across cultures, even though this may not necessarily mean the uniform diffusion of a shared, more 'rational' or 'scientific' way of seeing? The following investigation of making and seeing images explores the conjunction of these with materiality, memory, authorship, and notions of the self to arrive at a conception of vision that can embody each of these facets of experience. It does not proffer a narrative organised around an opposition between a predetermined, normative 'Renaissance model' of the individual, a unique 'Western self' as canonised within histories of art and culture by writings such as those of Jacob Burckhardt, and the absence of such a model elsewhere.[21] At the same time, it eschews explanations that elicit 'alternative' paths of development for Europe and Asia, each choosing its 'own' routes through imperial, regional, or local formations. Instead – taking a cue from recent revisionist research on the emergence of modernity under the aegis of the European Renaissance – it would be more useful to note that the discursive construction of European (early) modernity as pioneering and in bleak contradistinction to its 'others', including its 'medieval' predecessors, was achieved by erasing its own histories of formative exchange with these. Such relationships predated the Renaissance, but also nurtured it.[22] In other words, the European Renaissance and its creations, far from arriving as fully formed, autonomous carriers of the modern in other regions of the world, were themselves unceasingly transcultured through long-distance relationships. Transcultured histories and transitions to modernity, as the following discussion will show, can at the same time be discontinuous, episodic, or locally contingent.

The Assembled Image

The next two images from North Indian courts raise a number of questions to take this enquiry further. The first, a painting dated to the late seventeenth century featuring an imperial pastime, (Plate 2.2), opens up several pictorial units and planes simultaneously to the viewer. In the immediate foreground, we witness, together with the haloed emperor on horseback and his surrounding courtiers and attendants, a lively performance of male and female acrobats, each one out to impress with a unique demonstration of skill, as agile as it is artistic.

---

21 Peter Burke, 'Representations of the Self from Petrarch to Descartes', in Roy Porter (ed.), *Rewriting the Self: Histories from the Renaissance to the Present*, London/New York: Routledge, 1997, pp. 17–28.

22 Farago (ed.), *Reframing the Renaissance*; Daniel Savoy (ed.), *The Globalization of Renaissance Art: A Critical Review*, Leiden: E. J. Brill, 2017; Sheriff (ed.), *Cultural Contact*; Natalie Z. Davis, *Trickster Travels: A Sixteenth Century Muslim Between Worlds*, New York: Hill and Wang, 2007; Thomas F. Earle and Kate J. P. Lowe (eds), *Black Africans in Renaissance Europe*, Cambridge, UK: Cambridge University Press, 2005; Joaneath A. Spicer (ed.), *Revealing the African Presence in Renaissance Europe*, Baltimore: Walters Art Museum, 2012.

The viewer joins the emperor and his retinue to gaze onto the colourful feat; at the same time, the painting allows our gaze to travel over and above the performance in the foreground into a complex of palatial structures – a labyrinth of buildings, gateways, terraces, turrets, and pavilions connected by winding pathways. We get a glimpse of scattered groups of people both within and outside the precincts of the palace complex, while the vista extends further into the distance beyond the architecture to a river animated by the movement of boats. Still further in the distance we can observe a landscape of green, undulating hills, populated with buildings, groups of people including equestrian noblemen and standard bearers carrying a banner, the whole enclosed by segments of fortifications. We are presented with a panoramic view, which both zooms into activities in the immediate foreground as well as allows an entry through a bird's-eye into spaces at the interior of a built complex and stretches outwards to a distant horizon. The use of such encompassing views was a compositional device introduced by newly arrived European images, mainly Flemish and North European paintings and engravings, which created panoramic views through perspectival vision, and had become available to North Indian artists since the late sixteenth century.[23] However, unlike the European models, the page we are looking at is not organised according to a single vanishing point; instead, it contains many views from different perspectives and different planes, which are plotted onto a single composition, and allow the viewer access to details of each unit that are far more visible on the pictorial plane than they would be in reality. The multiplicity of positions available to the viewer means that the painting does not lay down or control his or her bodily relationship to the page; it allows free movement across the painted surface rather than a fixed position. Absorbing detail – figural interactions, architectural units, the fluid textures of nature – is as much a temporal experience. In the end observing, recalling, re-telling form a composite mode that seeks to problematise the act of seeing itself. This phenomenon of presenting a field with potentially multiple vignettes rather than one coherent spatial unit, or of combining different or contrasting pictorial modes and plotting multiple temporalities onto a single plane, was to become a feature of South Asian manuscript painting over the coming century, from the high noon of pictorial production at the Mughal courts under the patronage of the Emperors Jahangir and Shah Jahan (r. 1628–1658), to experiments of painters from the regional centres.[24]

The second image dates to a century and a half earlier – it is a painting by the artist Madhu Khanazad, which was produced in the court workshop of the Mughal emperor Akbar (r. 1556–1605) at Lahore in 1595 (Plate 2.3). It belongs to a Persian manuscript, the *Khamsa*

---

23 Ebba Koch, 'The Hierarchical Principles of Shah Jahani Painting', in: Milo C. Beach, Ebba Koch and Wheeler M. Thackston (eds), *King of the World: The Padshahnama, an Imperial Manuscript from the Royal Library*, London: Azimuth Editions, 1997, pp. 130–43.

24 See for instance examples from the Deccan: *Chand Bibi Playing Polo*, Golconda c. 1725, National Museum, New Delhi; *Chandi Bibi Hawking with Attendants in a Landscape*, Deccan c. 1700, both reproduced in Deborah Hutton, 'Portraits of "A Noble Queen": Chand Bibi in the Historical Imaginary', in Aitken (ed.), *A Magic World*, pp. 50–63, figs. 1 and 4.

of the poet Nizami Ganjavi (1141–1209).[25] The text was first composed in Iran at the turn of the thirteenth century and underwent many re-editions. Three hundred years later a new, and this time richly illustrated, edition was produced in North India. In this particular episode, Aflatun, the Persian name for Plato, forms part of the circle of Greek philosophers at the court of Alexander – or Sikandar, as he is called in Persian. To outdo his rival Aristu (Aristotle), Aflatun invents an instrument based on the laws of universal harmony, on which he plays soul-stirring music that can attract wild animals and charm them to the point of intoxication. In the words of the poet Nizami: when he played on it 'neither did the young wolf attack the sheep nor did the fierce lion pay attention to the wild ass'.[26] Nizami's commentary became the basis for an earlier interpretation of this image, when it was read as an example of a cultural transfer of Orphic notions of universal harmony grafted onto Solomonic ideals of perfect justice symbolised by the peaceful concord of animals; according to this reading, the ideal was then adapted by the Mughal rulers to ideologically frame notions of kingship.[27] Without undermining this earlier view, let us look at this image from another perspective, drawing attention to some of its features that have remained unexplained in earlier interpretations. I refer here to aspects, which go beyond the literary requirements of the text and are therefore unique to the visual representation of the subject, a characteristic that marked the practice of court artists both in Iran and North India.[28] To begin with, the musical instrument which Aflatun plays has been described in the text as an *arghanun*, an organ whose creation is credited to the tenth-century philosopher Al Farabi; it was made by stretching a gazelle skin perfumed with musk over a gourd to which strings were set.[29] In Madhu Khanazad's painting the instrument is a European pipe organ, based on a real example that had made its way to North India through one of many networks of object exchange, and which in the painted image comes to function as a sign of cultural difference. This is reinforced by a further characteristic of the painted image. Embedded in the organ is a collage of coloured drawings, each one proclaiming its specific cultural moorings: the bust of a man, whose hat is a marker of his European identity; below is the image of an artist painting a European; on the left above, a Christian scene, either a nativity or the annunciation, several examples of which were available to and copied by local artists; and below a drawing of

25 Barbara Brend, *The Emperor Akbar's Khamsah of Nizami*, London: British Library, 1995; Karin Ådahl, *A Khamsa of Nizami of 1439: Origin of the Miniatures, a Presentation and Analysis*, Uppsala: Almqvist and Wiksell, 1981.

26 Brend, *The Emperor Akbar's Khamsah of Nizami*, p. 58.

27 Robert Skelton, 'Imperial Symbolism in Mughal Painting', in: Priscilla P. Soucek (ed.), *Content and Context of Visual Arts in the Islamic World*, University Park: Penn State University Press, 1988, pp. 179–91; Ebba Koch, *Shah Jahan and Orpheus: The Pietre Dure Decoration and the Programme of the Throne in the Hall of Public Audiences at the Red Fort of Delhi*, Graz: Akademische Druck- und Verlagsanstalt, 1988, p. 29.

28 Artists did not execute paintings as literal illustrations of textual accounts. See John Seyller, *Pearls of the Parrot of India: The Walters Art Museum Khamsa of Amir Khusraw of Delhi*, Baltimore: Walters Art Museum, 2001, pp. 112–13.

29 Koch, *Shah Jahan and Orpheus*, p. 29.

Majnu in the desert communing with animals (Plate 2.3a, detail).[30] This particular mode of engagement with migrant images and traditions constitutes a practice of referencing or citation from different visual traditions – both the local and the distant – as a particular form of incorporation, one which motions towards difference and juxtaposes without assimilating or erasing that difference. That which is appropriated is not fully absorbed, but simply made visible by juxtaposing with a different pictorial mode. Little attention is paid to a coherent narrative; on the contrary, the inserted elements disrupt the narrative even as they remain alien to it.

The phenomena described in both the images above – of juxtaposing either seemingly incongruous modes of vision or of single elements used as pictorial codes – all recognise mobility as an evident and crucial factor. The image, understood in its materiality as an object in the process of becoming, is made through assembling multiple components that belong both to the moment and space when they are brought to converge as well as to other space-times. Yet the properties of such an assembled image are not limited to their discreet component parts but produced by the interaction between them. According to Kajri Jain, such an understanding of an assemblage is a productive concept for thinking about images because of its 'open-ended capacity to work historically across multiple registers of analysis that are ultimately materially driven'.[31] Inherited art historical readings of what I have, drawing on this understanding, termed an 'assembled image', are however premised on a different set of assumptions built into the history of the discipline. Art history's formation as a modern discipline, together with the modern university where it was located, was accompanied by a 'return' to the Renaissance. Cast as a canonical formative moment of Western art, a historical juncture when claims to art's modernity were seen to crystallise against a medieval background of cult objects and artisanal production, the Renaissance came to serve as a privileged object of art historical knowledge.[32] The pictorial crux of art's modernity was located within the naturalist-perspectival mode of illusionism, based on certain forms of recession and organisation of space around a single vanishing point together with the use of techniques like *trompe l'oeil* and *sfumato* – claimed as a modern, rational form of sight and of plotting the world by repudiating a 'medieval way of seeing'. Following a linear logic, modern vision is then believed to have travelled to other regions of the world as a fully formed and self-confident mode. The encounter with local regimes of visuality has been frequently characterised in terms of partial absorption or of a failure to attain the full technical mastery required by illusionist forms. An art historical discourse about the 'difficulties' experienced

---

30 A similar organ with collaged motifs of European figures – a nobleman and an angel – features on the lower edge of a *hashiya* of one of the folios of Jahangir Album conserved in the Berlin State Library (see below); reproduced in Ernest Kühnel and Hermann Goetz, *Indische Buchmalerei aus dem Jahangir-Album der Staatsbibliothek zu Berlin*: Scarabaeus Verlag, 1924, fol. 1a, p. 28. For the connection between Plato and Majnun, see Molly E. Aitken, *The Intelligence of Tradition in Rajput Court Painting*, New Haven: Yale University Press, 2010, pp. 166–67.

31 Jain, *Gods in the Time of Democracy*, p. 12.

32 Margaret Iversen and Stephen Melville, *Writing Art History: Disciplinary Departures*, Chicago: University of Chicago Press, 2010, pp. 15–16.

by North Indian artists in creating figures in space that would make for spatial coherence is marked by a consensus around the idea of failure to attain a perfect pictorial vision and underlines much of the writing on the subject. Such a position in the historiography of South Asian pictorial practices of pre-colonial court cultures goes back to colonial writings of the twentieth century – with some echoes in recent times.[33]

Among the founding figures of the modernist genealogy of Western art history was Erwin Panofsky, whose pivotal essay of 1927 (given as a talk in 1925), 'Perspective as Symbolic Form', provided the scholarly apparatus with which to make an essentially modern epistemological balance between subject and object theoretically explicit.[34] For Panofsky, the advent of perspective – 'the transformation of psychophysiological space into mathematical space … an objectification of the subjective',[35] representing vision as disembodied and distant – was at the same time the advent of a reflexive self-awareness about the nature of art. In other words, this reflexivity opened the door for a serious study of art's history: the moment of grasping perspectival vision was also the moment that art history as a discipline became possible.[36] While Panofsky's construct was subjected to critical revision in later years by Maurice Merleau-Ponty and Hubert Damisch as well as in discussions within film studies,[37] its powerful narrative of origins has – till recent revisionist moves to rethink the Renaissance in a critical global frame – profoundly shaped Western scholarship's engagement with art outside of the West. The historical juncture when artists in Europe, beginning with Cézanne and continuing with the Cubists, Expressionists, and Surrealists, staged a powerful revolt against the pictorial principles of naturalist art, coincided with the introduction of art schools providing teaching of academic art and 'modern' methods of figural drawing as well as the intro-

33 For a discussion of the context in studies of the European Renaissance that was one factor in generating normative art historical values, see Monica Juneja, 'Reading Culture through Art – Jacob Burckhardt in the Twenty First Century', in Andreas Beyer, Susanna Burghartz and Lucas Burkart (eds), *Burckhardt: Renaissance*, Göttingen, Wallstein Verlag, 2021, pp. 174–90, esp. p. 184ff. Discussions of Mughal painting go back to Percy Brown, *Indian Painting under the Mughals, AD 1550 to AD 1750,* Oxford: Clarendon Press, 1924; Basil Gray, 'The Mughal School', in: Barrett and Gray (eds), *Painting of India*, pp. 76–114. More recently, Ebba Koch has interpreted this play with contrary aesthetics in Mughal painting as expressions of 'hierarchical principles' within imperial ideologies; others have read this phenomenon as a failure to absorb fully a level of technical mastery required by illusionist forms: Koch, 'The Hierarchical Principles'; Milo C. Beach, 'The Gulshan Album and its European Sources', *Museum of Fine Arts Bulletin*, vol. 63, 1965: 63–91; Jeremiah P. Losty, 'Towards a New Naturalism: Portraiture in Murshidabad and Avadh, 1750–1780', in Barbara Schmitz (ed.), *After the Great Mughals: Painting in Delhi and the Regional Courts in the 18th and 19th Centuries*, Mumbai: Marg Publications, 2002, pp. 3–55.

34 'Perspektive als symbolische Form', lecture delivered in 1924 at the Warburg Library, Hamburg, published as Erwin Panofksy, 'Die Perspektive als symbolische Form', in: Fritz Saxl (ed.), *Vorträge der Warburg-Bibliothek 1924–25*, Berlin: Teubner, 1927, pp. 258–330; a modern English translation *Perspective as Symbolic Form*, trans. Christopher S. Wood, New York: Zone Books, 1991.

35 Panofsky, *Perspective as Symbolic Form*, p. 66.

36 Iversen and Melville, *Writing Art History*, pp. 122–23.

37 Maurice Merleau-Ponty, 'Le doute de Cézanne' (1945), in: *Sens et non-sens*, Paris: Gallimard, 1996, pp. 13–33; Hubert Damisch, *L'origine de la perspective*, Paris: Flammarion, 1987; Iversen and Melville, *Writing Art History*, Chapter 6.

duction of art history in the distant colonies.[38] Canons, which were destabilised under the aegis of artistic modernism in Western Europe, transported a 'hyperreal'[39] conception of the West to Asian contexts and continued to remain an entrenched basis of historiography; these were then absorbed within indigenous nationalist approaches to art historical writing, once colonial texts had been purged of the crassest of anti-colonial judgements.[40]

Let me now return to the examination of pictorial practices with a view to addressing issues that look beyond the above framework. In what follows, the images I will discuss could be regarded as a condensation of temporal moments, which then act as a space to make difference – or heterogeneity, to use James Clifford's term[41] – visible; the image acts as a site upon which to negotiate and theorise about its self-constitution through transculturation. The Jesuit missions were initially the principal agents involved in the transmission of visual and material artefacts – engravings, paintings, crucifixes – from centres in Europe to locations in Asia, Africa, and Latin America; the images that we view as vehicles of Western visual practices were shaped by Christianity on its global routes via its missions. These were primarily engravings produced at centres such as Antwerp, and included the famous Polyglot Bible as well as Flemish, German, and Italian prints whose production was anchored in a context of Christian devotional imagery. They were intended as a source of Christian narratives in keeping with the Council of Trent's conviction that images possessed the power to capture 'the visual senses and lead man to recognition of a higher truth'.[42] In other words, such images were about visualising Christian doctrine and closing the gap between faith and reason. From that perspective, the seemingly fluid connection between real and pictorial space was meant to mirror the heavenly in earthly terms along an articulated continuum, though equally subject to interruptions and disjunctures, which also emanated from the devotional character of the representations.

A couple of examples illustrate this. The print *Saint Matthew and the Angel* (fig. 1) refers to the truth of the Gospel signified by the writing of the word by St Matthew, a motif read in the South Asian context through the filter of archetypal debates, both scholarly and theological, about truth and falsity. The second example is an engraving by Raphael Sadeler of

38 Partha Mitter, *Art and Nationalism in Colonial India 1850–1922: Occidental Orientations*, Cambridge: Cambridge University Press, 1994; Tapati Guha-Thakurta, *Monuments, Objects, Histories: Institutions of Art in Colonial and Post-Colonial India*, New Delhi: Permanent Black, 2004.

39 The term was coined by Dipesh Chakrabarty, 'Postcoloniality and the Artifice of History', in: *Provincializing Europe: Postcolonial Thought and Historical Difference*, New Delhi: Oxford University Press, 2001, p. 37.

40 For a discussion of this historiography, Monica Juneja, 'Das Visuelle in Sprache übersetzen? Der wissenschaftliche Diskurs und die Polyvalenz indischer Bilder', *Zeitenblicke*, vol. 7 (2), 2008, http://www.zeitenblicke.de/2008/2/juneja/index_html (accessed June 2020).

41 James Clifford, *Routes: Travel and Translation in the Late Twentieth Century*, Cambridge MA: Harvard University Press, 1999, p. 3.

42 Ebba Koch, 'The Influence of the Jesuit Missions on the Symbolic Representations of the Mughal Emperors', in Christian W. Troll (ed.), *Islam in India: Studies and Commentaries*, New Delhi: Oxford University Press, 1982, pp. 14–29, reprinted in Ebba Koch, *Mughal Art and Imperial Ideology*, New Delhi: Oxford University Press, 2001, pp. 1–11, here p. 8; Gauvin A. Bailey, *The Jesuits and the Grand Mogul: Renaissance Art at the Imperial Court of India, 1580–1630*, Washington DC: Smithsonian Institution, 1998.

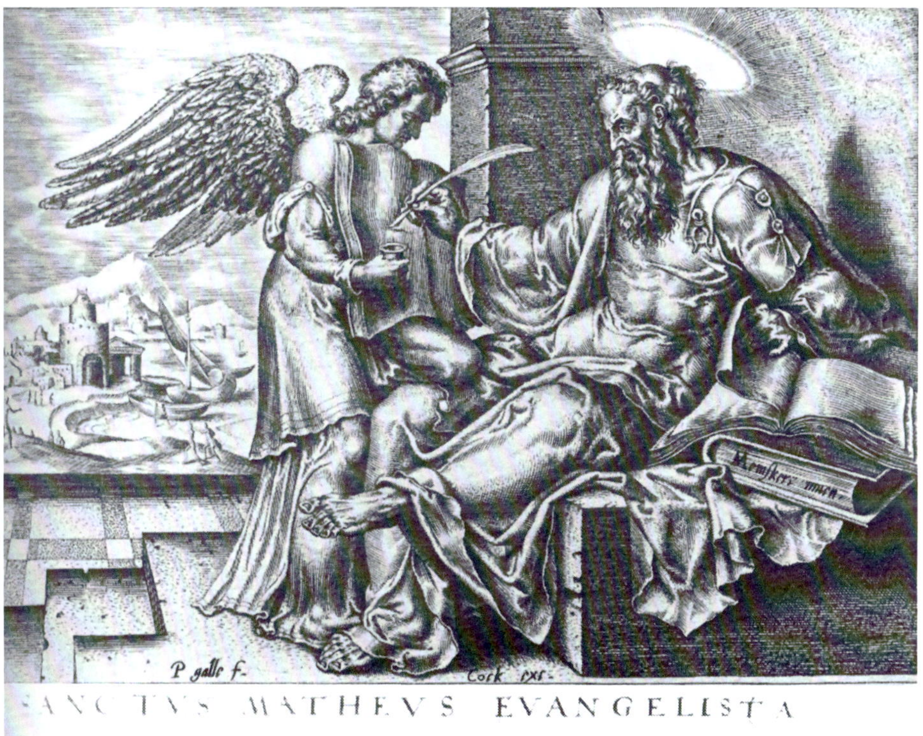

1 Philips Galle after Maarten van Heemskerk, *Saint Matthew and the Angel*, engraving, 1562, Amsterdam Rijksmuseum

a painting by the Flemish artist Martin de Vos – *Dolor* – which pays homage to Albrecht Dürer's *St Jerome in His Study* and portrays the contemplative life of a Christian saint (figs. 2 and 4). Both these prints provide examples of attempted spatial illusion, which is, however, only partially accomplished technically. In both prints, by Galle and Sadeler, breaks in the lines of recession are observable. In the first, the artist effected a break both in terms of space and scale: the inner space, treated as a fragment of the spectator's space, deploys the qualities of trompe l'oeil that inscribe it with a projective, intrusive quality. The wall abruptly breaks to suggest an aperture, a window with a receding view of the outside showing miniaturised figures, buildings, and boats which, though they ignore scale, could represent a painted view. The figures of the saint and the angel do not face the window/image or even register an awareness of it; rather, it is the spectator's eye that is meant to take in both fragments at one glance. A similar feature is evident in the Sadeler print, which effects a demarcation of inner and outer space, each subject to a different treatment. The interior features a large painting of the Last Judgment in the background, demonstrating that perspectival space went hand in hand with religious connotations. Both these prints break up the picture plane into fragments, making each the product of a distinct pictorial mode, a phenomenon in Flemish art

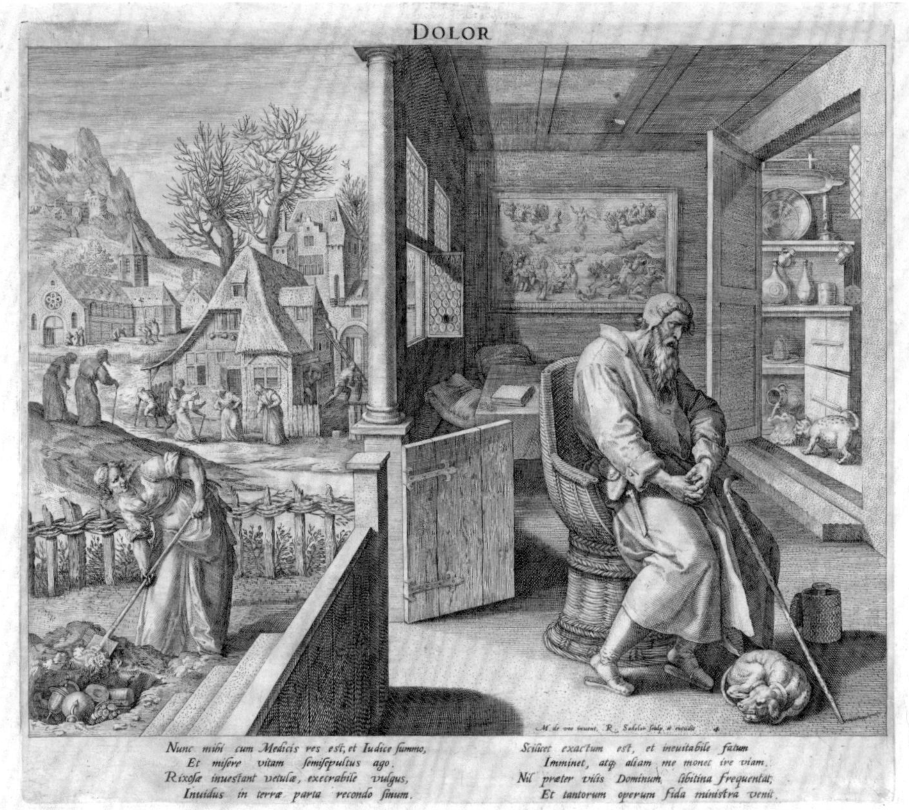

2 Raphael Sadeler after Maerten de Vos, *Dolor*, engraving 1591, New York, Metropolitan Museum of Art

that Victor Stoichita has designated as 'splitting' or the production of antitheses. Stoichita's analysis of the interactions between such split-levels in paintings and prints from Northern Europe reads these breaks as intrinsic to the Christian contexts of these images: antitheses are frequently a device of allegorisation and transmission of Christian truths. Initially condemned by contemporary theorists as 'pictorial heresies', this mode of theorising pictorial practice acquired considerable resonance in North European painting and its printed replicas.[43] The use of the window/niche/painting in the image of artists from the Jahangir album (Plate 2.1) – as in other examples where court artists pick up the motif – plays on different significations of the window in a new context. For instance, the window designated an opening into the inside world, an internal mirror through which to filter the outside world and see the immanence of God, an analogy that is frequently used in Islamic mystical texts, and to be discussed in the following section.

43 Stoichita, *The Self-Aware Image*, pp. 3–16.

Illusion and Beyond

Access to the reception of migrant images in the North Indian court ateliers requires piecing together stray references from existing sources and, above all, recovering the praxis of artists through their painted work. The latter – as will emerge below – allows us to observe that no one mode of representation was singled out for its narrative superiority or optical exactitude and which therefore required mastering a set of techniques to be universally applied. Rather, the visual characteristics of the newly arrived European images were perceived as representing an alien (coming from *firang*)[44] or specifically Christian mode of pictorial practice, a distinct visuality classified in such terms, one that could be acquired through copying and deployed to present subjects considered Western/Christian. Certain motifs – such as the window with the baroque curtain – came to function as codes for Western subjects and pictorial modes, as seen in this rendering of the Mughal artist Kesu Das of the subject of *Saint Matthew and the Angel* (Plate 2.4).[45] The awareness of different modalities of seeing and translating the 'seen' into image was inscribed within the few textual accounts available on the art of painting in the courts of North India. For example, the chronicler, philosopher, and court historian Abu'l Fazl Allami (1551–1602) draws up a chronological sequence of artists and the pictorial modes they stood for: he ascribes the highest respect to the Persian master Bihzad, then refers to the 'magic making' of the European artists, who possessed the quality of making 'inanimate objects appear to come alive'.[46] These and other responses to European images in the South Asian courts and the pictorial effects they achieved were wide-ranging and ambivalent. Naturalistic representation exercised enormous fascination: engagements with it through practices of copying, juxtaposing, or creating playful reversals display an intrinsic attraction to the enabling potentialities of naturalistic visual regimes – the 'magical' power to which Abu'l Fazl and Jesuit accounts refer. At the same time, illusionist ways of seeing, when relocated in South Asia, entered a field of opposing pulls because vision itself – in the Asian contexts I examine – was implicated in a set of ostensibly contradictory theological and literary discourses. In these expositions, the image was perceived both as a space of desire and yet as having a seductive power that could lead to a form of capitulation leaning dangerously close to idolatry.[47]

---

44 Abu'l Fazl Allami, *A'in-i Akbari*, trans. H. Blochmann, 2 vols., Delhi: Low Price Publications, 2001 (1927), vol. 1, pp. 102–3.

45 Among other examples of this usage: *The Disputing Physicians*, folio from *Khamsa* of Nizami, by Miskina, reproduced in Brend, *The Emperor Akbar's Khamsa*, figs. 3, 11; or a leaf from an album commissioned by Jahangir featuring the Virgin and Child by the painter Basawan (painted c. 1590 subsequently included by Jahangir in the album), San Diego Museum of Art. I have discussed this image at some length in: 'The Breast-Feeding Mother as Icon and Source of Affect in Visual Practice – a Transcultural Journey', in: Kumkum Roy (ed.), *Looking Within, Looking Without: Exploring Households in the Subcontinent through Time*, Delhi: Primus Books, 2015, pp. 105–33.

46 Abu'l Fazl Allami, *A'in-i Akbari*, vol. 1, pp. 113–15.

47 On the tangled question of idolatry and image making in Islam, Finbarr B. Flood, 'Between Cult and Culture: Bamiyan, Islamic Iconoclasm and the Museum', *The Art Bulletin* vol. 84 (4), 2002: 641–59, here 643ff. Jamal J. Elias, *Aisha's Cushion: Religious Art, Perception and Practice in Islam*, Cambridge MA:

This discussion of representation and emulation within a transcultured artistic practice acknowledges no stable 'Western' aesthetic against which 'responses' could be confidently plotted, and yet it does not rule out a consideration of the different ontologies at work that underpinned ways of seeing and representing the world. In the early modern Eurasian context investigated here, questions of artistic representation rested on an edifice of philosophical and theological questions – a vast subject awaiting detailed research – which I will briefly refer to here. Discussions on art-making, illusionism, and their philosophical underpinnings can be extracted from a few, yet useful, sources within the Persianate literary sphere, whose products were a shared resource among the elites of imperial courts across Central and South Asia during the centuries following Mongolian invasions.[48] Among these texts, prefaces to albums (*muraqqa*) of loose paintings, drawings, and calligraphy, compiled under the patronage of rulers and leading courtiers, were a repository of insights on images, their makers and viewers.[49] Though written as prescriptive texts in a literary idiom resistant to easy decipherment, the album prefaces, according to David Roxburgh, allow us access to 'a culture's view of the procedures, principles, and practices of art and give some idea of its criteria of judgment'.[50] Among the most important of album prefaces and the subject of a close reading by Roxburgh, was the preface to the Bahram Mirza Album, completed in 1544–45. It was authored by Dust Muhammad, an artist and calligrapher at the Safavid court who in 1555 travelled to India on the invitation of the emperor Humayun, and was crucial to creating the atelier for manuscripts and albums under Akbar.[51] Besides the genre of album prefaces, a handful of treatises on the lives of calligraphers and painters, together with a larger number of shorter biographical notices, form a further source to be tapped.[52] And not least, though again replete with oblique references and complex allusive devices, poetic works, have been fruitfully researched to get a grasp of conceptions of image making in the Persian-Islamicate cultural domain.[53]

Harvard University Press, 2012; Silvia Naef, *Bilder und Bilderverbot im Islam: vom Koran bis zum Karikaturstreit*, Munich: Beck Verlag, 2007.

48 I use the term 'Persianate' as an adjectival construction (analogous to 'Islamicate', coined by Marshall G. Hodgson, as distinct from 'Islamic'), to refer to transcultured products of regional cultures, all drawing on a Persian language or literary tradition. This follows the usage in Richard M. Eaton, *India in the Persianate Age 1000–1765*, Penguin Random House: London/New Delhi, 2019.

49 The practice of writing prefaces for albums goes back to late Timurid times (fifteenth century) and proliferated under the Safavids. A few Mughal albums, too, have prefaces written by calligraphers. An incisive study of a seminal Safavid album is David J. Roxburgh, *Prefacing the Image: The Writing of Art History in Sixteenth-Century Iran*, Leiden/Boston: E. J. Brill, 2001.

50 Roxburgh, *Prefacing the Image*, p. 2.

51 Stuart C. Welch, *The Emperor's Album: Images of Mughal India,* New York: Harry N. Abrams, 1987, p. 15.

52 For instance, Qadi Ahmad, *Calligraphers and Painters* (c. 1606), Eng. trans. V. Minorsky, Washington DC: Freer Gallery of Art, 1959.

53 Discussed in Priscilla B. Soucek, 'Nizami on Painters and Painting', in: Richard Ettinghausen (ed.), *Islamic Art in the Metropolitan Museum of Art*, New York: Metropolitan Museum of Art, 1972, pp. 9–22. Also Necipoğlu, 'The Scrutinizing Gaze', where the author investigates several genres of texts, including descriptions of monuments, studies of optics, and philosophical works.

Anecdotes, mythical stories, and biographical vignettes – often stories within stories – animate the different genres of texts; from these tales, didactic nuggets could be extracted relating to the legitimacy of painting, to criteria for defining a 'licit' image, and to distinctive traditions of picture-making across regions – the Persianate, Chinese, or European. Dust Muhammad's preface, for example, transmits a seminal foundational myth of the art of portraiture – a story titled 'The Chest of Witnessing' – with a view to reassure makers of images that 'depiction is not without noble lineage'.[54] Two ambassadors, so the account goes, were sent by the first caliph, Abu Bakr, to the court of the emperor Heraclius of Byzantium. During the meeting, Heraclius demonstrated to the assembled group a chest with several thousand compartments, each containing a portrait (*surat*) of a prophet, beginning with Adam and ending with the Prophet Muhammad. He explained to them that the chest with portraits painted on silk was created by God, in response to Adam's keenness to see God's progeny, the prophets. Subsequently, the king Alexander took the chest from Adam's treasury and carried it on his travels; he then passed it on to the prophet Daniel who made the copies, now in possession of the Byzantine emperor.[55] Tracing the origin of the art of depiction to God offered a path towards affirming the legitimacy of image-making. At the same time, however, the authors of album prefaces, who frequently cast God in the role of a scribe and artist (*musawwir*) wielding a pen/brush and surrounded by the tools of book-making – paper, ink pot, vermillion, white – had to walk a tightrope between the use of metaphor and the danger of 'anthropomorphizing the attributes of God'.[56] This meant having to introduce qualifications in order to distinguish the divine creative process from that of the manual labour of human practitioners.[57] Such a tension – between a theological and philosophical caution against a humanised divinity that could be worshipped as such, and the captivating power of images – runs through most accounts. The story of the chest of portraits can be read as an effort to deal with this ambivalence; it further served to discredit the celebrated tale of Mani, the founder of Manichaeism and a gifted artist, frequently held up as an exemplar of unsurpassed skill in creating true-to-life images.[58] The oft-cited story of Mani, circulated by way of the *Iskandar Nama*, one of the books of the *Khamsa* by the poet Nizami referred to above, recounts the travels of the artist who, upon his arrival in China, was deceived by the appearance of a pond made of perfectly polished glass: trying to fill his pitcher, he ended up breaking the glass. In revenge, Mani painted a completely naturalistic dead dog with its entrails torn out beside the real pond, which prevented the villagers from coming there to get their daily supply of water.[59] In this context, Dust Muhammad makes an important distinction

---

54 Roxburgh, *Prefacing the Image*, p. 174.
55 Summarized from Roxburgh, *Prefacing the Image*, pp. 171–74.
56 David J. Roxburgh, *The Persian Album, 1400–1600: From Dispersal to Collection*, New Haven: Yale University Press, 2005, p. 191.
57 Roxburgh, *Prefacing the Image*, pp. 190–91.
58 Soucek, 'Nizami on Painters', p. 11.
59 *Mani Paints a Dead Dog* by Sur Gujarati, from *Khamsa* of Nizami, reproduced in Brend, *The Emperor Akbar's Khamsah*: figs. 33–34, pp. 48–49. For an earlier rendering of the subject, Soucek, 'Nizami on Painters', pp. 10–11.

between a process of 'visual perception' and the 'visual nature' of an image in its relationship to phenomenal things in the world – a distinction that was equally an ethical one between licit and illicit representation.[60] The conception of an image within these expositions is akin to an intellectual activity, a 'composite sense', in the words of Priscilla Soucek. The images received by the eye are merely impressions (Persian: *nishan*), the starting point of vision; the latter however supersedes the purely physiological to be nurtured by the imagination (*khayal*).[61] Dust Muhammad further differentiates between an artist's skill (*hunar*) and his imagination – success lay not merely in the skilful performance of the hand but in the creative powers of the imagination.[62] An optical reflection of the world could be a site of illusion, the truth of vision lay in the image filtered through the artist's mind.[63] In 'reproducing' an object, the artist transformed an image impressed on his mind in a way that it could not be regarded as equivalent to what the eye saw in the world. Early Islamic texts resorted to the use of pairs of similar but non-identical images as a pedagogical device wherein the viewer was encouraged to critically compare the images on paper with other sources of knowledge in order to abstract a 'mental' image of a phenomenon.[64] The distinction between 'appearance' or 'outer form' (*zahir, surat*) and 'truth' or 'inner meaning' (*batin, manavi*), which was articulated in Islamic mystic thought and poetry, was further elaborated in the Indian context by thinkers such as Abu'l Fazl who put forward arguments about writing and painting. While seeing and knowing stood as the axes along which the critique of painting per se was expressed, Abu'l Fazl assures the reader of his history that Emperor Akbar was an excellent judge of both and therefore capable of using 'outer form' to lead to 'inner meaning'.[65] Going beyond mere eulogy, the court historian built up an argument in a way that negotiated theological tensions while providing an explanation for Akbar's patronage of painting and above all his deep interest in a wide range of new art forms, notably European paintings and prints, the 'rare forms' used by 'the painters of *firang*', as he referred to them.[66]

It would appear that intellectual stances and beliefs such as those described above, circulated and made up a shared universe across Asia and the Mediterranean, all cautioning against the slippery gap between truth and illusion. The Hindu cosmos, for instance, was governed by the belief that while the gods had the power to confuse the real and the illusory (*maya*), devotees were constantly challenged to distinguish one from the other. This message was conveyed by a painting from the court of Bikaner, drawn from the text *Bhagavata Purana*, whose narrative on the life of Krishna was transmitted through recitations over

---

60 Roxburgh, *Prefacing the Image*, p. 186.

61 Soucek, 'Nizami on Painters', pp. 14–15. Soucek also recounts the story, also from the *Khamsa*, of the gifted painter Shapur who worked from memory to create a portrait of the beautiful Shirin.

62 Necipoğlu, on the other hand, argues that creative imagination of the artist/artisan and his productive capacity were mutually reinforcing, 'thereby testifying to the elevated productive and perceptual capacities of humankind', Necipoğlu, 'The Scrutinizing Gaze': 30.

63 Roxburgh, *Prefacing the Image*, pp. 187–88.

64 Persis Berlekamp, *Wonder, Image and Cosmos in Medieval Islam*, New Haven: Yale University Press, 2011.

65 Abu'l Fazl Allami, *A'in-i Akbari*, vol. 1, p. 103.

66 Ibid., pp. 102–3.

generations of devotees.[67] The painting depicts the story of Krishna who responds to a prank played by the God Brahma by creating a group of perfectly simulated young cowherds and their flock within a natural and architectural setting whose life-like appearance manages to deceive the world. In this case, the artist seems to be no longer governed by the necessity of drawing upon naturalistic pictorial means as a language to portray exclusively a Christian subject. The mastery of techniques of illusion and *sfumato*, attained over a century and a half since their arrival at the Mughal centres from whence migrant artists carried them across regional courts, was skilfully used in this instance to draw attention to philosophical questions about vision. In other words, multiple and contrasting regimes serve to problematise the dangers of *maya* or illusion to create naturalistic effects, which are meant to deceive. It can be argued that it is the availability of contrasting modes that enables the creation of a transformed conception of pictorial space.

Drawing upon Michel de Certeau's designation of space (*espace*) in literary-cum-urban topographies[68] as an intersection of mobile elements – as opposed to the stability of a place (*lieu*) – pictorial space too, as the above examples reveal, can function as a polyvalent unity of opposing orders. Space is no longer univocal or stable; its inclusion of multiple 'vectors of direction'[69] allows it to bring narrative together with iconic functions and in the process introduce a fresh dynamic into an image brought to life through words and recitation, as is the case for a large number of paintings that accompany narratives, such as the *Bhagavata Purana*. Artists of many of these works continue to draw upon a sub-stratum of iconic practices that date as far back as an early Buddhist representation of the *jātaka* tales where linear narrativity is renounced in favour of indexical signs that serve as reminders of the Buddha's presence.[70] Yet they are now able to infuse its iconicity with a fresh dynamic wherein the narrative content can evoke a variety of memories, actions, and emotions. David Shulman has discussed the notion of *bhavana* in the context of literary creation, which enables the use of thought processes to make what is imagined efficacious.[71] Similarly, Michael Meister has drawn our attention to layered, processual relationships built into images/objects following from the interaction between image and ritual. The term 'iconoplasty' coined by him refers to a fluidity of forms and 'the transformational characteristics of meanings attached to forms in the same period by different users synchronically and over longer durations (diachronically)'.[72] Studies of transculturation within image making in early modern South Asia can draw

---

67 Reproduced in Aitken, *The Intelligence of Tradition*, fig. 1.8 and pp. 30–31.

68 Michel de Certeau, *L'invention du quotidien: Arts de faire*, Paris: Union générale d'éditions, 1980, pp. 208–10.

69 De Certeau, *L'invention du quotidien*, p. 208.

70 Robert L. Brown, 'Narrative as Icon: The Jātaka Stories in Ancient Indian and Southeast Asian Architecture', in: Juliane Schober (ed.), *Sacred Biography in Buddhist Traditions of South and Southeast Asia*, Honolulu: University of Hawaii Press, 1997, pp. 64–109; Vidya Dehejia, *Discourse in Early Buddhist Art: Visual Narratives of India*, New Delhi: Munshiram Manoharlal, 2005.

71 David Shulman, *More than Real: A History of the Imagination in South Asia*, Cambridge MA: Harvard University Press, 2012.

72 Michael W. Meister, 'Image Iconopraxis and Iconoplasty in South Asia', *RES: Anthropology and Aesthetics*, No. 51 (Spring), 2007: 13–32, here 15–16.

productively on such analytical tools that conceptualise the image as processual rather than static, embodying multiple times – and at the same time an object whose meanings depend on the material processes of its making and use.

Material Mimesis

When investigating cultural constructs of vision, the interactive moments are also about the encounter between the material and the visual. The enquiry involves, in the first place, questioning the notion of an image as exclusively visual: in the South Asian context where seeing was one element of a 'corpothetic' sensibility,[73] we need to address the interface between the material, visual, aural, and sensorial, as palpable objects from distant shores were transposed onto the two-dimensional plane of an image, be it painted from a crucifix, a globe, or an hourglass, or cut-out from prints and pasted, redrawn, relocated, or reframed. Among the image-objects mediating the processes of transculturation that this chapter investigates, prints – engravings and woodcuts – played a generative role. They arrived in large numbers through the commercial ports of Surat and Diu or were brought by travellers and emissaries to the court, but above all by Jesuit missionaries. Heralding a new mobility of images across geographic and temporal boundaries, as well as across media, the print was more than a simple substitute for an already existing work in another, more highly valorised medium, such as painting or sculpture. It functioned as an active agent in the new settings to which it travelled. The 'knowledge' that its narrative content was intended to disseminate may or may not have been assimilated according to the expectations of its makers. Instead, it served as a locus for material creativity and inventiveness – as a template for a new image, or as a movable element that could be extracted, re-affixed and juxtaposed to another fragment, inducing productive slippages and novel insights. A mutable image-object, the engraving or the woodcut came to occupy a nodal position in a web of relationships between cultural worlds and reference systems wherein it never ceased to draw attention to the dual nature of the image as something both internal and external to the human subject.[74]

Mobile materiality in the form of images as objects induced a form of cultural self-fashioning that involved, alongside of cognitive skills, bodily routines and the senses. Furthermore, these transactions with alterity and mimesis were not confined to courtly patrons who commissioned and pored over the finished works: artists, irrespective of individual faiths,

Recent writing has thrown valuable light on the connoisseurship of Sanskrit and Hindu aesthetics at the Mughal court. Translations of texts commissioned by imperial patrons include a work on *rasa* (aesthetic theory/experience), which could serve as a source of political affect. See Audrey Truschke, *Culture of Encounters: Sanskrit at the Mughal Court*, New York: Columbia University Press, 2016, Chapter 2.

73 The term is borrowed from Christopher Pinney, 'Piercing the Skin of the Idol', in: Christopher Pinney and Nicholas Thomas (eds), *Beyond Aesthetics: Art and the Technologies of Enchantment*, Oxford: Berg Publishers, 2001, pp. 157–78. See also Diana L. Eck, *Darśan: Seeing the Divine Image in India*, New York: Columbia University Press, 1996, who describes seeing as 'a kind of touching', p. 9 and Chapter 2.

74 Hans Belting, *Bild-Anthropologie: Entwürfe für eine Bildwissenschaft*, Munich: Fink Verlag, 2006 (3rd edition), p. 11ff.

training, or identification with particular styles, revealed the capacity to copy, emulate and dialogue with different styles, each of which was classified and labelled. Notes on the margins of manuscripts, paintings, or preparatory drawings often record the names of the artists involved in the production of a work; sometimes they even state the number of days spent painting each image as well as list occasional instructions from the patron conveyed via librarians or those in charge of the workshops (*taswirkhana*).[75] The evidence of the artists' names shows that paintings that appear stylistically irreconcilable were created by the same hand and testify to the ability and actual practice of artists to work in more than one idiom at any given time. This intriguing evidence, according to John Seyller, raises doubts about the tendency in art historical writing to ascribe 'individual' styles to court painters.[76] And yet, the history of patronage associated with ideals of connoisseurship cultivated by patrons, in particular Emperor Jahangir, appears to have fostered a cultivation of individual pictorial styles. Under Jahangir's patronage, certain master artists (*ustad*) were encouraged to develop recognisable areas of expertise: Mansur is mentioned frequently in the *Jahangirnama* as a painter with remarkable skills in portraying plants and animals, Abu'l Hasan and Bishan Das are named as imperial portraitists, Govardhan a painter of holy men and musicians.[77] This does not exclude the possibility, however, of works by each of these artists crossing the confines of the genres for which they were proclaimed as experts; nor did it keep them from experimenting with a combination of expressive idioms.[78] From a transcultural perspective, such fluid patterns can be used to destabilise dichotomous models of relationalities, which alternated between complete absorption and resistance or refusal.[79] Instead of flattening difference or even ignoring its sharp edges or disjunctures, transregional migratory practices appear to have generated fresh perceptions and representations involving recognition, an effort to fix, name, classify, and ultimately domesticate difference. Yet even the move to control meaning did not preclude a dialogical engagement; rather, it depended on and partook of it.

75 John Seyller, 'Scribal Notes on Mughal Manuscript Illustrations', *Artibus Asiae*, vol. 48 (3–4), 1987: 247–77, here 261.

76 Seyller, 'Scribal Notes'.

77 Wheeler M. Thackston (ed. and trans.), *The Jahangirnama: Memoirs of Jahangir, Emperor of India*, Oxford/ New York: Oxford University Press, pp. 268–69, 314, 319.

78 For instance, the exquisite rendering of a plane tree with squirrels that bears the name Abu'l Hasan (inscribed on the back), otherwise known for his painting of royal portraits and court scenes, London, British Library, see Plate 6.1. Another example is a late work by Govardhan painted in a 'Timurid' idiom and portraying Timur together with a parasol bearer on horseback, c. 1620–40, Dublin, Cheater Beatty Library, reproduced in Elaine Wright, *Muraqqa: Imperial Mughal Albums from the Chester Beatty Library Dublin*, Alexandria, Virginia: Art Services International, 2008, cat. 40A, p. 307.

79 This model of argumentation marks Hans Belting's study *Florenz und Bagdad*, where discussions of Asian regions are trapped in essentialisms as the complex histories of engagement with European imagery in these regions have not been investigated. Contrary to Belting's assumptions, artists, patrons and writers on art in the Eurasian regions following the Mongol conquest did not eschew the question of images; rather, they confronted it directly, discussed its legality and juxtaposed it with Western modalities of image-making, as I have discussed above for the case of North India. Among critical responses to Belting are Necipoglu, 'The Scrutinizing Gaze'; Claire J. Farago, review in *Renaissance Quarterly*, vol. 65 (3), 2012: 879–81; Frank Büttner, review in *Kunstchronik*, vol. 62 (2), 2009: 82–89; David Roxburgh, 'Two-point Perspective: On Hans Belting's *Florence and Baghdad*', *Artforum*, vol. 50 (8), 2012, pp. 61–64.

Material interaction with pictorial vision found a home within albums produced by artists and calligraphers for their patrons. An album was an assemblage of calligraphy, drawings, prints, stray paintings, or fragments thereof, arranged on folios, while folios in turn were compiled to produce an album. The album functioned as a central unit for the collection and display of images. The earliest albums date to the fifteenth century, they were patronised by Timurid rulers in Herat and are mostly preserved in the library of the Topkapi Palace Museum in Istanbul. Among the more famous albums, carefully planned by a single artist and calligrapher was the Safavid album of Bahram Mirza, compiled by Dust Muhammad in 1554 and whose preface I referred to in the preceding section. For the Mughals, who traced their descent to the Timurids, the artistic legacy of that dynasty, continued in the achievements of the Safavids, had a strong appeal. When Dust Muhammad migrated to the Mughal court on the invitation of the emperor Humayun, it is likely that his talents as a maker of albums were put to use in the Mughal *taswirkhana*. Unlike their Safavid counterparts, Mughal albums were not chronologically fixed or unchanging entities; rather, they continued to grow and undergo internal reorganisation from patron to patron. Among the famous Mughal albums – still intact today – is the Gulshan album (*Muraqqa-i Gulshan*), which derives its name from Gulshan/Gulistan Library in Tehran, where it is conserved.[80] It contains folios assembled for the emperors Humayun (r. 1530–1540, 1555–1556) and Akbar and underwent several additions and alterations under Jahangir. A companion volume, named the Berlin album (again because now conserved in the State Library of the Prussian Cultural Foundation in Berlin) and containing material dating from 1590 to 1618, was initiated for Akbar and enlarged for Jahangir.[81] The changing fortunes of the Kevorkian album, begun under Jahangir and continuously augmented, altered, and refashioned until the early twentieth century, when it was acquired at an auction by the New York collector, Hagop Kevorkian, make the album a palimpsestic object, a site to record different dynastic memories.[82]

The Persian term for album, *muraqqa*, means patchwork and refers to the cloak worn by mendicants or Sufis with patches taken from the garments of revered saints.[83] Albums, too, were created according to a practice of literally reusing picture fragments or pictures to compose new images or to collect them within a loosely bound volume, by physically cutting out chosen segments from existing paintings to be pasted on to single folios. The album brought together paintings – or cut-outs of them – from Persia, Northern Europe, Turkey, the Deccan and juxtaposed them to highlight their culturally alien qualities in a way that preserved the visibility of plurality while seeking to grasp and master it. Albums of paintings from Northern India furnish instances of the ways in which the album could become a site for compiling migrant images, either cut out and re-located or, more often, first copied by local artists from

---

80 Mohammad-Hasan Semsar, *Golestan Palace Library: A Portfolio of Miniature Paintings and Calligraphy*, Tehran: Zarrin and Simin Books, 2001. Also Milo C. Beach, 'The Gulshan Album and the Workshops of Prince Salim', *Artibus Asiae*, vol. 73 (2), 2013: 445–77.

81 On the Berlin album, Kühnel and Goetz, *Indische Buchmalerei*.

82 The trajectories of the Kevorkian album have been discussed by Welch, *The Emperor's Album*, pp. 11–30.

83 Roxburgh, *The Persian Album*, pp. 181–82; Wright, *Muraqqa*, p. xvii.

other sources and then cut and pasted. This was an aspect particular the making of albums in South Asia where, unlike their Safavid counterparts, patrons, artists, calligraphers, and all those involved in the production of folios to be compiled into an album drew on a more variegated repertoire of materials.[84] These included Persian and Turkish paintings, and drawings, European prints and paintings, Deccani works, and Mughal copies and adaptations of all of these, together with contemporary and earlier Mughal works. Images and fragments were drawn from diverse sources and placed together on pages of albums with each page becoming a space for multiple 'stories'[85] revealing an explicit eschewal of a single, linear narrative (Plates 2.5 and 2.6). Instead, the simultaneity of times and regimes enabled through acts of abstracting, relocating, and juxtaposing, of painting over to smooth edges, and of layering, is constitutive of a new pictorial space in which the agency to map the world is enacted through the modes of seeing it. The physical act of cutting, reassembling, and pasting – the act of combining which at the same time keeps the elements separate – works to suggest geographical and cultural distance and simultaneously a voyage through the haptic relationship with the material across this distance; boundaries are delineated, crossed, and reset.

In his preface to the Bahram Mirza Album, Dust Muhammad uses the term *jāmakhāna*, an analogy from architecture, to describe the album: the term referred to a room whose walls were embedded with small mirror fragments, a frequent feature in Persianate palace complexes, where persons standing in the room saw their fractured reflections.[86] An album too was considered one such locus of reflection and multiplication, in view of its contents as well as its forms that included collaged views, different colours, inks, interspersed calligraphy and disjunctive formats that created a tension between cohesion and disintegration and demanded of its viewers an act of re-contextualisation and an augmented comprehension. The analogy of broken reflections rather than a coherent mirror image implied that only those endowed with special powers of visual perception could make sense of the work – a specially privileged group of viewers who would not confuse what they see with what is made.[87] Mughal albums, while they resorted to copying, did not fail to draw attention to their own materiality, to the tactile processes of cutting, pasting, and recomposing, as transitions between fragments often remained tangible on the surface of the image-object. The 'frame' of the folio – the elaborate margins or borders (*hashiyas*) with archetypal figures sourced from a variety of texts – had the function of holding the folio with its component elements together. The borders, as in this example from the Gulshan album, were often replete with references to craftsmen making paper, calligraphers at work, a manuscript stand, or a pot containing gold leaf burnishing; their subject is the production of paintings, manuscripts

---

84 According to Roxburgh, Safavid and Timurid albums drew mainly on Chinese materials. The Bahram Mirza Album, for instance, had only two European works, one of which was removed from the album in the early twentieth century, see Roxburgh, *Prefacing the Image*, p. 196.
85 De Certeau uses the term 'récits', *L'invention du quotidie*, pp. 205–7.
86 Roxburgh, *Prefacing the Image*, p. 184.
87 Ibid., p. 189.

and albums (Plate 2.7).[88] The frame then becomes a space where the coming into being of an image as an act of production is made visible; it articulates a process which illusionism effaces from the painted surface. Material mimesis of the kind we encounter here complicates what we understand by imitation and emulation; it involves a mediation between different worlds, visual modes and symbolic systems. Mimetic desire, according to Taussig, does not necessarily rely on the power of that which it usurps or apes, but enters into a relationship to induce reflection on the instability of received knowledge, making the image into a charged object.[89] The album could be seen therefore as a discursive site to which the viewer was expected to bring, together with the gift of true cognition, his own historical knowledge and memory, to be able to compare and judge different modes of image-making. One highly didactic example is a folio from the Gulshan album that demonstrates four diverse modes, and at the same time references to different spaces and times, of portraying the human, male body – the Persianate, early and later Mughal and the European, the latter a copy of an engraving of Adam and Eve after the Fall by Jan Saedeler, subsequently cut out and visibly pasted on to the folio.[90] While the art historical narrative transmitted by Persian album prefaces, so dexterously recuperated by Roxburgh, builds on biography and a relationship between successive masters in a tradition, the materially mimetic Mughal albums made difference and variety within pictorial practice visible and tangible; they did so less by placing these in a linear order, than through juxtaposition and comparison. As images engage with images within the folios of the albums, it is for the viewer to in turn to engage with their engagement.

As tangible expressions of the ideals of connoisseurship, and a celebration of the love to collect, classify, and canonise through selection, albums were conspicuous for their opulent materiality. Their precious bindings differentiate between the textures of leather, lacquer, embossed surfaces on the exterior, and a radiant gold sunburst (*Shamsa*) as frontispiece. Viewing the album could often be a solitary, exclusive and introspective experience embodied in posture and gesture – a human form bent over the manuscript stand or holding the miniature album within joint palms, to pore over each detail of the page, a self-contained stance shutting out the world beyond. This was more likely in the case of Mughal albums in view of their size that did not come close to the gigantic folios of Timurid counterparts.[91] Narrative images – like the example from *Bhagwata Purana* cited above or the occasional single folio from a Persianate literary context[92] – were viewed with a prior oral knowledge of the content and were often, in the case of Hindu devotional texts, sung or recited, which was the aural filter through which seeing took place. The object-quality of the two-dimensional album page was highlighted through a further, purely material dimension: the use of colour as palimp-

---

88 Further examples are to be found in the Berlin album, see Kühnel and Goetz, *Indische Buchmalerei*, fol. 18a, p. 20.
89 Taussig, *Mimesis and Alterity*, Chapter 4.
90 Reproduced in Beach, 'The Gulshan Album and its European Sources': 89.
91 Rizvi (ed.), *Affect, Emotion*, pp. 4–5.
92 See for example the single folios from the *Shahnama* in the Berlin album, e.g. in Kühnel and Goetz, *Indische Buchmalerei*, fol. 14a.

sest. While colour, which in the Latourian sense comprises a range of raw substances that are transported across distances, can be transformed and sublimated into aesthetic effect,[93] pigment, given its chromatic materiality, can make the painted surface a field of force. The picture becomes a surface through which to experiment with the indexicality and materiality of colour. In the paintings studied here, colour is used in many possible ways: either as a translucent watery surface to suggest the insubstantiality of distant landscapes or in opaque layers to render faces as resistant to emotive tremor (like the over-painted faces of deities), alternatively in conjunction with other materials such as beetle wings to render the glistening effects of jewellery or to evoke the life of the dark night. Pigment, described by Natasha Eaton as 'affective material',[94] could impart to the image a sensuous presence that exceeds utilisation and simply asserts itself as resistant matter. Chromatic surfaces – silver and especially gold – both echoed and rendered tangible the innumerable references to precious metals in literary genres.[95] The resplendent materiality of gold adorning album pages challenged the notion of an image as illusion by asserting its value as a precious object by making its thingness palpable. The use of gold, which prevailed across the Eurasian empires, in the form of gold dust used in manuscripts,[96] underwent a transformation in the workshops of the Indian courts where it was used as liquid paint created through the melting of gold leaf.

Memory Chains

A painting of large dimensions titled *Princes of the House of Timur* and dated to around 1550, that is, to the reign of the second Mughal emperor Humayun, portrays a lush garden setting populated with a large number of personages – servants, courtiers, and guests. It shows a ruler in Central Asian dress seated in a pavilion and receiving a visitor in audience.[97] The picture, interestingly, has been considerably overpainted, most probably in the seventeenth century, to incorporate the figures of Akbar, Jahangir, and Prince Khurram (the later emperor Shah Jahan), probably also his brothers, the princes Khusrau and Parviz, while the seated courtiers have been labelled as the sons and grandsons of Timur. A large number of the figures of the crowded scene have also been retouched: while their original pose and costume remain unchanged, their faces have been remodelled to conform to the more naturalistic manner of

93　Michael Serres and Bruno Latour, *Conversations on Science, Culture and Time*, Ann Arbor: University of Michigan Press, 2008.

94　Natasha Eaton, 'Notes from the Field: Materiality', *The Art Bulletin*, vol. 95 (1), 2013: 14.

95　Cited in Natasha Eaton, 'Nomadism of Colour: Painting, technology and Waste in the Chromo-zones of Colonial India ca. 1765–ca. 1860', *Journal of Material Culture*, vol. 17 (1), 2012: 65.

96　Sheila S. Blair, 'Color and Gold: The Decorated Papers used in Manuscripts in Later Islamic Times', *Muqarnas*, vol. 17, 2000: 24–36, here 27.

97　The painting, housed in the British Museum, is on cloth, measures 108 by 108 cm, and bears the name of the artist Abd-al Samad. Its numerous aspects have been studied in the volume Sheila R. Canby (ed.), *Humayun's Garden Party: Princes of the House of Timur and Early Mughal Painting*, Mumbai: Marg Publications, 1994.

painting faces in Mughal works of the early seventeenth century.[98] What emerges as a result of this dramatic material recasting is a scene now carefully constructed to present a dynastic genealogy, as it was perceived during the first half of the seventeenth century. In other words, we witness an intervention that goes far beyond the 'repair' of an older painting, to visualise afresh the ruling dynasty's visual memory. Images functioned as a *lieu de mémoire* not only through their referencing of previous and existing artistic traditions, but also equally through their nurturing of narratives to be cast as memory. Making and seeing were as much a way of remembering, of connecting past and present, wherein the image participated in a temporal chain of connections through memory. Memory here functions on two registers – as an affective act of remembering, of placing oneself in a temporal sequence and partaking of a shared history, as well as a discursive mode of producing a narrative. It is based on the principle of storage and recall that was held to underpin the conception of an image, the 'composite sense' referred to above, by which the seen was transferred from the eye to the mind to be stored and later recalled.[99]

A mode of creating memory chains, more popular than the example of material recasting described above, unfolded through the circulation of archetypal themes and stories that were retold and pictorially re-performed through fresh rendering, so that they remained deeply inscribed in the psyche of those who commissioned, made, and viewed images. The magic of Alexander's name, for instance, had clearly captured the Islamicate world since the inclusion of the romance of his life in the *Iskandar Nama*, one of the books of Nizami's *Khamsa*, mentioned earlier. In the countless stories that circulated through the Persianate regions, Alexander emerges not only as a world conqueror, but also as a man in search of knowledge, seeking encounters with holy men. In this apocryphal cycle of stories, his mastery of the world is equalled by his awareness of the human condition. Artists illustrating the various iterations of the *Iskandar Nama* resorted to chosen mnemonic devices to guide remembrance. Particular components of an image employ a condensed system of reference for the image to be able to speak beyond summing up a given episode. Such content, as goes beyond that which is ostensibly portrayed, is supplied by those charged with remembering; it is an act that both demands an informed observer familiar with tales retold, as well as works to evoke emotion and cement an affective link in a memory chain that extends across time and space. In contexts where stories are shared orally, mnemonic devices speak not exclusively to internalised remembrance: seeing by generating recognition becomes a spring to communication. Mnemonic devices play on the familiar to bring forth one more variant of the story being (re-)told, in an act of archiving as well as renewing.

The story of Alexander visiting a hermit – a personification of philosopher and saint – in front of a cave, accumulated during the course of its peripatetic journeys meanings that resonated with several compelling concerns of medieval and early modern empires. These

---

98 See John Seyller, 'Recycled Images: Overpainting in Early Mughal Art', in: Canby (ed.), *Humayun's Garden Party*, pp. 49–80, here pp. 49–64.
99 Soucek, 'Nizami on Painters', p. 14.

condensed around a set of oppositions – between the ruler of a temporal realm and a luminary of the spiritual domain, between the royal palace and the hermit's mountain cave, between darkness and light – for which artists devised mnemonic signs within their pictorial creations. The painted prototype of this scene from the *Iskandar Nama* that became a model for subsequent iterations of the subject was a work by Bihzad illustrating Nizami's epic.[100] Here, Alexander is portrayed as a likeness of the ruler of Herat who, having turned his back to worldly desires, kneels by night at the feet of an ascetic at the entrance of a cave. The night sky is lit by a crescent moon in the upper section, while torchlight illuminates the space below. Though the pictorial language, in keeping with the conventions of Persian painting, is that of a shadowless art held together by gleaming, enamel-like colours, the work is replete with allusive devices to communicate that which lies beneath its optical surface. The carefully composed scene is dominated by a castle held by thieves; the fortifications overlook rocks, swarming with hidden demons. An overarching plane tree, the tree of life, resplendent in autumn foliage, frames the dark opening of the cave with a hermit seated in meditation while a brook flows from its roots. Elements organised around the pictorial axes formed by castle and cave include soldiers and attendants who look upon the scene. Michael Barry reads the attendants in the vicinity of Alexander's horse as allegorical personifications of the three 'troublesome companions' of the soul – Wrath, Fancy, and Lust.[101] A further layer of meaning to the opposition between darkness and light – personified by the ruler of the daylight world and the visionary seer of the night – is furnished by the Sufi paradox of black light (*nur-i siyah*), symbolised by the deep blackness of the cave. This refers to an inner darkness which, as opposed to common outward darkness, is luminous beyond all light and stands for an unfathomable divine essence.[102] Elements such as the cave, the fortified ramparts of the castle, the plane tree, the flowing brook, and the ruler's three companions, all came to function as mnemonic motifs for future renderings of this subject across space and time. Such citations abounded in sixteenth and early seventeenth century productions in Safavid Iran and extended to a range of themes and stories – for example, a flourishing plane tree overlooking an outcrop of rocks bristling with dry tree stumps was a familiar conceit.

The *Iskandar Nama* manuscript of 1494 containing Bihzad's canonical work subsequently made its way to the imperial Mughal library as an heirloom of the Eastern Timurids. Its presence there in the early seventeenth century is attested to by an inscription in Jahangir's hand attributing the authorship of the painting to Bihzad.[103] The literary theme of Alexander and the hermit and the mystical symbolism of the cave were no doubt a familiar subject within Indo-Persian poetry: during the fourteenth century, the poet Amir Khusrau of Delhi had produced his iteration of the Alexander romance, of which illuminated versions were commissioned under the patronage of the Mughal rulers. The archetypal image of Alexander visiting

---

100 Panted in Herat, 1494–85, London, British Library, reproduced in Michael Barry, *Figurative Art in Medieval Islam and the Riddle of Bihzâd of Herât (1465–1535)*, Paris: Editions Flammarion, 2004, p. 252.
101 Barry, *Figurative Art*, p. 300.
102 Ibid., p. 320, traces this idea to medieval Neoplatonized Christian mysticism.
103 Ibid., p. 257.

an ascetic appeared in numerous variations and permutations within courtly productions of the Indian subcontinent well into the eighteenth century.[104] Islamicate rulers of India since the Sultans of Delhi had cast themselves as heirs to Alexander, the conqueror of India; in addition the Mughals partook of the legacy of the Timurid rulers of Samarkand and Herat where the ritual practice surrounding the deference of rulers to spiritual figures was deeply entrenched and found eloquent expression in literary and pictorial creations. Narratives – visual, oral, and literary – all participated in constituting a transcultural historical memory that connected empires and communities across distances. Even as Bihzad's composition structured along the cosmic axis of cave and castle continued to function as the archetype, it underwent significant variations and adaptations in response to the cultural economies of the court and shrine that characterised Islamicate formations in South Asia. An early version of the theme was created by Abd-al Samad, the well-known Safavid master who had migrated to India during Humayun's reign, and who occupied an eminent position in the atelier of Akbar. The illustration to Nizami's story of Alexander and the hermit created by him in 1585 retains several of the Bihzadian mnemonic elements – the luxuriant plane tree curving above the rocky outcrop and rooted in the brook of life, the lean frame of the hermit set against the black cave, holding his hand out in exposition to the deferential, youthful prince, and the allegorical figures Wrath, Fancy, and Lust.[105] It is remarkable that the artist creates no place in his composition for the fortified castle in the background, allowing instead the natural setting to encompass the image. A subsequent rendering of the tale – this time an illustration of Amir Khusrau's iteration of the Alexander romance – by Akbar's artist Basawan introduces its own set of local variations, while adhering to the archetypal compositional formation (Plate 2.8). The meeting between Alexander, dressed like a Mughal emperor, and the 'hermit', now identified as Plato, takes place during the daytime under a sky that furnishes the artist with the opportunity to experiment with subtle atmospheric effects. Small, rich local detail – the playful presence of animals and birds, a servant bent over a simmering pot on a wooden fire, an attendant filling his jug with water from the fount of life and above all, the marble and sandstone architecture, so characteristic of Mughal palaces – serves to anchor the narrative in a context which strives to define the relation between court and shrine in its own terms. A distinct feature of a large number of variations of this iconographic archetype in which Alexander is invariably personified by a Mughal ruler and the hermit more often than not a Hindu ascetic, is the disappearance of a fortified castle inhabited by thieves/demons. Instead, the landscape recedes into the distance, cloaked in atmospheric mist, with the buildings of a distant town shimmering through it. At times, stray people can be discerned, who in spite of their miniscule size are easily identifiable as Europeans, from their hats and billowing pantaloons.[106] This rendering of distant cityscapes was clearly a 'Western' mode directly

104 Ibid., p. 374. In Amir Khusrau's iteration of Nizami's tale, the hermit was identified as Plato.
105 *A Prince Visiting a Hermit*, by Abd al-Samad, c. 1585–90, private collection, reproduced in, B.N. Goswamy and Eberhard Fischer, *Wonders of a Golden Age: Painting at the Court of the Great Mughals*, Zurich: Museum Rietberg, 1987, p. 47, no. 14.
106 *Prince and Hermit*, by Miskin, c. 1585, private collection, reproduced in Barry, *Figurative Art*, p. 382.

transplanted from paintings of Christian themes in a Flemish idiom,[107] and the presence of identifiable figures could be read as a code – similar to the baroque curtain in other works – to mark this fragment of the assembled image as executed in the style of *firang*.

Among the most striking of Mughal variations of the Bihzadian model is perhaps the well-known painting by the artist Govardhan of Jahangir visiting the Hindu ascetic Jadrup, painted as an illustration to a description of this visit recorded by the emperor in his memoirs. Interestingly, the emperor describes his journey as a boat trip followed by a solitary walk to the sage's dwelling, which has been rendered by the artist as a cave of black light.[108] The painted image however shows the ruler accompanied by a retinue of courtiers portrayed with such exactitude that they have been identified as leading officials of the kingdom, among them Jahangir's father-in-law Itmad-ud Daulah.[109] On the one hand, Jahangir describes the entrance of the Hindu ascetic's cave as akin to an Islamic prayer niche (*mihrab*), on the other the three-tiered compositional arrangement of the scene resonates with that of innumerable court scenes produced within the same ateliers.[110] Court and shrine crystallise in this rendering as two faces of a single imperial ideal. Creating historical memory involved both activating recollection and anticipating fresh possibilities. The pictorial transactions we just observed conceptualise memory as an act of mimetic encounter with the past in a way that allows that past to retain its recognisability and yet enables actors of the present to participate in a lived temporality, to make way for exploring the unexpected and uncharted.

The Artist's Art

How did image makers, when imagining and recreating the world in early modernity, strive to find their place in it? Scholarly efforts to push the boundaries of traditional art history have led to a search for expressions of authorship and subjectivity within artistic and literary productions of the early modern court cultures of Asia, even as they are careful to eschew a narrative that ascribes normative singularity to notions of selfhood rooted in European humanism. For the literati of the early modern Islamicate world, life stories other than hagiographies, written in the first person, and whose authors did not hesitate to express their innermost feelings, had begun to proliferate from the sixteenth century. Access to such voices has enabled scholars today to make 'the premodern speak' in ways that entangle the collective with the

---

107 This was a characteristic feature in scenes of the Crucifixion copied by Mughal artists. See for example, the single leaf painting mounted as album page, c. 1600, private collection, reproduced in Goswamy and Fischer, *Wonders of a Golden Age*, p. 40, no. 10; another album leaf attributed to Kesu Das portraying a Crucifixion, adapted from a European engraving, London, British Museum, reproduced in J. M. Rogers, *Mughal Miniatures*, London: British Museum, 1993, p. 68, no. 44.

108 Jahangir's *Memoirs* (trans. A. Rogers), cited by Barry, *Figurative Art*, p. 379.

109 Identified by Ivan Stchoukine, cited by Barry, *Figurative Art*, p. 378.

110 Observed by Kavita Singh, *Real Birds in Imagined Gardens: Mughal Painting between Persia and Europe*, Los Angeles: The Getty Research Institute, 2017, p. 44.

individuated.[111] What did the practice of image-making as a mode of knowing the world and reflecting on its expanse imply for the artist's self-awareness? In the absence of first-person narratives by artists, or even extensive biographical information, traces of possible meanings of authorship need to be recuperated from within the works themselves. While the rhetoric of image production accessible to us is cast in a language that privileges the patron's eye rather than the artist's hand, looking through the cracks within the available corpus of textual and visual sources has brought forth some fresh signs – the traces of an artist's presence, his name or his portrait – that have been read as tangible evidence of authorship.[112] The widely held vision of the painter in early modern South Asia, transmitted by earlier histories and which characterised him as a nameless craftsman confined within the twin prisons of patronage and caste, has long lost its tenacity. Research of the past years has unearthed the names of a large number of artists, attempted to decipher their 'signatures' and cull facts about their employment from inscriptions and marginal notes within manuscript folios. And yet, what does the appearance of a large number of individual names, at times concealed within the corners of a page, at times confidently proclamatory, signify within a particular culture of making and viewing images? What kind of individual presence can we plausibly invest the work with, when we study a particular artist's production? The search for the locus of authorship, for the self-awareness of the artist of his role in the historical canon he partook of, leads us back into the mechanics of image-making, shaped as it was by transregional encounters.

Evidently, the modernist notion of authorship ascertainable through identifying the artist's gestural 'trace' within his work is not the most useful lens with which to approach the issues outlined above. At a purely material level, the technique of burnishing a final painting to bring the entire surface together meant that individual touches were effaced from the pigment's surface, rendering it unreadable for conventional signs of an artist's facture. Yet, at the same time, the emperor Jahangir's description of his advanced skills as a connoisseur that enabled him to discern the artist's presence through characteristic and repeated elements such as the inflection of eyebrows, the rendering of hands, ears, drapery, drawing, or compositional arrangement,[113] points to a field of forces marked by different pulls, a set of tensions between different understandings of and claims to mastery. Methods of image production as well as the normative framework within which it was contained render the relationship between an individual artist, the patron, and the work of art a complex one.

111 Taymiya R. Zaman, 'Instructive Memory: An Analysis of Auto/Biographical Writing In Early Mughal India', *Journal of the Economic and Social History of the Orient*, vol. 54 (5), 2011: 677–700, here 694; See also Rizvi (ed.), *Affect, Emotion*, pp. 7–9; Azfar Moin, 'Peering through the Cracks in the *Baburnama*: The Textured Lives of Mughal Sovereigns', *Indian Economic and Social History Review*, vol. 49 (4), 2012: 493–526.

112 Sussan Babaie, 'Chasing after the Muhandis: Visual Articulations of the Architect and Architectural Historiography, in: Rizvi (ed.), *Affect, Emotion*, pp. 21–44; Marianne S. Simpson, 'Who's Hiding Here? Artists and Their Signatures in Timurid and Safavid Manuscripts', in: Rizvi (ed.), *Affect, Emotion*, pp. 45–65.

113 Thackston (ed. and trans.), *The Jahangirnama*, p. 268.

In an extensive exposition of categories of authority, the *Akhlaq-i Nasiri*, a celebrated treatise on ethics and conduct authored in the thirteenth century by the philosopher Nasir-ud-Din Tusi, speaks of a particular kind of authority enjoyed by an individual who 'is capable of imagining the end from within himself and has the (practical) understanding for the discovery of dimensions'. Such authority places him clearly above those who do not possess a similar faculty though, Tusi continues, 'once he [i.e. the one not endowed with superior understanding] has learnt the laws of the craft (in question) from the first individual, he becomes able to carry the craft into effect'.[114] It is remarkable that the painter commissioned to illustrate this long and complex set of postulates about the 'basis of the virtuous city' and those fit to wield authority in it, chose to do so by portraying the interior of a royal *kitabkhana* (lit. house of books; it included both the imperial library and workshop for the production of manuscripts) with painters and calligraphers at work (Plate 2.9). A bird's-eye perspective takes us into various levels of an elaborate architectural complex complete with cross-axial watercourses forming a miniature *chahar bagh* that stands for the rivers of Paradise, details all redolent with imperial symbolism. The placing and treatment of individuals also visualises hierarchies – between the master instructing a scribe, the master artist and two painters under his charge, the artisan burnishing a sheet of paper at a lower level on the edge of the image to the right, and finally the attendants. All confirm this as a view from the highest echelon representing a world of ordered relationships. The rich detail conveys industrious activity and a lively exchange of ideas and instruction, while unmistakably transmitting the message of the text about authority and hierarchy. Symbolic size and placing clearly point to the figure on the top right, dignified by age, as the *ustad* or master artist/craftsman. He is seated on the highest platform, while the other senior figure, dressed in a yellow *jama* and a brown shawl and placed diagonally opposite, instructs the painter who bends forward to listen.[115] At the left, on the same level though somewhat isolated, sits another young man contemplating a drawing. The two bands of calligraphy reproduce the lines of Tusi's text that refer specifically to the authority of the master endowed with superior knowledge, while a

114 G. M. Wickens (trans.), *Nasirean Ethics*, by Nasir ud-Din Tusi, cited in Goswamy and Fischer, *Wonders of a Golden Age*, p. 120.

115 The seating positions may also be read as a reference to the prevailing hierarchy between calligraphers and painters in the court workshops. Both groups were indispensable to the production of illuminated manuscripts, theirs was a relationship of collaboration at the same time as a competition for favours of the patron. According to Abu'l Fazl, calligraphers held the highest social standing among all groups involved in manuscript making, as the art of writing was considered more elevated than that of painting. Abu'l Fazl Allami, *A'in-i Akbari*, vol. 1, p. 103.

In her discussion of Persianate visual cultures among early modern Turko-Mongol dynasties Necipoğlu refers to frequent interactions among different groups – poets, painters and calligraphers – as well as to the possibility of a single person exercising more than one function. See Necipoğlu, 'The scrutinizing Gaze': 29–30. According to Porter the royal *kitabkhana* at the Persianate courts was organised around a collaborative relationship between calligraphers and painters, see Yves Porter, 'From the "Theory of the Two Qalams" to the "Seven Principles of Painting": Theory, Terminology and Practice in Persian Classical Painting', *Muqarnas*, vol. 17, 2000: 109–18, here 112.

miniscule entry on the bottom of the page, too fuzzy for clear decipherment, has been read as referring to the painter 'Sajnu'.[116]

Such a model of workshop production meant that the artist named on the colophons of painted folios was the person who oversaw the entire painting, assigned tasks to other members of the workshop and himself executed those elements considered the most difficult and therefore demanding particular expertise. The latter included drawing and overall compositional design (*tarah*) as well as the depiction of the most important face(s) (*chehra-i nami*). Colouring (*amal* or *rang amizi*) was likely to be done by another painter of the workshop, followed by burnishing, applying gold, and designing the margins (*hashiyas*). As the latter acquired growing importance within the overall design of the folio, master artists frequently intervened in their creation. A painted folio – as observed earlier in this chapter – was an assemblage of several components, sometimes designed separately before being transferred to the surface of the page, and therefore a product of several hands, especially the colouring. Till the end of the sixteenth century, most manuscript and album folios kept a record of the division of work that went into the making of a single image – this has come down to us through inscriptions mostly recorded by the librarian or another official of the *kitabkhana* on the margins or reverse of the page.[117] During the seventeenth century and later, the practice of recording collaborative work declined in favour of citing a single artist, whose name was frequently inscribed by no less than the emperor's hand.[118] With the increased production of single sheet folios for albums, the practice of one artist's name being attached to the work gained currency. The size of the atelier too became smaller under Jahangir, whose preferred group of artists often accompanied him on travels, including campaigns.[119] The organisation of image-making as a form of co-production within a workshop was a practice instituted along the lines of a similar model of pictorial production under the Timurid and Safavid rulers; as mentioned earlier, migrant artists from the Safavid court were instrumental in creating the first Mughal ateliers. The evolution of the system to privilege a notion of the master artist (*ustad*), each associated with a predilection for specific themes and expressive modes, even as the practice of co-production continued to prevail, speaks for the enhanced valorisation of connoisseurship within a given imperial structure of artistic production. The

116 Goswamy and Fischer, *Wonders of a Golden Age*, p. 120.

117 Drawing on methods adapted from the digital humanities, Yael Rice has provided statistical evidence from the late sixteenth century that attests to the high frequency of a collaborative practice of authorship among artists, especially when producing the densely illustrated narrative paintings commissioned by the emperor Akbar. See Yael Rice, 'Workshop as Network: A Case Study from Mughal South Asia', *Artl@as Bulletin*, vol. 6 (3), 2017: 50–65.

118 Several examples can be cited here: Jahangir inscribed Bihzad's name on the painting of Alexander visiting the hermit by night discussed above; or an inscription by Shah Jahan can be identified on a standing portrait of the nobleman, Shahnawaz Khan, painted by Hashim, c. 1615–20, now in the Minto album, Chester Beatty Library, Dublin, reproduced in Wright, *Muraqqa*, p. 315, no. 42. A further example has been cited in Rizvi (ed.), *Affect, Emotion*, p. 12.

119 Susan Stronge, 'Jahangir's Itinerant Masters', in: Mahesh Sharma and Padma Kaimal (eds), *Themes: Histories, Interpretations: Indian Paintings: Essays in Honour of B. N. Goswamy*, Ahmedabad: Mapin Publishing, 2013, pp. 125–35.

connoisseur's eye could claim the special power to discern talent and endow its bearer with high-sounding titles such as Wonder of the Age (*Nadir-ul Zaman*) or Golden Pen (*Zarin Qalam*).[120] Imperial etiquette prescribed that the self-description of the artist be cast in self-abnegation and humility in the face of his powerful patron: the same artist whom the emperor designated as Wonder of the Age would in his inscriptions describe himself as *ghulam* (slave), *banda-i dargah* (servant of the exalted house), *kamtarin* (the lowliest), *khak-i pa* (dust of the patron's feet) and so on. Pictorial self-representations on the other hand, frequently seek to bypass this rhetoric of subservience to confer a quiet dignity on the unique skills with which the artist – and he alone – could transform earthly materials – pigment, ink, paper – into transcendent aesthetic value. Such representations (see Plate 2.1) invariably portray image production by placing the materials, tools of work as well as their product, a painting or a bound manuscript, caringly across the picture plane.[121] We are thus left with the question of how and where to recover a notion of artistic agency and authorship within this complex, yet fluid constellation.

Both artists and patrons seem to have shared an awareness of their role in the historical canon; this involved knowledge of earlier precedents and of prevailing diverse idioms, especially Christian imagery that continued to migrate to the court ateliers, and the acumen to create genealogies for which the album emerged as the chosen format. The pride of an artist lay in a virtuosity that enabled him to master a range of pictorial traditions – from the Persianate to different phases of the Mughal, and the European. Authorship therefore can barely be conceived of outside of a mimetic culture involving a range of possible transactions: imitation, emulation, citation, of re-contextualising and re-historicising, above all, a culture of knowing and being able to transmit. One well-known example of the many such prevailing practices relates to the famous painting by Bihzad of two camels fighting;[122] it was admired and copied in the Safavid court before it made its way to the Indian subcontinent.[123] A copy dating to sometime around 1590 was prepared by Abd-al Samad, the Iranian artist at the Mughal court. Interestingly this is a mirror-reverse copy of Bihzad's image that has been embellished with additional landscape details. Moreover, it is painted in a different aesthetic idiom that gives more substance and volume to the bodies of the animals and men who populate the image, it elevates the horizon line and pays greater attention to three-dimensionality

120 Thackston (ed. and trans.), *The Jahangirnama*, pp. 268–69.

121 Another eloquent example is the colophon (self-)portrait (1610) from the *Khamsa* of Nizami. The manuscript was copied in 1595–96 by the calligrapher Abd-al Rahim, known as *Anbarin Qalam* (Ambergris Pen). The artist, Daulat, painted the double portrait of himself and the calligrapher at work, with the tools of their respected trades lovingly placed across the foreground plane. London, British Library, reproduced in Brend, *The Emperor Akbar's Khamsah*, p. 64.

122 Bihzad, *Fighting Camels*, c. 1535, today in the *Muraqqa-i Gulshan*, Gulistan Palace Library Museum, Tehran.

123 An ink and watercolour copy by an unnamed Iranian artist, late sixteenth to the early seventeenth century, is preserved at the Metropolitan Museum of Art, New York, https://www.metmuseum.org/art/collection/search/450602 (accessed June 2020). Reproduced in Marie Swietochowski and Sussan Babaie, *Persian Drawings in the Metropolitan Museum of Art*, New York: The Metropolitan Museum of Art, 1989, pp. 46–47, no. 18.

and colour tonalities of the landscape and clothing.[124] This was clearly a product of the artist's engagement with European art during the years he spent at Akbar's court, and that he acknowledges here as a mode of painting deserving of emulation, together with the work of the celebrated Iranian master. Apart from exhibiting the skill of the artist in re-historicising an existing model, such a procedure assumes, in the words of Roxburgh, 'a contract of communicability',[125] by which the viewer partly anticipates and is partly educated by a dynamic wherein an artist inserts himself into a chain of tradition, even as he carries it forward. Some two decades later, in 1608, Jahangir commissioned his artist Nanha to prepare a copy of Bihzad's work with the intention of mounting both original and copy on two facing album folios. This version, inscribed by Jahangir, was instead painted in the 'Persian style', aspiring to be an exact replica of the deceased master's work, and thereby challenging the discerning connoisseurial eye to distinguish one from the other.[126]

The abundant presence of European engravings at the Mughal court brought forth its own harvest of copies-as-adaptations, further attesting to the range of imitative practices which artists sought to master. The linearity of the graphic medium of print resonated with the aesthetic value, which all Persianate images attached to line and drawing (*tarah*). An engraving could be easily appropriated as *tarah* and replicated through the customary use of a pounce, as was done when copies were made and then pasted on to album folios. Additionally, a print could serve as the basis for a painting executed by a court artist by using a copy of the engraving as *tarah*. An exquisite rendering of the meeting of the Virgin Mary and her cousin Elizabeth by an unnamed Mughal artist transforms the print on which it was based into a resplendent painting exuding warm emotion that becomes legible when the image is recast in the medium of paint (Plate 2.10, fig. 3). The young Mary, having received the Angel Gabriel's tidings, is skilfully portrayed with a hovering smile, holding the hand of Elizabeth, who solicitously moves her face close as if whispering a confidence. The painter, it appears, sought to exhibit his virtuosity in the careful rendering of garments and the softly articulated features of the figures. In an intriguing reversal, the younger Mary, who on the engraving is unmistakably the figure on the right, is dressed in gold and lilac, colours that are traditionally not hers, whereas the canonical Marian combination of blue and red has been instead assigned to Elizabeth. The artist has taken further liberties with the landscape setting by giving it a lushness and animating it with flowers, birds, and a bubbling brook, rather than retaining the arid-looking foreground of the engraving. Such a mode of artistic conversation between a print and a painting can be said to invest painterly skill with the power of creative

124 Private Collection, reproduced in Asok K. Das, 'Transformation in Jahangir's Taswirkhana', in: Canby (ed.), *Humayun's Garden Party*, pp. 135–52, here p. 140.

125 David Roxburgh, 'Kamal-al Din Bihzad and Authorship in Persian Painting', *Muqarnas*, vol. 17, 2000: 119–46, here 136.

126 Jahangir's inscription on the right-hand corner reads: 'Allahu Akbar. This work of Ustad Bihzad was seen and copied by Nanha Musawwir according to my orders. Written by Jahangir, son of Akbar Badshah Ghazi in the year 1017 (1608–09)', cited in Das, 'Transformation in Jahangir's Taswirkhana', p. 142. The copy is preserved together with Bihzad's original as two facing folios of the *Muraqqa-i Gulshan*, Gulistan Palace Library Museum, Tehran.

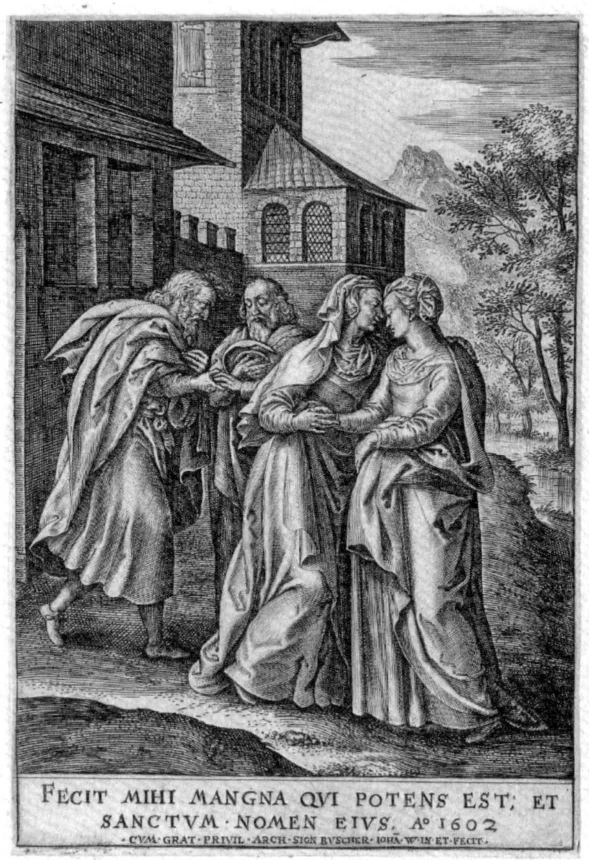

3   Johannes Wierix,
The Visitation, engraving,
1602–03

repetition or reiterative transformation, making the production of images nothing less than a transmedial, intersubjective process.

Two examples with which this chapter concludes afford us a rare insight into gestures of self-positioning on the part of artists, a fleeting sense of how they perceived their own skills and chose to represent these – together with their individual persona – perhaps as an indexical trace within a work's matrix. The first example counts among the most enigmatic and is at the same time possibly the most frequently reproduced painting from among the prolific number that emanated from the North Indian courts; its repeated appearance in anthologies and exhibition catalogues of Mughal painting, on book covers and posters, has led one scholar to characterise such visibility as a 'commodification' of the image (Plate 2.11).[127]

127 Valerie Gonzales, 'Confronting Images, Confronted Images: Jahangir versus King James I in the Freer Gallery Mughal Group Portrait by Bichitr (circa 1620)', in Frank Peter, Sarah Dornhof and Elena Arigita (eds), *Islam and the Politics of Culture in Europe: Memory, Aesthetics, Art*, Bielefeld: Transcript Verlag,

Though scholarship has engaged with different aspects of this work, uncovering the facets of meanings ascribable to it, it has invariably been treated as an imperial portrait of the emperor Jahangir by the artist Bichitr.[128] Let us try, instead, to explore its underlying layers: being both a portrait of the emperor (and other kings) as well as a self-portrait of the artist, such a painterly inflection gives the image an inbuilt ontological instability through the fissures of which a reflection on the act of image-making and the agency of the artist become readable. In this image of c. 1620 painted for the *Jahangirnama*, the Mughal emperor is seated on an hourglass throne, while he offers a book to a Sufi, Shaikh Hasan Chishti, ignoring the other, more 'worldly', figures placed in a descending row along the left edge of the picture space. These are the Ottoman sultan of Turkey, the English monarch, James I, and, interestingly, the painter of this miniature, Bichitr, who positions his self-portrait at the end of this line of kings. The presence of the two foreign rulers and their role in a mythical claim of the Mughal ruler to universal kingship has already been written about, together with an elaboration of the iconographic sources that went into the rendering of their persona.[129] The seated figure of Jahangir is framed by an enormous refulgent aureole that embodies both sun and crescent moon and so fixes the event within a moment of the eternal present. The radiance of the sun and moon aureole framing the persona of the enthroned ruler spells a notion of infinite time which, however, in this image exists in a state of tension with a competing notion of temporality symbolised by the hourglass: a Christian symbol of death, transformed into an insignia of Mughal universal kingship and relocated within the space of this extraordinary image. Its original meanings, however, continue to shimmer through the dense accoutrements of a *Pax Moghulica*. For the artist has deployed the language of naturalistic representation to draw our attention to the sands of time which have almost run out. In a gesture as if to exorcise the inexorable flow of time, two cupids inscribe directly upon the hourglass the words: 'O Shah, may the span of your life be a thousand years.' Death is the all-encompassing horizon that organises the experience of time; it generates the efforts presented in the image to overcome finite time. The work is replete with further sources of dissonance that I will not elaborate here,[130] except for pointing towards the destabilisation of its normative compositional

2013, pp. 219–35, here p. 233. The painting has been reproduced on the splendid cover of Thackston (ed. and trans.), *The Jahangirnama*; it also features on the cover of Singh, *Real Birds*. It has been reproduced in several anthologies and collections, too numerous to list here.

128 The work's iconography has been discussed by Richard Ettinghausen, 'The Emperor's Choice', in: Millard Meiss (ed.), *De Artibus Opuscula: Essays in Honor of Erwin Panofsky*, New York: New York University Press, 1961, pp. 98–120; Milo C. Beach, *The Imperial Image: Paintings for the Mughal Court*, Washington DC: Freer Gallery of Art, 1981, pp. 89–90; more recently, Monica Juneja, 'Jahangir auf der Sanduhr – Überlegungen zur Lektüre einer Visualität im Spannungsfeld zwischen Eigenem und Fremdem', in: Gerhard Schneider (ed.), *Die visuelle Dimension des Historischen*, Schwalbach: Wochenschau Verlag, 2002, pp. 142–57; Monica Juneja, 'Translating the Body into Image: The Body Politic and Visual Practice at the Mughal Court in the Sixteenth and Seventeenth Centuries', in Axel Michaels and Christoph Wulf (eds), *The Body in South Asia – Image, Ritual, Performativity*, New Delhi: Routledge, 2009, pp. 235–60; Gonzales, 'Confronting Images'; Singh, *Real Birds*, pp. 63–66.

129 Ettinghausen, 'The Emperor's Choice'; Beach, *The Imperial Image*: 89–90; Juneja, 'Jahangir auf der Sanduhr'.

130 Discussed in Juneja, 'Jahangir auf der Sanduhr'.

symmetry generated by the placing of four figures in vertical succession along the left margin of the image. No longer firmly structured along a central axis, such an asymmetrical image renders visible a series of tensions – between political power and religious authority, between competing imperial powers – and ends up undermining the harmony of a utopian *Pax Moghulica.*

The last and smallest of the four figures making up the left margin of the work is the painter himself, the person lowest in the social and religious hierarchy of those portrayed in the painting. He displays a product of his metier, a painting showing two horses and an elephant, and by placing himself in the line of kings can proclaim his own status as symbolic king of the arts. The artist, in addition, has put his signature to the painting on the top of the little stand, supported by a two-headed caryatid, at the foot of the throne. Its position just below the throne opening suggests that it served as a step to reach the high throne platform. The gesture of placing his name at the feet of his patron would be immediately read as a visualisation of the trope whereby artists cast themselves as *khak-i pa*, the dust at the feet of their patron. The stepping stool of sorts evokes, at the same time, another image – its outline, the caryatid notwithstanding, with its circular upper surface is that of an inverted imperial dynastic seal that contained the names of the Mughal emperors and their Timurid ancestors.[131] This kind of a seal was used on royal ordinances and diplomatic missives, whereas seals whose imprints we encounter on the colophons of manuscripts and paintings are either square or oval in shape.[132] The circular genealogical seal that was clearly a mark of imperial authority features symbolically in iconic paintings, such as in the image of Jahangir standing on the globe and shooting the head of his enemy Malik Ambar, or in a painting of Shah Jahan holding a dynastic seal.[133] That the artist Bichitr inscribed his name on the circular surface that evokes a dynastic seal, the location of imperial genealogies, opens his gesture to an alternative reading, much in line with the ontological dissonances built into this work. By additionally locating his persona on the margins of the image, an unusual instance of a painter, in the hierarchically regulated system in which this miniature was created, he apparently sought to share the pictorial space of his patron, albeit at its lowest edge. The framed picture he holds up contains a reference to his art both as creation and at the same time as a salaried activity; an elephant or horses stood for a reward to painters in the service of the Mughal court, who were paid as foot soldiers.[134] Vision, intended to assure immortality, then comes

131 For an extensive discussion, Annabel T. Gallop, 'The Genealogical Seal of the Mughal Emperors of India', *Journal of the Royal Asiatic Society,* vol. 9 (1), 1999: 77–140.

132 Wright, *Muraqqa*: 220–223; John Seyller, 'The Inspection and Valuation of Manuscripts in the Imperial Mughal Library', *Artibus Asiae*, vol. 57(3/4), 1997: 243–349, illustrated 257ff. See also imprint of the seal on Plate 2.12 below.

133 The genealogical seal can be seen in Mughal paintings, e.g. Jahangir Shoots the Head of Malik Ambar, c. 1616–20, reproduced in Wright, *Muraqqa*: No. 50, p. 345, detail of seal on p. 222. The painting dating to the emperor Shah Jahan's first regnal year, portrays him holding a dynastic seal, London, British Museum, reproduced in Rogers, *Mughal Miniatures*: No. 69, 101. For further examples, Gallop, 'The Genealogical Seal'.

134 At the end of the section on the art of painting, in the *Ain-i Akbari*, Abu'l Fazl states: 'The pay of foot soldiers varies from 1,200 to 600 dāms', Abu'l Fazl, *Ain-I Akbari*: vol. 1, 115; On the reward of an elephant

to rest on a mundane transaction between artist and patron for painted mythologies. A central prerequisite of viewing as a sacral, embodied vision,[135] a notion that the Mughals incorporated via court ritual (*jharoka darśan*) into their visual representations, was the invisibility of the artist, the effacing of all traces of his painterly activity. By making his presence and his hand visible, the artist transforms vision into an act of representation. From the point where the viewer becomes a participant in the process through which a mythic vision comes into being, the dissolution of that vision is already under way.

The second example, too, chooses to orient its narrative with death as the vanishing point. This is a work of the artist Farrukh Beg, done in 1615, when he was seventy years old (Plate 2.12). The deeply seated ambivalence that infuses the work begins with the subject itself. Often designated as a portrait of an old Sufi, which is its ostensible subject, the work is replete with references to the artist's persona, his biography and – not least – his skill in making images.[136] These visual signs have led Stuart Cary Welch to designate the image as a 'psychic self-portrait' of the artist.[137] Identifying (self-)portraiture through the lens of Renaissance Humanism in a context where a physical 'likeness' does not equate with mimetic rendering is no doubt a slippery task.[138] Yet, teasing out the components of this complex image from its numerous references – textual as well as visual – reveals it as a highly autobiographic image and therefore plausibly something of an overlap between a portrait and a self-portrait, wherein the person of the artist fuses with that of a Sufi, whose figure in turn was drawn from a representation of a Christian saint. Indeed, this image has grown out of multiple entanglements and crossings of traditions and practices that make it a site of intense transcultural negotiations. The initial impulse for the painting can be traced to a work of the Flemish artist Martin de Vos, entitled *Dolor*, which in turn was a homage to Albrecht Dürer's work *Saint Jerome in his Study* (fig. 4). Farrukh Beg's familiarity with de Vos was mediated through an engraving by Raphael Sadeler that had made its way to the Mughal atelier from Antwerp (fig. 2). In addition, the engraving by Dürer portraying Saint Jerome (*Der heilige Hieronymus im Gehäus*) representing the contemplative life of a Christian saint as well as a reprint of his *Melancholia I* was equally accessible to court artists in the seventeenth century.[139]

to the arist Bishandas, Thackston (ed. and transl.), *Jahangirnama*: 319; Abu'l Fazl lists 'robes, horses and trays of muhrs and rupis' as a suitable award for the artist Farrukh Beg, cited in Robert Skelton, 'The Mughal Artist Farrokh Beg', *Ars Orientalis*, vol. 2, 1957: 393–411, here 393.

135 Pinney, 'Piercing the Skin of the Idol'.
136 See Asok K. Das, 'Farrukh Beg: Studies of Adorable Youths and Venerable Saints', *Marg*, vol. 49 (4), 1998, special issue, 'Mughal Masters: Further Studies': 96–111, here 110; Skelton, 'The Mughal Artist': 406; John Guy and Jorrit Britschgi, *Wonder of the Age: Master Painters of India 1100–1900*, Ahmedabad: Mapin India, 2011, p. 66, no. 23.
137 Stuart Cary Welch, *India: Art and Culture 1300–1900*, New York: Metropolitan Museum of Art, 1985, p. 224.
138 I have discussed this in Monica Juneja, '"Likeness" as a Migrating Concept – Artfully Portraying the Universal Ruler in Early Modern South Asia', *Histoire de l'Art*, vol. 82 (1), 2018, special issue, 'Asie-Occident': 55–70.
139 Welch, *India*, p. 224.

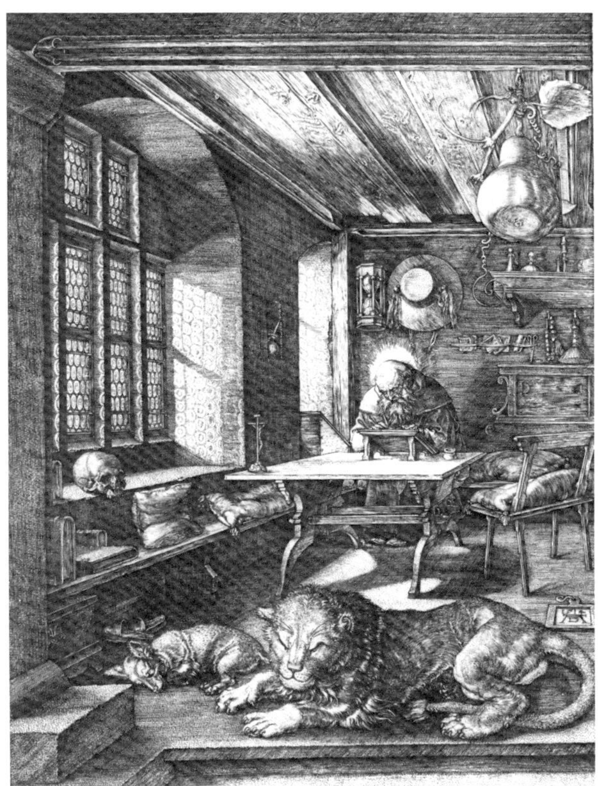

4   Albrecht Dürer, *Saint Jerome in his Study*, engraving, 1514

Farrukh Beg's life history too offers an instance of cultural entanglement, having migrated from Central Asia to North India, thence to the Deccan and finally back to the Mughal court, where he spent his last years. Such itinerant habits were not unusual for his times, motivated by a constant search for new and generous patrons.[140] The painter's early career was spent in Shiraz, Khurasan, and then Kabul. In 1580, he was employed by the Mughal emperor Akbar as a member of the imperial workshop of painters. The arrival of European works of art at the Mughal court meant that the Persianised idiom practised by Farrukh Beg declined in importance, leading him to migrate further south in the search of new patrons. He spent many years at the court of the Sultan of Bijapur, and returned in 1609, on the invitation of Akbar's successor Jahangir, to the Mughal capital of Agra.[141] This painting, possibly his last work, was according to Seyller the sole instance in which Farrukh Beg made a 'direct copy' of a European work,[142] yet in a manner that engaged with several sources, resulting in a complex example of transcultural negotiation that grafted visual references to his biography onto a

140 John Seyller, 'Farrukh Beg in the Deccan', *Artibus Asiae*, vol. 55 (3–4), 1995: 319–41, here 340.
141 Skelton, 'The Mughal Artist': 403.
142 Seyller, 'Farrukh Beg in the Deccan': 339.

selection of materials. The former, distributed across the picture field, include the miniature album of paintings with the red and gold lacquer binding, together with a pair of spectacles, an object often deployed by calligraphers and painters as a signature of their profession (see Plate 2.1). The motif of the cat stalking a puddle of spilt milk, taken from the Sadeler engraving, has been reconfigured in this image as a reference to the artist's activity: it refers to one of the important material dimensions of image-making for which cat's hair was a cherished material out of which the finest paint brushes, sometimes of a single hair, the *ekbaal qalam*, were made. Referencing the material aspects of art production functioned as a recognisable trope within the self-representation of artists and calligraphers, as has been observed earlier in this chapter. It referred to the power wielded by the artist alone, the skilled use of material substances to create immaterial aesthetic value. Contemporary texts often drew a parallel between this creative process and the way the Sufi used bodily experience to reach God.[143] Further references in the image by Farrukh Beg to his biography and stage in life are fused with Qur'anic symbols: the suggestion of a walled garden evokes the image of Paradise, as do the wine carafes, appropriated from the Flemish engraving and recast as a recognisable form of funereal imagery, frequently placed on the walls of mausolea in the Persianate world. The purplish glow of the stones on the wall is a reference to Bijapur, where Farrukh Beg spent many years of his life. It echoes the colour that stones on sacred tombs in Bijapur took on in the warm, late afternoon light, and which was a favourite trope of Deccani painters.[144] The animals are partly taken from de Vos and Dürer, for example, the sleeping dog, an animal associated with erudition as well as melancholy. The motif of the goat suckling its young, on the other hand, an addition by the artist, recurs in many variants in Mughal painting to draw attention to the cycles of life and changing generations – a reference again to the artist's own advanced stage in life.

Beyond appropriating and relocating symbols and motifs, the image is the product of a dialogical encounter between the artist and the works of Dürer and de Vos. Dürer's extraordinary artistic achievement lay in the way he used the engraver's burin and the graphic medium to recreate material textures: of wooden planks, of walled surface, of animal fur, of organic greenery. Farrukh Beg's response, akin to the pattern of a literary-cum-musical mode of improvisation in Indo-Persian tradition,[145] is to translate Dürer's particular mode of rendering texture into paint and colour: he accomplishes this using a single haired brush (*ekbaal qalam*) and paint, as in the treatment of the animal skins. Each hair of the dog, for example, was highlighted by a fleeting golden stroke. Further instances of the selective use of

---

143 Abu'l Fazl, *Ain-I Akbari*: vol. 1, p. 115.

144 See for instance the painting of c. 1610, attributed by Keelan Overton to the Bijapur artist Ali Riza, who had worked closely with Farrukh Beg, showing the ruler Ibrahim Adil Shah II visiting a Sufi shrine, today in the Bodleian Library, Oxford, MS Douce Or.b2(1), fol. 1a. Reproduced in Milo C. Beach, Eberhard Fischer and B.N. Goswamy (eds), *Masters of Indian Painting*, 2 vols., Zurich: Artibus Asiae Publications, 2011: vol. 1, p. 378.

145 According to Roxburgh the practice of men of letters engaging through verbal responses to a visual work, often through verbal improvisations that took the form of a dialogue within a literary gathering, a *majlis*, was widespread in Timurid and Safavid courtly circles, see Roxburgh, 'Kamal-al Din Bihzad': 122.

new representational practices can be observed in the brushwork of the wicker chair, in the graining of the wood panels of the desk and cabinet, and not least in the subtle and mottled painterliness of the stones, tree-trunk, and foliage. The billowing sleeves, the cuffs, and swelling folds of the Sufi painter's robe create further connections with Düreresque practice, as for example in *Melancholia*. We might speculate whether the idea of an artist as creator, a figure of loneliness and saturnal melancholy, has managed to seep in through the layers of this portrait where artist and Sufi/Christian saint merge into each other. The pictorial organisation of the image registers, on the other hand, a refusal of Albertian perspective that Dürer strictly adhered to in his work. Farrukh Beg's composite portrait gestures for a moment in the direction of the principle separating inner and outer space that marked the Saint Jerome portraits in their several variants, including the one by de Vos that provided the initial impulse for the present work. Here, however, a separation is barely suggested by the extension of the wall from one end of the picture frame to the other, only then to be discarded in favour of a wondrous and highly ambiguous space traversed by a fantastic, infinitely expanding tree populated by colourful birds that enters into the lonely space of the Sufi artist and subjects it to a different sense of spatial order. The placement of the tree follows a frequent compositional usage in Persian painting – that of the overarching plane tree to stand for the tree of life (see above), underscoring Farrukh Beg's roots in Shiraz and Khurasan, where he started his life as a court artist and managed – unlike most of his other counterparts – to retain, through his peripatetic life, a loyalty to Persianate idioms.[146] Yet the tree, unlike any other ever painted by a Persian, Mughal, or European artist of the time, is a product of a unique fantasy. Its bright red, orange, yellow, and green foliage burgeoning into cabbage-like shapes, rejects any concern for botanical observation or anthropocentric exactitude that had become the norm when representing plant and animal life, especially under the patronage of the emperor Jahangir. This unusual work, that in many ways is a condensation of a lifetime's experience, is also a statement about the artist's positioning in a field regulated by the predilections of changing patrons, and his struggle to retain a sense of his own constancy. Interestingly he is able to do so in a work that, by negotiating with different modes of image-making and their signifying processes, uses the mimetic to generate a surplus of meaning and thereby creates an ontological instability similar to what we encountered in Bichitr's attempt to alternate between margins and the centre.

Art historical practice today, confronted with the challenge of theorising plurality, has tended to alternate between the poles of human universals and radical cultural relativism. The disciplinary move away from recounting a history of style and towards relocation in the somewhat amorphous field of visual culture proceeds – often implicitly – on the assumption that vision, conceived of as solely optical perception, forms an anthropological constant. By charting the routes through which a range of media and materials travel, intersect, and at times collide, the above account has argued for investigating visual practice – the study of images, their making and seeing – as a site of transculturation. It has proceeded on the

146 Seyller, 'Farrukh Beg in the Deccan': 341.

assumption that regions and cultures that participated in a connected history of early modernity partook of a willingness to engage with alterity – with different ontologies, cosmologies, geographies, desires. More importantly, it addresses these issues as shared historical questions, even as it zooms into the contingencies of local and regional practice, acknowledging thereby the possibility of speaking across disparate intellectual and territorial domains.

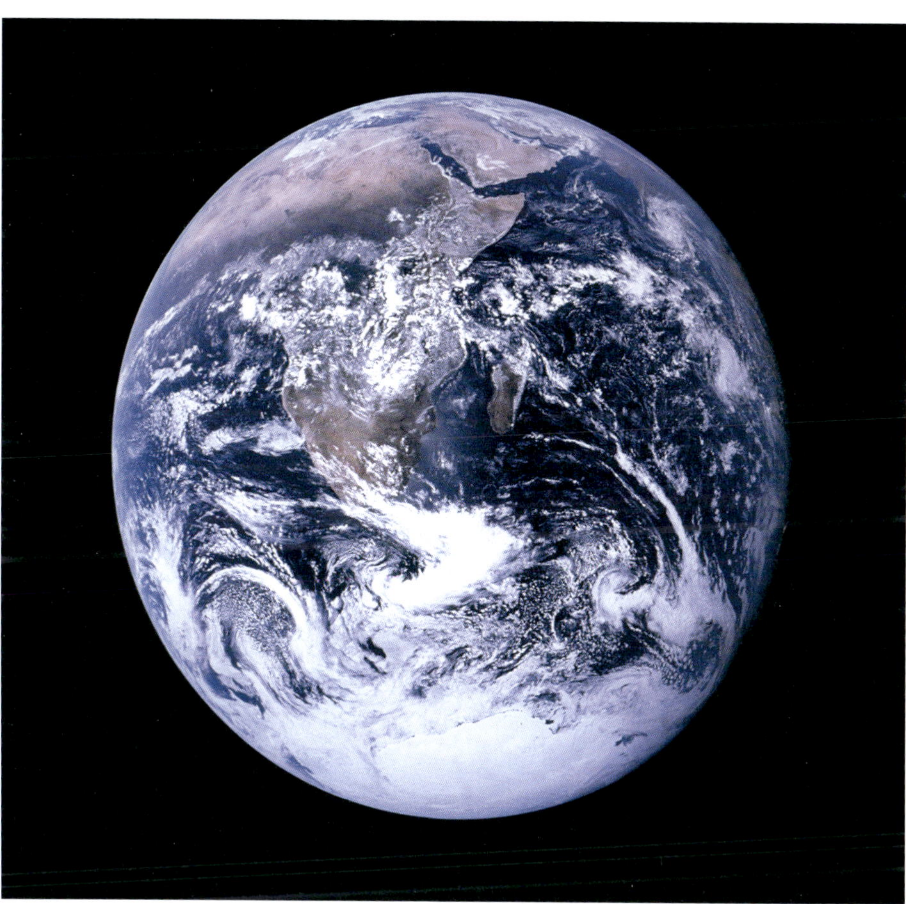

1.0 *The Blue Marble*, photograph by Apollo 17 crew taken on December 7, 1972.

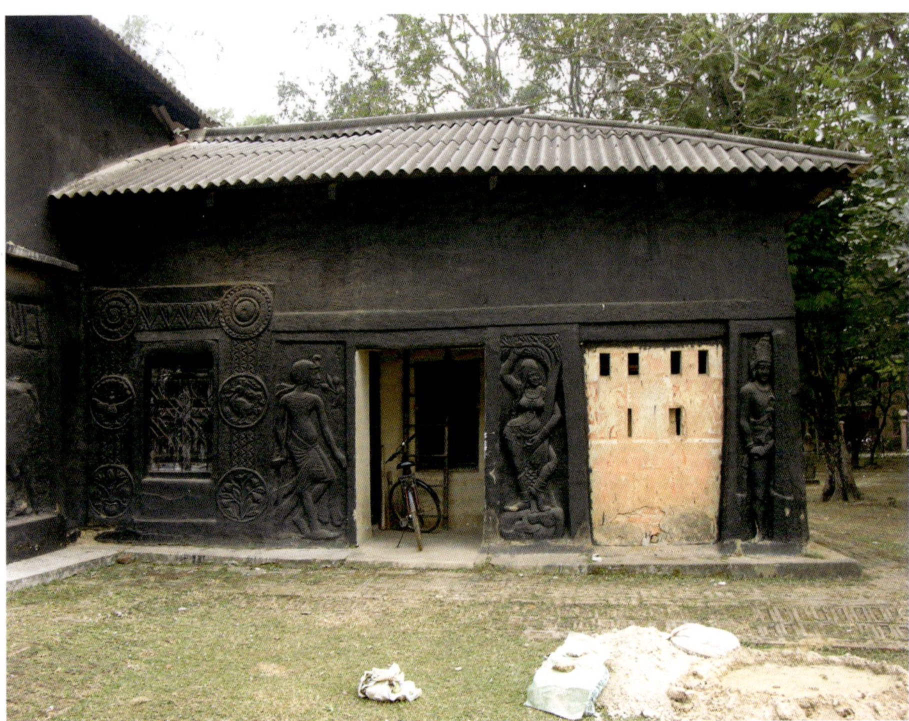

1.1 *Kalo Bari (Black House)*, 1934, conceived by Nandalal Bose and Binode Behari Mukherjee. Kala Bhawan, Visva Bharati Campus, Santiniketan, India.

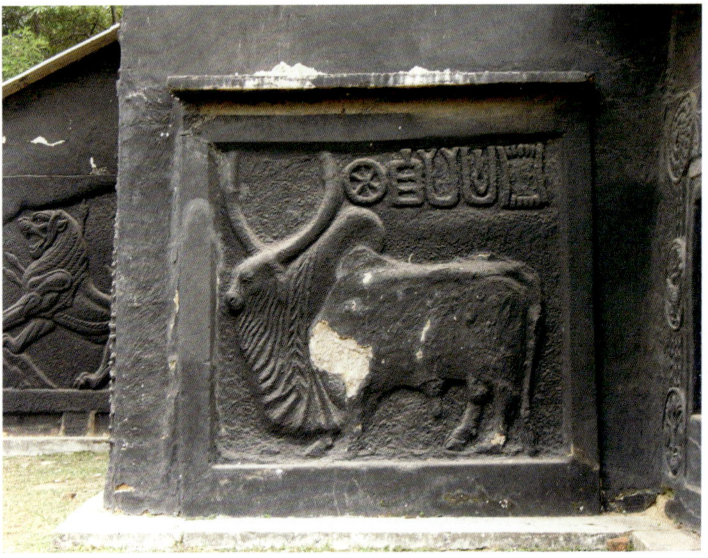

1.1a *Kalo Bari (Black House)*, detail. Seal from Indus Valley.

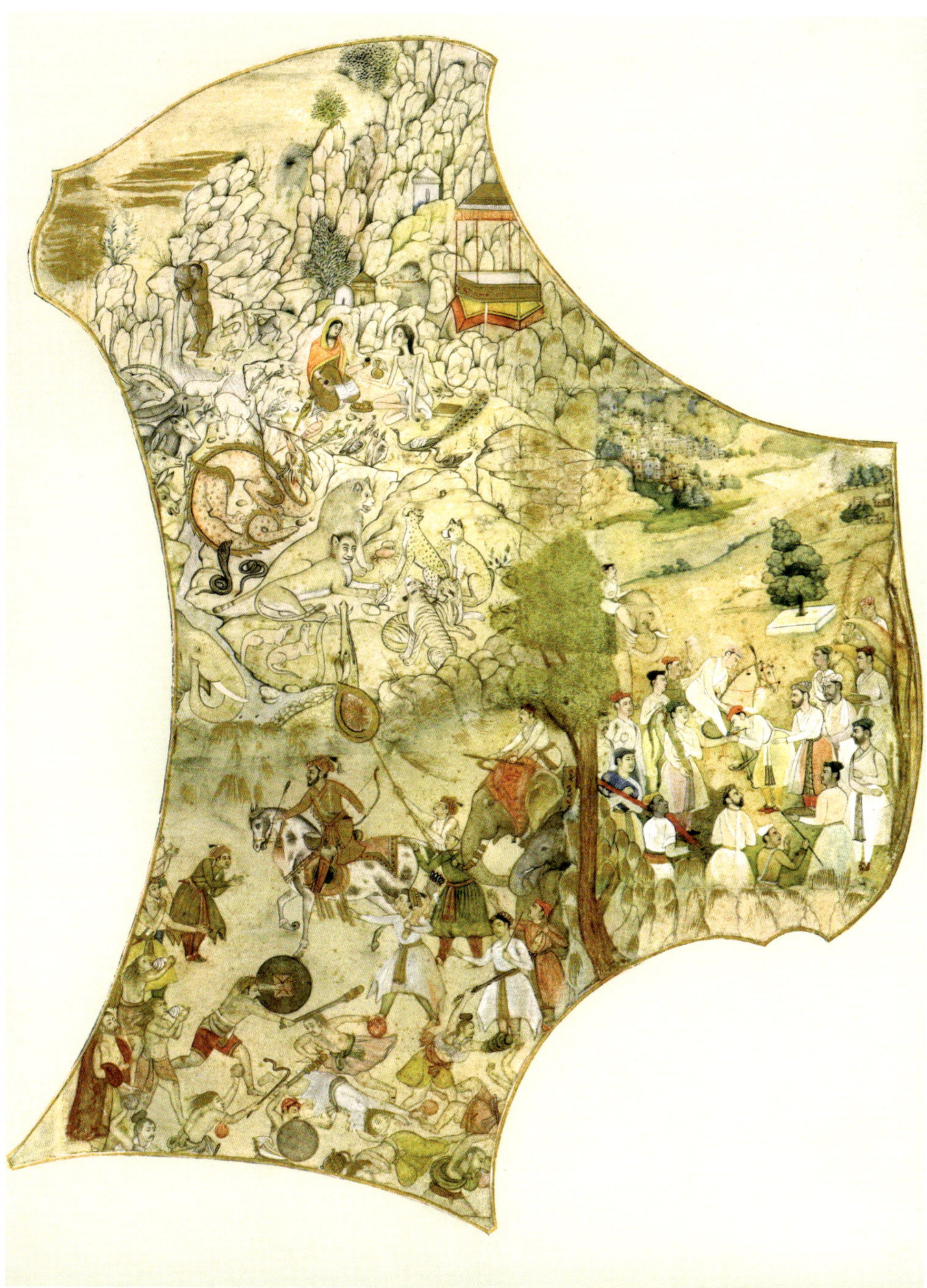

1.2 Millionenzimmer, Schloss Schönbrunn, Vienna, reconstruction (detail) of a cartouche containing collaged fragments of Mughal miniature paintings. Reconstructed by Josef Strzygowski, 1923.

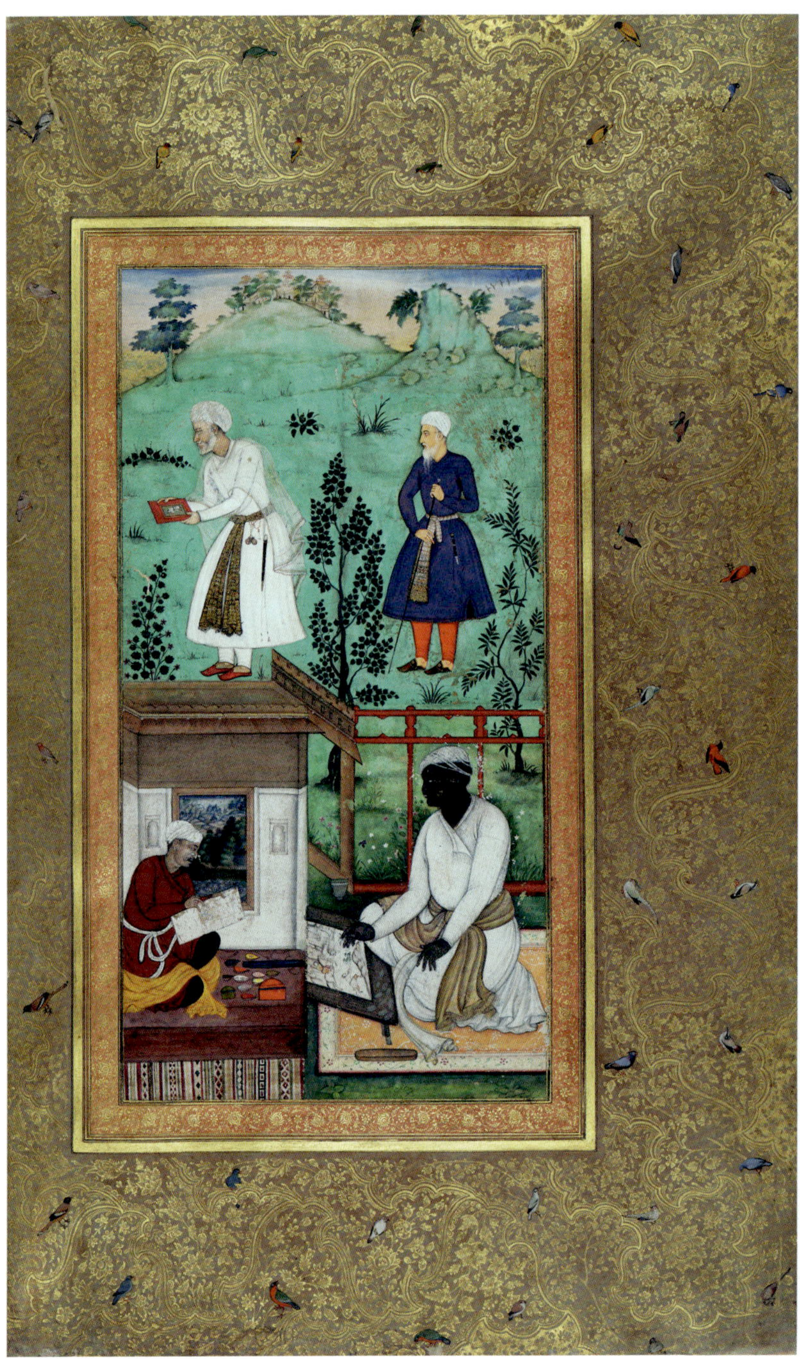

2.1   Jahangir Album, single folio showing artists at work, early 17th century, gouache on paper. Berlin, Staatsbibliothek Preußischer Kulturbesitz.

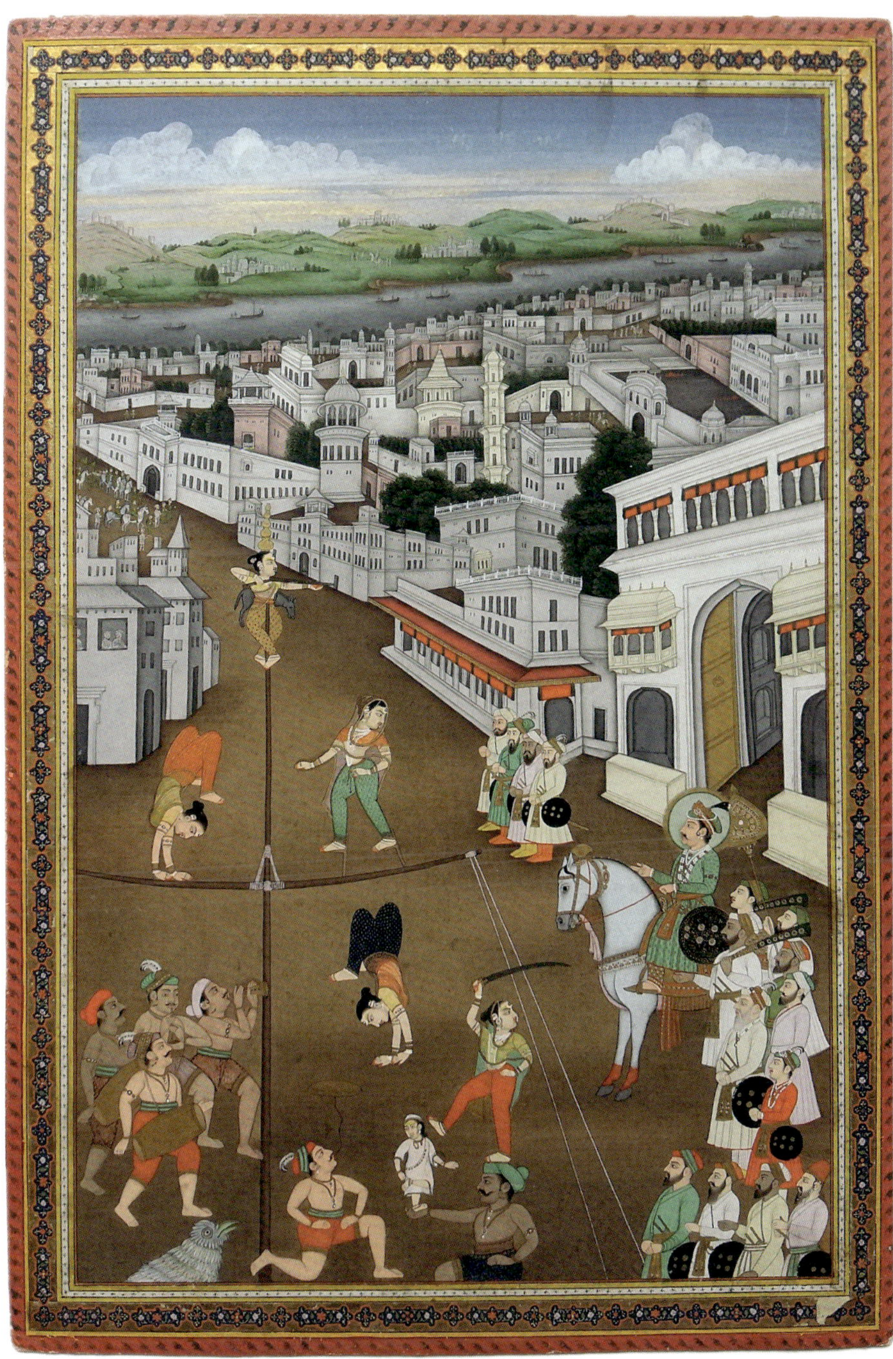

2.2   Single folio, showing acrobats performing to the Emperor and his retinue, late 17th century, Mughal. Berlin, Museum of Asian Art.

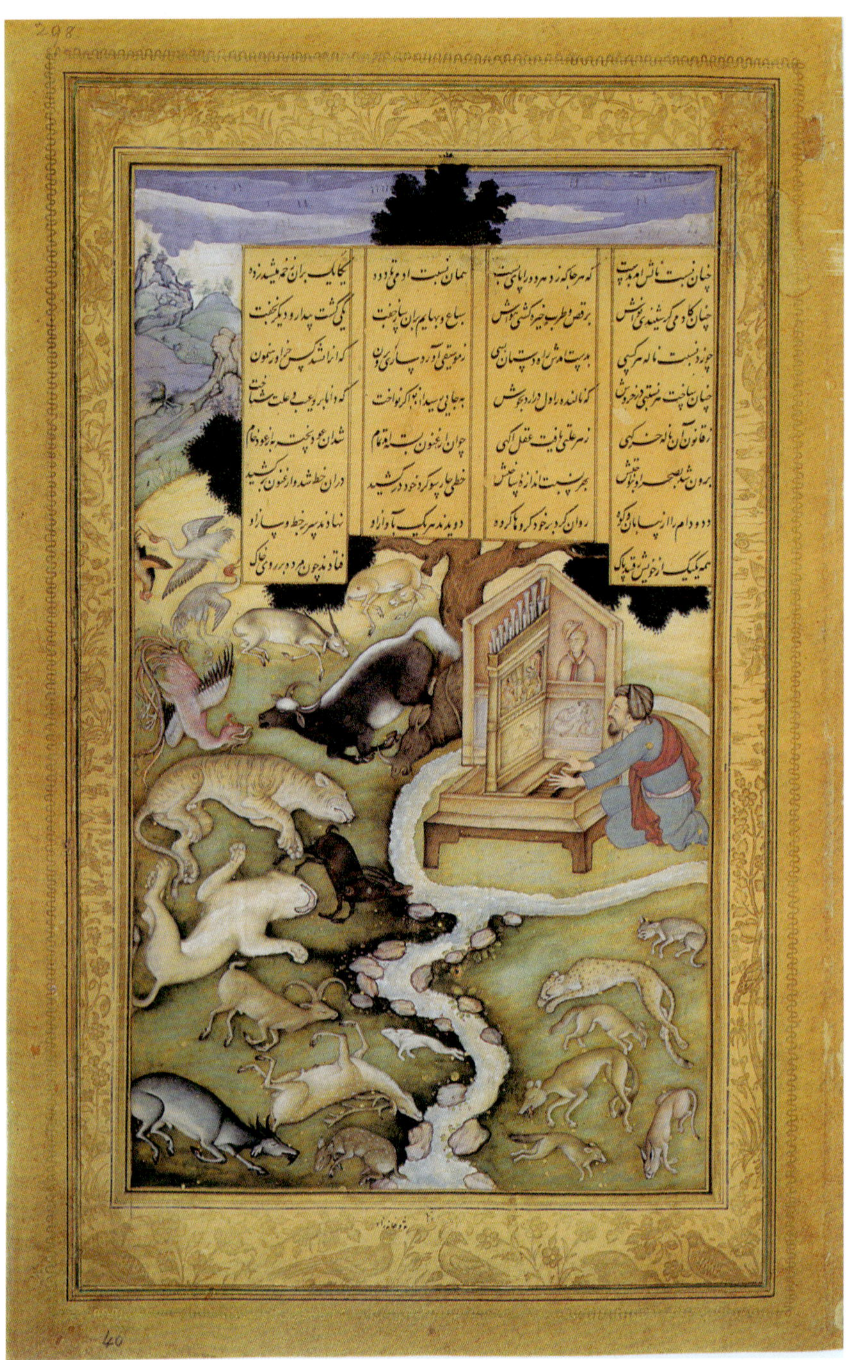

2.3　Folio from *Khamsa* of the poet Nizami Ganjavi, painted by Madhu Khanazad, showing Aflatun (Plato) playing music to the animals, 1595, gouache on paper. London, British Library.

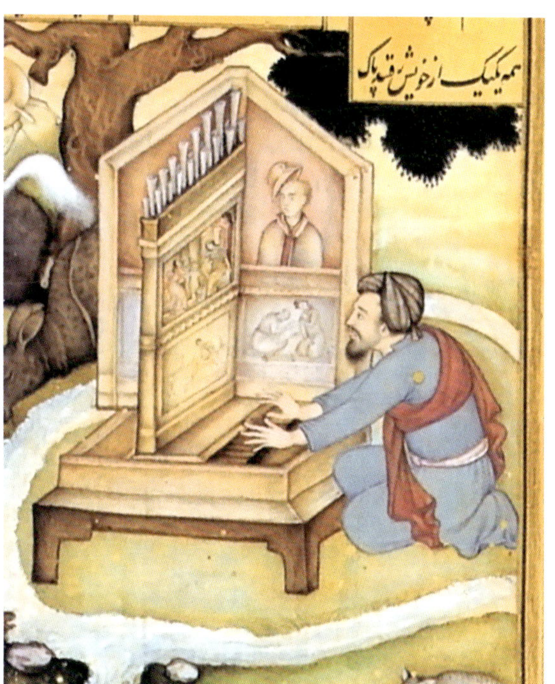

2.3a   Detail of 2.3

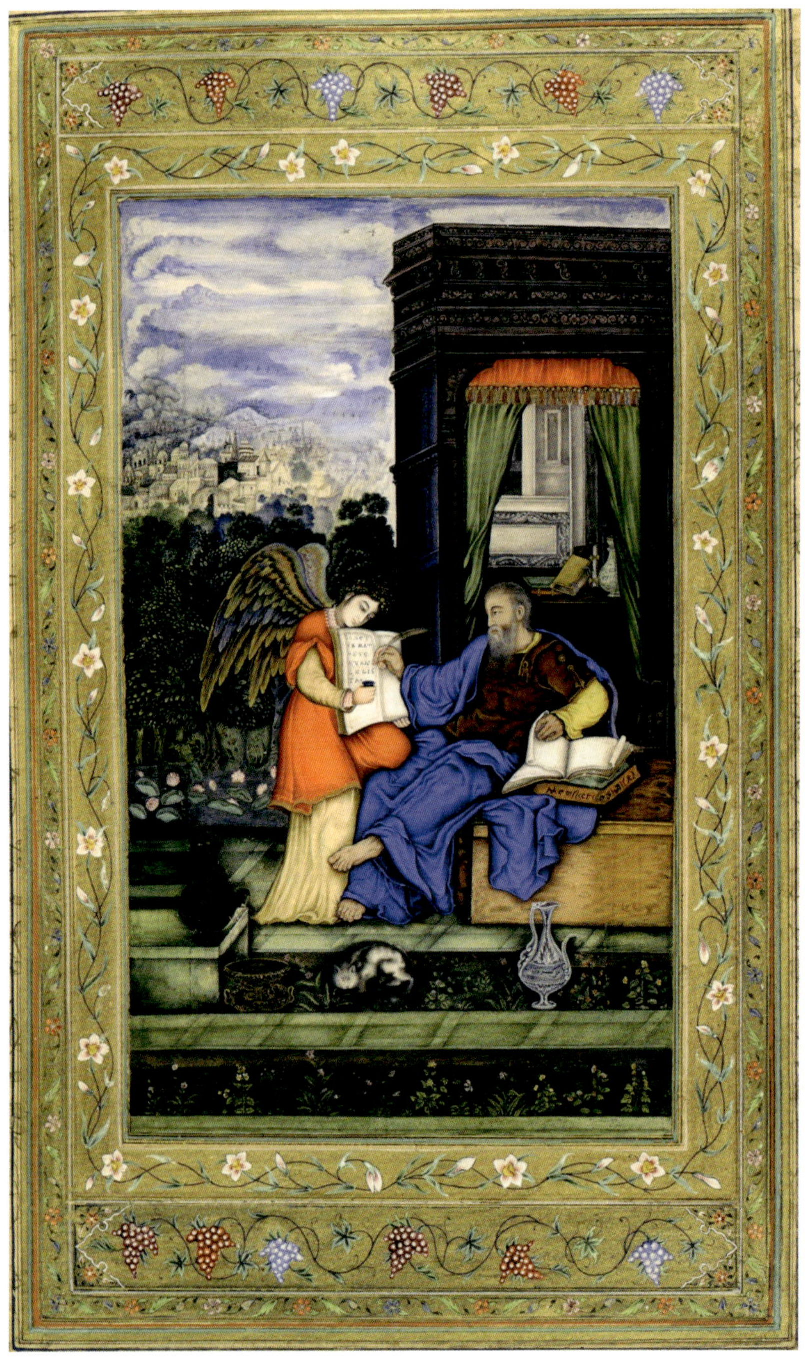

2.4   Single folio showing Saint Matthew and the Angel, painted by Kesu Das, 1588, gouache on paper. Oxford, Bodleian Library.

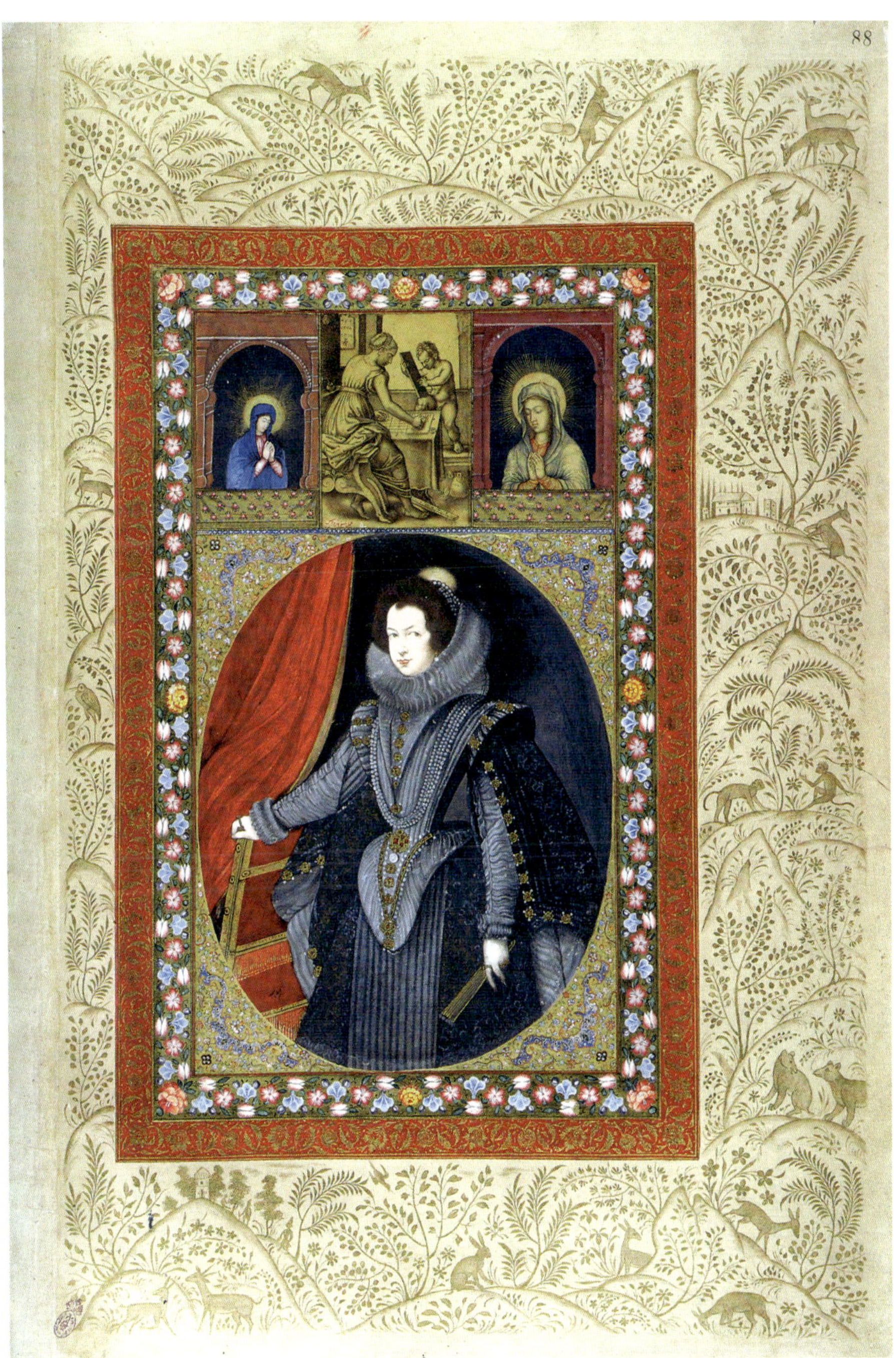

2.5 Folio from Saint Petersburg Album, composed of four fragments, early 17th century. St. Petersburg, Russian Academy of Sciences, Institute of Oriental Studies.

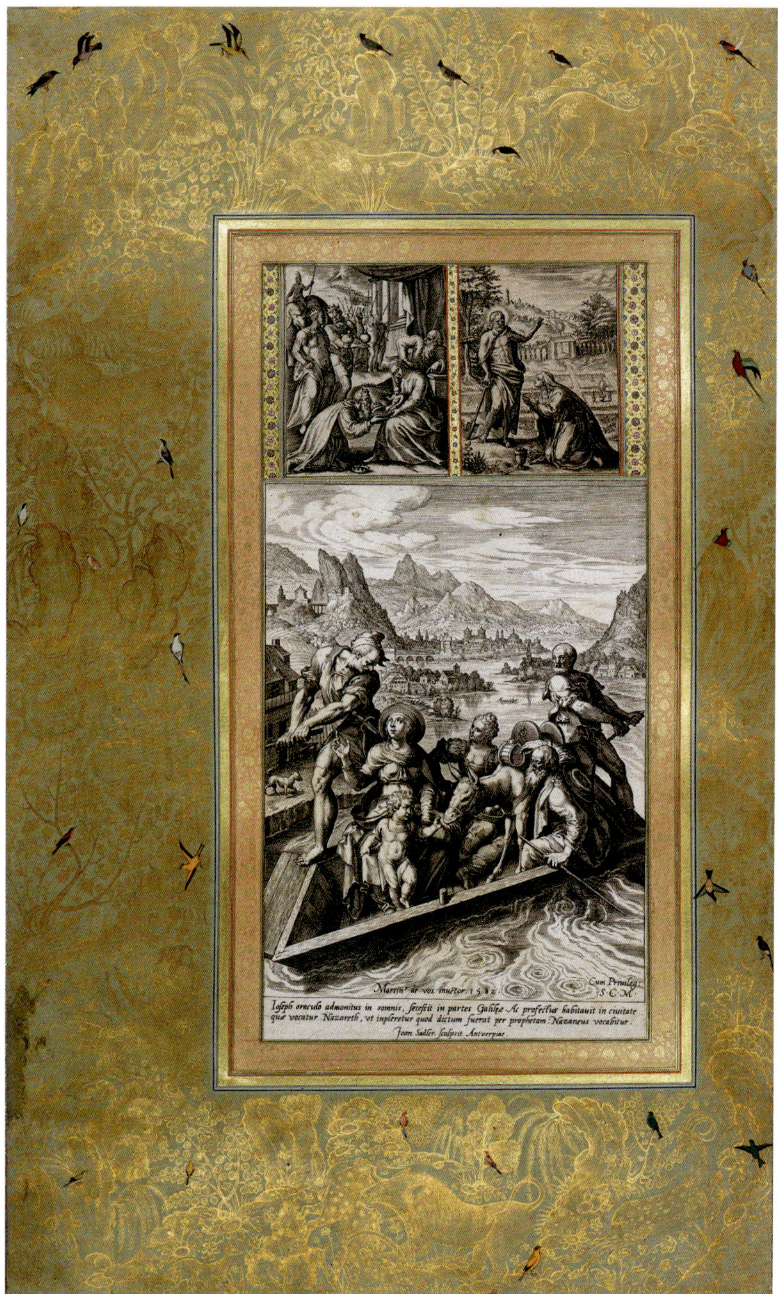

2.6   Page from Jahangir Album, composed of three fragments of engravings showing
Adoration of the three kings (top left), Christ and Maria Magdalena (top right),
and Holy Family on the way to Nazareth (below).
Staatsbibliothek zu Berlin, Stiftung Preußischer Kulturbesitz.

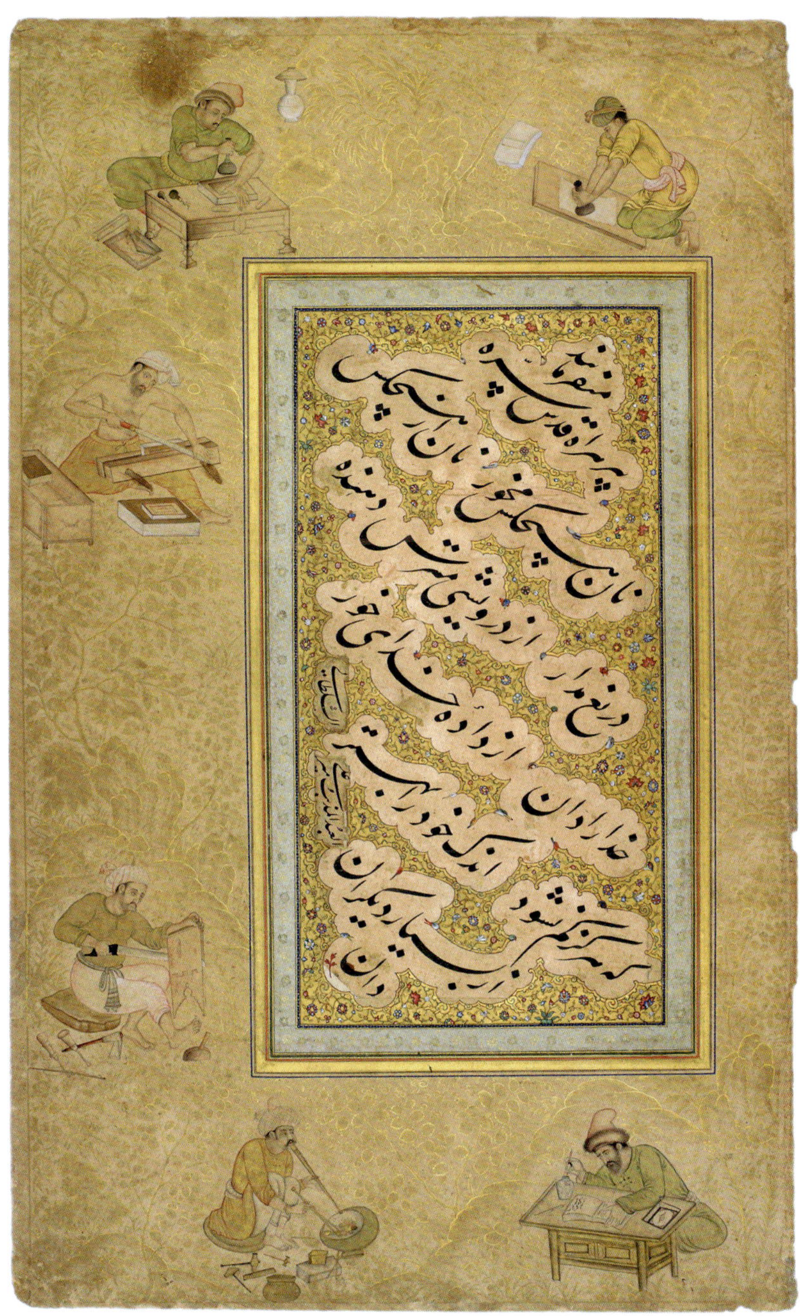

2.7   Folio from Gulshan Album, the painted margins of which represent
the stages of manuscript production, c. 1600, gouache, ink and gold on paper.
Washington D.C., Freer Gallery of Art, Smithsonian Institutions.

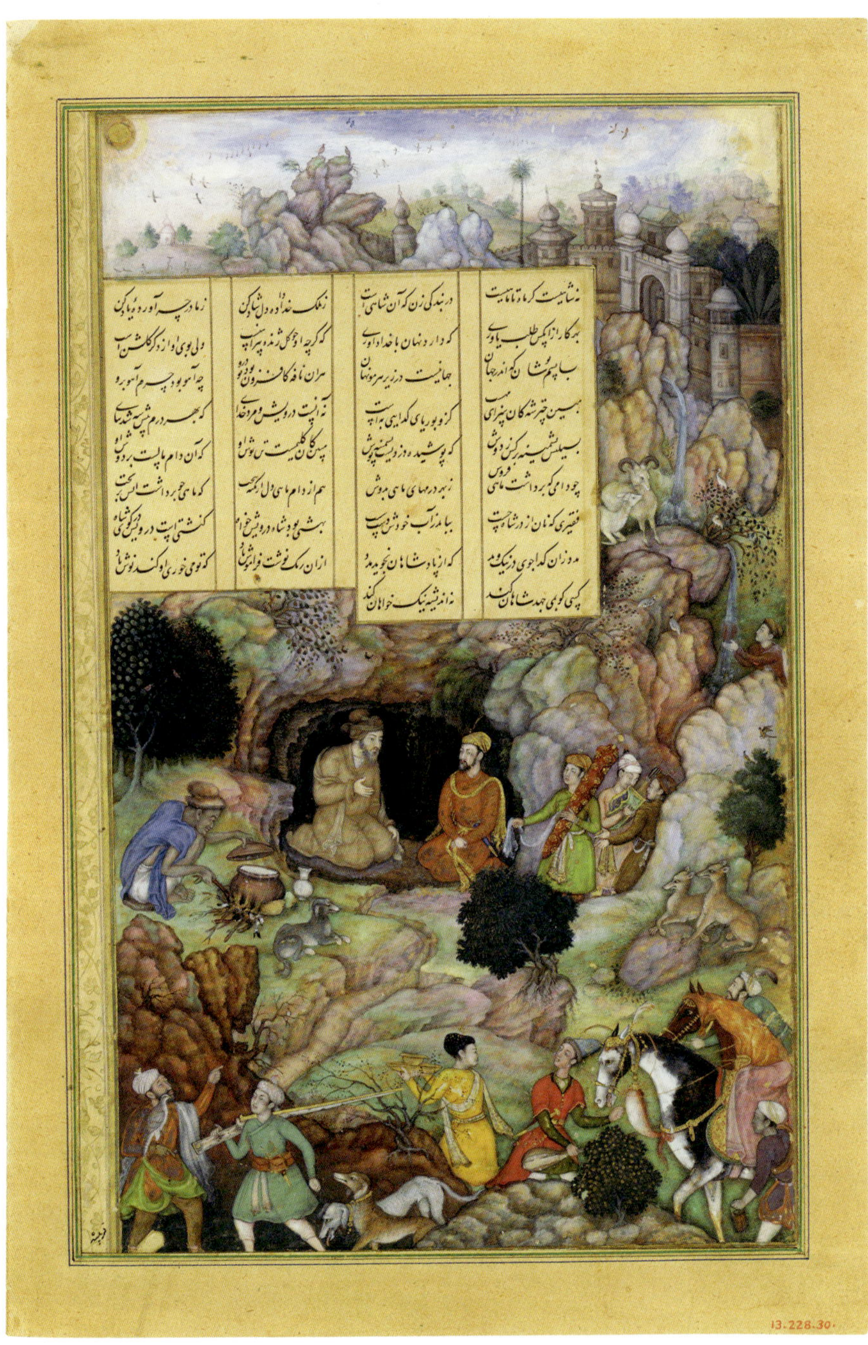

2.8　Folio from Khamsa of Amir Khusrau Dihlavi depicting Alexander visiting the cave of the sage Plato, painted by Basawan, 1597–98, gouache, ink, gold on paper. New York, Metropolitan Museum of Art.

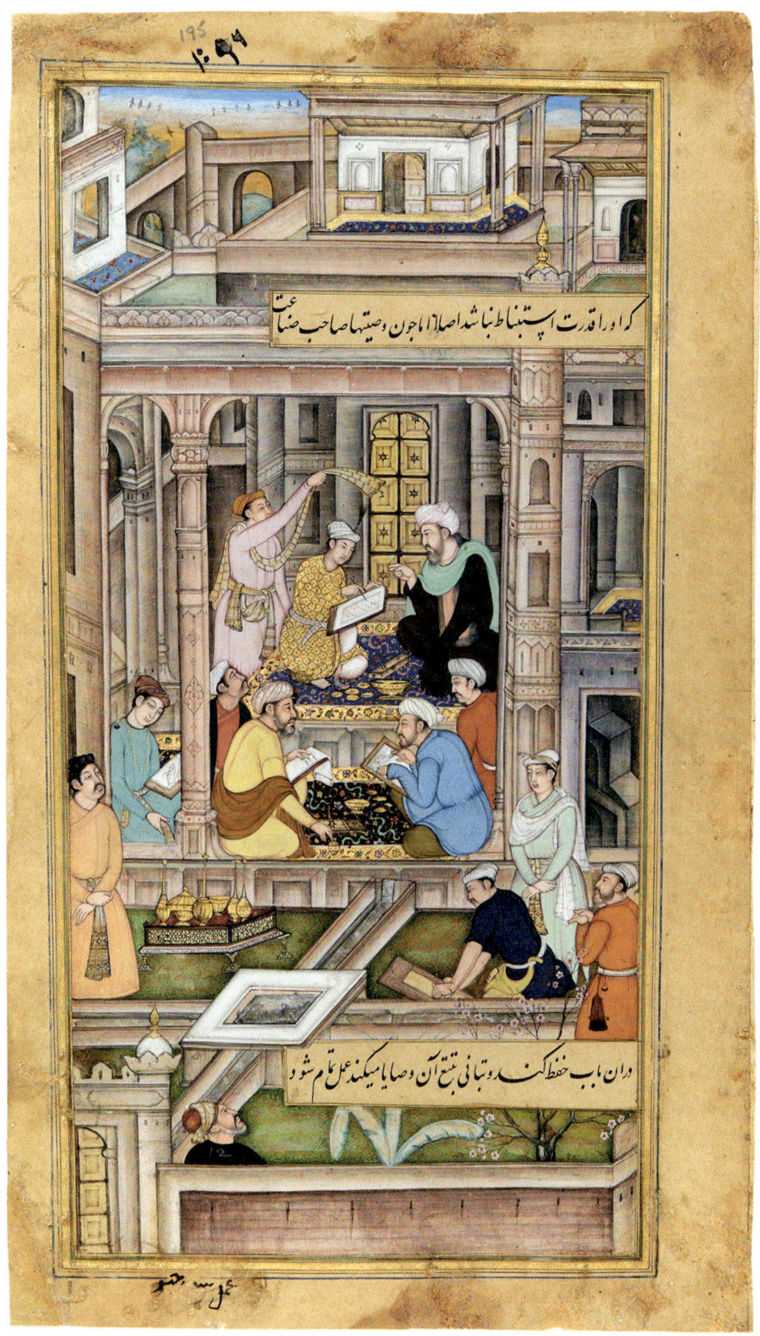

2.9   Folio from *Akhlaq-i Nasiri* by Nasir-ud-Din Tusi showing the interior of a royal kitabkhana with painters and calligraphers at work, c. 1590–95, gouache on paper. Toronto, Aga Khan Museum.

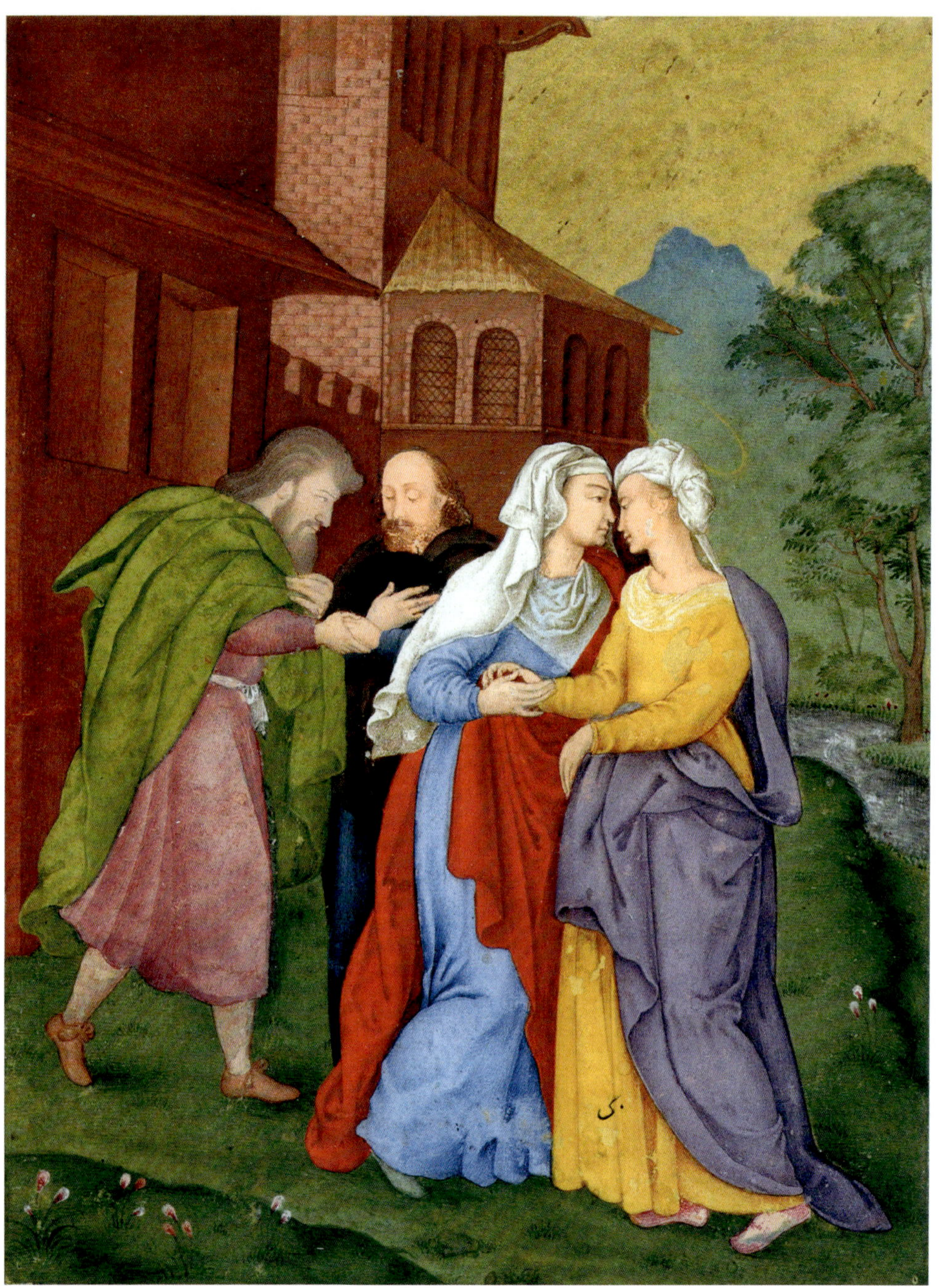

2.10 Single folio mounted on album page, painting based on an engraving by Johannes Wierix, *The Visitation*, by a Mughal artist, c. 1600–10, gouache, gold on paper. Zurich, Museum Rietberg.

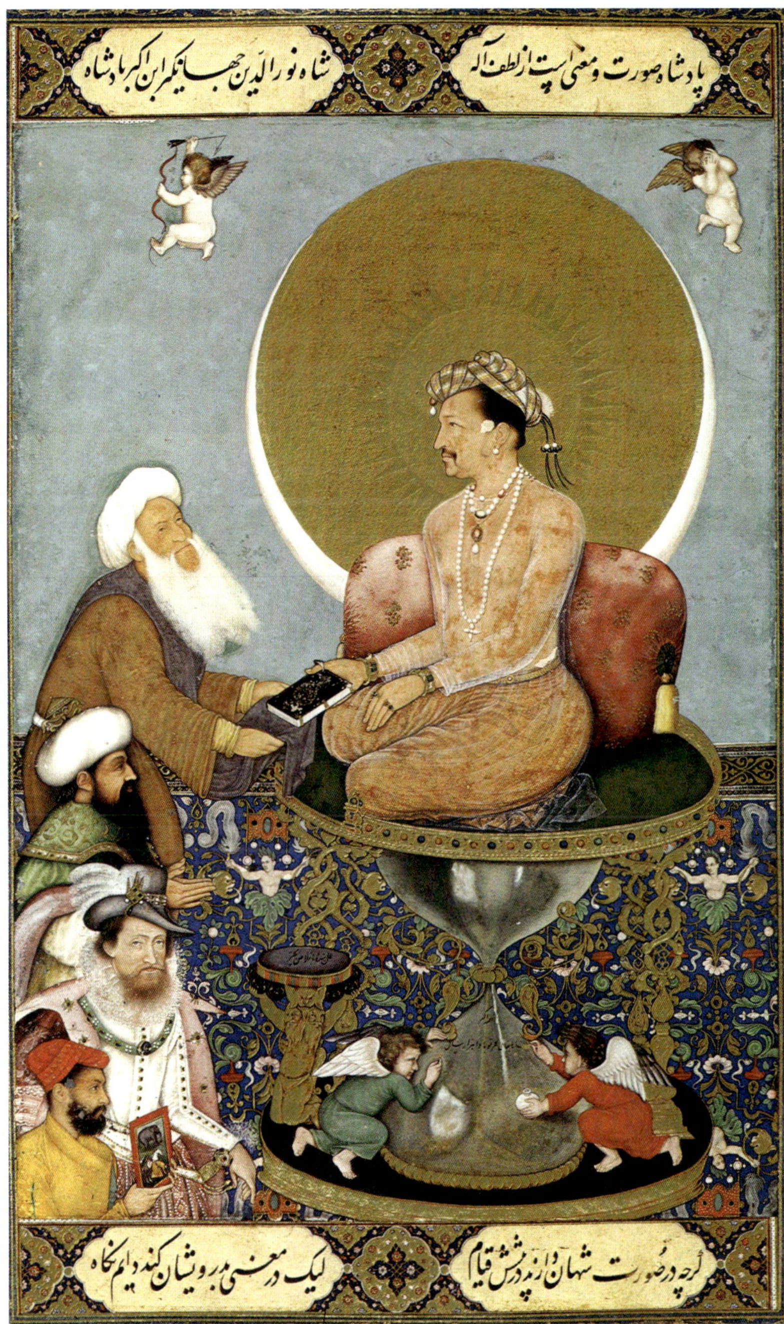

2.11   Folio from *Jahangirnama* portraying the Emperor Jahangir seated on an hour-glass throne offering a book to a Sufi saint, by Bichitr, c. 1620, gouache, ink, gold on paper. Washington D.C., Freer Gallery of Art, Smithsonian Institutions.

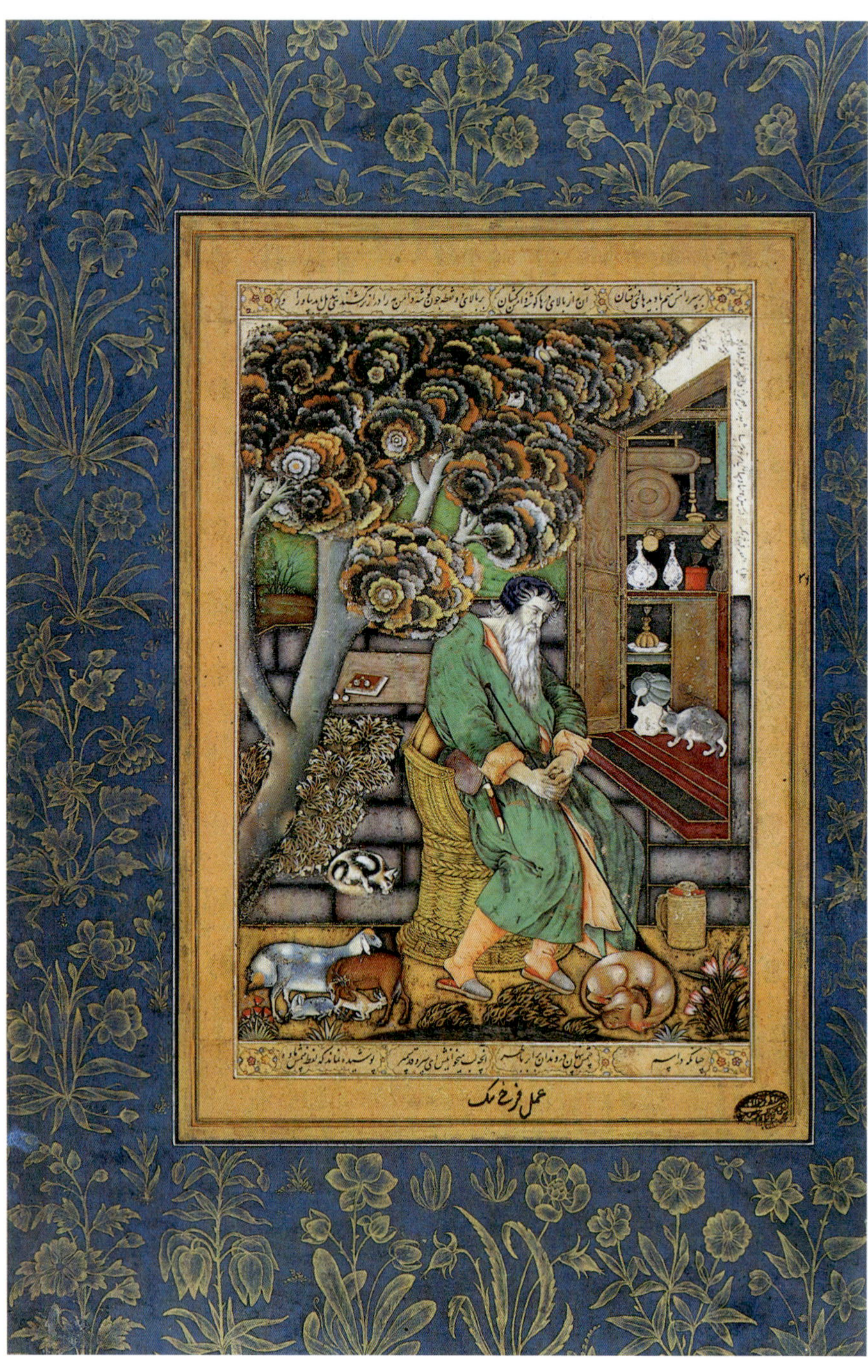

2.12   Single folio by Farrukh Beg portraying an old Sufi, c. 1615, gouache, ink, gold on paper. Qatar, Museum of Islamic Art.

CHAPTER THREE
TRAVERSING SCALE(S)
Transcultural Modernism with and Beyond the Nation

'[T]here is no inherent reason why the West/non-West opposition should determine the geographic perspective of modernity, except for the fact that it definitely serves to establish the putative unity of the West, a nebulous but commanding positivity whose existence we have tended to take for granted for such a long time… the West is particular in itself, but it also constitutes the universal point of reference in relation to which others recognize themselves as particularities.' – Naoki Sakai[1]

'[T]here is no crime bigger in the world of art than for an artist to limit his art within a specific piece of land.' – Kamel el-Telmisany[2]

Perhaps no other subject has brought forth so much writing and rewriting as has cultural modernity; yet in spite of the innumerable, diverging proclamations to de-centre, provincialize, pluralise or replace it, a consensus prevails over modernity's inbuilt structural dependence on a referent outside of it, 'a pre- or nonmodern in relation to which the modern takes its full meaning'.[3] Since the European Enlightenment, becoming modern from an earlier state of being non-modern has come to be conceived as a linear process of coming-of-age, of attaining autonomy. Such a vision rested on a Hegelian understanding of a perfectible human nature that enables individuals and civilisations to grow and be transformed into mature entities by dissociating development from the laws of nature.[4] Taking forward Sakai's thoughts cited above would mean considering the 'West' more as a geopolitical category through which the historical predicate of modernity is translated into a geographical one. This in turn implies that its relationship with other regions of the world is transformed through colonialism,

---

1   Naoki Sakai, 'Modernity and its Critique: The Problem of Universalism and Particularism', in: Naoki Sakai, *Translation and Subjectivity: On 'Japan' and Cultural Nationalism*, Minneapolis: University of Minnesota Press, 1997, pp. 153–76, here pp. 154–55.
2   Kamel el-Telmisany, 'Al-insāniyyah wa al-fann al-hadīth', *al-Tatawwur*, 2, 1940: 47–48, cited and translated by Sam Bardaouil, *Surrealism in Egypt: Modernism and the Art and Liberty Group*, London: I. B. Tauris, 2017, p. 47.
3   Michel-Rolf Trouillot, 'The Otherwise Modern: Caribbean Lessons from the Savage Slot', in: Bruce M. Knauft (ed.), *Critically Modern: Alternatives, Alterities, Anthropologies*, Bloomington: Indiana University Press, 2002, pp. 220–37, here p. 222.
4   Saurabh Dube (ed.), *Handbook of Modernity in South Asia: Modern Makeovers*, New Delhi: Oxford University Press, 2011, p. 19.

migration, new technologies of communication, and global organisation of labour, producing social subjects across the world who redefine the enunciation of the 'modern'. To take an example from a colonial context, prescriptive understandings of what it meant to the colonised to become modern underwent processes of translation and recasting, the effects of which, in spite of being occasionally theorised, more often than not end up being studied as regional specialisations. One of many such examples is Anand Pandian's ethnographic study of a Tamil settlement in colonial South India. Pandian has explored the transculturation of a colonial concept following its encounter with vernacular literary traditions wherein the meanings of 'maturation' or 'ripening' and their association with modernity do not obey the separation between cycles of nature and human development in the way they were elaborated in the Hegelian model of history as the realisation of universal reason.[5] In this account of colonial South India, natural phenomena and human development remain interdependent and mutually constitutive, instead of subscribing to an explanation wherein 'the maturation of one [must] entail a necessary transcendence of the other'. Such an understanding of development, moreover, does not detach human progress from 'situations of encounter, accident, and chance', nor does any clear value judgement attach itself to the process, to spell incompleteness, retardation, or failure.[6]

This is but one of many instances that allow us to reasonably argue for a modernity that is migrant and mutable, continuous and at best contingent. Its location stands for a distinct cultural ecology, for one possible 'habitation', to borrow from Dipesh Chakrabarty.[7] Even as the 'West', in the words of Dilip Gaonkar, 'remains the major clearinghouse of global modernity'[8], the recognition that it no longer offers the sole template for the unfolding of culture is now scarcely a matter of debate. The revived interest in modernity and the many sites on which it has been invoked, enacted, or self-consciously performed – religion, medicine, governmental technologies, advertising, art – is less about the opposition between the modern and the postmodern, and more a preoccupation with site-based studies, deep histories, and local contingencies. Much continues to happen worldwide in the name of the modern; its self-reflexive edge allows individuals to make themselves modern, as opposed to be being made so from the outside; becoming modern offers the license to play, refract, and refigure, it enables belatedness to be turned into an opportunity by the latecomer. Can the study of local sites avoid the pitfalls of recounting exclusively local histories, or the trap of continuing to take national cultures as closed units, even as in several regions beyond the West the nation was the terrain on which the struggle for emancipation from the colonial yoke was waged and won? This chapter addresses the challenge of bringing regions and nations into

---

5 Anand Pandian, 'Ripening the Earth: On Maturity and Modernity in South India', in Dube (ed.), *Handbook of Modernity*, pp. 157–69, here p. 158. See also Anand Pandian, *Crooked Stalks: Cultivating Virtue in South India*, Durham: Duke University Press, 2009.

6 Pandian, 'Ripening the Earth', p. 168.

7 Dipesh Chakrabarty, *Habitations of Modernity: Essays in the Wake of Subaltern Studies*, Delhi: Permanent Black, 2002.

8 Dilip P. Gaonkar, 'On Alternative Modernities', *Public Culture*, vol. 11 (1), 1999: 1–18, here 1.

a more dynamic, non-hierarchical, and, importantly, non-homogenizing relationship with each other, arguing that this cannot be adequately handled without simultaneously delving into localities and negotiating multiple scales – the local, regional, national, and global. The national within this context emerges for large sections of the once colonized regions of the world as a double-edged tool within the making of the modern: historically a mobilizing force for reclaiming sovereignty and channelizing modernist energies, the nation by the very logic of its formation ends up replicating those temporalities and hegemonic representational modes it sought to overturn.

Modernism, a cognate of modernity, historically reaches back to the mid-nineteenth century in Europe; transcultured from its inception, it extends into our times as a global phenomenon. The term as used in this chapter refers exclusively to artistic modernism – in other words, a conceptual designation that encompasses art movements across the globe extending from the late nineteenth till after the mid-twentieth centuries. Each of these experimented with a range of new forms in response to historical phenomena associated with modernity: broadly, industrialisation, urbanisation, war, and decolonisation. The global spread, and at the same time uneven temporal unfolding, of art movements termed modernist renders it difficult to attach these to a fixed chronological slot, or even to read them as a specific style or genre of art. Aesthetic modernism is informed by the epistemology of modernity, even as accounts of its global articulations do not follow any single, stable narrative. The widely accepted account of that which has been characterised as the 'European model of a strong opposition between socioeconomic modernity and aesthetic modernism' cannot be said to have translated seamlessly into other contexts.[9] Modernism in its nineteenth and early twentieth century phases was a product of a world of artistic and cultural exchange enabled by commerce, colonialism, and travel. At no point of its history, however, could the 'European modern' be read as a process begun and finished in Europe and thence ready to export to the rest of the world. If modernity, as Timothy Mitchell underlines, was brought forth from Europe's interaction with far-flung regions in Asia, the Caribbean, or the Ottoman Empire,[10] so must the emergence of modernist art be placed within the context of industrialisation and colonialism, whose global connections and complex political and cultural determinations made that emergence possible.

The transregional spatialities of modernist experiments, which emerged from projects and processes involving actors and institutions across continents, means that any discussion of the subject needs to work simultaneously within, beyond, and even bypassing the national space by engaging with the 'play of scales'.[11] The concept of scale has been intensely

---

9   Andreas Huyssen, 'Geographies of Modernism in a Globalizing World', *New German Critique*, vol. 34 (1), 2007: 189–207, here 193.

10   Timothy Mitchell, 'The Stage of Modernity', in: Timothy Mitchell (ed.), *Questions of Modernity*, Minneapolis: University of Minnesota Press, 2000, pp. 1–34, in particular pp. 2–5.

11   Jacques Revel, *Jeux d'Échelles: La micro-analyse à l'expérience*, Paris: Gallimard et Le Seuil, 1996. Also Jacques Revel, 'Microanalysis and the Construction of the Social', in Jacques Revel and Lynn A. Hunt (eds), *Histories: French Constructions of the Past*, New York: The New Press, 1998, pp. 492–502.

discussed among social scientists studying modern globalisation, as well as by historians in response to the challenges of writing global histories. For the latter group of scholars, this involves being able to effectively integrate the study of macro-level structural phenomena with questions attentive to differentiations around class, gender, or ethnicity that unfold on specific sites.[12] A transcultural perspective on scale, even as it builds on the insights that have preceded it, is careful to eschew polarities of macro- and micro-perspectives that risk essentialising these divides, particularly as they tend to work with predetermined spatial units. The transcultural move to 'traverse' scale, as it features in this account of artistic modernism on the Indian subcontinent, means inserting its subjects and questions within practices that signal to reciprocally constitutive trans-scalar relationships. Artistic modernism in any one regional context, this chapter argues, was shaped through a dynamic between the singularity and specificity of that site and its connectedness to other sites, distant and not so distant. Viewed in this perspective, the specificity of a given context – here South Asia – is read not as a product of its boundedness or in terms of an ideal of local authenticity, but in terms of the particularities characterising its connective relationships with other places, which impart life to its artistic experiments. A place, a region, or a nation no longer forms a closed context; context itself emerges as processual, constituted by transcultural interactions across other places and spaces, between individuals, knowledge, and artistic practice. Such an approach allows us to dismantle the monolith of a normative modernism with its universalising claims and retell the histories of global modernist art as non-linear, as an interrelated assemblage of often contradictory, uneven social and discursive practices, thus making hitherto submerged meanings and representations visible and globally intelligible. Negotiating scale – between the regional, the national, the local, and the global – by attending to the fluidity of each level, allows us to bring global processes of transmission and translation, resonance and refusal in sync with individual sites and their histories.

Art history, in addition, pays attention to scale as a social construct and form of self-positioning of the actors involved. Scale frequently forms a field of tension between the perspective

---

12   For a discussion of scale from a social science perspective, see the essays in E. Summerson Carr and Michael Lempert (eds), *Scale: Discourse and Dimensions of Social Life*, Oakland: University of California Press, 2016. Theorisations by historians include Sebastian Conrad, *What Is Global History?*, Princeton: Princeton University Press, 2017, p. 129ff.; Sebouh D. Aslanian, Joyce E. Chaplin, Ann McGrath and Kristin Mann, 'How Size Matters: The Question of Scale in History: AHR Conversation', *American Historical Review*, vol. 118 (5), 2013: 1431–72. Responding to impulses from micro-historical approaches of the 1980s and 1990s, global history strives to fruitfully combine these with the investigation of macro-level phenomena: see Francesca Trivellato, 'Is There a Future for Italian Microhistory in an Age of Global History?', *California Italian Studies*, vol. 2 (1), 2011: n.p.; Angelika Epple, 'Globale Mikrogeschichte. Auf dem Weg zu einer Geschichte der Relationen', in: Ewald Hiebl and Ernst Langthaler (eds), *Im Kleinen das Große suchen: Mikrogeschichte in Theorie und Praxis*, Innsbruck/ Vienna: Studien Verlag, 2012, pp. 37–47; Maxine Berg, 'Global History: Approaches and New Directions', in: Maxine Berg (ed.), *Writing the History of the Global: Challenges for the 21st Century*, Oxford: Oxford University Press, 2013, pp. 1–18. The foundational texts of Italian micro-history include Carlo Ginzburg, 'Clues: Roots of an Evidential Paradigm', in: Carlo Ginzburg, *Clues, Myths, and the Historical Method*, Baltimore: The Johns Hopkins University Press, 1989, pp. 87–113; Giovanni Levi, 'On Microhistory', in: Peter Burke (ed.), *New Perspectives on Historical Writing*, Cambridge: Polity Press, 1991, pp. 93–113.

of actors and the processes in which they are involved. Looking at scale as process rather than product allows bringing in multiple perspectives on objects of knowledge, to grapple with how scales are produced and used to structure relationships.[13] A region or even a nation can be perceived as a 'locality' from the viewpoint of the agents, for whom it may be a site to be recuperated, for instance from an empire, or serve as an anchor against fragility, seen as resulting from phenomena on a macro-scale. Viewed in this light, scale belongs to a mental geography, a set of projections that draw attention to how transcultural relationships impinge on subjectivities. In the studies discussed below, artistic subjectivity relocates concepts of the nation within an imagined realm: the nation could be recast as allegory or syncretic vision, it could be both local and transgress boundaries. However, the slippage between 'art' and its 'history' signals towards the tension between the nation as ground of emancipation in cultural memory, and as a constricting ideological frame, complicit in the production of the 'authentic' and the 'native', to contain the discipline. A theory of transculturation therefore does not constitute its units of analysis to coincide with a single place or region or nation, but to follow the logic of the interactive relationships related to the object being investigated. Tracking the course of processes brings together spatial extension with in-depth analysis, making it necessary for the scholar to negotiate multiple scales together with the co-existence of present and past times.

The following investigation of different facets of modernist art – with its central focus on the Indian subcontinent – uses a transcultural conceptualisation of scale to rethink this history as a relational account that unfolds across region, locality, nation, and the world. The chapter moves between individual actors, institutions, forms, and conceptual categories, to relativise the primacy of any one scalar unit, and instead to plot artistic modernism on a matrix of intersecting, mutually inflecting vectors of social and discursive practices. While each of the constituent elements of this history elucidated below participates in shared global concerns, other levels of observation reveal particular aspects that are at once singular and connected. A transcultural story of modernist art moves beyond widespread notions of 'multiple' or 'alternative' or 'vernacular' modernisms, to instead consider modernist experiments in South Asia in conjunction with other regions of the world, often treated as isolated studies. This in turn enables us to discard a predefined periodisation of artistic modernism, a tenacious legacy of Euro-American experiences, by which modernism transited to a postmodernist stage by the middle of the twentieth century. Attending to continuities and discontinuities across time and space necessitates acknowledging the simultaneity of multiple temporalities, depending on places and people.

---

13 See, for instance, Bruno Latour, *Reassembling the Social: An Introduction to Actor-Network-Theory*, Oxford/New York: Oxford University Press, 2005; Anna L. Tsing, *Friction: An Ethnography of Global Connection*, Princeton: Princeton University Press, 2005; for a synoptic overview of the field, E. Summerson Carr and Michael Lempert, 'Introduction: Pragmatics of Scale', in: Carr and Lempert (eds), *Scale*, pp. 1–21.

Shared Horizons, Resonant Microhistories

The story of artistic modernism can no longer be presented as a single chronicle of diffusion; neither does this history possess a singular temporality. Yet one of the persistent blind spots in the recounting of that story – an account that concluded in 1945 – has been the exclusion of a large number of global sites of modernist experiments that had emerged after the end of the Second World War, following the decline of European artistic power to set the agenda of modernism. Copious amounts of new material uncovered by recent scholarship are vital to redrawing the map of global modernism, directing at the same time our attention to both the multiplicity of accounts as well as the historical unevenness of institutional developments shaping the syntax of artistic modernity. A recent exhibition curated by the late Okwui Enwezor, Ulrich Wilmes, and Katy Siegel on post-war art after 1945 took on the ambitious task of translating and compressing the gains of young scholarship from across the world into the medium of an exhibition, in order to tell a story of a continuing, connected, multivalent, and, not least, uneven artistic modernity.[14] The modern, including its dominant iterations in the United States and Europe, was made visible, in the words of Katy Siegel, 'as a knot of mutually inflecting histories ... both local and a matter of mutual exchange'.[15]

Many histories of modernism during the 1940s take as their starting point the issue of *Life* magazine of 8 August 1949 that provocatively queried whether Jackson Pollock was 'the greatest living painter in the United States'.[16] These were the years that ostensibly saw the centre of the art world shift from a war-ravaged Europe to New York City, a time of which Serge Guilbaut wrote: 'New York stole the idea of modern art'.[17] The juncture represented at the same time the crystallisation of a geography of modernism plotted along a Paris-Berlin-Vienna axis that then extended to New York, from where its articulations supposedly travelled to distant corners of the world. Today, some seventy years later, our atlas of modernist art has been enriched by countless micro-stories unearthed by scholars from innumerable sites across the globe. These include Shanghai, Mexico City, Bombay (today Mumbai), Tehran, Ljubljana, Cairo, Dakar, Tokyo, São Paulo, Lahore, Lagos, Moscow, Beirut ... the list goes on.[18]

---

14 The exhibition *Postwar: Kunst zwischen Pazifik und Atlantik, 1945–1965* took place at the Haus der Kunst in Munich from 14 October 2016 to 26 March 2017, with catalogues in German and English. All citations here are from the latter: Okwui Enwezor, Katy Siegel and Ulrich Wilmes (eds), *Postwar: Art between the Pacific and the Atlantic, 1945–1965*, Prestel: Munich, 2016.

15 Katy Siegel, 'Art, World, History', in Enwezor et al. (eds), *Postwar*, pp. 42–57, here p. 45.

16 Dorothy Seiberling, 'Jackson Pollock. Is He the Greatest Living painter in the United States?', *Life*, 8 August 1949. See, for instance, Preminda Jacob, 'Between Modernism and Modernization: Locating Modernity in South Asian Art', *Art Journal*, vol. 58 (3), 1999: 48–57.

17 Serge Guilbaut, *How New York Stole the Idea of Modern Art: Abstract Expressionism, Freedom and the Cold War*, trans. Arthur Goldhammer, Chicago: University of Chicago Press, 1983.

18 The investigation of artistic modernism from regional perspectives beyond Euro-America is an expanding field. A few landmark publications that also problematise the global dimensions of the subject: Kobena Mercer (ed.), *Cosmopolitan Modernisms*, Cambridge, MA/London: Institute of International Visual Arts, 2005; Kobena Mercer (ed.), *Discrepant Abstraction*, Cambridge, MA: MIT Press, 2006; Christian Kravagna, *Transmoderne: Eine Kunstgeschichte des Kontakts*, Berlin: b_books, 2017; Partha Mitter, 'Interventions: Decentering Modernism: Art History and Avant-Garde Art from the Periphery',

In the light of such findings, it is no longer plausible to hold on to a now notoriously historicist or Greenbergian account of modernist art that presents Euro-America as its original locus and central axis, from where its achievements are said to have spread to far-flung peripheries that brought forth imitations of its expressive forms. Each of the stories above presents us with a vigorous modernism, not reducible to stylistic content, informed but not determined by counterparts in Paris, Vienna, or Berlin. Back in 2005, Kobena Mercer referred to 'the limitations of our available knowledge about modernism's cross-cultural past'.[19] Today, the challenge facing art historians and curators is not the lack of knowledge, but the task of meaningfully writing those modernist initiatives and experiments that unfolded in global locations beyond the New York-Paris corridor into the disciplinary matrix of art history and museum display. What kind of an art historical framework do we require that will enable us to go beyond simply adding unknown modernist artists to an existing canon or, alternatively, relegating regional articulations of the modern to the isolated domains of individual 'area

with responses by Alastair Wright, Rebecca M. Brown, Saloni Mathur and Ajay Sinha, *The Art Bulletin*, vol. 90 (4), 2008: 531–74; Monica Juneja and Franziska Koch (eds), 'Multi-Centred Modernisms – Reconfiguring Asian Art of the Twentieth and Twenty-First Centuries', themed section, *Transcultural Studies*, vol. 2 & 3, 2010–11; Piotr Piotrowski, 'Towards a Horizontal History of the European Avant-Garde', in: Sascha Bru and Peter Nicholls (eds), *European Avant-Garde and Modernism Studies*, Berlin: De Gruyter, 2019, pp. 49–58. A synoptic account of Asia is John Clark, *Modern Asian Art*, Honolulu: University of Hawai Press, 1998, and more recently John Clark, *The Asian Modern*, Singapore: National Gallery, 2021. Studies on regional sites include: Geeta Kapur, *When Was Modernism? Essays in Contemporary Cultural Practice in India*, New Delhi: Tulika Books, 2007; Partha Mitter, *The Triumph of Modernism: India's Artists and the Avant-Garde 1922–1947*, London: Reaktion Books, 2007; Rebecca M. Brown, *Art for a Modern India 1947–1980*, Durham, NC: Duke University Press, 2009; Iftikhar Dadi, *Modernism and the Art of Muslim South Asia*, Chapel Hill: University of North Carolina Press, 2010; Nada Shabout, *Modern Arab Art: Formation of Arab Aesthetics*, Gainesville: University of Florida Press, 2007; David Craven, *Art and Revolution in Latin America: 1910–1990*, New Haven: Yale University Press, 2002; Ming Tiampo, *Gutai: Decentering Modernism*, Chicago: University of Chicago Press, 2011; Alicia Volk, *In Pursuit of Universalism: Yorozu Tetsugorō and Japanese Modern Art*, Berkeley: University of California Press, 2012; Sonal Khullar, *Worldly Affiliations: Artistic Practice, National Identity and Modernism in India 1930–1990*, Oakland: University of California Press, 2015; Sam Bardaouil, *Surrealism in Egypt: Modernism and the Art and Liberty Group*, London: I. B. Tauris, 2017; Piotr Piotrowski, *In the Shadow of Yalta: Art and the Avant-Garde in Eastern Europe 1945–1989*, London: Reaktion Books, 2009; Klara Kemp Welch and Cristina Freire (eds), 'Artists' networks in Eastern Europe and Latin America', themed section, *ARTMargins*, #2 (1), 2012: 3–13; Mohamed Elshahed, 'Egypt Builds: A Revaluation of the History of Modernism', in: Georg Schöllhammer and Rubin Arevshatyan (eds), *Sweet Sixties: Specters and Spirits of a Parallel Avant-Garde*, Berlin: Sternberg Press, 2014, pp. 137–49; Alexandra D. Seggerman, 'Mahmoud Mukhtar: "The First Sculptor from the Land of Sculpture"', *World Art*, vol. 4 (1), 2014: 27–46; Elizabeth Harney, *In Senghor's Shadow: Art, Politics, and the Avant-Garde in Senegal, 1960–1995*, Durham, NC: Duke University Press, 2004; Salah M. Hassan, *Ibrahim El-Salahi: A Visionary Modernist*, Seattle: University of Washington Press, 2012; Hans Belting and Andrea Buddensieg, *Ein Afrikaner in Paris: Léopold Sédar Senghor und die Zukunft der Moderne*, Munich: C. H. Beck, 2018; Iftikhar Dadi and Suheyla Takesh (eds), *Taking Shape: Abstraction from the Arab World, 1950s–1980s*, New York: Grey Art Gallery, 2020; Chika Okeke-Agulu, *Postcolonial Modernism: Art and Decolonization in Twentieth Century Nigeria*, Durham, NC: Duke University Press, 2015; Joshua I. Cohen, *The 'Black Art' Renaissance. African Sculpture and Modernism Across Continents*, Oakland: University of California Press, 2020.

19   Mercer (ed.), *Cosmopolitan Modernisms*, p. 7.

studies'? Can we bring to the term modernism a less formalistic intonation and open it to accommodate experimental, at times disparately so, ventures?

There has no doubt been considerable critical engagement, primarily from postmodern and postcolonial positions, with narratives of artistic modernism since the time Serge Guilbaut and others wrote about the New York scene. Such appraisals have laid bare its teleology and value judgements about art; they have pried opened the structures and values of the modern to expose its triumphalist and universalising claims, its unmarked nature and implicitly masculinist framework.[20] Postcolonial critiques continue to identify Eurocentric paradigms within the historiography of modernism, while seeking to replace notions of 'export' and 'derivativeness' with concepts such as those of mimicry or cultural translation.[21] More recently, approaches informed by the multiculturalism of our globalised present have left their mark on the study of artistic modernism in two ways: these can be described as artistic pluralism and presentism. Studying modernism as a global phenomenon has frequently been interpreted as the production of a plurality of modernisms that then have designations such as multiple modernisms, or local, regional, vernacular, or national – Japanese, Brazilian, Turkish, or Slovenian – modernisms, or alternative modernisms.[22] To this list of proliferating modernisms the latest addition is even an 'absent' modernism, a recent position taken by Hans Belting, whose conceptualisation of the 'global contemporary' points to those non-Western cultures that, in his view, 'were never modern' and were catapulted into the world of global contemporary art.[23] All of these include the somewhat demeaningly labelled 'non-West' as a series of interesting but ultimately distant modernisms – recognised, dignified, and reified as culturally different. Inclusion by dignifying as different and yet distant only re-inscribes the framework that understands modernism in terms of originary centres and assimilative peripheries, or which subjects its history to a form of linearity wherein the

20 See, for example, Hans Belting, *Art History after Modernism*, Chicago: University of Chicago Press, 2003; Griselda Pollock, *Avant-Garde Gambits, 1888–1893: Gender and the Colour of Art History*, London: Thames and Hudson, 1993; Griselda Pollock, *Differencing the Canon: Feminist Desires and the Writing of Art's Histories*, London: Routledge, 1999; Viktoria Schmidt-Linsenhoff (ed.), *Weiße Blicke: Geschlechtermythen des Kolonialismus*, Marburg: Jonas Verlag, 2004; Viktoria Schmidt-Linsenhoff, *Ästhetik der Differenz*, 2 vols., Marburg: Jonas Verlag, 2010. More recently, a survey account authored by several prominent art historians connected to the *October* journal is an ambitious attempt to integrate critiques of modernism, and gesture in a more inclusive direction. See Hal Foster, Rosalind Krauss, Yves-Alain Bois and Benjamin H. D. Buchloh, *Art Since 1900: Modernism, Antimodernism, Postmodernism*, London: Thames and Hudson, 2004. For critiques of this survey, Mitter, 'Decentering Modernism': 531–32; Piotrowski, 'Towards a Horizontal History', pp. 49–50.

21 See Viktoria Schmidt-Linsenhoff, 'Das koloniale Unbewusste in der Kunstgeschichte', in: Irene Below and Beatrice von Bismarck (eds), *Globalisierung – Hierarchisierung: Kulturelle Dominanzen in Kunst und Kunstgeschichte*, Marburg: Jonas Verlag, 2005, pp. 19–38; Homi K. Bhabha (ed.), *Nation and Narration*, London: Routledge, 1993; Homi K. Bhabha, *The Location of Culture*, London: Routledge, 1994; Mercer (ed.), *Cosmopolitan Modernisms*.

22 See for example, Mark Wollaeger (ed.), *Oxford Handbook of Global Modernisms*, Oxford: Oxford University Press, 2013, with chapters organised according to national or ethnic classifications.

23 Hans Belting, Andrea Buddensieg and Peter Weibel (eds), *The Global Contemporary and the Rise of New Art Worlds*, Cambridge MA: MIT Press, 2012, pp. 28–29.

non-West is perpetually in a temporal moment of 'catching up'.[24] A plurality of modernisms or modernities – multiple, local, regional, alternative, vernacular, or peripheral – that are like parallel lines that never meet, only reaffirms the normative status of modernist art along the West European-North Atlantic axis.

A second approach that has framed the discussion of art of the early twentieth century stems from a form of presentism that we encounter in accounts of contemporary art. The contemporary, understood frequently as post-1989, has been designated as a point of rupture: contemporaneity is celebrated for its creation of a 'global art world'[25] (discussed in Chapter Four, 'Beyond Backwater Arcadias') characterised by the dissolution of borders, a process that the world both participates in and has effected, and for making cultural difference and diversity a feature of everyday life. Positing a progression from the modern to the contemporary in terms of collapsing distance is more likely a product of contemporary art's obsession with novelty, corresponding to global capitalism's constant need for new commodities. Accounts of contemporary art tend to overlook the period classified as modern, dismissing much of its art as of questionable quality, as belated or derivative, and of a troublingly nationalist political orientation that appears at odds with the contemporary post-1989 global spirit. Such a perspective ends up suppressing memories of transcultural encounters during the past in order to keep novelty alive. Art history as a history of exchange and transcultural relationships – as I have been arguing throughout – did not begin with the globalisation of the present. Negotiating cultural difference was rarely an incidental or aberrant feature of artistic production in earlier historical periods; indeed, individual histories of modernism show it to be a structural, even desirable characteristic of movements both in Europe and beyond, including the highly ambivalent character of modernity under the aegis of colonialism.[26]

The task of tracking the routes of transcultural modernism can build on impulses from postcolonial literary studies that have paid special attention to the nexus between modernism and the colonial experience.[27] Simon Gikandi describes modernist literary production as an 'intense … site of encounter between the institutions of European cultural production and the cultural practices of colonized people', as a 'dynamic', mutually constitutive relationship.[28] The encounter between European artists and intellectuals and their counterparts from the colonies, though marked by asymmetries of power in which the colonial subject was located in a space of unfreedom, nonetheless enabled creativity on both sides: it was in such

24 See the response by Rebecca M. Brown, 'Provincializing Modernity: From Foundational to Derivative', *The Art Bulletin*, vol. 90 (4), 2008: 555–57.

25 Hans Belting and Andrea Buddensieg (eds), *The Global Art World: Audiences, Markets and Museums*, Ostfildern: Hatje Cantz, 2009.

26 See note 18.

27 On a transcultural approach to artistic modernism, see Monica Juneja, 'Alternative, Peripheral or Cosmopolitan? Modernism as a Global Process', in: Julia Allerstorfer and Monika Leisch-Kiesl (eds), *Global Art History: Transkulturelle Verortungen von Kunst und Kunstwissenschaft*, Bielefeld: Transcript Verlag, 2017, pp. 79–108.

28 Simon Gikandi, 'Preface: Modernism in the World', *Modernism/Modernity*, vol. 13 (3), 2006: 419–24, here 421.

an encounter that modernist art and literature acquired a critical edge. Viewed in this light, modernisation in the garb of colonial exploitation paradoxically brought forth a modernity and its cognate modernism as a co-production of the West and its global, colonised subjects. The revolt against the artistic and literary orthodoxies of bourgeois culture in Europe was made possible through an intensive engagement with the objects, practices, and philosophies of the colonised other, whereas the same encounter opened the space through which colonial hegemony could be undermined and the 'other' acknowledged as a self-reflecting subject. The expansive direction of art history during the recent years that has resulted in the widespread inclusion of regions and artists within the modernist repertoire has by its logic made it necessary to engage theoretically with the multifarious, lively artistic systems and networks that have come to light. Many of these worked with a keen awareness of a world emerging out of violent conflict following war, decolonisation, exile, the experiences of racism, and the struggle for autonomy. Frantz Fanon, an impassioned spokesperson of national liberation and emancipation from racist oppression, did not perceive nationalism as an end in itself or national identity as a fixed attribute – rather he saw these as a necessary step towards a more radical liberation of consciousness.[29]

The years following 1945 saw a far-reaching reorganisation of the map of global modernism. While an internationally prominent American art sustained by abstraction, popular culture, and mass media attained hegemony in the North Atlantic West, emergent nations in Asia, Africa, the Middle East as well as those of the newly formed Eastern bloc in East and Central Europe, all experimented with fresh paradigms of artistic modernity anchored within their specific histories to mirror the changed terms of geopolitical dialogue across the world. The Cold War had divided the world into two ideological spheres – the countries aligned under the Warsaw Pact to the Soviet Union and those of Western Europe allied with the United States through the North Atlantic Treaty Organization. Synchronically with this bipolar division, a number of newly independent nations of Asia and Africa, as well as former Yugoslavia, formed a third group, the Non-Aligned Movement that refused co-optation with one or the other of the power blocs, preferring to remain as its name, non-aligned. Such far-reaching changes in the world order generated innumerable debates that sought to link issues of aesthetics and form with cultural questions of autonomy, subjectivity, humanism, international solidarity, or regionalism. The idea that art and artists had a role to play in a period of instability, of recovery and self-definition through new subjects and experiments with form and materials was crucial to the shaping of artistic modernity.[30] Andreas Huyssen reminds us that whenever and wherever modernism arrived, it did so at the threshold of a not yet fully modernised world, where 'old and new were violently knocked against each

---

29   Frantz Fanon, *The Wretched of the Earth*, London: Penguin Books, 1967, pp. 166–67.

30   See Seng Tan and Amitava Acharya (eds), *Bandung Revisited: The Legacy of the 1955 Asian-African Conference for the International Order*, Singapore: NUS Press, 2008; Dipesh Chakrabarty, 'Legacies of Bandung: Decolonization and the Politics of Culture', in: Saurabh Dube (ed.), *Enchantments of Modernity: Empire, Nation, Globalization*, London, New Delhi: Routledge, 2009, pp. 264–87; Atreyee Gupta, 'After Bandung: Transacting the Nation in a Postcolonial World', in Enwezor et al. (eds), *Postwar*, pp. 632–37.

other'.[31] Such an experience of transition gave modernism its critical, creative potential, which unfolded according to regional and local contingencies. Representational strategies, vocabularies and practices were generated by the subjectivities of the actors involved; stylistic considerations in a narrow sense and taken in isolation – for instance the ideologically charged, almost clichéd conflict of the 1940s between abstraction and figuration – do not allow us to access the meanings of this productivity. Artists in different regions of the world invariably worked with, and within, the language of dominant international forms and practices, yet could and did resist their formal canonicity. Uncovering these tracks and crafting a fresh narrative would mean undoing traditional art history's concern with primordiality – with establishing who said or did what first. Interrupting a sequential model of artistic chronology suggests that modernism beyond the North Atlantic West is not simply other or qualitatively inferior, but a different way of seeing: one that draws us back to that which is familiar and taken to be universal, and that urges us to look at it again.

The groundwork for many of the mid-century initiatives towards consolidating international solidarity under the aegis of decolonial thought was to an extent already being laid during the interwar period of the 1920s; these years saw the emergence of new visions of a world order following disillusionment with the measures of the League of Nations that allegedly ended in reaffirming imperialist constellations.[32] Artistic and scholarly movements were one important component of the new structures of transcontinental anti-colonial networks of this period – a notable example was the literary and artistic renaissance, which brought forth Pan-Africanism.[33] The Harlem Renaissance, a particularly significant articulation of this cultural efflorescence, was enriched by numerous encounters and exchanges among activists, literary figures, and artists located in New York and Paris and who, in turn, were connected to counterparts in Africa and the Caribbean islands. Journals like *Les Continents* (Paris, founded in 1924) and *Opportunity: A Journal of Negro Life* (New York, founded in 1924) or the more recent journal *Revue du Monde Noir* (founded in 1931), were crucial to creating a nexus between black politics of liberation and a transcontinental modernist aesthetic.[34] In South Asia, a similar cosmopolitan design was reflected in the syllabus of the newly founded university Visva Bharati in Santiniketan, and an exhibition of expressionist art from the Bauhaus held in Calcutta in 1922 – both will be further discussed below.[35] An expressive example of these global dynamics was the exhibition *La Verité sur les Colonies* (The Truth about the Colonies), which opened in Paris in 1931 and was conceptualised as a counter-exhibition to the *Exposition Coloniale Internationale* (International Colonial

---

31 Huyssen, 'Geographies of Modernism': 190.

32 See essays in Sebastian Conrad and Dominic Sachsenmaier (eds), *Competing Visions of World Order: Global Moments and Movements, 1880s–1930s,* New York: Palgrave Macmillan, 2008.

33 Andreas Eckert, 'Bringing the "Black Atlantic" into Global History: The Project of Pan-Africanism', in: Conrad and Sachsenmaier (eds), *Competing Visions*, pp. 237–57.

34 Kravagna, *Transmoderne*, pp. 45–46.

35 On Santiniketan, R. Siva Kumar, *Santiniketan: The Making of a Contextual Modernism*, New Delhi: National Gallery of Modern Art, 1997; on the Calcutta exhibition, Mitter, *The Triumph*, pp. 14–15.

Exhibition) of the same year celebrating the apogee of the French Empire. *La Verité sur les Colonies* was an enterprise co-produced by Surrealists in and beyond France together with artists and other members of anti-colonial organisations such as the *Ligue de Défense de la Race Nègre* that advocated political independence for French colonies in Africa and the Caribbean, or the Vietnamese *Comité de Lutte*.[36] Both exhibitions, the colonial and its counter-model, drew attention to the problematics of culturally appropriating 'indigenous arts' (*les arts indigènes*) – sculptures from Africa and Oceania – for different purposes. While the colonial exhibition used these to establish the superiority and the 'nobility' of colonial methods of conserving the heritage of peoples, considered intellectually and scientifically ill-equipped to do so themselves, for the Surrealists who lent their collections of African, Native American, and Oceanic objects to the counter-exhibition, such works infused with simplicity showed the way to undermining bourgeois tastes and values in the arts.[37] In one sense the groups that came together to organise the *Verité des Colonies* often ended up working within the same paradigms that they sought to subvert, notably in their reading of cultural objects and practices as signs of 'cultures' per se. Even so, this enterprise proved to be an important catalyst within programmatic moves by the proponents of Pan-Africanism to reclaim labels such as '*nègre*', anticipating thereby the tenets of *Négritude* of a decade later. *La Vérité des Colonies* in this sense did pave the way for the strengthening of ties between artistic circles in Paris and poets and painters such as Aimé Césaire and Wifredo Lam.[38]

Waves of decolonisation that followed in the mid-twentieth century did not bring a form of closure, as the oft-repeated phrase 'end of empire' in imperialist historiography proposes; rather, formal emancipation from colonial rule meant a redrawing of relationships between imperial nations and their former colonies. One determining factor in such renegotiation was an accelerated migration of former colonial subjects – Asian, African, Caribbean, West Indian, South American – to European cities, where they sought exile or opportunities to live, work, study, practise as artists. Taking Britain as an example, Sarat Maharaj has evocatively described this experience of migration from the so-called peripheries as 'Congacropolis … a flood that laps at the Acropolis, soon to submerge its commanding heights'.[39] Arrivals to Britain – artists in particular – came expecting a land of opportunity where their careers as artists would thrive, but were soon confronted with marginalisation, structures of othering, and a general climate of decolonisation hostile to migration in the reverse direction.[40] 'Black

---

36 See Jody Blake, 'The Truth about the Colonies, 1931: Art Indigène in the Service of the Revolution', *Oxford Art Journal*, vol. 25 (1), 2002: 37–58; also Jack J. Spector, *Surrealist Art and Writing, 1919–1939. The Gold of Time*, Cambridge: Cambridge University Press, 1997.

37 Blake, 'The Truth about the Colonies': 48–49.

38 Kravagna, *Transmoderne*, p. 48.

39 Sarat Maharaj, 'The Congo is Flooding the Acropolis: Art in the Britain of Immigrations', *Third Text*, vol. 5 (15), 1991: 77–90, here 81–82.

40 See Rasheed Araeen, 'The Other Immigrant: The Experiences and Achievements of Afro Asian Artists in the Metropolis', *Third Text*, vol. 5 (15), 1991: 17–28; Leon Wainwright, *Timed Out: Art and the Transnational Caribbean*, Manchester: Manchester University Press, 2011; Kobena Mercer, 'Ethnicity and Internationality. New British Art and Diaspora-Based Blackness', in *Travel and See: Black Diaspora Art Practices Since the 1980s*, Durham, NC: Duke University Press, 2016, pp. 186–206.

Art', a blanket term used to collectively describe a mix of voices and art in Britain produced in the shadow of unwelcome migration, swelled into a stream of modernism that called into question long-standing myths of purist Englishness, while coining a 'suitcase language … through squashing together regular, received words, images, contexts … geared to signify the clashing, colliding worlds of experience thrown together … WestIndianBlackBritishAsian'.[41] Yet, the so-designated Black Art did not position itself outside of the modernist mainstream; it was constitutive of a transcultured, metropolitan modernism that reclaimed its critical potential to produce counter-images, to resist being pushed to the margins. In one respect, it shared with high modernism the drive to overthrow the canonicity of the classical Greek ideal embodied by the 'Acropolis'.[42] Like modernist experiments that unfolded across the globe in the 1950s, to which migrant artists in Britain formed and retained their connections, Black Art showed a preoccupation with rethinking the human through an anti-colonial, anti-racist lens, conjoined with a focus on agency, which often prevailed over the abjection or trauma infusing art-making in a Europe ravaged by war and fascism. Blackness – as I will discuss below – resonated both as a literal and metaphoric category in the work of modernist artists across the world, as resistance to whiteness, but also as refusal to comply with expectations that artists choose between social and artistic identity, the traditional and the modern, between abstraction and realism.[43]

Within such shared horizons, individual studies of modernism have tended to privilege a locational approach that takes a particular site as its starting point, from which to delve into deep histories as well as explore connections and resonances with regions across space. Such microhistories can be a useful way of creating a mental map of modernism as a global and relational process, of tracing the course of art that travelled the way people and things did, to describe a process that is not linear or seamless, but one that is uneven and even erratic.[44] Chronology can no longer provide the single key to signposting the modern on the map of art history. During the recent years, makers of exhibitions have responded to this impulse and used microhistories as a curatorial device to make tangible a global matrix of shared concerns and local artistic initiatives.[45] The exhibition *Museum Global*, which ran in Düsseldorf during the winter of 2018–19, allowed visitors to follow the logic of the individual

41   Maharaj, 'The Congo is Flooding': 81.
42   Ibid.
43   Citing Fanon, Okwui Enwezor signals to Blackness as a sign within *Négritude* as well as in the Civil Rights movements in the United States, see Enwezor et al. (eds), *Postwar*, p. 32.
44   The notion of microhistory was introduced in the 1970s by social historians in Italy and France. See Revel, *Jeux d'Échelles*; Ginzburg, 'Clues: Roots of an Evidential Paradigm'; Levi, 'On Microhistory'.
45   The exhibition *Museum Global: Mikrogeschichten einer ex-zentrischen Moderne* at the Kunstsammlung Nordrhein-Westfalen, Düsseldorf (10 November 2018–3 October 2019) was the product of a collaborative project between the museum's team and the Chair of Global Art History at the HCTS, Heidelberg. The sites of modernist art it explored to relate micro-stories included: Tokyo, Moscow, São Paulo, Mexico City, Shimla, Beirut and Zaria. See Kunstsammlung Nordrhein-Westfalen (ed.), *Museum Global: Mikrogeschichten einer ex-zentrischen Moderne*, Weyertal: Wienand Verlag, 2018. The following discussion of the exhibition draws on my essay, 'Mikrogeschichten: Die Routen des transkulturellen Modernismus', in: *Museum Global*, pp. 27–46.

stories it featured, and in doing so to uncover the tracks of barely acknowledged networks, of sites of interaction, of journals and universities, all of which force open the binaries positing the West against the rest. Surrealism in North Africa, the New Negro Movement, the CoBrA group, Mexican muralism, or the Harlem Renaissance, are only a few among an increasingly visible number of examples that show modernist art as having been from its inception a multi-centred, always and already transcultured phenomenon, whose actors dynamically engaged with its sites in Europe without, however, presuming the universality of the models they encountered.[46] It becomes possible to identify resonating concerns, even as not all artists everywhere may have had personal encounters or participated in overarching networks. Yet their responses to shared or similar problems and constellations allow us to speak of resonance or indirect reception rather than direct encounters. Resonant microhistories are more than a fractured plurality of stories; they are particular though already global, reveal synchronicity and coevalness, where belatedness or derivative practices were assumed. At the same time, they allow us to take a closer look at regional singularities, to underline that transcultural interaction did not follow a straight, single, or foreseeable path. Instead, we become aware of a modernism shaped by the distinct problematics of modernity in local, regional, or national contexts across the globe, whose actors at the same time understood its cultural articulations as embedded in a quintessentially international movement.

Each of the case studies featured in the exhibition *Museum Global* took as its starting point a site beyond Europe, to then unravel specific issues and conditions of the particular locality, where modernist ideas became a productive domain of confrontation and negotiation. The concerns of individual actors were less related to appropriating the normative authority of 'Western' models; rather they were focused on dealing with the situational problematics of their own contexts. This can be observed, for example, in the study of Japanese modernist experiments of the early twentieth century that featured in the show: Yorozu Tetsugorō's (1885–1927) modernist work *Nude Beauty* of 1912, which belonged to the same time frame as Cubism or the works of Matisse and the *Blaue Reiter*, engaged in an experimental practice of citation and translation of these sources, in search for an answer to the fraught question of Japan's place in the modern art world. The work's connections to Post-Impressionist art became palpable within the exhibition display through its juxtaposition to Ernst Ludwig Kirchner's *Girl with a Japanese Parasol* (1909), a painting that belongs to the museum's permanent collection.[47] The artist and his work were drawn into debates on difficult issues of censorship, the role of art institutions, the reappraisal of tradition, and the transgressive

---

46 On Surrealism, Bardaouil, 'Surrealism in Egypt', in: Sam Bardaouil and Till Fellrath (eds), *Art et Liberté: Umbruch, Krieg und Surrealismus in Ägypten (1938–1948)*, Paris: Editions Skira, 2016; on the New Negro Movement and the Harlem Renaissance, Kravagna, *Transmoderne*; Cornelia Kogoj and Christian Kravagna, *Das amerikanische Museum: Sklaverei, schwarze Geschichte und der Kampf um Gerechtigkeit in Museen der Südstaaten*, Vienna/Berlin: Mandelbaum Verlag, 2019; on CoBrA, Marion von Osten and Sarat Maharaj, 'Der Überschuss des Globalen', *Texte zur Kunst*, vol. 23 (91), 2013: 133–51, here 135–41.

47 See Maria Müller-Schareck, '"Ich beabsichtige, meinen eigenen Weg auszubauen": Moderne am Beispiel des Malers Yorozu Tetsugorō', in *Museum Global*, pp. 72–90.

function of art that characterised Japan's transition to modernity during the first half of the twentieth century.[48] In the case of Japan, as in many other microhistories narrated here, the nation as site and framing unit did not exclude an engagement with the world. Likewise, for the Progressive Artists Group of Bombay, about which more follows later in this chapter, modernist art was anchored in the locality, committed to the community of the nation, and at the same time looked beyond the frontiers of the nation towards Mexican muralism, Expressionism, or *Négritude*. The Artist's Centre, the name given to the room in which the group met, functioned as more than a gallery space. Starting as a refuge for artists and critics from Austria and Germany escaping the Holocaust, it soon became a node in a network of sites that included cities in India and art centres around the world.[49] The sense of purpose attached by its members to the modernist movement was to create a community that cut across scales – the local, the regional, the national, and the international. Both in the case of Japan as well as India, the nation was equated less with a territorial or political formation, that is the nation-state; rather, it could be imagined as a utopian idea from which a dialogical modernism could take shape. In Japan, modernist experiments navigated different and shifting visions of how to define Japan's position in the world. While Yorozu's project of creating a 'universal and cosmopolitan' art was to be reconciled with the objective that envisaged Japan as a contributor to global civilisation, later developments in the 1930s brought forth a vision wherein Japan would 'lead the world' and its modernist art would surpass anything produced in the West.[50] Finally, in both India and Japan, modernist art was confronted not only with the challenge of accommodating cultural difference within a local framework, but also with the problem of dealing with difference within the sameness assumed to mark its home space. In India, modernist art praxis underwent shifts as visionary dreams for the future of a new-born nation gave way to a searing critique of invented traditions, following regular eruptions of ethnic and religious violence. Early modernist celebration of the nation-space had bypassed the deep paradox attached to the traumatic birth of the nation that was also a partitioning of that space into the nation-states of India and Pakistan, followed by Bangladesh in 1971. Emergence of the new premised on a truncation of the old was as much a globally resonant product of the upheavals following war and decolonisation – as studies of Israel and Palestine, North and South Korea, East and West Germany, Sudan and South Sudan, Ireland and Northern Ireland, China and Taiwan show. Experiences of forced migration, loss, recovery, and resettlement in each of these contexts have brought forth a surge of creativity and fresh reflections on the conditions and possibilities of art as 'undisciplined' praxis, as artists drew on personal histories and memories that at the same time touched

48   Alicia Volk, *In Pursuit of Universalism: Yorozu Testsugorō and Japanese Modern Art,* Berkeley: University of California Press, 2010.
49   Karin Zitzewitz, *The Art of Secularism: The Cultural Politics of Modernist Art in Contemporary India,* London: Hurst Publishers, 2014, pp. 78–86.
50   Volk, *In Pursuit of Universalism*, p. 208.

upon universal human concerns of home and belonging, tradition and transgression.[51] Placing examples such as the above next to each other shows how the underpinnings of the modern resonated across space and yet were far from being stable or seamless.

As long as art history continues to uphold a canonical language of taste and criticism, large chunks of modernist history and practice will remain illegible. For the fascinating microhistories of modernism to be inscribed within the larger narrative of modern art, the discipline needs to disconnect style from fixed location. The exhibition spaces – at Munich and Düsseldorf – described above showed up as a good place to bring this fresh impetus to the ambitious enterprise of refiguring canonical narratives.

Shifting Scale – Art, Nation, Region

Studying global modernism as a connected ensemble of resonant microhistories means looking at intersections, entanglements, and divergences. It also means, as outlined at the beginning of this chapter, negotiating scales beyond the poles of the local and the global to navigate multiple scales, indeed, to grapple with scale from the perspective of actors for whom it becomes a mode of self-positioning. Such an approach requires a certain critical distance from given, often overused scalar distinctions such as macro and micro and focus instead on the dynamics of making and negotiating scales within specific social constellations. Scale as a tool of transcultural investigation helps track and describe rather than catalogue or classify. A more open approach serves, in turn, to relativise polarised positions that studies from non-European perspectives have on their part occasionally set up as a foil against which to plot the more 'contextual' or regionally particular modernist quest of movements beyond the 'global West'.[52] Rather, the negotiations surrounding the mapping of the historical on to the formal or subjective emerge as a hallmark of modernist art everywhere, whose individual, frequently uneven dynamics need to be unravelled.

When engaging with the challenges modernist art from beyond the North Atlantic West poses to conventional narratives, recent studies have questioned in particular modernism's historicist temporality in conjunction with a diffusionist paradigm. At the heart of many

51 The term has been used by Irit Rogoff, see 'Interview with Irit Rogoff by Hammad Nasar', in: Iftikhar Dadi and Hammad Nasar (eds), *Lines of Control: Partition as Productive Space*, London: Green Cardamom, 2012, 101–10, here p. 108. The exhibition of the same name featured, in addition to the Indian subcontinent, studies of Sudan, Korea, Palestine and the frontier between the United States and Mexico. See also, Monica Juneja, 'Migration, Dispossession, Post-Memorial Recuperations: An "Undisciplined" View of the Partition of the Indian Subcontinent', in: Burcu Dogramaci and Birgit Mersmann (eds), *Handbook of Art and Global Migration: Theories, Practices, and Challenges*, Berlin: De Gruyter, 2019, pp. 298–314.

52 One such example is the opposition set up between Greenbergian 'pure form' as a 'hallmark of post-1945 Western art' and that of India described as 'a double text of the personal and public, the formal and the contextual', see Sanjukta Sunderason, 'Making Art Modern, Re-visiting Artistic Modernism in India', in: Dube (ed.), *Handbook of Modernity*, pp. 245–61, here p. 246. Such an opposition is now increasingly being called into question as an ideological postulate rather than a reflection of the everyday practices of artists.

discussions, however – and this is especially characteristic of those 'third-world modernisms' that emerged in entanglement with movements of emancipation from colonial rule – is the seemingly paradoxical relationship between the transcultural affinities and connections of modernist art and an artistic subjectivity whose quest for self-expression was mediated through the nation. Several studies have forcefully argued that decolonisation and post-colonial nationhood were constitutive for the emergence of modernist art outside of Euro-America.[53]

Writings on South Asian art of the twentieth century uphold – in nuanced variations – this influential paradigm, to propose a modernist sensibility formed by the cultural politics of decolonial nationhood.[54] In a 'deeply politicized'[55] artistic modernism inflected with cultural projections of the nation, the latter was a space subjectively constituted, in a scalar sense, as 'locality' to be wrenched back from the global constellation of empire. Endeavours to define the relationship of modernism to the nation veer towards viewing the former as a series of practices, while the latter remains something of a causal force. It is within this context that the modernist category of 'art' becomes legible, as a category oscillating between autonomy, that is 'for its own sake', and a powerful medium in the articulation of national sovereignty.

The encounter with modern paradigms of 'art' and the 'artist' in the context of a colonised society was accompanied by changes in patterns of patronage, practice, and pedagogy. Together with a heightened self-consciousness that hinged on individuality, identity, and affiliation across scales, the transition from the nineteenth to the twentieth century in South Asia also produced a special discursive and institutional space for art in middle-class society. In their new privileged status and modernised conceptions, the twin notions of art and the artist lent themselves to ideological assimilation within an agenda of anti-colonial nationalism. At

---

53   The conjunction of the national and the modern in the context of India has been eloquently put forward by Geeta Kapur, *When Was Modernism? Essays on Contemporary Cultural Practice in India*, New Delhi: Tulika Books, 2000; see also more recently, Saloni Mathur, 'Ends and Means: A Conversation with Geeta Kapur', *October*, 171, 2020: 115–38. Taking his cue from Kapur and Elizabeth Harney before him, Chika Okeke-Agulu asserts that 'modernism and political ideology in the context of decolonizing nations were not mutually exclusive discourses', Okeke-Agulu: *Postcolonial Modernism*, p. 2; Harney, *In Senghor's Shadow*.

54   The persuasive stance taken by Kapur was reinforced by important studies that investigated modernist institutional formations and practices within the framework of nation-building: Tapati Guha-Thakurta, *The Making of a New 'Indian' Art: Artists, Aesthetics and Nationalism in Bengal, c. 1850–1920*, Cambridge: Cambridge University Press, 1992 (repr. 2008); Partha Mitter, *Art and Nationalism in Colonial India 1850–1922: Occidental Orientations*, Cambridge: Cambridge University Press, 1994; Tapati Guha-Thakurta, *Monuments, Objects, Histories: Institutions of Art in Colonial and Postcolonial India*, New Delhi: Permanent Black, 2004. Recent, more differentiated positions have been put forward by Rebecca M. Brown and Sonal Khullar. While Brown's survey cuts across different media to insist on a global history of modernism that acknowledges the constitutive role of colonialism, Khullar makes an eloquent argument for the 'worldly' connections of Indian artistic modernism. At the same time, she takes the binary between 'East and West' seriously, asserting 'East and West were marshalled as formal and social attributes in art history's most crucial debates on naturalism and abstraction, line and color, art and crafts, masculinity and femininity, nature and culture'. See Brown, *Art for a Modern India*; Khullar, *Worldly Affiliations*, p. 12.

55   Kapur, *When Was Modernism*, p. 301.

the same time, their existence was contingent on an emerging 'field of cultural production',[56] a world inhabited by critics, buyers, collectors, exhibitors, journalists, art schools, and the expanding possibilities of mechanical reproduction. Together these facets formed a matrix of intersecting forces in which a clear nexus between an overarching national consciousness and modernist art production was not always easy to identify, as it was regularly interrupted by pulls from regional sites – Calcutta (today Kolkata), Madras (today Chennai), Mysore, Santiniketan, Bombay, Baroda (today Vadodara) – each invested in nurturing its own literary and intellectual culture as a response to a homogenising imagination of a 'national modern'. In addition, some of these sites – as some examples discussed below will show – nurtured connections beyond the national frame, transcending the colony-coloniser divide, even as the self-determining nation stood for a utopian ideal. The transition to artistic modernity in South Asia may best be described as a complex interplay wherein migrant understandings of the artist as an autonomous, creative individual came to be transcultured during their endeavours to drive roots in a terrain where court, bazaar, and bourgeois public jostled with each other. Within art production both the court and the bazaar remained locations where artistic modernity unfolded, while they experienced and adjusted to transformed institutional patterns, to the emergence of new styles and material techniques together with the growing emancipation of the artist from the twin cages of caste and artisanship.[57]

The process of redefining the artist as working outside of established systems of patronage unfolded in the wake of new pedagogies and institutional structures. The introduction of art education saw the establishment of four British art schools from the 1850s to the 1870s – Madras, followed by Calcutta, Bombay, and Lahore. Teaching at these schools focused on the applied and industrial arts with the aim of equipping artists with vocational and technical

---

56   Pierre Bourdieu, *The Field of Cultural Production: Essays on Art and Literature*, Cambridge: Polity Press, 1993.

57   Investigations of these phenomena as they unfolded on different regional sites include: on Bengal, Guha-Thakurta, *The Making of a New 'Indian' Art*, and Mitter, *Art and Nationalism*; on Madras, Shivaji K. Panikkar, 'Reading the Regional through Internationalism and Nativism: The Case of Art in Madras, 1950 to 1970', and Ashrafi S. Bhagat, 'The "Madras Art Movement" and the Lineages of Abstraction', both in Shivaji K. Panikkar, Deeptha Achar and Parul D. Mukherji (eds), *Towards a New Art History: Studies in Indian Art*, New Delhi: D. K. Printworld, 2003, pp. 105–21 and 229–241 respectively; also Ashrafi S. Bhagat, 'Modernity in the South: An Overview', in Gayatri Sinha (ed.), *Art and Visual Culture in India 1857–2007*, Mumbai: Marg Publications, 2009, pp. 206–17; on Mysore, Janaki Nair, *Mysore Modern: Rethinking the Region under Princely Rule*, Minneapolis: Minnesota University Press, 2011; Deeptha Achar and Pushpamala N. (eds), *Mysore Modernity, Aesthetic Nationalism: The Art of K. Venkatappa*, New Delhi: Routledge (forthcoming 2023); on Baroda, Gulammohammed Sheikh (ed.), *Contemporary Art in Baroda*, New Delhi: Tulika Books, 1997; Priya Maholay-Jaradi (ed.), *Baroda: A Cosmopolitan Provenance in Transition*, Mumbai: Marg Publications, 2015; on Bombay, Yashodhara Dalmia, *The Making of Modern Indian Art: The Progressives*, New Delhi: Oxford University Press, 2006; Zitzewitz, *The Art of Secularism*: Chapter 3; Partha Mitter, 'Indian Artists in the Colonial Period: The Case of Bombay', in: Sinha (ed.), *Art and Visual Culture*, pp. 24–39; on artists' collectives, Shukla Sawant, 'Artist Collectives in the Age of Anxiety, 1940–1950', in Sinha (ed.), *Art and Visual Culture*, pp. 136–49; on popular art, Kajri Jain, *Gods in the Bazaar: The Economies of Indian Calendar Art*, Durham, NC: Duke University Press, 2007; on the period of transition between the Mughal and British empires, Natasha Eaton, *Mimesis across Empires: Artworks and Networks in India, 1765–1860*, Durham, NC: Duke University Press, 2013.

training, together with the rudiments of academic art conventions. Art pedagogy aimed, at one level, to produce skilled artisans, who as draughts people, surveyors, engravers, decorators, and lithographers would serve important, expanding public functions. In addition, art education was meant to 'improve the taste of the native people as regards beauty of form and finish in articles of daily use among them'.[58] A uniform syllabus based on that of the School of Industrial Arts in South Kensington was initially devised for all the art schools. It soon became clear, however, that the schools were attended, not by artisans – who could neither afford to, nor did they take to academic art – but instead by young male students from middle-class, literate social groups. This led in the course of time to the transformation of the schools into institutions of fine arts, and ultimately, as in the case of Bombay, into academies.[59] The third quarter of the nineteenth century saw the introduction of Victorian academic art, naturalism, oil and easel painting as part of an ideology that elevated art as a carrier of moral lessons. History painting, valorised by the British Royal Academy as a genre that raised art above manual dexterity, was introduced in India as a medium to bring about the moral improvement of colonial subjects.[60] In a lecture titled 'The Fine Arts in India' delivered in 1871 to the Native Literary Christian Society of Madras, the governor of the presidency, Lord Napier, highlighted the power of naturalist idioms to effectively render episodes and characters from Indian mythology.[61] For educated Indian artists and their public, history painting proved to be an equally welcome choice: an art steeped in historicism offered an ideal medium for a recreation of the nation's ancient past.

Processes shaping the formation of the professional artist, not always smooth, need to be unravelled within the interstices of structures of patronage and the emergence of art criticism, but also in conjunction with a broadening market that encompassed collectors as well as a growing middle-class public whose avid interest in art found satisfaction through mechanically reproduced images. Such processes can usefully be charted through the course of individual careers. The artist Ravi Varma (1848–1906) emerges here as an identifiable protagonist in the Indian artist's passage to the modern. Described as 'a gentleman artist in the Victorian mould',[62] the course of Ravi Varma's career helps capture a particular moment of transition within the relationship between painting, a public for art, and the changing role of the artist in South Asia. The preceding century, since the 1760s, was marked by the presence in India of itinerant Western academic artists – such as Tilly Kettle (1735–1786) or Thomas Hickey (1741–1824) – whose work came to stand for what in the nineteenth century was considered an advanced 'rational' form of art, and which gradually brought with it a change

---

58 *Imperial Gazetteer of India: The Indian Empire* (1909), cited in Sinha (ed.), *Art and Visual Culture*, p. 10.

59 Mitter, 'Indian Artists in the Colonial Period', p. 26.

60 The nexus between history painting and civic virtue was extensively fleshed out in art theory in England from mid-eighteenth century onwards, as surveyed in John Barrell, *The Political Theory of Painting from Reynolds to Hazlitt*, New Haven: Yale University Press, 1986.

61 Cited in Ratan Parimoo, *The Paintings of the Three Tagores: Abanindranath, Gaganendranath, Rabindranath: Chronology and Comparative Study*, Baroda: Maharaja Sayajirao University, 1973, p. 30.

62 Kapur, *When Was Modernism*, p. 145.

of taste among patrons and a growing middle-class intelligentsia.[63] Yet, these artists inhabited a parallel world, as none of them participated in the official art education introduced during the mid-nineteenth century. Ravi Varma, born into a princely family of Travancore and educated in Indian classics as well as traditional Tanjore painting, picked up the tenets of the neoclassical academic style from Western itinerant artists. The story of his life, told and retold, has a hagiographic ring: his apprenticeship of oil and easel painting was acquired, so the legend goes, by being allowed to watch the Dutch painter, Theodore Jensen, a visitor to the court of Travancore, at work.[64] Elevated to the status of a self-taught prodigy, Varma has been eulogised as having succeeded in mastering the coloniser's language, which he then proceeded to rework into an idiom with which to recreate 'authentic' narratives of Indian tradition – illustrations of history and the epics, or portraits of regional feminine types, all brought alive through the magic of naturalism. Circulating works of Western artists in colonial India had contributed to a growing familiarity with European art among the Indian elite, who had begun collecting such works, mainly oils, watercolours, or engravings. The latter were a main source through which European art of the Renaissance and neoclassical works of the nineteenth century could be accessed, though several copies in oil of masterpieces, such as paintings by Rembrandt, also found their way into private collections. According to Mitter, Ravi Varma saw examples of paintings from the Royal Academy in British magazines of art.[65] It is through similar channels that he acquired familiarity with French Salon artists, such as Adolphe-Guillaume Bouguereau (1825–1905), Louis and Gustave Boulanger (1808–1867 and 1824–1888) whose work had captured his interest.[66] Equally important was the inspiration Varma derived from Orientalist art and scholarship. For instance, his knowledge of ancient Hindu art was drawn almost entirely from *The Hindu Pantheon* by Edward Moor, a pioneer work in the British 'discovery of Hinduism'.[67] With the help of a traditional narrator – a practice that goes back to indigenous regional schools of painting of the seventeenth and eighteenth centuries – the artist was able to select appropriate themes from literary classics and mythological texts that he transformed with the help of naturalistic idioms and the tactile materiality of oil into sumptuous, sentimental figures, a 'blend of Kerala and Guercino'.[68] Ravi Varma's paintings offer a transcultured ensemble of rhetorical postures and expressions – *mudras* and *abhinaya* – derived from the conventions of classical dance dramas of Kerala, combined with the plasticity and powers of simulating textures and surfaces – flesh, textiles, jewels, marble – or atmospheric effects such as radiant light and translucent shadows, all made possible by the rich density of oil paint. While the subjects he painted were quintes-

---

63 Mildred Archer, *India and British Portraiture, 1770–1825*, London: Sotheby Parke Bennett, 1979; Eaton, *Mimesis across Empires*, Chapter 1.

64 Kapur, *When Was Modernism*, p. 148; Mitter, *Art and Nationalism*, pp. 184–85; Rupika Chawla, *Raja Ravi Varma: Painter of Colonial India*, Ahmedabad: Mapin Publishers, 2010, pp. 35–36.

65 Mitter, *Art and Nationalism*, pp. 186–87.

66 Kapur, *When Was Modernism*, p. 148.

67 Partha Mitter, 'The Artist as Charismatic Individual: Raja Ravi Varma', in: Rebecca M. Brown and Deborah S. Hutton (eds), *Asian Art*, Oxford: Blackwell, 2006, pp. 167–76, here p. 170.

68 Ibid., p. 171.

sentially Indian, drawn from across the length and breadth of the subcontinent, their titles, such as *Sisterly Remembrance, Expectation, Begum at Bath, Woman with a Fruit, A Family of Gypsies*, and *Here Comes Papa*, retained the sentimental flavour of academic Salon paintings.

In addition to being a history painter, Varma owed his success as a professional artist to his reputation as a fashionable painter of portraits for members of the upper-caste elites of Indian society. He employed agents who helped him secure commissions from all over India. His glittering career demonstrated not only the striking success of Victorian academic art in India, transcultured to produce a 'national' style, but equally the professionalisation of an artist whose business acumen and family connections helped him create a pan-Indian network of viewers and customers. Viewed with equal enthusiasm by the colonial elite, his eminent status brought him an invitation to represent India at the World Columbian Exhibition in Chicago in 1893. A striking aspect of Varma's modernity as a professional lay in the calculated marketing strategy through which he set out not only to satisfy the artistic tastes of an influential and privileged clientele, but equally to respond to the consumerist desires of a middle-class public for whom buying original works of art remained an unaffordable dream. The striking illusionist language of his painted human dramas lent itself to the production of high-quality reproductions made possible by the emergence of printing technology. Together with his brother Raja Varma, and with the help of a German technical assistant, he set up in 1894 the Ravi Varma Fine Art Lithographic Press in Lonavla, near Bombay, that produced oleographic prints of the artist's epic paintings, or his portraits of nationalist leaders and figures from Hindu mythology.[69] Though after his death, this genre of work was dismissed as imitative and lampooned as kitsch, its highly coded, densely saturated object world merged into other emerging genres such as film and calendar art, to become a factor in cementing an 'imagined community' across the subcontinent, well into following decades and into the era of television. Questioning the universal applicability of Walter Benjamin's subsequent prediction that mechanical reproduction entailed a loss of aura, Christopher Pinney argues for an altered form of the 'auratic' made possible by the new technologies of chromolithography and photography. Pinney signals to the dependence of many of Ravi Varma's paintings on photographic referents – paintings were first reproduced as photographs before they served as prototypes for the mass production of oleographs at the Lonavla press.[70] With its continuous accumulation of both cultic and affective value, the mechanically reproduced image came to be valorised as an efficacious mode of circulating trust and faith. 'Gods in the Bazaar', to cite Kajri Jain, were perceived less as problematic embodiments of commodification, rather they acted as signs of the desirability of production and circulation. The fluidity between the realms of art, mass culture, and religion, as embodied in these image-objects, Jain has

---

69   Mitter, 'Indian Artists in the Colonial Period', 31.

70   Christopher Pinney, 'Mechanical Reproduction in India', in: Sinha (ed.), *Art and Visual Culture*, pp. 72–83, here pp. 75–76. See also Erwin Neumayer and Christine Schelberger (eds), *The Diary of C. Raja Ravi Varma: Portrait of an Artist*, New Delhi: Oxford University Press, 2005.

persuasively argued, reformulated pre-colonial entanglements of commerce, religion, and sociality within the aesthetic of an emergent national consciousness (Plate 3.1).[71]

The narrative of success associated with a figure like Ravi Varma, whose career brought significant connotations to the identity of the artist in the transition to modernity, however, needs to be read with, and against the trajectory of further instances, if we are to get a sense of existing faultlines within the emergent modernist formation. These reveal how processes of transition and transculturation, far from following a seamless path, often faltered within an agonistic mix of opposing structures inhabiting a common universe. Let us look at another example, the figure of K. Venkatappa (1886–1965), an artist who traversed the worlds of artisanal tradition and modern art practice, moving between nationalist Calcutta, princely Mysore and middle-class Bangalore.[72] Almost four decades apart in age, the paths of the two artists crossed briefly at the Mysore court, where Ravi Varma, on the invitation of the ruler, spent several short periods during the years between 1902 and 1905. Venkatappa, born to a *chitragara* family – a low placed caste of traditional workers skilled primarily in gold leaf painting – served at the court together with several other artists, all from lower-caste artisanal backgrounds; patronizing such castes was considered an ideal way of preserving traditional artistic skills. Ravi Varma, on the other hand, was commissioned to paint a series of nine paintings for the Durbar Hall of the newly constructed palace, for which he was opulently remunerated.[73] Varma worked in the elite medium of oil with a growing interest in the possibilities opened up by photography, both media standing for the modernizing ambitions of a particular region. His aristocratic origins coupled with his reputation as an artist no doubt play a role in the status he came to enjoy – yet this example draws attention to seemingly opposed currents that constituted the dynamics of producing the modern. The age-old institution of caste could lend itself to re-reading as a modern category; members of hereditary artisan castes, once trained at the art schools in European academic norms, would become important actors in the making of a 'regional modernism'. As one of the beneficiaries of this opportunity, Venkatappa joined the school of industrial arts in Madras, following which he was sponsored by the Mysore court in 1909 to study at the Government School of Arts in Calcutta, where he spent seven years. Calcutta brought the artisan-painter exposure to the emerging nationalist aesthetic of the so-designated Bengal School[74] and to a cultural milieu that was coterminous with that of the Bengali *bhadralok* (lit. respectable people) – an

71 Jain, *Gods in the Bazaar.*

72 Nair, *Mysore Modern,* Chapter 5. The artist's life and work is also the subject of a forthcoming collection of essays, Deeptha Achar and Pushpamala N. (eds), *Mysore Modernity.*

73 In 1905–06, Ravi Varma was paid 25,000 rupees for this commission. By comparison palace artists earned in the vicinity of 10 rupees a month. Their duties ranged from varnishing paintings to painting the Mysore coat of arms on carriages or painting portraits of members of the royalty from photographs for distribution to institutions across the state. See Janaki Nair, 'Drawing a Line: K. Venkatappa and his Publics', *Indian Economic and Social History Review,* vol. 35 (2), 1998: 179–210, here 182; Nair, *Mysore Modern,* pp. 172–73.

74 The Bengal School refers to an art movement with its centre in Kolkata, associated with emergent Indian nationalism (*swadeshi* movement) and let by Abanindranath Tagore. It will be further discussed in the following section of this chapter.

emergent Bengali middle-class – where Venkatappa, by virtue of his class and caste as well as his provincial origins was not fully equipped to integrate. Calcutta also introduced him to a modern art establishment of critics, journalists, exhibitors, and middle-class patrons, all closely involved in the activities of the Bengal School artists, notably Abanindranath Tagore (1871–1951) and his pupils. Venkatappa's training there taught him to reject large-scale oils in the academic style of Varma, to work instead with watercolours in a flat idiom and drawing on the miniature tradition.[75] Back in Mysore after the end of his scholarship, Venkatappa accepted a commission to decorate the palace walls; he also took to painting landscapes or miniature portraits on ivory for private customers. The remaining years of his life were consumed by the travails of juggling a long and bumpy relationship with a royal patron on the one hand, and bourgeois buyers on the other. His career can be described as a protracted struggle to extricate his artistic persona from its location within an artisan caste and cultivate instead the habitus of an individual, autonomous, even idiosyncratic modern artist.

The Government School of Arts in Calcutta had brought an awareness to the artisan-painter, Venkatappa, of the extraordinary cultural capital vested in 'art' as profession, and which was unavailable to those trapped in the hereditary frame of caste. He sought to use this acquired capital by distancing himself from common employees of the palace, by mystifying the labour of artistic creation and, not least, fashioning himself as an artist by cultivating the persona of an eccentric genius, alienated and melancholic, the latter a characteristic he drew from his study of European painting traditions.[76] Grafted on to these traits, and meant to be read as unmistakable signs of male artistic genius, was the indigenous notion of carefully cultivated abstinence, both material and sexual (*brahmacharya*), resonant of anti-colonial nationalism associated with iconic figures such as Gandhi and Vivekananda.[77] At the same time, Venkatappa's life as an artist was enacted within rather than outside of the coordinates of an emerging art world of critics, journalists, and buyers, all crucial to the legitimation of a work as art. Remarkably, the courts of justice – owing to the artist's predilection for litigation – served as a democratic stage where he struggled to defend, even build up his reputation as an artist. Venkatappa's dealings with prospective buyers, recorded in his diary, testify to his reluctance to sell his work for what he considered 'very poor prices'[78], with the

---

75   While at Calcutta he had the opportunity to illustrate, along with the artist Nandalal Bose, Abanindranath Tagore's treatise on Indian aesthetics, *Shadanga or The Six Limbs of Painting: Some Notes in Indian Artistic Anatomy*, 1914. See Parul D. Mukherji, 'Anatomy Lessons from *Shadanga*: Abanindranath Tagore and T. Venkatappa's Shaping of a New National Self', in: Achar and Pushpamala N. (eds), *Mysore Modernity* (forthcoming).

76   Achar and Pushpamala N., 'Introduction', in *Mysore Modernity* (forthcoming).

77   A watercolour by the artist titled *Veeneya Huchchu* (*Mad after Veena*) and acquired by the Mysore Gallery in 1924, can be read as a self-portrait of sorts. It presents the artist as a gaunt figure in an ascetic's garb, placed between the muses of art and music. The composition is dominated by a disproportionately large *veena* (a stringed musical instrument) that extends diagonally across the picture space; the artist kneels in devotion in front of the *veena*, turning his back to the frail, drooping forms of muses of art and the bust of his mentor, Abanindranath Tagore, placed on top of a tall pedestal. The painting is reproduced in Nair, *Mysore Modern*, p. 178, fig. 43.

78   Entry in the artist's diary, 14 July 1926, cited in Nair, *Mysore Modern*, p. 181, n. 95.

intent to underline the importance of fair value for artistic work as a hallmark of autonomy. Similarly, and here his stance contrasts with artists such as Ravi Varma or the Bengal School, his refusal to permit printed reproductions of his works in popular magazines and the daily press was grounded in an acutely felt dissatisfaction with the quality of reproduction that in his eyes did little justice to his artistic achievement.[79] While relatively isolated among his contemporaries in the field of art, Venkatappa was much courted by leading intellectuals of his time including poets, literary scholars, scientists, all of who saw him as an exponent of a specifically regional idiom of nationalist art, a spokesman of a 'Kannada nation'.[80] This important aspect in the consecration of an artist speaks for the complex field of forces – regional, national, vernacular, institutional, and disconnected from factors of individual style – within which the categories modern art and the artist came to be negotiated.

Encounters – Persons, Institutions, Narratives

In an admirable endeavour to provide a synoptic overview of modernism in Asia during the twentieth century that at the same time takes into account cultural processes specific to individual locations, John Clark has argued that the parameters of the arts in colonial India were 'constructed on political lines', constituted from their inception by anti-colonial nationalism. In his view, artistic modernism resisted and challenged all that was 'non-indigenous', looking back to an 'authentic' and 'mythological past of purity or spiritual plenitude'.[81] Choosing to spotlight the Bengal School in the early decades of the twentieth century, Clark further asserts that the 'modern movement', characterized as such by contemporaries, was more a form of 'neotraditionalism' that drew its impetus not from the urge to link 'formal innovation to an articulated world view', but from a 'fundamentally anti-humanist stance' that positions the 'Indian' against the 'European' in the realm of art.[82] Any attempt to characterise the course of artistic modernism in South Asia as a distinctive mode ends up being a vexed process, as its several currents and divergent trails are not reducible to a single or coherent stylistic transformation, even less to a straight 'anti-West' stance. Experiments and understandings of what it meant to be 'modern' unfolded on several sites that included Calcutta, Bombay, Madras, Mysore, and Baroda; artists at each location articulated their preferences for a particular formal language.[83] A careful study, even of Bengal, made possible by existing research, brings

79 According to Nair, he threatened to file lawsuits against those responsible for reproductions that 'grossly misrepresented' his work, see *Mysore Modern*, p. 188.

80 Nair cites the lawyer, politician and independence activist, C. Rajagopalachari who, on seeing Venkatappa's landscapes hailed him as the 'Turner of India', *Mysore Modern*, p. 193.

81 Clark, *Modern Asian Art*, p. 20.

82 Ibid., pp. 80–81.

83 Of these centres Bengal (includes Calcutta and Santiniketan) is probably the most extensively researched. In addition to Mitter, *Art and Nationalism*; Mitter, *Triumph of Modernism*; Guha-Thakurta, *The Making of a New 'Indian' Art*; Guha-Takurta, *Monuments, Objects*; Siva Kumar, *Santiniketan*; Parimoo, *Paintings of the Three Tagores*; see more recently Sanjukta Sunderason, *Partisan Aesthetics: Modern Art and India's Long Decolonization*: Stanford: Stanford University Press, 2020. On the institutional network of newspapers, literary salons and semi-private spaces, Swati Chattopadhyay, *Representing Calcutta: Modernity,*

forth a more nuanced picture than Clark's reductive stance suggests. The lively art scene of Calcutta, portrayed by Partha Mitter as 'a public battle of styles',[84] was indeed formed of different groups who positioned themselves as opposing currents. Selective Westernisation, perceived by members of the rising Bengali middle-class as a path to self-improvement, brought forth a crop of artists practising what was termed the 'Western style', that is, academic oil painting. Art lovers were regularly exposed to reproductions of European art works published – also in colour – in journals such as *Prabasi, Modern Review, Bharati,* or *Sahitya,* all of which played a leading role in the visual education of a growing and avid group of would-be connoisseurs. Works by Western masters such as Raphael, Titian, Greuze, Murillo, Rodin, and the like rubbed shoulders with those of lesser-known but no less propagated Victorians – all considered appropriate to inducing morally uplifting sentiment among their viewers.[85] Artists, in their turn, who endeavoured to adopt the tenets of Western naturalism, akin to what we saw in the work of Ravi Varma, produced works that – predictably – were not mirror images of post-Renaissance or nineteenth century European art, but hybrids of different kinds.

The expansion of the above trend brought with it an inevitable cultural counter-position, defined by the movement of 'Indian-style painting',[86] a nationalist art movement that in retrospect was named the Bengal School, centred around Abanindranath Tagore, the nephew of the poet and Nobel laureate Rabindranath Tagore (1861–1941), and a widening circle of artists, writers, critics, and patrons, with an institutional locus in the Indian Society of Oriental Art founded in 1907. Such a cultural assertion, it must be observed, was less inward looking than might appear at first; it was profoundly nurtured by a century of European Orientalist research that became a channel through which cultural nationalists could create a historical perspective on 'Indian tradition'. The production of such a national framework for art and culture was therefore as much a transcultural co-production as it was an act of confrontation. In the arts, this meant a rejection of academic realism – an explicit anticolonial gesture – and a revival of indigenous values and forms, even as the nationalist reading of 'tradition' turned out to be selective, at times polemical, and more often than not slippery. Two prominent architects of such reading, E. B. Havell (1861–1974), the principal of Calcutta's Government School of Art from 1896 to 1906, and the cultural theorist and philosopher Ananda K. Coomaraswamy (1877–1947), drew their inspiration chiefly from the anti-industrial critique of the Arts and Crafts movement spearheaded by the Victorian art critic John Ruskin (1819–1900) and the socialist activist and designer William Morris (1834–1896). The artistic practice of the Bengal School was not entirely revivalist or anti-syncretic, as Clark would have it,[87] but sought to open up tradition to diverse Asian elements, a move sustained by regular exchanges with Japan and the presence of Japanese and Chinese artists

---

Nationalism and the Colonial Uncanny, London: Routledge, 2005, pp. 13–650. The following synthetic account draws on this output.

84 This is part of the title of Chapter 9 in Mitter, *Art and Nationalism.*

85 Ibid., p. 350ff.

86 Parimoo, *Paintings of the Three Tagores,* p. 74.

87 Clark, *Modern Asian Art,* pp. 80–81.

in Bengal. However, it must be observed that the short-lived vision of a Pan-Asian movement sealed on the basis of opposition to a European civilising mission could not form the basis of a robust 'Asian modernity'. Its main proponent, the Japanese scholar and director of the Imperial Art Academy in Tokyo, Okakura Kakuzō (1863–1913, also known as Okakura Tenshin), espoused a potentially ultra-nationalist vision of Eastern spirituality that was at odds with Rabindranath Tagore's more cosmopolitan stance against colonialism.[88] Art practice, on the other hand, chose to follow more syncretic paths. Abanindranath Tagore was trained under European artists and even as he abandoned oils in favour of watercolours, his work retained elements of realism, modifying these through selectively assimilating elements from Mughal, Japanese, and Persian modes. It is not insignificant that his predilection for East Asian or Persian art fed on the very qualities – pictorial flatness and less inhibited use of space – whose magnetic pull was felt equally by Western modernists in the late nineteenth and early twentieth centuries. Scholarship on modernist art of this period thus ends up confronting several paradoxes, when its organising trope builds primarily on stylistic analysis contained within a sealed regional enclave. More importantly, a recourse to style alone risks falling into the trap of earlier positions that viewed modern art produced outside the West as second-hand variations of a European canon. A more fruitful path to pursue might be to look at actual dynamics of encounter in which artistic idioms are entwined with the role of persons and institutions. Christian Kravagna has highlighted histories of 'contact', of reciprocal invitations and meetings of individuals across the boundaries of the colonial world, as a particularly productive dimension of modernisms beyond the Euro-American mainstream.[89]

'Every culture assumes only as much of a foreign influence as is fit for it. … Indian art never effected any change in the development of European art, nor did European art leave any considerable traces in India. But those epochs deserve notice, where parallel results appear without any connection or influence, but produced by an inner affinity.'[90] This affirmation forms the opening lines of an article authored by the Austrian scholar, Stella Kramrisch (1896–1993), who emerged as an influential figure within the transcultural story of contact referred to above. The article just cited was written shortly after her arrival in India in 1921; it was published the following year in *Rupam*, the prestigious journal of the Indian Society of Oriental Art. After having completed her doctorate on early Buddhist art from Sanchi and Bharhut under the supervision of Josef Strzygowski and Max Dvořák at the University of Vienna, Kramrisch met Rabindranath Tagore in London in 1919, where she continued her scholarly pursuits as wartime émigrée. It was on Tagore's invitation that she moved to the newly founded university Visva Bharati at Santiniketan in 1921. In the years that followed,

---

88 Okakura is said to have visited India twice within an interval of ten years during the last decade of the nineteenth century, see Parimoo, *Paintings of Three Tagores*, pp. 57–59; Okakura's book *Ideals of the East* has been discussed in ibid.; see also Rustom Bharucha, *Another Asia: Rabindranath Tagore and Okakura Tenshin*, New Delhi: Oxford University Press, 2006; Clark draws our attention to the subsequent fascist turn taken by Pan-Asianism in Japan, *Modern Asian Art*, p. 81.

89 Kravagna, *Transmoderne*.

90 Stella Kramrisch, 'Indian Art and Europe', *Rupam*, no. 11 (July), 1922: 81–86, here 81.

Kramrisch became an important scholarly voice who took on the role of a cultural mediator to make the 'inner affinity' she discerned between Indian and European art traditions visible and graspable to audiences in Europe and India through regular acts of cross-cultural translation. Her extraordinary and long career, relatively understudied, was equally exceptional in its bringing together the role of scholar and curator.[91] In 1922, Stella Kramrisch lectured to artists and students at Kala Bhawan, the newly formed art school of the Visva Bharati, on the art of Europe from the Gothic to Impressionism and Post-Impressionism. Modernism at Santiniketan at this time was primarily informed by East Asian art; at the same time, it drew impulses from the indigenous folk and craft aesthetic of Bengal.[92] Into this context Kramrisch introduced modern European art together with a language of formalist art criticism with which to write the story of traditional as well as modern art. This vocabulary found its way into her prolific writings on a range of subjects, from ancient Indian sculpture to the Cubist forays of Gaganendranath Tagore (1867–1938), and left a lasting impact on emergent art critical writing during the nineteen twenties and thirties.[93] Kramrisch's years in Vienna had instilled in her a deep interest not only in ancient Indian art, but equally in contemporary art movements, especially avant-garde movements like Cubism and Expressionism that challenged the formal conventions of academic art and 'developed out of the need of the moment, and no artist in whom the present is alive can escape their formulae'.[94] This statement emanates from the 'Catalogue of the Fourteenth Annual Exhibition' of the Indian Society of Oriental Art; one section of the show, in particular, comprising of modernist works from Germany, was curated by Kramrisch to allow Indian artists direct access to contemporary European art.[95] No doubt an extraordinary event, the show is now being celebrated as a high point of modernist internationalism, an 'encounter of the cosmopolitan avant-garde'.[96]

---

91   A biographical essay together with a selection of Kramrisch's writings can be found in Barbara Stoler Miller (ed.), *Exploring India's Sacred Art: Selected Writings of Stella Kramrisch*, Philadelphia: University of Pennsylvania Press, 1983; reprinted New Delhi: Indira Gandhi National Centre for the Arts, 1994. All citations are from the Indian reprint. A recent work exploring Kramrisch's life and scholarship through a feminist lens is Jo Ziebritzki, *Stella Kramrisch: Eine Kunsthistorikerin zwischen Europa und Indien: Ein Beitrag zur Depatriarchalisierung der Kunstgeschichte*, Marburg: Büchner Verlag, 2021.

92   R. Siva Kumar, 'Shantiniketan: A World University', in: Regina Bittner and Kathrin Rhomberg (eds), *The Bauhaus in Calcutta: An Encounter of the Cosmopolitan Avant-Garde*, Ostfildern: Hatje Cantz, 2013, pp. 109–16, here pp. 110–11.

93   Joseph M. Dye III, 'A Bibliography of the Writings of Stella Kramrisch', in: Stoler Miller (ed.), *Exploring India's Sacred Art*, pp. 35–48.

94   Stella Kramrisch, 'Exhibition of Continental Paintings and Graphic Arts' (1922), reprinted in Bittner and Rhomberg (eds), *The Bauhaus in Calcutta*, p. 2.

95   Contrary to a long-held view that the initiative to organise a show of works from the Bauhaus came from Rabindranath Tagore (see Mitter, *The Triumph of Modernism*, pp. 16–17), archival documents, including Kramrisch's correspondence with Johannes Itten, have now established beyond doubt that she was the one who initiated and conceptualised the show, see Kris K. Manjapra, 'Stella Kramrisch and the Bauhaus in Calcutta', in: R. Siva Kumar (ed.), *The Last Harvest: The Paintings of Rabindranath Tagore*, Ahmedabad: Mapin Publishing, 2011, pp. 34–40, here p. 34.

96   As proclaimed by the subtitle of Bittner and Rhomberg (eds.), *The Bauhaus in Calcutta*. This publication emerged in the context of an exhibition held in Dessau in 2013 and is discussed in the following paragraphs.

The Calcutta Bauhaus exhibition of 1922, as it is frequently referred to, has been valorised – both in art historical accounts as well as in global curatorial projects – as a foundational moment in the story of modernist art on the Indian subcontinent.[97] The event of 1922 was resurrected in 2013 by a collaborative curatorial and scholarly project to reconstruct the Calcutta exhibition at the Bauhaus Foundation in Dessau with a view to reframing the history of this avant-garde German institution as a global and cosmopolitan undertaking.[98] An ambitious experiment of this kind raises a number of questions about what is at stake in such an act of 'restaging',[99] as it draws our attention to the dynamics as well as limits of the label 'transcultural modernism'[100] when applied here in an unqualified manner. The Calcutta exhibition, opened in December 1922, brought some 250 works from Weimar to Calcutta: these comprised primarily of prints, woodcuts, and watercolours by leading artists of Expressionist and Abstract currents including Lyonel Feininger, Wassily Kandinsky, Sophie Körner, Gerhard Marcks, Georg Muche, Oskar Schlemmer, Paul Klee, and not least Johannes Itten, who was responsible for the selection of exhibits and organisation of their transfer at the German end. The works, exhibited in the rooms of the Indian Society of Oriental Art in the heart of colonial Calcutta, were intended from the start, not only for exhibition, but also for sale to interested buyers.[101] Detailed information on the curatorial aspects of the show remains elusive; the exhibition catalogue, which had for a long time been untraceable, now reveals that a broad cross-section of Indian artists from Calcutta featured in the event.[102] Their work, the description and examples from the *Rupam* review suggest, was informed by varying interpretations of what it meant to be 'modern', yet did not reveal an overt resemblance or even affinities with the formal language or pictorial concerns of Bauhaus modernism. What they ostensibly shared was the rejection of academic, naturalist art, though more often from a nationalist rather than formalist stance, as the eclecticism displayed by the exhibits leads us to infer. One factor that might have connected artists from Calcutta and Santiniketan to the spirit of the Bauhaus was a commitment of the artist to working with 'craft', or a return to a romanticised notion of a pre-modern past. The latter ideal characterised the early phase of Bauhaus modernism before its programme shifted to more rationalist forms and media that included photography, film, or metal sculptures and furniture; for Calcutta 'Indian style' artists in turn, recovering the pre-modern past spelt a clearly anti-colonial stance. Thus, the two groups could be brought together by a curatorial hand, even as their motivating impulses

97 Mitter's story, *The Triumph of Modernism,* takes this exhibition as its starting point.

98 Bittner and Rhomberg (eds), *The Bauhaus in Calcutta.*

99 The term has been used by Saloni Mathur, 'The Exhibition as "Re-Job": Reconstructing the Bauhaus in Bengal', in Bittner and Rhomberg (eds) *The Bauhaus in Calcutta*, pp. 191–99, here p. 191.

100 Regina Bittner and Kathrin Rhomberg, 'The Bauhaus in Calcutta: World Art since 1922: On the Topicality of an Exhibition', in *The Bauhaus in Calcutta*, pp. 65–84, here p. 83.

101 Manjapra, 'Stella Kramrisch and the Bauhaus in Calcutta', p. 34.

102 It is somewhat surprising that Bittner and Rhomberg only obliquely refer to the catalogue of 1922. An extensive review of the exhibition – in all likelihood authored by Kramrisch – names several of the participating Indian artists and contains six reproductions of exhibited works. See Anon., 'The Fourteenth Annual Exhibition of the Indian Society of Oriental Art', *Rupam*, no. 13 (Jan–June), 1923: 14–18.

differed and their understanding of modernist form remained pictorially dissimilar. At the Indian Society of Oriental Art, the two groups of works were displayed in adjacent but separate rooms. Kramrisch, whose curatorial intention was driven by the urgency of showing to an Indian public of artists and art lovers that European modern art did not mean academic realism alone, sought to join the two groups of work by observing that the exhibiting artists on both sides had been trained in art academies but were all 'driven by sheer inner necessity to abandon their lifeless scheme'. She continued 'the transformation of the forms of nature in the work of an artist is common to ancient and modern India and Europe as an unconscious and therefore inevitable expression of the life of soul and artistic genius'.[103]

While the event of 1922 made visible the dividing line within the Calcutta art world between the practitioners of a 'Western style' and those who rejected this current, the direct impact of European Expressionist and Abstract art, often inspired by esoteric teachings, on the artists who saw these works cannot be recuperated on a formal register. One exception might be Gaganendranath Tagore, the elder brother of Abanindranath, whose work, primarily in the realm of satire and print making, is held to have turned to painting in a Cubist style directly following the Bauhaus exhibition. The work of this 'Indian Cubist', as Stella Kramrisch described him, is said to have transformed cubism by infusing it with 'emotion', by turning a 'static order into an expressive motive'.[104] Yet, it must be observed that Kramrisch's article, which appeared in July 1922, preceded the Bauhaus exhibition by some months; it suggests therefore that Gaganendranath's interest in Cubist art predated the show, which however would have propelled that interest further resulting in the intense productivity of the artist during the years immediately following the 1922 event. A postcard of the previous year, featuring a watercolour image of a street view in Cubist mode by Gaganendranath, which he sent to the artist Roopkrishna in Lahore, carried the message: 'I am practising Cubism and this is the result.'[105] Ratan Parimoo's survey of the artistic trajectories of the 'three Tagores' suggests that Gaganendranath turned to Cubism via stage scenography. The arrangement of sets – often conceived of in terms of overlapping and receding planes – attracted the artist to the work of Russian scenographists who were among the first to adapt Cubist and Constructivist ideas to stage decor.[106] Gaganendranath's preoccupation with designing for the stage was equally linked to the role of light – lighting on the stage involved casting beams of light on principal characters that when criss-crossing each other created the effect of faceted planes to form an integrated complex. He then proceeded to experiment with these phenomena in paintings composed of intersecting planes of light juxtaposed with shadows. The occasion to see original works in a Cubist idiom was no doubt an inspiring trigger for a number of sophisticated exercises in creating a pictorial structure where intersecting planes, the

103 Ibid.: 18.
104 Stella Kramrisch, 'An Indian Cubist', *Rupam*, no. 11 (July), 1922: 107–09, here 109.
105 The postcard, which R. Siva Kumar dates to 1921, is part of the collection of the Victoria and Albert Museum, London, reproduced in Bittner and Rhomberg (eds), *The Bauhaus in Calcutta*, p. 44. R. Siva Kumar, *Paintings of Gaganendranath Tagore*, Kolkata: Pratikshan, 2015, p. 292.
106 Parimoo, *Paintings of the Three Tagores*, p. 102.

play of light and shadow, were also combined with spatial recession (Plate 3.2). The untitled ink and grey wash on paper consists of shafts of intense light that cross to create planes; their juxtaposition with shadows produces not a flat surface design, akin to the experiments of French Cubists, Picasso and Braque, but a spatial structure in which shades of black become recesses that suggest volume of the built structure. Gaganendranath, though stimulated by the work of pioneering Cubists, conceived of his experiments as chalking an independent path to more effectively pursue his artistic goals of evoking emotions through an exploration of mood and atmosphere, while being no longer dependent on naturalist methods.[107] His encounter with Feininger's work that featured in the Calcutta exhibition is likely to have inspired him to draw in colour and produce chromatic rhythms, a predilection that Parimoo attributes to work of Robert Delaunay as well.[108] Colour brought with it a new sense of light and materiality, and an enhanced kaleidoscopic experience. In an article of 1925, Kramrisch refers to Gaganendranath's paintings as the 'crystallized world of [a] storyteller's imagination',[109] pointing thereby to a path away from pure abstraction, and instead a commitment to connecting the literary and narrative to the exploration of a new formal syntax. The artist's career was unfortunately cut short in the later 1920s following a paralytic stroke that meant spending the last ten years of his life in near oblivion.

Of the European modernist works that travelled from Weimar to Calcutta, only one – a painting by Sophie Körner – was sold; the buyer was none other than Rabindranath Tagore. The remaining works, though returned to Weimar, are no longer traceable.[110] The 2013 exhibition at Dessau was therefore more in the nature of an attempted simulation than a precise reconstruction of the 1922 show. While the latter provided Rabindranath Tagore and Stella Kramrisch 'a platform … [to] advance their progressive views in favour of internationalism in the visual arts', its long-term transformative implications remain ambivalent.[111] Kramrisch's endeavours to introduce a vocabulary of formalist criticism, though a step towards bringing the study of Indian objects into the realm of 'art', did not always encounter positive resonance within the immediate circle of artists and scholars at Santiniketan or Calcutta, where she moved in 1923.[112] More than anything else, the visibility of European modernism following the Bauhaus exhibition worked to highlight an unstable constellation of agonistic pulls marked by the simultaneity of dialogical response and retraction into an 'Indianness' that

107 As stated by the artist during an interview by K. H. Vakil of the *Bombay Chronicle*, 30 June 30 1926, in: Parimoo, *Paintings of the Three Tagores*, Appendix I (C), p. 162.

108 Ibid., p. 104.

109 Stella Kramrisch in *The Englishman*, 29 January 1925, in *Paintings of the Three Tagores*, Appendix I (A), p. 160.

110 Manjapra, 'Stella Kramrisch and the Bauhaus in Calcutta', p. 37.

111 Saloni Mathur points out that many of the works exhibited at Dessau had earlier featured in an exhibition of 1991 at the Los Angeles County Museum of Art, also a reconstruction, this time of the notorious show, *Entartete Kunst* (Degenerate Art) mounted by the Nazi cultural establishment in 1937. Mathur, 'The Exhibition as "Re-Job"', pp. 196–97.

112 Sanjukta Sunderason, 'In Search of a New Visual Culture' (in conversation with Tapati Guha-Thakurta, Regina Bittner and Kathrin Rhomberg), in: Bittner and Rhomberg (eds), *The Bauhaus in Calcutta*, pp. 93–100, here p. 95.

equally staked its claim to 'modernity'. A word of caution is therefore in order in the face of an eager, unequivocal valorisation of what was no doubt an unusual event, as a harbinger of a transcultural 'avant-garde'.[113] The Bauhaus Calcutta exhibition of 1922 furnishes an example of how transcultural processes, while propelled by the humanist-cum-vanguard spirit of individual actors, falter in the face of cultural difference – contingencies of local practice and faultlines within sites where they unfold – and the intended aims of individual initiatives prove to be at best partially realisable. This in turn raises questions about the criteria scholarship deploys to judge the long-term effects of such processes. Our evaluation often tends to rest, at least in part, on specific intellectual predilections and philosophical convictions; instead, examples such as this one urge us to further nuance our vocabulary as we unpack the morphology of transculturation, to be able to speak more precisely and plausibly across disparate contexts. From a reverse perspective, recent scholarship on the Bauhaus movement has, responding to the call of the times, sought to highlight this as a 'global' movement;[114] however, the assimilation of the Calcutta event in the historiography of the Bauhaus has remained confined to being a story of a one-way diffusion. The subsequent history of the Bauhaus was marked by internal disarray and deepening differences, for instance between Johannes Itten and Walter Gropius about the future orientation of the school, leading to Itten's resignation in 1923. The defamation and persecution of the movement as part of the Nazi campaign of the 1930s to exterminate 'degenerate' art, meant its dispersal as its leading members migrated to other continents, and its re-inscription in new contexts, for example that of modernism in post-war America.[115] Against this background, there has been no engagement to date with the implications of a travelling show to Calcutta for the larger history of the movement.

Kramrisch's role as a cultural mediator over the years she spent in Calcutta came to focus almost entirely on the scholarly project of building Indian art history as an intellectual discipline shaped by inputs from history, archaeology, iconography, and religion. The ambition to make 'Indian art' knowable encompassed both East and West: Kramrisch brought her scholarly skills, acquired primarily at the University of Vienna, followed by a stint in England, and enriched by her direct encounter with sites, practices, and objects in India, to the study of a wide range of subjects on art and aesthetics. Her prolific writings furnished an art historical narrative no longer dependent on ethnological or antiquarian studies, which characterised contemporary perspectives both in the German-speaking regions of Europe as well as in India. In the latter context, such an enterprise involved an important taxonomic shift. At the time of Kramrisch's arrival in India, a large number of actors from a range of professional groups were involved with Indian objects: archaeologists, anthropologists, photographers, makers of plaster casts on the one hand, and collectors, officials, and keepers of antiquities

---

113 Bittner and Rhomberg (eds), *The Bauhaus in Calcutta*; Mitter, *The Triumph of Modernism*.
114 Jürgen Waurisch (ed.), *Bauhaus Global*, Berlin: Gebr. Mann, 2010; Marion von Osten and Grant Watson (eds), *Bauhaus Imaginista: A School in the World*, London: Thames and Hudson, 2019.
115 Barry Bergdoll and Leah Dickerman (eds), *Bauhaus 1919–1933: Workshops for Modernity*, New York: Museum of Modern Art, 2009.

in museums on the other. The status accorded to these objects, however, remained a subject of controversy. Discussions took place primarily within a colonial context of collection, administration, and knowledge production; the terms used to designate the objects ranged from idol to artefact or from antiquities to curiosities, depending on their provenance and their individual trajectories.[116] The category of art, or fine art, belonged to a securely guarded domain, whose keepers were not yet ready to accord Indian objects an entry.[117] Among the leading colonial scholars, James Fergusson spoke disparagingly of the attributes of Indian sculpture and architecture, except when it revealed Graeco-Roman influence, while his contemporary and collaborator, James Burgess, claimed that 'high art had never been with the Hindu, as with the Hellenic race, a felt necessity for the representation of their divinities'.[118] A discipline fixated on classical Greek civilisation continued to provide the normative framework within which aesthetic quality was evaluated. The contestations surrounding the concepts deployed to write about Indian objects and images surface in a frequently cited incident that took place at a meeting of 13 January 1910 at the Royal Society of the Arts in London. E. B. Havell, a passionate spokesman for the aesthetic value of Indian objects, which he ascribed to their 'spiritual qualities', set out to counter widespread prejudices of British observers in relation to these objects. He was in turn countered by George Birdwood, a referee of the Indian section of the South Kensington Museum (later the Victoria and Albert Museum), who pointed to a Buddha image and derogatively compared it to a 'boiled suet pudding', an 'uninspired brazen image, vacuously squinting down its nose to its thumbs, and knees, and toes'.[119] Even more influential than the writings of Havell was the erudite oeuvre of Ananda K. Coomaraswamy that drew on philosophy and religion as sources for deciphering the deeper significance of art.

Kramrisch's writings of this time were among the earliest to bring formalist art history, in which she had been trained, to the study of Indian objects, to be dignified as art and placed within a global canon. In 1924, three years following her arrival in India, she published a monograph in German, *Grundzüge der Indischen Kunst* (Elemental Features of Indian Art).[120]

---

116 See Richard H. Davis, *Lives of Indian Images*, Princeton: Princeton University Press, 1997, Chapter 3.

117 The project of colonial scholars in India was overwhelmingly antiquarian rather than art historical. See Monica Juneja (ed.), *Architecture in Medieval India: Form, Contexts, Histories*, New Delhi: Permanent Black, 2001; Guha-Thakurta, *Monuments, Objects*. Painting too was generally read as a mirror of society that 'gives you a perfect idea of the customs, manners and the dress of men and women ... also of their birds, trees and plants', William Watson, cited in Bernard S. Cohn, *Colonialism and Its Forms of Knowledge: The British in India*, Princeton: Princeton University Press, 1996, p. 99.

118 Cited in Pramod Chandra, *On the Study of Indian Art*, Cambridge MA: Harvard University Press, 1983, p. 46.

119 Cited in Davis, *Lives of Indian Images*, pp. 177–78. As late as 1935, George Birdwood, who emerged as an ardent spokesman for the 'decorative arts' of India, remarked on the absence of 'sculpture' and the 'fine arts' in India, a deficiency that he attributed to the 'monstrous shapes of the Puranic deities', which rendered them 'unsuitable for the higher forms of artistic representation'. George C. M. Birdwood, *The Industrial Arts of India*, 2 vols., London: Chapman & Hall, 1880, vol. 1, p. 125. For a systematic history of these attitudes, Partha Mitter, *Much Maligned Monsters: History of European Reactions to Indian Art*, Oxford: Clarendon Press, 1977; Cohn, *Colonialism*, Chapter 4.

120 Published by Avalun-Verlag at Hellerau (near Dresden) in 1924.

Based on materials drawn from two thousand years of Indian art, beginning with early Buddhist sculpture and extending to eighteenth century painting, the relatively slim book (141 pages with 48 plates) presents us with a dense analysis of such 'basic features' of Indian art that animate objects across time and space. The narrative is not organised chronologically but discusses objects and concepts under the themes of myth and form, nature, space, and rhythm.[121] Though Kramrisch drew on Strzygowski's method of *Wesensforschung* (study of essences), she did not subscribe either to his speculative theories about a Nordic centre in opposition to the Mediterranean or to his critique of philology (discussed in Chapter One, 'The World in a Grain of Sand'), and instead harnessed the study of Sanskrit aesthetics, especially the *Citrasutra* of the *Visnudharmottara Purana* to her study of art forms.[122] Further methodological inspiration for the *Grundzüge* came from the work of her other mentor at Vienna, Max Dvořák: in analogy to his distinction between the naturalistic and idealistic realms of art, Kramrisch introduced the concepts *dṛṣṭam* and *adṛṣṭam,* manifest and unmanifest, as two poles whose relationship animates the entirety of Indian art through the presence of divine nature in its forms. The book's purpose can be defined as an identification – arrived at through a conceptual analysis of individual objects – of the unique 'Indianness' that inheres in works across time, something that is first felt and then seen. Art historical analysis comprised therefore of extracting this essential quality, expressed in myriad relations of line, surface, volume, and other elements of visualisation. The *Grundzüge*, in spite of its being written in German, was reviewed in several languages, and enjoyed a mixed reception.[123] While a critic writing for the *Burlington Magazine* was dismissive of the book as a whole, arguing that Indian art was 'more illustrative comment than an art itself', and destined to remain 'within the limits of the sensual sentimentality of [Indian] literature', reviews by Havell and other Orientalists acknowledged the merits of the work, which they located in such concepts and principles that the author was able to extract from different sources to plausibly endow objects with the status of art.[124] *Grundzüge der indischen Kunst* was published with the Avalun Verlag, a small publishing house founded in Vienna in 1919 and that in 1923 relocated to Hellerau, a garden city on the outskirts of Dresden. Built on the model of Ebenezer Howard's garden cities, Hellerau attracted colonies of artists, reformers, critics of uncontrolled industrial urbanism and provided one important context for a reception of Kramrisch's account of Indian art.[125]

Not all of Kramrisch's writings, however, were addressed to an exclusive circle of European readers with an interest in Oriental studies. On the invitation of Curt Glaser, a scholar

121 For a detailed discussion of this work, Ziebritzki, *Stella Kramrisch*, p. 55ff.

122 In 1928, she published a commentary on the *Citrasutra*, a treatise on image making within the *Visnudharmottara Purana*, see Dye, 'Bibliography', p. 37.

123 Discussed in Ziebritzki, *Stella Kramrisch*, pp. 74–77.

124 Review by S. P., *The Burlington Magazine for Connoisseurs*, vol. 47 (269), 1925: 109; Review by E. B. Havell, *Rupam*, nos. 27–29 (July–October), 1926: 74–77; Review by Karl With, *Artibus Asiae*, vol. 1 (2), 1925: 157–58.

125 Ziebritzki draws our attention to the importance of this context for the reception of the book, *Stella Kramrisch*, p. 77ff.

of East Asian art, she contributed a chapter on Indian art to the sixth volume of Anton Springer's *Handbuch der Kunstgeschichte*, begun in 1929.[126] Titled *Die Aussereuropäische Kunst* (Non-European Art), this concluding volume was addressed, like its companions in the genre of *Weltkunstgeschichte* discussed in Chapter One, to connoisseurs, scholars of art history as well as an educated reading public, so as to respond to what Glaser described as a growing interest in 'non-European art', an interest underpinned by the desire to break free from a Mediterranean classical canon.[127] The expanse of the non-European world was broken up into six chapters – East Asia, India, the Islamic World, Africa, Native America, and the Malayan-Pacific – whose individual authors were divided equally between art historians and museum directors in charge of anthropological collections. Though Kramrisch's chapter on India, slightly over a hundred pages and with illustrations built into the text, was organised – unlike the *Grundzüge* – in seven chronological units spanning a thousand years, (conforming to the pedagogically oriented format of the Handbook), her account manages to integrate the study of shifting visual, textual, and cultural contexts with a conception of art that permeates all her work: art as material transformed by creative process into a sacred object. Such an approach registers a significant departure from the established concerns of *Weltkunstgeschichte*, which strove to locate the 'origins' of art in order to establish a relationship between art and the stages of development of humankind. Indian art, Kramrisch sought to demonstrate, was neither reducible to 'ornament', nor to be studied as a source of unspoilt forms that promised a new beginning for Western modernism. Her account approached the subject as a distinct field that merited serious study using methods identical to those deployed for investigating European art; this linked her to a small circle of German art historians, who had begun to view art of the 'world' as a separate cultural category, as more than an object of archaeological enquiry and not to be conflated with religion or anthropology. All the chapters of this particular volume of Springer's *Handbuch* share the assumption that art outside of Europe experiences a decline of creativity with the advent of modernity, in the wake of a close relationship with the West that often meant a 'capitulation' to modern European styles.[128] Kramrisch's chapter is no exception to this position; even as she continued to show an interest in contemporary developments during her sojourn in India and wrote occasionally on the subject, her scholarship turned primarily to the domain of the pre-modern, to ancient aesthetics and the study of Hindu sculpture and temple architecture, where she located the primordial principles of aesthetic production. Her magnum opus, *The Hindu Temple*, represents a crystallisation of her synthetic approach that viewed the temple as a symbolic image of the cosmos realised through the integrity of architectural forms, sculptures, myths, ritual

126 Anton Springer, *Handbuch der Kunstgeschichte*, vol. VI, Leipzig: Alfred Kröner Verlag, 1929. See also the discussion in Ziebritzki, *Stella Kramrisch*, p. 85ff.
127 Curt Glaser, 'Vorwort', in: Springer, *Handbuch*, p. VII.
128 In his chapter on Chinese art, Glaser speaks of a penchant for eclectic copying: Curt Glaser, 'Die Chinesische Kunst', in: Springer, *Handbuch*, pp. 120–21. Similarly, Ernst Kuhnel describes the 'destitute rigidity' ('hilflose Erstarrung') that set into Ottoman building styles following its 'capitulation' ('Kapitulation') to Western idioms; Ernst Kuhnel, 'Die Islamische Kunst', in: Springer, *Handbuch*, p. 525.

practice, and metaphysical conceptions, as they are visualised in the eye and mind of the worshipper.[129] Like her contemporary Ananda Coomaraswamy, the formative role of Islamic traditions and practices that came in the wake of centuries of migration from West and Central Asia, find no place in Kramrisch's oeuvre; though unlike Coomaraswamy her approach was less scholastic or dependent on abstract metaphysics and more rooted in concrete objects and images – visual, material, and literary. The prolific scholarly production of this Viennese scholar, the import of which is yet to be fully assessed, can be seen as providing a blueprint for nationalist art history in the years following the emergence of India as an independent nation-state. Her formalist methods, which replaced anthropology to dignify objects as art, proved useful in taking the art of the erstwhile colony out of the zone of 'otherness'. The discourse of difference that pervades Kramrisch's understanding of Indian art proved to be equally attractive to Indian scholars seeking to rebut the colonial castigation of its inadequacies. Nationalist scholarship, too, searched for the primordial sources of artistic creativity in an ancient Hindu past, while subjecting a more recent, millennium-long Islamic presence to erasure; it privileged the transcendentalist dimension of art production and strove to place artworks within an indigenous knowledge system waiting to be excavated from aesthetic or philosophical texts. Nationalist art history in this sense was as much a product of transculturation with approaches and methods of the discipline formed elsewhere, which had unfolded through a history of 'contact'.

The Politics of 'Significant Form'

'Today we paint with absolute freedom for contents and techniques, almost anarchic; save that we are governed by one or two sound elemental and eternal laws of aesthetic order, plastic coordination and colour composition. We have no pretensions of making vapid revivals of any school or movement in art.'[130] This manifesto-like statement made by the artist Francis Newton Souza (1924–2002), one of the founding members of the Progressive Artists Group (also referred to as the PAG), featured in the catalogue of the first exhibition of the group in Bombay in 1949. Founded two years earlier to coincide with the end of colonial rule in South Asia, the PAG has gone down in the art history of the Indian subcontinent as marking a foundational moment in the story of modernism that was at the same time a shift of its creative centre from Bengal – Calcutta and Santiniketan – to Bombay. Another of the PAG's leading artists, S.H. Raza (1922–2016), spoke of the shared search for 'significant form' as the primary urge that gave this movement its radical edge.[131] By dissociating art production from other agendas – national, social, or revivalist – both Souza and Raza stake a claim for the autonomous language of form as a legitimate ground for an aesthetics through which the

---

129 Stella Kramrisch, *The Hindu Temple*, 2 vols., Calcutta: University of Calcutta, 1946.
130 Francis Newton Souza, *Progressive Artists Group*, Catalogue of the first PAG Group Exhibition, Artists Centre, Bombay, 7 July 1949, cited in Dalmia, *The Making of Modern Indian Art*, p. 43.
131 Raza in an interview with Yashodhara Dalmia, Bombay, January 1991, cited in Ibid., p. 147.

transition from subjection to freedom could be imagined. Viewed through a global lens, the developments on the Indian subcontinent resonate with a rethinking of artistic paradigms taking place at numerous sites within a world recovering from the trauma of war and fascism, at the same time witnessing the dismantling of colonial empires and the emergence of independent nation-states in Asia and Africa. Critiques of Western Humanism came from divergent perspectives – from profound civilisational doubts experienced in the aftermath of devastation and genocide in Europe, or from decolonial analyses of liberal Humanism's complicity in upholding colonial violence. These positions found articulation in the domain of art, be it in Nigeria or Egypt or Vietnam or Indonesia: everywhere cultural sovereignty and individual autonomy conjoined in a productive tension to seek out artistic and literary forms adequate to articulating the aspirations of a modern, culturally confident self. Okwui Enwezor refers to an 'artistic worldliness' that inhered in diasporic and decolonised subjectivities as they charted new paths of aesthetic discourse.[132]

On the Indian subcontinent, the 1940s were an eventful decade marked by turbulent anti-colonial struggle culminating at once in independence and the traumatic partition of the subcontinent into the separate nation-states of India and Pakistan in 1947. In the years before, 1943 saw a devastating famine in Bengal, followed some three years later by Communist-led peasant uprisings in Telengana in the region of Andhra Pradesh. This was a juncture when politics entered visual frames more violently to destabilise the 'modern', once tied to nostalgia for the past, and now making a bid for critical dialogue. That culture had a crucial role to play in the movement for national sovereignty, which sought to free an enslaved economy and bring about a modicum of social justice, is an awareness that materialised in the creation of several groups who chose to call themselves 'progressive' or of the 'people' – the Progressive Writers Association of 1936, the Progressive Painters' Association in Madras of 1944, the Indian Peoples' Theatre Association of the same year, and of course the Progressive Artists' Group of 1947. Of these the last has been singled out and celebrated as 'the fountainhead of Indian modernism',[133] as a movement that engaged openly and creatively with currents of European modernism, especially Cubism and Expressionism, while at the same time looking towards Mexican muralism or *Négritude*. The PAG's emergence at an important transitional moment in the history of a new-born nation, when it could respond to the challenge of bringing together formalist invention with the production of a new sovereign community of citizens, contribute no doubt to its being revered as a 'national vanguard'.[134] Photographs, as this one (fig. 1), reproduced in almost every account of the Progressive Artists' Group, have further buttressed such canonisation.[135] Taken in 1950, on the occasion of

<hr>

132 Okwui Enwezor, 'The Judgment of Art: Postwar Art and Artistic Worldliness', in Enwezor et al. (eds), *Postwar*, pp. 20–41, here p. 36.

133 Chaitanya Sambrani, 'The Progressive Artists' Group, in: Gayatri Sinha (ed.), *Indian Art: An Overview*, New Delhi: Rupa & Co., 2003, pp. 97–111, here p. 97.

134 The term has been used by Sambrani, ibid., p. 98.

135 The photograph has been reproduced in several works: Dalmia, *The Making of Modern Indian Art*, fig. 20; Zitzewitz, *The Art of Secularism*, fig. 3.5; Khullar, *Worldly Affiliations*, fig. 48; Zehra Jumabhoy and Boon

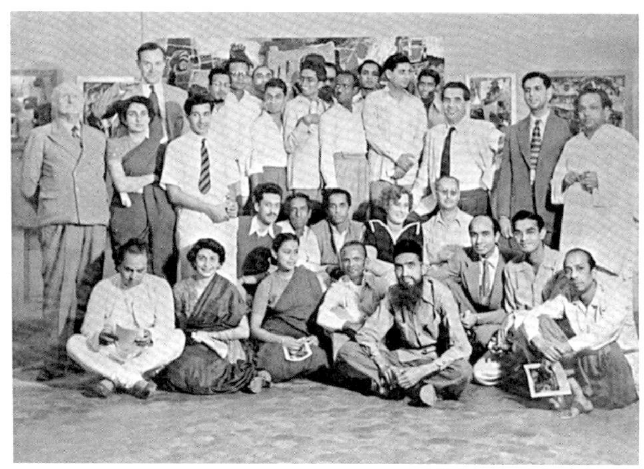

1 The Progressive Artists' Group,
   Art Centre, Bombay 1950

the first solo exhibition of one of its members, the artist M. F. Husain (1915–2011), the picture purports to document the formation of the PAG as a collective enterprise of a small group of Indian artists and critics with the support and encouragement of Jewish émigrés from Central Europe who had sought exile in Bombay during the 1930s, having escaped from the Nazi regime. We see a mixed group of Indians and Europeans – artists, critics, connoisseurs, and gallery owners – exuding optimism and solidarity, assembled in the somewhat cramped space of an exhibition gallery. The paintings hanging on the walls in the background are recognisable as the work of Husain, seated in the first row (fifth from left). The owner of the gallery, Kekoo Gandhy (1920–2012) (standing, second from right, wearing a striped tie) was one of independent India's earliest gallerists who helped to give shape to the infrastructure of an emerging art world.[136]

The Progressive Artists' Group was formed when six young men, all migrants to Bombay, came together and positioned themselves as a radical, anti-establishment group in the art world.[137] It is significant that its members were seen to personify the plurality of India's society: Husain and Raza were Muslims, Souza a Christian, and K. H. Ara (1915–1985) came from a *dalit* community. The two other members were Sadanand Bakre (1920–2007) and Hari Ambadas Gade (1917–2000). Their social and economic backgrounds lent weight to their bid for a universal, emancipatory modernism. The Europeans in the photograph above include Rudolf von Leyden (1908–1983) and Walter Langhammer (1905–1977), both art critics as

Hui Tan (eds), *The Progressive Revolution: Modern Art for a New India*, New York: Asia Society, 2018, fig. 41.

136 Zitzewitz, *The Art of Secularism*, pp. 78–81.

137 Zehra Jumabhoy intriguingly mentions the presence of a female artist, Bhanu Rajopadhye Athaiya, within the group, whose name appeared once in a catalogue of 1953, and who apparently soon gave up painting to become a costume designer. Though two of her works have been reproduced in the Asia Society exhibition catalogue of 2018, her relationship to the PAG remains inconclusive, see Zehra Jumabhoy, 'A Progressive Revolution? The Modern and the Secular in Indian Art', in: Jumabhoy and Tan (eds), *The Progressive Revolution*, pp. 18–19, and figs. 1 and 2.

well as artists, who had migrated to India and now worked for the *Times of India*, the former as art critic and the latter as art director. Langhammer and his Jewish wife held an informal art salon at their home for young artists. Emmanuel Schlesinger (1896–1964) was the owner of a pharmaceutical firm and an art collector, who, having had to leave his collection behind in Germany, emerged as a patron of contemporary art. He was among the first to collect Husain's work, enabling him to practise as full-time artist.[138] The connoisseurship brought by the exiles from Central Europe introduced the restless artists of the PAG to the powerful languages of European modernism, catalysing their enthusiasm into productivity. The group and its associates were united in their opposition to fascism, as they were in the faith that art could repair the damages wrought by recent upheavals. Together they partook of the excitement of decolonisation, energised by a newfound agency and an experimental mood within a closely-knit community of artists and critics. The Progressives saw themselves as an intellectual force vital to the life of a young nation at a historical moment when its cultural mandarins sought instead to privilege an ancient past as the most authentic embodiment of its heritage. Modernist works were rather easily dismissed as 'Western, rootless … and sterile'.[139] Characterised by a 'translational vitality',[140] Bombay modernism survived on a meagre budget, minimal infrastructure, and through the support of individual sympathisers. The latter aspects too made for a special bonding of the PAG into a collective of bohemian artists living on the edge of poverty. Such explicit self-fashioning drew heavily on the romantic habitus of European modernism, notably its valorisation of rebellion per se and its deeply masculinist ethos.

The new 'national modern' that became the hallmark of the PAG was formed out of a two-fold critique – a castigation of the academism disseminated by the colonial art schools, in particular the Sir Jamshetjee Jeejeebhoy School of Art in Bombay (known as the J. J. School of Art), as well as a rejection of the revivalist modernism being practised in several regions under the influence of artists from Calcutta and Santiniketan, who had travelled to various cities to work in art schools there.[141] Both these institutional sites served as trigger for rebellion, which also had a personal dimension: Souza who had joined the J. J. School of Art in 1940 and later became a member of the Communist Party of India, was expelled for participating in a demonstration against the policies of the school's principal Charles Gerrard.[142] Even as the artists of the PAG chose to experiment with the vocabularies of Post-

---

138 Geeta Kapur, 'Maqbool Fida Husain: Folklore and Fiesta', in: Geeta Kapur, *Contemporary Indian Artists*, New Delhi: Vikas Publishing, pp. 117–45, here p. 121.

139 In the words of the artist Gieve Patel, cited in Khullar, *Worldly Affiliations*, p. 101.

140 The term was used by Homi Bhabha, 'India's Dialogical Modernism: Homi Bhabha in Conversation with Susan S. Bean', in: Susan S. Bean (ed.), *Midnight to Boom: Paintings in India after Independence*, London: Thames and Hudson, 2013, pp. 23–36, here p. 24.

141 Teaching at the J. J. school of Art followed conventional tenets of academic styles, though the decade 1937–47 under the principalship of Charles Gerrard saw the introduction of Indian design and Post-Impressionist currents, see Sambrani, 'The Progressive Artists' Group': 102.

142 Geeta Kapur, 'Francis Newton Souza: Devil in the Flesh', in *Contemporary Indian Artists*, pp. 1–46, here p. 6.

Impressionist styles, notably an exuberant version of Central European Expressionism that has infused their works, their appropriations were selective – as I will show below. At the same time, experimental fervour was extolled by the group as an opening to distinctively individual paths towards a realisation of 'significant form' that would enable a discursive re-imagination of a national culture after empire. Yet the emphasis on 'nationness'[143] was an open one, turned both inwards as well as looking outwards. The nation, affectively perceived as locality, was an entity of one's own that had been recuperated from the global constellation of empire. At the same time, the cultural articulations of this act of retrieval were embedded in an international movement; no contradiction was felt in creating an art for the nation that was at the same time cosmopolitan. The interrelatedness of the nation with the world found an echo in the internationalism of politics in the 1950s, especially as it took shape during the conference of non-aligned nations held at Bandung in Indonesia in 1955. This important meeting helped foster a set of affinities across national interests, thereby inspiring a collective consciousness among young independent nations anxious to find a place in the international world order.[144] For artists like M. F. Husain and his peers, the nation provided an ancient past, a body of myths and iconic anchors that could be invoked as civilisational ethos, as a cultural resource, which, however, had to be successfully translated into modernist idioms to occupy a worldly aesthetic space.[145] Husain's copious oeuvre that extends across four generations, till his death in 2011, is devoted to excavating the many facets of a nation-space – the rural, the urban, the symbolic, figurative, and heroic. His works are populated by figures of Hindu mythology – gods, goddesses, characters from the Hindu epics, the *Ramayana* and *Mahabharata* – and their spirited horses that he infused with a vigour inspired by the ink drawings of the Chinese artist, Xu Beihong.[146] Husain's canvases conjoin rural life – its bullock carts and rustic figures – with the bustle of the small-town bazaar. Further, the faces and personae of contemporary history — its saints, politicians, and film stars – all shaped his vision of being an artist of and for modern India. Such choices of subject and idiom possibly account for Husain's relatively early international recognition at a time when non-Western modernisms were invisible globally. He became a significant presence in a transnational art

143 The term is from Homi Bhabha, 'Introduction: Narrating the Nation', in: Homi Bhabha (ed.), *Nation and Narration*, London: Routledge, 1990, pp. 1–7, here p. 2.

144 Gupta, 'After Bandung'; Sonal Khullar speaks of a 'postcolonial worldliness' as a mode of asserting belonging to a national and international community in a way never possible under colonialism, *Worldly Affiliations*, pp. 21–22.

145 On the artistic oeuvre of M. F. Husain, Kapur, 'Maqbool Fida Husain'; Dalmia, *The Making of Modern Indian Art*, Chapter 5; Sumathi Ramaswamy (ed.), *Barefoot across the Nation: Maqbool Fida Husain and the Idea of India*, London: Routledge, 2010; Zitzewitz, *The Art of Secularism*, Chapter 1; Khullar *Worldly Affiliations*, Chapter 3. In 1948, Husain and Souza had travelled to Delhi to see the exhibition *Masterpieces of Indian Art* that offered a rich repository of traditional forms, which unceasingly inspired their citational practice, see Susan Bean, catalogue entry in *Midnight to Boom*, p. 86. On the Delhi Exhibition, Tapati Guha-Thakurta, 'Marking Independence: The Ritual of a National Art Exhibition', *Journal of Arts and Ideas*, nos. 30–31, 1997: 89–114; Kavita Singh, 'The Museum is National', in: Saloni Mathur and Kavita Singh (eds), *No Touching, No Spitting, No Praying: The Museum in South Asia*, New Delhi: Routledge, 2015, pp. 107–131, here pp. 127–28.

146 Bean, *Midnight to Boom*, pp. 86–87.

world many years before the 'global turn', after his *Mahabharata* project shot him into fame at the São Paulo Biennial in 1973.

While the modernist canon has devoted much discussion to the tension between abstraction and figuration, reading it also as a way of denoting larger frictions – between West and East, capitalism and communism, or between Western abstraction and non-Western representational content – the actual dynamics of art-making show that artists' practices were rarely as fixed as the names for them were in the discourse. Within the PAG, the 'progressive' was singled out in the group's manifestos to stand for untrammelled freedom to experiment with form, and yet their pictorial choices worked against the dominance or isolation of formalism, and to rethink instead the political, the personal, the popular, and the everyday as dynamically expressed in paint, colour, and facture. The preoccupation with the human subject – the human form in various states from the heroic-statuesque, the voluptuous, to the deprived pushed to the edge of precarity – remained central, signalling to their concern with notions of agency and predicament. The qualities as well as subjects that artists of the PAG selected from European modernist idioms were among those 'already institutionalised in the West'[147] rather than the more radical avant-garde positions that came with Surrealism or the Dada; for their choices were framed by an agenda that looked to the future not by reflecting on ideological or material structures of the past. Even the annihilating violence wrought by the partition of the subcontinent, the tragic other face of freedom from the colonial yoke, was more often than not bypassed in order to uphold the heady promise of growth and optimism. Their prolific works responded to the magnetic pull of dark, intense, contrasting hues, thick impasto, and the powerful compositional vectors of expressionist works, such as those of Emile Nolde, Max Beckmann, Egon Schiele, Oskar Kokoschka, or Georges Rouault, which could be translated into primordial archetypes of persons, objects, animals, and movements and welded into a decorative whole. Husain, for instance, developed an unmistakeable signature style with which to typologise Indianness, deploying a modernist language of flattened, contained forms frequently plotted in frieze like compositions. The PAG's choice of subjects – the modern city, monumentalised peasants, workers and prostitutes, or the marginal figure of the ragpicker, and above all the celebration of the feminine as a nurturing force for a male artist's creativity – were all a direct legacy of a European canon, ready to be infused with local personae, sensibilities, and stories. The intense modernist preoccupation with the female nude lent itself to easy assimilation within an 'Indian' tradition of erotic religious art – for artists such as Akbar Padamsee (1928–2020), Ara, Souza, and especially Husain, sensuous femininity was a paean to the fecundity of Indian visual culture.[148] A celebration

---

147 Kapur, *When Was Modernism*, p. 366.

148 Souza, Padamsee and Husain all faced court cases on charges of obscenity; Husain subsequently was accused of 'hurting religious sentiments'. In all these instances the defence of the artists used the art historical evidence of Indian 'tradition' to counter the charges of obscenity. See, for instance the full text of the judgement in the Padamsee case, published by Mulk Raj Anand, the editor of *Marg*: 'Judgment in the Trial of Akbar Padamsee for Alleged "Obscene' Paintings"', *Marg*, vol. 7 (4), 1954: 90–91. Also Zitzewitz, *The Art of Secularism*, p. 86.

of the rural and the marginal as a counter-image of the industrialised urban – a representational trope characteristic of much of nineteenth-century European art[149] – resonated with a Gandhian valorisation of the village. A condensation of this translational praxis is *Zameen*, an early work by Husain, whose title stands for both Earth and Land. The painting on canvas extends horizontally over a width of some five and a half meters, taking on the quality of a frieze (Plate 3.3). It is a non-narrative ensemble of compartments, two-dimensional forms, emblems, and pictographs brought together in a self-consciously experimental idiom. Its vivid details – a peasant tilling the land with a pair of bulls, a woman winnowing grain, a dancer, a kite, a woman churning milk, another giving birth, religious symbols such as the wheel, the hand evoking Fatima, the footprint, associated with the Buddha, Vishnu, and the Prophet Muhammad – are both an inventory and components of a mythology of the young nation. A more enigmatic work of the same time and in a similar format, *Man* (of which we get a glimpse in the photograph of his show; see fig.1) is about the modernist conception of the artist and art making that transforms material into myth. Its central, dominating figure, painted in black with an uncanny green eye, echoes the pose of Auguste Rodin's thinker – a creator, like the artist. Surrounding him is an ensemble of plaques with signs and figures from Hindu iconography symbolising a panoply of forces – divine as well as infernal – all woven together in an intense contest of colours. It is a perplexing image, demanding to be decoded; at the same time, it is one that allows the viewer to bypass the figural complex and read it as an ensemble of colours, shapes, compartments, of juxtapositions and swirling movements.[150]

The transcultural encounter between the PAG and their European mentors, though it has acquired the hues of a foundation legend, was more in the nature of a powerful catalyst that channelised the creativity of six individuals and their associates to generate extraordinary productivity. This in turn gave Bombay modernism a unique place within both art historical accounts as well as in the repositories of museums across the world. Today, the works of its artists fetch high prices on the art market. The collective life of the group itself did not endure beyond a decade, after three of its artists migrated to metropolitan centres – London, Paris, New York – turning their backs to the 'developmental nationalism'[151] of the Nehruvian years that, though it valorised culture in the service of the nation, privileged genres such as murals and public sculpture at the expense of an infrastructure congenial to more individualistic, experimental forms of creativity. While Husain continued to paint unceasingly and succeeded in connecting his art to India's public culture – till he was targeted by right-wing Hindu nationalists in the 1990s[152] – Souza and Raza left for London and Paris respectively.

---

149 Monica Juneja, *Peindre le paysan: L'image rurale dans la peinture française de Millet à Van Gogh*, Paris: Editions du Makar, 1998.

150 The painting, part of the Herwitz collection at the Peabody Essex Museum in Salem, has been reproduced in Bean, *Midnight to Boom*, p. 89, plate 4. It has been discussed by several scholars: see Geeta Kapur, 'Modernist Myths and the Exile of Maqbool Fida Husain', in: Ramaswamy (ed.), *Barefoot Across the Nation*, pp. 21–53, here pp. 22–24; Dalmia, *The Making of Modern Indian Art*, pp. 102–03; Bean, *Midnight to Boom*, p. 86; Khullar, *Worldly Affiliations*, pp. 94–96.

151 The term has been used by Gupta, 'After Bandung', p. 635.

152 This aspect has been extensively dealt with by the essays in Ramaswamy (ed.), *Barefoot across the Nation*.

With his move to London in 1949, Souza became a participant in the postcolonial journey of migrant artists from the former colonies of Asia, Africa, and the Caribbean into the western metropolitan world, to what Sarat Maharaj describes as a Britain 'after the floods'.[153] This was a transformative conjuncture in the story of twentieth century modernism when individual histories, mapped across (post) empire and former colony in a connective, mutually constitutive relationship, created possibilities of dismantling notions of stability and conformity within established orders entrenched in national units. Souza's early years in Britain were marked by isolation and poverty, as his work encountered little interest in the art world there.[154] Reviews of his work were couched in orientalist tropes of the exotic or belatedness, characteristic of art critical responses to the productions of artists belonging to Asian, African, or Caribbean diasporas in Britain. The now-familiar argument that recognition as a 'modern' artist was inaccessible to non-white members of the art world who aspired to situate themselves within a domain predicated on their exclusion, however needs to be relativised by paying attention to the artistic modes and strategies of immigrant artists engaged in myriad forms of critique, often through an initial complicity with the materials and idioms that such critique sought to destabilise.[155] From the start of his artistic career as member of the PAG, Souza's work was a kaleidoscope of multiple iconographic references – the sculptural language of the nude body appropriated from Hindu iconography, the jagged planes of Expressionist idioms, the tortuous as well as sublime aspects of religion proffered by Christian art, and not least the turn to still life that hovers in the interstices of a European bourgeois genre and a feeling for the sacred. The artist's continued, deeper exploration of transcultural praxis as a way of identifying with his new location, ran counter to the expectations of metropolitan viewers and critics anxious to 'read' diasporic identities through references to a single locus of origin. For Souza, Christianity was a bridge that connected him to other diasporic communities, in particular artists from the Caribbean. Yet, it was also more than that: the image of Christ as an incarnation of the tragic was a path that enabled the artist to intervene in the post-war crisis of humanist values. Souza's relocation to England in the immediate aftermath of wartime devastation and the horror of concentration camps brought him into the midst of passionate debates about the European sources of humanism, including philosophical moves – be it the thought of Nietzsche or Existentialism – to rethink the humanist legacy through the lens of the 'dreadful memories' of mass annihilation, as Jean-Paul Sartre wrote in 1948.[156]

153 Maharaj, 'The Congo is Flooding the Acropolis': 90.
154 Kapur, 'Francis Newton Souza', p. 11.
155 This argument about denied recognition has been put forward by Araeen, 'The Other Immigrant'; also Gilane Tawdros, 'Running with the Hare and Hunting with the Hounds', in: Mora J. Beauchamp-Byrd and M. Franklin Sirmans (eds), *Transforming the Crown: African, Asian and Caribbean Artists in Britain 1966–1996*, New York: Caribbean Cultural Center, 1997, pp. 58–62, cited in Leon Wainwright, 'Francis Newton Souza and Aubrey Williams: Entwined Art Histories at the End of Empire', in: Simon Faulkner and Anandi Ramamurthy (eds), *Visual Culture and Decolonisation in Britain*, Aldershot: Ashgate Publishing, 2006, pp. 101–26, here p. 103–04.
156 Cited in Sarah Wilson, 'New Images of Man: Postwar Humanism and Its Challenges in the West', in Enwezor et al. (eds), *Postwar*, pp. 344–49, here p. 345.

Artistic preoccupation with the question of what defines the human found expression in the myriad, obsessive engagements with the human body, sculpted, painted, or drawn. The exhibition *New Images of Man*, curated by Peter Selz for the Museum of Modern Art, in New York City in 1959, staged this new dialogue of forms, signalling to the renewed centrality of a figurative mode.[157] The enquiry into the failure of Western civilisation unfolded in another vein among spokespersons in former European colonies: discourses of *Négritude* as well as Frantz Fanon's impassioned work *Black Skin, White Masks* reclaimed for the once colonised the ethical right to bring forth their vision of humanity.

For Souza, having grown up in the midst of Goa's pageant-like church imagery, a locally transcultured Christianity – with its primordial paradoxes of suffering, guilt, and the promise of grace – came to be an enduring force shaping his life and art.[158] Even as his innumerable paintings and drawings of a suffering Christ were injected with unrelieved affliction, even rancour, Christianity remained for the artist a vital source of humanism – in Christianity man was meant to be the image of God and God himself became man. In the wake of the anguished debates of his time, Souza's rendering of Christ (Plate 3.4) imbibed some of Nietzsche's rage coupled with a castigation of colonialism's degradation of humanity. The crucified Christ has been turned into a black, spindly figure as if cobbled together with thorny pieces of wood, with grotesquely jutting white teeth, a signature trope in the artist's religious imagery. Flanked by two men – one of who is surmised to be Saint John – clad in patched shirts of red and green, this deformed triad borders on the edge of caricature rather than invite compassion. Souza's handling, reminiscent more of the Romanesque vision of an avenging God than the gentleness of the Gothic, resonates with the similarly brutal treatment of religious themes by his contemporaries Francis Bacon (1909–1992) and Graham Sutherland (1903–1980) to articulate the deeply disturbed psychic representation of the human subject that haunted the imaginations of post-war generations.[159] London afforded Souza the opportunity to study Goya's works in the National Gallery; from these as much as from Nietzsche came the compulsion to engage with another face of Christianity – the theme of hypocrisy tied to clerical authority. The artist's rendering of Christian saints bristles with ambivalence. Saint Sebastian, ironically titled *Mr Sebastian*, dons a dark suit and tie very much in the style of the numerous caricatural portraits of 'gentlemen of our times' painted by the artist – face without a forehead, bearded, bulging eyes, and the signature protruding razor-teeth.[160] Arrows that had once pierced the saint's innocent body and provide the clue to his martyrdom, are now stuck with a vengeance into the 'gentleman's' black face and neck.

157 See Peter H. Selz (ed.), *New Images of Man*, New York: Arno Press, 1959; also Wilson, 'New Images of Man' p. 348.

158 He wrote: 'My beginnings were small and secret and growth was by contact with Christ', in: 'Notes from my Diary', cited by Kapur, 'Francis Newton Souza', p. 17.

159 Enwezor reads Blackness as a reference to racist violence in the United States, 'The Judgment of Art', p. 30.

160 Francis Newton Souza, *Mr. Sebastian* (1955), oil on cardboard, New Delhi, Kiran Nadar Museum of Art. Wainwright terms the representation 'a saint secularised', in: 'Francis Newton Souza and Aubrey Williams', p. 108. For examples from the 'gentlemen of our times' series, see Rob Dean and Giles Tillotson

These and other works brought Souza favourable critical attention during the 1950s – he participated in group exhibitions, while the newly opened Gallery One hosted a solo show of his work, generating sales and reviews by eminent critics such as John Berger and Edward Mullins.

The mid-1960s brought forth a series of 'black paintings', anchored within a complex network of artistic practices that characterised a global modernism of the post-war years. Several readings of these enigmatic works have been proffered. While Enwezor locates them in the discursive frame of a 'blackness constituting a resistance to an idealizing and blinding whiteness'[161], Aziz Kurtha conjectures these works to be a homage to Goya's *Pinturas Negras* of the last years of his life, around 1819.[162] The connection between blackness, civil rights movements, and the resistance to racial segregation and violence has been frequently sought for within works of artists investigating the tensions between humanism and colonialism,[163] yet the subject of racism has only rarely found a place in Souza's oeuvre. In the context of one particular painting, *Negro in Mourning*, that stands apart from so much of his other work in that it exudes a deep empathy and melancholy for its subject, the artist does refer to the period of heightened racism when it was painted to suggest a gesture of mourning for a victim of racist violence.[164] Souza's works in the *Black on Black* series emerge above all as a formalist experiment in their refusal to choose between the unproductive binary of abstraction and figuration, and instead to deliberately combine figuration with facture.[165] The 1960s saw similar experiments in black among Expressionist artists such as Robert Rauschenberg and Ad Reinhardt as an act of exploring the limits of the visible.[166] By allowing the figure and

(eds), *Modern Indian Painting: Jane and Kito de Boer Collection*, Ahmedabad: Mapin, 2019, figs. 78, 79, 80, 81, 85.

161 Enwezor, 'The Judgment of Art', p. 32.

162 Aziz Kurtha, *Francis Newton Souza: Bridging Western and Indian Modern Art*, Ahmedabad: Mapin, 2006, p. 39.

163 Enwezor, 'The Judgment of Art', p. 32–33; Homi Bhabha, 'Remembering Fanon: Self, Psyche, and the Colonial Condition', in: Enwezor et al (eds), *Postwar*, pp. 350–55.

164 The work, part of the collection of the Birmingham Museums' Trust, is reproduced on: https://www.sothebys.com/en/articles/shelley-souzas-elegy-to-a-negro-in-mournings (accessed 10 January 2021). Shelley Souza cites her father's message to the Birmingham Museum and Art Gallery of 16 October 1997 as follows: 'Although I wasn't involved in any unpleasantness over skin colour and have never been, prejudice is a fact of life. Being born in India I know better. But the black man, the negro, had the worst of it. In fact, it was in London that I became aware of this black-white discrimination. Much of it had to do with sex. It was dangerous for a black man, a negro, to be seen with a white woman!' The artist's statement draws attention to the nuances within practices of racial segregation that distinguish between brown and black. Though he experienced racism in postwar Britain, he also saw himself as an empathetic observer of 'black-white discrimination'.

165 In 1966, London's Grosvenor Gallery hosted a solo exhibition of Souza's works entitled *Black Art and Other Paintings*; in 2013, it featured many of these monochromatic works in a fresh show, *FN Souza, Black on Black*. https://www.grosvenorgallery.com/exhibitions/126-fn-souza-black-on-black-frieze-masters/overview/ (accessed 20 January 2021).

166 See the catalogue of the exhibition at Haus der Kunst, Munich: Stephanie Rosenthal (ed.), *Black Paintings: Robert Rauschenberg, Ad Reinhardt, Mark Rothhko, Frank Stella*, Ostfildern: Hatje Cantz, 2006. A recent essay on Souza's Black Paintings, which appeared after this manuscript was completed, examines the intersections of 'the politics and poetics of color' within the larger context of postwar conditions,

the ground to merge and interpenetrate, the black paintings demand of the viewer an intense act of looking, almost an act of excavation of the resistant forms deeply ensconced in the thick impasto of black-on-black paint. The works – though immediately suggestive of a classic melancholy – were at the same time a demonstration of tremendous skills both as painter and as draughtsman. They are also designed as a challenge to techniques of mechanical reproduction, demanding light at particular angles in order to be able to penetrate through the layers of paint and get a glimpse of the images concealed in the dark depths. At once a palpable material surface and a metaphysical proposition, a painting acts as a space that refers to another space, challenging, exhorting the viewer to grasp figure and ground in their complex organic unity. These works, no doubt an important conceptual development within Expressionism, already gestured in the direction of art across the Atlantic. Indeed, soon after this exhibition, which was strangely bypassed by art criticism in the mid-sixties, Souza left England for the United States where he spent the remainder of his life, returning to India shortly before his death in 2002.

A Migrant Concept – Primitivism

The last section of this chapter on artistic modernism as a transcultural phenomenon turns to one of its most resilient tropes – primitivism – that has not relinquished its hold over the imaginations of scholars and curators. If modernity is defined according to the principle that the present always stands for a more advanced stage than that which came before it, if to be modern logically means having progressed beyond the non- or the pre-modern, articulations of modernity are then predicated on the concept of the timeless, the non-historical, also designated as the archetypal primitive. Even as the primitive, in other words that which is resistant to history, has always already inhabited the regime of the modern, its prolific representations have shown the primitive to be an unstable, chameleon-like concept. Dealt with from several disciplinary positions across the humanities and social sciences, the concepts primitive/primitivism have come to form one of the most passionately discussed facets of modernity and its cognates, literary and artistic modernism.[167] The subject continues to preoccupy the art world today, not least because many of the arguments between art historians, anthropologists and curators have re-emerged within the debates on contemporary art, said to be undergoing an 'ethnographic turn' in the wake of the unprecedented visibility that accrues to cultural difference in global exhibition circuits.[168] Placed against the existing, dense corpus of writing, the ensuing thoughts seek to direct our attention to the work primi-

see Atreyee Gupta, 'Francis Newton Souza's Black Paintings: Postwar Transactions in Color', *The Art Bulletin*, vol. 103 (4), 2021: 111–137.

167 I have avoided placing the terms primitivism and primitive in quotes, though these are clearly intended to stand for ascriptions throughout the discussion in this section.

168 Though the epithet 'primitivism' is eschewed in contemporary discussions following the notoriety attached to it after the MoMA exhibition of 1984 discussed below; instead art critical writing today speaks of 'ethnic' or 'Indigenous' art, as will be further elaborated in Chapter 5.

tivism as a migrating concept does to weave artistic modernism into a set of braided histories across time and space.

The following account will track one segment of the many global journeys of a key concept by drawing on insights from a transcultural conceptual history – an initiative to extract the canonical *Begriffsgeschichte* from its national confines and investigate the formation of concepts as implicated in transcultural processes.[169] Such a perspective seeks to unravel the unfolding possibilities when concepts migrate and take roots in different settings, to examine processes of appropriation and resignification – but also ambivalent reproduction – following the delinking of concepts from their 'original' moorings. The conceptual approach is vital to art history, for it signals to issues that otherwise fall by the wayside owing to the exclusions effected by the discipline's taxonomic protocols – as will be evident in the discussion of primitivism's journeys across three continents traced below, signalling to the foundational place the concept occupies in the history of artistic modernism. Conversely, an art historical perspective, when grafted to a history of concepts, aims to fix the meaning of a concept beyond exclusively lexical definitions by bringing these into play with the efficacy of the visual and the material within the dynamics of meaning making and conceptual formation. A methodologically refined conceptual history would then account for multiple modalities of signifying, by integrating practices of argumentation brought forth by visual media, material objects as well as institutional practices.

In 1937, the American art historian Meyer Schapiro defined 'primitivism' as an attitude of modern artists who sought and found 'an intimate kinship' with the imagery of 'primitive peoples without a recorded history', peoples whose pictorial creativity was held to approximate 'spontaneous animal activity … self-contained … without dates or signatures, without origins or consequences except in the emotions'.[170] Well into the nineteenth century, the art historical use of the term primitive had related to a set of north European neo-classical painters of the early nineteenth century.[171] The late nineteenth century, however, also witnessed a rapid shift of its point of reference in the direction signalled by Schapiro, occasioned by the increasing presence of and preoccupation with objects from across the non-European world in European collections. Within art history, the conceptual shift was in turn expedited by a burgeoning scholarly engagement across disciplines with prehistoric societies, datable to

169 This perspective informed a cross-disciplinary research group ('Towards a Global History of Concepts') at the Heidelberg Cluster Asia and Europe to question the premise of a canonical conceptual history, as proposed by Reinhart Koselleck and J. G. A. Pocock, that such a history could only be written in national terms. For a similar approach see Margrit Pernau and Dominic Sachsenmaier (eds), *Global Conceptual History: A Reader*, London: Bloomsbury, 2016.
170 Meyer Schapiro, 'The Nature of Abstract Art', *Marxist Quarterly*, vol. 1 (1), 1937: 77–98, reprinted in *Modern Art 19th and 20th Centuries: Selected Papers*, New York: George Braziller, 1978, pp. 185–211, here pp. 200–01. Aesthetic modernism thus effected a shift in the meaning of the word 'primitive' from the backward to the primal or natural. It also introduced its cognate 'primitivism' that was imbued with a processual dynamic, and thereby endowed with a potential for reinvention and renewal in the course of its transcultural journeys.
171 See Andrée Hayum, 'The 1902 Exhibition, Les Primitifs flamands: Scholarly Fallout and Art Historical Reflections', *Journal of Art Historiography*, vol. 11 (2), 2014: 1–20.

the second half of the nineteenth century and which expanded exponentially in the early twentieth. The ideologically charged term primitive, with its connotations of backwardness or depravity, rapidly morphed into a capacious conceptual container for diverse visual traditions – African, Oceanic, Native American, even Asian and ancient Egyptian – that liberal elites of the modern West had come to admire as primordial, non-classical, unspoilt, or mystical, and whose inventive visual grammars came to permeate modernist painting and sculpture. Even as Schapiro ascribed the appeal of the primitive to its allegedly mythical, timeless quality, he was among the few scholars of his time to establish the historical nexus between the modern artistic phenomenon of primitivism and European imperial subjugation of peoples cast as primitive, whose arts paradoxically underwent an unprecedented aesthetic valorisation by those complicit with acts of colonial depredation.[172] Such a historicisation, however, receded into the background of scholarship: though the latter continued through the twentieth century to focus on the myriad practices of artistic primitivism, these were treated as a decontextualised set of preferences. The question of primitivism's complicity with colonialism resurfaced only in 1984, in the controversial debates triggered by the now infamous exhibition on the subject curated by William Rubin and Kirk Varnedoe for the MoMA in New York. Titled *Primitivism in 20th Century Art: Affinity of the Tribal and the Modern*, the show relied on juxtaposition and visual resemblance between the chosen objects: modernist paintings, whose artists were named and dates specified, placed alongside of 'tribal' objects treated as nameless and timeless, with the intent to establish the reciprocal affinity announced by its curators. The ensuing protracted and often polemical discussions brought to the fore a cluster of critical positions informed by postcolonial and postmodernist theory – the charge of asymmetrical treatment of objects, of the evacuation of history from the presentation, or the underlying epistemic violence wrought by the curatorial move to treat 'tribal artefacts' as modern art works displayed in glass cases.[173]

Subsequent accounts of the modernist revolution in art forms, even as they problematised the ethics of cultural appropriation that was complicit with colonialism, continued to regard the European discovery of archaic objects from Africa and Oceania as having enabled a moment of modernism that overturned inherited aesthetic norms. However, even the most critical discussion of artistic modernism has generally remained confined within a bounded domain of 'art' and of individual artists, or at best has forged links with related movements

172 Schapiro, 'The Nature of Abstract Art': 200.

173 William Rubin (ed.), *'Primtivism' in 20th Century Art: Affinity of the Tribal and the Modern*, 2 vols., New York: Harry N. Abrams, 1984. Critical responses include: Thomas McEvilley, 'Doctor Lawyer Indian Chief: "Primitivism" in 20th Century Art at the Museum of Modern Art in 1984', *Artforum*, vol. 23 (November), 1984: 54–60, reprinted in Thomas McEvilley, *Art and Otherness: Crisis in Cultural Identity*, New York: McPherson and Co., 1992, pp. 27–56; James Clifford, 'Histories of the Tribal and the Modern', *Art in America*, vol. 73 (4), 1985: 164–77, 215; Hal Foster, 'The "Primitive" Unconscious of Modern Art', *October*, vol. 34 (Autumn), 1985: 45–70; Yves-Alain Bois, 'La pensée sauvage', *Art in America*, vol. 73 (4), 1985: 178–88; Rasheed Araeen, 'From Primitivism to Ethnic Arts', *Third Text*, vol. 1 (1), 1987: 6–25; Simon Gikandi, 'Picasso, Africa and the Schemata of Difference', *Modernism/Modernity*, vol. 10 (3), 2003: 455–80.

in literature or music. In addition, the scathing critique of the New York exhibition brought with it a hardening of a modern institutional separation of the spaces where 'high art' and 'ethnological objects' were each conserved, displayed and thereby vested with signification and value: the two rarely met, apart from the one brief, notorious moment at the MoMA in 1984.

One among the many faces of modernity is the acquisitive quality of collecting – by colonial administrators, archaeologists, anthropologists, missionaries, travellers, scholars – that has meant that since the Renaissance hordes of objects from all over the world filled the repositories of ethnographic collections and museums. Travelling, buying, and collecting acquired a particularly feverish character in the wake of colonialism, driven by the concern that modernisation was leading to a rapid disappearance of remnants of the past that needed to be safeguarded and preserved. In its delineation of a 'developmental history of art' corresponding to evolutionary classification schemes to characterize the world's cultures from the 'savage' to the 'civilised', the practitioners of a *Weltkunstgeschichte*, as discussed in Chapter One ('The World in a Grain of Sand'), provided the world of art with a conceptual language to describe these objects. It is in this context that the concept of the primitive as an art historical category acquired a discursive fixity, a term that became a key concept to define the temporal competence of modernist culture at the turn of the century – artistic modernism's *alter ego* as Kobena Mercer put it.[174] Unpacking the conceptual formation of artistic primitivism therefore calls for overcoming taxonomic principles of separation, themselves a product of modernist ideology, and for plotting art production onto a historical field that it shared with related phenomena, all engaged in producing artistic knowledge about the world by paying attention to close material relationships with migrant objects. The mobile materiality of such objects made their reframing as objects of knowledge possible – of knowledge produced by scholars, curators, and artists. Modernist experiments, such as Cubism and Expressionism, are best viewed as a nodal-point in an Ariadne-like web, to borrow from Bruno Latour, making up a shared matrix of transactions through which art and art historical knowledge about the world and about the sites of display were produced. This means that the modernist artistic revolution was coterminous and entangled with other phenomena that have been relegated to distinct institutional and scholarly spaces: the textual production of knowledge about the primitive, above all the writing of *Weltkunstgeschichte*, and the building of ethnological collections. And finally, a transcultural gaze directs our attention to the primitive as a phenomenon that is re-appropriated and recast at those sites beyond the modern West, which were cast as locations of the primitive.

The relationship between the primitive and the modern in the field of making and interpreting art needs to be read in conjunction with theorisations of the primitive as a figure of thought across various fields of knowledge and disciplines at the close of the nineteenth and the early decades of the twentieth century. Making the primitive the subject of representational knowledge was a condition for the production of modernist histories and

---

174 Mercer, *Cosmopolitan Modernisms*, p. 42.

subjectivities.[175] Broadly viewed, two lines of argument can be singled out from the large number of intersecting positions within this corpus of writing. The first subscribed to the notion of affinity between the 'life of the mind of prehistoric cultures and the inner life of the present', as the historian Karl Lamprecht expressed it in 1901.[176] Similarly, the artist Wassily Kandinsky, for whom the contemporary crisis of culture had encouraged the discovery of this spiritual kinship, posited such an inner affinity between modernism and the urges of 'unspoiled pure artists' of societies considered primitive.[177] The second approach, more clearly informed by evolutionist theory, took a relativist position that placed the primitive as a distinct epoch on the scale of evolution, one with its own mental life and laws. The writings of the French philosopher Lucien Lévy-Bruhl proposed the notion of 'other thinking', also described as primitive, pre-logical, savage, or mystical. Translated into German and English and widely circulated, these studies of the primitive mind characterised it as incapable of differentiating or analysing phenomena, and instead a mentality that chose to ascribe a magical character to events.[178] This in turn implied that primitive artistic creation, considered unique, was endowed with autonomous meaning and therefore had to be analysed in the context of its own time. The evolutionist-cum-relativist position, which also corresponded to the cultural relativism in American anthropology whose foundations were laid by the writings of Franz Boas resonated with the writings of exponents of a *Weltkunstgeschichte*, discussed in Chapter One.[179] Their art historical understanding was reinforced by Wilhelm Worringer's concept of empathy, which argued that the assumption of a 'psychic unity of mankind' formed a precondition for being able to understand the artistic creation of an entirely different mental world. According to Worringer, intuition and 'historical divination' of a researcher played an important role in the investigation of style.[180] In an article published in the *Reallexikon für Vorgeschichte* in 1927, the historian Herbert Kühn summarised the discussion on primitive art by positing that an absolute standard of beauty in the sense of idealised nature could no longer be held as valid; rather the concept of art could

175 This is a vast subject to which anthropologists, psychologists, philosophers, sociologists, and historians of prehistoric societies have contributed. For a survey of primarily German-language texts, see Doris Kaufmann, '"Pushing the Limits of Understanding": The Discourse on Primitivism in German *Kulturwissenschaften*, 1880–1930', *Studies in History and Philosophy of Science*, vol. 39 (3), 2008: 434–43.

176 Karl Lamprecht, 'Fragen moderner Kunst', *Neue Deutsche Rundschau*, vol. 12 (2), 1901: 734–41, cited in Kaufmann, 'Pushing the Limits': 436.

177 '[U]unsere Sympathie, unser Verständnis, unsere innere Verwandtschaft mit den Primitiven. Ebenso wie wir suchten diese reinen Künstler nur das Innerlich-Wesentliche in ihren Werken zu bringen.' Wassily Kandinsky, *Über das Geistige in der Kunst insbesondere der Malerei* (1911), Bern: Benteli Verlag, 2009, p. 25. See also David Pan, *Primitive Renaissance: Rethinking German Expressionism*, Lincoln: University of Nebraska Press, 2001, pp. 100–20.

178 Lucien Lévy-Bruhl, *La mentalité primitive* (1922) was published in German as *Die geistige Welt der Primitiven*, Munich: F. Bruckmann, 1927; and *L'âme primitive* (1927) as *Die Seele der Primitiven*, Vienna: Braumüller, 1930; cited in Kaufmann, 'Pushing the Limits': 437.

179 Franz Boas, *Primitive Art*, New York: Dover, 1927, was the first general scholarly work on the subject in English to make a case for understanding primitive art as an expression of the degree of complexity of the society that produced it.

180 Cited in Kaufmann, 'Pushing the Limits': 438–39.

be best characterised as 'the formed expression of the relationship of oneself to the world'.[181] Such a conclusion found resonance among artists of the contemporary avant-garde – from Expressionism to Dadaism to Surrealism – for whom the wholeness of culture, ruptured in other spheres of life, could still be captured within the realm of art through the inclusion of the pre-logical, mystical or primitive.[182] For proponents of *Weltkunstgeschichte* such as Ernst Grosse or Karl Woermann, difference dignified as pure expression could coexist with civilisational hierarchies.

The artistic appropriations of such diverse conceptual understandings of the primitive were, likewise, far from uniform or consistent – indeed the argument that the modernist artistic revolution unfolded in symbiotic relationship to modernity's *alter ego* needs considerable nuancing.[183] The famously liberating encounter with objects from Africa and Oceania held to have been experienced by artists in the early twentieth century has become the subject of many art historical mythologies; while Picasso is the most prominent example of such legend-making, this also applied to Expressionist artists in Germany, whose relationship to the primitive was more mediated and followed diverse and individual trajectories. Ernst Ludwig Kirchner (1880–1938), for instance, had declared having discovered art of the South Seas in the Ethnological Museum at Dresden, where he was a student of architecture. Kirchner's experience of primitive art, however, owed less to a direct aesthetic encounter, and was instead mediated by textual accounts of primitive art. He encountered these, for instance, in two older, important texts that were seminal reading for the students of architecture and had also been a subject of contemporary art historical discussions – Gottfried Semper's (1803–1879) *Der Stil* and Owen Jones' (1809–1874), *Grammar of Ornament*.[184] Semper had insisted on the universal validity of certain formal principles and referred to 'the art of all times and peoples' in this context to establish his point. Jones, in turn, opened his study with a profusely illustrated chapter, 'The Ornaments of Savage Tribes', in which he argued that the urge to create, shared by all humans, savage and civilised, finds its purest expression in ornament. The 'evidence of the mind', in Jones' words, was more transparently discernible in the 'ornament

181 'Nicht mehr kann der Maßstab der "Schönheit" im Sinne der idealisierten Natur gelten, der Begriff Kunst scheint m.E. am bestimmtesten gefaßt, wenn man ihn bezeichnet als den gestalteten Ausdruck der Beziehung vom Ich zu Welt', Herbert Kuhn, 'Primitive Kunst', in Max Ebert (ed.), *Reallexikon der Vorgeschichte*, vol. 10, 1927–1928, pp. 264–92, here p. 269.
182 Pan, *Primitive Renaissance*, p. 98ff.
183 The literature on the subject is too abundant to recapitulate here. Some overviews include Susan Hiller (ed.), *The Myth of Primitivism: Perspectives on Art*, London: Routledge, 1991; Pan, *Primitive Renaissance*; Joshua I. Cohen, 'Fauve Masks: Rethinking Modern "Primitivist" Uses of African and Oceanic Art', *The Art Bulletin*, vol. 99 (2), 2017: 136–65; Jack D. Flam and Miriam Deutsch (eds), *Primitivism and Twentieth-Century Art: A Documentary History*, Berkeley: University of California Press, 2003. A theme issue of the *Journal of Art Historiography* edited by Wilfried van Damme and Raymond Corbey points to the increasing elasticity of the concept of the primitive and the ongoing scholarly engagement with it: *Journal of Art Historiography*, vol. 12 (June), 2015. The following account will focus on the conceptual entanglement between textual and visual sources and delineate the transcultural journeys of the concept, drawing on pertinent interventions in the field.
184 L.D. Ettlinger, 'German Expressionism and Primitive Art', *The Burlington Magazine*, vol. 110 (April), 1968: 191–201, here p. 192.

of a savage tribe than in the innumerable productions of a highly advanced civilisation. Individuality decreases in the ratio of the power of production'.[185] In addition to the writings of Semper and Jones, the survey texts by Grosse and Woermann, the latter being the director of the art gallery and print room in Dresden, were available and widely read among artists and students. Many of the examples discussed by Woermann in *Geschichte der Kunst aller Zeiten und Völker* came from the Dresden ethnological collection and it is clear that the colour plate illustrating the decorated roof beams from the island of Palau were seminal to Kirchner's discovery of the primitive, since elements of their design were adapted by him in the wall decorations of his Dresden studio and then reappeared several times as fragments in other illustrations.[186] What apparently attracted Kirchner and possibly other artists of the *Brücke* group to primitive art was less its formal quality and more the 'spirit' of the art, valorised as 'work from natural desire or instinct … free from restraint or rule', an idea Kirchner echoed when he wrote: 'The way of translating an experience into a work of art is free.'[187] His admiration was more a product of the kinship he imagined to exist between his own artistic impulses and methods and those of the South Sea islanders.

Studies of German Expressionism in the early twentieth century reveal primitivism as a double-edged resource, inevitably imbricated within the ambivalence that marked the avant-garde's position towards the question of modernity in a post-Second World War Germany. In the case of Emil Nolde (1867–1956), this ambivalence predates the war, as his engagement with primitivising idioms had informed his treatment of religious subjects during the first decade of the twentieth century. Nolde probably first encountered objects from Africa and Oceania at the Museum Folkwang – then located at Hagen – whose director, Karl Ernst Osthaus (1874–1921) had been assiduously building up a collection of non-European art during the years before the outbreak of war.[188] Nolde's painting of 1909, *Pentecost*,[189] conveys the religious ecstasy of the apostles by transforming their faces into radiant masks. Later works – based on 'copies' he made of objects in the Ethnological Collection in Berlin – veer towards still life, in which masks, now objects hung against a background, are animated by human emotions – laughter, surprise, slyness – to occupy an uncanny, liminal space between object and feeling. By replaying the cabinet style of the museum wherein artefacts were juxtaposed in crowded cases and rendered, in the artist's view, lifeless and cultureless, the painting appeared to convey a sense of life trapped in a modern European historicist apparatus. It provided an articulation in paint of his critique of ethnographic curating as a mode of 'killing

185 Owen Jones, *The Grammar of Ornament*, London: Quarich, 1910, pp. 13–18, here p. 14.
186 Ettlinger, 'German Expressionism': 195. Ettlinger also draws our attention to the reappearance of Palau motifs on decorative borders of subscriber cards and lists for members of the Brücke, which served as a logo of sorts, ibid., figs. A and B.
187 Cited in ibid.: 195.
188 Rainer Stamm, 'Weltkunst und Moderne', in: Hartwig Fischer and Uwe M. Schneede (eds), *'Das schönste Museum der Welt': Museum Folkwang bis 1933*, Göttingen: Steidl, 2010, pp. 27–46.
189 1909, Berlin, Nationalgalerie, reproduced in Jill Lloyd, *German Expressionism: Primitivism and Modernity*, New Haven: Yale University Press, 1991, fig. 204.

objects' through 'massive heaping'.[190] Nolde's invocation of the primitive throughout these years, which he idealised as an antidote to the fragmentations of modernity, led to the appropriation of the concept in the cause of a *völkisch* nationalism that he had embraced as part of his anti-modern critique. Primitive art, or *Urvölkerkunst* as the artist referred to it, lent itself to easy idealisation as a natural counter-image to the modern industrial world, art valorised as an outcome of an unmediated and organic relationship between producer and the object. The primitive thereby came to serve Nolde as a channel to connect with his own ideas about the rebirth of the German spirit and German art.[191] His combination of conservative subjects and the avant-garde style in which they were rendered is in itself symptomatic of the debates that rocked German modernism in the early twentieth century.[192]

The conceptualisation of the primitive took yet another turn, as Nolde continued his journey from the ethnological museum to the heart of German colonial enterprise that brought a direct encounter with the societies designated as primitive. In 1913–14, the artist took part in a major medical expedition sent by the German Colonial Office to investigate the causes of population decline in the German colony of New Guinea. The political economy of the colony was primarily dependent on German firms who employed indentured labour to produce plantation crops and mine phosphate for the world market. High death rates among the recruited labour population provided the impetus for racial and eugenic studies in the colony, following the anthropologist Richard Thurnwald's explanation that detailed racial knowledge would allow colonial powers 'to use every racial type according to its ability'.[193] Nolde's task on the expedition was to paint different racial types, as skin colour was recognised as a significant racial marker – though secondary to measurement – to allow differentiation between different groups of labourers: the inhabitants of the South Pacific, the Chinese, and the Black population. Primitivism thus shifted from the act of drawing

190 '[D]urch ihre Masse tötende Ansammlung', Emile Nolde, *Jahre de Kämpfe, 1902–1914*, Flensburg: Wolff, 1957, cited in Andrew Zimmerman, 'From Natural Science to Primitive Art: German New Guinea in Emil Nolde', in: Cordula Grewe (ed.), *Die Schau des Fremden: Ausstellungskonzepte zwischen Kunst, Kommerz und Wissenschaft*, Stuttgart: Franz Steiner Verlag, 2006, pp. 279–300, here p. 296.

191 Nolde's autobiography, *Jahre der Kämpfe*, written in the early 1930s and published in 1934, was about the years preceding the First World War, and put together on the basis of letters and diaries. Looking back on these years, he expresses his critique of the internationalist tendencies of the art world, objecting to its dependence on French models and its commercialism and opposed to this his own anti-materialist, spiritual and inner Germanic art. See Bernhard Fulda, 'Noldes Autobiografie: Das verkannte Genie im Kampf um die deutsche Kunst', in: Bernhard Fulda, Christian Ring and Aya Soyika (eds), *Emil Nolde: Eine Deutsche Legende*, 2 vols., Munich: Prestel Verlag, 2019, I, pp. 69–75. According to Lloyd, however, writing during the 1930s, a time when Nolde's nationalist affiliations and his commitment to a 'Germanic' mission of art became sharper and more explicit, it is open to what extent these ideas were projected backwards in time, see Lloyd, *German Expressionism*, p. 162. In 1912, Nolde had planned a book *Die Kunst der Urvölker* (The Art of the Primitives) that he however never completed; see Zimmerman, 'From Natural Science to Primitive Art', p. 296.

192 Discussed by Lloyd, *German Expressionism*, pp. 162–66.

193 'Nutzung jedes Rassenschlags nach seiner Leistungsfähigkeit', Richard Thurnwald, 'Die eingeborenen Arbeitskräfte im Südseeschutzgebiet', *Koloniale Rundschau*, vol. 2, 1910: 607–32, here 632. Also, Andrew Zimmerman, 'Primitive Art, Primitive Accumulation, and the Origin of the Work of Art in German New Guinea', *History of the Present*, vol. 1 (1), 2011: 5–30.

inspiration from local objects that would transform the modernist idiom, to the production of racial knowledge about the Indigenous peoples who became the objects of painting. The knowledge about human types presented in Nolde's watercolours draws primarily on colour rather than line, shape, or dimension – realism therefore re-entered the representation of the primitive. The artist frequently resorted to the use of complementary colours to emphasise a particular aspect of skin tone – for instance, he often used green, either as background or in details of clothing or jewellery to highlight the reddish tones of a subject's skin.[194] The subjects of Nolde's paintings were for the most part labourers – contracted or imprisoned – transported to New Guinea for projects of the colonial government; his account of the expedition records his discomfort with the brutality of colonial practices he witnessed, lamenting the damage colonialism caused to Indigenous societies. He valorised his painting (comparing it to that of Gauguin) as a compensation of sorts, a 'spiritual deed' that gave expression to the 'inexhaustible richness of primitive natural life', even as this 'deed' participated in the same colonial project.[195] In the words of Andrew Zimmerman, Nolde's 'primitive art' and the colonial project of 'primitive accumulation' were intrinsically connected. In the economic realm the primitive functioned as a 'space traversed by racial and ethnic divisions'.[196] For the artist, works of art formed a domain where 'historical truth' was intended to be made visible, where art itself was endowed with the potential of founding a world in which new forms of labour could be instituted. The primitive, in turn, was transformed into a mystical attribute of that art.

The denial of history or 'coevalness', to draw from Johannes Fabian,[197] to those Indigenous societies where the primitive was located, emerged as a shared ideological premise of artistic primitivism across its diverse articulations. The indentured workers portrayed by Nolde, for instance, had long been extracted from the *Urzustand* ascribed to them and harnessed to colonialism's capitalist modernity, in the service of which they formed a dislocated, globally mobile force that laboured in plantations, mines, and docks. In Nolde's perception, however, they comprised – as opposed to the more Europeanised groups in New Guinea's populace he had despised – the 'authentically primitive', for like many other Europeans, he read the poverty and abjection caused by colonialism as a residue of a precolonial condition.[198] An

---

194 Reproductions in Emil Nolde, *Welt und Heimat: Die Südseereise 1913–1918, geschrieben 1936*, Cologne: Dumont, 1965, p. 54; Lloyd, *German Expressionism*, figs. 269–70, and Zimmerman, 'Primitive Art', figs. 1–4.

195 In his travel diaries Nolde wrote: 'Das Kolonisieren ist eine brutale Angelegenheit. … Wenn, von den farbigen Eingeborenen ausgesehen, eine Kolonialgeschichte einmal geschrieben wird, dann dürfen wir weißen Europäer uns verschämt in Höhlen verkriechen.' And further: 'Gar keinen anderen bildenden Künstler weiß ich, außer Gauguin und mir selbst, der aus der unendlichen Fülle des Urnaturlebens Bleibendes brachte. Und was haben z.B. die Engländer in ihren großen vielartigen Kolonien an Urwesen vernichtet für immer, ohne meines Wissens irgendeine geistige Tat vollführt zu haben, welche etwas die Zerstörung entschuldigen könne.' Nolde, *Welt und Heimat*, pp.57–58, 89.

196 Zimmerman, 'Primitive Art': 25.

197 Johannes Fabian, *Time and the Other: How Anthropology Makes its Object*: New York, Columbia University Press, 1983.

198 Nolde, *Welt und Heimat*, p. 93.

ahistorical and pristine condition was equally associated with particular objects, especially masks and statues – a material category often brought together under the label of 'fetish' – held to have been catalytic in releasing those energies that then effected a radical breakthrough in the language of form. Such ascriptions figure in a central way within foundation myths of modernist creativity. One of art history's most widely disseminated legends relates to Picasso's painting *Les Demoiselles d'Avignon*, completed in 1907, that has come to stand par excellence for the canonical breakthrough achieved by Western modernism. In 1937, thirty years after the completion of the work, Picasso is said to have described to André Malraux his uncanny experience during a visit to the Trocadéro museum on a Sunday afternoon in June 1907: the epiphany following his encounter with 'fetishes … [those] magic things' that unleashed his creativity. The *Demoiselles d'Avignon*, he claimed, 'must have come to me that very day'.[199] The conversation was published only in 1974, following Malraux's death and was reprinted and canonised by Rubin during the MoMA exhibition of 1984 as a 'turning point' in the artist's production and the history of modernism as such.[200] The myth resurfaced in 2017 – critical research during the intervening years notwithstanding – in the exhibition *Picasso primitif* curated by Yves Le Fur at the Musée du Quai Branly in Paris; the visitors to the exhibition were offered a two minute-long montage of digitised archival photographs of the old ethnographic galleries at the Trocadéro, played across a concave wall, to enable them to simulate the artist's visit.[201] While it has been long known that by the summer of 1907 work on the *Demoiselles* was well under way, with the artist having made several preparatory sketches, critiques of the MoMA show additionally pointed out that the large number of African objects chosen by Rubin for the exhibition, to argue for their striking formal resemblance to Picasso's art, had mostly entered European collections some decades later.[202]

A more productive procedure than identifying purely morphological similarities between works selected without verifying their historical trajectories, might be to uncover the paths through which knowledge about the objects and their producers and collectors actually travelled. The authorities – anthropologists, art historians, curators, or artists – who read these objects as articulations of a mystical, preconscious mentality depended in turn for their knowledge on another group of border crossers or cultural brokers, such as missionaries or colonial administrators located in Africa – or ethnologists such as Leo Frobenius (1873–1938) – with whom they were in contact and whose information carried the authority of being first-hand.[203] The attitudes of these different actors to colonial practices might have varied, in that some of these information brokers had adopted critical stances to overt acts

---

199 André Malraux, *Picasso's Mask*, London: Macdonald and Jane's Publishers, 1976, pp. 10–11.
200 Rubin, *'Primitivism' in 20th Century Art*, vol. 1, 254–55.
201 *Picasso primitif* curated by Yves le Fur, Paris, Musée du Quai Branly, 28 March – 23 July 2017. Catalogue Yves Le Fur (ed.), *Picasso primitif*, Paris: Flammarion, 2017.
202 Clifford, 'Histories of the Tribal and Modern'; Joshua I. Cohen, 'Picasso and Primitive Art: Paris, Kansas City and Montreal', *The Burlington Magazine*, vol. 159 (November), 2017: 944–45.
203 See Suzanne Marchand, 'Leo Frobenius and the Revolt Against the West', *Journal of Contemporary History* 32 (2), 1997: 153–70; Gikandi, 'Picasso, Africa': 475–76.

of colonial appropriation or violence, as we saw in the case of Nolde, yet they did so without questioning the epistemological foundations of the knowledge they were complicit in generating. What they shared in common was the concern to overlook the transformative effects of colonialism on the societies through which they travelled. More recently, Suzanne Preston Blier's excavation of the sources of Picasso's famous painting, even as it endorses the view that Picasso was attracted to African figures because of their magical power, proposes that he drew primarily upon illustrations from Leo Frobenius' *Die Masken und Geheimbünde Afrikas* while seeking models for his work. In other words, rather than the figures at Trocadéro, it was the coloured drawings of African masks based on photographs Frobenius took during his travels in west and central Africa that were the principal pictorial source for the *Demoiselles*.[204] In the course of his investigations Frobenius, too, was determined to search for that which was still untouched by the 'foreign'; from here ensued narratives about the native mind, a mentality that was outside of rationality, entrenched in myth. The fetish came to serve as a code to access the musealised object in Western collections, as its meanings and uses disseminated and were picked up by academic anthropology, psychology, and world art history.[205] Such interweaving of bodies of knowledge is seminal to the production and subsequent readings of art works.

Coevalness can now be restored to the narrative of modernism, also by drawing on research of scholars – especially of African art – who have explored the histories of the works considered formative for European modernists and showed them to be equally embodied contemporaneous African responses to colonial modernity. While information brokers of the early twentieth century, like those mentioned above, set out to search for those aspects of primitive cultures that could be construed as immemorial or unchanging, recent research shows the vast numbers of objects that we associate with modernism to have in fact been participants within local production systems, and intended primarily though not exclusively for European buyers. The history of sculptural objects can be traced to an early modernity that predated colonialism: artistic creativity flourished in the regions along Africa's Atlantic coast in the wake of trade and urbanisation, in turn creating the syncretic spaces conducive to artistic production.[206] Colonial relationships accelerated these processes by drawing the regions within the vortex of an industrialised global economy that meant on the one hand larger and more distant markets, and on the other more intensified cultural encounters locally. Merchants who placed orders in the colonies – mainly French and Belgian – in turn participated in intricate commercialised collection networks that connected distant localities with art dealers and gallerists in Europe, and from there to New York in the first two decades of the twentieth century. Segments of what is a long and tortuous story involving collectors, dealers, theoreticians, and critics were narrated by Yaëlle Biro in the exhibition

---

204 Suzanne Preston Blier, *Picasso's Demoiselles: The Untold Origins of a Modern Masterpiece*, Durham, NC: Duke University Press, 2019, pp. 111–16.

205 See Gabriele Genge (ed.), *Art History and Fetishism Abroad: Global Shiftings in Media and Methods*, Bielefeld: Transcript Verlag, 2014.

206 Cohen, *The 'Black Art' Renaissance*, p. 6.

African Art: New York and the Avant-Garde at the Metropolitan Museum of Art (2013–14). Galleries such as Alfred Stieglitz 291 and Marius de Zayas' Modern Gallery were among the first to build on the trade in African art as early as 1914, after the locus of trade had shifted from Paris to New York following the outbreak of war.[207] Piecing this material together with related research by scholars of African art makes it possible to affirm that so much of what was termed primitive art was commissioned and produced in the colonies during the early twentieth century for Western markets, whose thirst for it appeared unquenchable.[208] Indeed, as Zoë Strother drawing on Fabian points out, commodification of sculpted objects within the African colonies, was a prerequisite of collecting rather than its consequence. Colonial transformation in the Central African regions during the early twentieth century brought with it the professionalisation of sculpture – Frobenius was among the earliest to sneeringly remark that the Black person found carving a more 'pleasant' activity than other forms of forced labour, such as tapping rubber.[209] The integration of African sculpture within the global market however also meant assigning Western values to the objects, which in the case of masks, statues, and other works meant rendering them nameless and timeless, often helped on by artificial ageing induced by middlemen. It was only on the presumption that a work, bearing the label 'African mask', emanated from a precolonial, tribal past and was a product, not of an individual artist's hand, but born out of a sense of collective self, that it could be situated into the category of the primitive and a corresponding market value be assigned to it. In this art world, in the words of Strother, 'it is the *buyer* who replaces the artist as visionary, who is able … to recognize aesthetic value in the unassuming artifact'.[210]

The charge of epistemic violence levied against the curators of the MoMA exhibition of 1984, for having imposed 'modernist' categories of 'art' and the individual artist onto cultures for which art presumably did not exist as a distinct category, and in which formal change could therefore not be credited principally to individual artists,[211] can thus be turned on its head. For their part, Rubin or Varnedoe, too, failed to acknowledge the status of works from Africa or Oceania as coeval, modern works; rather, they read the aesthetic-cum-affective

---

207 Elena Martínez-Jacquet (ed.), *African Art, New York and the Avant-garde* (special issue *Tribal Art Magazine*), 2012. See also Yaëlle Biro, 'Avant Charles Ratton: Commerce et diffusion des arts africains aux années 1920', in: Sophie Laporte (ed.), *Charles Ratton: L'invention des arts 'primitifs'*, Paris: Editions Skira, 2013, pp. 42–57. Also Yaëlle Biro, *Fabriquer le regard: Marchands, réseaux et objets d'art africains à l'aube du XXème siècle*, Dijon: Les presses du réel, 2018. A large number of the objects on display in the section on primitivism in the exhibition *Icônes d'art modern: La collection Chtchoukine* (Fondation Louis Vuitton, Paris, October 22, 2016–March 5, 2017), featuring the collection of the Russian textile magnate and passionate collector of modernist art Sergei Stchoukhine, were also produced in the twentieth century. Among the dealers who supplied Stchoukhine his works was Joseph Brummer, proprietor of Maison Brummer in Paris (1908–1914) that also spread his activities to the United States.
208 Zoë S. Strother, *Inventing Masks: Agency and History in the Art of Central Pende*, Chicago: University of Chicago Press, 1997; Zoë S. Strother, 'Gabama a Gingungu and the Secret History of Twentieth-Century Art', *African Arts*, vol. 32 (1), 1999: 18–31; Sidney L. Kasfir, *African Art and the Colonial Encounter: Inventing a Global Commodity*, Bloomington: Indiana University Press, 2007.
209 Cited in Strother, 'Gabama a Gingungu': 30.
210 Ibid.: 31 (italics in original).
211 This was among the criticisms made by McEvilley, 'Doctor Lawyer Indian Chief', pp. 43–45.

power of the 'tribal' objects as a proof of the artistic achievement of modernist masters.[212] In effect, both the exhibition and its numerous critics were complicit in inventing the concept of the primitive by an act of suppressing the modernity of African art already intertwined with that of the West. European artists, in turn, who drew on the visual grammars of the so-called primitive arts, unknowingly assimilated the modernity of those grammars to infuse vigour into Western modernism. The conceptual trajectory of primitivism weaves various elements of its story into a single fabric of modernity and commodification. Rather than a story of survivals of a disappearing past crying to be salvaged, we have an account of global actors in a shared and entangled historical present.

Modernist art and art history, to recapitulate, were two faces of the same coin, which crossed many borders as they migrated across the globe. This included travelling to those sites beyond the modern West that were cast as locations of the primitive or placed on different stages of the civilisational *scala*. If modernity as a connecting label implies an equally shared temporal principle by which alterity, whatever its location and texture, can be translated into the absence of coevalness, it becomes important to unpack the possibilities and paths of transculturation built into different articulations of the modern and its relation to the primitive. Different stories can be told about a reconfigured primitivism; these draw attention to the potential of the concept to be transformed into a resource, but also to the deep epistemic ambivalence that surfaces within acts seeking to return coevalness to the concept. Ruth Phillips has argued that the double-edged quality of modernism as a global movement makes it necessary to distinguish between a 'negative sociological primitivism' advanced by cultural evolutionists, often in complicity with colonialism, and a 'positive aesthetic primitivism' that, because it looks to the arts of non-Western people for aesthetic inspiration, could be reclaimed as heritage by those peoples to whose ancestral traditions the arts belonged. In an investigation of Indigenous societies in North America, Australia, and New Zealand, where modernist experiments unfolded through encounters of local societies with intellectuals who had fled Central Europe under Nazi rule, Phillips draws our attention to a dynamic that forced open 'certain key contradictions embedded within European aesthetic primitivism', in the end overturning its asymmetries.[213] Investigations of other regions – Africa or South Asia – show different processes at work, revealing the potential of the concept to be enabling and emancipating, alternatively as reproducing the power structures built into it.

Scholars of African modernism, when telling the story of European engagement with African art, itself predicated on the latter's nascent modernity, have continued the narrative further to configure it as a global story by adding fresh layers to it. In the 1920s and 1930s, Paris had become a centre of Black activism and critical discourse, which had brought forth the *Négritude* movement among a French speaking African diasporic intelligentsia. By co-opting canonical figures of modernist art, notably Picasso, into the repertoire of an emergent African

212 Rubin, 'Modernist Primitivism. An Introduction', in: *'Primitivism' in 20th Century Art*, vol. 1, pp. 1–81.
213 Ruth B. Phillips, 'Aesthetic Primitivism Revisited: The Global Diaspora of "Primitive" Art and the Rise of Indigenous Modernisms', *Journal of Art Historiography*, vol. 12 (June), 2015: 1–25, quotes 2, 8.

modernism, leading personalities such as Léopold Senghor (1906–2001) sought a 'worldly positioning' for African heritage as well as an opportunity to unmoor tradition from any neatly delimited regional or ethnic sphere.[214] In several newly independent nations across the continent, modernist art practices gained remarkable support from young national governments; at the same time artists and writers continued to dialogue with a number of international currents – these included, in addition to *Négritude*'s humanism, the more radical, critical theory of Frantz Fanon and the anticolonial internationalism of French avant-gardes such as the Surrealists. By bringing Indigenous art and modernist practice within an expansive pan-African dynamic, a modernism that was considered autochthonous and at the same time international allowed formerly colonised peoples to recover and reorganise the continent's material culture into a rich visual archive. For artists and art critics of the Harlem Renaissance, or for the sculptor Ernest Mancoba (1904–2002), the appropriations of the European avant-garde pointed – in an entirely non-teleological manner – to a set of 'formal and social possibilities associated with art making' that crystallised into ideas and practices delinked from racial determinism.[215] The 'black art' movement in Cohen's conceptualisation emerged as a framework of solidarity, while 'prompting the West to reckon with its cultural debts'.[216] As a reconfigured notion, so-designated Black art was able to supplant many of the assumptions around 'primitive art' and instead open a discursive space for a non-centric global modernism.

Turning to South Asia, also caught in the throes of modernity with all its paradoxical tensions, the transcultural conceptual trajectory of the primitive has to be tracked in conjunction with the contradictions of a decolonising national formation. Partha Mitter has narrated a story of the ironic appropriation of primitivism by local actors and institutions on the Indian subcontinent who sought to make the primordial civilisational attributes of the concept serve as a critique of colonialism. Building on the analysis of David Pan, Mitter has argued that 'the Indian discourse of Primitivism' could effectively turn the notion on its head, to then undermine the foundations of 'Western progress'.[217] Mitter discusses several variants of the primitive – these include artists, such as Amrita Sher-Gil (1913–1941), statesmen like Gandhi, and institutions such as Rabindranath Tagore's university at Santiniketan – in what ends up as a romanticised, somewhat overly accommodating use of the concept. The argument proffered is that adopting the idea of the primitive as a mode of civilisational critique of the modern West enabled it to function as an act of resistance to colonialism, an appealing position echoed by Mercer.[218] It has also been endorsed by Ruth Phillips, who uses this reading as a lens to examine the unfolding of 'Indigenous Modernisms'.[219] In the following analysis that focuses on one

214 Cohen, *The 'Black Art' Renaissance*, p. 3; Harney, *In Senghor's Shadow*; Belting and Buddensieg, *Ein Afrikaner in Paris*; Elizabeth Harney, 'The Densities of Modernism', *South Atlantic Quarterly*, vol. 109 (3), 2010: 475–503. The following sketch summarizes some of this research.
215 Cohen, *The 'Black Art' Renaissance*, pp. 192–94; also, Christian Kravagna, 'Encounters with Masks: Counter-Primitivism in 20th Century Black Art', in: Genge (ed.), *Art History and Fetishism*, pp. 189–204.
216 Cohen, *The 'Black Art' Renaissance*, pp. 191–95.
217 Mitter, *The Triumph of Modernism*, pp. 29–35.
218 Mercer (ed.), *Cosmopolitan Modernisms*, p. 9.
219 Phillips, 'Aesthetic Primitivism Revisited'.

of the iconic modernist art works discussed by Mitter and others, *Santhal Family* (Plate 3.5) by the artist Ram Kinkar Baij (1906–1980), and said to represent a 'subaltern' primitive consciousness, I will endeavour to unpack some of the unresolved dilemmas that inhere in such an approach. A more fine-tuned method indebted to transcultural conceptual analysis, which allows us to investigate the morphologies of relationships and their often paradoxical or contradictory workings, can suggest further possibilities of reconfiguring a concept beyond artistic intentionality, also eschewing the poles of colonial pejoration and subaltern resistance. Instead, I argue, a transcultured primitivism within the South Asian context of colonialism and nation-building is caught in a mode of ambivalent reproduction.

For Mitter, any artist or institution who sought the 'rural as refuge' qualified for the epithet of primitive; Santiniketan, therefore, the site of the university, Visva Bharati, created by Rabindranath Tagore, and its art school, Kala Bhawan, founded in 1919, became in Mitter's words a location of 'environmental primitivism'.[220] Located on a rural stretch, on extensive lands originally owned by Tagore's grandfather, the wealthy entrepreneur Dwarkanath Tagore, the university and its art school were conceived as a locus of cultural resurgence wherein art and art education played a central part. Art as it was practised at Santiniketan sought a robust relationship to the larger life surrounding it – to nature, rural communities, and their creative skills brought together under the label of 'craft'. The quest for a non-historicist, yet autochthonous art brought forth a modernism based on a sense of place and a commitment to local experiential reality, a 'contextual' yet non-insular modernism as it has been famously described.[221] During these years of anti-colonial fervour coupled with the absence of modern amenities, the cosmopolitanism of Santiniketan lay, according to Siva Kumar, in its intellectual pursuits rather than its lifestyle.[222] A few small buildings and large open spaces marked its expanse. It was here that the sculptor Ram Kinkar Baij (often referred to as Ram Kinkar) began to fill the campus grounds with on-site sculptures, innovative in their subjects and highly personal in their language, and therefore considered a radical departure from the classical forms of sculpture within the Indian subcontinent.

Ram Kinkar, originally from a low-caste peasant background, came to Kala Bhawan in 1925, at a juncture where the art school had – thanks to the contribution of Kramrisch (discussed above) as well as the creation of a photo archive of world art – turned from its earlier pan-Asian orientation towards interacting with modernist currents from other parts of the world, especially Europe. His search for a modernist sculptural language beyond Indic historical styles and not dependent on traditional structures of patronage, led him to many formal sources – Auguste Rodin (1890–1917) mediated through the work of Antoine Bourdelle (1861–1929), who in turn had been a teacher of Marguerite Milward (1873–1953), a visiting artist at Santiniketan; in addition, the work of German sculptors such as Wilhelm Lehmbruck (1881–1919)

---

220 Mitter, *The Triumph of Modernism*, p. 78.
221 R. Siva Kumar, *Santiniketan: The Making of a Contextual Modernism*, New Delhi: National Gallery of Modern Art, 1997.
222 R. Siva Kumar, 'Shantiniketan: A World University', p. 111.

and Ernst Barlach (1870–1938), coupled with Soviet-style Socialist Realism, all left their mark on the artist's exploration of the labouring human body. Years of hardship under colonialism following from bonded labour, famine, and war, directed Ram Kinkar's creativity to an increasingly politicised terrain. At the same time his interaction with Marguerite Milward, who initiated him into post-Rodinesque sculpture, is likely to have introduced Ram Kinkar to an anthropological perspective on peoples and objects. In addition to her interactions with the Santiniketan art world, Milward was closely associated with contemporary anthropologists, above all Verrier Elwin.[223] Between 1935 and 1938, she journeyed through the Indian subcontinent making sketches and sculptures of the heads of men and women for a collection of 'ethnic types'. These works, praised during their time for their accuracy as anthropological data, occupy the interstices of anthropology and art, ethnography and portraiture.[224] The gaze Ram Kinkar brought on to peoples such as the Santhals was therefore infused with a mix of modernist artistic and ethnographic sensibility.

The Santhals, the subject of the artist's monumental sculpture of 1938, *Santhal Family*, were a tribal group, inhabitants of the East Indian regions of Bihar and Bengal contiguous to the Nepal border. Under the administration of the East India Company, the Santhals were physically and territorially segregated and fenced in so that they could no longer interact directly with other sections of Indian society – their autarky made them fit post facto the classification in later colonial censuses as 'scheduled tribes'.[225] In the second half of the nineteenth century, English and Norwegian missionaries studied their language and produced ethnographic accounts of their customs and objects, many of which have now been musealised in collections across the world. In 1855, the Santhals rebelled against colonial exploitative modes of revenue extortion and practices such as bonded labour, in which Bengali moneylenders and upper caste Hindu landowners – *zamindars* – were complicit. The rebellion (*hul*), a dramatic event, became part of not only Santhal lore, but also of Bengali popular traditions and innumerable history books and literary accounts.[226] The revolt was brutally suppressed by the Company and martial law imposed on the entire tribal belt. English accounts criminalised it as an uprising of primitive, pre-civilisational violence: a print in the *Illustrated London News* showing 600 Santhals attacking a small group of colonial sepoys carries all the tropes of a primitivist rendering (fig. 2). Within the colonised society too, inscribing the *hul* into history books involved a particular mode of representation: to

---

223 See Ramachandra Guha, *Savaging the Civilized: Verrier Elwin, His Tribals and India*, Chicago: University of Chicago Press, 1999, pp. 101–102.

224 Mark J. Elliott, 'Sculptural Biographies in an Anthropological Collection: Mrs Milward's Indian "Types"', in: Kate Hill (ed.), *Museums and Biographies: Stories, Objects, Identities*, Woodbridge: Boydell Press, 2012, pp. 215–28.

225 Daniel J. Rycroft, *Representing Rebellion: Visual Aspects of Counter-Insurgency in Colonial India*, New Delhi: Oxford University Press, 2006; Daniel J. Rycroft, 'Santalism: Reconfiguring the Santal in Indian Art and Politics', *The Indian Historical Review*, vol. 33 (1), 2006: 150–74; Prathama Banerjee, *Politics of Time: 'Primitives' and History-Writing in Colonial Society*, New Delhi: Oxford University Press, 2006, pp. 14–15.

226 Banerjee, *Politics of Time*, Chapter 4.

THE ILLUSTRATED LONDON NEWS

196   [Feb. 23, 1856.

THE SANTHAL INSURRECTION.

ATTACK BY 600 SANTHALS UPON A PARTY OF 50 SEPOYS, 40TH REGIMENT NATIVE INFANTRY.

territory, had settled down, cleared away the forest, and cultivated the land.

The migration commenced about 1830; and in 1838, their numbers attracting the notice of Government, an officer was appointed to superintend their movements, to watch their interests, to induce them to clear away the forests in the Bhangulpoor District, and eventually to collect the land tax exacted from them as well as from their neighbours, the Zemindars.

In July last intelligence reached the quiet little station of Bhangulpoor that a band of armed Santhals had decapitated a police-officer in the hills; had wounded several policemen; and were plundering the neighbouring villages. The intelligence, delivered with every semblance of truth, and backed by most minute circumstantial and corroborative evidence, was disbelieved, from the simple fact that the Santhals had up to that moment borne the character of being the most truthful, faithful, gentle, and harmless race in India. Rapid and repeated messages, however, pouring in one after the other, soon confirmed the truth of the first report; and it was too soon discovered that this race of men, naturally the most cowardly and harmless of the human race, were all of a sudden turned into the cruelest, boldest, and most bloodthirsty wretches that ever disgraced the face of the earth. Such a transition and effect was too sudden not to have some deep-seated cause, which I will describe hereafter. In the mean time troops were sent against them; but these troops, being composed of the natives of a tribe very similar to themselves, they fled upon the first attack of the Santhals. Regular troops were then poured in upon all sides; and, after some fighting and scouring the jungles, hanging the rebels, and capturing the chiefs, we may hope that the matter is at an end, and that the Santhals have been taught a lesson they will never forget.

The Portrait of Seedhoo Manghee, the chief and miserable origin of the insurrection, was taken whilst he was in prison at Bhaugulpoor, immediately after his capture. He is a short, thin, active little fellow, very unlike a Santhal in appearance. He exulted over his performances, and spoke unreservedly about all he had done. He gloried in the orders he had given for numerous executions of Zemindars, police officials, and others; in the numerous villages he had plundered and then burnt, and in the general devastation and misery he had caused; he declared that he was now a great man—that his name was well known, even all the way down to the banks of the Damoodah river, an insignificant stream seventy miles from the scene of his atrocities. Upon being confronted with an official—I believe in the service of a Zemindar—Seedhoo exclaimed "What! you here? Why, I ordered your execution ten days ago!"

(Continued on page 200.)

2   The Santhal Rebellion, *Illustrated London News*, 1856

paraphrase Prathama Banerjee, the act of narration transformed an unprecedented and contingent act into a 'causated' event, reconstituting it within a structure of historicist knowledge.[227] For the literate colonised, history writing – the notion of historicity – was the path towards constituting themselves as a modern nation with a narrative of its unique civilisational achievements. Within this trajectory, modern technologies of producing the historical were by their temporal logic dependent on the timeless, that which was resistant to modern history, a logic that replicated itself through the production of what Banerjee calls the 'primitive within'.[228] At the same time, however, the proximity of such 'real-life primitives', for instance the Santhal tribes, required their assimilation within a national community without having to take recourse to a colonial anthropological mode.

Tagore's Santiniketan, where members of a scholarly elite assumed the mantle of pedagogical leadership, was configured as a site of cultural renewal from within a rural setting; it

227 Ibid., p. 20.
228 Ibid.

was the locus of an immediate encounter with the Santhals, who in the decades following the *hul* were drawn into a market economy as agricultural labourers or mill workers. Identified as the 'intrepid subaltern from Santiniketan',[229] Ram Kinkar's humble, rural background is invariably invoked to sustain accounts of the cultural power of his work: the artist has been cast as 'uniquely positioned' to represent this marginal group without having to face 'the charge of exoticising his subject'.[230] The sculptural ensemble *Santhal Family* has thereby been singled out as a capacious modernist experiment built on a left-leaning humanist, empathetic, non-hierarchical relationship with dispossessed subjects for whom the artist made place within the politicised genre of public statuary.[231] Kapur reads the work as embodying 'radical affect' that imparts to the oppressed and marginal an iconic presence within the national.[232] For Ram Kinkar, the primitive, instead of being distant and unseen, was indeed close at hand, allowing responsible appropriation. The larger than life-size ensemble portrays a family on the move – a peasant couple with two children and a dog, companionably strutting along the side. The young woman holds one child against the left flank of her body, supported by her arm, while the second child, sitting on the front basket of the weighing scales balanced by the man on his shoulder, peeps out from between its bamboo poles. The minimal accessories – the weighing scale, a basket poised on the woman's head with a rolled mat on top – suggest a ritual of rural communities who carry agricultural produce to sell at the market in exchange for money to buy other basic commodities. The erect bodies of the two adults move purposefully forward in a rhythmic, synchronised movement, looking into the distance with an air of quiet resolve (fig. 3). They are portrayed heading in a western direction – towards sunset and home. A similar poetically charged empathy pervades another work of the same year, *Mill Call* (1938), also on the campus grounds, that catches the lightning movement and energy of two female figures running to work at the mill on hearing the call of the siren. Both works are an example of the artist's exploration of a modernist sculptural vocabulary as well as his use of particular materials that give the work its rough, corrosive texture. Ram Kinkar chose a cement-concrete for all his sculptures, which he produced out of locally available lateritic granules and gravel from degraded lands, mixed with just enough cement to bind the mix and give the surface a granular feel. To attain the complexity of the ensemble, he first created a skeleton of iron pipes and steel wire, over which he cast fistfuls of the mixture, smoothing and shaping the whole while it was in the process of drying.

On one level, Ram Kinkar Baij's engagement with the Santhals, seen as confronting the Western discourse of the primitive, can be read against that discourse in the light of his palpable moves to bring back coevalness to the concept. References to the market, to industry, to the modern temporal rhythms of workers' shifts in mills, all work to locate his subjects

229 Kapur, *When Was Modernism*, p. 271.

230 Grant Watson, 'Introduction', in: Anshuman Dasgupta (ed.), *Santhal Family: Positions around an Indian Sculpture*, Antwerp: MUKHA, 2009, pp. 3–7, here p. 3.

231 Mitter, *The Triumph of Modernism*, p. 98; R. Siva Kumar, 'Ram Kinkar Baij and Modernism's Dual Commitments', in: Dasgupta (ed.), *Santhal Family*, pp. 14–19; Rycroft, 'Santalism', p. 153.

232 Kapur, *When Was Modernism*, p. 342.

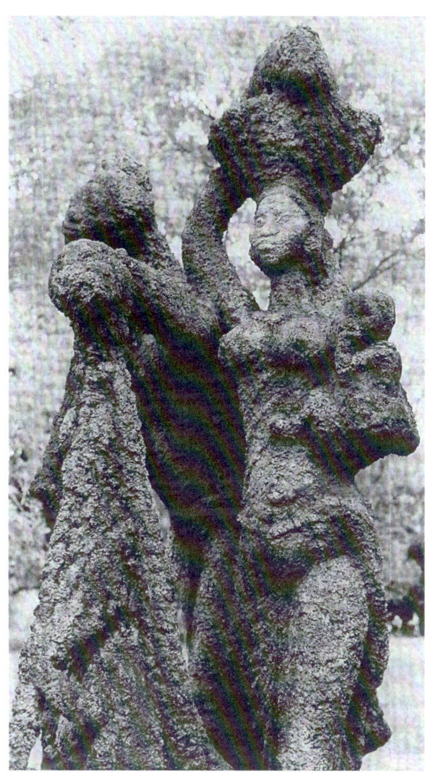

3   Ram Kinkar Baij, *Santhal Family*,
sculpture, 1938, detail

in historical and industrial time and thereby undo the colonial stigmatisation of this group by freeing it of threatening alterity. And yet, the recourse to history asks for the work to be resituated, beyond the intentionality of the individual artist, within the paradoxes of national formation and the claim to modernity. Tropes such as mobile labour and a money economy enabled an imagination of disenfranchised groups such as the Santhals as spatially integrated within the nation. At the same time, history – the path through which the colonised could reclaim for themselves the modernity denied to them by colonialism – depended on a domain of knowledge that could be conceived of as distinct from and incommensurable with 'god' or the 'supernatural' or contingent, attributes ascribed to those non-contemporaneous peoples – peasants, tribals – who made up the national fabric.[233] Referring to the different ways of knowing the historical happenings surrounding the Santhal uprising, Chakrabarty underlines such difference as a condition of possibility for definitions of the modern subject.[234] Art as a domain of historical knowledge partook of a narrative of national history, requiring

233 Dipesh Chakrabarty, 'Minority Histories, Subaltern Pasts', in: *Provincializing Europe: Postcolonial Thought and Historical Difference*, Princeton: Princeton University Press, 2000, pp. 97–113, here 103. Also, Banerjee, *Politics of Time*, who builds on this argument.
234 Chakrabarty, 'Minority Histories, Subaltern Pasts', p. 113.

constant negotiation with the obstinate presence of the 'primitive within'. Art production and the person of the artist hinged on the principle of representational knowledge that acquired unprecedented predominance in modernity. A product of colonial modernity, the artist aspired to become a member of a literate elite at a remove from subalternity; his status was now defined by creativity, as one who brings his gaze to the objects that are transformed into art. For all the sympathies that Ram Kinkar Baij experienced towards his subjects, who were also the objects of representations, and the intention to infuse temporal coevalness into the concept of the primitive notwithstanding, otherness and distance remained inherent to a national project through the issues of class and history. In Tagore's Santiniketan, a nationalist cultural elite, by prescribing that the artist eschews a demeaning closeness to the market, further underlined the vitality of art and the artist to a civilisational project.

In an article published in 1965, a student of Ram Kinkar Baij, the artist K. G. Subramanyan used the term 'primitive' to refer to the predicament of the modern artist for whom 'old myths' and 'anthropocentric religious systems' no longer served the present. The postcolonial artist's search for a language within an independent nation made him, in Subramanyan's words 'the primitive[s] of a new age'.[235] For Subramanyan the new primitivism meant a return to tradition while revitalising it in a fresh symbiosis, by using it as a wedge to overcome colonial taxonomies imposed on a living aesthetic system.[236] In postcolonial India of the 1960s and 1970s, primitivism came to be harnessed to the articulation of cultural nationalism. Steered by the state towards a form of multiculturalism that celebrates difference by aestheticising it, it resulted in a frequent showcasing of cultural diversity through festivals, costumes, music, cuisine, and, not least, art. One of the issues modern artists faced in a young postcolonial nation was the expectation that their art make their cultural identity visible on different scales – national as well as belonging to a particular linguistic or caste group: that their art provide the visible 'evidence' of that society's multiculturalism. (This aspect is discussed in the following chapter.) As a key modernist concept, the primitive retained its resilience owing to its potential to serve different agendas. When replicated and deployed in the service of the nation, it actively participated in the exoticisation and musealisation of identities – folk, tribal, or minority cultures – which were also hierarchies in relation to the mainstream national. Within art history, as it is practised across the globe, the concept has proved useful through its ability to buttress the modernist narrative that places the individual artist at the pinnacle of a productive process – a process which unfolds through 'exorcising' the primitive, that radical, threatening otherness through the artist's creative power. Finally, it contributes to reinforcing art history's epistemic premises that link the notion of style to a single region, stabilise the mobility of objects and forms and locate the artist's work in a space that detaches it from all transcultural referentiality. This appears to be a cornerstone of primitivism's conceptual staying power.

235 K. G. Subramanyan, 'The Artist on Art', *Lalit Kala Contemporary*, vol. 3, 1965: 13–15, here 13.
236 Discussed in Khullar, *Worldy Affiliations*, Chapter 4.

CHAPTER FOUR
BEYOND BACKWATER ARCADIAS
Globalised Locality and Contemporary Art Practice

'Contemporaneity, the sensation of being in a time together … is the tug we feel when our time pulls at us. But sometimes one has the sense of a paradoxically asynchronous contemporaneity – a strange tug of more than one time and place – as if an accumulation or thickening of our attachments to different times and spaces were manifesting itself in the form of some unique geological oddity, a richly striated cross section of a rock, sometimes sharp, sometimes blurred, marked by the passage of many epochs.' – Raqs Media Collective[1]

The widespread use of the term 'contemporary' to describe the art of the day seems at first glance self-evident, and yet the past three decades have produced scores of discussions, publications, questionnaires, all striving to pin down the historicity and dynamics of what has emerged as a slippery signifier.[2] Finding a conceptual frame adequate to contain the unmanageable volume of works treated as contemporary art, and dispersed over a field that is de-centred, networked, and multi-local, is particularly challenging for an art historical scholarship wedded to fixed geographical and temporal units that have been organised along the axis of evolving 'styles'. The vitality of innumerable histories in constant and simultaneous translation continues to be perceived as both a 'cacaphonic mess'[3] as well as an expression of a fresh and expansive dynamism. Over the years, a consensus appears to have been formed

<hr>

1   Raqs Media Collective, 'Nowhere and Elsewhere', in: Julieta Aranda, Brian K. Wood and Anthony Vidokle (eds), *What Is Contemporary Art? An Introduction*, Berlin: Sternberg Press, 2010, pp. 40–57, here pp. 44–45.
2   In 2009, the editors of *October* issued a questionnaire to examine and specify various dimensions of the heterogeneous practices being brought under the label of the contemporary, see *October*, 139 (Fall), 2009: 3–124. Contributions on the subject have also been brought together in Aranda, Wood and Vidokle (eds), *What Is Contemporary Art?* Similar questions were posed in '13 Thesen zur Gegenwartskunst', *Texte zur Kunst*, no. 74 (June), 2009: 4–136. Voices from the Global South have been assembled by the Asia Art Archive in *Field Notes 01 – The And: An Expanded Questionnaire on the Contemporary*, April 2012, https://issuu.com/asiaartarchivehk/docs/fn01_the_and_eng (last accessed 20 September, 2020). For an overview of discussions, Terry Smith, *Art to Come: Histories of Contemporary Art*, Durham, NC: Duke University Press, 2019; Terry Smith, Okwui Enwezor and Nancy Condee (eds), *Antinomies of Art and Culture: Modernity, Postmodernity, Contemporaneity*, Durham, NC: Duke University Press, 2008; Geoff Cox and Jacob Lund, *The Contemporary Condition: Introductory Thoughts on Contemporaneity and Contemporary Art*, Berlin: Sternberg Press, 2016.
3   Aranda, Wood and Vidokle (eds), *What Is Contemporary Art?*, p. 8.

around what is now considered to be the quintessentially 'global' quality of the contemporary, made palpable through the emergence of art worlds across the planet, driven by forces of globalisation and vitalised by their own energies. The 'global contemporary', as it was christened some three decades back, signals towards a radically new current, with the intent to distinguish it from the art worlds of modernity, whose systems of value and structures of authority transported through their master narratives, so the argument goes, could no longer prevail. The ensuing provincialization of Euro-American conceptions of what counts as an art world, once art from 'elsewhere' is accorded a viable presence within an uneven yet in principle a shareable world order, is a trope characteristic of much writing on art since the late twentieth century. Its most articulate spokespersons have been Hans Belting, Andrea Buddensieg and Peter Weibel, who ran the Global Arts and the Museum project at Karlsruhe, in south Germany, for almost a decade.[4] By shifting the focus from 'what' to 'where', when querying the phenomenon called contemporary art, Belting and the members of his group centre-staged geography and locatedness in a globalised art world to propose an artistic practice that is plural, differentiated, and one that defies a single universalist perspective.

A large number of curators and cultural theorists from across the spectrum have affirmed such an understanding, as the following sample of voices shows. Terry Smith speaks of 'today's art to come' as an art that increasingly moves towards wordliness or, drawing on Édouard Glissant, *'mondialité'*, art that could partake of a 'coeval commons'.[5] Similarly Okwui Enwezor's oft cited 'will to globality' to refer to a widespread, shared ground of common questions and affinities among those who do not or yet cannot subscribe to the dogma of globalisation, points to an understanding of the self that realises itself through collaboration across boundaries.[6] Migration, mobility, travel are the keywords that make up the coordinates of the 'Altermodern', a notion coined by Nicolas Bourriaud to cast the contemporary as an altered modern constituted by alterity, an entity that is neither centred on the West

---

4   The project Global Art and the Museum, located at the Hochschule für Gestaltung in Karlsruhe, ran from 2006 to 2014. It included a Graduate School and organised regular summer academies to bring together scholars, curators and art practitioners from across the world. Its outstanding publications include: Peter Weibel and Andrea Buddensieg (eds), *Contemporary Art and the Museum: A Global Perspective*, Ostfildern: Hatje Cantz, 2007; Hans Belting and Andrea Buddensieg (eds), *The Global Art World: Audiences, Markets, and Museums*, Ostfildern: Hatje Cantz, 2009; Hans Belting, Jacob Birken, Andrea Buddensieg, Peter Weibel (eds), *Global Studies: Mapping Contemporary Art and Culture*, Ostfildern: Hatje Cantz, 2011. Belting and Buddensieg also curated the exhibition *The Global Contemporary and the Rise of New Art Worlds* that ran from September 2011 to February 2012 at the Zentrum für Kunst und Medien (ZKM), Karlsruhe and produced an opulent catalogue, see Hans Belting, Andrea Buddensieg and Peter Weibel (eds), *The Global Contemporary and the Rise of New Art Worlds*, Cambridge MA: MIT Press, 2013.

5   Smith, *Art to Come*, p. 327.

6   Okwui Enwezor, 'The Black Box', in *Documenta 11: Platform 5*, Ostfildern: Hatje Cantz, 2002, p. 42, cited in Ranjit Hoskote, 'Biennials of Resistance: Reflections of the Seventh Gwangju Biennial', in: Elena Filipovic, Mareike van Hal and Solvieg Øvstebø (eds), *The Biennial Reader*, Ostfildern: Hatje Cantz, 2010, pp. 306–21, here p. 312.

nor inflected by nationalist concerns, but takes the global as its starting point.[7] While both Marsha Meskimmon und Nikos Papastergiadis mine the contemporary for its 'cosmopolitan aesthetics', for Patrick Flores it embodies a privilege that allows the subject to 'participate in the project of emancipation'.[8] At the same time, however, concerns have been expressed about the framing of the globalised contemporary, in ways that make it legible only within a European or American context: for example, through signposting contemporary art as a time that succeeds modernism – a linear sequence that overlooks the dynamics of modernist art practices at sites beyond the Paris-New York axis.[9] Chika Okeke-Agulu cautions against a horizontal art history that ends up flattening local and regional particularities and discrepant intellectual traditions, homogenising troubling difference, to then bring back master narratives of 'old regime art history' through the back door.[10] The editors of the questionnaire 'What Is Contemporary Art', in turn apprehend that by mobilising peripheries as 'centers in their own right', the contemporary art system ends up 'atomizing' its innumerable components.[11] More recently, David Joselit has added a critical note to ongoing discussions of global contemporary art by positing that 'globality' implies the necessity of adopting an international style, which both appropriates and represses indigenous modes of creativity. He characterises this process as a 'synchronization' of divergent histories and genealogies 'with one another, as well as with Western modernism'.[12]

This chapter takes a 'periphery-in' approach by drawing attention to those sites of cultural action crucial to contemporary art that loosen the rigid linearity of narratives segregating contemporaneity from the modern. Such vibrant peripheries – the account below shows – produce both novel art as well as a critical discourse, and therefore demand a fresh optic to theorise the context within which artistic projects as well as conceptual insights are born. Continuing the discussion of the previous chapter, this story of contemporary art throws light on the shifting relationship between art production, nation, and locality in postcolonial South Asia; the quest for artistic selfhood is equally placed in relation to global circuits, which open up new possibilities of transcultural co-production and at the same time bring forth fresh hierarchies. The region becomes the locus of a transcultural avant-garde, the latter now detached from its provincial European moorings and conceptually reinvigorated as it travels

7   Nicolas Bourriaud, *Altermodern: Tate Triennial*, London: Tate Publishing, 2009, cited in Atreyee Gupta, 'On Territorialty, Temporality, and the Politics of Place', in: Asia Art Archives, *An Expanded Questionnaire on the Contemporary*, pp. 73–80, here p. 76.

8   The term has been used by Nikos Papastergiadis, *Cosmopolitanism and Culture*, London: Polity Press, 2012. Also, Marsha Meskimmon, *Contemporary Art and the Cosmopolitan Imagination*, London: Routledge, 2010. Patrick Flores, 'Errant in Form', in: Asia Art Archives, *An Expanded Questionnaire on the Contemporary*, pp. 22–23, here p. 22.

9   Gupta, 'On Territoriality', pp. 75–76.

10   Chika Okeke-Agulu, 'Globalization, Art History, and the Specter of Difference', in: Alexander Dumbadze and Suzanne Hudson (eds), *Contemporary Art: 1989 to the Present*, Chichester: Wiley-Blackwell, 2013, pp. 447–56, here p. 454.

11   Aranda, Wood and Vidokle (eds), *What Is Contemporary Art?*, p. 8.

12   David Joselit, *Heritage and Debt: Art in Globalization*, Cambridge, MA: MIT Press, 2020, pp. xxi–xxii, and Chapter 2.

to new loci. Drawing on the work of a handful of artists, the chapter fleshes out how a more politicised engagement with the dilemmas of the contemporary – induced by the crisis of liberal democracies, mass migration, and the spectacular regimes of global capitalism – has made contemporary art practice in a postcolonial nation-state a domain to explore forms of identity beyond the nation. The selected themes addressed here – history, memory, and time; the body politic; and participatory art – are galvanised by transcultural affiliations, even as they use globalised locality to develop fresh codes and media initiatives. Singling out the work of individual artists is not intended as a return to a biographical, more often than not celebratory mode of art history that treats the work of the single artist as the pinnacle of a creative process. Rather, facets of an artist's work are brought into relationship with other works and concepts in vectors that invite further exploration.

Signposting the Present

Though spread over a spectrum of positions, many of the views presented in the flurry of writings mentioned above celebrate the dissolution of master narratives and the new regimes of visibility put into place within the world of contemporary art. They mostly share the premise that contemporary globalisation has brought to us a fresh historic moment, a radical break with earlier artistic practices, constituted by unprecedented global connectivity. Such a collapse of distance, it is implied, has in addition been enabled by a revitalised multiculturalism that recognises the plurality of cultural experience. When unqualified, such an affirmation can involuntarily end up as a form of presentism that works in insidious ways to reaffirm earlier canons, such as those of modernism, whose monocultural authority continues to be accepted as given. As the previous chapter argued, the prolific scholarly engagement with modernist art on sites across the globe, even as it highlights the still unwritten histories of the field, has reconfigured it in ways that go beyond bringing hitherto neglected currents into an existing canon: rather, the study of artistic modernism as a field of transculturation has begun to plot individual stories onto a common matrix to show connections, to uncover synchronicity and coevalness. This research has further drawn our attention to the longevity of modernist traditions in many regions of the world through the twentieth century, and to the unfolding of symbiotic relationships with global practices, to perhaps engender and dynamise the experiments we consider to belong to contemporary art.[13] When narrating the story of modern/contemporary art in South Asia for example, one is obliged to discard the idea of

---

13   See, for instance, the numerous contributions to the catalogue of the exhibition curated by Okwui Enwezor and Katy Siegel on postwar art at the Haus der Kunst in Munich (October 14, 2016 to March 26, 2017), Okwui Enwezor, Katy Siegel and Ulrich Wilmes (eds), *Postwar: Art between the Pacific and the Atlantic 1945–1965*, Munich: Prestel Verlag, 2016. Also, Sonal Khullar, *Worldly Affiliations: Artistic Practice, National Identity and Modernism in India 1930–1990*, Oakland: University of California Press, 2015; Saloni Mathur, 'Ends and Means: A Conversation with Geeta Kapur', *October*, 171 (Winter), 2020: 115–38, esp. 125–26.

an art scene marked by an orderly succession of one generation and its practices by another.[14] Rather, at any given moment since the second half of the twentieth century and into the present, at least four generations of practicing artists can be identified – these range from some of the founder figures of modernist art during the mid-twentieth century to a generation of art school graduates catapulted into the global circuit of biennials. They have all been simultaneously active, as the examples discussed below will show, and have participated in debates over questions of medium or idiom and the direction of art in general. Unravelling complex and entangled temporalities in the making of the modern/contemporary is a task that awaits a transculturally framed investigation. Instead of positing a progression from the modern to the contemporary in terms of collapsing distance, a transcultural perspective could be more usefully deployed to examine the specific dynamic between distance and proximity, between contradiction and affinity that operates within individual and different historical periods and at different sites across the globe. Further, it urges us to ask what the blurring of difference, induced by contemporary globalised conditions of migration, travel, and media connectivity, entails in terms of transactions with cultural difference? What are the new hierarchical modes that are created to deal with these? Where can we observe continuities within disciplinary and institutional hierarchical principles of the last century and this one, and which new boundaries are created following the dissolution of older ones? Underlying these questions is the assumption that negotiating cultural difference is not an aberrant or incidental feature of artistic production in earlier historical periods; rather we need to test the hypothesis that takes it to be a structural, even normative characteristic for any period we investigate.

Once we discard our understanding of contemporary art as a description of no more than a heterogeneous mix of artworks produced within the duration of a particular present – however that present is defined – we need to provide a discursive frame to render the epithet critically intelligible. According to Peter Osborne, the contemporary stands in the first place for 'a claim for its significance in participating in the actuality of the present'.[15] In the realm of art-making it articulates the self-consciousness of those within, who affirm it as a critical form of living the historical present that appropriates the past, in order to be invested in envisioning possibilities for the future that await realization. And yet, at the present juncture contemporaneity turns out to be an impossibly diversified form, the geopolitics of which is interlocked in myriad histories, temporalities, and subject positions. For Osborne, then, it is but an 'operative fiction' through which we attribute a sense of unity to the present that

---

14 This tends to be implicit in generalising positions like those of Joselit, and Belting before him, that ascribe to global contemporary art an overweening epistemic violence, in that it allegedly succeeds pre-modern 'indigenous' modes that it both appropriates and represses. It might be useful here to pay more attention to a variety of modernist experiments that unfolded within the context of colonialism and yet forged links beyond the colony-coloniser divide: see Joselit, *Heritage and Debt*; Hans Belting, 'From World Art to Global Art: View on a New Panorama', in Belting, Buddensieg and Weibel (eds), *The Global Contemporary*, pp. 178–85.

15 Peter Osborne, *Anywhere or Not at All: The Philosophy of Contemporary Art*, London: Verso, 2013, p. 2.

encompasses disjunctive temporalities that we can never fully grasp.[16] In view of its encompassing scope, contemporary art, it would seem, can no longer denote a style, or a period, or even an ideological position other than a commitment to 'return to a present where we have never been'.[17] Even as such a perspective advances the proposition that there is no homogenous global contemporary, and any attempt to fix a signpost for art ends up in a dysfunctional exercise, 1989 brought forth the affirmative claim that the fall of the Berlin Wall does exactly serve that end. This claim has gained considerable ground since then.

The events of 1989 and their aftermath brought with them a sense of global renewal, articulated in a flurry of terms announcing a post-ideological, post-ethnic, post-historical, even post-political condition, while art, at the same juncture, is said to have become fully 'contemporary', that is, an active component of a shared present. The proliferation of biennials, art fairs, and mega-exhibitions in and beyond Euro-America since 1989 that featured works of artists from distant corners of the world meant that global contemporary art could be characterised as a freely circulating, ahistorical, non-situated, and economically exploitable mass.[18] Even as critical responses to such an interpretive framework that unquestioningly links aesthetic changes to the geopolitical shifts of 1989 have since then come from several positions, 1989, when adequately historicised, can serve as a pragmatic landmark for a discussion of factors at a global scale that have undoubtedly impinged on art production.[19] The fall of the Berlin Wall brought with it the end of Cold War polarities, followed by the emergence of a host of nation-states on the ruins of the erstwhile Soviet Union, and in turn the eastward expansion of the European Union. Further, this juncture marked the end of Apartheid in South Africa as well as the reaffirmation of China's communist identity following the Tiananmen Square massacre. The euphoric belief in the transformative force of economic globalisation – the growth of transnational corporations, neoliberal economics, the heightened role of accelerated information technologies, and the culture industries[20] – accompanied the emergence of a global system of cultural production, perceived as having enabled transcultural collaborations wherein 'location … liberated itself from geography'.

16 Osborne, 'The Fiction of the Contemporary', in *Anywhere or Not at All*, pp. 15–35.

17 Giorgio Agamben, 'What Is the Contemporary', in: *What Is an Apparatus*, Stanford: Stanford University Press, 2009, p. 52.

18 Hans Belting, 'Contemporary Art as Global Art: A Critical Estimate', in Belting and Buddensieg (eds), *The Global Art World*, pp. 38–73; also, Belting, Buddensieg and Weibel (eds), *The Global Contemporary*.

19 Critical positions on 1989 as chronological signpost include: Ruth Simbao, 'What global art and current (re)turns fail to see: A modest counter-narrative of "not-another-biennial"', *Image and Text*, 25, 2015: 261–86; Maria Hlavajova and Simon Sheikh (eds), *Former West: Art and the Contemporary after 1989*, Cambridge, MA/Utrecht: MIT Press/BAK, 2017; Michaela Ott, 'Die kleine ästhetische Differenz', *Texte zur Kunst*, 23 (91), 2013: 101–09; Parul D. Mukherji, 'Art History and its Discontents in Global Times', in: Jill H. Casid and Aruna D'Souza (eds), *Art History in the Wake of the Global Turn*, New Haven: Yale University Press, 2014, pp. 88–106, here pp. 94–95; Christian Kravagna, 'Für eine postkoloniale Geschichte des Kontakts', in Christian Kravagna, *Transmoderne: Eine Kunstgeschichte des Kontakts*, Berlin: b_books, 2017, pp. 35–57.

20 Stuart Hall describes these as characterising the 'fourth phase of globalization'. Stuart Hall, 'Creolization, Diaspora and Hybridity in the Context of Globalization', in: Okwui Enwezor (ed.), *Creolité and Creolization: Documenta XI Platform 3*, Ostfildern: Hatje Cantz, 2003, pp. 185–98, here pp. 193–94.

These unfolded through a range of formats including travelling exhibitions, symposia, collective publications, artists' residencies, and research projects, all celebrated as 'intense occasions of collegiality' and 'a new, redeeming solidarity'.[21] The discussion of the contemporary has now shifted from the issue of visibility gained by art from beyond the West in the exhibition circuits and scholarly accounts of the 'mainstream' to querying the conditions that make such visibility possible.[22] The new geo-aesthetic maps of globally networked art worlds that figured prominently in the Karlsruhe exhibition curated by Hans Belting and Andrea Buddensieg cannot be read as an unproblematic dissolution of hierarchies without examining the nature of relationalities that connect the luminous nodal points distributed across the surface of cartographic representation. 1989 and its aftermath threw into relief a number of vexed questions, not least the challenge of connecting across scales: of retaining regional and local anchors without becoming hostage to the global, further the challenge to those discursive infrastructures and production systems of a neoliberal economy whose workings both revealed and accentuated the unevenness of regions and localities. Art practice in the new millennium geared itself to a fresh set of urgencies, as the euphoria of the early 1990s celebrating an effortless, even naturalised 'flow' of materials, goods, capital, and human resources, together with dissolving national and cultural boundaries, gave way to critiques of neoliberal economics and politics, their disregard of human sovereignty and evasion of environmental responsibility.

Today, three decades following the end of the Cold War, earlier polarities that had shaped the cartographies framing our scholarship, have once more been overwritten by urgent contemporary ones: continuing migration from West Asia and Africa following war and ecological crises has breached even recent divisions between the Global North and the Global South. The presence of large immigrant communities in the midst of Western societies has generated discussions on citizenship and its nexus with culture: the meanings of citizenship as a juridical category that secures rights within a national framework while at the same time working as a tool for the bio-political regulation of illegality, are now being freshly theorised.[23] In contemporary postcolonial societies too – India, Indonesia, Nigeria, Iran, and most recently, Israel – narratives of citizenship and belonging are ceaselessly being debated, reconstituted, and endangered, as they take on majoritarian hues and punitive forms, while forcing allegiance to an officially fabricated cultural past and a synoptic vision of the future.

---

21 Nancy Adajania and Ranjit Hoskote, 'Notes towards a Lexicon of Urgencies', in: *Independent Curators International Research*, October 2010.

22 Discussed in Monica Juneja, 'Global Art History and the "Burden of Representation"', in: Belting et al., *Global Studies*, pp. 274–97.

23 See Etienne Balibar, *Citizenship*, Cambridge: Polity Press, 2015; Saskia Sassen, *Territory, Authority, Rights: From Medieval to Global Assemblages*, Princeton, NJ: Princeton University Press, 2006. Both Sassen and Balibar argue for a new model of 'co-citizenship' or 'shared citizenship' that is non-territorial, goes beyond being an institution determined by the nation-state, and includes solidarities that transcend borders of single nations. See also Giorgio Agamben's theorisation of the refugee as a figure of 'a new historical consciousness' that allows us a glimpse of a future beyond the nation-state founded on an exclusion of non-citizens. Giorgio Agamben, 'Beyond Human Rights', in: *Means without End: Notes on Politics*, Minneapolis: University of Minnesota Press, 2000, pp. 14–25, here p. 14.

These issues assume an urgency for art that strives to function as a domain of symbolic action, as an arena of political and creative practices, of affirmative, performative citizenship rather than a simply reactive aesthetic. By constructing imaginative possibilities that await potential realisation, by envisaging a political horizon for the subject and community that challenges the monocultural exclusivity on which dominant versions of collective belonging are based, artistic practice is now being conceptualised as a terrain to 'open up the transformative potential of dislocation that decenters the very basis of national identity'.[24] A set of shared urgencies cutting across the global divide, while particularised when viewed through the lens of local histories and memories, challenges scholarship to unravel the simultaneous, unevenly unfolding, yet mutually entangled articulations of contemporary art. A narrative account of contemporary art can no longer map the conjuncture of a closed system; it rather needs to look for that which joins individual elements and localities, even as it takes into account the dynamics of their situatedness. For instance, it can draw attention to those emerging networks of collaborative practice that have produced an expanded vision of the legacies and global futures of modernism.[25] Narratives of history, place, and displacement have come to occupy a central position in the definition of contemporary culture. Artists today locate themselves *in* 'the contemporary', as its co-producers rather than as members reacting from the outside. They work more closely within civil society, in conjunction with local communities, activists, curators, and technicians, while establishing lateral connections and shaping new models of agency and responsibility. Transcultural connections among cultural activists have meant that artists, while retaining a grounded and visceral relationship to their localities, constantly strive to make their work speak to concerns that transcend the local and the national. Experiments within localities in turn bring forth – born out of their particular situatedness – examples and insights that necessitate an enlarged, recalibrated lexicon of concepts such as authorship and participation that would refine prevailing understandings of contemporary art practice, reconfiguring what the global might stand for.[26]

The belief in contemporary art's utopian potential to solder a global citizenry around a discourse of universal rights makes it necessary to ask how art situates itself within a national context. In many regions of the world, today's postcolonial citizen, committed to a polyvocal, historicised contemporaneity, has emerged empowered through an anti-colonial struggle that had informed modernist enterprises. The nation, the ground on which that struggle was waged, continues to be a site of production for art that confronts the divergent, often totalis-

---

24 T. J. Demos, *The Migrant Image: The Art and Politics of Documentary during Global Crisis*, Durham, NC: Duke University Press, 2013: xix.
25 See contributions to Enwezor, Siegel and Wilmes (eds), *Postwar*.
26 I will elaborate on this through a case study on participatory art in the final section of this chapter. Similar issues feature in Atreyee Gupta, 'The Global, the Local, the Contemporary, the Collaborative: *Ghari/Ghar Pe/At Home*, Dharavi, Mumbai, 2012', in: Deborah S. Hutton and Rebecca M. Brown (eds), *Rethinking Place in South Asian and Islamic Art, 1500–Present*, London: Routledge, 2017, pp. 78–93; Reiko Tomii, 'How to Build a World Art History on Stones: Robert Smithson', 'Horikawa Michio, and 1960s Art in Japan', in: Melanie Trede, Mio Wakita and Christine Guth (eds), *Japanese Art: Transcultural Perspectives*, Leiden: E. J. Brill, (forthcoming 2023).

ing forces at work within a globalisation whose workings are as coercive as they are enabling. The nation is at the same time a ground of contested positions: marked by ethnic stratification, replete with multiple living traditions and historical memories, it is simultaneously the terrain of pernicious and majoritarian nationalism. How does contemporary art negotiate the transformative potential of a 'global public sphere' and at the same time resist the marginalisation of region and nation?[27] The question becomes increasingly pertinent as the aura of national affiliation remains the condition of visibility and participation accorded to art production of societies of the Global South within international exhibition circuits. The phenomenon by which exhibitions from 'elsewhere' are curated as a national survey coincides paradoxically with the emergent multicultural ethos that has prompted liberal democracies in the West to become more 'inclusive' by according more space to the work of non-European artists. As a progressive political imperative, multiculturalism is characterised by an affirmation of cultural diversity as value per se. It celebrates cultural difference as a form of plenitude in which diversity exists side by side, wherein all styles and beliefs, more often than not identified by national labels, are considered equally valid and where the prerogative of judgment is frequently ceded to the art market. By the turn of the twentieth century, cultural marginality was no longer a matter of invisibility; rather one where an 'excess of visibility', as Jean Fisher puts it, made cultural difference into a readily marketable commodity.[28]

The prominent landmark exhibition that secured the visibility of non-Western art in a metropolis of the First World was the show *Magiciens de la Terre*, curated by Jean-Hubert Martin and his team for the Centre Georges Pompidou, Paris, in 1989. Animated by a democratic urge to showcase the art of the world by attributing to all objects a creative and conceptual parity, *Magiciens* generated an intense debate about the polarity it ended up producing between a Western avant-garde and timeless 'magic-driven' artworks of cultures, which have not been objects of 'contamination' by the West.[29] And yet the 'productive provocation'[30] produced by the show's bold topography did, in the long-run, shake up the prevailing taxonomies of metropolitan art history and have provided impulses for a more critical globality that continue to be thrashed out in discussions since, as the following chapter will elaborate.

27 The term is Okwui Enwezor's, cited by Geeta Kapur in her conversation with Saloni Mathur, 'Ends and Means', pp. 122–24. Enwezor has emphatically qualified the contemporary as 'postcolonial', arguing that the world was charged with a 'postcolonial condition' that has transformed subjectivities and works as a generative force for aesthetic practices, see Okwui Enwezor and Chika Okeke-Agulu (eds), *Contemporary African Art Since 1980*, Bologna: Damiani, 2009, Chapter 2.

28 Jean Fisher, 'The Syncretic Turn: Cross-Cultural Practices in the Age of Multiculturalism', in: *Theory in Contemporary Art Since 1985*, eds Zoya Kocur and Simon Leung, Malden: Blackwell, 2008, pp. 233–41, here p. 235.

29 The term, used by Jean-Hubert Martin, has been cited by Rasheed Araeen, 'Our Bauhaus Others' Mudhouse', *Third Text*, vol. 3 (6), 1989: 3–16, here 9. The special issue of the journal was devoted entirely to a discussion of this controversial exhibition. The terms of the debate will be discussed in detail in the following chapter, which engages with the implications of this show for the writing of global histories of art.

30 As Geeta Kapur puts it; see Geeta Kapur, 'Curating in Heterogeneous Worlds', in: Dumbadze and Hudson (eds.), *Contemporary Art*, pp. 178–91, here p. 179.

The years since the 1990s saw a spurt of exhibitions, all carrying the label 'India', generating thereby tricky questions of curatorial representation.[31] When art is made to function as a surface from which a primordial national, ethnic, or religious identity could be read off, it ends up being locked into the frame of ethnicity, rather than allowing the exhibition space to be transformed into a meeting ground for a plurality of visual grammars and languages of artistic address. Despite the burden of expectation this places on the artists, capitulation to spectacles of exotic difference built into the visual culture of global capitalism and multiculturalism has not been the only, not even the overwhelming response among them. Even as art was meant to stand for an entity 'India', located in the Global South, the works themselves registered a refusal to valorize the 'local' against an overpowering 'global'. Instead, while feeling its way to defining a more complex politics of place, art has sought to prod aesthetic theory and criticism towards finding the conceptual tools necessary to grasp the intrinsic transcultural characteristics of contemporary art production without giving in to the deceptive lure of 'authenticity'.

Another signpost, a transitional moment in the history of exhibitions of contemporary art from India in institutions of Western Europe, can be located in 2008, when the travelling exhibition *Indian Highway*, curated by a trio comprising Julia Peyton-Jones, Hans-Ulrich Obrist, and Gunnar Kvaran, opened in London's Serpentine Gallery. *Indian Highway*, whose title spells both mobility and technology, epitomised mobility in more than one sense: it journeyed from London to Oslo, Herning, Lyon, Rome, and thence to Beijing, the only site in Asia.[32] Further, it marked the moment when contemporary art from India had become mobile: unhindered by the legal restrictions applicable to objects classed as heritage, such art could travel to wherever it was sought after; it was seen and sold at art fairs and in galleries across the world. The exhibition featured a galaxy of artists spread over different generations – ranging from the iconic founding figure of Modernism, M. F. Husain (1915–2011) to a generation born in the 1970s – whose collective presence appeared 'festive in its diversity', and whose practice worked in its collectivity to unsettle canonical certainties through a simultaneous engagement with a plurality of aesthetic modes and discursive stances.[33] At the same time, however, *Indian Highway* found itself grappling with the challenges that an exhibition defined as an overview of a nation's art brings with it. As an exhibition bearing a national label, it was ostensibly meant to 'inform' viewing publics at different venues about the entity 'India'; at the same time, we read it as a project conceptually committed to being with the times, to celebrating the spirit of globalisation, articulated in curatorial statements

31 To name a few examples: *Indian Highway* (2008, London, Oslo, Herning, Lyon, Rome, Beijing, see below); *The Empire Strikes Back – Indian Art Today* (London, 2010), *New Narratives – Contemporary Art from India* (Chicago, Kansas, New Brunswick, 2007–08), *The Matter Within – New Contemporary Art of India* (San Francisco, 2011), *India: Art Now* (Arken, 2012–13), *Mémoires des futurs – Modernités indiennes* (Paris, 2017), *The Progressive Revolution – Modern Art for a New India* (New York, 2019).

32 Kathleen Madden and Sam Philips (eds), *Indian Highway – the Catalogue*, London: Koenig Books, 2008; a recent ethnographic study of the exhibition is Catherine Bublatzky, *Along the* Indian Highway: *An Ethnography of an International Travelling Exhibition*, London/New Delhi: Routledge, 2019.

33 Ranjit Hoskote, 'Signposting the Indian Highway', in: *Indian Highway*, pp. 190–93, here p. 193.

through terms such as 'exchange', 'dialogue', or 'reciprocity'.[34] The former agenda was bolstered through an array of cultural programmes that accompanied the show – they ranged from literature, dance, and performance to lectures and food festivals, all conforming to habits of cultural consumption that they in turn shaped or reinforced. While art critical reports of the show abounded with buzzwords such as 'hybridity' or 'blending', they also struggled with the tyranny of the diverse labels they had to negotiate – Indian, global contemporary, or Indian contemporary? The outcomes of the *Indian Highway* as an epitome of a globally circulating praxis have been measured according to different yardsticks. Its long-term effects have been judged as boosting the process of making contemporary Indian art a marketable commodity: India as a cultural reference for art objects made it into a 'desirable brand' within the dazzling array brought forth by neoliberal capital.[35] Such pivotal agency ascribed to the art market has been further detected in the fresh roles the market has assumed, those of 'producing the discourse through web-resources, auction catalogues, and books ... building the archive of modern and contemporary art'.[36] Ascriptions along these lines have in turn been eloquently countered by the assertion that the *Indian Highway* was an important milestone in generating a culture of 'responsible and responsive encounter' ... a catalyst that gave art practice 'strategic and imaginative freedom' to unfold beyond the 'radar range of the market'.[37] Even as India did not figure on the exhibition's itinerary, its resonance led to transformations in urban infrastructures within Indian localities that have worked in different directions, making visible the contingent conditions of the contemporary. While galleries, artists' associations, or institutions such as the India Art Fair have proliferated in urban settings, it has also meant that much of contemporary art – in spite of its forays into sites beyond the gallery – has come to be insulated within exclusive spaces that draw a clear boundary between the institutions of art and other genres of visual or material creation.[38] In the final analysis, the importance of this show lies no less in the historical perspective it opened up by examining the pitfalls and promises of a one-nation show and thereby allowing us a vantage point from which to critically rethink the nation as a frame.

The opportunity to do so was seized by Ranjit Hoskote who, when he accepted the commission to curate the first 'national' Indian pavilion at the Venice Biennale of 2011, deployed this canonical site as a laboratory to deliberate on whether the 'idea of India'[39] could be pushed beyond its existing limits.[40] The Venice Biennale, the oldest and most canonical of biennials

---

34 Bublatzky, *Along the* Indian Highway.
35 Manuela Ciotti, 'Post-colonial Renaissance: "Indianness", Contemporary Art and the Market in the Age of Neoliberal Capital', *Third World Quarterly*, 33 (4), 2012: 633–51, here 637.
36 Kavita Singh, 'A History of Now', *Art India*, 15, 2010: 26–33, here 32.
37 Hoskote, 'Signposting', pp. 191, 193.
38 On the emergence of genres beyond the gallery and studio, and their claims to the status of 'art', see the study by Tapati Guha-Thakurta, *In the Name of the Goddess: The Durga Pujas of Contemporary Kolkata*, Delhi: Primus Books, 2015.
39 The title of a well-known book: Sunil Khilnani, *The Idea of India*, New Delhi: Penguin Books, 2004.
40 It is pertinent however to point to prior exhibitions that transcended national units and were conceived of as a counterpoint to those of Western curators, while remaining in conversation with them. Back in 1996, the Thai curator Apinan Poshyananda mounted an impressive exhibition titled *Contemporary Art*

and one that continues to be organised around the principle of nationality, has accumulated aura and authority through its longevity and periodicity; it was in a sense an ideal site for a curatorial intervention to show another path to producing 'a centrifugal diffusion of dissidence'.[41] The intriguing title of the pavilion *Everybody Agrees: It's About to Explode* makes one pause at the ambiguous 'it' that might refer to the nation-state, to contemporary art, to the art market, or to myths about these entities. Hoskote assimilated the transcultural history of the exhibition space at the Venice Arsenale to his project, in which each of the four artistic positions presented could be opened up to explore the potential extension of national identity across plural anchors of belonging.[42] According to this conception, the national survey was built around a set of questions rather than answers, to view the nation as a conceptual entity rather than a territorially bound unit.

While anti-colonial nationalism – as we saw in the last chapter – had conceptualised the nation as locality, to be wrenched back from the global constellation of empire, the local within contemporary art does not stand for a backwater arcadia. The remaining sections of this chapter will flesh out the ways in which a conception of locality can be made to extend outward into a global space of the imagination, and to negotiate multiple scales. It will do so around a selected group of themes that resonate transculturally to shape so much of contemporary art practice: history, memory, and time; the body politic; and participatory art. This sampling of case studies within a globalised locality has been brought together under the umbrella of a transcultured avant-garde. In doing so I take my cue from Geeta Kapur, who has persuasively argued for delinking the concept of the avant-garde from the logic of a Euro-American master narrative and to harness it to the 'hitherto unlogged initiatives' of

of Asia: *Traditions/Tensions* that chose Asia as a frame. See Apinan Poshyananda, *Contemporary Art in Asia: Traditions – Tensions*, New York: Abrams, 1996. In a similar vein, the *West Heavens* project curated by Chaitanya Sambrani and Johnson Chang sought to focus on intra-Asian relationships whose genealogy Sambrani traces to the pan-Asian ideal of early twentieth century scholars such as Okakura Kakuzo, Rabindranath Tagore and Ananda Coomaraswamy. See Chaitanya Sambrani, 'An Experiment in Connectivity: From the "West Heavens" to the "Middle Kingdom"', in: Michelle Antoinette and Caroline Turner (eds), *Contemporary Asian Art and Exhibitions: Connectivities and World-Making*, Acton: ANU Press, 2014, pp. 89–107, here pp. 89–91. Also, Johnson Chang and Chaitanya Sambrani, *Place, Time, Play: Contemporary Art from the West Heavens to the Middle Kingdom*, Hong Kong: Hanart TZ Gallery, 2012. An exhibition on Indian art, also curated by Sambrani and that problematised the national frame, together with questions of locality and belonging, was *Edge of Desire*, a show that between 2004 and 2006 travelled from Australia to New York, Mexico City and Mumbai. See Chaitanya Sambrani, *Edge of Desire – Recent Art from India*, London: Philip Wilson Publishers, 2005. The exhibition *Midnight to Boom* curated by Susan Bean at the Peabody Essex Museum in 2013, took a cross-generational approach, and though with a focus on painting, draws our attention to the plurality of media that marks modernist and contemporary art in South Asia. See Susan S. Bean, *Midnight to Boom: Painting in India After Independence*, London: Thames and Hudson, 2013.

41   Nancy Adajania and Ranjit Hoskote, 'Notes Towards a Lexicon of Urgencies' https://curatorsintl.org/journal/14896-notes-towards-a-lexicon-of-urgencies (last accessed 21 September 2020).

42   See the curatorial essay by Ranjit Hoskote, 'Everyone Agrees: It's About to Explode', *Seminar*, 2014, http://www.india-seminar.com/2014/659/659_ranjit_hoskote.htm (last accessed 21 September 2020).

regions beyond the West.[43] Rooted in Marxist aesthetic theory, the avant-garde – conventionally read as standing for any experimental stance, an agential force within art and above all a rejection of existing institutions of the art world – has been the subject of intensive debates; after a long-standing prediction of its death, it has been now discarded as an obsolete historical and aesthetic proposition.[44] In her response to Foster, Kapur not only drew attention to the non-specific character ascribed to the prevailing concept coupled with its narrow geopolitical frames, she argued in addition that 'if the avant-garde is a historically conditioned phenomenon and emerges only in a moment of real political disjuncture, it will appear in various forms in different parts of the world at different times.'[45] Viewing it as a '*template* for radical disruption'[46] allows both the theory and practice of art to reanimate its potential to understand art's discursive economy in a historically informed way, perhaps to fracture the notion into several related shards or nuggets that could then be reused in transgressive ways. As a mobile concept the avant-garde no longer retains its dependence on the metanarrative of modernism's progressivism; it has been re-appropriated in a 'Third-World' context of a struggle to undermine the modernist antinomy of tradition and modernity, while being cautious of the burdens that a doctrinal patrimony can impose on cultures seeking to redefine themselves.[47] Yet, its theoretical potential has hardly been fully tapped in critical art history of the Indian subcontinent, Kapur's enabling propositions notwithstanding.[48] Rescripting it as a historicised concept might be one step towards making the contemporary a critically intelligible category. The avant-garde in its recalibrated, transcultured forms can appear as a mode of dismantling assimilative hegemonies, be these national allegories or old and new imperialisms; it emerges as a zone of possibility rather than a model of progress or utopia,

43 Geeta Kapur, 'Dismantled Norms: Apropos an Asian/Indian Avantgarde', in: *When Was Modernism? Essays in Contemporary Cultural Practice in India*, New Delhi: Tulika Books, 2001, pp. 365–413, here p. 374.

44 A seminal text is Hal Foster, 'What's Neo about the Neo-Avant-Garde?', *October,* no. 70 (Fall), 1994: 5–32. For a formulation of the larger problematic, Peter Bürger, *Theory of the Avant-Garde*, Minneapolis: University of Minnesota Press, 1996; Renato Poggioli, *The Theory of the Avant-Garde*, Cambridge, MA: Bellknap Press, 1968; Andreas Huyssen, 'The Search for Tradition: Avant-Garde and Postmodernism in the 1970s', *New German Critique*, vol. 22 (Winter), 1981: 23–40. The discussion, following Kapur, has been carried forward by introducing perspectives outside of the Euro-American context: Elizabeth Harney, 'Postcolonial Agitations: Avant-gardism in Dakar and London', *New Literary History*, vol. 41 (4), 2010: 731–51; Saloni Mathur, 'A Response to Kapur's "Proposition Avant-Garde"', *Art Journal*, vol. 77 (1), 2018: 90–94; Rachel Weiss, 'Some Thoughts after Kapur and Mathur', *Art Journal*, vol. 77 (1), 2018: 95–101. See also the article by Ann Gibson, 'Avant-Garde', in: Robert S. Nelson and Richard Shiff (eds), *Critical Terms for Art History*, Chicago: University of Chicago Press, second edition 2003, pp. 202–16.

45 Foster had dismissed the postwar 'neo-avant-garde' as simply a series of 'paradigm repetitions', see Foster, 'What's Neo about the Neo-Avant-Garde?': 5. Kapur, 'Dismantled Norms', p. 374.

46 Geeta Kapur, 'Proposition Avant-Garde: A View from the South', *Art Journal*, vol. 77 (1), 2018: 87–89 (italics in original), also cited (without italics) in Mathur, 'A Response': 91.

47 Weiss underlines the importance of the Havana Biennial as a place of live encounter and interaction that brought forth the possibility of using the notion of avant-garde outside of the Western canon, see Weiss, 'Some Thoughts'.

48 In the context of the Havana Biennial, Kapur, in a conversation with Rachel Weiss, commented on the 'aversion' to the term in India 'due to its tight association with dominating Western discourses', Weiss, 'Some Thoughts': 95.

or a stance of universal negation. By building on interactive languages that draw on memory, citation, or bricolage, a regenerated avant-garde seeks to dovetail issues of medium with argument instead of a surrender to a 'freewheeling libertarianism' that posits one against the other in order to protect art from 'any argumentative relationship to the past or the future'.[49] The following sections, as they draw our attention to the emergence and expansion of sites of cultural action beyond the West crucial to contemporary art, explore how these have recast the premises of an avant-garde as it becomes global.

Re-collecting – Contemporary Pasts

Old Arguments on Indigenism, an oil painting of 1989 by Nalini Malani (b. 1948), is a multi-layered reflection on the transcultural genealogies of the artist's work – its transparent quality is equally articulated by the material surface of the work.[50] By invoking two artists of an earlier generation, Amrita Sher-Gil and Frida Kahlo, the painting posits a relationship built on shared concerns and art practices. Working in gendered art worlds, the three artists are united by a particular self-consciousness that propels them towards the use of indigenous sources in their work, acknowledging simultaneously a shared critical stance towards the patriarchal underpinnings of that, which was glorified as tradition. Scattered across the painting are objects/icons associated with each of the artists – a woman with an exposed, bleeding spine, a sculpted figure, probably from a temple, a seated peasant girl, together with fleeing victims of violence who populate Malani's works, bearing their troubling signs such as severed limbs and prosthetic bodies. Malani has placed herself in the background, a shadowy presence, paintbrush in hand, observing. Five years later, Atul Dodiya's (b. 1959) self-portrait, *The Bombay Buccaneer*, is similarly replete with vignettes that reference different art historical sources.[51] The work can be described as a hybrid of art history and popular culture: the protagonist poses like a film star in Bollywood style, the lenses of his glasses mirror brightly coloured portraits of two pop artists-cum-mentors, David Hockney and Bhupen Khakhar, a Ralph Lauren logo of a polo player on the lower edge spells upper class consumerism. The overall tone is ironic, at the same time the image is an exploration of media and assemblage, acknowledging the genealogical strains of this form of art-making. The work of both artists, Malani and Dodiya, is conspicuously referential. While Malani delves into a globally dispersed archive of myths and literary narratives to pick her protagonists from Euripides, the Ramayana, Saadat Hasan Manto, Christa Wolf, or Heiner Müller, Dodiya

---

49 The expressions are from Kobena Mercer, 'The Cross-Cultural and the Contemporary', in: *Travel & See: Black Diaspora Art Practices since the 1980s*, Durham, NC: Duke University Press, 2016, pp. 262–76, here pp. 268–70.

50 Beth Citron writes of the artist having 'integrated transparency and layering into oil painting', see Bean (ed.), *Midnight to Boom*, p. 206. The work has been reproduced in the exhibition catalogue (plate 67, p. 209) and figures in 'India's Dialogical Modernism: Homi Bhabha in Conversation with Susan S. Bean', in: ibid, p. 28. See also Kapur, *When Was Modernism?*, p. 23.

51 Also reproduced in Bean (ed.), *Midnight to Boom*, plate 63, p. 201; for a discussion between Bhabha and Bean, p. 31.

experiments with a gallery of art historical figures across time that features, among others, the Mughal painter Ustad Mansur, Piero della Francesca, Duchamp, Picasso, Beuys, Jasper Johns, Gerhard Richter, or Bhupen Khakhar. Both artists continue a tradition characteristic of one strain of Indian artistic modernism, which conceived of itself as both cosmopolitan as well as rooted in the nation;[52] yet they carry this consciously dialogical engagement a step further to read art practice as a form of radical self-reflexivity that segregates transcultural hospitality from a celebration of nationalism.

Both Malani and Dodiya are situated in Mumbai; while a generation separates them in age, both have responded in their work to different aspects of the precarious urbanity of the mega-city with its confident rising middle-classes, its popular culture, at the same time its corruption and deepening class conflict. The 1990s left the city torn by religious violence, followed by the rise of xenophobic nationalism, which included renaming Bombay Mumbai in 1995, and marked the end of its century-old cosmopolitanism. Nation building in South Asia during and following decolonisation was seized by dilemmas that laid bare the fissures within the mythical imagined community. The discarding of the colonial yoke was at the same time the truncation of the national body. The trauma of partition had brought with it more than a million dead following the eruption of violence, together with the forced dis-placement of 10 to 12 million people. Yet 1947 was not a single event that terminated with the formation of independent nation-states. Its repressed memories continued to reverberate in postcolonial South Asia, to explode once more in the events of the turn of the century – the destruction of the Babri Mosque in Ayodhya (North India) in 1992 by activists of the Hindu right, the genocide of the Muslims in the western province of Gujarat ten years later, the continued production of jingoistic nationalism to mark the triangular relationship between India, Pakistan, and Bangladesh.[53] A transculturally oriented art practice in South Asia from the 1990s onwards has eschewed the celebratory triumphalism of a neoliberal economic and technological globalisation, even as it continues to be enthused by the possibilities of transcultural collaborations, which a connected world has opened up. More importantly, a persistent questioning of the nexus between the nation-state and culture has informed sig-nificant artistic initiatives, a sampling of which will be examined here. Indeed, a coupling

---

52 See M. F. Husain's work, *Man*, reproduced in Bean (ed.), *Midnight to Boom*, plate 4, p. 89; for an extensive discussion of Husain's art, Sumathi Ramaswamy (ed.), *Barefoot Across the Nation: Maqbool Fida Husain and the Idea of India*, London: Routledge, 2011; Khullar, *Worldly Affiliations*, Chapter 2. Husain's work in the context of the Progressive Artists' Group has been discussed in the previous chapter, 'Traversing Scale(s)'.

53 Recent studies of artistic responses to the Partition of the subcontinent include Bhaskar Sarkar, *Mourning the Nation: Indian Cinema in the Wake of Partition*, Durham, NC: Duke University Press, 2009; Iftikhar Dadi and Hammad Nasar (eds), *Lines of Control: Partition as Productive Space*, London: Green Cardamom, 2012; Natasha Ginwala (ed.), *My East is Your West: A Collateral Event at the 56th Venice Biennale*, New Delhi: Harper Collins, 2016; Alice Correa and Natasha Eaton (eds), *Partitions Special Issue, Third Text*, vol. 31 (2/3), 2017; Monica Juneja, 'Migration, Dispossession, Post-Memorial Recu-perations. An "Undisciplined" View of the Partition of the Indian Subcontinent', in: Burcu Dogramaci and Birgit Mersmann (eds), *Handbook of Art and Global Migration: Theories, Practices, and Challenges*, Berlin: De Gruyter, 2019, pp. 298–314.

of the promise of unbridled economic growth with the vision of a rejuvenated nation that has fuelled populist energies and turned governance into an instrument of coercion, forms the backdrop against which much of contemporary art unfolds.[54] Opening the history of the nation to fresh questions, to narrate the story of the nation so as to reconceive it as a transculturally constituted, polyphonous entity, requires a recourse to history and the archive that has come to inform art-making. Yet the work of art and artists to re-collect memories, lost or repressed, is confronted with an official culture of memory that mobilises a mythic past to the politics of majoritarian nationalism. Negotiating the faultline between imposed nativist memories and those transgressive moments of hope that have suffered erasure is a dialectic that contemporary art across the globe continues to juggle.

Debates about remembering the violent past – be it the Holocaust, the politics of Apartheid in South Africa, state terror in countries of Latin America, the Tiananmen Square massacres in China, or the genocide of Muslims in Bosnia – transcend the national contexts in which they generally originate, making the retrieval of history and memory a transculturally formed preoccupation among artists, as their work – and the artists themselves, often living in exile – circulates globally.[55] This in turn has led scholarship and exhibitions to probe, at a global level, the relationship between contemporary art and the archive.[56] 'Archive fever', as Enwezor, citing Jacques Derrida, describes the surging artistic engagement with the archive, involves recognising it as both resource, a repository to access the past, as well as a regulatory discursive system holding out the promise of taxonomic order. While film and photography, those 'critical instruments of archival modernity'[57] have been the primary media and channels of retrieval, the notion of the archive as an artistic storehouse has continued to expand to include literary narratives, myths – a sedimented bedrock of tradition – alongside of a mix of objects drawn from personal collections. Taken together, these have made the archival idea resilient in the hands of contemporary artists who have transformed its resources into aesthetic principles and have used archival legacies to connect art-making and historical narration.

Among the most prominent responses to the archival idea was Marcel Duchamp's *La boîte-en-valise* (1941–68), a miniaturisation of his corpus of works, codified into an archival

54 This concatenation has been persuasively fleshed out by Ravinder Kaur, *Brand New Nation: Capitalist Dreams and Nationalist Designs in Twenty-First Century India*, Stanford: Stanford University Press, 2020.

55 Two books by Andreas Huyssen on the politics of memory and its relationship to art and architectural practice are: *Twilight Memories. Marking Time in a Culture of Amnesia*, London: Routledge, 1995; and *Present Pasts: Urban Palimpsests and the Politics of Memory*, Stanford: Stanford University Press, 2003. See also Sharon MacDonald, *Memorylands: Heritage and Identity in Europe Today*, London: Routledge, 2013.

56 Hal Foster, 'An Archival Impulse', *October*, no. 110 (Fall), 2004: 3–22; Ingrid Schaffner and Matthias Winzen (eds), *Deep Storage: Sammeln, Speichern, Archivieren in der Kunst*, Munich: Prestel, 1997; Okwui Enwezor (ed.), *Archive Fever: Uses of the Document in Contemporary Art*, Göttingen: Steidl, 2008.

57 Enwezor (ed.), *Archive Fever*, p. 12.

system cum mobile museum in a suitcase.[58] Small-scale facsimiles of the artist's work were placed in a box, made to slip into a valise. The work was both an attempt by the artist to save his works from oblivion, while also an ironic comment on the museum as institution, the artwork as artefact, and on the myth of a monographic artistic identity. About half a century later, Atul Dodiya, whose early work wrestled with the anti-art impulse of Duchamp, created *Broken Branches*, an installation that draws on the notion of the archive that he conjoins to the early modern *Wunderkammer*, to coax a miscellany of objects and images into a story of the present and its pasts (Plate 4.1). *Broken Branches* is a room-size installation of cabinets, closely modelled on the display vitrines of the Gandhi Museum in Porbandar, a small town in the region of Saurashtra in Gujarat where Gandhi was born and from where the artist's family comes. The work, created for the exhibition *Home-Street-Shrine-Bazaar-Museum* curated by the artist Gulammohammed Sheikh for the Manchester Art Gallery in 2002, was a direct response to the pogrom of the same year orchestrated by the Hindu Right against the Muslim community of Gujarat that had left thousands killed, maimed, or traumatised.[59] The glass-fronted cabinets resonate in many directions – they are a reminder of early modern cabinets of curiosities, later appropriated by artists of the modernist avant-garde such as Jeff Koons, Matthew Barney, and above all Joseph Beuys, whose work has served Dodiya as a repository of references – a transcultural archive – to draw on.[60] Additionally, the design of Dodiya's cabinets exudes a clearly colonial flavour – such glass-fronted cases were a staple framing and display device for ethnographic objects and archaeological finds in museums established during the early decades of the twentieth century and that have lingered on in provincial sites such as the Porbandar Gandhi museum. The iconic figure of Gandhi – a symbol of compassion and non-violent resistance – forms one main, though implicit, point of reference in the aftermath of genocidal violence. While Dodiya's installation displays a fascination with the archival idea as a facet of memory, the objects that make up this meditation on mourning and damage – the latter both bodily and spiritual – work more in an allusive, evocative, even elusive manner, rather than add up to the discursive logic of a conventional archive. The assemblage of photographs and objects is subject to no single taxonomic arrangement; its eclectic

---

58 Reproduced in Enwezor (ed.), *Archive Fever*, p. 15. For an extensive discussion, T. J. Demos, *The Exiles of Marcel Duchamp*, Cambridge, MA: MIT Press, 2007.

59 It was also shown in the following year in New York, at Bose Pacia Modern, see Peter Nagy, 'Atul Dodiya: A Gargantuan Responsibility', in the exhibition catalogue, *Atul Dodiya: Broken Branches*, Bose Pacia Modern, New York, 2003 (n.p.). The work has also been discussed by Geeta Kapur, 'Mortal Remains', in: Charles Merewether and John Potts (eds), *After the Event: New Perspectives on Art History*, Manchester: Manchester University Press, 2010, pp. 132–55, here pp. 140–46.

60 For an enumeration of Dodiya's sources, see Ranjit Hoskote, 'Atul Dodiya: An Encyclopaedist's Desire for the World', in idem (ed.), *Atul Dodiya*, Munich: Prestel, 2013, pp. 12–87, here 65–67. The artist makes his archive the subject of another work, using the same device of a glass case, *Meditation (with Open Eyes)*, 2011, Tate Modern, which features on the cover of this book. The case contains an assemblage of portraits – photographs of Robert Rauschenberg, Louise Bourgeois, Gerhard Richter, Joseph Beuys, Pablo Picasso, Rabindranath Tagore and a few others – and objects including copies of art works and figurines, citations. Two of the cabinets acknowledge the dialogue that Dodiya's work has carried out with that of Piet Mondrian, whose painting *Composition B (No. II) With Red* has been displayed next to Dodiya's cabinets.

mix perforates the membrane of public and private memories. Grainy newspaper photographs of Gandhi laying a foundation stone, of Gandhi and Jinnah in animated exchange, a 1970s photograph of the Arte Povera artist Mimo Palladino in Manhattan, scenes of villagers fleeing a flood, a one-year-old orphan girl robbed of her corneas[61] – all attest to the artist's assiduous documentation of many years. Photographic testimonies share space with etchings – Dürer's *Holy Family* – with watercolours, prints of birds from an atlas of natural history, family photographs – Dodiya's father with a diseased, distended stomach, a symptom of the acute ascites of which he died, the artist's daughter playing with a bone – further, with workmen's tools, an open lexicon and bric-a-brac such as a wooden toy model of a woman with a *chakki*, a reference to childhood memory encapsulated in an unforgettable watercolour from an earlier work, *Tearscapes*.[62] A recurring motif that runs through the display cases are the visible signs of the human toll claimed by violence that maims a society – bones, handmade prostheses, amputated limbs, and crutches, all placed in poignant propinquity with birds poised in graceful flight.

Broken Branches, as Peter Nagy puts it, 'could accommodate the multiple references inferred by home, street, shrine, bazaar and museum'.[63] The artist's seemingly improvised, random collation of diverse materials, also described as 'an encyclopaedia without index',[64] consciously disrupts the discipline from which the archive derives its authority as a repository that enables the retrieval of history. The work instead plays with the *objet trouvé* or readymade,[65] and subjects its inbuilt instability engendered by the simultaneous claims projected on to it, to a transcultural process of re-historicisation, to then use it to record the tragic failure of Gandhi's utopian vision. Coined by Marcel Duchamp and canonised by his *Fountain* of 1917, the readymade involved an act of reframing an object – whose selection was a matter of 'visual indifference'[66] – and which at the same time involved an ontological shift by blurring the distinction between a work of art and a commodity. For Dodiya, some

61 This is a reference to an earlier work of the artist, *Sharda* (2001), cited in Hoskote, 'Atul Dodiya', p. 58.

62 Dodiya speaks of *Woman with a Chakki* as follows: 'she is inspired by an old woman who was my next door neighbour. She had been widowed at the age of 18 and was already the mother of 4 children by then. She worked to support her family, making pickles and other eatables. She had a large handmill, a chakki, and all her life she worked on it.' Cited in Ranjit Hoskote and Nancy Adajania (eds), *Atul Dodiya: The Dialogue Series*, Mumbai: Popular Prakashan, 2011, p. 90. On the *Tearscapes* series, Sumathi Ramaswamy, 'The Wretched of the Nation', *Third Text*, vol. 31 (2/3), 2017: 213–37.

63 Nagy, 'Atul Dodiya', n.p.

64 Hoskote, 'Atul Dodiya', p. 67.

65 In my discussion of Dodiya's work I use the terms *objet trouvé* and readymade interchangeably, though our attention has been drawn to the divergent legacies of each of these terms, see for instance Margaret Iversen, 'Readymade, Found Object, Photograph', *Art Journal*, vol. 63 (2), 2004: 45–57. My discussion of Dodiya's re-historicising of the notion shows that his appropriation encompasses a set of valences that renders such a distinction redundant.

66 In a talk he gave at the Museum of Modern Art, New York in October 1961, Duchamp declared: 'A point I want very much to establish is that the choice of these "readymades" was never dictated by esthetic delectation. This choice was based on a reaction of visual indifference with at the same time a total absence of good or bad taste … in fact a complete anesthesia (sic.).' Marcel Duchamp, 'Apropos of "Readymades"', in: Michel Sanouillet and Elmer Peterson (eds), *The Writings of Marcel Duchamp*, New York: Oxford University Press, 1973, pp. 141–42, here p. 41.

nine decades later, the choice of the *objet trouvé* was far from being a matter of artistic indifference; it was shaped by the object's absorption of the pastness of the present, by its potential to allow re-collection. Dodiya's readymades – sepia-toned photographs, a construction worker's tools, a leg brace – bearing traces of use (deviating in this respect from Duchamp's urinal), are both material residue of and witness to history. While Dodiya distances himself from the work of negation performed by Duchamp's readymades in order to test the limits of the work of art, the objects he chooses do expand the idea of medium in the Duchampian sense, though this expansion goes beyond the art institution and opens the work even wider to find a place for subjectivity and sociality. In the seemingly random assemblage brought together within the glass cases of *Broken Branches,* each object evinces the passage of time in that it stands for a physical condensation and sedimentation of memory – a reminder of utopia, loss, damage, and makeshift repair. Their togetherness enables the formation of new, seemingly incongruous, inner relationships; it hints at unanticipated readings, reframing the relationship between objects and the archive. In the final analysis, the authority to narrate history is now delegated to the viewer.

'Memory sculpture' is a term coined by Andreas Huyssen to designate a kind of sculpture or installation 'not centred on spatial configuration alone, but that powerfully inscribes a dimension of localizable, even corporeal memory into the work'.[67] Huyssen considers this genre as a transcultural phenomenon, produced by artists in India, South Africa, Latin America, or countries of the former Soviet bloc – Vivan Sundaram, William Kentridge, Doris Salcedo, or Miroslaw Balka are some artists studied by Huyssen, whose concerns reciprocally resonate within a globally connected art world.[68] Memory sculpture remains clearly distinct from the public monument or memorial in that it embodies lived, private memories, collective or generational, rather than standing for official memory. It performs 'memory work that activates body, space and temporality, matter and imagination, presence and absence in a complex relationship with the[ir] beholder'.[69] The installation *Broken Branches* qualifies as a member of this genre, not least owing to the circumstance that it addresses the individual, or uses the private, taxonomically non-quantifiable archive to address the community; its place is in the gallery rather than in a public square. More than any other historical figure on the Indian subcontinent, Gandhi has been appropriated for commemorative purposes by innumerable organisations across the political spectrum. His image appears on postage stamps,

67 Huyssen, *Present Pasts*, p. 110.
68 Andreas Huyssen, 'The Memory Works of Vivan Sundaram', in: Deepak Ananth and Anna Schneider (eds), *Vivan Sundaram: Disjunctures*, Munich: Prestel, 2018, pp. 88–101; Andreas Huyssen, 'Doris Salcedo's Memory Sculpture: *Unland: The Orphan's Tunic*', in *Present Pasts*, pp. 110–21; Andreas Huyssen, *William Kentridge and Nalini Malani: The Shadow Play as Medium of Memory*, Milan: Edizione Charta, 2013.
On Vivan Sundaram's forays into history and the archive, see Kapur, 'Mortal Remains'; Vivan Sundaram, *History Project*, New Delhi: Tulika Books, 2017; Ananth and Schneider (eds), *Vivan Sundaram: Disjunctures*; Saloni Mathur, 'The Edifice Complex', in: *A Fragile Inheritance: Radical Stakes in Indian Contemporary Art*, Durham, NC: Duke University Press, 2019, pp. 72–95.
69 Huyssen, *Present Pasts*, p. 111.

currency notes, hangs on the walls of public offices and schools; roads are named after him, the site of his assassination has been made into a national monument. *Broken Branches* defies this official culture of memory, even as it urgently seeks to secure the past from the pervasive threat of amnesia: the work's allusions to Gandhi's visible, ubiquitous public persona are sparse, implied rather than explicit.[70] The old, often discarded or forgotten materials and their arrangement within the installation signals towards an understanding of memory as (re-)collection, as indissolubly linked to the materiality of things and bodies in time and space. The assembled elements are neither votive objects nor a martyr's memorabilia, even as they induce mourning and feelings of human loss. Their non-spectacular textures together with their dense propinquity within a glass case resist the lure of quick consumption, to demand instead deep, sustained looking before their associations can be grasped and absorbed. Remembering here is both specific – the aftermath of the recent religiously driven massacre – as well as an enduring process, wherein the viewer is pressed into dialoguing with the work, forming associations, reading analogies, and not least unravelling the artist's private gesture of world-making that understands his art as transcultural co-production.[71]

The contemporary artist's recourse to the archive – and by extension to the museum – has emerged as a powerful and widespread trope, in and beyond South Asia, in the face of intensifying culture wars and fundamentalist violence. Yet the implications of the strategies adopted in different instances vary, as I will discuss while examining a set of recent works by the artist Jitish Kallat (b. 1974), who has both drawn on archival documents and located his work within the collection of a museum of history. Kallat, an artist of the generation following Dodiya's, delves into the archive to retrieve seminal historical documents, which while endlessly republished in textbooks, have degenerated into meaningless abstractions, and which he transforms into dramatically material artworks. In a series titled *Public Notice* large installations stage the texts of speeches by Jawaharlal Nehru, Mohandas Karamchand Gandhi, and the religious reformer and philosopher Swami Vivekananda, to have them revisited and contemplated as text rather than heard as powerful oration.[72] The first work of the series, made in 2003 following the genocidal violence in Gujarat, returns to Nehru's speech 'Tryst with Destiny' delivered from the ramparts of Delhi's Red Fort on the midnight

70 A number of contemporary artists have responded to an urge to return to the figure of Gandhi. In 1999, Dodiya devoted a series of watercolours titled *An Artist of Non-Violence* to the persona of Gandhi. Others include Gulammohammed Sheikh, G. R. Iranna, Tallur L. N. A recent work on the subject of Gandhi in the artistic imagination is Sumathi Ramaswamy, *Gandhi in the Gallery: The Art of Disobedience*, New Delhi: Roli Books, 2020.

71 Dodiya's works are replete with reflections and dense citations that pay homage to artists across time and region – Piero della Francesca, Dürer, Duchamp, Beuys, Jasper Johns. In his words, 'being an artist, the whole span of art matters to me', in: Hoskote and Adajania (eds), *Atul Dodiya: The Dialogue Series*, p. 53, see also pp. 27, 93. His concept of art as transculturally co-produced is expressed in *Meditation (with Open Eyes)*, 2011, see above.

72 'Public Notice' is an administrative term, used often to designate directives or information to be disseminated, or proclamations of policy. For a description of the series, opulently illustrated, see Suhanya Raffel, 'Ruminations on the Grammar of a Universe: Back to the Future', in: Natasha Ginwala (ed.), *Jitish Kallat*, Ahmedabad: Mapin Publishing, pp. 202–33.

of 14 August 1947 to commemorate the birth of an independent India. The artist transcribed the words of the speech in inflammable rubber adhesive material onto five acrylic mirrored panels. Each alphabet was then set on fire, so that in the end Nehru's words, now charred, were branded onto the mirror's surface that in turn was distorted from the heat and sent back warped reflections of viewers as they moved across the panels, stopping by to decipher the text. This gesture, akin to a cremation of prophetic words, was repeated in a second variant of the theme, this time to invoke the act of exhumation. *Public Notice 2* of 2007 dwells upon a speech by Gandhi delivered on the eve of the historic Dandi March (also known as Salt March), when Gandhi and seventy-eight of his followers marched over twenty-four days from the Sabarmati Ashram in Ahmedabad to the coastal village of Dandi. Here, Gandhi gathered salt grains on the seashore in defiance of the British tax and monopoly over the sale and distribution of salt. The letters and words of Kallat's large installation were formed of 4,479 pieces of fibreglass bones that evoked a display of exhumed archaeological specimens, now cleaned and systematically arranged on a museum shelf. In the words of Chaitanya Sambrani, 'Kallat's "bones" are both reminders and remainders'.[73] The fusion of salt, speech and bones has strong bio-political overtones reminding us that politics is inseparable from living bodies, from the right to life and self-determination. The third work of the series was staged on the steps of the grand staircase of the Art Institute of Chicago, where the speech given by Vivekananda to the World's Parliament of Religions on 11 September 1893 in the same building was reproduced in LED lights on the steps.[74] The content of the speech calling for tolerance and the end of religious fanaticism resonated profoundly at a time when India and the rest of the world were being torn apart by religious strife and xenophobic nationalism. The coincidental date of 11 September led the artist to inscribe one more layer of memory within the body of his work by making his words appear in the five colours used by the Homeland Security Advisory System in the United States to signify levels of terrorist threat. Finally, *Covering Letter* (2012), a video projection through a wall of fog, is the text of a letter written by Gandhi to Adolf Hitler, dated 23 July 1939, urging him to reconsider his violent plans of war.[75] The mist surrounding the text echoes the futility of Gandhi's words in the war-mongering climate of the times. All these works have temporality inscribed within them as they propel the visitors of these installations into another time and place, during their slow journey through the lines of text in a gallery space, far removed from a setting of the past, while meditating on the relevance of the words they read to the troubled present. Yet these works also dramatise the material of art, holding on to the emphatic notion of the object that does not dissolve in an act of return to the performance of speech. It is the object that enacts the process of memory.

73   Chaitanya Sambrani, 'Of Bones and Salt: Jitish Kallat's *Public Notice 2*', in: Art Gallery of New South Wales & Sherman Contemporary Art Foundation, *Jitish Kallat: Public Notice 2*, Art Gallery of New South Wales: Sydney 2016, pp. 11–17, here p. 13.
74   See Madhuvanti Ghose (ed.), *Jitish Kallat: Public Notice 3*, Chicago: Art Institute of Chicago, 2011.
75   Sambrani, 'Of Bones and Salt', p. 17, reproduced in Raffel, 'Ruminations on the Grammar', pp. 214–15.

Contemporary art's return to history coupled with the self-reflexivity that induces a questioning of art history and its institutions has resulted in artists being invited to work within museums and intervene within its spaces, which are also spaces that produce and stabilise social memory. Even as such a move continues to gain popularity in many places and museums of the world, its workings and long-term implications remain rooted in a wide range of considerations, depending on the genre and particular history of the museum in question. In general, artists are urged to consider the museum and its collection as an archive and a place of 'fieldwork', of experiment and display; they are invited by museum curators to invest old objects with new interpretations, to excavate, even counteract difficult histories, to 'disorient the frames'[76] of the museum and question the understanding of heritage built into its collection and its pedagogy.[77] The Bhau Daji Lad Museum of the city of Mumbai, formerly the Victoria and Albert Museum, is among the museums that have in the recent years opened their doors to contemporary artists, inviting them to respond to the museum's archival holdings and its collections as well as its institutional histories with a view to introducing 'more nuanced and inclusive counter histories'.[78]

In 2011, Jitish Kallat created a set of works to be inserted within the setting of the museum – in its long central hall, built in Victorian style as well as within its display cases. One more work involved re-working an image from the museum's restoration archive.[79] *Circa* is a sculpture comprising 120 pieces erected as an ensemble resembling a bamboo scaffolding that a resident of any Indian city would immediately associate with a construction site. The work occupied the centre of the long, resplendent Victorian hall of the museum, enclosing the marble statue of Prince Albert within its frame. Cast in pigmented resin and steel and bound together by coir ropes, the individual poles turn out, on closer observation to be sculpted surfaces inscribed with images of animals caught in acts of procreation or of devouring each other. These motifs, we learn, have been extracted from the animal reliefs that populate the neo-Gothic archways and capitals of the entrance porch of Mumbai's major commuter railway terminus, the Victoria Terminus (renamed Chhatrapati Shivaji Maharaj Terminus).[80] Also within the hall, set among the glass vitrines displaying museum objects, is another life-size, painted black lead and steel sculpture, *Annexation*, a title that unmistakeably references

76 Ranjit Hoskote, 'The Afterlife of the Past, the Mimesis of Climate: Jitish Kallat's Interventions in the Space and Time of the Museum', in: Ginwala (ed.), *Jitish Kallat*, pp. 234–71, here p. 237.

77 The opening of the museum and its collections as a space of 'fieldwork' for contemporary artists was a curatorial initiative launched by Clémentine Deliss at the ethnological museum of Frankfurt whose name was changed to *Weltkulturenmuseum* (Museum of World Cultures). For a discussion of this programme, Clémentine Deliss (ed.), *Object Atlas: Fieldwork in the Museum*, Berlin: Kerber Verlag, 2012.

78 Tasneem Z. Mehta, the current director of the museum, in *Verve Magazine*, 13 March 13, 2018, https://www.vervemagazine.in/arts-and-culture/why-you-must-catch-asymmetrical-objects-at-the-dr-bhau-daji-lad-mumbai-city-museum (last accessed 22 September 2020).

79 Hoskote, 'The Afterlife of the Past'. These works have also been described on the artist's website: https://jitishkallat.com/works/circa-fieldnotes/ (last accessed September 22, 2020).
    The following account summarises the above descriptions before it engages with some of Hoskote's conclusions.

80 See https://jitishkallat.com/works/circa-fieldnotes/ (last accessed 22 September 2020).

the colonial order, of which the museum too is seen as a product.[81] The overblown sculpture is modelled on an old-fashioned Primus, a kerosene stove, widely used in Indian middle-class kitchens, before liquid petroleum gas became readily available for domestic consumption. Here too, the entire surface is densely populated with hundreds of animals and grotesque creatures culled from the same Victorian source, once more caught in primal acts of gorging food, biting, preying on each other. Hoskote reads these works as an allegory of urban precarity and the 'dog-eat-dog aggressiveness' it breeds.[82] The logical consequence of such a mode of existence is violence and rioting, which is the subject of another installation, *Anger at the Speed of Fright*, composed of sixty-two painted figures, each some fifteen centimetres in height, as if in mimicry of clay figurines of regional types that form part of the museum's display. Kallat's figures fill a vitrine close to ground level, granting the museum visitor a surveyor's view from above. They make up a scene of public violence that includes goons armed with bricks or metal rods, ready to strike, policemen threatening the troublemakers, ordinary citizens, victims fallen to the ground. The work is clearly a rendering of rioting and street violence that had become a frighteningly regular feature of everyday life in a city sundered apart by extremist violence.[83]

To read these insertions into the exhibitionary regime of the museum as 'seismic tremors',[84] as an interpretation of history that forcefully injects a dystopian present within an institutional space committed to conserving the past, is at one level a plausible interpretation of their content. Yet its ambivalent effects make it necessary to query the epistemic implications of the curatorial move to temporarily bring contemporary art into a museum that houses historical and ethnographic collections. To posit that contemporary art, given its ability to challenge the illusion of historical stability embedded within what allegedly continues to be a 'sanctum of Victoriana',[85] needs to be brought in to infuse life and relevance into a former colonial museum, assumes in turn that the museum has remained frozen in its colonial habitus. Founded in 1857 by George Birdwood as a museum of national history, economy, geology, industry, and arts, the museum, now renamed after another of its founding members, Sir Bhau Daji Lad, has been consciously recalibrated in the postcolonial present to emancipate it from its colonial legacy. It was reopened to the public in 2008, after intensive renovation that restored its original Palladian architecture and resplendent Victorian interior. The decision to do so is informed, less by a celebratory impulse to monumentalise the colonial past, and more the need to historicise the museum's identity without whitewashing its history – the latter a trend increasingly encountered among populist regimes.[86] If the museum in colonial

---

81 Hoskote, 'The Afterlife of the Past'.
82 Ibid., p. 247.
83 See https://jitishkallat.com/works/anger-at-the-speed-of-fright-1/ (last accessed 22 September 2020).
84 Hoskote, 'The Afterlife of the Past', p. 249.
85 Ibid.
86 On the restoration of the museum building, see Tasneem Z. Mehta, *A Unique Partnership: The Restoration and Revitalisation of the Dr. Bhau Daji Lad Mumbai City Museum*, Mumbai: Dr. Bhau Daji Lal Museum Trust, 2009, pp. 43–45.

India was marked as a tool to control, educate, and civilise, during the postcolonial period it increasingly became a locus of an official culture of the nation, though, in general, the appropriation of the institution for nationalist ends was not always easily achieved. The process has registered shifts from the Nehruvian era that foregrounded the dictum 'Unity in Diversity' to the contemporary period marked by religious revivalism and cultural nationalism.[87] The Bhau Daji Lad Museum sees itself as a museum of the city of Mumbai with a civic function – a space of participation and citizenship, both 'pedagogical' and 'performative', in the sense described by Dipesh Chakrabarty.[88]

The task of questioning the 'objectivity' of a museum's classificatory order, for instance by dismantling tenacious dichotomies such as art/artefact, fine art/craft, and by recasting object histories as histories of making, of the transcultural migration of makers, knowledge, and materials, are all challenges that the Bhau Daji Lad Museum continues to grapple with as part of its agenda to develop a new aesthetic lexicon for its collections.[89] While the incorporation of contemporary art within this agenda might effectively serve as a supplemental aesthetic for the museum's overarching strategy of reanimating its narratives, we need to keep our feelers primed for tensions built into the premise that makes the contemporary artwork and artist a privileged bearer of criticality, of the responsibility to 'emancipate the objects of the museum from the narratives into which they are embedded'.[90] The artwork, when inserted within the existing museum display, deploys the freedom it possesses as art to introduce the present into old collections and thereby create fresh knowledge; yet, what are the histories that such knowledge suppresses through the act of overwriting? While the visitor is meant to revisit the museum objects equipped with a perspective furnished by the contemporary artist's intervention, to what extent is the former able to share in the assumption about what art is and the license it enjoys to jolt the collections out of their 'hushed serenity[91]? One immediate impact of juxtaposing the contemporary and the historical is that, even as the intention behind such a placing may be to dissolve the art/artefact divide, an inbuilt asymmetry becomes palpable and gets perpetuated: in other words, the makers of a large number of objects housed in glass cases continue to remain unnamed, the collection itself is rendered indeterminate, while the

In India the last decades have seen innumerable debates on the issue of removing material signs of the colonial past from the urban setting – beginning with the removal of the statue of George V from the canopy in the heart of New Delhi, the renaming of roads, and the most recent project of the present government to 'refurbish' major parts of Lutyen's Delhi by replacing colonial buildings that house, for instance the National Museum or the National Archives and the Secretariat complex, by what the historian Narayani Gupta calls a 'Modernist-Brutalist Burj Dubai concoction', Narayani Gupta, 'The Age of Replacement', *The Indian Express*, 19 September 2019.

87   Saloni Mathur and Kavita Singh (eds), *No Touching, No Spitting, No Praying: The Museum in South Asia*, London and New Delhi: Routledge, 2015, pp. 6–7. The essays in the volume bring to light the immensely variegated and continuously proliferating landscape of museums in India and underline the difficulty of generalising about their intellectual agenda or curatorial strategies, even as these unfold against a larger background of nationalism, globalism, religion, and late capitalist modernity.

88   Dipesh Chakrabarty, 'Museums in Late Democracies', *Humanities Research*, vol. IX (1), 2002: 5–12.

89   See Mehta, *A Unique Partnership*, pp. 124–75.

90   Hoskote, 'The Afterlife of the Past', p. 237.

91   The description is from Hoskote, 'The Afterlife of the Past', p. 256.

authority to interpret both past and present is vested in the work of the contemporary artist whose position is reaffirmed within a modern system of art that places the singular artist at the pinnacle of creativity. It might be salutary to remember that both the categories – the musealised object and the modernist work of art – were constituted together through a set of representational practices and technologies that do more than simply display them. Delegating the task of interpreting a collection to a contemporary artist, who enjoys the freedom to subvert its narratives, also ends up naturalising the practices and histories that made such art possible. The museum and its exhibits are epistemological authorities that constitute systems of value – to be able to convey its message, an artwork inserted into a display vitrine stakes a claim to the same authority that it seeks to undermine. During the recent years museum curators in South Asia, even as they are confronted with the pressures of a state-mandated national culture on the one hand and the divergent claims to representation by a number of social communities on the other, have engaged in creative, even audacious experiments, to challenge the ideas of authenticity or wholeness of cultures, meant to be read off objects, collected and exhibited since time immemorial.[92] Though an elaboration of the strategies that museums might devise to 'make appropriate objects tell "inappropriate" stories'[93] is beyond the scope of this discussion, unlocking the critical potential of contemporary art, when brought into conversation with historical collections, could be a promising prospect. To realise its promise, the terms of that conversation would need to be recast, so as to rest on greater reciprocity while questioning inherited aesthetic and institutional frames. For instance, creating an assemblage of the historical and the contemporary might productively be steered towards such 'counter histories'[94] able to bring to light diverse acts of making and curating – be it an installation, figurines in a glass case, a woven rug or a lithograph – as a site of distributed agency, unravelling thereby a host of assumptions surrounding notions of art, the artefact, and the singular artist.[95]

Performing the Body Politic

In *Who Sings the Nation-State?* Judith Butler cites a remarkable instance where unregistered Latin American immigrants to the United States took to singing the US national anthem in Spanish as a performative act of declaring 'a non-nationalist or counter-nationalist mode of belonging'.[96] Such a radically different form of group belonging, in Butler's words, posits a 'collectivity that comes to exercise its freedom in a language or a set of languages for which

---

92   Mathur and Singh (eds), *No Touching, No Spitting, No Praying*, Introduction and the reports under the section Museum Watching.
93   Gyan Prakash, 'Museum Matters', in Bettina M. Carbonell (ed.), *Museum Studies: An Anthology of Contexts*, Chichester: Wiley-Blackwell, 2012, pp. 317–23, here p. 322.
94   Mehta, *Verve Magazine*.
95   I will return to this issue in the last section of this chapter.
96   Judith Butler and Gayatri C. Spivak, *Who Sings the Nation-State? Language, Politics, Belonging*, New York/Calcutta: Seagull Books, 2007, pp. 58–59.

difference and translation are irreducible'.[97] The performative gesture that installs plurality within a political entity constituted by notions of linguistic and cultural homogeneity leads Butler to conclude that 'there can be no radical politics of change without performative contradiction'.[98] This section builds on the notion of public discursive demonstration as a destabilising mode of collective being, to investigate art-making as one such site from which the yet unforeseen possibilities within the presumed monolith of the nation-state can be made visible and palpable. In examining art's potential to know 'otherwise', the following analysis zooms into the intersection of gender, sexuality, and ethnicity on the one hand, and the dialectic of freedom and the unfree on the other, which constitute the core of the national idea. Drawing on the concept of an embodied 'corporeal-materialist aesthetic' elaborated within feminist studies, I further signal towards the importance of gender as a category within a global/transcultural paradigm, and its role as a lens to make entangled differences intelligible within a work of art.[99] Such an approach, as Marsha Meskimmon underlines, enables us to grasp the implosive dynamics of performance within a production of knowledge that eschews the subject-object/artist-model binaries implicit within Cartesian dualism, to reconfigure a concept of agency conjoined with ethical responsibility.[100]

The case study elaborated within this section zooms into the work of the artist Pushpamala N. (b. 1956) whose spirited experiments with a genre designated as photo-performance have attracted considerable critical attention.[101] Trained as a sculptor, the artist shifted to photography and performance in the 1990s, reinventing herself as an ethnographer in search of readymades: a repertoire of floating images, from which she chooses favourites to constantly

97 Ibid., p. 62.

98 Ibid., p. 66.

99 Marsha Meskimmon, 'Art Matters: Feminist-Corporeal Materialist Aesthetics', in: Hilary Robinson and Maria Elena Buszek (eds), *A Companion to Feminist Art*, Chichester: Wiley-Blackwell, 2019, pp. 353–67. Also, Donna Haraway, 'Situated Knowledges: The Science Question in Feminism and the Privilege of Partial Perspective', *Feminist Studies*, vol. 14 (3), 1988: 575–99.

100 Meskimmon, 'Art Matters', p. 354.

101 The artist Pushpamala N. studied at Baroda and is based in Bangalore. Her work – in particular her experiments with different media and genres such as cinema, photography and performance – has been the subject of considerable critical writing. See Geeta Kapur, 'Gender Mobility: Through the Lens of Five Women Artists', in Maura Reilly (ed.), *Global Feminisms: New Directions in Contemporary Art*, London: Merrell, 2007, pp. 79–96; Ajay Sinha, 'Pushpamala N. and the "Art" of Cinephilia in India', in: Christiane Brosius and Roland Wenzlhuemer (eds), *Transcultural Turbulences: Towards a Multi-Sited Reading of Image Flows*, Heidelberg: Springer Books, 2011, pp. 221–48; Latika Gupta, 'Pushpamala N. And Clare Arni', in: Jodi Throckmorton (ed.), *Postdate: Photography and Inherited History in India*, Berkeley: University of California Press, 2015, pp. 100–11; Parul D. Mukherji, 'Self in Stills, Conflict Within the Frame: In Conversation with Pushpamala N.', in: Gayatri Sinha (ed.), *Voices of Change: 20 Indian Artists*, Mumbai: Marg Publications, 2010, pp. 62–75; Pushpamala N. and Claire Arni (eds), *Native Women of India: Manners and Customs*, exhibition catalogue, Bangalore: India Foundation for the Arts, 2004; Marta Jakimowicz, 'The Self Versus Self-Images and the Cliché', in: *Pushpamala N: Indian Lady*, New York: Bose Pacia, 2004, n.p.; Sharanya Murali, 'An Eye for an Eye: The Hapticality of Collaborative Photo-Performance in *Native Women of India*', *Theatre Research International*, vol. 44 (2), 2019: 118–34; Monica Juneja and Sumathi Ramaswamy (eds), *Motherland: Women and Nation in Pushpamala N's Photo-Performances*, New Delhi: Roli Books, 2022. This body of critical writing has brought forth a number of conceptual terms to describe the work of the artist: mimicry, mimesis, masquerade, cinephilic practice.

reinvent her persona. The term photo-performance has come into usage, not to describe the embodied performance of the artist or a performance made only for its remediation. Rather, it stands for a work that takes as its point of origin a pre-existing photograph, which Pushpamala then 'performs,' re-staging and remediating it through a co-production with a photographer. Her early projects were conceived and executed together with Claire Arni (b. 1962), a photographer born in Scotland who has spent most of her life in South India. In addition, Pushpamala and Arni worked together with a team of designers and technicians who produce the theatrical settings that animate the work. The starting point of photo-performance is always a concrete image, most frequently one that has been reproduced in print and circulates through media and market networks – be it a calendar image, a reproduction of a museum exhibit, a photograph of a film star or a politician from the cover of a glossy magazine. In this construction, the artist's role can be likened to that of a modern consumer who picks and chooses from a vast array of circulating images. Pushpamala then proceeds to re-enact the image by 'entering it' with her performative body – here a Benjaminian approach comes to be grafted onto the idea of performative mimesis: 'One is inside the image, not just outside, looking.'[102] The re-enactment, captured by the photographer's lens, then becomes one more photograph in a stream of ever-proliferating, constantly circulating, fabricated images. As such, the work points to the art image's tendency towards reproduction, and directs our attention to the tangled question of the differing value accorded to the original versus its copies – a distinction that came with Western modernity and has been transcultured within art historical thinking globally. Once photographed, the performative body of the artist becomes a still image, disconnected from the primary performative activity. Even as the artist experiments with genres, notably the cinematic and the theatrical, it is the logic of still photography that ultimately prevails.

By bringing together performance and body, the concept of the performative self enables a notion of selfhood to unfold through a body that operates on multiple registers – the physical, the psycho-emotional, and the self-reflexive. The significance of corporeality to subjectivity, the integral entanglement of body and mind together with the mutuality of subjects and objects, as elaborated in corporeal aesthetics, makes this way of art-making go beyond illustrating, representing, or symbolising its subjects/objects, to make the work a hypothetical proposition about something that could potentially be. Even as the artist remains invariably present 'under the image' of the figure she re-enacts, these chosen figures, according to Marta Jakimowicz, do not represent her alter egos; rather they are an instance where 'the feminine

---

102 This oft-cited assertion of the artist is recorded in 'Native Women. Pushpamala N. and Claire Arni in Conversation with N. Rajyalakshmi', in *Native Women of India*, pp. 135–40, here p. 135. See also Sinha, 'Pushpamala N.' for an explication of Benjamin's approach to art as a 'way of seeing the inside of things', pp. 221–22. On performing mimesis, see Parul D. Mukherji, 'Who Is Afraid of Mimesis? Contesting the Common Sense of Indian Aesthetics through the Theory of "Mimesis" or Anukaraṇa Vâda', in: Arindam Chakrabarty (ed.), *Indian Aesthetics and the Philosophy of Art*, London: Bloomsbury, 2016, pp. 71–92.

has to confront the feminist'.[103] Photo-performance is a journey to enter, explore, probe; further to comprehend, interpret, and almost always to play out with a mix of sympathy, at times empathy with the subject, as well as irony evoked by a range of practices, not least the making and circulation of images.

Placing the self inside the image allows the artist to unpack the message of a pre-existing representation through the intrusion of her own persona – her body, her emotions, and her intellect. In this way, the form of photo-performance acts to deconstruct icons and typologies. Socially ingrained representations that make up a staple of visual culture have been among the popular subjects chosen for this form of iconic interruption: for example, colonial strategies of classification, enumeration, and hierarchisation of Indigenous peoples – an obsession with labelling that continued in postcolonial India to create popular stereotypes in the fraught domains of gender, caste, and religion. In the ambitious project titled 'Native Women of South India – Manners and Customs' (2000–2004), Pushpamala, together with Arni, took up these themes directly – themes that, though rooted in colonial times, persist in today's postcolonial nation.[104] One frequently reproduced example from this project is *Toda* (fig. 1), which cites a colonial trope by re-enacting a nineteenth century documentary photograph of a native woman from the Andaman Islands being subjected to biometric measurement (fig. 2).[105] The checkerboard grid in the background represents a scientific scale against which people in various parts of the world, previously unknown to Euro-American explorers, were measured, identified, categorised, and made visible and knowable. While the colonial photograph shows a naked figure, the artist chooses to remain clothed in her re-enactment. In doing so, she draws attention to the predicament of the colonial subject whose nudity served to act out the colonial fantasy of primitivism. The same subject – as we see in other photographs of the series – was likely to be imbricated in other colonial civilising projects, such as schooling or evangelisation, with her body thereby shaped by a uniform or a nun's habit.[106]

Elaborating on the workings of corporeal-materialist aesthetics, Meskimmon designates the dynamics of art-making as 'subjectivity-in-process', a mutuality through which 'a mutable material subject' emerges.[107] In other words, the collaborative process of making a work – in this particular instance a photo-performance – engenders a shared subjectivity that further undermines an essentially masculinist and modernist conception of the artist. Pushpamala's photo-performance involves an elaborate production setup, a

---

103 Jakimowicz, 'The Self Versus Self-Images' , n.p.

104 See exhibition catalogue, Pushpamala and Arni (eds), *Native Women*. In addition, the project, whose title mimics conventional anthropological surveys, has been discussed by Sinha, 'Pushpamala N.'; Murali, 'An Eye for an Eye'; Sambrani (ed.), *Edge of Desire*, pp. 70–75; Juneja and Ramaswamy (eds), *Motherland*.

105 From the collection of Maurice Vidal Portman (1860–1935), a colonial administrator whose photographs, many commissioned by the British government as well as the British Museum, of the inhabitants of the Andaman Islands are now part of the museum's digital collection. See https://www.britishmuseum.org/collection/object/EA_As-Portman-B30-15.

106 For example, in Pushpamala and Arni (eds), *Native Women of India*, p. 53 (right).

107 Meskimmon, 'Art Matters', p. 358.

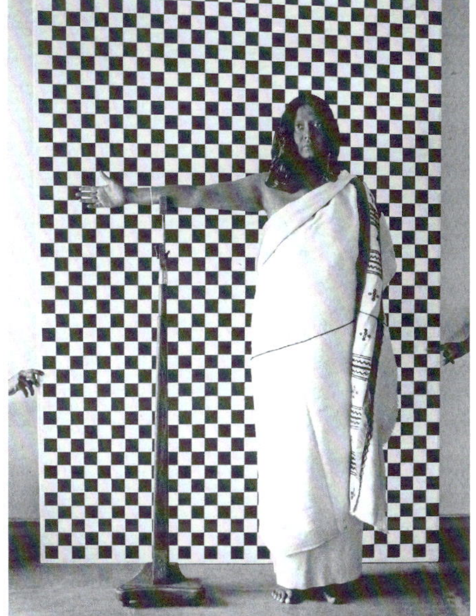

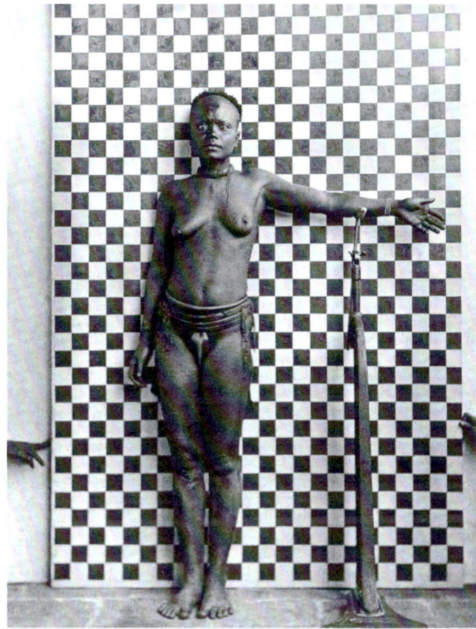

1   Pushpamala N. *Toda*, Photograph, 2004

2   Maurice V. Portman, *Female Andamanese*, photograph, 1890s

co-production comprising scenic artists, costume designers, and lighting experts, working in concert to create a spatio-temporal reconfiguration of a flat image. To convincingly render Pushpamala's life-size, three-dimensional painted tableau, details of the original image are recreated with the help of commercial products, including rented professional theatre accessories and a variety of visual technology – all of which are obtained in the local bazaars of Bangalore and Delhi. *Native Women* includes one section titled 'The Process Series' that meticulously documents the production at every step;[108] the photographs and notes are, in the words of the artist who describes her collaborative enterprise in graphic detail, 'important images in themselves. … I began looking at the photographic studio with its inherent play of equipment, crew and chaos, as a set piece in itself.'[109] To work against 'looking at it as perfect art work'[110] the seams of the work are visibly built into the work itself, whose often improvised quality that is a product of distributed participation remains palpable. For instance, there is no attempt to paper over details such as the hands holding up the checkerboard screen simulating a grid in *Toda*, or the makeshift curtains and the papier-mâché

108 Pushpamala and Arni (eds) *Native Women of India*, pp. 115–33.
109 Ibid., p. 136.
110 Ibid., p. 140.

tiger in a personification of Mother India.[111] Opening the work to 'making the costume show where it does not entirely fit'[112] reiterates the trace of corporeal presence as it emerges between subjects and objects. Even as *Toda* articulates political empathy with the colonial subject, returning the gaze of the coloniser's lens is contingent on the collaborative process between Pushpamala and Arni that the image indelibly records. The collaboration between the two women posits a different relationality between the people facing and operating the camera: it is both dialogue and intersubjective encounter, and finally a material process that ends in a photograph, both a circulating object and a discursive entity.

Pushpamala N.'s engagement with 'Indianness' in its unending manifestations and all its contradictions have inevitably led her to dissect the creation of national stereotypes or iconic modes of representing the nation. The study of personifications of the nation, either as goddess or as cartographic image or allegory, figure prominently in her repertoire.[113] In the following paragraphs I engage with one such (re-)enactment, though of an image that leads the artist away from the terrain of the 'native' to venture into a transcultural engagement, an act of becoming intimate with a political ideal that stakes a proud claim to universality. I refer here to her spectacular embodiment of Eugène Delacroix's iconic painting *Liberty Leading the People*, a photo-performance that has surprisingly remained in the shadows, compared to the otherwise prolific critical writing on her work (Plates 4.2, 4.3).[114] Liberty, a virtue grafted onto the nation while it at the same time transcends national frames, has known abundant personifications in contexts of nation-building. One genealogical strain of Delacroix's image can be traced to representations of the democratic body politic that proliferated in the wake of the revolutionary ferment that swept through France and Europe during the late eighteenth century. A density of symbolic accretions made the image of liberty assimilable through recognisable attributes: the red Phrygian cap of a liberated slave, broken chains, a bundle of fasces, the triangle of equality, the charter of the rights of man and the citizen, the crown of laurel leaves for the virtuous citizen, the multi-headed hydra of despotism trampled over by the figure of liberty wielding the club of Hercules (Plates 4.4, 4.5). Even as they lacked individuality, these allegorical representations were imbued with a controlled, yet tactile erotic content, domesticated by classicising idioms. Such images of the female body carry an ever-present tension between a stable juridical entity, be it the nation or liberty, that the female ideal promises to secure, and the actions of real women in the private and public spaces of a given society, a tension between normative female virtue and the possibility of its disruption.

---

111 On the latter, Romita Ray, 'The "Clumsy" Lion? Disruptions and *Darshan* in Pushpamala N's Imaging of Mother India', in: Juneja and Ramaswamy (eds), *Motherland*, pp. 44–57, fig. 4.2; also, Murali, 'An Eye for an Eye'.

112 Jakimowicz, 'The Self Versus Self-Images'.

113 See contributions to Juneja and Ramaswamy (eds), *Motherland*.

114 See Monica Juneja, 'Inside/Out: Pushpamala N's Embodiment of Liberty', in: Juneja and Ramaswamy (eds), *Motherland*, pp. 70–81. The following discussion in this section draws largely on that essay.

The model of liberty that Pushpamala N. has chosen to impersonate has a double-edged quality that brings the underlying tension between a virtuous and threatening sexuality to the surface. Delacroix's *Liberty* is a powerfully built figure who leads a revolutionary insurrection. Her muscular arms wield a rifle and a tricolour as she strides across a barricade of stones trampling over bodies of the dead and wounded, accompanied by armed comrades and the smoke of battle. The work caused a scandal, above all owing to the distinctly proletarian sexuality of the figure of Liberty, scathingly referred to in contemporary critiques as a fishwife, a lower-class courtesan, a woman of the streets with visible layers of dirt congealed on her bare torso.[115] Its blurring of the roles of the virtuous woman and the prostitute allowed her to both inspire and threaten. Pushpamala's impersonation that was produced for the exhibition *Paris-Bombay-Delhi* at the Centre Pompidou in Paris (2011), is immediately striking for the economy of detail it effects. It dispenses with the barricade of human bodies, with a few stones retained as a minimalist gesture that works to heighten the iconicity of the larger than life-size figure of Liberty. The sets for the performance included a smoke machine; on the photograph, the smoke becomes a source of white light that envelops the figure of Liberty like an aureole.

Part of a series of three pictures, named *The Harcourt Series*, the re-enactment of *Liberty* needs to be read in conjunction with its pendant, a black-and-white photograph titled *The Slave and her Slave*, for it is the reciprocity of the two images that brings forth the full force of the re-enactment (fig. 3).[116] The second photograph mimics an Orientalist work – an anonymous engraving adapted from one among the numerous works of Jean-Auguste-Dominique Ingres on the subject of an odalisque with her slave. As all works of its genre, this one too is replete with civilisational messages: the odalisque – a concubine of the Turkish sultan – is portrayed, as in Orientalist paintings, as a white woman being served by a Black slave. It is the figure of the latter, the second slave, that Pushpamala 'enters': her performative persona joins Liberty to the slave, making them appear as two faces of the same coin. The unmistakable reference is to the fundamental contradiction built into modern democracy at the moment of its inception that made explicit its exclusions. As is well known, slavery was a hotly debated matter among political elites and intellectuals, and shares the same historical space as discourses about liberty. Liberty, or the freedom to pursue economic interests that depended on enslaved populations of the world, emerged as the most persuasive argument against the abolition of the slave trade during the late eighteenth and nineteenth centuries. The slave condition is constitutive of the contradiction between freedom of property and freedom

---

115 Monika Wagner, 'Freiheitswunsch und Frauenbild: Veränderungen der "Liberté" zwischen 1789 und 1830', in: Inge Stephan and Sigrid Weigel (eds), *Die Marseillaise der Weiber: Frauen, die Französische Revolution und ihre Rezeption*, Berlin: Argument-Verlag, 1989, pp. 7–36, here p. 13.

116 The title of the series refers to the Harcourt studio in Paris with whom the artist collaborated to produce these photographs. The history of the studio goes back to 1934, when it was founded by the Lacroix brothers. It is particularly known for its black-and-white glamour photographs of celebrities.

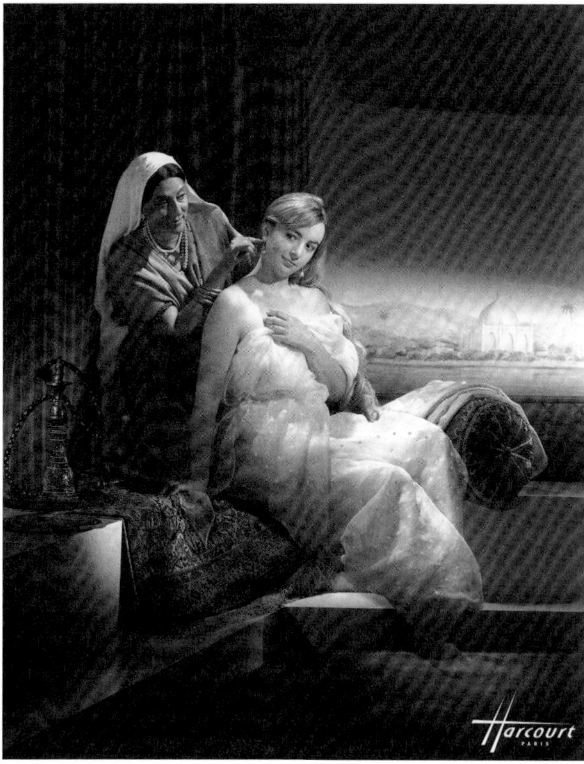

3   Pushpamala N., *The Slave and her Slave*, Harcourt Series, photograph, 2009

of person.[117] The double embodiment restages a concept of individual liberty ensconced in classical liberal theory that is contingent on the subjection or self-subjection of sections of humanity, at home and afar, that are by the same definition unfree.

The performative conjunction, which Pushpamala effects between the figures of liberty and the slave, works to re-anchor the circulating icon in its conditions of production. The racial economy of the works, describable as hybrids of an icon/ethnic type and a self-portrait, entails a two-fold 'crossing of the "colour line"'[118] by the artist, as she embodies in turn a white and a Black woman. Importantly, this act of transgression intersects with a moment of discursive instability surrounding systems of signification that seek to fix and naturalise difference within societies, to then decide on who can belong to the body politic. The cultural theorist Sara Ahmed defines the 'stranger' as an entity produced through relations of proximity within multicultural societies of the present. Being an alien is then a matter of

117 Susan Buck-Morss, *Hegel, Haiti, and Universal History*, Pittsburgh: University of Pittsburgh Press, 2009, p. 21ff. Also, Achille Mbembe, 'Necropolitics', *Public Culture*, vol. 15 (1), 2003: 11–40.
118 The expression has been adapted from Cherise Smith, *Enacting Others: Politics of Identity in Eleanor Antin, Nikki S. Lee, Adrian Piper and Anna Deavere Smith*, Durham, NC: Duke University Press, 2011, p. 3.

inhabiting a certain body; racial difference, among other attributes, enables processes of recognition to designate those 'outsiders inside', whose presence makes it necessary to demarcate spaces of belonging, to police the borders of habitable domains.[119] During the years when Pushpamala's works above were being assembled and exhibited, France was seized by violent upheavals ascribed to migrant communities, relegated to ghettos on the outskirts of Paris. The problem of ontologising the 'alien' as a way of being in the world, to then exclude those labelled as such from rightfully belonging to the nation, is, however, not an issue confined to France, but – as mentioned above – an intensely debated question in several Western as well as postcolonial societies. Contemporary discourses of globalisation and multiculturalism, despite their effort to assimilate those considered unassimilable, end up, paradoxically, reinforcing existing boundaries through their prioritising of group identity, or the emphasis on becoming, even as they seek recourse to liberal concepts such as hybridity or in-betweenness. The process of demarcating boundaries within the 'we' of a nation can reopen the prior histories of bodies marked as alien – re-enactment of such histories through artistic intervention is one path to re-scripting the stories told within the narrative of the nation. A relationship of intimacy and sociality fostered through performatively 'entering' an alien body involves the production of meaning through the very fluidity of self-definitions that ensues. It challenges the construction of selves through stable binaries to disrupt existing ontologies.

Let us return to Delacroix's *Liberty* and its double. For all the outrage provoked by the artist's rendering of the female allegory, techniques of mechanical reproduction made it possible to domesticate its troubling sexual force. By delinking the head from the body, the image proliferated through postage stamps and bank notes and came to be imprinted on the memory of its users as a form that has the iconicity of a ruler's profile on a coin (Plate 4.6). This makes Delacroix's work an eminently reproducible image, a profile that spells the absence of reciprocity, a distant face that can be gazed at but does not look back. If we compare this with Pushpamala's impersonation, the difference in the profile that veers towards a three-quarter view of the face reminds us of the physical and material presence of the artist (Plates 4.6a, 4.6b). A trace of subjectivity returns through the gaze, through the gentle, knowing smile hovering on her lips, bringing back that which was evacuated to produce the icon. The photo-performance produces an effect of oscillation, in that the viewer looks at it, registers immediate recognition, to be succeeded by doubt and then recognises the photograph as a double – an oscillation effect between credibility and its limits. Can the production of iconic interruption, while becoming the double of an image by entering it, open it up to a new context of actions and relations? An aesthetic that fissures the singularity of an icon to bring forth a form of excess has the power, as I have argued above, to trigger a debate about history and belonging within a national collective by disrupting inherited narratives that can now be overwritten. Our visual imagination of Liberty is unlikely to ever be the same.

---

119 Sara Ahmed, *Strange Encounters: Embodied Others in Postcoloniality*, London and New York: Routledge, 2000, p. 3ff.

To ask how the act of becoming an icon's double might open it to new contexts, the enquiry needs to proceed to another register. We need to go beyond reading the symbolic content of images – to put aside ways of *representing* liberty in images – to ask how images and their production have been declared a *site* of liberty. Modernity has ascribed to art the quality of autonomy, that which makes it distinct from religious faith and accords to it a license to appropriate, provoke, and critique; to become a space of freedom, a playfield of experiment. All these attributes allow the image to assume a distance from lived experience, a secluded space that art or the image inhabits, which is distinct from the realm of life. As such, images find themselves at the centre of culture wars of the present, fought over issues of their permissibility and their accepted limits. The riots that broke out across the Islamic world in the autumn of 2005, over the Danish newspaper *Jylands Posten*'s publication of cartoons depicting the Prophet Mohammed is one example reminding us of the encompassing nature of such discourses.[120] Another example, drawn from South Asia, is the violent controversy surrounding the person and work of the modernist artist, Maqbool Fida Husain, who became an embattled figure in the 1990s.[121] Where images foster an agonistic intimacy, they also become a trigger of violence or themselves an object of violence. Not only has the relationship between art and freedom been repeatedly shaken up, but this troubled relationship leads us to ask whether images can then mediate between freedom and its opposite.

The issue of artistic autonomy is caught in a set of contrary pulls. Recognising art as a free and self-determining entity forming the basis of a democratic social order brought with it the incessant drive to overcome the separation between art and life, to expose the conditions of art's autonomy. Critical avant-garde movements of the twentieth century were propelled towards expansive inclusion – aesthetic autonomy meant any material could be used as art, any subject considered fit for it, any form employed. At the same time, the avant-garde's urge to negate art's exceptionality opened the way to exposing the material conditions of art-making through movements such as conceptual, site-specific, participatory, socially-engaged art, as well as institutional critique – this aspect will be further discussed in the following section on participatory art. Performance in particular – enacting an icon with one's own flesh-and-blood body – embodies a new, sensuous yet critical form of art that at the same time strives to bridge the gap between art and life. Equally essential to defining the nature of the link between artistic practice and its outside is the issue of work. To stabilise the autonomy and exceptionality of art, the modern usage of the term is premised on a separation of 'aesthetic' concerns from 'utility', of art from craft, individual creation from collective manufacture.[122] Here, too, the avant-garde's call to abolish art as a distinct activity was a call to restore art to life, to the activity of working out its proper meaning. Contemporary art

---

120 See Saba Mahmood, 'Religious Reason and Secular Affect: An Incommensurable Divide?', *Critical Inquiry*, 35 (4), 2009: 836–62.

121 For a scholarly discussion of this controversy, see the essays in Ramaswamy (ed.), *Barefoot Across the Nation*.

122 Larry E. Shiner, *The Invention of Art: A Cultural History*, Chicago: University of Chicago Press, 2001, pp. 5ff.

practice continues to juggle this terrain between dependence on infrastructural networks for its very existence and survival, and the special relationship that a cult of the artist presupposes between doing, making, and being.[123] At no time in the recent decades have the faultlines and abysses that make up the contemporary art world surfaced with such poignancy as in the ongoing pandemic. Not only has it exposed the vulnerability – individual and collective – of large numbers of practitioners in the arts, theatre, film, music, who found themselves excluded from state support measures granted to 'workers' and essential services, the dramatic weakening of infrastructural sustenance has produced its own forms of precarity.

Pushpamala's embodiment of Liberty generates an ongoing ripple of reflections, even as it strives to call attention to its making. The spectacular visual quality of the image notwithstanding, we recognise its dependence on teamwork and studio photography. These in turn draw our attention to artifice, stylisation, the 'simulacral', theatricality, aestheticisation that bring forth the entire sensuous process of 'being self and the other at the same time',[124] defying the binary between subject and object, artist and model. Moving from the outside in and back, the work – in the end a photograph – joins the stream of other freely circulating works, dependent on digitality and caught in a globally shared web of market relations, to circulate among diverse publics, to both shake up and reaffirm favourite typologies.

The year Pushpamala's photo-performance was exhibited at the Centre Pompidou in Paris, the artist Danh Võ (b. 1975) exhibited *We the People* at the Kunsthalle Fridericianum in the German city of Kassel, also a performative deconstruction of another famous icon. The first thing that caught the visitors' attention on entering the exhibition space was a disarray of objects – part of an outsized copper foot, the folds of a robe, a fragment of a torch, part of a broken chain, fingers, together with several other pieces, difficult to identify – casually lying on the floor or leaning against the walls (Plate 4.7). These were drawn from among the 267 odd pieces that replicated in full scale the component parts of Frédéric Auguste Bartholdi's *Statue of Liberty*, 46 metres tall, standing on Liberty Island in New York Harbour.[125] The individual pieces were, however, created with the explicit intention of not reassembling the parts to recover the allegorical whole – their mode of placement at the numerous sites across the

123 On the seminal function of infrastructure – with reference to contemporary art in South Asia – see Karin Zitzewitz, 'Infrastructure as Form: Cross-Border Networks and the Materialities of "South Asia" in Contemporary Art', *Third Text*, vol. 31 (2/3), 2017: 341–58.

124 Pushpamala N. in an online conversation with the group of authors who contributed to Juneja and Ramaswamy (eds), *Motherland*, 1 August 2020.

125 The Kassel exhibition *July, IV, MDCCLXXVI* that ran from 1 October to 31 December 2011, was curated by Rein Wolfs. Its title – *July 4, 1776* – is the date on which the United States signed its Declaration of Independence. It is inscribed in Roman numerals on the stone tablet held by Liberty in her left hand. The artist Danh Võ migrated with his family as a political refugee from Vietnam to Europe at the age of four. After several years in Denmark, he now lives and works in Berlin and Mexico City. The work *We the People* has been discussed in Anne R. Petersen, *Migration into Art: Transcultural Identities and Art-Making in a Globalised World*, Manchester: Manchester University Press, 2017, p. 14ff. See also Mirjam Varadinis and Catherine Schelbert, 'Zerbrochene Freiheit = Shattered Freedom', *Parkett*, no. 90, 2012: 204–06. For an account of the artist's biography and work, Nora Taylor, 'Hunter-Gatherer or the other Ethnographer? The Artist in the Age of Historical Reproduction', *Journal of Material Culture*, vol. 27(1), 2022: 10–29.

globe where they were exhibited, obstructed rather than facilitated the imagination of putting them back into a replica of the statue. Like Pushpamala's performative entry into an icon, Võ's dismemberment of it too plays on ambiguity and oscillation, in what he describes as an act of making the familiar unfamiliar.[126] Like the original statue, these works, too, were made out of copper sheets. Their production in China, in collaboration with a team from Basel's Kunstgiesserei, stood for, and was contingent on globalised capitalism of the present. Though vastly apart in size and format, the works of both artists were geared to mobility, to travel in order to become something else. Both creative ensembles, despite their showy surface appearance, reveal traces of their making, addressing thereby their own production and circulation.

One thread linking both the artistic acts of transcultural dismemberment and recreation lies in the title of Danh Võ's distributed artwork: its evocation of the opening sentence of the Constitution of the United States of America, 'We the People', raises the question of who this 'we' might be. If 'we' refers to those who share a social and political world, where is this world to be located, in a national space or a global one, or the world of museum visitors? How do spectators of the work, scattered like its individual pieces, relate to each other to form a possible imagined we? Both artists see inclusion not simply as a matter of integrating their work into a pre-existing, inherently recursive history of art; rather, they use it to enter that field from a peripheral position and to reflect critically on its systems and hierarchies seeking to impose a sense of order on the world.

Participatory Art – Emplacement between the Metropolitan and the Vernacular

'[T]he creative act is not performed by the artist alone; the spectator brings the work in contact with the external world by deciphering and interpreting its inner qualifications and thus adds his contribution to the creative act.'[127] Marcel Duchamp's proclamation of 1957 announced a democratisation of creativity that would recast a work of art as an ongoing process generative of aesthetic polysemy, rather than remaining a single, finished product. As observed in the previous section, the redistribution of creativity through socially engaged participatory art was an outcome of art's urge to uncover its conditions of making. Studies of contemporary art recognise participation as an open form of praxis, wherein the distinction between viewers, participants, and actors is blurred: a form that enables political and artistic modes of articulation to blend into each other. Our understanding of this mode of art-mak-

---

Liberty Enlightening the World, to cite the full name of the work, was a gift of France to the United States on the centenary of its independence. It was installed and inaugurated in 1886. The colossal statue was transported in some 200 cases containing individual pieces to be assembled on site.

126 See 'Danh Vo Interview: A Question of Freedom', YouTube video, 22 January 2015, uploaded by Louisiana Chanel, https://www.youtube.com/watch?v=1ELmm-jNkLs (accessed December 2021).

To further cite the artist: 'Personally I think the icon of the Statue of Liberty has been raped enough, too many people have been claiming whatever stupidity on what freedom might or might not be.'

127 Marcel Duchamp, 'The Creative Act', in: Sanouillet and Peterson (eds), *The Writings of Marcel Duchamp*, pp. 138–40, here p. 140.

ing has been built upon what has become a set of canonical writings, starting with thoughts on relational aesthetics put forward by Nicolas Bourriaud, which then engendered intensive discussions including the critical position taken by Claire Bishop – both continue to define the parameters of what we know as relational or participatory art.[128] Drawing on a series of fascinating case studies from a particular context – that of Europe post-1989 – Bishop extracts a broad characterisation of participatory praxis, even as she continues through the course of her study to nuance and refine it. Her characterisation can be summarised as follows: while the artist works as a collaborator rather than a creator, a co-producer of 'situations' rather than discrete objects, the work of art emerges more as process than end product, as continuous and with no clear beginning or end.[129] In addition, Bishop conceives of participatory art as a 'delegated' and 'dematerialised' performance, involving a delegation of power by the artist to those 'outside of the artistic fold', thereby relocating authenticity away from a singular artist. This also opens art as space of risk and ambiguity, with unpredictable results. At the same time, in Bishop's view, participation becomes a move to undermine institutional authority provoked by 'amateurism' or 'institutional perversion'.[130] The question about the extent to which participation or relational practices end up delinking themselves from visual art, rejecting the inventive quality of art itself, remains an unresolved issue in the discussion.

The following account takes a fresh look at the logic of dematerialisation ascribed to the process of democratisation implicit within participatory art; it does so from the perspective of an experiment located on a site of the avant-garde beyond Euro-America. It engages with a particular foray into participatory art from South Asia in which the artist in question, Atul Bhalla (b. 1964), conjoins the conceptual, the vernacular, and the material within a symbiotic relationship. We have here an experiment that steps out of and unfolds beyond the domain of art institutions, without however entirely severing the bond with these. It resorts to, as Bishop's study proposes, a mode of delegated performance in that it seeks a form of sharing, whose results are largely unforeseen, to however end in the re-materialisation of the process, thereby urging us to rethink the canonical parameters of relational art practice. Indeed, mutuality and materiality are from the start not opposing poles within this experiment; rather co-production unfolds in their interstices to reaffirm the place of the work within the art institution, whose authority art-making does not de-legitimise, even as it seeks to undermine the hegemony of a particular division of labour, or redefine artistic labour as conjoining ethics, risk, and pleasure.

Atul Bhalla's work takes a journey of 'thinking with the river' as its starting point. The river is the Yamuna that flows through the city of Delhi, where Bhalla lives and works, and provides the core of his incessant engagement with water. The artist's work on water alternates between different stances. At times, it explores the meanings of water with all cultural

---

128 Nicolas Bourriaud, *Esthétique Relationelle*, Dijon: Les Presses du Réel, 1998; Claire Bishop, 'Antagonism and Relational Aesthetics', *October*, vol. 110 (Fall), 2004: 51–79.

129 Claire Bishop, *Artificial Hells: Participatory Art and the Politics of Spectatorship*, New York: Verso, 2012, p. 2.

130 Ibid., p. 237.

markers kept out. It is about feeling, drinking, wading, about water as fog, mist, steam, or tears; here, he speaks of water on a planetary register and of a primal and shared biology.[131] On other occasions Bhalla's concerns shift from the planetary to the local, to the river deeply embedded in a cultural context. His concern centres on the ways in which the city has turned its architectural back to the river, now choked with effluents. Walls hide it from public view; people have no access to it because of barricades, the only access being through death – to the cremation grounds located on the banks of the river. Pointing to the 'disconnect' between the city and the river, one of Bhalla's projects involved questioning inhabitants of the city that he plastered with stickers querying: 'Have you ever seen the Yamuna?' or 'Have you ever touched the river?' The 'Yamuna Walk' project recorded the artist's wanderings along a stretch of fifty-six kilometres following the course of the river through Delhi and beyond.[132] The five-day trek sought to recuperate the lost relationship between a once sacred river and the life of the city suffering from the effects of extreme pollution and uncontrolled urbanisation. His images show that the worship of the Yamuna as goddess does not secure the river from the brutality that follows when both corpses and medical waste are consigned to its waters. Engaging with Bhalla's projects signals our attention to the confrontational matrix within which art's attempts at self-renewal through projecting into the outside world encounter capitalist development's appropriation of the historical function of aesthetics to convert it into a *dispositif*.[133] Today, the riverbank of the Yamuna is rapidly changing from a 'non-place' to prized real estate for public and private corporations. The ambition of the state of Delhi and many of its privileged citizens to make the city qualify as 'world-class' have during the past decade materialised in a flurry of construction projects – such as luxury high-rise apartments as part of a complex to house athletes and officials during the Commonwealth Games of 2010.[134] Earlier, a ninety-acre complex within the flood plains was – after illegally evicting farmers settled there – converted into a gigantic complex, a religious theme park comprising the Akshardham temple, a lake, gardens with musical fountains, a multiplex cinema, a food court, and a Centre for Applied Research in Social Harmony.[135] The riverfront development that aspires to emulate the aesthetic values of Western modernity visible in riverfront cities like London or Paris, though it appears benign, elides key issues, both social and ecological. Its model of gated communities and demarcating exclusive spaces through gentrification creates a structure of 'inclusive exclusion' that sets it out on a course of collision with partici-

---

131 Atul Bhalla, 'You Always Step into the Same River!', in: Sugata Ray and Venugopal Maddipati (eds), *Water Histories of South Asia: The Materiality of Liquescence*, New Delhi/London: Routledge, 2020, pp. 276–93.

132 Atul Bhalla and Maliha Noorani, *Yamuna Walk*, Seattle: University of Washington Press, 2012.

133 Josephine Berry, 'Everyone is Not an Artist: Autonomous Art Meets the Neoliberal City', *New Formations*, nos. 84/85, 2015: 20–39.

134 Amita Baviskar, 'What the Eye Does Not See: The Yamuna in the Imagination of Delhi', *Economic and Political Weekly*, vol. 46 (50), 2011: 43–53.

135 Saloni Mathur and Kavita Singh, 'Reincarnations of the Museum: The Museum in an Age of Religious Revivalism', in: Vishakha Desai (ed.), *Asian Art in the 21st Century*, New Haven: Yale University Press, 2007, pp. 149–68; Sanjay Srivastava, 'Urban Spaces, Disney-Divinity and Moral Middle Classes in Delhi', *Economic and Political Weekly*, vol. 44 (26/27), 2009: 338–45.

patory art practices, even as it co-opts the latter's methods and uses the aesthetic as a mode of compensation.[136]

Bhalla's project *The Wake* dates to 2013 and brings the artist's ongoing preoccupation with water together with his interest in wood, which is both a receptacle of water and a material with which boats were once made. This interest ties his work to communities who live in symbiosis with the river and work with their hands, their knowledge, and their materials, as they pass on embodied knowledge from one generation to the other. Entering into a relationship with them becomes a journey to investigate layers of time and history, a journey that the artist narrates step by step, not knowing where it would end; what it would bring forth was entirely uncertain, unforeseen. Both narration and process constitute the work *The Wake*.[137]

Viewed today as a site-specific installation at the Heritage Transport Museum in Gurgaon, *The Wake* is best described as a composite of process, engagement with materials and expertise, and a story of forming ties through the participatory act of making, an act that, however, rematerialises in a body of objects. The process is reminiscent of the dialectic between 'Site' and 'Nonsite' within Land Art.[138] Bhalla began his journey in early 2012 in search of a community of boat-makers with embodied knowledge of constructing a *Pattaya*, a particular transport boat, made by nailing together long wooden planks, characteristic of the lower Ganges basin (Plate 4.8). His travels took him to the village of Ghani on the banks of a tributary of the Ganges, to a community of boat builders, more specifically an extended family of boatmen. *The Wake* is also about Bhalla's assimilation into this community of different generations and closely-knit kinship ties. The participants in the project were Subhash, the father of a family, his son Ram Mohan, and the latter's maternal uncle, Mamaji, addressed respectfully as is the custom using the Hindi word for this relationship. Their collective enterprise began with acquiring the right wood from the neighbouring forest, the requisite materials and tools, such as long, square nails made by artisans in the village, who used no synthetic waterproofing material (Plate 4.9). Detailed and finely tuned calculations of size and proportion that drew upon stored knowledge of elders in the family were a further requisite to produce the boat whose size was designated according to the number of buffaloes it could carry. The entire process that extended over more than two months was both collaborative and investigative – an attempt on the part of the artist to live through by actively participating in long-established contexts, to reconnect with practices and knowledge that were not yet dead, and, not least, to connect the actors and those who embodied that knowledge to another set of places and institutions. The notion of emplacement used in the sub-heading of this section refers to the 'challenge of formulating experimental belonging' in a chosen

---

136 Berry, 'Everyone is Not an Artist'.
137 The following account of the work of Atul Bhalla draws, unless otherwise cited, on several exchanges with the artist during his residency at the HCTS hosted by the Chair of Global Art History within the framework of an Erasmus Plus exchange programme in June–July 2019.
138 Priya Pall, 'The Wake', in: *Atul Bhalla: You Always Step into the Same River*, New Delhi: Vadehra Art Gallery, 2014, pp. 39–43.

location that requires engaging with communities, histories, and memories on new sites to forge new relationships around it.[139]

Once constructed, the boat was transported to the river, overruling thereby the museum's insistence that a museum object needed to be untouched by water. This was an act of collective consummation, a reference to the boat builders' lives embedded in a spiritual and symbiotic relationship with nature. Actions and rituals carried out in the landscape were extensively documented and made part of the final installation – in an act of registering shared authorship and participatory process. Following its installation in the museum of transport, the idiom of the site sought to communicate and intensify the experience of making. A grid of interspersed courts and voids generate a network of visual connections: the museum levels are vertically connected to create full-height voids from the topmost down to the lowest level, enabling different views of an exhibit. While the view from below reveals the underside of the boat and fragmented reflections through mirror-clad beams, viewing it at eye-level, while walking around the installation results in the loss of the dramatic or spectacular, leaving the viewer to engage with the work without embellishments.[140] The exhibit is presented through the accompanying documentation as a form and process of co-production that eschews subsuming different authorships and collectively embodied labour and art of making within the creation of a singular artist.

Before returning to issues of collaborative praxis, let us look at another work by the same artist. The installation entitled *Chabeel* was created in 2006 for an urban art festival in Delhi named 48 °C, a designation that refers to one of the hottest summers the city had known. It was created in a historical part of the old walled city of Delhi known as Kashmiri Gate, which in the seventeenth century was the Mughal capital Shahjahanabad. Maps show that until the mid-nineteenth century the river had flown close to the old city wall. Today, it is more or less inaccessible, separated by a heavily trafficked road, and barely noticeable from the ramparts of the citadel. Bhalla's installation was intended to draw attention to the way the city had become visually and materially disconnected from the waters that had once gushed close to it. The Punjabi word *chabeel* refers to a custom in north-western India of giving free drinking water to travellers and passers-by during the hot summer months. Such an act worked towards building a community, as believers carried it out in the name of God. In a move to reanimate this practice, the work took the form of a giant white jerrycan – a container used to transport water – faced with white tiles, that was also turned into a kiosk, from which the artist dispensed water, filtered from the Yamuna, to thirsty visitors in recyclable paper cups (Plates 4.10, 4.11). People were requested to leave their cups at the counter; the dregs of water left behind were mixed with sand from the river and cement to produce solidified small blocks of concrete. These mini-monuments were then collected in the *Chabeel* with the intent of creating a larger monument to the river, co-produced by each passer-by. On leaving the

139 Adajania and Hoskote, 'Notes Towards a Lexicon of Urgencies'.
140 Pall, 'The Wake'.

kiosk, each person was given a sticker to take home that asked: *Have you seen the Yamuna? Have you ever touched the river?*

The idea of co-production here is tied to the indigenous notion of *jooth*, a Hindi word to describe a concept that in Bhalla's words is a 'very Eastern concept'. *Jooth* stands for a bodily trace of a person left on a glass or a vessel from which he or she would have drunk or eaten something – and is marked by the person's saliva, 'your DNA', as the artist put it.[141] In Hindu practice, the idea of *jooth* is tied to the imagination of ritual purity and pollution: once a person has drunk or eaten from a vessel, no one will use it till it is cleansed, in the case of certain lower or 'untouchable' castes, the vessel remains indelibly polluted. The artist's conception here involved treating each person's waste or *jooth* as part of a participatory act which, once rematerialised into an object, would solidify as an inextricable part of the monument to the river. The participants in this process were acutely aware of the exclusivity of their own waste and of its merging into the collectivity of a monument.

In an effort to pluralise our understandings of participatory art and relational aesthetics, this account has sought to argue for a less oppositional, instead, a more symbiotic understanding of the process. Participation, it argues, no longer needs to rest on 'delegation' to 'those outside of the artistic fold', or 'amateurism';[142] rather, it draws both its dynamism and its quality of the unforeseen from a move to break out of the inside/outside divide. In doing so, it works to open up institutional spaces by extending participatory possibilities to those excluded; in the long term such a process would work towards transforming the epistemic foundations of both, the sites of making and exhibiting art as well as of the canonical discourses that make sense of these. The work of Atul Bhalla – to take the example elaborated here – consciously seeks to conjoin the conceptual to the artisanal, the material, and the vernacular. His is a pursuit of an understanding built into art-making of South Asia, a conception that had been relegated to the margins, first in the wake of advancing modernist ideologies and, more recently, as a consequence of globalised forms of labour harnessed to the production of gigantic artworks for public spaces.

In another context I have argued in favour of introducing an 'artisanal epistemology' – defined as an ensemble of technical and manual skills, technical procedures, and material practices – as a pillar of art history.[143] This would take us beyond the individual artist whom art history tends to canonise as the pinnacle of creativity, and propel us instead to look for a more distributed agency.[144] Such an approach can show the way beyond the existing compass

<hr>

141 Atul Bhalla, oral presentation, University of Heidelberg, June 2019; see also Venugopal Maddipatti, 'Water in an Expanded Field: Art, Thought and Immersion in the Yamuna River: 2005–11', in: Hutton and Brown (eds), *Rethinking Place*, pp. 60–77, here pp. 63–66.

142 Bishop, *Artificial Hells*, pp. 237–38.

143 The term has been borrowed from Claire Farago, 'Artisanal Epistemologies and Artless Art of Post-Tridentine Painting', in: Camilla S. Paldam and Jacob Wamberg (eds), *Art, Technology and Nature: Renaissance to Postmodernity*, Farnham: Ashgate Publishers, 2015, pp. 117–32.

144 Monica Juneja, 'Crafts and the Spiritual' (with an excerpt from Ananda K. Coomaraswamy, *The Indian Craftsman*), in: Beate Söntgen and Julia Voss (eds), *Why Art Criticism? A Reader*, Berlin: Hatje Cantz, 2022, pp. 52–61.

of the discipline and its hierarchy of genres that has migrated to regions of the non-European world, often in the wake of colonialism. Art histories in younger postcolonial nations have frequently ended up assimilating existing distinctions, such as art versus artefact that downgrade or exclude many historically and aesthetically significant kinds of objects and practices from consideration – challenging scholarship today to find plausible ways of unsettling these. The above discussion of a sampling of Atul Bhalla's work suggests that 'dematerialised practice' as a founding principle of participatory art, in the sense that Bishop deploys it, can work towards privileging an exclusive – confined to a particular region – understanding of the nexus of participation, aesthetics, and criticism. Making materiality central to the experience of art – to its production and reception – helps pluralise our understanding of concepts such as vision, and make art history more capacious for synaesthetic notions of sight.[145] An understanding of seeing beyond the purely ocular is among the notions that continue to prevail in different world cultures.

As stated above, this experiment in participatory art steps out and unfolds beyond the domain of art institutions, only to relocate the act back into the world of art. Atul Bhalla's engagement with vernacular practices of making culminates in their rematerialisation into co-produced musealised objects. What does this mean for the possibility of institutional critique, said to be built into the notion of the participatory? Once more, it may be useful to look at the trajectory of institutional critique as the idea took root in localities beyond the West. Our established understanding of the canonised, formative moment of such critique – avant-garde modernism – reads it in terms of a privileging of technical advancement and an attack on established institutions and academic codes of art. Such an understanding, drawing as it does exclusively upon Euro-American metropolitan definitions, does not consider the transculturation of the avant-garde as it found roots on sites beyond the West. Modernist experiments at sites without established and complex institutional frameworks required creating new institutions rather that rebelling against non-existent ones – institutions such as journals, exhibition spaces, art schools, and cultural foundations. Here, institutional 'critique' from the outset involved working with and beyond institutions.

At the same time, we are aware that institutional critique itself has not remained static since its founding moment in any part of the world; it has undergone reinvention and generational shifts in response to changing and difficult contemporary conditions. The crisis of liberal democracies across the globe, the critique of neoliberal capitalism and of its concomitant evasion of both social and environmental responsibility, together with a growing artistic internationalism that inhabits the fluid space between art and activism – have all meant that institutional critique is now being reinvented across continental distances. Critique today has taken the form of what Gerald Raunig defines as 'instituent practice', a practice that in his words 'thwarts the logic of institutionalization', invents new forms of instituting that do

145 See Chapter Two.

not oppose institutions, but 'flee from institutionalization and structuralization'.[146] The strategies and competencies of art here, according to him, can be deployed to spur on a general reflection on the problems of institutions. Shifting our gaze back to present day South Asia and the work of contemporary artists – including Atul Bhalla – shows these to be also part of a global circuit, as a result of which they develop transcultural networks of affinity that cut across national boundaries, often built around shared predicaments.[147]

At a local level, critique takes the form of a practice of radical social questioning, which however does not necessarily adopt a position of distance from institutions. Critique grows from a conjoining, often indirect, of political positions and social movements – in the Indian context one important terrain would be caste as a basis of skilled and unskilled labour – but without renouncing a belief in artistic competence, in the inventive power of artistic creation to envisage the possibilities of an alternative yet unforeseen future, and without setting aside possibilities within an art field. Rather, the attempt to live a different form of artistic labour and make place within institutions defined by their exclusivity seeks to visualise and materialise and re-valorise this labour as and through the object. The classical avant-garde dictum that there can be art without the artwork is turned on its head even as the formalisation of the work or its processes move in and out of an institutional field.

And yet, participatory art's ongoing attempt to forge interrelationships through radical questioning and responsive emplacement, a practice that construes the regional and local so as to make it globally intelligible, simultaneously confronts the appropriation and use of its very idea of itself by the political and economic regimes of globalised modernity. The modernist dictum of autonomous art freed aesthetic practice from traditional constraints, so that any material or subject or form has come to be considered appropriate to art-making. Participatory art was one among those novel ways of 'redistributing the sensible'[148] enabled by the new freedom to expand infinitely, transcending paradoxically the divide between art and life that inheres in the idea of autonomy. The same concern with life and its conversion into a source of value, shared by the 'biopolitical orientation' of modern political institutions, places art-making on a matrix shared with capitalism and the modern state.[149] That the use of art for culture-led regeneration with the intention to heal social wounds, works at the same time to exacerbate these is evident in the colonisation of urban imagination through a particular aesthetic vision for the Yamuna riverfront in Delhi. The processes that have rendered the riverfront recognisable as a place of value – a spectacular skyline, appealing scenery, cultural performances – are equally anchored within a set of values that belong to aesthetic modernity, even as 'participation' is now recast as consumption for an exclusive public. For all its strivings to produce alternative realities through embodied, rematerialised practice,

---

146 Gerald Raunig, 'Instituent Practices: Fleeing, Instituting, Transforming', in: Gerald Raunig and Gene Ray (eds), *Art and Contemporary Practice: Reinventing Institutional Critique,* London: MayFly Books, 2009, pp. xiii–xviii, and 3–12, here p. xvii.
147 Adajania and Hoskote, 'Notes Towards a Lexicon of Urgencies'.
148 Jacques Rancière, *The Politics of Aesthetics: The Distribution of the Sensible,* London: Bloomsbury, 2013.
149 Berry, 'Everyone is Not an Artist'.

contemporary relational art remains entangled within a struggle with parallel regimes of modernity that deploy the notion of creativity – the latter end up being constitutive of art's function to challenge, resist and redistribute.

Writing on different inflections of contemporaneity, Kobena Mercer identifies a 'dividing line' within global contemporary art 'between a worldly impetus to aesthetic invention that engages with past, present, and future and an equally inventive attitude toward form, medium, and materials'.[150] According to him, art produced in the wake of 'the transnational turn' is less preoccupied with the 'spectacularism or retro-sensationalism'[151] characteristic of a certain stream of contemporary art driven by the cultural economies of consumption. The artistic experiments discussed in this chapter – I have argued – all eschew a presentist visual culture of easy consumption cast in the language of market formalism; yet, they do not submit to a schematic dividing line between argumentative content and questions of medium and form. Instead, they self-consciously conjoin aesthetics and politics, the cognitive and the affective. Their works, tethered to particular histories, are addressed to and inscribed in wider regional and global contexts through the aesthetic means and media they choose to deploy. The principle of an avant-garde, harnessed to a fresh set of situations and locations, can be said to disavow technologically driven models of progress to consider art as a move beyond representation, as a shift from an ontology of being to a mode of becoming. The Benjaminian notion of *Denkbilder*, thought images, could be extended here to encompass thinking/making that which has not yet come to be, a proposition in advance of its potential realisation, one whose transformative force ought not to be underestimated. I am tempted to conclude this chapter, as I started, with one more terse observation by the Raqs Media Collective: 'A contemporaneity that is not curious about how it might be surprised is not worth our time.'[152]

150 Mercer, 'The Cross-Cultural and the Contemporary', p. 266.
151 Ibid., p. 270.
152 Raqs Media Collective, 'Nowhere and Elsewhere', p. 47.

CHAPTER FIVE
WHEN ART EMBRACES THE PLANET
The Contemporary Exhibition Form and the Challenge of Connected Histories

'[Artists'] ability to accommodate change makes art relevant, current, vital. Like the work of its artists, a dynamic and living culture is also flexible and aware of choices. This is the key to survival.' – Frank LaPena[1]

'Opting for change is indeed a willed act of transgression. … Curiously urban art promoters and votaries of purity have common stakes in the staticity and ethnicity of tribal art.' – Gulammohammed Sheikh[2]

Swirling patterns of cloud move across the planet in Neil Dawson's work *Globe* (1989), suspended twenty-five metres from above the Centre Pompidou in Paris during the summer of 1989 as it greeted visitors to *Magiciens de la Terre*, named the 'first worldwide exhibition of contemporary art'[3] (Plate 5.1). In its eschewal of cognitive detail, *Globe* echoes the pictures of the planet Earth taken by astronauts from a distance in space, described in the opening pages of this book (Plate 1.0), and on which it was modelled. Indeed, one of the earliest reviews of *Magiciens de la Terre* featured a photograph of the 'blue planet' as its key visual, conjoining thereby the affective power of this icon to the encompassing scope of the 'whole earth show'.[4] The curators of what has become a landmark event, not least because of the continuing debates it has triggered, inflected their use of the term 'mondial' (translated as both global as well as worldwide) with a planetary consciousness. They did so by invoking the notion of the earth (*terre*), in an incidental invocation of Heidegger, who described a work of art as a 'world

---

1 Frank LaPena, 'The Fourth World', in: National Museum of the American Indian (ed.), *The Path We Travel: Celebrations of Contemporary Native American Creativity*, Washington DC: Smithsonian Institution and Fulcrum Inc., 1994, pp. 1–22, here p. 21.
2 Gulammohammed Sheikh, 'The World of Jangarh Singh Shyam', in: Jyotindra Jain (ed.), *Other Masters: Five Contemporary Folk and Tribal Artists of India*, New Delhi: Crafts Museum, 1998, pp. 17–34, here p. 20.
3 The exhibition *Magiciens de la Terre* took place in Paris, at the Centre Pompidou and the Grande Halle de la Villette, from 18 May to 14 August 1989. The *Petit journal* accompanying the show, referred to the curatorial statement designating it as the 'première exposition mondiale de l'art contemporain', cited in Lucy Steeds et al. (eds), *Making Art Global (Part 2): 'Magiciens de la Terre' 1989*, London: Afterall Books, 2013, p. 24.
4 Eleanor Hartney, 'The Whole Earth Show', *Art in America*, vol. 77 (7), 1989: 91–97.

on uninscribed earth'.[5] To read the world as the 'whole earth' connotes a terrestrial sphere which is a source of life; together with water, air, and fire, it is one of the four stable elements that have constituted the universe in human thought since time immemorial. The world conceived of as *terre* rather than *monde* gives it, on the one hand, a quality that is planetary rather than spatial. On the other, the earth is also an attachment, a place of dwelling, a territory, a soil, all of which spell rights, power, and not least struggle. It is therefore no coincidence that many of those chosen to participate in the exhibition nurtured intimate ties to land and place, and their art carried memories of struggle and loss – as will be discussed further below. *Magiciens de la Terre*, described variously as a 'global', 'planetary', or 'whole earth' show thus manages to scramble the different categories via the multiple registers it works on. Its gestalt as an exhibition also places it squarely within the institutional context of an artworld; this made it 'a springboard'[6] and forum for novel encounters, as well as for debates on representation, curatorial privilege, and geopolitical hierarchies. Perhaps another photograph of Earth from the same source, which strikes a different, discordant note, might be an instructive example here. Also taken by astronauts of the NASA, this extraordinary image zooms into a single region of the planet to show the floodlit fence that is the border separating India and Pakistan, thereby directing our attention from abstraction to a significant reality of a globally connected world.[7] The detail showing one of the most militarised borders of the world is a statement about the proliferation of barriers and barricades that on a daily basis thwart human mobility in defiance of a euphoric celebration of multinational 'flows' of capital, culture, information, and, not least, people. A globally connected world, navigated by actors and institutions, emerges as one where borders are being simultaneously crossed by some and reinforced for others. A space of encounter between a multiplicity of languages, of practices and forms, all continuously engaged in 'translating' each other, reminds us that cultures, past and present, live in a permanent and fluctuating, at the same time, uneven relationality with each other.

In the domain of contemporary cultural institutions, the exhibition space and curatorial practice have emerged as one such site of encounter with cultural difference, or of a struggle to embrace the planet. The years following 1989 have seen an upsurge of interest in 'global shows' whose aim is to keep with the times by giving place to the work of artists from 'elsewhere' within the world formed by the Western art system. Such an act of 'cultural hospitality', as the director of the 1993 Venice Biennale, Achille Bonito Oliva put it, was induced by an awareness of multiple obligations felt by Western nations in a rapidly globalising post-

<hr>

5   Cited in Gayatri C. Spivak, 'Looking at Others', in: Steeds et al. (eds), *Making Art Global (2)*, pp. 260–66, here p. 261.

6   The term has been used by Jean-Marc Poinsot, 'Review of the Paradigms and Interpretative Machine, Or the Critical Development of "Magiciens de la Terre"', in: Steeds et al. (eds), *Making Art Global (2)*, pp. 94–108, here p. 94.

7   Reproduced in Saloni Mathur, 'Partition and the Visual Arts: Reflections on Method', *Third Text*, vol. 31 (2/3), 2017: 205–12, here 205.

Cold War world.[8] Expansion, or inclusion, emerged as a privileged compensatory mode and institutional strategy to meet the challenges of the global. Has the swing of the pendulum within cultural institutions and exhibitions from 'xenophobia to xenophilia'[9] engendered a discursive space to remap cultural geographies and theorise the disjunctive condition of contemporaneity, or does it merely answer global capitalism's need for new commodities? How do moves to include art from beyond the West within metropolitan exhibition circuits mesh with processes under way within those distant art worlds now sought to be drawn into the global matrix? The following discussion of these issues will focus on the famous – also much maligned – exhibition of 1989 announced by Dawson's *Globe*: *Magiciens de la Terre*, conceptualised as the first planetary show of contemporary art that at the same time sought to challenge the conventions of exhibition making within the narrow confines of the art world and its modernist taxonomic frames. Curated by Jean-Hubert Martin (b. 1944), then director of the Musée de l'Art Moderne at the Centre Pompidou in Paris, the show aspired to create a display in which cultural differences could coexist without a homogenising agenda. In spite of the unprecedented volume of critical writing that emerged – and the ongoing discussions – in response to this landmark show, it becomes necessary to revisit the exhibition together with its widespread critical reception that overwhelmingly argues along a polarised axis, overlooking the role of multiple localities and contexts beyond the metropolitan centre in shaping an emergent global exhibition practice.[10] In an endeavour to recuperate those dimensions of this transcultural encounter that get written out of narratives about centres that connect to peripheral regions of the globe, this chapter follows the exhibition's bold topography across continents to one of those sites where the works and artists that travelled to Paris were anchored. Further, by examining their post-*Magiciens* lives, it urges us to read objects, their producers, and curators coevally. Instead of flattening their historical trajectories by invoking the sole agency of continuing (post)colonial epistemic violence, the following account argues for restoring to multiple sites their specific historicity. The case of South Asia, which this chapter fleshes out, serves here as an example of a possible locus from which to attempt a connected history of a global exhibition, whose transcultural dynamics are lost in accounts that singularly address the metropolitan centre, even if to castigate its cultural biases.

8 Cited in Helmut Draxler (ed.), *Andrea Fraser, Christian Philipp Müller and Gerwald Rockenschaub: Österreichs Beitrag zur 45. Biennale von Venedig 1993*, Cologne: König, 1993, pp. 185–203, here p. 187.

9 The expression has been used by Irit Rogoff, 'Hit and Run – Museums and Cultural Difference', *Art Journal*, vol. 61 (3), 2002: 63–73, here 66.

10 A consolidated bibliography of the exhibition's reception was compiled by the Centre Pompidou: *Fortune Critique de l'Exposition: Magiciens de la Terre: Bibliographie selective.* (Downloaded in December 2017. The link is unfortunately no longer active.) An overview of the art critical and art historical responses to the show is Jean-Marc Poinsot, 'Review of the Paradigms and Interpretative Machine'.

The 'Magic' of 1989

The now quasi-canonical narrative of global art has successfully positioned *Magiciens de la Terre* as a key event to signpost the beginnings of an art world that accorded visibility to art from the peripheries; its date stands for a turn to inclusivity that brought with it a proclaimed intention to dismantle systemic forms of privilege and discrimination. Hans Belting and Andrea Buddensieg connect this event to the formative geopolitical developments of 1989 – the fall of the Berlin Wall, the neoliberal globalisation of capital, followed by the proliferation of biennial art shows across the globe, all of which are firmly held to have irreversibly transformed the map of contemporary art.[11] From the perspective of the curatorial team of *Magiciens de la Terre*, which had started planning the show in 1984, a time when the dramatic events of 1989 that would bring about the dissolution of cold war divisions were still unforeseeable, the project was conceived in another, more nationally charged, context.[12] First, it was intended to be part of the galaxy of cultural events planned to mark the bicentennial of the French Revolution of 1789. Celebrating the universal ideals of liberty and human rights as an achievement of the French nation was clearly a national agenda to which Jean-Hubert Martin sought to give a global inflection by inviting artists of the world to be part of a show animated by a spirit of universal fraternity. His explicit aim was to include artists on an individual basis, freeing them from the obligation of standing for a nation. Additionally, Paris as location was meant to reinforce the national claims of France as a new centre for contemporary art from the world, thereby reclaiming the place that New York had held since the late 1940s, when it 'stole the idea of modernism' from a Europe battered by the damages of war.[13]

As the most important point of his agenda, Jean-Hubert Martin announced that his aim was to correct the problem of 'one hundred percent of exhibitions ignoring eighty per cent of the earth';[14] in other words, the exhibition was intended to give visibility and recognition to the world's art that was never accorded to it before. According to the curatorial team, the choice of artists was consciously meant to transcend established taxonomic distinctions between the so-called 'fine' arts and 'folk' traditions, distinctions sanctified by colonial practices and which have continued to be upheld in modern museums, in turn classified into ethnological or art museums, museums of so-called Indigenous or native art, or of decorative art. The exhibition's expansive embrace together with its spectacular scale made it an

11 Hans Belting, Andrea Buddensieg and Peter Weibel (eds), *The Global Contemporary and the Rise of New Art Worlds*, Cambridge, MA: MIT Press, 2013, p. 28.
12 The initial conceptual framework for the exhibition was drawn up by Jean-Hubert Martin in 1984, following discussions with Jan Debbaut, Mark Francis and Jean-Louis Maubant. The curatorial team he subsequently led included Mark Francis, Aline Luque and André Magnin, see Jean-Hubert Martin, *L'Art au large*, Paris: Flammarion, 2013, p. 17ff.
13 From the title of Serge Guilbaut, *How New York Stole the Idea of Modern Art: Abstract Expressionism, Freedom and the Cold War*, Chicago: University of Chicago Press, 1983.
14 See the Wikipedia entry for the exhibition, 'Magiciens de la Terre,', last updated 28 April 2021, https://en.wikipedia.org/wiki/Magiciens_de_la_terre.

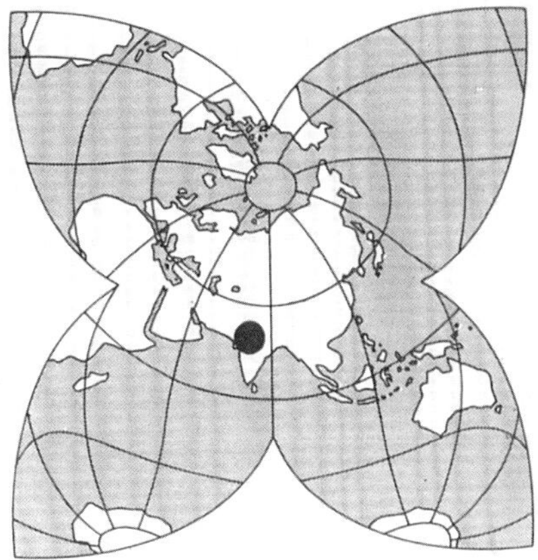

Jangarh Singh Shyam.
1962.
Patangarh, Madhya Pradesh
Inde.
Indien.
Vit à Bhopal.

1   Catalogue entry, *Magiciens de la Terre*

impressive feat of curatorship; these accounted for its visually exciting features, while at the same time emerged as a source of myriad inconsistencies within the concept of the exhibition, provoking much criticism. I will return to this aspect further below. By abandoning the nation or the region, and with them political considerations as identifying anchors, and instead presenting the artist as individual, the exhibition makers sought to reinforce a form of humanist equality and an equally humanist celebration of the exemplary individual. This stance was visualised in the exhibition catalogue, where a dot on a map – a flattened version of the globe – always at its centre, placed on the top right-hand corner of each artist's entry, identified his or her singular location on the planet (fig. 1). Yet, the decision to bring a more global mix of people into an exhibition and by extension to the field of artistic practice, to explore the possibilities of newer positions, was not without precursors going back to the late 1960s. One example is the exhibition *Live in Your Head: When Attitudes Become Form* curated by Harald Szeemann in 1969 at the Kunsthalle Bern, which adopted a two-staged curatorial process, similar to the making of *Magiciens*. In other words, artists were selected following curatorial research and travel to their sites of work, followed by the production of the work itself within the exhibition space, as a response to a new context.[15] In its worldwide

15   See Harald Szeemann, *Live in Your Head: When Attitudes Become Form: Works – Concepts – Processes – Information*, Bern: Stämpfli Cie, 1969. According to Geeta Kapur, Szeemann 'set the stage for the curator as collaborator and coproducer of artworks and exhibitions alike', see Geeta Kapur, 'Curating Across

purview, *Magiciens* came closest to the *Bienal de La Habana*, whose second iteration in 1986 hosted, in addition to artists from Latin America, participants from Asia and Africa, setting the global orientation for future iterations. However, as its then director Gerardo Mosquera has underlined, the *Bienal's* main thrust was towards involving artists in social and discursive events rather than commissioning works to be produced on site.[16] The Havana *Bienal* had discarded the national principle that informs the canonical Venice Biennale; in coupling this to a discursive frame with a view to bringing out the vital and productive messiness of the contemporary, its role in shaping future biennials post-1989 was perhaps more formative than that of *Magiciens*.

Magiciens de la Terre consciously positioned itself against prevalent models of exhibitions, in vogue since the nineteenth century. These included, first, colonial exhibitions and world fairs that sought to reconstruct cultures through representations of their constitutive elements such as architecture, mock rituals, human and animal displays, and, of course, material objects, all placed within re-enacted original settings. The *Exposition Coloniale* held in Paris during the summer of 1931 was one such example. Secondly, *Magiciens* conceived of itself as a postmodern response to the more recent model of an exhibition of silent objects, notably *Primitivism in 20th Century Art* of 1984,[17] where unnamed 'primitive' works were juxtaposed to modernist masterpieces as evidence of the universality of the modernist canon. In fact, much of the conceptualisation of *Magiciens* took place in the midst of continuing and widespread controversial discussions surrounding the *Primitivism* show. For Martin and his team a primary concern was to exhibit works from Euro-America next to those from other continents in a manner that would do away with cultural hierarchies and value judgements. Where *Primitivism* had denied objects from Africa and Oceania identity and temporality by leaving them anonymous and undated, *Magiciens* resolved to treat all exhibits in exactly the same manner – by levelling hierarchies, obliterating context, allowing each artwork to appear without an ostensible ideological framework. The answer to the Greenbergian formalism underpinning *Primitivism* was provided by 'Malraux's brand of humanism'.[18] Inclusion meant the presence and visible involvement of artists, as individual actors and subjects.

Agonistic Worlds', in: Parul D. Mukherji, Naman P. Ahuja and Kavita Singh (eds), *Influx: Contemporary Art in Asia*, New Delhi: Sage Publications, 2013, pp. 158–81, here p. 160. Steeds, in turn, traces the sources inspiring *Magiciens* back to the 1936 international Surrealist exhibition at London, as well as to André Breton's home and studio in Paris, and further to the Fourth Biennial of Sydney, directed by William Wright in 1982. Martin had curated the French pavilion there and provided its director with valuable input. There was a considerable overlap of artists between the Biennial and *Magiciens*. At Sydney too, French and Aboriginal artists prepared their work side by side, see Lucy Steeds, '"Magiciens de la Terre" and the Development of Transnational Project-Based Curating', in: Steeds et al. (eds), *Making Art Global (Part 2)*, pp. 24–92, here pp. 30–33.

16 Gerardo Mosquera, 'The Third Bienal de la Habana in its Global and Local Contexts', in: Rachel Weiss et al. (ed.), *Making Art Global (Part 1): The Third Havana Biennial 1989*, London: Afterall Books, 2011, pp. 70–79, here pp. 72–73.

17 Held at the MoMA, New York and curated by William Rubin and Kirk Varnedoe, discussed in Chapter Three.

18 As put by Yves Michaud, who views both as different faces of universalism, see Yves Michaud, 'Doctor Explorer Chief Curator', *Third Text*, vol. 3 (6), 1989: 83–88, here 86.

As opposed to the Hegelian view implicit in the 1984 show, of a universal modernity whose achievements spread from Western centres to remote peripheries, in 1989 the pendulum had swung to an absolute relativism that eschewed questions of quality.[19] The two-volume catalogue accompanying the MoMA exhibition had a heavy didactic slant that compellingly put forward the curatorial interpretation of the exhibits; the catalogue of the *Magiciens*, on the other hand, was conspicuous for its minimalistic approach that abstained from providing scholarly information or critical interpretation of the works. It sought instead to produce a richly visual work accompanied by the biographies of the artists, while leaving the visitors with little additional orientation, not even adequate bibliographic information.[20]

The works of some 106 artists from across the world and spread over two exhibition venues in Paris were exhibited in a loose arrangement that dispensed with the didacticism of text panels or slide shows, the only context being the exhibition design itself. The bold, idiosyncratic mix of individuals and works that defied conventional classificatory systems confronted the exhibition makers with the dilemma of language and cultural categories. The egalitarian principle of establishing those who work outside of the Western art system on the same footing as those who work within it, led to the curatorial decision to eschew terminology associated with modernism. In particular, terms such as 'art' and 'artist' were dropped so as not to impose one more Western category on individuals who in the earlier colonial system were labelled craftsmen or referred to by the names of their tribes or regions. All were now poetically named magicians – drawing on the 'magie de l'art' – instead of artists.[21] Martin and his team were of the view that a magician was an individual who could escape the determinations of a specific art system or context; this would give him or her an unfettered agency and be both an emancipatory and egalitarian form of address for all. The volley of criticism that the title brought on included charges of occultism or the equation of an artist with a trickster,[22] though the exhibition's web page denied associations with shamanism or supernatural practices, arguing instead that the curatorial concept identified the 'creative impulse' as a common denominator.[23] That the title of the show echoed with Frantz Fanon's *Les Damnés de la Terre* (*The Wretched of the Earth*), was pronounced as coincidental; instead, as observed at the opening of this chapter, *terre* was conceived of as standing for the planet or the world; it further referenced Earth as land, locality, or physical matter, all aspects relevant

---

19 'The term "quality" has been eliminated from my vocabulary, since there is simply no convincing system to establish relative and binding criteria of quality when it comes to such a project.' This was stated by Martin to Benjamin Buchloh, see 'Interview: Benjamin H. D. Buchloh and Jean-Hubert Martin', *Third Text*, vol. 3 (6), 1989: 19–27, here 24.

20 The exhibition catalogue comes across as a collage of texts on artists, plans, and opulent images, with a few essays thrown in. See Jean-Hubert Martin (ed.), *Magiciens de la Terre*, Paris: Editions du Centre Pompidou, 1989.

21 Jean-Hubert Martin on exhibition website www.magiciensdelaterre.fr (no longer active). See also Martin, *L'Art au large*, pp. 18–19. In the Preface to the catalogue, Martin speaks of 'la magie derrière ces pratiques parfois d'apparence très matérialiste' (the magic that lies behind seemingly materialist practices), Martin (ed.), *Magiciens*, p. 9.

22 Jean Fisher, 'Other Cartographies', *Third Text*, vol. 3 (6), 1989: 79–82, here 81.

23 Martin (ed.), *Magiciens*, p. 9.

to many makers of art. The show in the final analysis was more than a simple display of works from across the world; not only did it stage globalisation as a theme, it was also, to cite Clémentine Deliss, 'about the representation of art and the manifestations one agrees to call art'.[24]

The Efficacy of Display

Spread over two sites – the galleries of the Musée d'Art Moderne at the Centre Pompidou and the expansive spaces of the Grande Halle de la Villette, the latter a converted cattle market and slaughterhouse – *Magiciens de la Terre* featured a spectacular array of works, where sheer numbers were matched by an exceptional formal and semantic diversity. Most artists made or installed their works on site; these were arranged not according to national or geographic principles, not even according to medium. In addition to canvas painting and sculpture, and a relatively small number of photographic works, media such as painting on paper or wood, wall or floor painting, and installation were meant to stand for a global range, though – as mentioned earlier – with minimal labelling. The loose curatorial framing of the exhibits, employing notions such as 'magical', 'spiritual', or 'individual creativity',[25] did not preclude practices radically antagonistic to these premises – the works of artists such as Hans Haacke, Barbara Kruger, Jeff Wall, Daniel Buren, and Krzysztof Wodiczko were among these. Haacke's site-specific intervention *One Day, The Lions of Dulcie September Will Spout Water in Jubilation* (1989),[26] to cite one example, transformed an existing but defunct fountain outside the building, originally made to commemorate Napoleon's Egyptian campaign of 1798, into a monument to celebrate the life and work of Dulcie September, a South African anti-apartheid activist who had been murdered in Paris the year before. The four sculpted lions of the fountain painted in gold, the shaft in the middle in green, and the basin filled with water dyed black, replicate the three colours of the ANC flag. However, such an oppositional stance was not exclusive to participants from the Western art system. The widespread criticism that the curators of the show selected Western artists on the basis of their adherence to late modernist as well as contemporary practices of conceptual and institutional critique, while works of artists from the so-called peripheries were a product of 'spiritual' impulses promising transcendence, did not entirely square with the evidence of the exhibits.[27] Stances radically opposed to the framing denominators of the exhibition permeated the works of a large number of artists across the regional spectrum: this was evident, for example, in Huang Yongping's *Reptiles* (1989), where the artist put French and Chinese communist newspapers

24 Clémentine Deliss, 'Conjuring Tricks: "Magiciens de la Terre"', *Artscribe International*, no. 77 (September–October), 1989: 48–53, here 49.
25 Martin (ed.), *Magiciens*, pp. 8–9.
26 Not reproduced in the exhibition catalogue, see however Belting et al. (eds), *The Global Contemporary*, p. 67.
27 Though this was a recurring critical point, see for instance, Buchloh, 'Interview', p. 21; Deliss, 'Conjuring Tricks': 50–51.

through two minutes of a washing machine cycle to produce paper pulp as the transmogrified matter of the international communist movement. Huang's installation was informed by several intellectual and artistic currents including traditional Chinese tomb architecture, Dada, Duchamp's readymades as well as ancient Taoist philosophy.[28] The installation *Mission/Missions: How to Build Cathedrals* (1987) by the Brazilian artist Cildo Meireles took recourse to an aesthetic of the opulent and the macabre while referencing Jesuit mission settlements in Paraguay, Argentina, and the south of Brazil between 1617 and 1767. By playing on sensory knowledge, the artist arranged the pillars of economy, the sacred, and the animal around an architecture of gold coins, communion wafers, and animal bones to expose the civilisational dynamics of the colonisation of South America.[29] While Alfredo Jaar's work *La Géographie, ça sert d'abord, à faire la guerre* (*Geography = War*, in Jaar's translation, 1989) led visitors into a maze of spaces and images that had emerged from his investigations of toxic waste dumped by Western corporations in Nigeria, the Zairean artist Chéri Samba showed pictures from modern media containing information on AIDS or violence against women.[30] In doing so, he situated his art practice squarely within the context of modern journalistic communication rather than an archaic spiritualism. The profusion of similar examples that coexisted with traditional forms such as *mandalas*, tantric drawing, or Aboriginal bark painting highlighted above all the open eclecticism of the show, assembled under the umbrella notion of a 'transhistorical experience of spirituality'.[31]

Responding to a questionnaire on the display of a work of art published in the *Cahiers du musée national d'art moderne* in 1986, Jean-Hubert Martin underlined the efficacy of display or *accrochage* (hanging) of a work in shaping our understanding of it in terms of 'the relations it establishes with other surrounding works'.[32] In other words, an exhibition consisted of an invitation to view and read a work in the setting of its display rather than returning to its moment and place of origin, remote from the exhibition context. An exhibition design to bring artworks into relationship with each other, to argue that an exhibition is more than the sum of its individual artworks, appears to have informed the curating of *Magiciens* some three years later. Of the works created 'in dialogue', the *Red Earth Circle* by the Land artist Richard Long and the floor painting *Yam Dreaming* by a collective of artists of the Australian Aboriginal Yuendumu community attracted the greatest attention, which included pulling up the curatorial decision to bring these together for its 'neo-colonialist' arrogance (Plate 5.2). Situated in the back space of the vast hall of La Villette, Long's large circle made of mud from the river Avon and applied to the dark wall was a spectacularly striking creation. It was paired with a large – equally striking – floor painting made on site by

---

28   See Martin (ed.), *Magiciens*, pp. 152–53.
29   Reproduced in ibid, pp. 196–97.
30   Ibid, pp. 222–23.
31   Buchloh, 'Interview', p. 21.
32   'Selon les relations qu'il établit avec les autres oeuvres environnantes!', in: Fabrice Hergott, 'Réponses au Questionnaire: "Accrocher une Oeuvre d'Art"', *Cahiers du Musée nationale d'art modern*, 17/18, 1986: 204–15, here 205.

the seven members of the Yuendumu led by Paddy Jupurrurla Nelson, made up of three separate motifs – a *Warna Jadiwarnpa* (snake), *Ngapa* (water), and a *Yarla* (brush potato) – and had a free-standing yam on a decorated pole near the centre. Earth, lived as land, dwelling, nurture, and, not least, rights, was the thread connecting the two. This pair was among the most striking exhibits, and the most extensively photographed ensemble. It has been unfailingly reproduced in the copious reviews of the exhibition since then and has thereby acquired an iconic status of sorts that spells the magnetic pull exercised by *Magiciens*, even among its sternest critics. Indeed, its visual power notwithstanding, the mode of pairing brought forth forceful criticism for allegedly creating a hierarchical, 'neo-colonial' relationship between the Long circle that took up the entire central back wall of the vast hall, dominating from above and afar, while the work lying on the floor beneath it was read as evocative of conquest and subordination.[33] The critic Jean Fisher compared the effect of *Red Earth Circle* to the rose window of Notre Dame, complete with lateral exhibits at a lower level or on the floor like subsidiary side chapels. In her eyes, this juxtaposition spelt an asymmetry that ran through the entire show: while the Christian symbolism of the rose window would have been familiar to most viewers, the cosmogonies of other traditions remained unexplained and therefore rendered silent.[34] And yet, as Lucy Steeds reminds us, such responses frequently depended on photographs, which, widely reproduced, constituted a visual memory of the exhibition long after it was over. While the pictures privileged a certain angle of viewing, the exhibition space offered several possible visual relationships, depending on the location of the viewer.[35] The artist Long – in a conversation with Steeds – described his interactions during the making of the work with Paddy Nelson and his co-workers as having been marked by mutual interest and rapport. Among the factors that joined them was the use of similar pigmented material, coming from different corners of the globe.[36] How crucial the process of making was to the content of the work became forcefully clear to him on a visit to the show a month later, when without the artists it appeared 'sad and empty'.[37]

The absence of rigid framing, the loose eclecticism of a curatorial vision that drew on sensibility and emotion, even the wondrous in art, ended up being both a source of discontent as it spelt a promise. The criticism that the exhibition offered its viewers no orientation 'to find out more about the relationship between the art works and the "real" world' is a legitimate one.[38] Neither did the curators give thought to making palpable the relationship of the exhibits to the transformations unfolding in the contexts whose associations the participants

---

33 Thomas McEvilley describes the placement of the painting on the floor 'as if conquered or raped'; 'Marginalia: Thomas McEvilley on the Global Issue', *Artforum*, vol. 28 (7), 1990: 19–21, here 19; Rasheed Araeen, 'Our Bauhaus Others' Mudhouse', *Third Text*, vol. 3 (6), 1989: 3–14, here 11.
34 Jean Fisher, 'Fictional Histories: "Magiciens de la Terre" – The Invisible Labyrinth', *Artforum*, 28 (1), 1989: 158–62, here 161.
35 Steed, '"Magiciens de la Terre"', pp. 71–72.
36 Ibid.
37 'The best time of it was being there when the show was being made', Richard Long in conversation with Lucy Steeds, 21 March 2008, cited in ibid, p. 78.
38 Deliss, 'Conjuring Tricks': 51.

brought with them to Paris. The '*functionally vague*'[39] criteria adopted by the curators was directed by their primary urge to explore the possibilities of display, the effects of absence or presence of copious information, and to thereby create a path towards the release of a fresh, radical, creative energy by allowing cultural producers to relate to each other within the exhibition space. Creativity here does not preclude collision or iconic interruption, as can be discerned in the encounter of a number of works that share the exhibition space, though not further problematised by the curators or the critics. While, once more, it might be naïve or illusory to conceive of, as Martin and his team seem to have done, the exhibition form as a clean slate that would allow for fresh articulations of form and content, its potential as a space of transcultural co-production cannot be altogether negated under the pretext of neo-colonialist asymmetry or by recourse to a reductionist discussion of exhibitions as identity struggle.[40] By refusing an opposition between 'us' and 'them', the exhibition emerged as a space that did away with the idea of belonging, and therefore staged itself as a ground open for objects and artists to forge new, even inadvertent relationships. Conjoining Long's *Red Earth Circle* to the Aboriginal earth painting employing sacred herbs and water, for instance, endowed Long's work with a meaning that, in another context, it may not have had, but for which it emerges as a stronger work.[41] The question also posed by Lewison in the other direction, that is, 'at what point do "third world" objects transcend the barrier between folk art and fine art', will form the crux of my arguments in the following sections.[42]

Magiciens de la Terre remains present in discussions of global art not least because of the exceptionally vocal response it provoked – in the form of newspaper reviews, interviews, and features, in addition to scholarly and art critical assessments. This has made it a starting point for a debate that continued long after the event. A detailed survey of the vast corpus of critical writing is beyond the scope of this discussion;[43] I will limit myself to drawing attention to a few main lines of criticism that provide the relevant backdrop and springboard for the subsequent sections of this chapter. While the exhibition itself shied away from critical theory, scholarly analyses of its professed shortcomings drew on a heavy dose of postmodern and postcolonial perspectives. Apart from the charge of lame curation, the absence of contextual information, or choice of a title that evoked 'conjuring tricks', the bulk of critiques castigated Martin and his team for their neo-colonialist, ethnocentric approach to 'curating cultures' of the so-called Third World. Several voices echoed Jean Fisher's charge of epistemic violence having been inflicted on non-European works by forcing them into a

---

39   The term has been used by Michaud, 'Doctor Explorer': 86 (italics in original).

40   See for instance Norman L. Kleeblatt, 'Identity Roller Coaster: From *Magiciens de la Terre* to Documenta 11', *Art Journal*, vol. 64 (1), 2005: 61–63. This particular issue of the journal is devoted to 'Identity Exhibitions'.

41   See Jeremy Lewison, '"Bilderstreit" and "Magiciens de la Terre": Paris and Cologne', *The Burlington Magazine*, vol. 131 (1037), 1989: 585–87, here 585.

42   Ibid. Artists' responses collected by Steed shows that the 'dialogue' invoked by Martin and so frequently decried as an illusion by his critics could have been experienced by several artists as productive, see Poinsot, 'Review of the Paradigms', p. 103.

43   For a survey of writings from within the Western art world, Poinsot, 'Review of the Paradigms'.

Western modernist framework of display,[44] by presenting ephemeral works or installations in a manner that 'could never succeed in doing justice'[45] to them. A key criticism of the show was its refusal to acknowledge the global dimension of modernism as a significantly inflected tradition beyond Euro-America. Martin's problematic stance towards the abundant artworks brought forth by worldwide modernist movements, leading him to dismiss these as derivative or 'contaminated' by the West, and to seek instead cultural 'authenticity' in traditions associated with practices labelled as 'ritual' or 'folk' or 'archaic', was chastised above all by Rasheed Araeen.[46] He and others following him rebuked the curatorial vision for privileging a selection premised on Orientalism and neo-primitivism that continued to exoticise cultures in the name of dignifying difference.[47] The argument is indeed a persuasive one, and the negative appraisal was no doubt exacerbated by Martin's unfortunate choice of language that framed his refusal to consider modernist works from the Global South as potential contributors to the show: in its English translation the term 'contaminated' bears connotations of discourses of racism, notorious for drawing upon similar bio-medical analogies and assumptions of purity. A noticeable trend in the critical reception of *Magiciens* is the tendency to address the framework of the exhibition and with it the person of the principal curator as an independent object of study, rather than to seize the challenge of engaging with the admittedly vast and diverse body of artworks, which not infrequently disrupt the framework intended to accommodate them. Here different forms of agency appear to be at work – with, and often against, each other: the loosely pluralistic curatorial conception, the efficacy of the artworks, and the exhibition design at two different sites, all brought forth in their mutual confrontation new and surprising articulations, such as the exhibition did not set out to propose.

44 Fisher, 'Fictional Histories': 160.

45 Deliss, 'Conjuring Tricks': 48; Gavin Jantjes charged the exhibition of practising inclusion through homogenisation; while Michael Brenson pointed to the 'layers of disjunctiveness' between art of non-Western origin and the site, designed for modernist works. See Gavin Jantjes, 'Red Rags to a Bull', in: Rasheed Araeen (ed.), *The Other Story: Afro-Asian Artists in Post-War Britain*, London: Hayward Gallery, 1989 (unpaginated); Michael Brenson, 'The Curator's Moment', *Art Journal*, vol. 57 (4), 1998: 16–27, here 23.

46 Araeen, 'Our Bauhaus': 9–14.

47 Araeen's critical stance was echoed by several other scholars and art critics: Catherine David, for example, reproached the curatorial vision of *Magiciens* for reinforcing preconceived ideas about the non-Western archaic as peripheral modern or a form of 'premodern rationalities', in: 'Roundtable: Global Tendencies: Globalism and the Large-Scale Exhibition', introduced by Tim Griffin, *Artforum*, vol. 52 (3), 2003: 153–63; 206–12, here 155. Also, Okwui Enwezor and Olu Oguibe, 'Introduction', in: *Reading the Contemporary: African Art from Theory to the Marketplace*, Cambridge, MA: MIT Press, 2000, pp. 9–14, here p. 9. Ranjit Hoskote, 'Kaleidoscopic Propositions: The Evolving Contexts of Contemporary Indian Art', in: Christian Gether et al. (eds), *India: Art Now*, Ostfildern: Hatje Cantz, 2012, pp. 54–62, here p. 58; James Clifford, 'The Others: Beyond the "Salvage Paradigm"', *Third Text*, vol. 3 (6), 1989: 73–77. Geeta Kapur reads the binary of Indigenous and avant-garde built into the curatorial paradigm of *Magiciens* as one that posits 'individual agency' against 'timeless consanguinity' and thereby overlooks 'the self-conscious breakthrough in language and politics' of modernism in non-Western societies, see Kapur, 'Curating Across Agonistic Worlds', p. 163.

The understanding of the exhibition as a text created by a single author underpinned a large number of interpretations of *Magiciens*, leading to a widespread view of it as a show that saw the rise of a powerful curator who makes the world a terrain of exploration in a benevolent spirit of producing conviviality among cultures and genres. Looking back some two decades later, Yacouba Konaté read this role as mirroring a colonial operation and wrote: 'He [the curator] plunges into the Africa of mysteries and ambiguities to discover creatures which nobody had sought. Then, taking them by the hand, he reveals them to their contemporaneity. The whole strategy of this big difference lies in this twofold operation: going back into the pre-modern to display the contemporary.'[48] While this criticism of the choice of artists from Africa might hold, it is difficult to apply in a consistent and systematic way to artists from other continents, whose practices, as examples from the show suggest, resonated with contemporary artistic languages across the globe, and many of whom would become regular participants in French and other Western exhibition contexts. And yet, discussions in this vein make us aware more than ever of the difficulty of coming to terms with the paradoxes built into an enterprise that was on the one hand emancipating in its questioning of the inward-looking taxonomies of Western art history, as well as in its resolve to accord conceptual parity to myriad creative acts across cultures. On the other, the project's intrinsically democratic urge remained trapped within an opaque notion of otherness. Perhaps a way to come to grips with this paradox might be to begin by asking: What remains distant or unsaid in the prolific narratives of and about the show? What would the writing of a connected history of a global exhibition like this one demand if it is to avoid the trap of telling this story from a singular perspective that effaces multiple subjectivities and regional histories that were active within it? How can we plot experiences and experiments both entangled and coeval onto a single matrix? What are the archives we need to tap to be able to address both the emancipatory potential of global connectivity as well as its oppressive aspects from positions not limited to the metropolis? Existing narratives of *Magiciens* have chosen to focus on a single site, a single institution, and a single curator whose strategies of selection and display they dissect. Casting actors from 'elsewhere' as passive objects of epistemic violence ends up replicating that which the curators of the exhibition have been reproached for: that is, for objectifying otherness by radicalising difference and implying the untranslatability and incommensurability of their art production in relation to a Western art system. The critical concern to dismantle the tenacious hegemony of the metropole can backfire if it does not address the postcolonial trajectories of those histories that were equally implicated within shared global circuits. The following sections of this chapter will move away from an exclusive engagement with debates firmly anchored within the discursive concerns of the Euro-American academy, and instead explore the transformations and emergent faultlines on those sites beyond Paris that came to be enmeshed with the making of this exhibition. Such an approach, the chapter argues, would be a step towards grasping more fully the globality of the contemporary exhibition form.

48   Cited in Poinsot, 'Review of the Paradigms', p. 105.

Curators, Artists, Native Informers

Looking back nostalgically to the *Exposition surréaliste d'objets* of 1936, Jean-Hubert Martin wryly observed that while André Breton and his team never invited a 'savage' to Paris, this was now possible half a century later, thanks to the shrinkage of the planet enabled by modern transportation and communication technology.[49] The choice of works for *Magiciens* as well as the method of their selection were among the aspects of the show for which the curatorial team was rebuked, on the grounds that it promoted the paradigm of *'curator as explorer'*[50] and thereby shifted the focus of an exhibition from the individual works to the project of gathering them. To move beyond the polemics of a debate that remains trapped within the Manichean mould of the West and the 'other', it is necessary to look at how the selection process unfolded in different parts of the world, at the transcultural connection between the French curator(s) and their 'native informers'; further to investigate the complex artworlds in which informers, artists, and their works were embedded. We still have to find an explanatory mode of reading the process of selecting and curating as an act that goes beyond the sole authorship of a Paris curator, and instead to unravel its entanglement with local, regional, and national processes and the role of multiple actors across the Europe-Asia divide. Can we identify the processes that were initiated through the show or accelerated after it was over? What can the post-*Magiciens* lives of actors and objects tell us about the workings of a planetary logic in local and regional contexts?

The curatorial team of *Magiciens de la Terre* divided the continents of the world among themselves, though each member made occasional trips to a region for which another curator was overall in charge. Trips to establish initial contacts at times included other experts – such as the anthropologist Carlo Severi or the curator Bernhard Lüthi.[51] For the selection of artists from India, Martin drew on the expertise of Yves Véquaud, the author of one of the earliest monographic studies on Mithila painting, a work which romantically projected this regional genre as a timeless tradition and veritable expression of an 'authentic Indian civilization'.[52] In addition, another specialist, Frank André Jamme, was commissioned to carry out research on tantric artists in India. The art critic and curator, Bernard Marcadé, a co-editor of the exhibition catalogue, also visited. The access to artists and the selection process in India was mediated by two main native informants, Jyotindra Jain (b. 1943), an eminent scholar and

---

49 Jean-Hubert Martin, 'Est-Ouest, Nord-Sud: nouveaux venus, nouveaux continents', in: Daniel Soutif (ed.), *L'art du XXe siècle, 1939–2002: De l'art moderne á l'art contemporain*, Paris: Citadelle & Mazenot, 2005, pp. 459–78, here p. 463.

50 The expression has been used by Johanne Lamoureux, 'From Form to Platform: The Politics of Representation and the Representation of Politics', Art *Journal*, vol. 64 (1), 2005: 64–73, here 66 (italics in original).

51 Steeds, '"Magiciens de la Terre"', p. 47.

52 Yves Véquaud, *L'Art du Mithila*, Paris: Les Presses de la Connaissance, 1976. German translation: *Die Kunst von Mithila*, Geneva: Weber, 1977, p. 11 (all citations are from this edition). The exhibition catalogue lists Véquaud as a member of the advisory team ('Chargés de Mission'), Martin (ed.), *Magiciens*, p. 4.

the then director of the National Crafts Museum in New Delhi, and Jagdish Swaminathan (1928–1994), artist and director of Roopankar Art Museum, Bhopal, in Central India. Both headed institutions that specialised in what was designated as folk art, distinct from the gallery circuit and museums for modernist and contemporary art. The general impression of the term 'folk' with reference to culture or aesthetic practice is that of a consensual, collective tradition of a time gone by, existing in a state of disjunction with the present.[53] In a postcolonial national context, as in India, folk culture became a central concern of nationalist ideology and therefore saw the creation of new institutional spaces for the preservation of that which was canonised as India's craft heritage.[54] State patronage in certain instances, as will be shown below, also worked to catalyse modern experiments in the domain of so-called folk art. It is in such a context that the role of Jain and Swaminathan as members of the cultural establishment, can be located: both were instrumental in bringing artistic production hitherto consigned to the domain of rural ethnography into an urban, institutional mainstream of state-sponsored projects.

Of the artists chosen for the Paris show by Martin's team in partnership with their local Indian collaborators, Baua Devi (b. 1942, accompanied by her husband and an assistant) came from Mithila, Jangarh Singh Shyam (1964–2001) belonged to the community of Gonds from Central India, while Jivya Soma Mashe (1934–2018) – who in the end did not make it to Paris – was a member of the Warli community from Maharashtra.[55] In addition, Raja Babu Sharma (b. 1956) and Acharya Vyakul (1930–2000) were practitioners of tantric art. Clearly, Martin and his team avoided choosing from a lively scene of modern and contemporary art, mainly urban based in cities such as Mumbai, Delhi, or Bangalore, and who were professionally trained in modern art schools, were part of collectives, networks, and gallery circuits. This was an art practice that Martin rather categorically dismissed as a remnant of colonial culture and imitative of mainstream culture of the West, for which he was, as recounted above, severely reproached. Rather, he set out, with the help of his local contacts, in search for the 'authentic' that he believed was to be found in the Indian villages – among groups that were not assimilated within mainstream urban art culture but continued to nurture their own forms of pictorial practice. It is important to clarify that Martin's stance was clearly not one of striving to salvage a timeless world, believed to be threatened with extinction. He, in a seeming paradox, viewed his chosen artists as both authentic and 'contemporary' – to him their practice was very much of the present. And yet the full import of according actors and practices contemporaneity meant that it was necessary to acknowledge that they were connected to, or partook of the same historical space as the institutions, strategies, and products of the art world of the time – even as they worked on the scale of the village or the small town.

<hr>

53   For a critical position, Barbara Kirshenblatt-Gimblett, 'Folklore's Crisis', *The Journal of American Folklore*, vol. 111 (441), 1998: 281–327.

54   Paul Greenough, 'Nation, Economy, and Tradition Displayed: The Indian Crafts Museum, New Delhi', in: Carol A. Breckenridge (ed.), *Consuming Modernity: Public Culture in a South Asian World*, Minneapolis: University of Minnesota Press, 1995, pp. 216–48.

55   Jivya Som Mashe is however represented in the exhibition catalogue, Martin (ed.), *Magiciens*, pp. 192–93.

This is an aspect that neither the curators of the show nor its critics fully grasped; its implications for the way to analyse global exhibitions have yet to be addressed.

The artists chosen for *Magiciens* were bearers of labels that seek to pin their identity: these include designations such as tribes or *adivasis*, which mostly go back to colonial censuses, or caste names.[56] They designate groups who had mainly inhabited non-urban spaces – forests, villages, the hills – and have a long history of marginalisation and impoverishment. The appropriation of forests and rivers as key sites of resources for modern industry – minerals, coal, hydraulic energy – under colonial rule, has continued in independent India with all its modernisation programmes. Faced with the dispossession of lands or the drowning of entire villages following the construction of large dams, sections of the population of these communities have – since the nineteenth century – migrated to urban areas, while drawn into the modern economy as workers in mines and factories or wage labourers in various governmental schemes. As we saw in Chapter Three, the notion of primitivism – both in its cultural-evolutionist iteration as well as its artistic variant – had migrated as the other face of modernity to sites across the globe. Colonial officials stamped the so-called tribal groups like the *adivasis* or the *santhals* as primitive, conjuring up either a savage force that had to be domesticated or, as the obverse of same coin, a romantic image of people lacking in forms of modern rationality, but possessing an instinctive wisdom and imagination. Stashed away into a different historical space as well as a different temporality, these groups continued to be the object of a politics of cultural nostalgia in postcolonial India. Colonial as well as post-colonial elites avidly collected cultural products of communities considered primitive, valorising their artefacts as examples of exceptional artisanal skills and reservoirs of traditional knowledge systems whose survival they sought to ensure. In the mid-nineteenth century, various tribal groups had emerged as insurrectionary forces against landlords and representatives of the colonial regime; since the late 1960s, their militancy acquired a socialist or Marxist-Leninist or Maoist ideological orientation, leading to a surge of armed uprisings against the policies of the postcolonial state. Struggles against dispossession of lands, for rights to resources, against displacement as a result of the construction of the Sardar Sarovar Dam, have continued through the 1990s, dispersed across the subcontinent.[57] Insurgency

---

56 The classification of certain marginal groups as 'tribes' in colonial censuses continues in independent India: roughly eight per cent of the population is officially classified in the Constitution as Scheduled Tribes. The term *adivasi* (Sanskrit for 'original habitants'), as an encompassing designation for this collectivity, is often used interchangeably with tribe, though the two are not identical. The former is a self-designation, used today as an autochthonous term and as an equivalent of the now globally widespread designation Indigenous. While tribe is generally avoided outside of official contexts, some communities accept the official designation, which entitles them to reservations and other privileges. See Amita Baviskar, 'Adivasi Encounters with Hindu Nationalism in MP', *Economic and Political Weekly*, vol. 40 (48), 2005: 5105–13, here 5106–07; Virginius Xaxa, 'Tribes as Indigenous Peoples of India', *Economic and Political Weekly*, vol. 34 (51), 1999: 3589–95.

57 Amita Baviskar, *In the Belly of the River: Tribal Conflicts over Developments in the Narmada Valley*, Delhi: Oxford University Press, 2004 (second edition); Ajay Skaria, *Hybrid Histories: Forests, Frontiers and Wildness in Western India*, Delhi: Oxford University Press, 1999; Nandini Sundar, *Subalterns and Sovereigns: An Anthropological History of Bastar, 1854–1996*, Delhi: Oxford University Press, 1997.

has added one more layer to the existing typology: the *adivasis* as heroic rebels, alternatively as a violent threat to political stability. Moreover activists for *adivasi* rights have frequently sought to naturalise the latter's connections to the environment by attributing to them a special ecological wisdom due to an innate, organic link to nature, together with an economy based on reciprocity and subsistence rather than competition and accumulation.[58] Such ascriptions that have extended over a *longue durée*, have produced contradictions and slippages, denying to these groups the capacity for autonomous and willed negotiations with the forces of change – including urbanisation, modern education, and the relationship to markets, all of which brought with them transformations in familial structures as well as those of cultural production. Let us therefore endeavour to uncover the tracks followed by two of the participating artists of *Magiciens*, Baua Devi and Jangarh Singh Shyam, whose lives carried the burden of such subaltern contexts;[59] their trajectories, as I will argue, were entangled in a shared contemporaneity connecting the village to the town, and to the metropolis, and at the same time existed in a conflicting unity with it.

The artist Baua Devi, from the village of Jitwarpur in Madhubani District in east Indian Bihar, has been a practitioner of what is today termed as the Mithila (as an adjective Maithil) school of painting, since she was twelve years old. The scholar and collector, Yves Véquaud, who chose not to identify the painters he studied by name in order to preserve their primordiality,[60] knew Baua Devi personally since the 1970s and was, together with Jyotindra Jain, instrumental in singling out her work for the exhibition in Paris. It is important at this juncture to recapitulate, albeit briefly, the story of transformation within which Baua Devi's career as an artist was enmeshed: the transformation that a form of domestic wall-painting linked to life-cycle rituals underwent in order to become a transportable object of collection, exhibition, and commodification.[61]

While authors such as Véquaud blandly refer to Mithila painting as a tradition some three millennia old, such a claim must, in view of the ephemerality of the genre, remain speculative. The earliest historical evidence available dates to the early twentieth century, when William G. Archer, then an official in the colonial civil administration, discovered these

58 Baviskar, 'Adivasi Encounters': 5109.
59 While Baua Devi, who came from Mithila in Bihar, does not belong to a tribal group or even a lower caste, the grinding economic poverty, ecological vulnerability, and tenacious patriarchal practices of the region account for placing her within a subaltern, marginalised group.
60 Véquaud, *Die Kunst von Mithila*, does not name any of the artists of the large number of works reproduced in the book.
61 The earliest study of Mithila painting was William G. Archer, 'Maithil Painting', *Marg*, vol. 3 (3), 1949: 24–33. The more recent transformations have been studied by Jyotindra Jain, *Ganga Devi: Tradition and Expression in Mithila Painting*, Ahmedabad: Mapin Publishing, 1997; Jyotindra Jain, 'Ganga Devi: Tradition & Expression in Mithila Painting', *Third Text*, vol. 3 (6), 1989: 43–50; Pupul Jayakar, *The Earthen Drum: An Introduction to the Ritual Arts of Rural India*, New Delhi: National Museum, 1980; Richard H. Davis, 'From the Wedding Chamber to the Museum: Relocating the Ritual Arts of Madhubani', in: Jan Mrázek and Morgan Pitelka (eds), *What's the Use of Art? Asian Visual and Material Culture in Context*, Honolulu: University of Hawai'i Press, 2008, pp. 77–99; Mani S. Singh, 'A Journey into Pictorial Space: Poetics of Frame and Field in Maithil Painting', *Contributions to Indian Sociology*, 34 (3), 2000: 409–42.

works and subsequently wrote about them. Practitioners of the art of painting in Mithila – done either on walls or floors of domestic/ritual spaces – refer to it as *likhiyā*, derived from the Sanskrit as *alekhya*, meaning both writing and painting, and which points to the story-telling function of the compositional ensemble.[62] Images and ceremonial diagrams thereby fuse within ritual settings, the most prominent of which was the *kohbar ghar* or wedding chamber, situated at the heart of a Maithil home, where a marriage was ritually consummated. The task of painting the walls and floor of the chamber in preparation for the wedding was an exclusively female domain, a collective practice involving women of the extended family across generations and organised according to a hierarchy of skill and seniority. Mud walls plastered with cow dung were primed with whitewash, followed by rice paste. The colours originally used were both mineral and vegetal, put together locally, but by the second half of the twentieth century were replaced by brighter, chemical pigments available in bazaars of neighbouring towns.[63] The process of painting proceeded from a chosen centre and radiated outwards, slowly covering the wall with a complex composition, an interwoven ensemble of geometric motifs, vegetal elements, and numerous living creatures – birds, fish, snakes, turtles, together with gods, goddesses, and humans. Every cranny of available space came to be filled with proliferating forms, because, to cite Jyotindra Jain, 'emptiness would be tantamount to infecundity'.[64]

The taxonomic shift that transformed Mithila painting from ritual activity to a work of art, endowed with an expressive power said to match that of Western modernism, took place in the first half of the twentieth century, very much in the terms that marked the discourse of primitive modernism. The principal actor involved here was William G. Archer who, in his capacity as a colonial administrator visiting the earthquake ravaged regions of Bihar in 1934, discovered this painted wealth in the interior domestic spaces of damaged homes, spaces to which he as a British male would in normal times never have had access. His response recorded in his memoirs exudes all the tropes of modernist epiphany experienced by the Western artist or connoisseur when face to face with the energies embodied in primitive objects: 'in these murals', he wrote, 'we somehow electrically met'.[65] Such reactions have, as discussed in Chapter Three, provided the stuff of foundation myths of the modernist revolution. For Archer, the paintings he witnessed were full of a 'savage forcefulness' that reminded him of 'the fanciful contortions of a Klee or Miro'.[66] In the following years, he carried out extensive surveys of the art, took photographs, and on returning to England, wrote an article on the subject, published in the 1949 issue of the journal of Indian art, *Marg*.[67] Archer was

62 Susan S. Wadley, '*Likhiyā*. Painting Women's Lives in Northern India', in: Susan S. Wadley (ed.), *South Asia in the World. An Introduction*, New York: M. E. Sharpe, 2014, pp. 241–60.

63 Singh, 'A Journey into Pictorial Space': 412.

64 Jain, *Ganga Devi*, p. 54.

65 William G. Archer, 'Into Hidden Maithila', in: William and Mildred Archer, *India Served and Observed*, London: BACSA, 1994, pp. 53–58, here p. 58. Archer's discovery has also been described by Davis, 'From the Wedding Chamber', pp. 82–84.

66 Archer, 'Into Hidden Maithila', pp. 54–56.

67 Archer, 'Maithil Painting'.

now the Keeper of the Indian Section of the Victoria and Albert Museum and instrumental in canonising Mithila painting, together with a number of other regional and tribal objects that he acquired for the museum and explicitly categorised as '*art*'.[68] A similar project – albeit in the form of a temporary exhibition – was curated by Stella Kramrisch at the Philadelphia Museum of Art in 1968, where she too strove to extricate 'folk' objects from the domain of 'crafts' and reposition them as art.[69] This enterprise represented a continuation of her scholarly perspective that goes back to her days in Calcutta (see Chapter Three), following which she continued to read these works as embodiments of sacrality wherein the ritual and artistic fused. Neither Archer nor Kramrisch showed interest in individual producers – the power of the works they observed was perceived as residing in their innate collective energy.

The individualisation of artists followed in the subsequent decades, once more catalysed by natural disaster and impoverishment. In this instance the intervening agency came from the Indian state, in the persona of Pupul Jayakar, the chairperson of the All India Handicrafts Board and confidante of the then Prime Minister, Indira Gandhi. Among the measures taken to provide relief during a severe famine in 1966 was a programme to revitalise the tradition of painting by encouraging women to paint on paper and thereby produce transportable works that could be appropriately framed, collected, and sold on the market. Inspired by Archer's article in *Marg*, Jayakar had earlier surveyed the region and was dismayed by the decline of a once rich mural tradition, now victim to the grinding poverty of its makers. What started as a famine relief project rapidly acquired momentum over the coming years, when Mithila art left the walls of village homes and was produced on paper and marketed in craft shops and galleries in major metropolitan cites in and beyond India. While some of the work continued to be deeply individual, with artists being singly identified, named, and recognised through awards, a large volume was mass produced, organised by middlemen, who commissioned unnamed artists in the villages – cutting across caste barriers – to churn out colourful renderings of deities, flora and fauna, and mythological stories. The role of state patronage together with interventions by individual curators, and not least the change of medium and scale have all brought this genre of work into the discursive domain of art history. Mithila painting has over the past decades become a subject of scholarly investigation by art historians and visual anthropologists, such as Véquaud (who was known in the villages as Bihko Fransi[70]), Caroline Henning Brown, or Mani Shekhar Singh, who have all done extensive field work in the region.[71] The shift of scale and context, according to Jyotindra Jain, has meant a freedom from constraints of making 'ritual-bound' images in a static space,

---

68   William G. Archer, *The Vertical Man: A Study in Primitive Indian Sculpture*, London: George Allen & Unwin, 1947, p. 10 (italics in original).

69   Stella Kramrisch (ed.), *Unknown India: Ritual Art in Tribe and Village*, Philadelphia: Museum of Art, 1968.

70   Jain, *Ganga Devi*, p. 16.

71   Caroline Henning Brown, 'Contested Meanings: Tantra and the Poetics of Mithila Art', *American Ethnologist*, vol. 23 (4), 1996: 717–37, cited in Davis, 'From the Wedding Chamber', pp. 81–82; Singh, 'A Journey into Pictorial Space'.

enabling individual experiments with themes and styles.[72] As individual artists began to sign their names, they also perceived this as a possibility to explore new subjects related to contemporary concerns or affecting their personal lives – images of the classic symbols of industrial modernity such as trains, airplanes, roller-coasters, which also impinged on their direct experiences of travel and relocation to urban settings.[73] The state policy of publicly recognising achievement through awards as well as by selecting artists to exhibit their works in shows abroad, has contributed to the renown of individual artists such as Jivya Soma Mashe, Ganga Devi (1928–1991), Sonabai (c. 1930–2007), and not least Baua Devi and Jangarh Singh Shyam, the two artists whose trajectories were interwoven with these developments.

Baua Devi, who had painted since her childhood and was married at the age of twelve, was discovered by Bhaskar Kulkarni, artist and aid worker for the Indian government sent by Pupul Jayakar to the region of Madhubani during the famine of 1966. Baua, at that time in her teens, still remembers how she found painting on paper a liberating experience, as it meant not having to wait as long for the paint to dry as when painting on mud walls. During the initial years, Kulkarni made regular trips to the village to collect work of the artists. Some years later Baua Devi was among those invited to paint a mural for the National Handicrafts and Handlooms Museum (also known as the National Crafts Museum) in New Delhi, of which Jyotindra Jain was the director between 1984 and 2001. In 1984, she received a National Award, while her work travelled to international exhibitions on Indian 'folk art' or 'crafts'.[74] Her prolific oeuvre, yet uncatalogued, ranges from paintings on paper of a small format to canvases of a height going up to six metres, and occasional murals. While her repertoire has retained its original range of themes, these have been continuously subjected to fresh pictorial experiments. One recurring subject is the legend of *nag kanya* (snake maiden), a creature with the torso of a young woman and the lower body of a snake. The reference here is to the snake goddess with its distinct iconography, however the artist's rendering draws inspiration from the forms of reptiles that inhabited her native region. Baua Devi's prolific work explores different episodes from the mythical life of this hybrid being. The theme also figured in one of her works exhibited in Paris (Plate 5.3).[75] A work that followed the September 11 attack on the World Trade Center in 2001 featured the *nag kanya* in excruciating

---

72　Jain, *Ganga Devi*, p. 9.

73　See for instance Ganga Devi's 'autobiographical works' on her travels to the United States and Japan, or her *Cancer Series*, in Jain, ibid, pp. 113–30. Baua Devi responded to the September 11 attacks through her painted work. On Mithila women painters' portrayal of dowry-related violence against women, Mani S. Singh, 'What Should Happen, but Has Not Yet Happened: Painterly Tales of Justice', *Contributions to Indian Sociology*, vol. 53 (1), 2019: 184–216. A compelling study of contemporary experiments – both pictorial and thematic – is Roma Chatterji, *Speaking with Pictures: Folk Art and the Narrative Tradition in India*, New Delhi: Routledge, 2012.

74　Catalogue of the Festival of India in the United States 1985–1986: *Aditi: The Living Arts of India*, Washington DC. Smithsonian Institutions, 1985; Saryu Doshi (ed.), *Pageant of Indian Art: Festival of India in Great Britain*, Bombay: Marg Publications, 1983; Lory Frankel (ed.), *Festival of India in the United States*, New York: Harry Abrams, 1985.

75　The catalogue reproduces three paintings on the same theme, all from Véquaud's collection, see Martin (ed.), *Magiciens*, pp. 128–29.

pain looking on to a dark world suffering from the aftermath of terrorist violence.[76] The process of institutionalisation through state-initiated projects took place under the aegis of a national vision to project a vigorous tradition of Indian crafts. The establishment of the All India Handicrafts Board headed by Jayakar was one step in the realisation of this vision, the National Crafts Museum and the institution of an annual National Craftsman award were all further measures in this direction, as were the international exhibitions intended to demonstrate the skills of craft-making. An institutional framing at the national level of the large corpus of work produced in non-urban sites outside of the gallery circuit as 'contemporary' and 'art' took place only in the 1980s, some years before Martin's visit to India. This was at the Roopankar Art Museum of the Bharat Bhavan, opened at Bhopal in 1982 and headed by the artist Jagdish Swaminathan. It was here that the young Jangarh Singh Shyam was first trained as a professional artist.

Jangarh Singh Shyam was a member of the community of the Pardhans, a sub-group of the Gonds, one of the largest tribes of Central India. He came from the tribal district of Patangarh, where the British anthropologist Verrier Elwin (see Chapter Three) had settled after marrying a local girl, who happened to be distantly related to Jangarh.[77] The Pardhans were musicians, genealogists, and storytellers of the Gonds. Their occupation over the centuries was to sing stories about their chief deity Bada Dev, or about the valour of the Gond kings, accompanied by music played on the *bana*, a three-stringed instrument venerated as a manifestation of the chief deity.[78] Performers by vocation, they lived on patronage accorded to them for their role as narrators of the collective memory of the community. With the dwindling of traditional structures of patronage in the twentieth century, the Pardhans were forced to take up farming or manual labour in their villages or in nearby towns. Jangarh, too, came from a region where inhabitants, dispossessed of land, worked as wage labourers. He grew up in extreme poverty, was forced to quit school at an early age, grazed buffaloes and sold milk in nearby towns. Unlike the women of Mithila discussed above, the Pardhans possessed no developed tradition of painting other than that of drawing ritual diagrams.[79] Jangarh himself was not trained in pictorial practices, in his spare time he enjoyed helping the women of the village who made clay relief patterns on the walls of their huts. While in his late teens, Jangarh was discovered by Swaminathan who, with his team, had set out to spot artistic talent in the remote villages. The young man moved together with his wife, Nankusia, to Bhopal to learn painting and graphic arts, and become an artist in the brave new world at Bharat Bhavan, with Swaminathan as his visionary mentor (fig. 2). In this instance too,

---

76 Vandana Kalra, 'Painting on the Wall', *Indian Express*, 13 October 2012, http://archive.indianexpress.com/news/painting-on-the-wall/1016026/3 (accessed February 2021).

77 I follow the practice of Pardhan artists being referred to by their first names. On Elwin's engagement with Gond art, John H. Bowles, *Painted Songs & Stories: The Hybrid Flowerings of Contemporary Pardhan Gond Art*, Bhopal: INTACH Bhopal Chapter, 2009, pp. 20–21.

78 Bowles, ibid, p. 18.

79 Udayan Vajpeyi, 'From Music to Painting. The Strange Yet Not-So-Strange Tales of Pardhaans', in: Monica Narula (ed.), *Frontiers: Sarai Reader VII*, Delhi: CSDS, 2007, pp. 212–20.

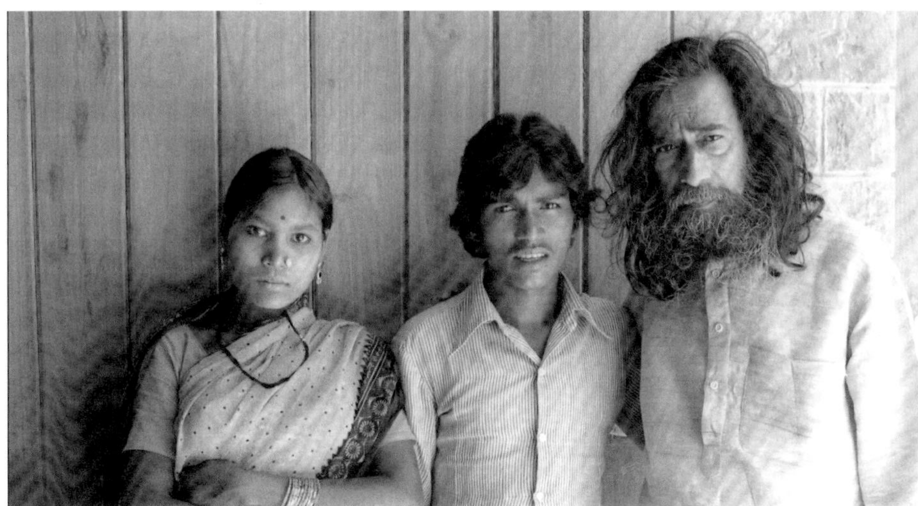

2　Jangarh Singh Shyam, Nankusia Shyam and Jagdish Swaminathan, photograph, 1987. Jyoti Bhatt, Asia Art Archive

institutional developments pushed by the postcolonial Indian state, and in which individual personalities played a catalytic role, propelled critical transformations. While the Bharat Bhavan complex at Bhopal in Central India was a government institution that aimed at including folk art of the large *adivasi* population of the region, to conserve and showcase it as one component of national heritage in a special wing of the Roopankar Museum of Fine Arts, the experiment took a radical turn under the direction of Swaminathan, a left-wing artist and vibrant personality who strove to bring to the institution an individual vision of indigeneity.

Art and Indigeneity – In the Interstices of the Nation and the Planet

Indigeneity, now a familiar globally circulating concept that seeks to replace the stereotype of timeless 'tribal cultures', nonetheless needs to be unpacked, given its frequent usage as a hold-all term that attempts to create a typology put together from around the world. The difficulty in arriving at a consensual understanding of the notion can be observed through the repeated attempts of the United Nations over several decades to arrive at a working definition of 'indigenous': a concept based on relationship to ancestral lands, cultural continuity, language, and, recently, the right to self-identification.[80] Historically the usage of the term goes back to colonial administration and anthropology, when Europeans designated the native inhabitants of the territories they governed as indigenes, the Latin etymology of which means

---

80　Christine Lalonde, 'Introduction: At the Crossroads of Indigeneity, Globalization and Contemporary Art', in: Greg A. Hill, Candice Hopkins and Christine Lalonde (eds), *Sakahān: International Indigenous Art*, Ottawa: National Gallery of Canada, 2013, pp. 13–20, here p. 15.

'born from within'.[81] Though grounded in a deep localism, indigeneity has come to denote a global spread. Yet it is important to point to its divergent valences in different contexts: for those in settler-colonies of Australia, New Zealand, North and South America, where the term initially gained prominence and has since taken strong root, indigeneity encompasses histories of invasion, expropriation, resistance, and survival, together with claims to 'first nationhood'. In the independent, postcolonial nations of Asia and Africa, on the other hand, the Indigenous, whose claims to being the original settlers often predates European colonisation by many centuries, are subject to specific national situations wherein residual colonial constructs come to be grafted onto the modernising agendas of a nation-state that produces its own dynamics of marginalisation and co-option. In both instances, the Indigenous has grown out of the primitive, even as it sets out to cast off that legacy. At the same time, scholarship on different regions has pointed to instances where artists have successfully reconfigured modernist primitivism for purposes of affirmation and resistance.[82] Transcending the different approaches to the subject is a shared understanding of indigeneity as 'a processual category that acknowledges its own historical instability':[83] marked by colonialisms, past and present, it continues to unfold along as yet undetermined pathways.

In India, organisations that represent tribal or *adivasi* groups claim Indigenous status on their behalf in the sense of these being descendants of the region's 'original' inhabitants, and therefore possessing first rights to ancestral land and its resources. As a signatory to several conventions of the United Nations to protect the interests of 'indigenous and other tribal and semi-tribal populations', the Indian government has, under the Fifth and Sixth Schedules of the Indian Constitution, placed the *adivasi*-populated regions of the country under special laws and procedures.[84] The Indian state's patronage of indigeneity, described as 'a new technique of governmentality',[85] can in one sense be read as a response to a dilemma remounting to an earlier phase of national formation involving the struggle for emancipation from colonial rule (see Chapter Three). The path through which a colonised elite could reclaim for itself the modernity denied to it by colonialism depended on a historical and temporal consciousness distinct from those groups – peasants, tribals – seen to form what Prathama Banerjee has termed the 'primitive within'.[86] At the same time the exigencies of an anti-colonial struggle

---

81 James Clifford, *Returns: Becoming Indigenous in the Twenty First Century*, Cambridge, MA: Harvard University Press, 2013, p. 13.

82 As examples from Canada and Australia show. See Ruth B. Phillips, 'Aesthetic Primitivism Revisited: The Global Diaspora of "Primitive Art" and the Rise of Indigenous Modernisms', *Journal of Art Historiography*, vol. 12 (June), 2015: 1–25; Elizabeth Harney and Ruth B. Phillips (eds.), *Mapping Modernisms: Art, Indigeneity, Colonialism*, Durham, NC: Duke University Press, 2018.

83 Harney and Phillips (eds), *Mapping Modernisms*, p. 16.

84 Baviskar, 'Adivasi Encounters': 5106.

85 Sandip K. Luis, 'Between Anthropology and History: The Entangled Lives of Jangarh Singh Shyam and Jagdish Swaminathan', in: Sasanka Perera and Dev Nath Pathak (eds), *Intersections of Contemporary Art, Anthropology and Art History in South Asia: Decoding Visual Worlds*, Cham: Palgrave Macmillan, 2019, pp. 139–79, here p. 141.

86 Prathama Banerjee, *Politics of Time: 'Primitives' and History-Writing in a Colonial Society*, New Delhi: Oxford University Press, 2006.

necessitated the assimilation of diverse elements of the nation's fabric within a national community without having to take recourse to a colonial anthropological mode. The ensuing relationship between nationalist elites and marginal groups was grounded in ambivalence and lived through fresh tribulations in postcolonial times. Modernisation programmes of an expanding economy in independent India meant a continued exploitation of individuals and communities situated along an 'internal frontier' – forest or agricultural areas converted into a site for mines, dams, and heavy industries.[87] The late 1960s and 1970s saw the spread of armed insurrectionary movements led, among others, by Maoist groups in several pockets of Eastern and Southern India; these were severely repressed during the national emergency imposed by Indira Gandhi's government in 1975, resulting in their dispersal and fragmentation. Struggles of the 1980s against dispossession and displacement, during the course of which a distinct *adivasi* identity was asserted, were shaped and strengthened by globally circulating discourses of Indigenous peoples.[88] The fourth Five-Year Plan starting in 1969 put forward a policy to systematically survey, conserve, and integrate craft traditions.[89] Against this background the move to elevate tribal cultures to a component of the nation's heritage can be read as part of the Indian state's 'indigenist project'.[90] For Jagdish Swaminathan, however, the newly established Bharat Bhavan with its Roopankar Museum of Fine Arts, offered a fertile experimental terrain for his own, more radical, paradigm of indigeneity that strove to question prevailing ethnographic models of creativity subsumed under homogenising rubrics such as folk tradition or craft.

A modernist artist, critic, and left-wing activist, Jagdish Swaminathan is best known as a founding member of the short-lived artists' collective named Group 1890, formed in Bhavnagar, Gujarat, in 1962.[91] During the group's first and only exhibition held at New Delhi in 1963, the notion of indigenism crystallised as an 'anti-imperialist platform' from which to critique technocratic ideas of progress. For Swaminathan, the eventual location of an artist embodying this ideal was 'the Indian tribal'.[92] His understanding of indigeneity drew upon the writings of Octavio Paz, the Mexican ambassador to India between 1962 and 1968, who wrote the catalogue text for the Group 1890 exhibition, and with whom Swaminathan

87 Baviskar, 'Adivasi Encounters': 5106.
88 Amita Baviskar, 'Indian Indigeneities: Adivasi Entanglements with Hindu Nationalism in India', in: Marisol de la Cadena and Orin Starn (eds), *Indigenous Experience Today*, Oxford: Berg Publishers, 2007, pp. 275–304, here p. 275.
89 Prathama Banerjee refers to this process of casting the Adivasi as a purely cultural being as part of a 'double-bind', see 'Culture/Politics: The Irresoluble Double-Bind of the Indian Adivasi', *The Indian Historical Review*, vol. 33 (1), 2006: 99–126.
90 Luis, 'Between Anthropology and History', p. 156.
91 Shruti Parthasarathy, 'Group 1890: The Journey of a Moment', in: Kishore Singh (ed.), *Group 1890: India's Indigenous Modernism*, New Delhi: DAG Modern, 2016, pp. 18–136.
92 Ashish Rajadhyaksha, 'The Last Decade', in: Gulammohammed Sheikh (ed.), *Contemporary Art in Baroda*, New Delhi: Tulika Publications, 1996, p. 215, cited in Katherine Hacker, '"A Simultaneous Validity of Co-Existing Cultures": J. Swaminathan, the Bharat Bhavan and Contemporaneity', *Archives of Asian Art*, vol. 64 (2), 2014: 191–209, here 200.

developed a close intellectual friendship.[93] While Paz's exposition of Mexican *indigenismo* that made up a state-sponsored project was a critical one, his empathy for indigeneity as a component element of Mexican national identity resonated deeply with Swaminathan's ideas.[94] When setting up the Roopankar Museum, the latter devoted an entire wing to 'folk and Adivasi' art, curated with the intent to allow these to exist in a shared contemporaneity with other displays. Contemporaneity, in the catalogue of the Roopankar collection, titled *The Perceiving Fingers* and authored by Swaminathan, was defined as 'a simultaneous validity of co-existing cultures'.[95] Repositioning *adivasi* art within the gallery space meant naming individual artists, keeping contextual information to a minimum, placing the rural and urban at par, and not least, initiating young painters from the rural hinterlands into work with modern paints on canvas, to be framed and displayed against white walls. And yet, Swaminathan's understanding of indigeneity was not without ambivalence. While Luis posits a distinction between the 'primitivism' of the early nationalist elite and the 'indigenism' of the post-Nehruvian era, designating the former as a *'cultural fantasy'*, a leftover of colonialism, and the latter a *'political project'* dear to a national intelligentsia,[96] the two were not always clearly separable. We observe this in the case of Swaminathan, whose empathetic and inclusive approach to the contemporaneity of a different artistic expression was infused by sedimented remains of primitivist thought. For Swaminathan the indigenous tribal continued in his 'sheer childlike joy'[97] to embody unspoilt innocence and vulnerability even as he could act as a self-conscious insurgent rebel. His art formed a 'sensuous reality', not subject to logical reason.[98] In his more programmatic statements, however, Swaminathan rejected ethnological models and terminologies such as primitive or tribal, preferring the term *adivasi*, which ascribed to its bearer the quality of an autonomous subject. Swaminathan's determination to realise the full potential of his project of according contemporaneity to the Indigenous led him to make the Bharat Bhavan a place of nurturing and fostering the artistic energies of the *adivasi* groups of the region. His interest in art was neither anthropological nor archival, but lay in what he termed its 'numinous function'.[99] An inclusive contemporaneity from which the primitive was not yet fully evacuated constituted a framework of thinking that connected Swaminathan to Jean-Hubert Martin, as did ideas positing the numinous or wondrous dimension of art, the belief in an innate individual creative impulse

93   Parthasarathy, 'Group 1890', pp. 63–66.
94   Luis cites a passage from Paz's *Labyrinths of Solitude* on the philosophy of time, which Swaminathan drew upon when developing his conception of contemporaneity between the primordial and the modern, see Luis, 'Between Anthropology and History', pp. 152–53.
95   Jagdish Swaminathan, *The Perceiving Fingers: Catalogue of Roopankar Collection of Folk and Adivasi Art from Madhya Pradesh, India*, Bhopal: Bharat Bhavan, 1987, p. 30. This well-known phrase features in the title of Hacker's essay, '"A Simultaneous Validity"'.
96   Luis, 'Between Anthropology and History', p. 140 (italics in original).
97   Cited in ibid, p. 145.
98   Swaminathan, *The Perceiving Fingers*, pp. 16–17.
99   Hacker, '"A Simultaneous Validity"': 202.

and the valorisation of archaic forms.[100] Both, Martin and Swaminathan, subscribed to the paradoxical view that it was precisely the ahistorical quality of *adivasi* – or other Indigenous art – that made it contemporary. As curators, they privileged a loose eclecticism that eschewed problematising politics of the present. *Adivasi* artists, including Jangarh Singh Shyam, whom Martin encountered during his visit to Bhopal in 1987, were to him at the same time contemporary as they were 'other', though neither he nor Swaminathan further reflected on the textures of otherness.

Recalling his practice of giving paper to *adivasi* artists who immediately took to drawing, Swaminathan wrote: 'What came flowing out of their fingers was unexpected and startling.'[101] Jangarh too, exposed in Bhopal to the world of modern art and artists, discovered the secrets of paper, canvas, poster colours, and acrylic paints, of drawing and printmaking. The *chatak*, or dazzling hues of synthetic pigments excited him intensely, as he confessed to Jyotindra Jain.[102] The new materials fired his imagination and accounted for an enormous productivity in the next two decades, till his career was tragically cut short in 2001. In view of his formidable production, it is difficult to pinpoint the hallmarks of his style rich in subtle, experimental variations, though the *Jangarh kalam,* or Gond style has now crystallised as an identifiable painterly phenomenon, as I will show below. Schooled in music and narrative poetry rather than a tradition of visual art, Jangarh's innate skills enabled the metamorphosis of songs into painting. Bada Dev and other deities, birds, snakes, animals, flowering plants, and trees – all those entities who populated the songs of the Pardhans, or existed as notes of music, took form as colourful images on canvas. The stories they tell are about the cyclical nature of all life, the cruelty of existence, also found in nature where animals feed on each other and birds of prey hover over the dead. During his years at Bhopal, Jangarh worked in different media ranging from simple pen and ink drawings on paper, minimalistic in style, to more ambitious acrylic paintings on canvas, silkscreen prints, large-scale murals, and terracotta sculptures. The eager response to modern urban materials and ways of working did not however negate a retention of the memory of the past and innate modes of expression. Much of the artist's expanding pictorial repertoire brought urban images to coexist with the village world, to be imagined through another filter – for example, the mural with an aeroplane in the Bhopal Legislative Assembly building that Jangarh was commissioned to paint is translated into an organic entity, as a gigantic bird or grasshopper, assimilated within a world of other flying creatures.[103] Several painted narratives showing a co-presence of deities, nature, and humans recapture the role of the Pardhans as narrators of the community's collective memory: this

---

100 In the manifesto of the Group 1890, Swaminathan described art as an innate need, a 'primal urge to create', cited in Parthasarathy, 'Group 1890', p. 76. See also Martin (ed.), *Magiciens*, pp. 8–11; Jean-Hubert Martin, 'The Death of Art – Long Live Art, 1986' (translation and reprint of an earlier curatorial statement of the author), in Steeds et al. (eds), *Making Art Global (Part 2)*, pp. 216–22, here pp. 216–20; Martin in Buchloh, 'Interview': 22.
101 Swaminathan, *The Perceiving Fingers*, p. 60.
102 Jyotindra Jain, *Jangarh Singh Shyam: A Conjuror's Archive*, Bangalore: The Museum of Art and Photography, 2018, p. 25.
103 Reproduced in ibid, fig. 29.

role asked to be reaffirmed as new visions of the future were becoming available with a velocity that threatened to overtake remembrance. In an unusual painting, autobiographical in content, the artist portrays a young boy playing the flute while the grazing cows and other surrounding animals appear to be intoxicated by the sweet music.[104] The image evokes a childhood memory of the young Jangarh whose task it was to tend to the cows while they grazed. Painted in dreamlike colours – shades of lemon and green and a splash of red – and populated with birds, bees, a snake, and other creatures, the story of animals being charmed by music resonates with legends of Krishna, Majnu, and even more distant tales of Orpheus and his lute that had made their way into the repertoire of Indian images since early modern times. For a Gond artist, individual memory folds into the collective and becomes a channel through which a community's experience could be inserted within life beyond the locality.

During his initial years at the Bharat Bhavan, Jangarh encountered the painted works of visiting Aboriginal artists from Australia, and it is possible that his turn towards experimenting with pattern was inspired through that interaction. He later also visited Australia, and in 1999 collaborated with two Aboriginal artists, Djambawa Marawili and Liyawaday Wirrpanda, who had been invited by Jyotindra Jain to the Crafts Museum. Together, four artists collaborated to produce a single large painting replete with creation myths and imagined geographies (Plate 5.4). It was, however, in his extraordinary pen-and-ink drawings that Jangarh's inventiveness emerged as a mature form: in the creation of an incredible range of textures within a minimalist medium and moving away from naturalist appearance. He developed unending distinctive patterns – meshes, scales, rows of ovals, bands of dots, comblines, veins, hatchings – to characterise a bird or an animal or a reptile, a leaf, a branch, or a cloud. Such patterning was also used 'to achieve an animating Gestalt', as Gulammohammed Sheikh put it,[105] and brought his art close to abstraction. A particularly skilled, mature drawing is a portrayal of *vichhi*, a scorpion that has a special place in Gond beliefs (fig. 3). Endowed with a toxic sting, the scorpion was perceived as 'a sorcerer's weapon to cast an evil eye on an enemy adversary'.[106] In Jangarh's pen-and-ink composition, the mysterious aura of the creature draws on the aesthetic power of the artist's patterns, both sensuous and full of virtuosity, which tantalisingly camouflage the scorpion's naturalistic appearance. Here the ethnological is translated into a modernist abstract form.

Building on Shelly Errington's observations about 'the death of authentic primitive art', Hans Belting has proposed the description 'post-ethnic' as a key with which to make sense of burgeoning contemporary art in societies outside of the Western hemisphere.[107] As Belting, understandably, does not delve into the specific paths of art production in individual regions, it is important here to draw attention to the partitioned worlds of the contemporary on the

---

104 Private Collection, reproduced in ibid, fig. 58.
105 Sheikh, 'The World of Jangarh Singh Shyam', p. 25.
106 Jain, *Jangarh Singh Shyam*, p. 81.
107 Hans Belting, 'Contemporary Art and the Museum in the Global Age', in: Peter Weibel and Andrea Buddensieg (eds), *Contemporary Art and the Museum*, Ostfildern: Hatje Cantz, 2007, pp. 16–38, here p. 22.

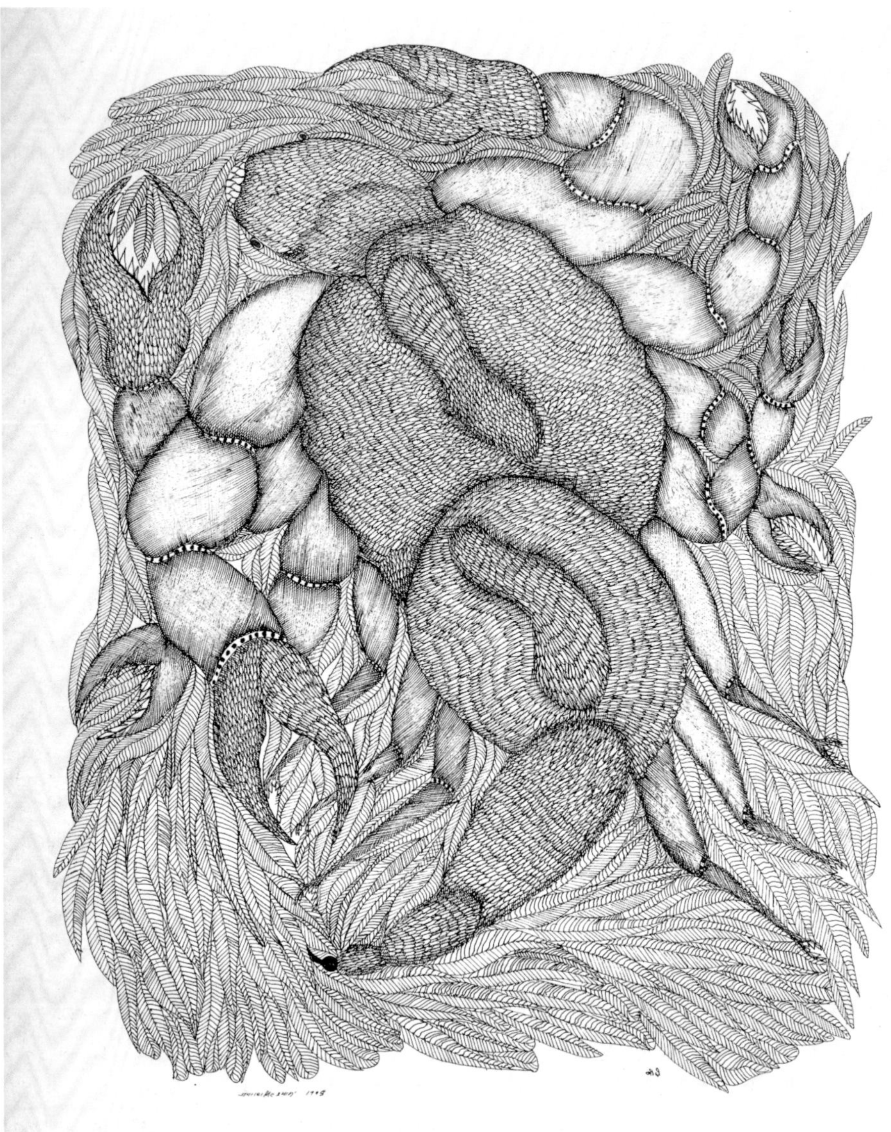

3   Jangarh Singh Shyam, *Vichhi, Portrait of a Scorpion*, pen-and-ink drawing on paper 1995. Museum of Art and Photography, Bangalore

Indian subcontinent. In spite of Swaminathan's inclusive conception of contemporaneity and his refusal of historically constituted oppositions between the modern and its other, the Roopankar museum reinscribed these divisions by demarcating a separate section for tribal and folk arts, distinct from that of the urban arts that housed works of recognised modernist artists from Vadodara, Mumbai, or Delhi. The trajectories of those practitioners who made up the former group – two examples of which have been sketched here – were marked by a set of transitions, personal and institutional, which they lived through over the years, and which positioned them likewise in a stream of modernism whose inventive possibilities they unceasingly explored from within an existing thematic repertoire. Their works, responding to the contemporary predicament through the filter of individual subjectivities, came to be framed and exhibited, bought and sold just as those of their urban counterparts. Yet they inhabited a world that ran parallel to that of mainstream contemporary art, even as the two constituted a coeval entity. Group exhibitions were held in separate venues: Jangarh had his first solo show in New Delhi at the Dhoomimal Gallery in 1984, which however received little notice among metropolitan artists. That apart, the venues where he and his companion artists showed their work consisted of craft fairs, such as the Surajkund *Mela*, a colourful affair that takes place in spring each year at Surajkund, on the outskirts of Delhi.[108] In 1988, Jangarh's work – together with that of the Warli artist Jivya Soma Mashe – was shown for the first time abroad. This took place as part of the state-sponsored Festival of India events that included a show *Art of the Adivasi* curated by Jyotindra Jain, and which travelled to four venues in Japan. The emergent faultline – expressed in Jangarh's frequent references to the *sheheri* (lit. 'of the city') artists present at the Bharat Bhavan, a group to whom he did not feel he belonged[109] – deepened after 1989, in spite of the fame and market success that participation in *Magiciens* brought.

Viewed against the background described above, it is evident that the selection for the Paris show of Baua Devi, Jivya Soma Mashe, and Jangarh Singh Shyam, collectively made by Jain, Swaminathan, and Martin, cannot be attributed to a 'neo-primitivist salvage paradigm'.[110] Far from being a group slated either to disappear against the weight of modernity or to suffer degradation through its forces, the artists they chose were embedded in contemporaneity, though dependent on state patronage and curatorial intercession. The three catalytic visionaries who mediated throughout shared a commitment grounded in a notion of inclusive egalitarianism, which was at once radical as it was somewhat naive. For the artists, the journey from the national to the global was a shift of scale rather than one of framework, the bewildering Francophone world notwithstanding; it was the outcome of an intervention in transformative processes well under way for some three decades, leading from the walls of the village home to the white cube of the metropolitan museum, and which were further galvanised by the recognition brought by this fresh opportunity. Similar processes, wherein indigenous artists have participated in experiments that seek a reflexive dialogue between local traditions and the world of modernist and contemporary art beyond the locality, have proliferated in several parts of the world, and thereby reinforce the stance of Martin and his Indian

---

108 Aurogeeta Das, *Jangarh Singh Shyam: The Enchanted Forest. Paintings and Drawings from the Crites Collection*, New Delhi: Roli Books, 2017, p. 34.

109 Cited in Jain, *Jangarh Singh Shyam*, p. 22.

110 This was one of the most frequent of criticisms levelled against the show, summarised by Poinsot, 'Review of the Paradigms', p. 98ff.

interlocutors. The Dreamtime artists of the Aboriginal Yuendumu community in Australia, who also participated in *Magiciens*, continue to evoke ancestral beliefs and creator-figures in their works, even as they have made their way into contemporary national and global art worlds. Together with using materials such as tree bark and earth, Dreamtime artists have taken to modern media such as acrylic on canvas, work in naturalistic as well as abstract idioms, even playing with the desire for the authentic while producing for a global market.[111] In a similar vein, Nicholas Thomas' study of the Papua New Guinean artist, Mathias Kauage, traces his move from the hinterland to the modern capital, his interactions with the urban modernist milieu, and practice in print workshops.[112] Issues of marginality remain a source of ongoing tension; yet to fix Indigenous practices in a pure and immobile state of attachment to place, overlooking histories of mobility, relocation, or connection to urban cultures, amounts to a denial of coevalness that leaves the back door open for colonial cartographies and temporalities. Indeed, *Magiciens de la Terre* stands out as a singular moment of coevalness, acknowledged by dissolving the borders separating different domains of contemporary art, albeit within the temporary frame of the exhibition space. The short-lived fate of this experiment soon became evident with subsequent developments at different ends of the spectrum. In Paris, Martin lost his position as director of the Musée d'Art Moderne in the Centre Pompidou soon after the show ended. Although he had negotiated for the works produced on site during the exhibition to be bought by the Paris museum after it was over, this commitment was not fulfilled. The museum instead donated the few works it had acquired to the Musée National des Arts d'Afrique et de l'Océanie, thereby reinforcing old divisions.

For the Indian artists, the *Magiciens* effect catapulted them into fame: they now drew the attention of the metropolitan art world, had to respond to growing market demands, and were exposed to different publics, also at home. Jangarh's post-*Magiciens* career pulled him into an international art circuit, an emergent art market for tribal art with galleries specialising in this genre, and a system of international residencies. Two years later he participated in a show at the Municipal Museum, Arnhem, then in 1993 in a travelling group exhibition in Australia, and in the same year in an exhibition devoted primarily to his work, titled *The Known and Unknown: Tribal Painting from Central India* at London. In 1998, Jyotindra Jain curated *Other Masters: Five Contemporary Folk and Tribal Artists of India* at the National Crafts Museum of New Delhi, while later in the same year Hervé Perdriolle included Jangarh's work in a show titled *Expéditions Indiennes: Art tribal et art populaire indiens contemporains* at the Musée des Arts Décoratifs in Paris. In 2010, the Musée du Quai Branly, also devoted to ethnographic objects, hosted a show *Autres Maîtres de l'Inde* co-curated by Jain. Perhaps the only exception to this emergent formation of separate spheres within the domain of contemporary art was the travelling exhibition *Edge of Desire: Recent Art in India* curated by

111 Peter Sutton (ed.), *Dreamings: The Art of Aboriginal Australia*, New York: Asia Society, 1988; Michael Eather (ed.), *Dreamtime: Zeitgenössische Aboriginal Art*, Klosterneuburg: Ed. Sammlung Essl, 2001.
112 Nicholas Thomas, '"Artist of PNG": Mathias Kauage and Melanesian Modernism', in: Harney and Phillips (eds), *Mapping Modernisms*, pp. 163–86.

Chaitanya Sambrani.[113] Though Jangarh's work occasionally did begin to feature in exhibitions of modern and contemporary art, it was primarily bracketed – together with the works of similar artists from other regions of the subcontinent, all of who were classed as tribal, – in shows and auctions of tribal and folk art.[114] The way to becoming a modern professional brought emancipatory possibilities together with continuing, hardening segregation; it also pulled the artist into the vortex of the 'global contemporary', driven by the 'great machine'[115] to produce art for a market whose hunger seemed insatiable. The artist's tragic death by suicide in 2001, while working for a private museum in Japan under conditions resembling bonded labour, is a poignant example of a struggle between the individual and the uncontrollable logic of the global art world.[116]

The early decades of the present century have seen a consolidation of the aspects delineated above. The recent boom in the market for Indian art has impacted the interest for Indigenous art, also internationally. The Pardhan tradition of painting, some three and a half decades young, has crystallised into a stream, or a school, the origins of which go back to the early years at Bharat Bhavan, when Jangarh had involved several members of his extended family and his community in the production of his works. Once apprentices, they have now emerged as important artists in their own right producing for an expanded market. The designation as a particular stylistic stream has also impacted exhibition practice: in 2006, the state government of Madhya Pradesh organised a show *Jangarh Kalam: An Exhibition of Gond Painting* at the Lalit Kala Akademi in New Delhi, in which paintings were displayed according to individual artists. Also in Delhi, a left-wing publishing house, Navayana, helped to organise a solo exhibition of the Pardhan sculptor, Sukhnandi Vyam in 2010.[117] Even as artists strove to create individual styles associated with their names, their formation as artists has continued to be organised along a traditional workshop model where young apprentices learn under the supervision of a master, till such point as they are ready to branch out on their own and claim an individual artist's status with a unique signature style. In addition, the handing down of skills from one generation to another within the family – a pattern that goes back to at least the sixteenth century – marks the practice of these contemporary artists.

---

113 The exhibition travelled between 2004 and 2006 from Perth, New York, and Monterrey to New Delhi and Mumbai. Sambrani made an explicit case for creating an exhibition model where 'folk, Adivasi, and visual popular culture' would be taken seriously as art, to recognise the 'ability of non-modernist work to participate in innovative contemporary practice on its own terms'. See Chaitanya Sambrani (ed.), *Edge of Desire: Recent Art in India*, London: Philip Wilson Publishers, 2005, pp. 14–15.

114 These have continued to proliferate, see for example the exhibition in two parts, *Now That the Trees Have Spoken* featuring Gond art organised at the Dadiba Pundole Art Gallery in Mumbai from 28 July–14 August and 17 August–7 September 2009. The term 'tribal art' has now emerged as an umbrella term used both in the art market as well as in museums. See the gallery website, https://www.pundoleartgallery.in/exhibition/now-that-the-trees-have-spoken-45 (accessed December 2020).

115 Kavita Singh, 'Jangarh Singh Shyam and the Great Machine', *Marg*, vol. 53 (2), 2001: 60–64.

116 The immediate factors that triggered this course have remained open to speculation, see Singh, 'Jangarh Singh Shyam'; Jain, *Jangarh Singh Shyam*, pp. 113–27 provides an extensive discussion with documents.

117 The show curated by Jaya Vivek, a Bhopal-based artist and former member of Swaminathan's team, ran from 16–22 September 2009. Both examples have been cited in Chatterji, *Speaking with Pictures*, pp. 1, 7.

For instance, Baua Devi, whose works have come to be avidly sought by collectors these past three decades since *Magiciens*, has trained all her children and daughter-in-law in the art of Mithila. Jangarh's family, both immediate – his wife Nankusia, son Mayank, and daughter Japani – as well as extended, are practising artists. Photographs of a family or a couple posing with their work testify to the emergence of a particular subjectivity in relation to their identity as artists, even a special sentiment of companionate conjugality centred on the work (Plate 5.5).

The field of Indigenous art in India is far from homogenous – the transition to a modern practice has responded to different categories of buyers within a growing market. While artists known by names, who enjoy the support of gallerists and auction houses specialising in 'tribal' or 'folk' styles, paint on canvas using acrylic colours, there is also a large-scale production of (unnamed) works on sheets of paper using water-based paints, sold to middle-class buyers looking for affordable originals as decor for their homes. The price spectrum is, not surprisingly, wide. Outlets for sales are state-run emporia, popular craft bazaars, such as the Dilli Haat in New Delhi, or the Tribes Shop set up by a cooperative federation under the Ministry of Tribal Affairs.[118] While embedded in the contemporary world, Indigenous art continues to depend on the mediating role of the state in connecting this production and individual artists who have gained prominence, to institutions of art, including the market. Art critical writing, in turn, has endeavoured to categorise this domain of contemporary pictorial practice that, according to Annapurna Garimella, exists as a growing 'informal sector' distinct from the more urbanised, anglophone gallery circuit of artists and curators. Drawing on the notion of vernacularity theorised by Kajri Jain, who deployed it to find a legitimate place for mass-produced, mostly sacred, images intended for a non-anglophone viewership, Garimella uses the term 'vernacular' to encompass a body of Indigenous art.[119] The label vernacular in this case is a curatorial gesture to mark a difference from contemporary high art to, as Roma Chatterji observes, 'incorporate [this genre] into the art world, albeit at a lower level'.[120] In resonance with Garimella's 'informal sector', Ranjit Hoskote has referred to this category of work as forming 'a third field of artistic production in contemporary Indian culture'.[121] However sympathetic they may be, such attempts to acknowledge this burgeoning domain while rejecting the tyranny of erstwhile labels, still participate in reaffirming the existing separation from what remains the mainstream contemporary.

---

118 The latter is mentioned in Rashmi Varma, 'Primitive Accumulation: The Political Economy of Indigenous Art in Postcolonial India', *Third Text*, vol. 27 (6), 2013: 748–61, here 749.

119 Annapurna Garimella, *Vernacular, in the Contemporary*, 2 vols., New Delhi: Devi Art Foundation, 2010–11; Annapurna Garimella, 'Aboriginalisthan in the Gallery', in: Hill et al. (eds), *Sakahān*, pp. 72–84. Jain has developed her concept of the vernacular in two major works: Kajri Jain, *Gods in the Bazaar: The Economy of Indian Calendar Art*, Durham, NC: Duke University Press, 2007; Kajri Jain, *Gods in the Time of Democracy*, Durham, NC: Duke University Press, 2021. See also Kajri Jain, 'India's Modern Vernacular – On the Edge', in: Sambrani (ed.), *Edge of Desire*, pp. 170–83.

120 Roma Chatterji, *Speaking with Pictures*, p. 8.

121 Ranjit Hoskote, exhibition brochure, *Now That the Trees Have Spoken* (see note 114).

Magiciens de la Terre, in the words of Okwui Enwezor, 'opened up a space for … articulating the relationship between the works made in the West and the non-West'.[122] Viewed in this light, its inclusion of art and artists from different parts of the world – Australia, South Africa, the Caribbean, Nigeria, Brazil, Ghana, Papua New Guinea – whom contemporary cultural theory has grouped under the rubric 'Indigenous', raised the thorny question about the constitution of contemporary art at a global level, and its potential to bridge or deepen faultlines. Having effected both an opening as well as a bifurcation of the terrain of the global contemporary, *Magiciens* was followed by an efflorescence of biennials and large-scale exhibitions, the opening of lavish, architecturally photogenic museums of contemporary art, accompanied by a spate of international journals on the subject. The visibility of Indigenous art within these global circuits has been at best sporadic, confined largely to artists from the Global North. An important exception, however, has been the Sydney Biennial, beginning with its iterations of 2010 and then 2012, which has built an integral Indigenous focus within its curatorial programme.[123]

By assembling the Indigenous, the global, and the contemporary within a single community of art makers held together by the loose common denominator of a creative impulse, the curators of *Magiciens* unwittingly paved the way for a category of the 'global Indigenous' to emerge during the post-*Magiciens* boom of global shows. The notion formed the animating principle of the exhibition *Sakahān* organised in 2013 by the National Gallery of Canada in Ottawa: for the curators of the show, global Indigenous served as an umbrella term for Indigenous art practices from across the divide of North and South, of settler-colonies and postcolonial nations.[124] *Sakahān*, which means to light a fire, was conceptualised, according to Rickard, as an endeavour to place Indigenous art production of the world on the exhibition map as a 'geo-political' presence rather than simply a 'geographic' one; it intended to counter the dismissive construction of Indigenous artistic articulations as 'local essentialism' within global contemporary art.[125] During the course of selection, the authors of the curatorial framework drew upon aspects they found to forge 'visual and conceptual connections' between artworks of Indigenous communities across the globe: 'self-representation, histories of encounters, the value of the handmade, transmigration between the spiritual, the uncanny and the everyday, homelands and exile, and personal expressions of the impact of physical violence and societal trauma', all within a 'fine balance between aesthetics and

<hr>

122 Interviewed by Paul O'Neill in *The Culture of Curating and the Curation of Culture(s)*, Cambridge, MA: MIT Press 2012, p. 59. Enwezor's own curatorial stance in Documenta XI however was diametrically opposed to that of Martin, one which devolved on a more discursive concept instead of Martin's 'top-down pluralism', ibid.
123 Jolene Rickard, 'The Emergence of Global Indigenous Art', in: Hill et al. (eds), *Sakahān*, pp. 54–60, here 55–56.
124 Lalonde, 'Introduction', p. 16.
125 Rickard, 'The Emergence of Global Indigenous Art', p. 55. The term 'local essentialism' she cites has been used by Gerald McMaster, 'Towards an Aboriginal Art History', in: W. Jackson Rushing (ed.), *Native American Art in the Twentieth Century: Makers, Meanings, Histories*, London: Routledge, 1999, pp. 81–96.

agency'.[126] Bringing Indigenous groups from across the world onto a common matrix on the basis of certain shared experiences can fructify in transcultural artistic collaborations as some of the bolder curatorial experiments of *Magiciens* pointed to. An exhibition across the North-South divide can certainly act as a productive space. And yet we need to be careful not to flatten regional experiences with their particular rough edges into a smooth category labelled global. In other words, the global cannot become an alibi for the separatist potential of the term in a given national context. For India, Amita Baviskar has drawn our attention to the circumstance that the *adivasi* invocation of indigeneity, inspired by globally circulating discourses, rested on a principle of cultural difference, on the basis of their being tied to a particular place, to its land and resources. While such a claim is a powerful weapon for mobilisation in times of struggle, it eschews a broader principle of citizenship and equal rights for all – the landless or migrants – and thereby produces its own exclusions. Today, Baviskar reminds us, Indigenous *adivasi* groups are being co-opted by fascist Hindu movements on the basis of a similar exclusion, that of religious minorities or migrants.[127] The tussle between what Peter Geschiere calls 'autochthons' and those labelled 'others', both citizens of the same nation, has emerged as a source of violent conflict in several nation-states of the present.[128] The call to global indigeneity can cut both ways.

Engaging with *Magiciens de la Terre* requires a sensitivity to the always already transcultured modernity of Indigenous art movements and groups. By showcasing the polyphony of the contemporary world, the show sought to open a radical prospect; by privileging a 'project-based'[129] approach over a national or cultural principle, it intended to create an uncluttered, catalytic space for transformative dialogue. However, by its refusal to build the context of the works within the curatorial concept, it overlooked the relationship between objects and the politics enveloping them, containing them instead within an opaque otherness. By choosing to be governed by visual criteria or 'artistic intuition alone', Jean-Hubert Martin and his team were inevitably trapped within a vague and idiosyncratic category that nonetheless carries unspoken cultural assumptions.[130] I have however tried to argue against a reductionist approach that views exhibitions as purely a struggle over identity, a dispute about inclusions and exclusions, and to instead unravel the transcultural dimensions of the show by entering it through one of the many peripheral sites that was no less constitutive of its dynamics. Planned as a project to celebrate the revolutionary birth of democracy in France, the concept of *Magiciens* seemed to have given in to the French principle of shunning identity politics on the basis of religion, ethnicity, or gender in the name of a benevolent national whole made up of allegedly equal individuals.[131] The assumptions of such a rhetoric

126 Lalonde, 'Introduction', pp. 18–19.
127 Baviskar, 'Adivasi Encounters': 5110.
128 Peter Geschiere, *The Perils of Belonging: Autochthony, Citizenship, and Exclusion in Africa and Europe*, Chicago: University of Chicago Press, 2009.
129 The term has been used by Steeds, '"Magiciens de la Terre"', p. 35.
130 Buchloh, 'Interview', p. 20.
131 Lamoureux, 'From Form to Platform': 68.

dovetailed with the agendas and their premises shared by the native informers whose collaboration shaped so much of the project. A similar national inflection informs the politics of multiculturalism subscribed to by many democracies of the world, in particular those caught in the drives of postcolonial nation-building: an affirmation of cultural diversity as a value per se. Art – and this applies to societies across Europe and Asia – especially outside of the mainstream is called upon to provide evidence of a society's multiculturalism. The use of difference, or diversity, to speak of a convivial plurality – as those involved in fixing the signposts of the Paris show naively sought to accomplish – suppresses the stories of objects and their producers as implicated in a deeply divided present. Though the makers of *Magiciens* cannot be taken to task for entirely ignoring the discursive and institutional context of art production in different sites of the globe – as this connected history has sought to show – the adoption of a pluralist approach without a degree of self-reflexivity disavowed the tangled ways in which these conditions played themselves out between the periphery and the centre. An initiative that aims to embrace the planet can intervene in these processes; without grasping the full import of their complexity, it can provide an emancipating impulse, while also deepening existing faultlines and opening the way to the oppressive mechanisms of a neoliberal globalisation. The aspiration to be planetary in scholarship, in turn, requires a methodological criticality that goes beyond the observation of inclusion per se to analyse the contemporaneity of different but contingent currents.

POSTSCRIPT
THE HUNTER AND THE SQUIRREL
Art History from the Global to the Planetary

'What if the idea that the Earth teems with other beings who act, communicate, tell stories, and make meaning is taken seriously?' – Amitav Ghosh[1]

The five meditations that make up this book draw on a theory of transculturation – to which they in turn give shape and depth – to explore key moments of an art history that can no longer be adequately approached, I have argued, through a facile globalism. Transculturation, which we read as a new ontology of culture, enables a radical critique of explanatory paradigms and disciplinary frameworks premised on a bounded understanding of culture. It equips us to question established chronological signposts, inherited teleologies, as well as art historical assumptions about medium, genre, quality, and connoisseurship. The hallmarks of this theoretical apparatus are its processual dynamism, its groundedness, reflexivity, attention to precise morphologies, and sensitivity to the contingent. By freeing connectivity from its reductive dependence on mobility, and by carrying it beyond its secondary function of linking putative units that pre-exist interaction and continue to survive it more or less unscathed, a theory of transculturation eschews considering oppositional categories such as Western and non-Western, or dominant and marginal, as a set of stable attributes. Instead, it urges us to analyse these as constituted through their specific transcultural formations, which renders each constantly mutable and renewably (co-)productive. By choosing to focus on a location designated in mainstream scholarship as peripheral, I have argued that developing a theoretical understanding, too, needs to be a transcultural exercise. In other words, my plea is to bring experiences, insights, concepts, and paradigms from the histories of regions, which continue to be segregated within scholarship and institutional domains as individual areas, centre-stage, so that they exert analytical pressure on established canons. While a theory of transculturation destabilises the nexus between the entities of nation and culture, its genealogy at the same time signals towards the tension between the nation as a ground of emancipation in cultural memory, and as a constricting ideological frame, com-

---

1   Amitav Ghosh, *The Nutmeg's Curse: Parables for a Planet in Crisis*, Chicago: University of Chicago Press, 2021, p. 197.

plicit in the production of the 'authentic' and the 'native', to contain the study of disciplines. Applied to art history, the studies investigated here attend to the slippage between art and its history, treating the nation as a friable construct. They use the uneven, often divergent regional affordances of that construct to dismantle the methodological nationalism informing narratives and paradigms predicated on the concept, while retaining the nation as a category of the imagination. The tension between the two valences of a single idea runs through many of the themes discussed here.

Infusing the global, when attached to art history, with a criticality enabled by a theory of transculturation allows us to reject both the presentism of the former as well as its reliance on the logic of economic globalisation. Such refusal, in turn, opens the door to a fresh set of questions that take us to domains beyond those explored in this book – the following pages of this postscript offer some thought on potential future directions. Contemporary critiques of neoliberal economics are now inextricably linked with one of the most pressing issues of our time: the climate crisis, which the novelist-cum-essayist Amitav Ghosh named 'a crisis of culture'.[2] Discussions of anthropogenic climate change propose that we collapse the long-standing humanist distinction between the natural sciences and the humanities in order to help address the future of an endangered planet. According to the advocates of this position, humanity now counts as but one member of a composite species encompassing all elements of the biosphere – animals, plants, minerals, rocks. The anthropologist Tim Ingold has argued for an 'ontogenetic' – that is, related to the fluxes and flows of materials entailed in making and growing – developmental system, wherein cultural forms arise in conjoint activity with the non-human, as part of an 'all-embracing matrix of relationships' that are mutually conditioning.[3] What does this move to dissolve the humanity-nature binary imply for scholarship in the humanities? Does the ontology of culture proposed by transcultural theory ask for yet another radical recalibration that acknowledges the oneness of living organisms – humans, plants, animals, insects, microbes? What does it mean for a transcultural critique of the conceptual premises and categories of art history, as elaborated in the foregoing pages, when its understanding of culture no longer rests on a nature-culture divide?

The relationships between art-making, art history, and political, social, or environmental change are neither direct nor causal. As an activity crafted by human artifice, art, though it cannot save the planet, can through its powers to represent, critique, and imagine, envisage futures not yet attainable, futures that are not those prescribed by neoliberal thought. Futures, to nail down a truism, cannot be made without thinking them. Art-making is always the product of an age, including one whose existence feels threatened; its conditions of production articulate this context, as much as they signal beyond it. Art history, in turn, is called upon to position itself in the discussions about the understanding of the new aggregate figure of the

---

2   Amitav Ghosh, *The Great Derangement: Climate Change and the Unthinkable*, Chicago: University of Chicago Press, 2017, p. 9.

3   Tim Ingold, 'Prospect', in: Tim Ingold and Gisli Palsson, *Biosocial Becomings: Integrating Social and Biological Anthropology*, Cambridge: Cambridge University Press, 2013, p. 8.

human, and what this implies for its own practice as one field of the humanities. In his much-cited theses 'The Climate of History', Dipesh Chakrabarty maintains that anthropogenic climate change has propelled the humanities towards the sciences in order to grasp the nature of the human, now recognised as a major geological and agential force in determining the climate of the planet.[4] While urging us to engage with what climatologists and paleobiologists posit about the human species, Chakrabarty is wary of a composite notion of species, which according to him elides the important distinction of how climate change impacts different sections of humanity, that is, those who propel it for their benefit and those who suffer its consequences.[5] The outcome of research conducted by biologists can no doubt broaden our understanding of the long-term impact of human actions, and in the process demonstrate the possibilities and limitations of human agency; yet, the humanities alone provide us with a distinct mode of self-knowledge rooted in realms of human life as religion, philosophy, literary and artistic creation. Questions addressed by the humanities about how to inhabit the planet anew and share its resources equitably, or how to remember it as an integral system for humans and non-humans alike, need to be investigated on human scales, even as these appear diminutive within the larger, deeper histories of natural reproductive life of the planet.

The inception of art history is inseparable from the constitution of 'art' as a powerful index of humanness. The formative discourses of the discipline were premised on the assumption that art served to distinguish between grades of humanity: admitting that the earliest human collectives possessed art was a way of recognising their humanity. Art history then, as Chapter One ('The World in a Grain of Sand') of this book has shown, was a discipline that enabled its practitioners and readers to position cultures of the world on the civilisational ladder. Writings of Humanists, coming in the wake of European expansion, had devised criteria by which art objects could be read either as a sign of creativity or of moral corruption. Claire Farago has, however, traced the historical roots of this discursive mode to the writings of Aristotle some two and a half millennia back. In both *Metaphysics* and *Politics*, the Greek philosopher posited a difference between human powers of cognition, based on reason and reminiscence, and the behaviour of animals, who supposedly act according to their inborn nature, without deliberation or intelligence.[6] The discourse aligning art-making with moral character was carried forward, as Farago further shows, by commentators over

---

4 Dipesh Chakrabarty, 'The Climate of History: Four Theses', *Critical Inquiry*, 35 (2009): 197–222; reprinted in Dipesh Chakrabarty, *The Climate of History in a Planetary Age*, Chicago: University of Chicago Press, 2021, pp. 23–48.

5 See Dipesh Chakrabarty, 'The Planet: An Emergent Humanist Category', *Critical Inquiry*, 46 (2019): 1–31; reprinted in Chakrabarty, *The Climate of History*, pp. 68–94. However, for a critique of Chakrabarty that considers his position as faltering, see T. J. Demos, *Against the Anthropocene: Visual Culture and Environment Today*, Berlin: Sternberg Press, 2017, pp. 48–49. In the article cited here, which appeared two years after Demos wrote, Chakrabarty's stance is more explicit.

6 See Claire J. Farago, '"The whole world in his hands": A Decolonial Approach to European Concepts of Art', in: Amelia Jones and Jane C. Davidson (eds), *A Companion to Contemporary Art in a Global Framework*, Oxford: Wiley Blackwell (forthcoming). I am grateful to the author for sharing her unpublished manuscript with me. Also David Summers, *Michelangelo and the Language of Art*, Princeton: Princeton University Press, 1981, cited by Farago, ibid.

several centuries – from medieval commentators, to scientific and philosophical movements of the seventeenth and eighteenth centuries, culminating in ideologies of capitalism.[7] The latter harnessed the notion of human exceptionalism to colonial enterprises, beginning with early modern capitalist expansion in the Americas, in that they denied to chunks of humanity the status of the human by assimilating them instead to the realm of 'Nature'.[8] Anthropocentrism, the other face of the same coin, came to be built into the definition of art as a product of a contest between nature and the human hand. Read as evidence of those human capacities denied to animals, it has been cemented as an unspoken bias and agenda of art history, in conjunction with other default preferences such as monoculturalism, nationalist categories, and fixed, linear chronologies. To what extent have these assumptions persisted at the heart of the discipline, now practised across the globe, and have constituted its languages and methods? The challenge for art history is to find new paths to working beyond these in order to uncover subterranean structures of thought that have remained suppressed or inarticulate. Can such structures provide an index to ways in which societies across the globe thought about their relation to forms of life on the planet, responded to climate crises, and conceived of art-making as a mode of relating to the world beyond the human, even as the act of making continued to envisage the human hand as endowed with 'magical'[9] force?

An art history directed towards the future faces the task of recuperating cosmologies and ontologies that do not subscribe to such Aristotelian concepts of humanity, which have led to their suppression. In order to make place within culture to be able to enclose, as well as to unravel the entwined relationships between the human and non-human worlds, disciplines – according to a growing school of post-humanist and radical materialist philosophy – are urged to take recourse to forms of thought that go beyond the human social and political, without however discarding these.[10] Discussions of human-driven climate change – subsumed under the concept of the Anthropocene[11] – have brought art history to a threshold that

---

7 Farago, ibid.

8 Jason W. Moore, 'The Rise of Cheap Nature', in Jason W. Moore (ed.), *Anthropocene or Capitalocene? Nature, History, and the Crisis of Capitalism*, Oakland: PM Press, 2016, pp. 78–115, here p. 79.

9 See Chapter Two above, note 46.

10 Bruno Latour, *Politics of Nature: How to bring the Sciences into Democracy*, Cambridge, MA.: Harvard University Press, 2004.

11 The concept of the Anthropocene, a contested term, designates a geological epoch marking the commencement of human impact on the Earth's ecosystems. By its definition, it stands for the enormous temporal or spatial scales of the earth and life sciences. There is no consensus on when to date the transition to the present era of anthropogenic climate change, which overtook the Holocene, in existence for about twelve millennia. While some scholarship dates this to the Industrial Revolution that accelerated the use of fossil fuels, other positions view the European expansion in the New World as a historical moment leading to an unprecedented, massive reorganisation of life on Earth wrought by colonialism's quests of land and extraction of natural resources. Writings on the Anthropocene – from a range of disciplinary positions – are too numerous to list here. An extensive survey of the field is provided by Demos, *Against the Anthropocene*. Some further references are Eva Horn and Hannes Bergthaller, *Anthropozän: Eine Einführung* (second, expanded edition), Hamburg: Junius, 2020; Heather Davis and Etienne Turpin (eds), *Art in the Anthropocene: Encounters among Aesthetics, Politics, Environments and Epistemologies*, London: Open Humanities Press, 2015; Moore, *Anthropocene or Capitalocene?*

looks beyond its comfort zone, challenging it to sharpen its tools, at the same time to look for new ones that would equip it to transcend anthropocentric perspectives. Visual and material cultures, especially in Asia and in conjunction with religious and philosophical thought, have been early to recognise life forms in their widest totality, to view them together with the laws of nature, and to consider the delicate equilibria existing between all living creatures of the world. And yet, both making art and writing about it are faced – like other disciplines in the humanities – with the tangled problem of how to overcome their deeply entrenched anthropocentrism. Learning to look at the human world also from non-human points of view is beset with the contradiction that human modes of knowing are invariably mediated by languages that are ultimately human. Strivings to transcend anthropocentric perspectives at the same time end up reinforcing the awareness of the disciplinary limits within which such efforts are necessarily circumscribed. The concept of the Anthropocene itself is caught in a paradox: its abstraction spells an unknown ecological peril difficult to render visible and palpable as form, image, or object. A similar paradox marks the notion of the human – an axis along which so much of art is aligned: human subjects facing an endangered future are both potential victims and perpetrating agents. They are a geological agential force that alone cannot control or entirely domesticate those menacing forces that have come into being as a consequence of human activities, such as the complex of capitalist industrialisation and an unrestrained extraction of the Earth's resources. Aesthetic practice and representation are challenged to find a way out of the tussle between abstract and concrete agency, as expounded by biologists, geologists, or post-humanists. How can histories of art and culture sharpen our conceptions of the human in its inextricable relationship to the non-human world, ultimately our conception of 'who we are, where we came from, and where we are going in the era of climate and ecosystem emergency'.[12]

Art history has begun to respond to the challenge of recalibrating the understanding of culture that underpins the discipline by taking a cue from the practice of contemporary artists, who have chalked their own paths to make sense of the dilemmas of the present, and to negotiate them. Recent years have witnessed the emergence of a segment of contemporary art that positions itself at the intersection of art-making, politico-ecological theory, and environmental activism. Its aesthetic does not privilege a white-cube setting alone. Rather, art production enters the domain of field research and participates in civil society solidarities. It moves within the institutionalized sites of the art system as well ventures into public spaces beyond it (see Chapter Four, 'Beyond Backwater Arcadias'). Such art gives expression to political-environmental imaginaries through a range of media: documentary photography and film, installation, video, and performance.[13] Much of its interventionist documentation

---

12   Claire J. Farago, 'The Future of the Past: What Comes After World Art History?', in Helen Westgeest and Kitty Zijlmans (eds), *Mix and Stir: New Outlooks on Contemporary Art from Global Perspectives*, Valiz: Amsterdam, 2021, pp. 395–400, here p. 400.

13   T. J . Demos, *Decolonizing Nature: Contemporary Art and the Politics of Ecology*, Berlin: Sternberg Press, 2016; also T. J. Demos, 'The Art and Politics of Ecology in India: A Roundtable with Ravi Agarwal and Sanjay Kak', *Third Text*, vol. 27 (1), 2013: 151–61.

draws attention to human extractive attitudes to nature, while recording places and moments of irreversible civilizational destruction. While contemporary art works within the framework of human scales and agential responsibility, it eschews the human as a universal category. Instead, it shows that the present ecological crisis is as much a crisis within human collectivities, as it is one between the human and the non-human. While taking care to restore to the non-human its integrity and ontological weight, such art is equally careful not to effect a dispersal or dilution of human responsibility. Within this proliferating field, the work of the South Asian artist and filmmaker Amar Kanwar (b. 1964) might be briefly cited here: *The Sovereign Forest* is an installation of films, objects, and texts, the latter including documents, newspaper reports, letters. It narrates the story of corporate mining in the East Indian region of Odisha and its impact on the ecosystem and the lives of communities, transformed through the unfettered violence of neoliberal economics in the name of a promise of economic prosperity.[14] Among other things, *The Sovereign Forest* points to how indigenous knowledge can undo the nature-culture binary that has become entrenched through the universalization of modernist dualism. For example, a vital element of the installation is an exhibit of 272 varieties of rice seeds displayed serially on small shelves labelled in Odia and mounted on the walls in the exhibition space. Each variety's name resonates with local cultural connections to family, life, and the cosmos. A small photo-text album tells us of the numerous varieties of paddy seeds that had once existed in Odisha and had assured high yields. It commemorates the work of Natbar Sarangi, an elderly organic farmer who had lived through the Green Revolution and ultimately rejected its chemical-intensive farming to return to the tradition of organic farming of his parents' and grandparents' generations, to achieve greater yields. The book archives Sarangi's recovered traditional knowledge, now in the process of being destroyed. Today, only twenty high-yielding varieties persist, all requiring large amounts of water and chemical fertilisers; they are also unable to withstand adverse weather conditions. The seed archive becomes a vocabulary of an extensive system of Indigenous crops, of knowledge, of heritage, and history. Kanwar's use of the archives as a tool of art-making follows its own set of protocols to produce forms of knowing not conflatable with mainstream disciplines. He uses archival resources – documents, photographs, letters, sale deeds – less as 'evidence' and more as a means to confront us with a different set of positions from which to witness and understand. Such an approach renders subjects of the humanities into sensory knowledge, transforms the empirical into the haptic. At the same time, the documentary photographs, interjected by and refracted through biographical and

14 The work, a collaborative enterprise of the artist with the media activist Sudhir Pattnaik and the designer Sherna Dastur, is ongoing since 2012, and was exhibited at the Samadrusti campus in Bhubaneswar, Odisha, till December 2016, when it had to close. See the exhibition catalogue, Amar Kanwar and Daniela Zyman (eds), *Amar Kanwar: The Sovereign Forest*, Berlin: Sternberg Press, 2014; Hans Dickel, 'Amar Kanwars *The Sovereign Forest* (2012) – Ein Wahrnehmungsfeld als "Parlament der Dinge"', in *Natur in der zeitgenössischen Kunst: Konstellationen jenseits von Landschaft und Materialästhetik*, Munich: Verlag Silke Schreiber, 2016, pp. 179–96; Rajesh James and Sathyaraj Venkatesan, *India Retold: Dialogues with Independent Documentary Filmmakers in India*, London: Bloomsbury Academic, 2021, pp. 37–45; Demos, *Decolonizing Nature*, Chapter 5.

autobiographical stories and memories, bring forth an archive that cannot be fully tested against the 'objectivity' of documentation. Instead, it evokes the incompleteness of public and private narratives – as Amar Kanwar expressed in a conversation with the art historian Emilia Terracciano, during an exhibition of this work at Yorkshire, a former mining region whose coal deposits had helped fuel Britain's industrial revolution and dynamos of its empire.[15] We learn to see the artist's archive as a surface of unrecorded subjectivities, but also as a place of shared dilemmas and politics transcending one place, or one nation-state. Returning sovereignty to the forest is also about returning it to each of its legitimate owners.

The theory of transculturation that forms the scaffolding of this book is premised on a refusal of methodological presentism; recalibrating art history within a more capacious notion of culture means having to offset similar tendencies within studies of climate change, which frequently use models to make projections for the future. As vital as this body of knowledge is to understanding the dynamics of natural phenomena, such methods unwittingly reinforce a perception that disconnects experiences of ecological fragility from the past, by situating the way we think about climate change in the present as well as directing our thoughts towards the future. Is climate migration, we might ask, exclusively a phenomenon of the present, or can our understanding be deepened by relating it to forms of displacement, human and non-human, in the past? Here again, contemporary artists have been quick to respond by evoking a now effaced pre-capitalist past as a lens through which to envision an endangered future. Since such a future still surpasses human understanding, the Anthropocene, a place of ecological foreboding, is rendered thinkable through ecologies and cosmologies it has left behind through recapturing that which was another time and place. We discover this past, to cite another example from South Asia, as a storehouse and resource in the work of Sheba Chhachhi (b. 1958), where the Anthropocene epoch acquires its form and chronicity by re-activating worlds that have been blurred, even suppressed by modernity. Her installations – *Winged Pilgrims, The Water Diviner* – draw on a vast repertoire from across Asia – animal congeries, birds, landscapes – no longer linked to a single locality.[16] They stand for historical memory that, when juxtaposed to the contemporary, comes to spell a ravaged civilisation. Digitality, a technology of the present, allows the artist to re-appropriate images and stories from pre-modern repositories to make them resonate in the present. The art historian, on the contrary, when handling pre-modern works, is required to relocate them within their historical relationships of a different time and place, and uncover the innumerable negotiations of the volatile divide between human and non-human domains in which they were implicated. This involves unravelling systemic dimensions of pre-modern formations and their distinct modalities of living with the instability, vulnerability, and unpredictability of the biosphere. How can art history enter such works of the past without the mediation of the contemporary,

<hr>

15 Emilia Terracciano, 'Disappearing Worlds', *The Caravan: A Journal of Politics and Culture,* February 2014: 106–13, here 110–11.
16 See the image on Volte.artm https://volte.art/artists/25-sheba-chhachhi/works/201-sheba-chhachhi-winged-pilgrims-a-chronicle-from-asia-2006-2008/ (last accessed April 2022).

and above all without falling into the trap of romantic nostalgia for the archaic? How can we access ontologies that bypassed those brought forth by European Antiquity or the Enlightenment? Such ontologies, often infused with the vernacular, are articulated through strategies of signifying and sacralising nature and place, of creating an ethics of the everyday that forged a nexus between the elements, the worlds of plants and animals with an expressive visual culture. Exploring this osmotic relationship takes us to the outer edges of art history's disciplinary terrain from where we can get a sense of a particular society's ecological imaginaries. Recent art historical forays into a transdisciplinary, ecologically framed art history have occasionally nurtured a belief in an originary, static nature, only unsettled by human intervention through capitalism and the colonisation of nature.[17] Writings exploring cultural dimensions of climate change in non-European, pre-modern contexts have sought to destabilise this assumption of ecological plenitude projected on to the past. They address questions of ecological fragility by attending to the ways theology, literary modes, and a distinct 'optical sensibility' produced a semiotics of nature, while making it an object of veneration, but also pleasure.[18]

Art history is thus urged to recuperate how image-making in the past was imbricated in issues of getting access to resources, the tasks of transforming barren land into habitable place, the quotidian experiences of sacrality, topography, fragilities, bonding, and sociability – all contained within larger scaffoldings of power, conquest, governance, and servitude. It would in addition need to explore understandings of image-making – as discussed in Chapter Two of this book – as a self-conscious material process that conceived of visual production as a celebration of non-human materiality. This would further mean engaging with the connectivity and relationality of the geological, vegetal, and human in conjunction with other time scales – the social, historical, mythological, theological, political, and, finally, microscales of the everyday. Given that art production is intrinsically anthropocentric, our access to the imagination of the natural world, to the conceptualisation of the non-human realm, takes place through a humanly configured medium; it is therefore governed by its protocols and conventions, and not least its subject positions. The challenge, therefore, is to find ways of entry into this medium which look beyond the discipline's explicit programme, even underneath its uppermost layers, to uncover some of its still unarticulated understandings and ecological imaginaries. Let us take a look at the following example, to outline part of the agenda and some open questions that a rich repertoire, animated by ontologies that do not obey Aristotelian norms of the human, brings forth.

The ostensible subject of this painting (Plate 6.1) of the early seventeenth century is a hunter climbing a plane tree chasing a squirrel that scampers up the trunk. Bathed in autumn

---

17 See for instance Nicholas Mirzoeff, 'Visualizing the Anthropocene', *Public Culture*, vol. 26 (2), 2014: 213–32.

18 The term has been used by Sugata Ray, *Climate Change and the Art of Devotion: Geoaesthetics in the Land of Krishna, 1550–1850*, Seattle: University of Washington Press, 2019, p. 47; see also Daud Ali and Emma Flatt (eds), *Gardens and Landscape Practices in Precolonial India: Histories from the Deccan*, London/ New Delhi: Routledge, 2012; Daud Ali, 'Gardens in Early Indian Court Life', *Studies in History*, vol. 19 (2), 2003: 221–52.

colours of red and gold, the tree is populated with sprightly red squirrels, who enjoy full visibility, thanks to the artist's treatment of the foliage. While each leaf is painted identically and as a distinct entity, the centre is left sparse in order to make room for the squirrels. Several particularities strike the viewer: the artist's reversal of scale wherein the squirrel escaping the hunter appears to be half the size of the human figure below. Further, the concern to celebrate a lifeworld beyond the human: the undulating terrain teems with different kinds of vegetation – flowering shrubs, grass, leafy plants emerging from the crevices of the rocks. The space itself is framed by rocks and punctuated by animals and birds – a ram, grazing gazelles, a fowl, cranes, birds in pairs perched on trees in the distance. Eschewing modes of naturalist rendering that South Asian artists had adopted from Flemish works (see Chapter Two, 'Making and Seeing Images'), the work seems to be consciously composed to highlight every detail of a world whose self-sufficient poise contrasts with the awkward efforts of the single human figure struggling to climb the tree. To start with, we might set aside conventional art historical modes of reading that focus on narrative, symbolic, and iconographic dimensions of the image; we might use the words land, earth, ground, field, or terrain, for example, instead of landscape, to denote the subject of the image. If we set out to test the hypothesis that productions of what art history terms landscape are not merely a representation of natural phenomena by a human hand, but an articulation of a relationship between humans and the world of plants, animals, and geological formations, in which the maker of the image acknowledges the presence of members of the non-human world together with their innate power and agency as co-producers of a lifeworld, how might we go about this? While a painted landscape stands inevitably for an anthropocentric perspective, one step would be to investigate ways of reading such images that help to uncover a more complex relationality – and a felt uncertainty about human mastery – built into the work that goes beyond the simple will to domesticate nature by transforming it into an image contained within a frame. What is the agency that the makers of these works ascribe to plants, trees, animals, rocks, and wasteland? How can we interpret the multiple temporalities within a single image that distinguish human time from seasonal, climatic, or geological time? What pictorial strategies do the image makers deploy? What are the art historical methods required to plausibly decipher the relationships between humans and nonhumans as co-producers of imagined lifeworlds that these visualisations subtly suggest? To begin with, we can explore a different mode of entering these images, one that takes the non-human elements as a starting point, to investigate the information they supply, as opposed to knowledge of which the result is a message of a world under control. Perhaps this could then provide the impulse to problematise the quiet, inconspicuous, marginal aspects of a work, which one often stumbles upon when travelling across the pictorial surface.[19]

---

19 Innumerable examples could be cited from within the repertoire of folio paintings from the North Indian courts: for instance the folio (painted by Payag in 1633) from the Windsor *Padshahnama* showing the siege of Qandahar where in a scene of dramatic battle we encounter an idyllic corner protected by luxuriant vegetation and a pair of rabbits silently absorbed with their reflection in a pool of water, seemingly untouched by the turbulence of human action surrounding them, reproduced in Milo C. Beach, Ebba Koch and Wheeler Thackston, *King of the World: The Padshahnama*, London: Azimuth, 1997, figures 18, 58.

In his critique of art historical conventions of reading landscape as a 'scopic regime of picturing land', Sugata Ray argues instead for 'new modalities that triangulate the relationship among human bodies, land and landscape'.[20] Ray's study of Braj introduces the notion of 'interspecies intimacy' following from deforestation.[21] Such relationships across species form an ancient ontology that can be encountered over several centuries, going back to the Buddhist association of the Bodhi tree with Enlightenment, as well as the intimate association of gardens, groves, and trees with the life of the Buddha.[22] Anthropomorphism, the ascription of human qualities to animals, another continuing trans-species relationship, served as a device for humans to create an affinity with the animal world, while ascribing an agential quality to its members. In societies where animals were both feared and worshipped, they entered the imagination as magical as well as tameable beings. Animals represented on the one hand dark, lurking fears of the world beyond the human; on the other, they were bred as well as worshipped and sacrificed. This seemingly paradoxical duality generated a need for mythologies that ascribed human characteristics to animals, or invented figures like Majnu who sought to communicate to them through words or music – in itself an admission of a human lack that needed the creation of mutuality through communicability and expressed a need for proximity. When artists of the seventeenth and eighteenth centuries rendered a world belonging to animals, it is humans who are shown to enter their space. The approach might be read as a sublimation of the nature-culture dichotomy within the ecological imagination that informs these works. The dynamics of such interspecies intimacy cannot be grasped through the methods of modern science. These are associations and relationships that occurred at given moments of time were recorded in works of the imagination and can only be approached by attending to the circumstances of their visual production. It is less a question of deciphering the human claim to be able to communicate with the non-human – animals, trees, mountains, or demons. Such claims elude dominant forms of reasoning today. Rather, we might try to recover lost ontologies and understand the reasons and modes of their suppression.

Arguing against a radical separation of epistemology from ontology, the feminist theorist and science studies scholar Karen Barad insists that we study 'practices of knowing in being'. In other words, knowing and, following from that, doing are inseparable from our being part of the world 'in its differential becoming'.[23] Viewed in this light, art-making in pre- and early modern societies of South Asia could be read as a domain within which trans-species relationships unfolded, as the materiality of making was perceived as a bridge to connect the

Another example: the intriguing parallel created by the turned profile of a resting goat and the peaceful repose of the face of the resting Virgin Mary in the *Madonna and Child*, painted at the end of the sixteenth century by Basawan, San Diego Museum of Art.

20 Ray, *Climate Change and the Art of Devotion*, p. 67.

21 Ibid., p. 117.

22 On gardens and vegetal aesthetics in Buddhism, see Akira Shimada, 'The Use of Garden Imagery in Early Indian Buddhism', in Ali and Flatt (eds), *Gardens and Landscape Practices*, pp. 18–38.

23 Karen Barad, *Meeting the Universe Halfway: Quantum Physics and the Entanglement of Matter and Meaning*, Durham: Duke University Press, 2007, p. 183.

art-maker, the work, and the world in a relation of interdependence, rather than ontological separation. The artifice of art becomes possible and thinkable only because the maker and his work are already of the world, because the outside and the inside fuse in the material body of the work. The relationship between the image-maker and his materials described in Chapter Two of this book already points in this direction, and would merit being further pushed to develop a paradigm that transcends the humanity-nature divide. Art history's overwhelming focus on finished 'works', as well as on their fortunes once they enter the world of art to continue their lives as treasures or objects to be contemplated, exhibited, and consumed, results in overlooking the other lives such works carry within them before becoming something else. In the worldview of their makers and those who prized them, the work – a painted page or a sculpted rock – was as much about living matter – its malleability, elasticity, resistance, or tensions. A painter's brush or vegetal paint was matter that had grown along with the animal or plant of which it was once an integral part and carried that life into the work it enabled. Finished images abound with frequently hidden references to such thinking, which they urge us to extract from their crevices. The squirrels in the painting above, for example, ask to be read as standing for more than a colourful, lively presence in an image seeking to record the life of the world beyond the human. This world was far from being a domain to be observed from the 'outside'. A squirrel's hair was prized by artists to make special brushes, often comprising a single hair – the *ekbaal qalam* – to delineate fine lines and nuances. Paint, too, carried with it a life and tactility drawn from its vegetal sources. The deep, luminous yellow we frequently encounter in the works studied (see Chapter Two, 'Making and Seeing Images') was a product of mango leaves fed to a cow, whose urine was collected and dried in the sun to leave a residue of colour that then transmuted into pigment known in colonial texts as 'Indian yellow'.[24] The merging and melding of plant and animal life with the materiality of the image might urge us to conceptualise art as a theory of making which assembles the components of the natural world, always already on their way to becoming something else, and connects them to conventions of cultural practice. It points to a reading of art as something organic, a process of becoming within which the human artist is one of many actors, a co-producer who conjoins his energies to the work of active materials – of plants, animals, stone, wood, paper, gold, marble, alabaster, textiles, and so the list goes on. From a geological point of view, the life of an artwork, a minuscular fraction of geological time, forms one constituent phase of a long cyclical relationship wherein the materials of the work all ultimately return to the domain they came from through natural processes of degeneration, even as conservationists and restorers engage in a perennial struggle to stem this process. While the maker has a conception of the work in mind, the latter comes into being only through

24 Also known as *purree*, the yellow pigment was used by colonial artists to capture the darker shades of flesh when portraying non-white subjects, till it was caught in controversy; for a riveting account of the shifting fortunes of this particular pigment, Jordana Bailkin, 'Indian Yellow: Making and Breaking the Imperial Palette', *Journal of Material Culture*, vol. 10 (2), 2005: 197–214.

an interplay of organisms, through what Tim Ingold has termed a *'morphogenetic'* process, blurring thereby the distinction between 'organism and artefact'.[25]

Even as we agree that humans have become a natural planetary force, a geological agent, to paraphrase Chakrabarty, our responsibility to understand the role of humans and societies in the age of the Anthropocene and act on these, though it requires the knowledge of science, also requires ethical decisions on other grounds. Biologists – in the words of Julia Thomas –'can help us understand our present predicament, but they cannot provide the political imagination to resolve it'.[26] To this we might add, nor do they possess the artistic imagination to think somatically, within an expanded understanding of culture that makes place for our relationship with the non-human world. Art history, one of the humanities, is potentially a discipline about unravelling the meanings of life and about what our lives should mean. For long riveted on the persona of the artist as the sole agency, and premised on monolithic understandings of culture, the crises of the present have brought it to a fresh threshold. A theory of transculturation, this book has argued, goes a long way in creating new frames for the discipline. The next challenge to be attended – and the agenda for a following book – is that of making place within culture for an organic relationship with the non-human world, thereby carrying the theory beyond anthropocentrism, even as, paradoxically, any work in this direction will by necessity unfold within an anthropocentric frame. Not only does the onus of making the Anthropocene intelligible remain human, and contingent on the human imagination and the human hand, so do the media through which production of knowledge takes place – as also the language and terms of its access – be it literary or artistic or scientific. Within this disciplinary scaffolding, we might be able to look for cracks where planetary consciousness intervenes to make space, in innumerable seemingly marginal and inconspicuous ways, to recognise other ontologies, for acknowledging a more distributed form of agency, and for using the idea of contingency to introduce the notion of co-production in the essentially anthropocentric act of image-making.

25 Tim Ingold, *Making: Anthropology, Archaeology, Art and Architecture*, London: Routledge 2013, p. 22 (italics in the original).
26 Julia A. Thomas, 'History and Biology in the Anthropocene: Problems of Scale, Problems of Value', *American Historical Review*, vol. 119 (5) (2014): 1587–1607, here 1605.

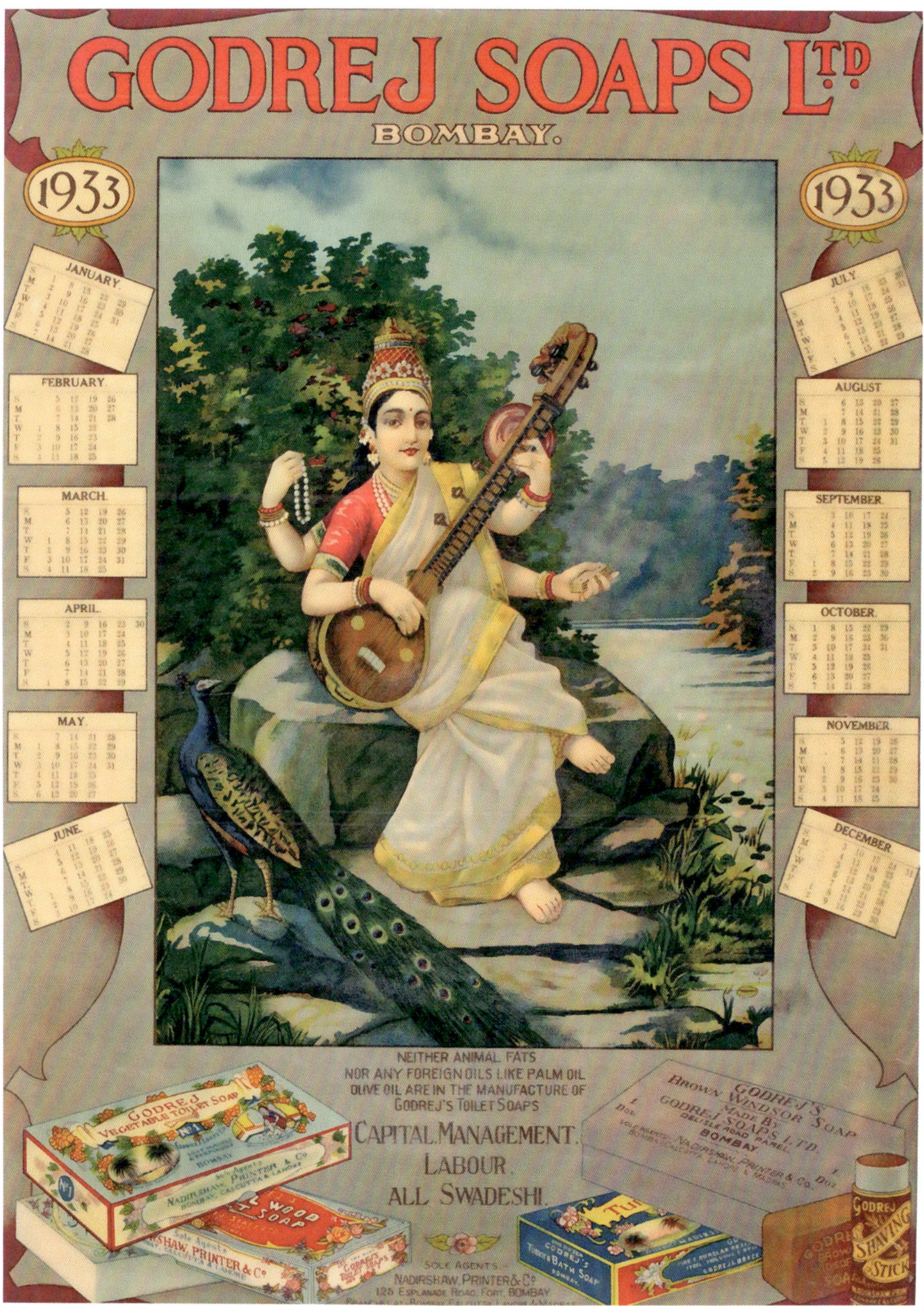

3.1   Godrej Soaps Calendar, oleograph after a painting by Ravi Varma, *Saraswati*, 1933.
Jane and Kito de Boer Collection.

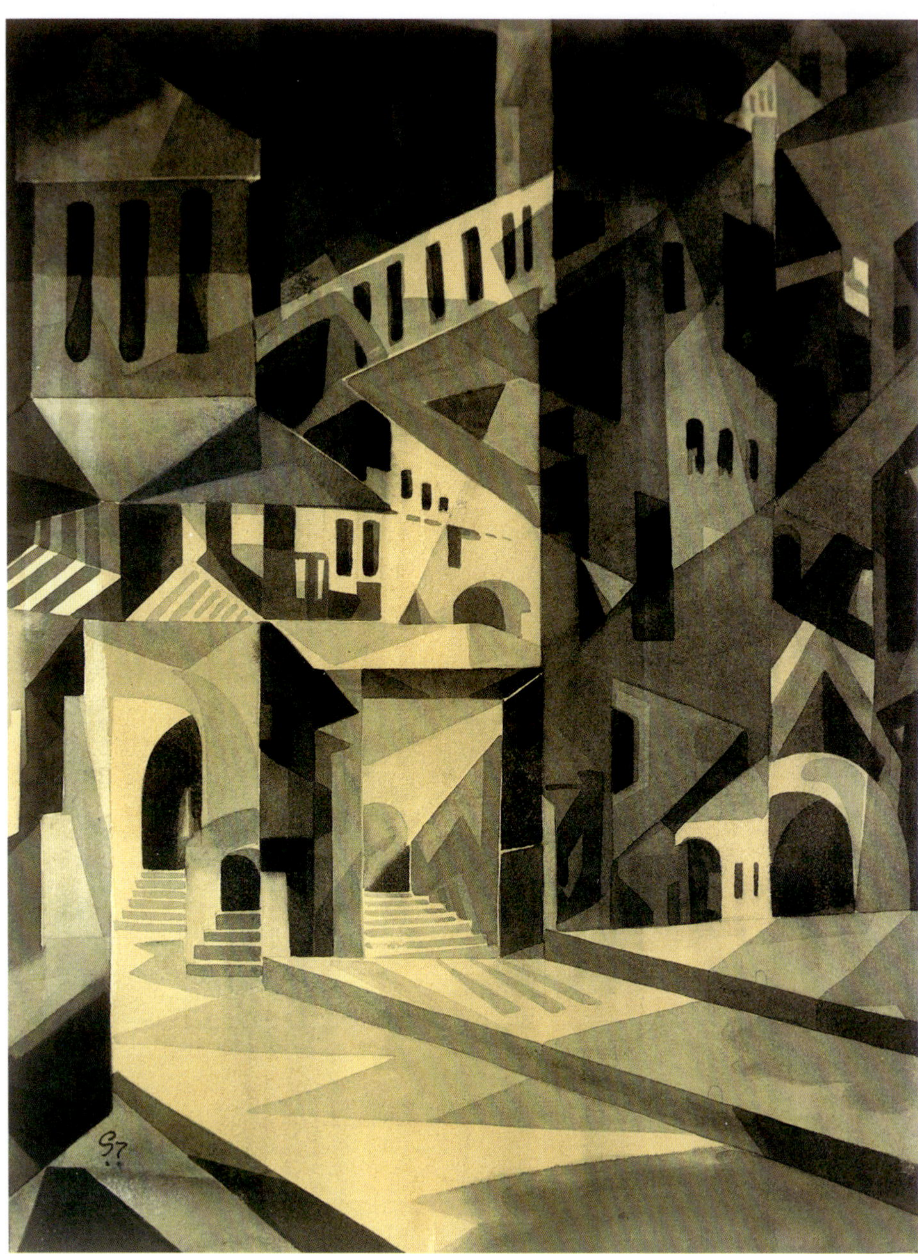

3.2   Gaganendranath Tagore, *Untitled,* 1924–25, ink and grey wash on paper.
New Delhi, Savara Foundation of the Arts.

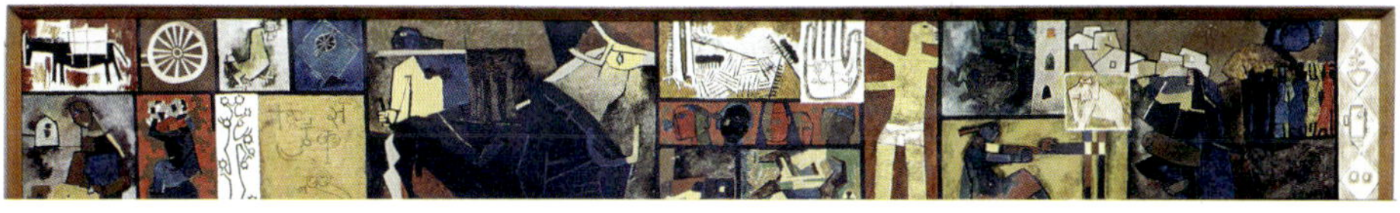
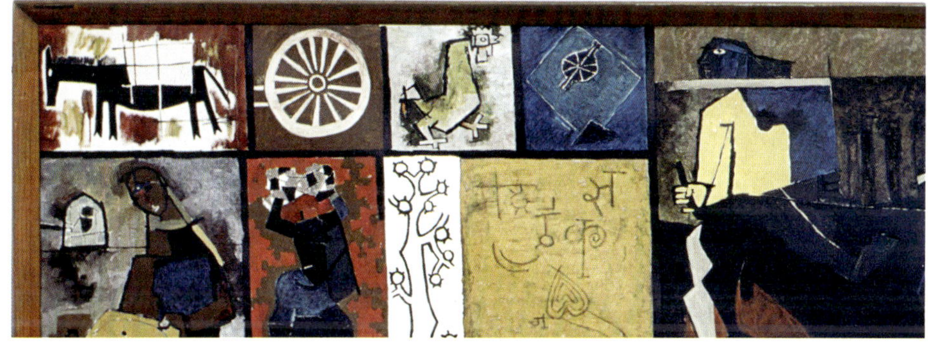
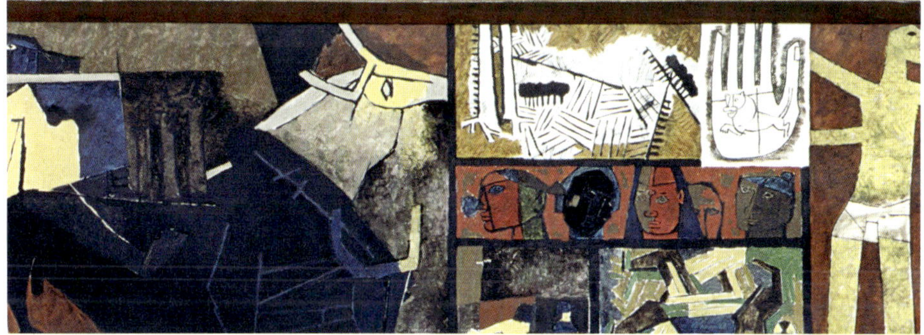
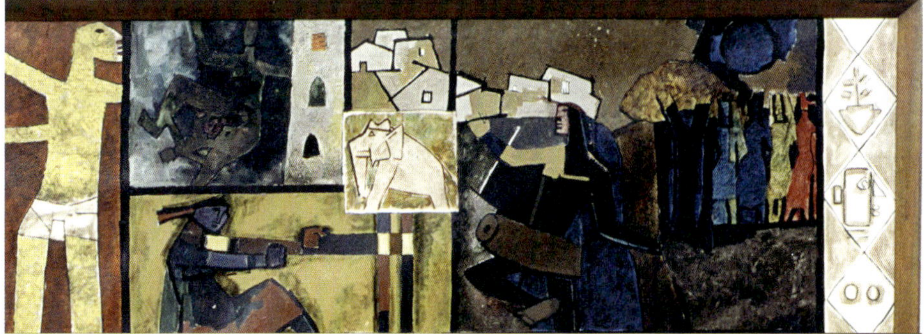

3.3   M. F. Husain, *Zameen*, 1954, oil on canvas. New Delhi, National Gallery of Modern Art.

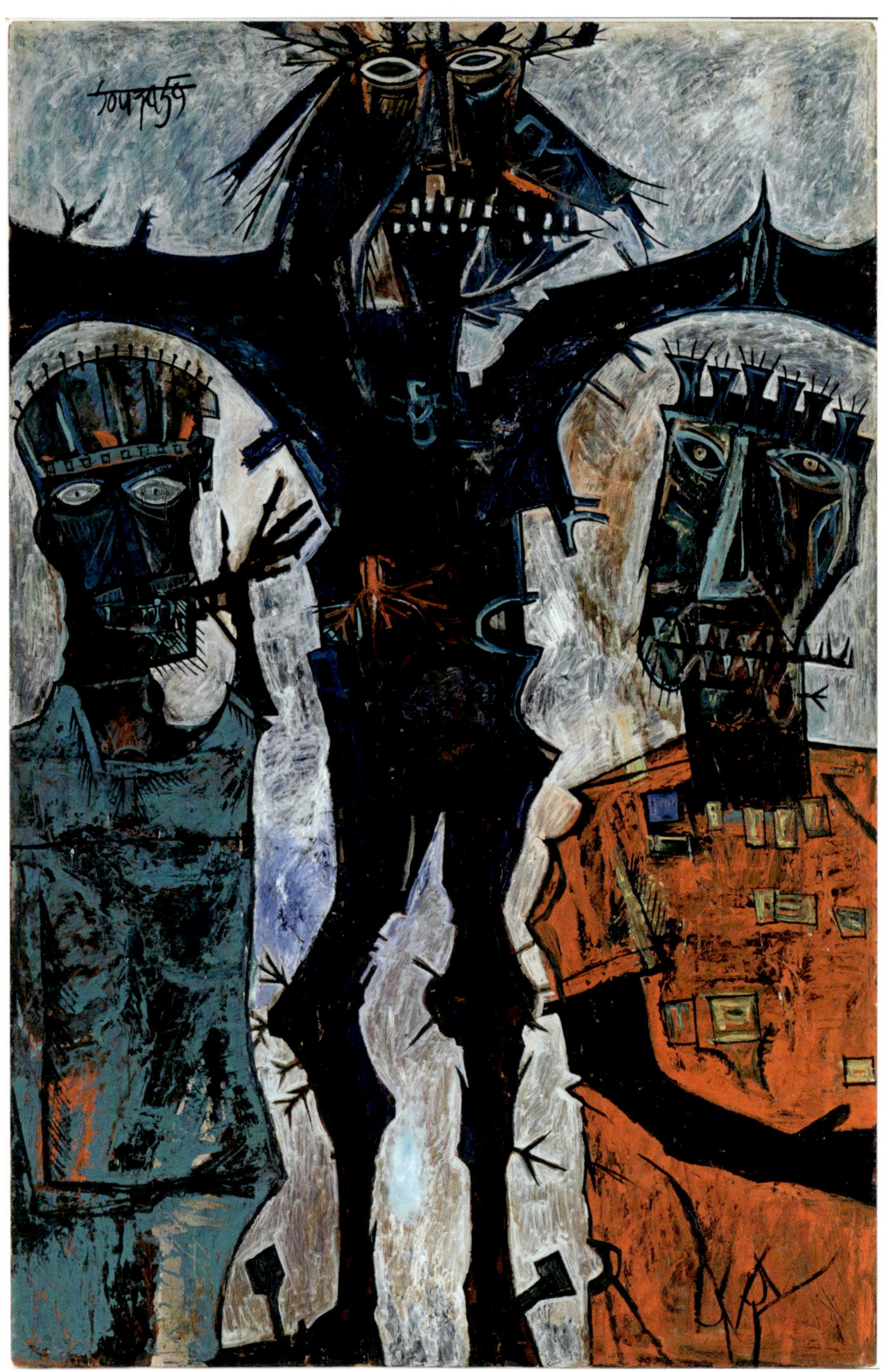

3.4   F. N. Souza, *Crucifixion*, 1959, oil on board. London, Tate Modern.

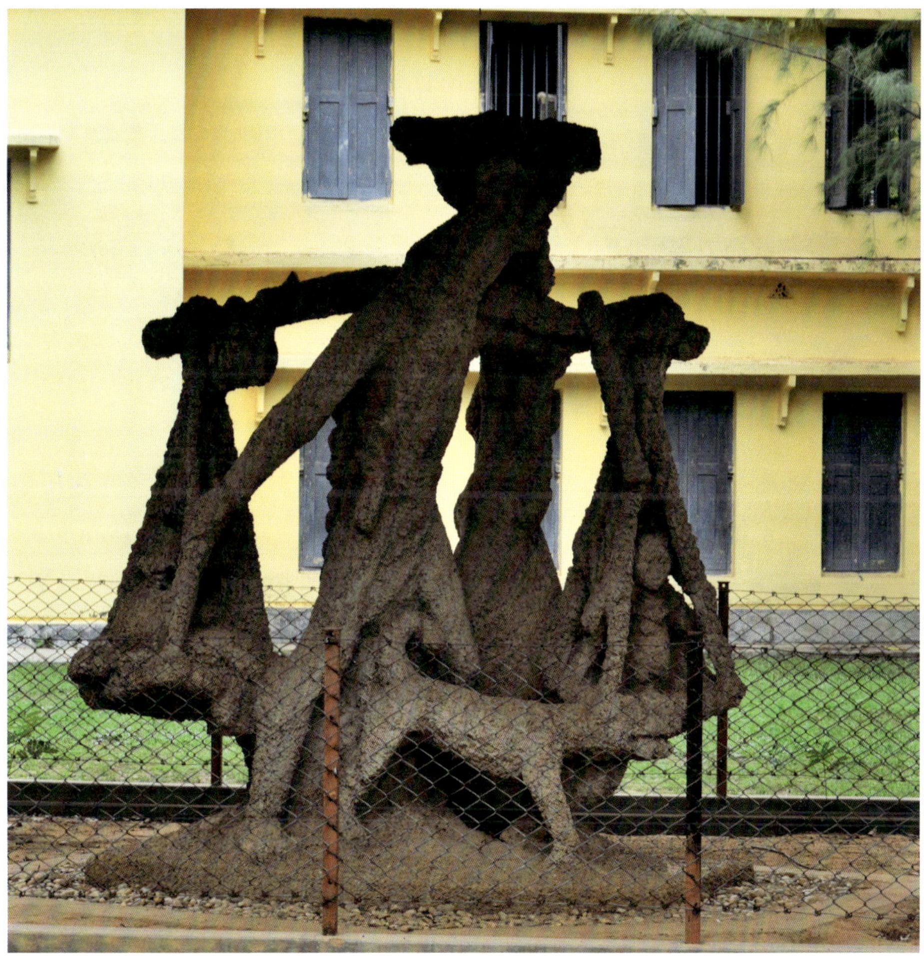

3.5   Ram Kinkar Baij, *Santhal Family*, 1938, on-site sculpture. Kala Bhavan, Santiniketan.

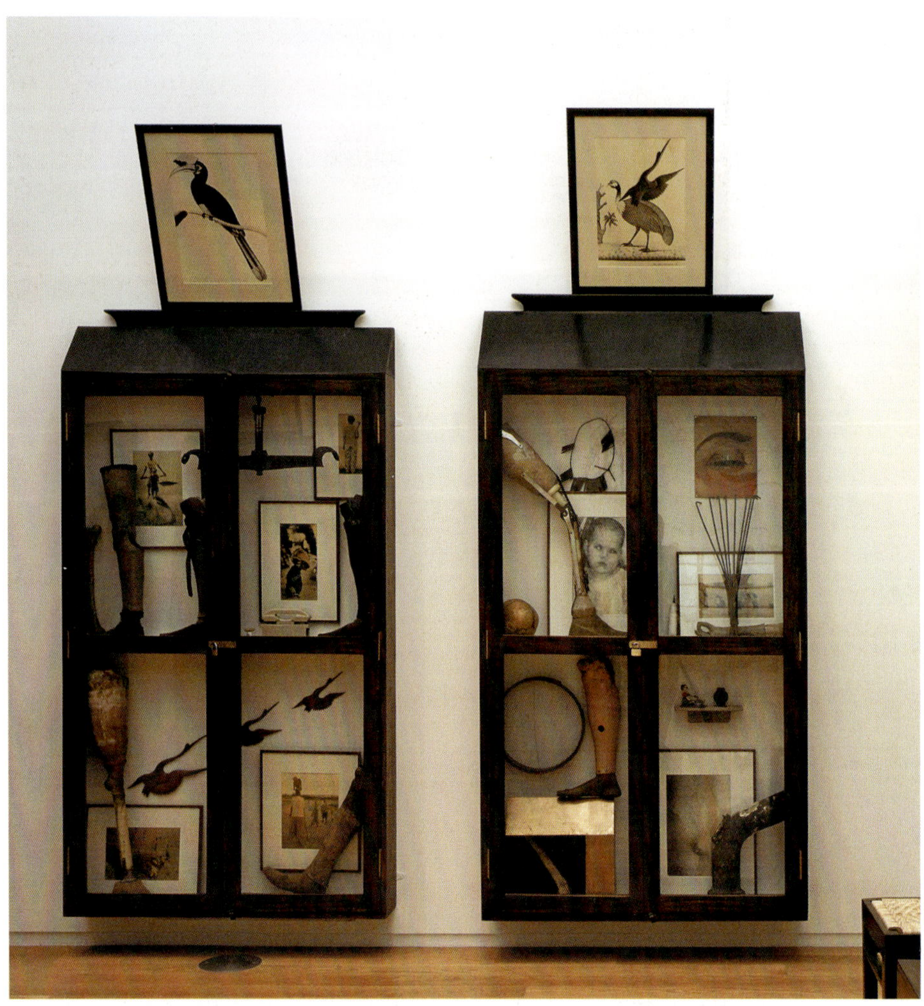

4.1   Atul Dodiya, *Broken Branches*, installation 2002.

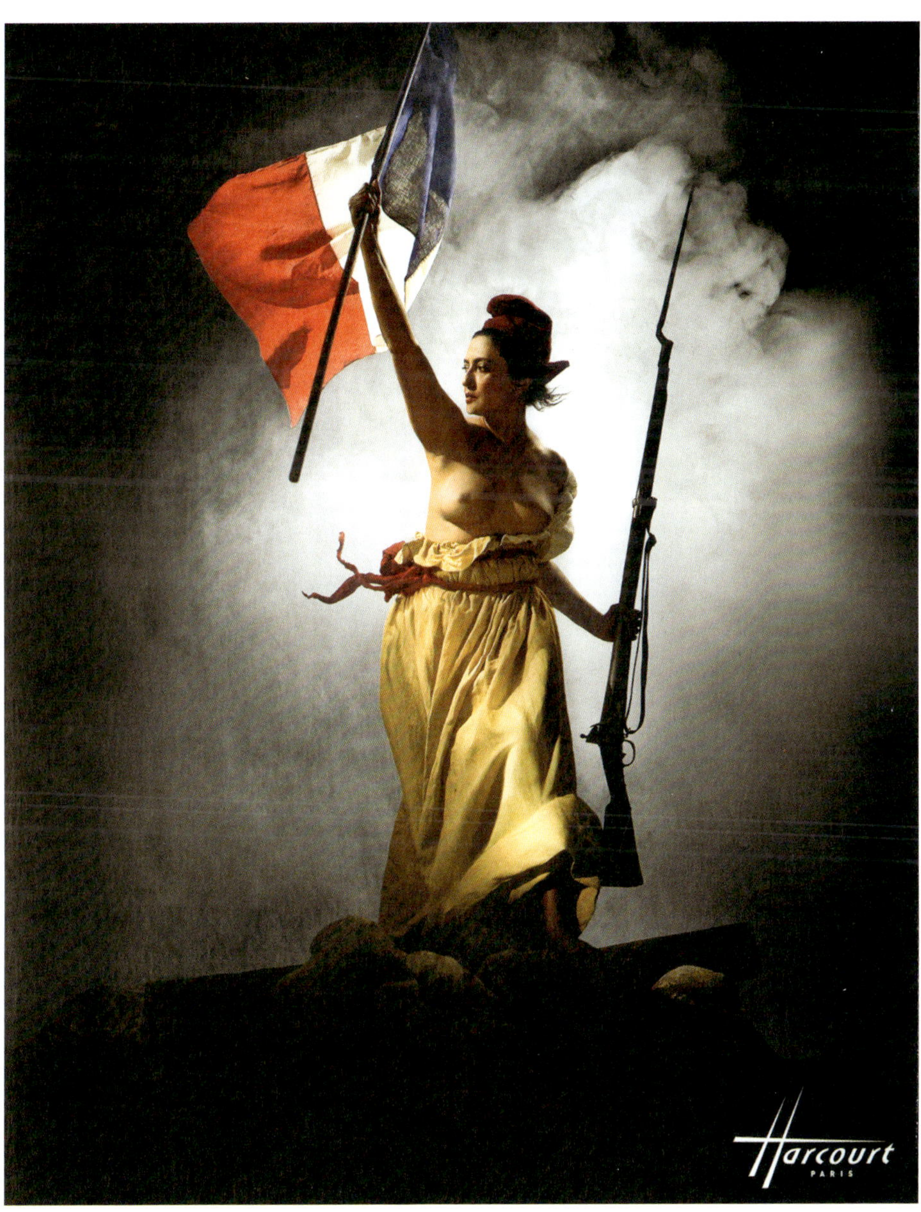

4.2   Pushpamala N., *Liberty (after Delacroix)*. Harcourt Series, photograph, 2009.

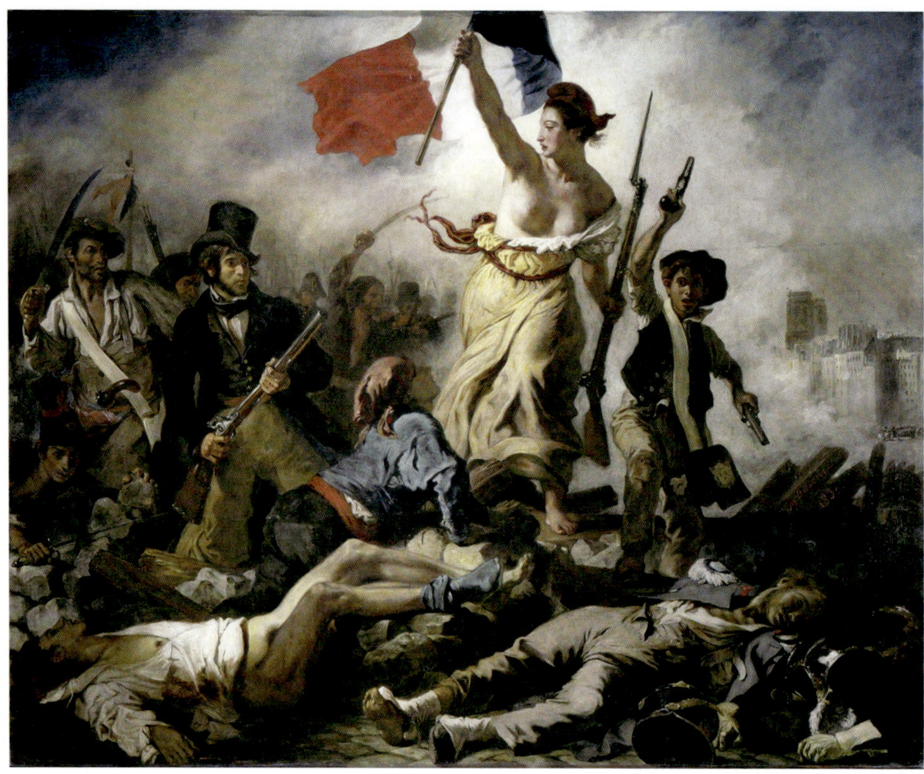

4.3   Eugène Delacroix, *Liberty Guiding the People*, oil on canvas, 1830–31. Paris, Musée du Louvre.

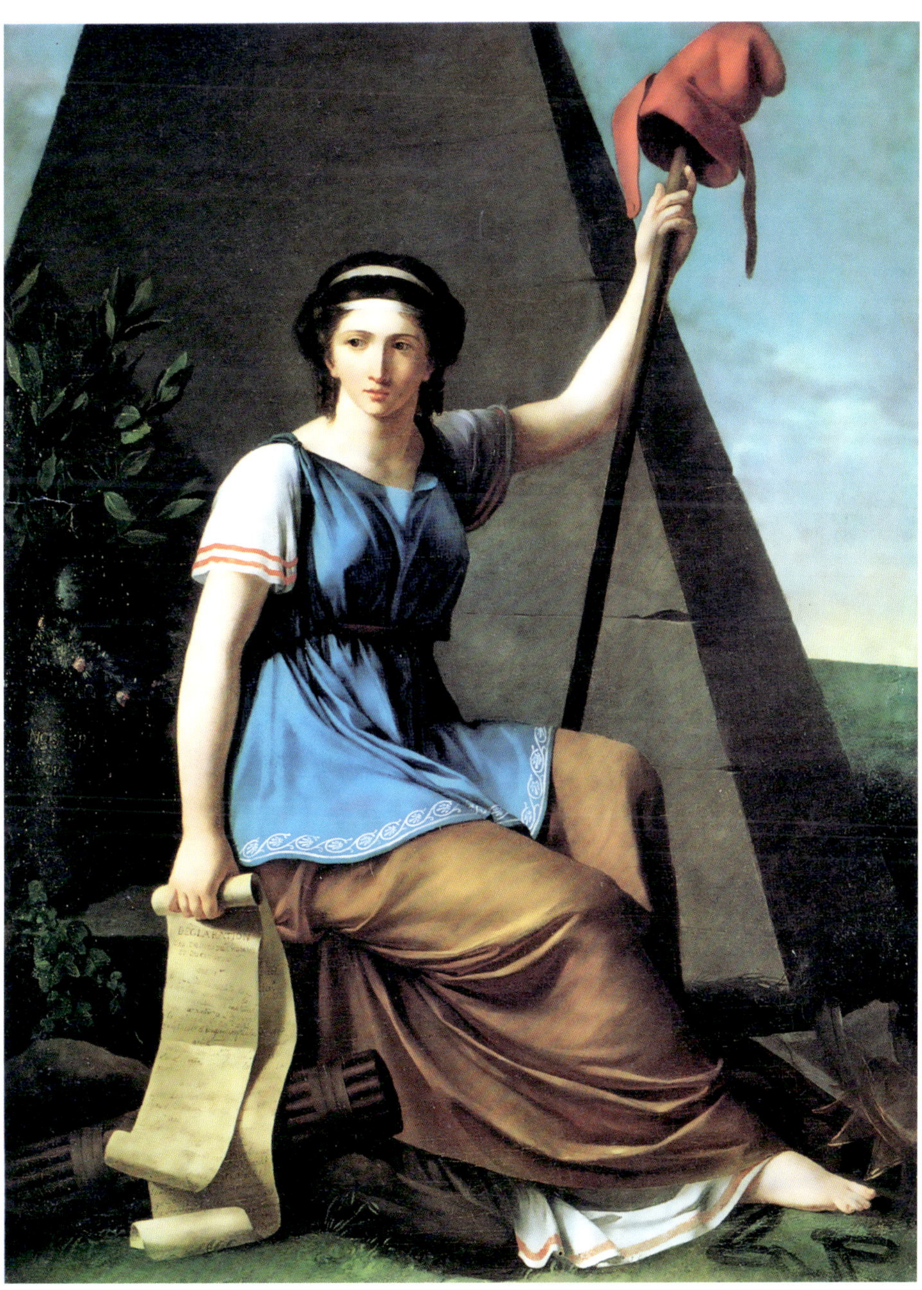

4.4   Nanine Vallain, *Liberty*, oil on canvas, 1793–94. Vizille, Musée de la Révolution Française.

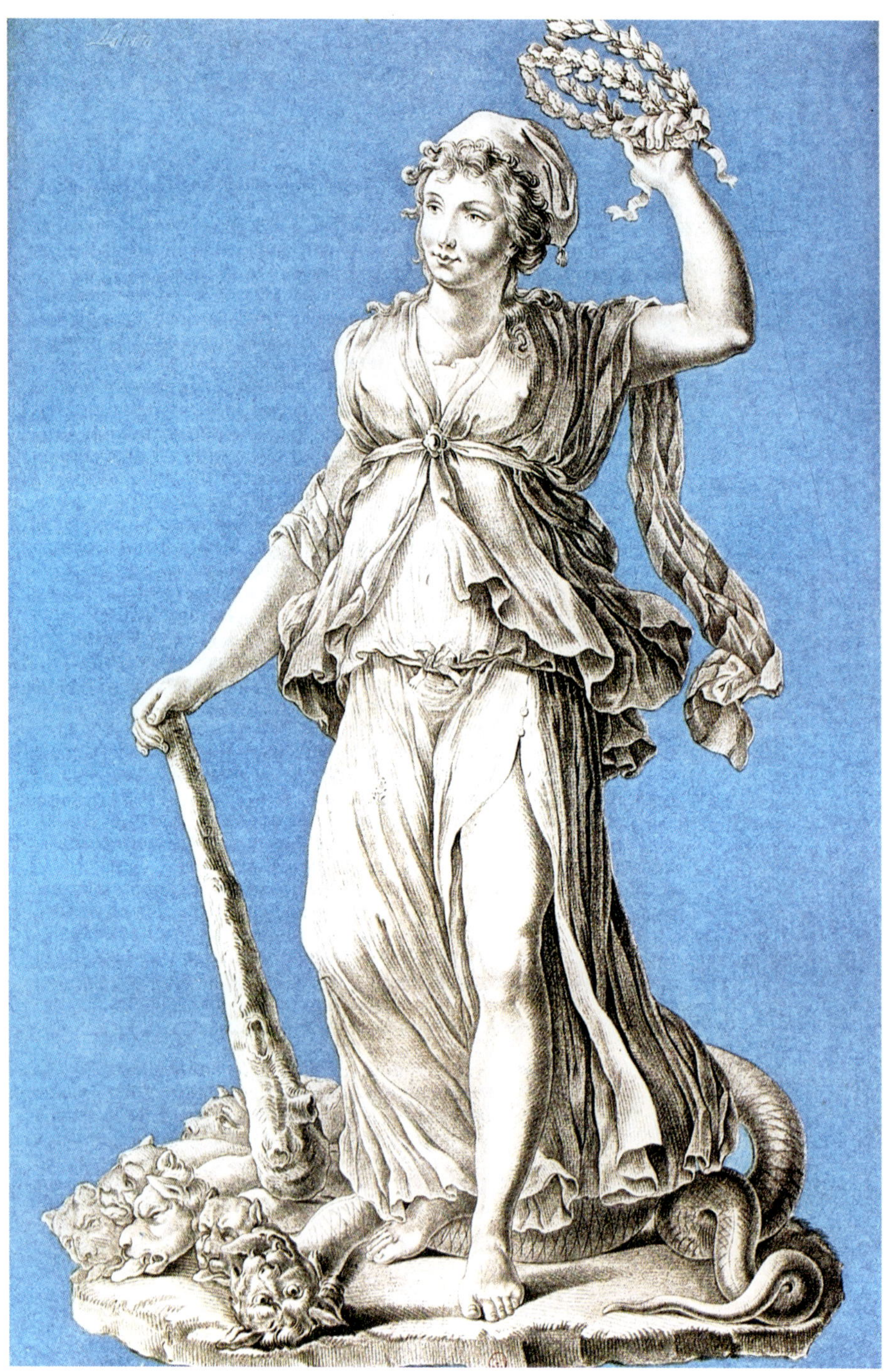

4.5 *Liberty*, coloured engraving by Carrée after a drawing by Leclerc, 1791. Paris, Musée Carnavalet.

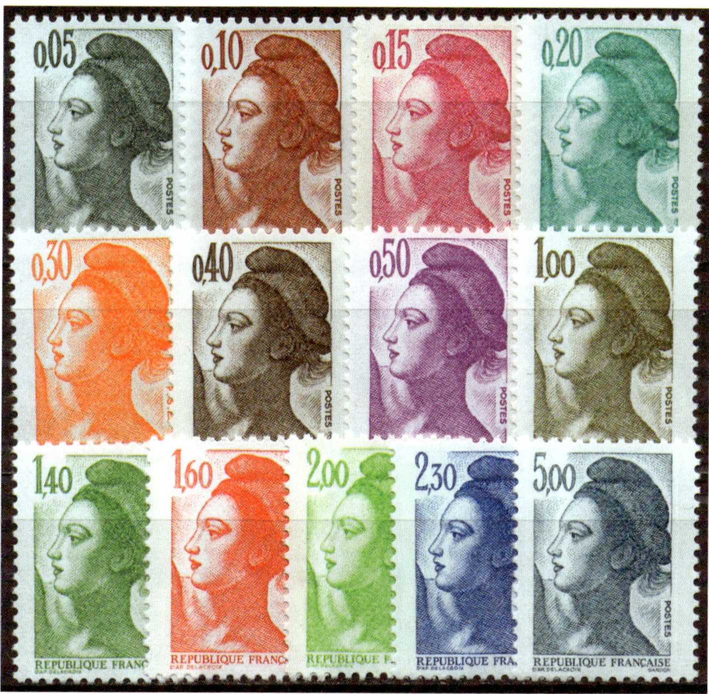

4.6   French postage stamps commemorating *Delacroix's Liberty guiding the People*.
Private collection.

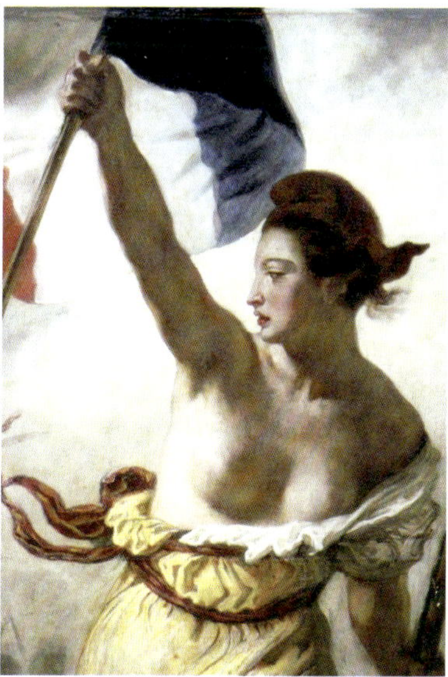

4.6a   Eugene Delacroix, *Liberty Guiding the People*, detail.

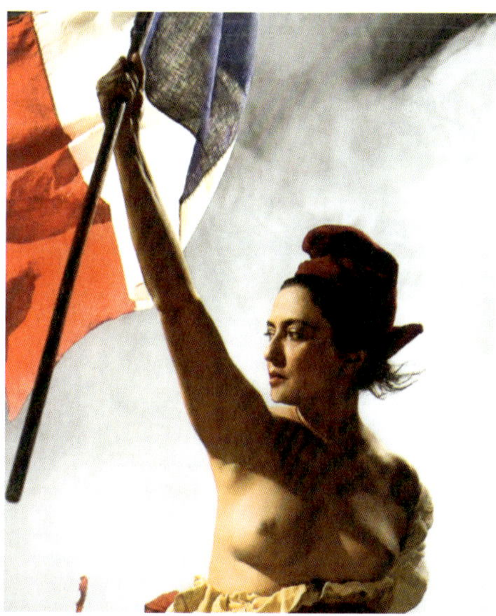

4.6b   Pushpamala N., *Liberty (after Delacroix)*, detail.

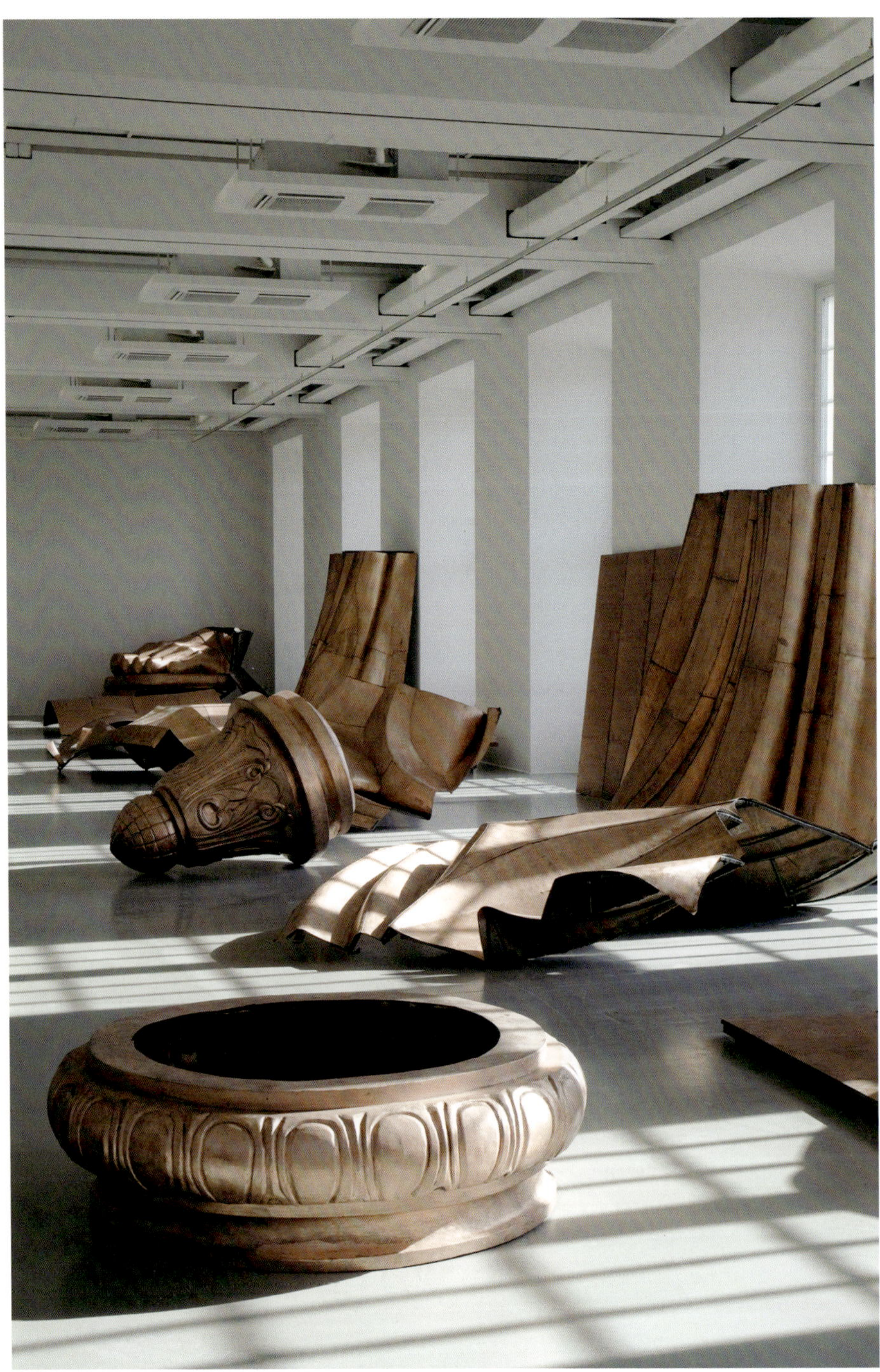

4.7 Danh Vō, *We the People*, installation 2011.

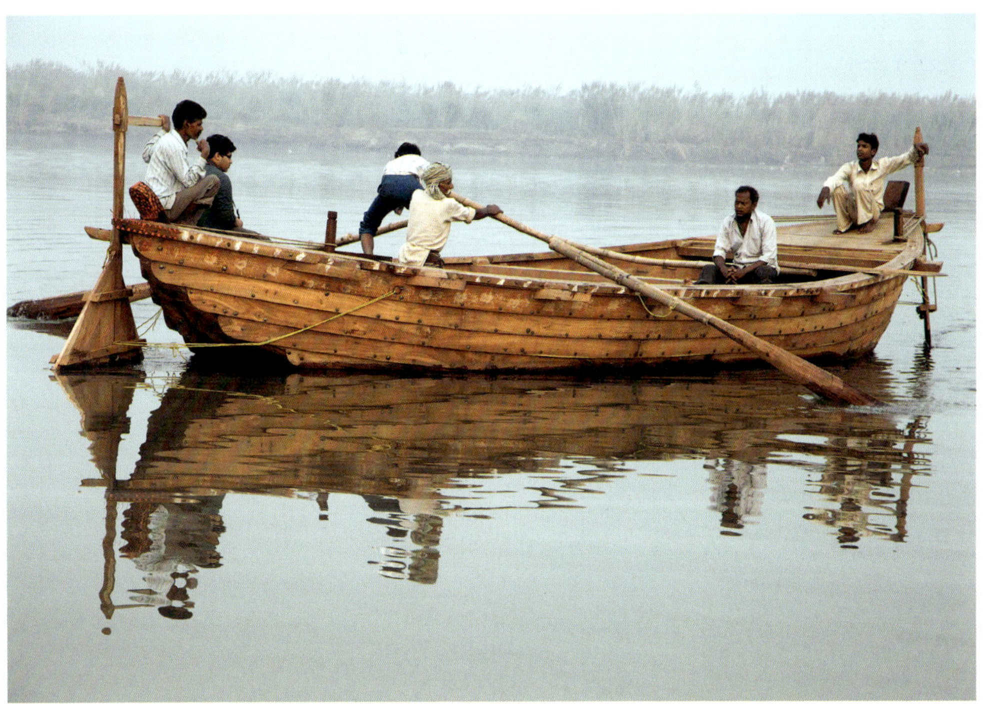

4.8   Atul Bhalla, Pattaya, photograph for *The Wake*, 2013.

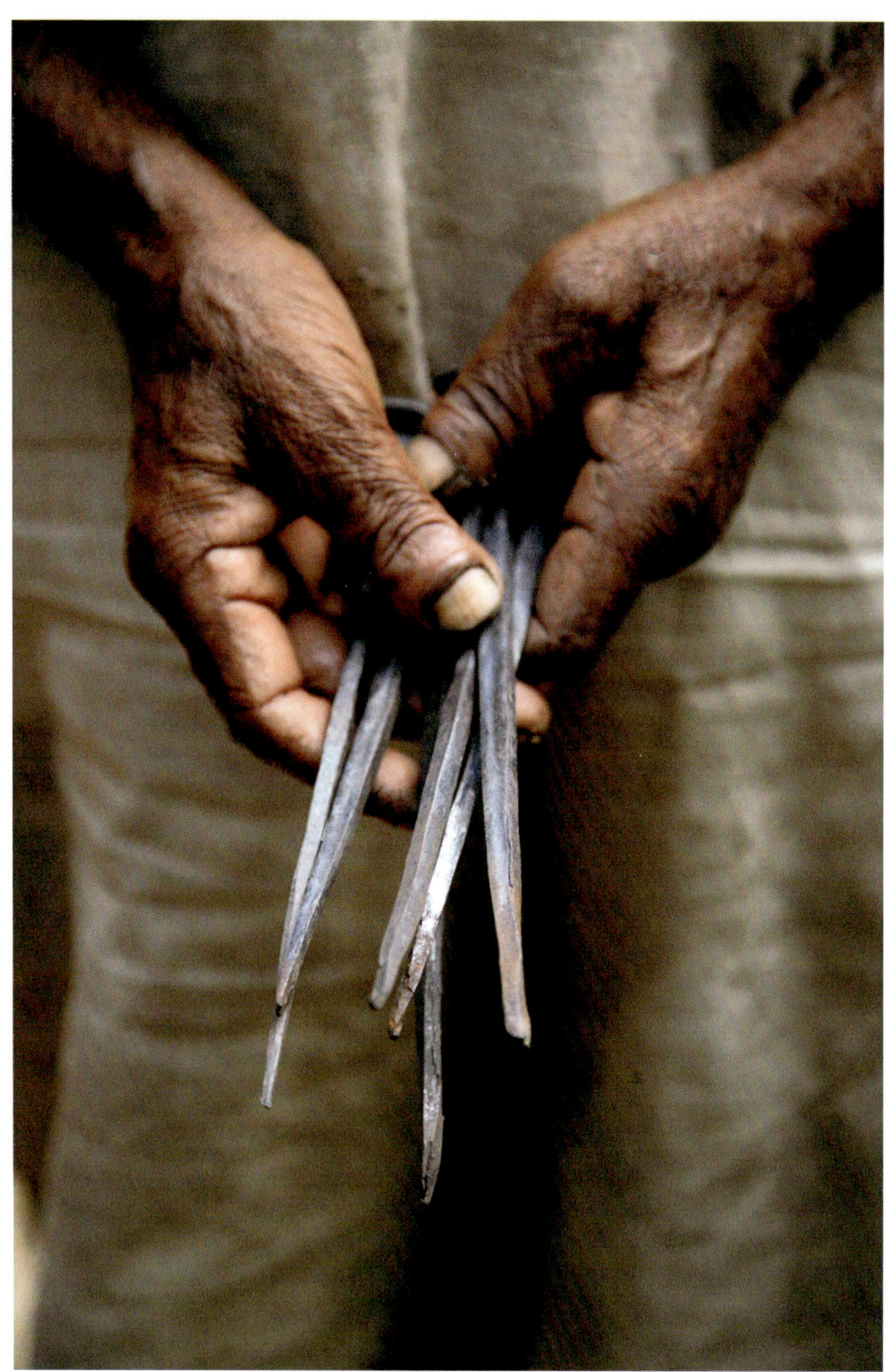

4.9   Atul Bhalla, Pattaya, photograph for *The Wake,* 2013.

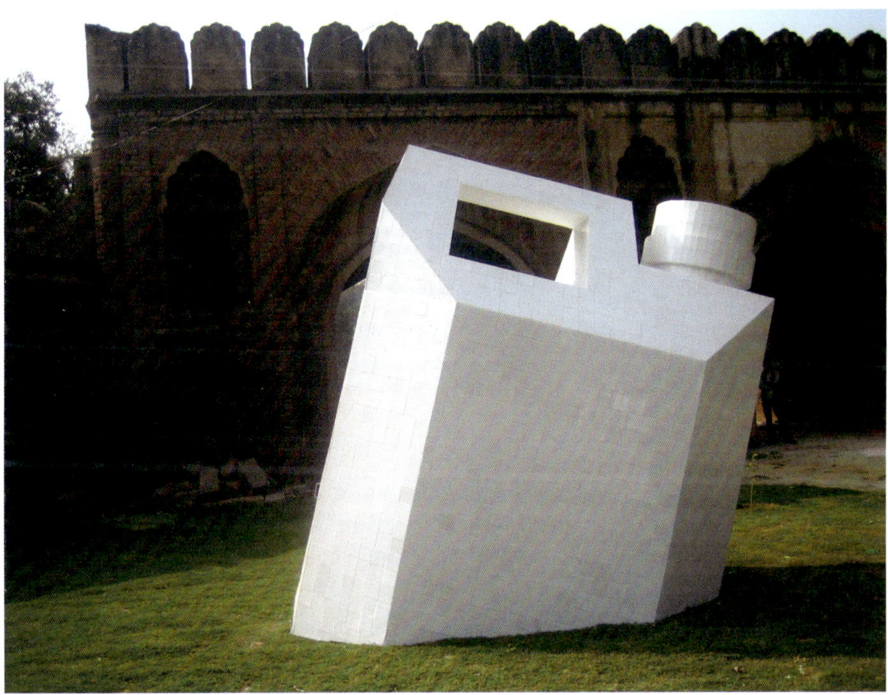

4.10   Atul Bhalla, *Chabeel*, installation, 2006.

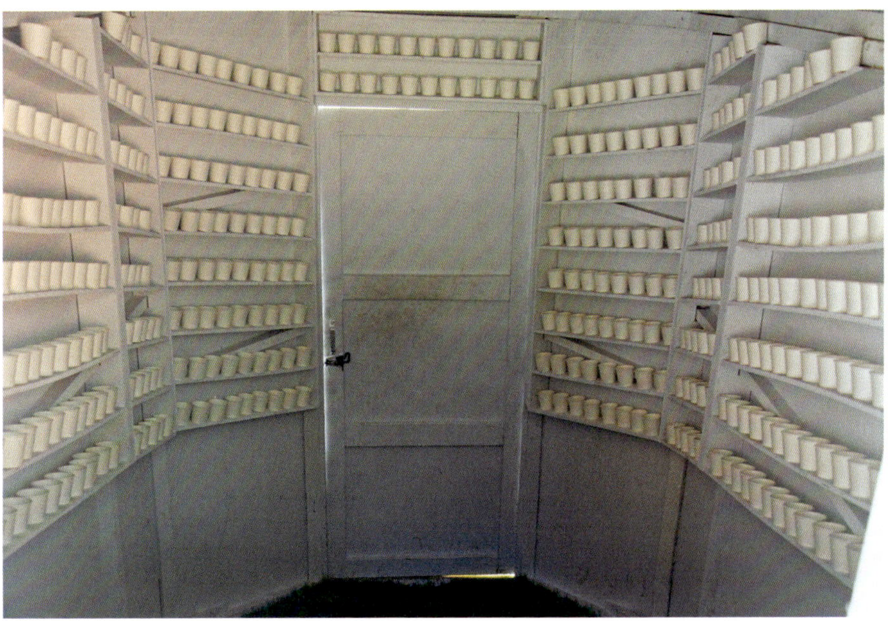

4.11   Atul Bhalla, *Chabeel*, installation, 2006.

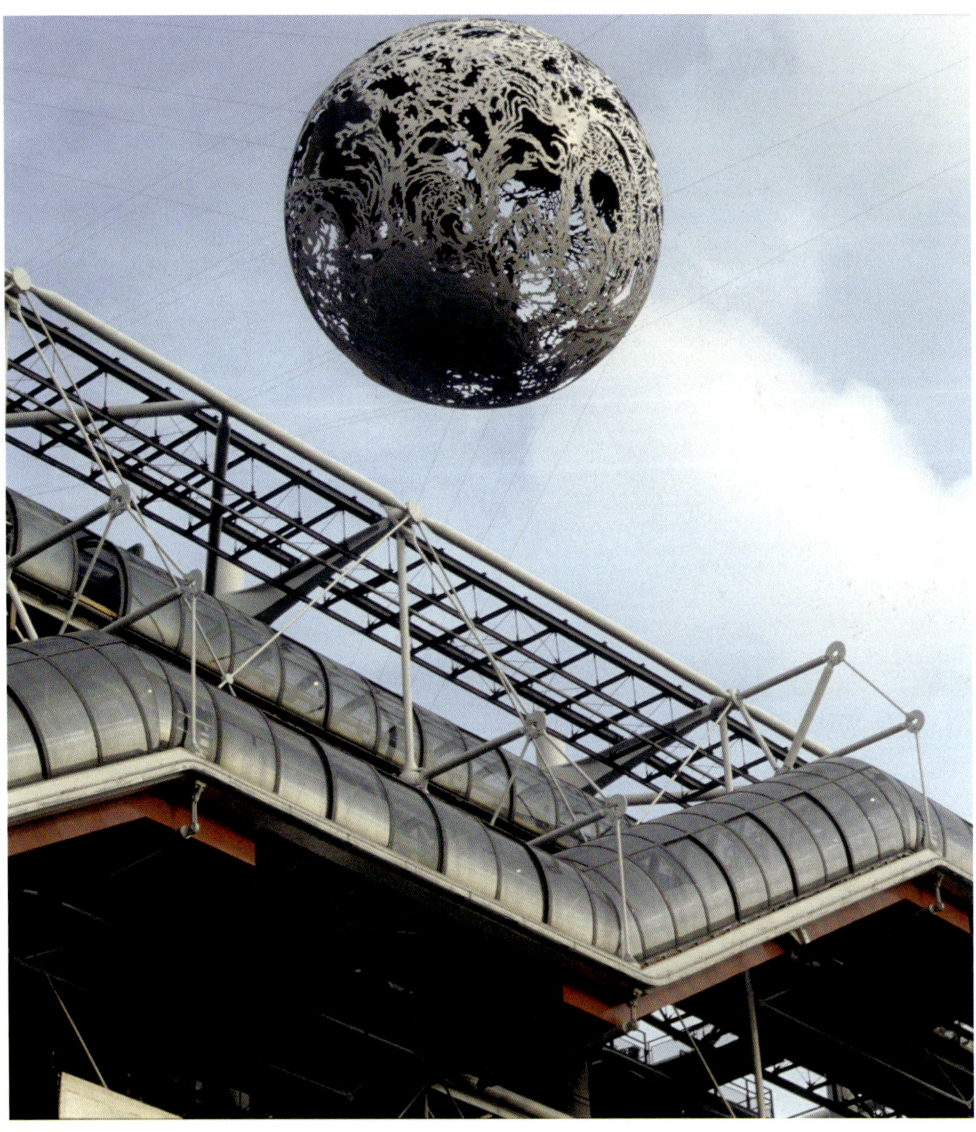

5.1   Neil Dawson, *Globe*, Sculpture and Installation, 1989.

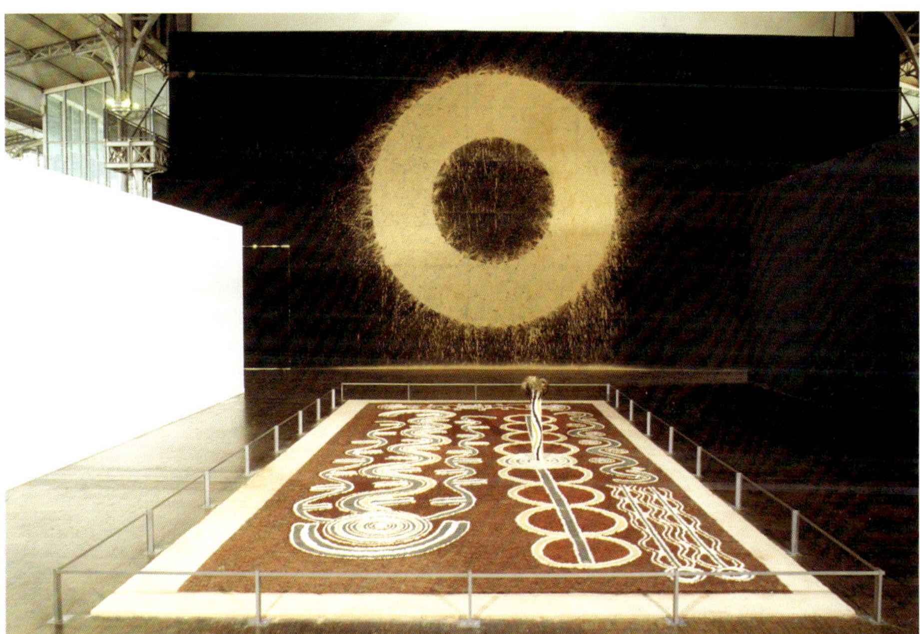

5.2   Richard Long, *Red Earth Circle*, Wall Painting (1989). On floor: Artists of Yuendumu community –
Francis J. Kelly, Frank B.J. Nelson, Paddy J. Nelson, Neville J. Poulson, Paddy J. Sims, Paddy J. Stewart,
Towser J. Walker, Yam Dreaming, Floor Painting, 1989.

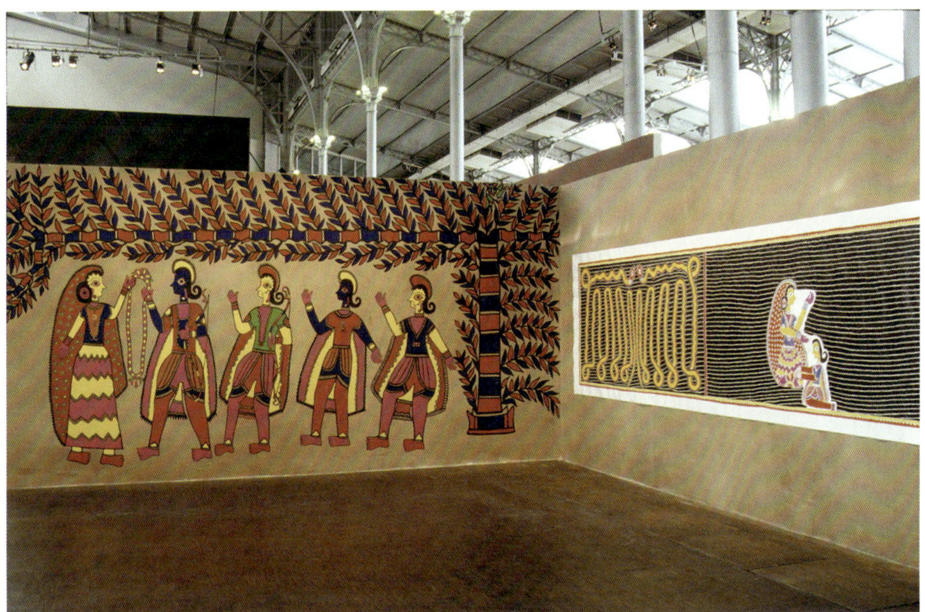

5.3   Baua Devi, *Snake*, Painting on Paper, 1989.

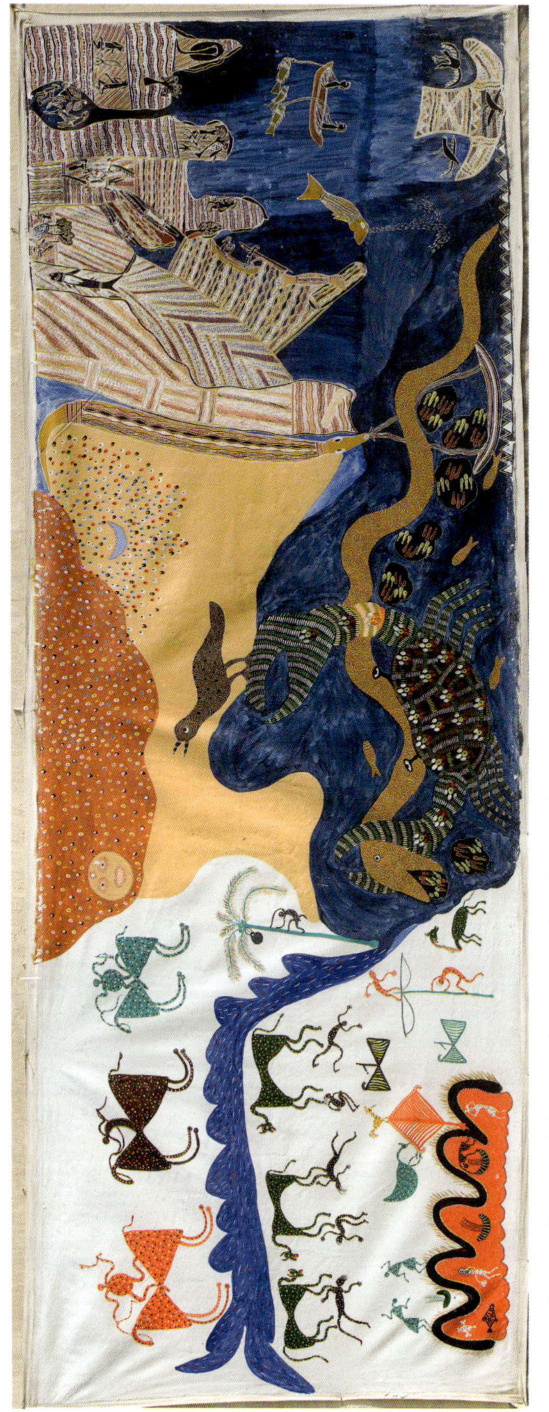

5.4 Jangarh Singh Shyam, Ladobai, Djambawa Marawili and Liyawaday Wirrpanda, Collaborative work between Indian and Australian artists, Acryllic Painting on Canvas, 1999. RMIT Gallery, Melbourne.

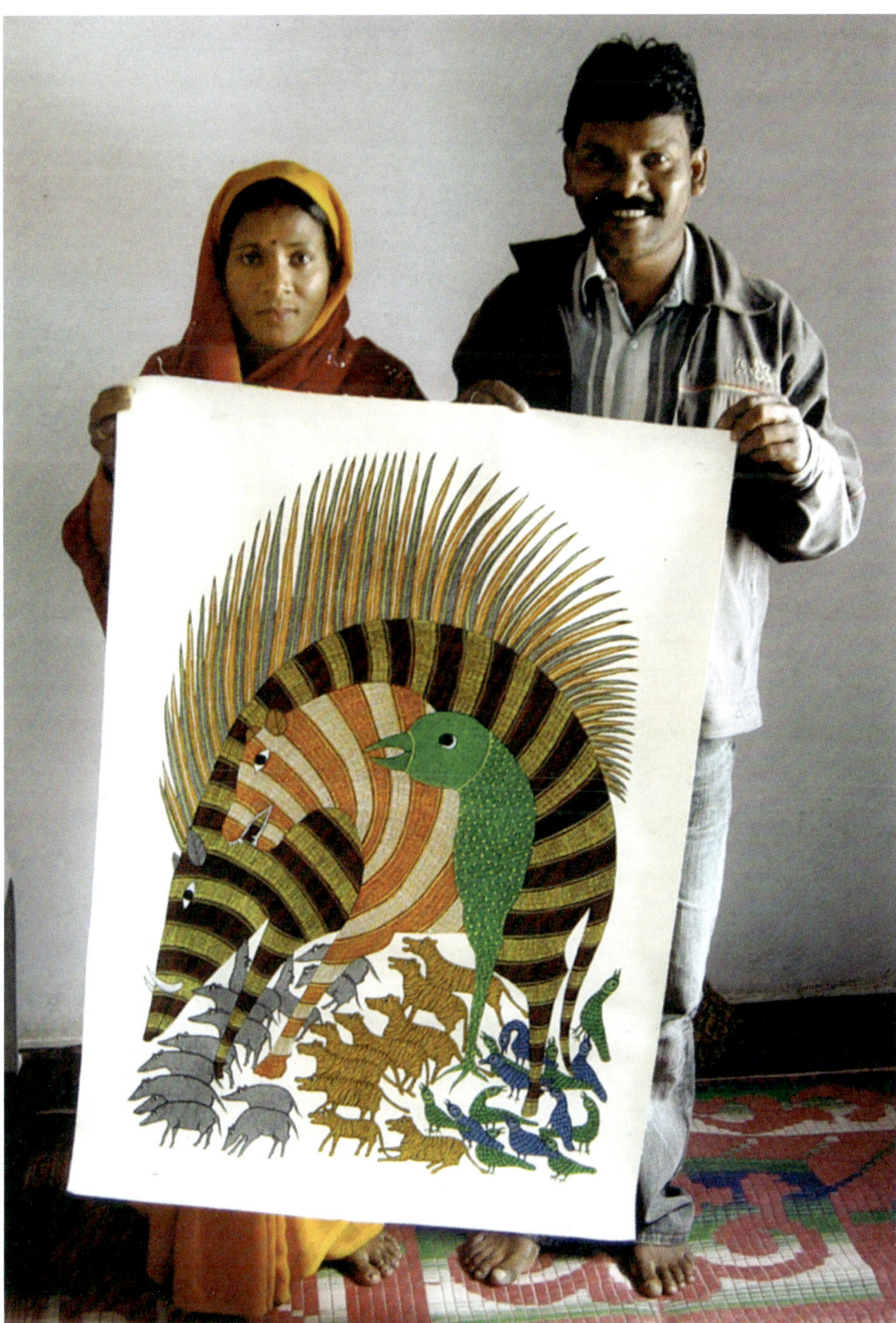

5.5   Sushila and Rajendra Shyam displaying their work at their home in Bhopal, Photograph, 2009. Private Collection.

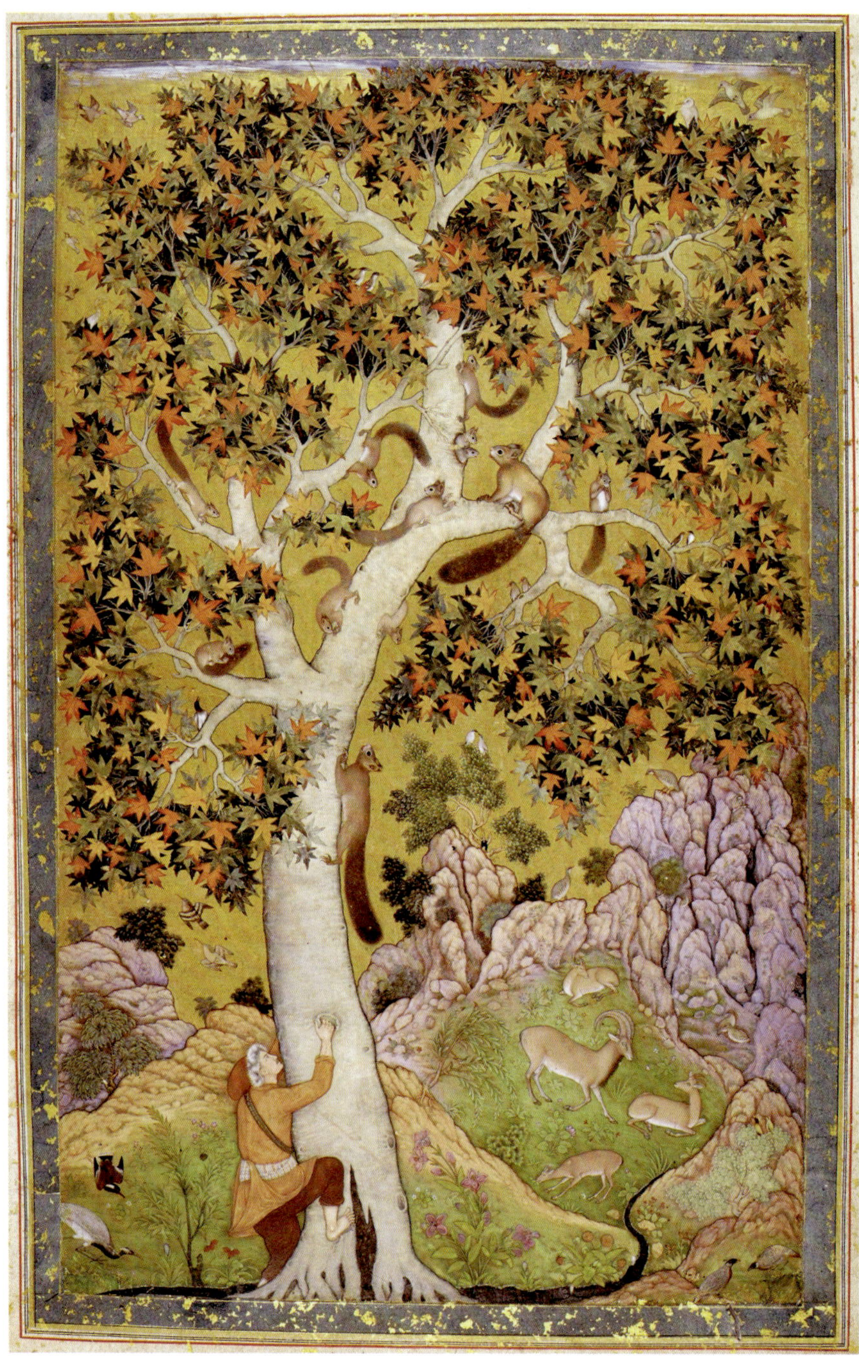

6.1   Single folio *Squirrels in a Plane Tree*, ascribed to Abu'l Hasan, 1605–08. Johnson Album, London, Victoria and Albert Museum.

BIBLIOGRAPHY

Anon., 'The Fourteenth Annual Exhibition of the Indian Society of Oriental Art', *Rupam*, no. 13 (January–June 1923): 14–18.

Allami, Abu'l Fazl, *A'in-i Akbari*, trans. H. Blochmann, 2 vols. (Delhi: Low Price Publications, 2001, 1927).

Abu-Lughod, Janet L., *Beyond European Hegemony: The World System A.D. 1250–1350* (New York: Oxford University Press, 1989).

Achar, Deeptha and Pushpamala N. (eds.), *Mysore Modernity, Aesthetic Nationalism: The Art of K. Venkatappa*, (London and New Delhi: Routledge [forthcoming 2023]).

Ådahl, Karin, *A Khamsa of Nizami of 1439: Origin of the Miniatures, a Presentation and Analysis* (Uppsala: Almqvist and Wiksell, 1981).

Adajania, Nancy and Ranjit Hoskote, 'Notes towards a Lexicon of Urgencies', *Journal of Independent Curators International Research* (1 October 2010), https://curatorsintl.org/research/notes-towards-a-lexicon-of-urgencies.

Agamben, Giorgio, *Means without End. Notes on Politics* (Minneapolis: University of Minnesota Press, 2000).

Ahmad, Qadi, *Calligraphers and Painters* (c. 1606), trans. V. Minorsky (Washington DC: Freer Gallery of Art, 1959).

Ahmed, Sara, *Strange Encounters: Embodied Others in Postcoloniality* (London and New York: Routledge, 2000).

Aitken, Molly E., *The Intelligence of Tradition in Rajput Court Painting* (New Haven: Yale University Press, 2010).

– (ed.), *A Magic World: New Visions of Indian Painting* (Mumbai: Marg Publications, 2016).

Ali, Daud, 'Gardens in Early Indian Court Life', *Studies in History*, vol. 19/2 (2003): 221–52.

Ali, Daud and Emma Flatt (eds.), *Gardens and Landscape Practices in Precolonial India: Histories from the Deccan* (London and New Delhi: Routledge, 2012).

Allerstorfer, Julia and Monika Leisch-Kiesl (eds.), *'Global Art History': Transkulturelle Verortungen von Kunst und Kunstwissenschaft* (Bielefeld: Transcript, 2017).

Amanshauser, Hildegund and Kimberly Bradley (eds.), *Navigating the Planetary* (Vienna: Verlag für moderne Kunst, 2020).

Anand, Mulk Raj, 'Judgment in the Trial of Akbar Padamsee for Alleged "Obscene' Paintings"', *Marg*, vol. 7/4 (1954): 90–91.

Ananth, Deepak and Anna Schneider (eds.), *Vivan Sundaram: Disjunctures* (Munich: Prestel, 2018).

Anderson, Benedict, *Imagined Communities: Reflections in the Origins and Spread of Nationalism* (London: Verso, 1983; 2016, revised ed.).

Appadurai, Arjun, *Modernity at Large: Cultural Dimensions of Globalization* (Minneapolis: University of Minnesota Press, 1996).

Araeen, Rasheed, 'From Primitivism to Ethnic Arts', *Third Text*, vol. 1/1 (1987): 6–25.

– 'Our Bauhaus Others' Mudhouse', *Third Text*, vol. 3/6 (1989): 3–16.

– 'The Other Immigrant: The Experiences and Achievements of Afro Asian Artists in the Metropolis', *Third Text*, vol. 5/15 (1991): 17–28.

Archer, Mildred, *India and British Portraiture, 1770–1825* (London: Sotheby Parke Bennett, 1979).

Archer, William G., *The Vertical Man: A Study in Primitive Indian Sculpture* (London: George Allen & Unwin, 1947).
– '"Hidden Maithila"', in William and Mildred Archer, *India Served and Observed* (London: BACSA, 1994), 53–58.
– 'Maithil Painting', *Marg*, vol. 3/3 (1949): 24–33.
Aslanian, Sebouh D., Joyce E. Chaplin, Ann McGrath and Kristin Mann, 'How Size Matters: The Question of Scale in History. AHR Conversation', *American Historical Review*, vol. 118/5 (2013): 1431–72.
Athanasiou, Athena, 'Formations of Political-Aesthetic Criticality: Decolonizing the Global in Times of Humanitarian Viewership. Athena Athanasiou in Conversation with Simon Sheikh', in Paul O'Neill, Simon Sheikh, Lucy Steeds and Mick Wilson (eds.), *Curating After the Global: Roadmaps for the Present* (Cambridge, MA: MIT Press, 2017), 71–94.
Azoulay, Ariella A., 'Potential History: Thinking Through Violence', *Critical Inquiry*, vol. 39/3 (2013): 548–74.

Babaie, Sussan, 'Chasing after the Muhandis: Visual Articulations of the Architect and Architectural Historiography', in Rizvi (ed.), *Affect, Emotion*, 21–44.
Bailey, Gauvin A., *The Jesuits and the Grand Mogul: Renaissance Art at the Imperial Court of India, 1580–1630* (Washington DC: Smithsonian Institution, 1998).
Bailkin, Jordana, 'Indian Yellow. Making and Breaking the Imperial Palette', *Journal of Material Culture*, vol. 10/2 (2005): 197–214.
Balibar, Etienne, *Citizenship* (Cambridge: Polity Press, 2015).
Banerjee, Prathama, *Politics of Time: 'Primitives' and History-Writing in Colonial Society* (New Delhi: Oxford University Press, 2006).
– 'Culture/Politics: The Irresoluble Double-Bind of the Indian Adivasi', *The Indian Historical Review*, vol. 33/1 (2006): 99–126.
Barad, Karen, *Meeting the Universe Halfway: Quantum Physics and the Entanglement of Matter and Meaning* (Durham, NC: Duke University Press, 2007).
Bardaouil, Sam, *Surrealism in Egypt: Modernism and the Art and Liberty Group* (London: I. B. Tauris, 2017).
– Bardaouil, Sam and Till Fellrath (eds.), *Art et Liberté. Umbruch, Krieg und Surrealismus in Ägypten (1938–1948)* (Paris: Editions Skira, 2016).
Barrell, John, *The Political Theory of Painting from Reynolds to Hazlitt* (New Haven: Yale University Press, 1986).
Barrett, Douglas E., *Studies in Indian Sculpture and Painting* (London: Pindar Press, 1990).
Barrett, Douglas E. and Basil Gray, *Painting of India* (Lausanne: Skira, 1963).
Barry, Michael, *Figurative Art in Medieval Islam and the Riddle of Bihzâd of Herât (1465–1535)* (Paris: Editions Flammarion, 2004).
Bauer, Stefan and Simon Ditchfield (eds.), *A Renaissance Reclaimed. Jacob Burckhardt's* Civilisation of the Renaissance in Italy *Reconsidered*, (Oxford: Oxford University Press, 2022).
Baviskar, Amita, *In the Belly of the River: Tribal Conflicts over Developments in the Narmada Valley* (Delhi: Oxford University Press, 2004, 2nd edition).
– 'Adivasi Encounters with Hindu Nationalism in MP', *Economic and Political Weekly*, vol. 40/48 (2005): 5105–13.
– 'Indian Indigeneities: Adivasi Entanglements with Hindu Nationalism in India', in Marisol de la Cadena and Orin Starn (eds.), *Indigenous Experience Today* (Oxford: Berg Publishers, 2007), 275–304.
– 'What the Eye Does Not See: The Yamuna in the Imagination of Delhi', *Economic and Political Weekly*, vol. 46/50 (2011): 43–53.
Beach, Milo C., *The Imperial Image: Paintings for the Mughal Court* (Washington DC: Freer Gallery of Art, 1981).
– 'The Gulshan Album and its European Sources', *Museum of Fine Arts Bulletin*, 63 (1965): 63–91.
Beach, Milo C., Ebba Koch and Wheeler Thackston, *King of the World: The Padshahnama* (London: Azimuth, 1997).
Beach, Milo C. and Jorrit Britschgi (eds.), *Masters of Indian Painting*, 2 vols. (Zurich: Artibus Asiae Publications, 2011).
Bean, Susan S. (ed.), *Midnight to Boom: Paintings in India after Independence* (London: Thames and Hudson, 2013).
Bell, Julian, *Mirror of the World: A New History of Art* (London: Thames and Hudson, 2007).

Belting, Hans, *Art History after Modernism* (Chicago: University of Chicago Press, 2003).
– *Bild-Anthropologie: Entwürfe für eine Bildwissenschaft* (Munich: Fink Verlag, 2006).
– *Florenz und Bagdad: Eine westöstliche Geschichte des Blicks* (Munich: Beck Verlag, 2008).
– 'Contemporary Art and the Museum in the Global Age', in Peter Weibel and Andrea Buddensieg (eds.), *Contemporary Art and the Museum* (Ostfildern: Hatje Cantz, 2007), 16–38.
– 'Contemporary Art as Global Art: A Critical Estimate', in Belting and Buddensieg (eds.), *The Global Art World*, 38–73.
– 'From World Art to Global Art: View on a New Panorama', in Belting, Buddensieg and Weibel (eds.), *The Global Contemporary*, 178–85.
Belting, Hans and Andrea Buddensieg, *Ein Afrikaner in Paris: Léopold Sédar Senghor und die Zukunft der Moderne* (Munich: C. H. Beck, 2018).
Belting, Hans and Andrea Buddensieg (eds.), *The Global Art World: Audiences, Markets, and Museums* (Ostfildern: Hatje Cantz, 2009).
Belting, Hans, Andrea Buddensieg and Peter Weibel (eds.), *The Global Contemporary and the Rise of New Art Worlds* (Cambridge, MA: MIT Press, 2012).
Belting, Hans, Andrea Buddensieg and Peter Weibel (eds.), *Contemporary Art and the Museum: A Global Perspective* (Ostfildern: Hatje Cantz, 2007).
Belting, Hans, Jacob Birken, Andrea Buddensieg and Peter Weibel (eds.), *Global Studies: Mapping Contemporary Art and Culture* (Ostfildern: Hatje Cantz, 2011).
Berg, Maxine (ed.), *Writing the History of the Global: Challenges for the 21st Century* (Oxford: Oxford University Press, 2013).
Bergdoll, Barry and Leah Dickerman (eds.), *Bauhaus 1919–1933: Workshops for Modernity* (New York: Museum of Modern Art, 2009).
Bergthaller, Hannes and Peter Mortensen (eds.), *Framing the Environmental Humanities* (Leiden: Brill, 2019).
Berlekamp, Persis, *Wonder, Image and Cosmos in Medieval Islam,* (New Haven: Yale University Press, 2011).
Berry, Josephine, 'Everyone is Not an Artist: Autonomous Art Meets the Neoliberal City', *New Formations*, nos. 84–85 (2015): 20–39.
Beyer, Andreas, Susanna Burghartz and Lucas Burkart, *Burckhardt.Renaissance: Erkundungen und Relektüren eines Klassikers* (Göttingen: Wallstein Verlag, 2021).
Bhabha, Homi K., *The Location of Culture* (London: Routledge, 1994).
– 'India's Dialogical Modernism: Homi Bhabha in Conversation with Susan S. Bean', in Bean, *Midnight to Boom*, 23–36.
– 'Remembering Fanon: Self, Psyche, and the Colonial Condition', in Enwezor et al. (eds.), *Postwar*, 350–55.
– (ed.), *Nation and Narration* (London: Routledge, 1993).
– 'Of Mimicry and Man: The Ambivalence of Colonial Discourse', *October*, Issue 28 (Spring 1984): 125–33.
Bhagat, Ashrafi S., 'Modernity in the South: An Overview', in Sinha (ed.), *Art and Visual Culture in India 1857–2007*, 206–17.
– 'The "Madras Art Movement" and the Lineages of Abstraction', in Shivaji K. Panikkar, Deeptha Achar and Parul D. Mukherji (eds.), *Towards a New Art History: Studies in Indian Art* (New Delhi: D. K. Printworld, 2003), 229–41.
Bhalla, Atul, 'You Always Step Into the Same River!', in Sugata Ray and Venugopal Maddipati (eds.), *Water Histories of South Asia: The Materiality of Liquescence* (London and New Delhi: Routledge, 2020), 276–93.
Bhalla, Atul and Maliha Noorani, *Yamuna Walk* (Seattle: University of Washington Press, 2012).
Bharucha, Rustom, *Another Asia: Rabindranath Tagore and Okakura Tenshin* (New Delhi: Oxford University Press, 2006).
– 'Somebody's Other: Disorientations in the Cultural Politics of Our Times', *Economic and Political Weekly*, vol. 29/3 (1994): 105–10.
Biedermann, Karl, 'Cultur', in Karl von Rotteck and Karl Welcker (eds.), *Das Staats-Lexikon: Encyklopädie der sämmtlichen Staatswissenschaften für alle Stände*, 14 vols. (Leipzig: Brockhaus, 1860), vol. 4, 227–39.
Birdwood, George C. M., *The Industrial Arts of India*, 2 vols. (London: Chapman & Hall, 1880).
Biro, Yaëlle, 'Avant Charles Ratton: Commerce et diffusion des arts africains aux années 1920', in Sophie Laporte (ed.), *Charles Ratton: L'invention des arts 'primitifs'* (Paris: Editions Skira, 2013), 42–57.
Bishop, Claire, *Artificial Hells: Participatory Art and the Politics of Spectatorship* (New York: Verso, 2012).
– 'Antagonism and Relational Aesthetics', *October*, Issue 110 (Fall 2004): 51–80.

Bittner, Regina and Kathrin Rhomberg (eds.), *The Bauhaus in Calcutta: An Encounter of the Cosmopolitan Avant-Garde* (Ostfildern: Hatje Cantz, 2013).

Black, Charlene V. and Tim Barringer, 'Decolonizing Art and Empire', *The Art Bulletin*, vol. 104/1 (2022) 6–20.

Blair, Sheila S., 'Color and Gold: The Decorated Papers used in Manuscripts in Later Islamic Times', *Muqarnas*, vol. 17 (2000): 24–36.

Blake, Jody, 'The Truth about the Colonies, 1931: Art Indigène in the Service of the Revolution', *Oxford Art Journal*, vol. 25/1 (2002): 37–58.

Blier, Suzanne Preston, *Picasso's Demoiselles: The Untold Origins of a Modern Masterpiece* (Durham, NC: Duke University Press, 2019).

Boas, Franz, *Primitive Art* (New York: Dover, 1927).

Bois, Yves-Alain, 'La pensée sauvage', *Art in America*, vol. 73/4 (1985): 178–88.

Bourdieu, Pierre, *The Field of Cultural Production: Essays on Art and Literature* (Cambridge: Polity Press, 1993).

Bourriaud, Nicolas, *Altermodern: Tate Triennial* (London: Tate Publishing, 2009).

– *Esthétique Relationelle* (Dijon: Les Presses du Réel, 1998).

Bowles, John H., *Painted Songs & Stories: The Hybrid Flowerings of Contemporary Pardhan Gond Art* (Bhopal: INTACH Bhopal Chapter, 2009).

Brend, Barbara, *The Emperor Akbar's Khamsah of Nizami* (London: British Library, 1995).

Brenson, Michael, 'The Curator's Moment', *Art Journal*, vol. 57/4 (1998): 16–27.

Brotton, Jerry, *The Renaissance Bazaar: From the Silk Road to Michelangelo* (Oxford: Oxford University Press, 2003).

Brown, Caroline Henning, 'Contested Meanings. Tantra and the Poetics of Mithila Art', *American Ethnologist*, vol. 23/4 (1996): 717–37.

Brown, Percy, *Indian Painting under the Mughals, AD 1550 to AD 1750* (Oxford: Clarendon Press, 1924).

Brown, Rebecca M., *Art for a Modern India 1947–1980* (Durham, NC: Duke University Press, 2009).

Brown, Robert L., 'Narrative as Icon: The Jātaka Stories in Ancient Indian and Southeast Asian Architecture', in Juliane Schober (ed.), *Sacred Biography in Buddhist Traditions of South and Southeast Asia* (Honolulu: University of Hawaii Press, 1997), 64–109.

Bublatzky, Catherine, *Along the* Indian Highway: *An Ethnography of an International Travelling Exhibition* (London and New Delhi: Routledge, 2019).

Buchloh, Benjamin H. D., 'Interview: Benjamin H. D. Buchloh and Jean-Hubert Martin', *Third Text*, vol. 3/6 (1989): 19–27.

– 'The Whole Earth Show: An Interview with Jean-Hubert Martin', *Art in America*, vol. 77/5 (1989): 150–59, 211, 213.

Buck-Morss, Susan, *The Dialectics of Seeing: Walter Benjamin and the Arcades Project* (Cambridge, MA: MIT Press, 1989).

– *Hegel, Haiti, and Universal History* (Pittsburgh: University of Pittsburgh Press, 2009).

Bunzl, Matti and H. Glenn Penny (eds.), *Worldly Provincialism: German Anthropology in the Age of Empire* (Ann Arbor: University of Michigan Press, 2003).

Burckhardt, Jacob, *Die Kultur der Renaissance in Italien* (Stuttgart: A. Kröner Verlag, 2009; orig. 1860).

– *Weltgeschichtliche Betrachtungen* (Munich: Beck Verlag, 2018; orig. 1868).

– 'Kunstgeschichte', in *Allgemeine deutsche Real-Enzyklopädie für die gebildeten Stände: Conversations-Lexikon*, 15 vols., 9th edition (Leipzig: Brockhaus, 1843–1848), vol. 8, 435–36.

Bürger, Peter, *Theory of the Avant-Garde* (Minneapolis: University of Minnesota Press, 1996).

Burke, Peter, 'Representations of the Self from Petrarch to Descartes', in Roy Porter (ed.), *Rewriting the Self: Histories from the Renaissance to the Present* (London and New York: Routledge, 1997), 17–28.

Büttner, Frank, Rezension von Hans Belting, *Florenz und Bagdad: Eine west-östliche Geschichte des Blicks*, *Kunstchronik*, vol. 62/2 (2009): 82–89.

Butler, Judith and Gayatri C. Spivak, *Who sings the Nation-State? Language, Politics, Belonging* (New York and Calcutta: Seagull Books, 2007).

Canby, Sheila R. (ed.), *Humayun's Garden Party: Princes of the House of Timur and Early Mughal Painting* (Mumbai: Marg Publications, 1994).

Carr, E. Summerson and Michael Lempert (eds.), *Scale: Discourse and Dimensions of Social Life* (Oakland: University of California Press, 2016).

Carrier, David, *A World Art History and its Objects* (University Park: Penn State University Press, 2008).

Casanova, Pascale, *The World Republic of Letters* (Cambridge, MA: Harvard University Press, 2004).

Casid, Jill H. and Aruna D'Souza (eds.), *Art History in the Wake of the Global Turn* (New Haven: Yale University Press, 2014).

Castells, Manuel, *The Informational City: Information Technology, Economic Restructuring and the Urban-Regional Process* (Oxford: Blackwell, 1989).

Certeau, Michel de, *L'invention du quotidien: Arts de faire* (Paris: Union générale d'éditions, 1980).

Chakrabarty, Dipesh, *Habitations of Modernity: Essays in the Wake of Subaltern Studies* (Delhi: Permanent Black, 2002).

– *Provincializing Europe: Postcolonial Thought and Historical Difference* (Princeton: Princeton University Press, 2000).

– *The Climate of History in a Planetary Age* (Chicago: University of Chicago Press, 2021).

– 'Legacies of Bandung: Decolonization and the Politics of Culture', in Saurabh Dube (ed.), *Enchantments of Modernity: Empire, Nation, Globalization* (London and New Delhi: Routledge, 2009), 264–87.

– 'Museums in Late Democracies', *Humanities Research*, vol. IX/1 (2002): 5–12.

Chandra, Pramod, *On the Study of Indian Art* (Cambridge, MA: Harvard University Press, 1983).

Chang, Johnson and Chaitanya Sambrani, *Place, Time, Play: Contemporary Art from the West Heavens to the Middle Kingdom* (Hong Kong: Hanart TZ Gallery, 2012).

Chatterji, Roma, *Speaking with Pictures: Folk Art and the Narrative Tradition in India* (New Delhi: Routledge, 2012).

Chattopadhyay, Swati, *Representing Calcutta: Modernity, Nationalism and the Colonial Uncanny* (London: Routledge, 2005).

Chawla, Rupika, *Raja Ravi Varma: Painter of Colonial India* (Ahmedabad: Mapin Publishers, 2010).

Cheah, Pheng, *What is a World? On Postcolonial Literature as World Literature* (Durham, NC: Duke University Press, 2016).

– 'What Is a World? On World Literature as World-making Activity', *Daedalus*, vol. 137/3 (2008): 26–38.

Chen, Kuan-Hsing, *Asia as Method: Toward Deimperialization* (Durham, NC: Duke University Press, 2010).

Ciotti, Manuela, 'Post-colonial Renaissance: "Indianness", Contemporary Art and the Market in the Age of Neoliberal Capital', *Third World Quarterly*, vol. 33/4 (2012): 633–51.

Clark, John, *Modern Asian Art* (Honolulu: University of Hawaii Press, 1998).

Clifford, James, *Returns: Becoming Indigenous in the Twenty First Century* (Cambridge, MA: Harvard University Press, 2013).

– *Routes: Travel and Translation in the Late Twentieth Century* (Cambridge, MA: Harvard University Press, 1999).

– 'Histories of the Tribal and the Modern', *Art in America*, vol. 73/4 (1985): 164–77, 215.

– 'The Others. Beyond the "Salvage" Paradigm', *Third Text*, vol. 3/6 (1989): 73–77.

Cohen, Joshua I., *The 'Black Art' Renaissance: African Sculpture and Modernism Across Continents* (Oakland: University of California Press, 2020).

– 'Fauve Masks: Rethinking Modern "Primitivist" Uses of African and Oceanic Art', *The Art Bulletin*, vol. 99/2 (2017): 136–65.

– 'Picasso and Primitive Art: Paris, Kansas City and Montreal', *The Burlington Magazine*, vol. 159 (2017): 944–45.

Cohn, Bernard S., *Colonialism and its Forms of Knowledge: The British in India* (Princeton: Princeton University Press, 1996).

Conrad, Sebastian, *What Is Global History?* (Princeton: Princeton University Press, 2017).

Conrad, Sebastian and Dominic Sachsenmaier (eds.), *Competing Visions of World Order: Global Moments and Movements, 1880s–1930s* (New York: Palgrave Macmillan, 2008).

Contadini, Anna and Claire Norton (eds.), *The Renaissance and the Ottoman World* (Farnham, Surrey: Ashgate Publishing, 2013).

Cook, Jill (ed.), *Ice Age Art: The Arrival of the Modern Mind* (London: The British Museum Press, 2013).

Coomaraswamy, Ananda K., *Rajput Painting: Being an Account of Hindu Paintings of Rajasthan and the Punjab Himalayas from the Sixteenth to the Nineteenth Century Described in Their Relation to Contemporary Thought*, 2 vols. (Delhi: Motilal Banarsidass, 1976; orig. 1916).

Coronil, Fernando, 'Introduction', in Fernando Ortiz, *Cuban Counterpoint: Tobacco and Sugar*, (1947), trans. by Harriet Onís (Durham, NC: Duke University Press, 1995), ix–lvi.

Correa, Alice and Natasha Eaton (eds.), *Third Text*, Special Issue: Partitions, Dissonance, Art – A case for South Asia, vol. 31 2/3 (2017).

Cosgrove, Denis, *Apollo's Eye: A Cartographic Genealogy of the Earth in the Western Imagination* (Baltimore: Johns Hopkins University Press, 2001).

Cox, Geoff and Jacob Lund, *The Contemporary Condition: Introductory Thoughts on Contemporaneity and Contemporary Art* (Berlin: Sternberg Press, 2016).

Craven, David, *Art and Revolution in Latin America: 1910–1990* (New Haven: Yale University Press, 2002).

Dadi, Iftikhar, *Modernism and the Art of Muslim South Asia* (Chapel Hill: University of North Carolina Press, 2010).

Dadi, Iftikhar and Hammad Nasar (eds.), *Lines of Control. Partition as Productive Space* (London: Green Cardamom, 2012).

Dadi, Iftikhar and Suheyla Takesh (eds.), *Taking Shape: Abstraction from the Arab World, 1950s–1980s* (New York: Grey Art Gallery, 2020).

Dalmia, Yashodhara, *The Making of Modern Indian Art: The Progressives* (New Delhi: Oxford University Press, 2006).

Damisch, Hubert, *L'origine de la perspective* (Paris: Flammarion, 1987).

Damme, Wilfried van, 'Ernst Grosse and the "Ethnological Method" in Art History', *Philosophy and Literature*, vol. 34/2 (2010): 302–12.

– '"Good to Think": The Historiography of Intercultural Art Studies', *World Art*, vol. 1/1 (2011): 43–57.

Damme, Wilfried van and Raymond Corbey (eds.), 'The European Scholarly Reception of "Primitive Art" in the Decades around 1900', *Journal of Art Historiography*, vol. 12 (June 2015).

Danto, Arthur, 'The Artworld', *Journal of Philosophy*, vol. 61/19 (1964): 571–84.

Das, Asok K., 'Farrukh Beg: Studies of Adorable Youths and Venerable Saints', *Marg*, special issue Mughal Masters: Further Studies, vol. 49/4 (1998): 96–111.

– 'Transformation in Jahangir's Taswirkhana', in Canby (ed.), *Humayun's Garden Party*, 135–52.

Das, Aurogeeta, *Jangarh Singh Shyam: The Enchanted Forest. Paintings and Drawings from the Crites Collection* (New Delhi: Roli Books, 2017).

Dasgupta, Anshuman (ed.), *Santhal Family: Positions Around an Indian Sculpture* (Antwerpen: MUHKA, 2009).

David, Catherine, 'Roundtable: Global Tendencies. Globalism and the Large-Scale Exhibition', introduced by Tim Griffin, *Artforum*, vol. 52/3 (2003): 153–63; 206–12.

Davis, Natalie Z., *Trickster Travels: A Sixteenth Century Muslim Between Worlds* (New York: Hill and Wang, 2007).

Davis, Richard H., *Lives of Indian Images* (Princeton: Princeton University Press, 1997).

– 'From the Wedding Chamber to the Museum: Relocating the Ritual Arts of Madhubani', in Jan Mrázek and Morgan Pitelka (eds.), *What's the Use of Art? Asian Visual and Material Culture in Context* (Honolulu: University of Hawaii Press, 2008), 77–99.

Davis, Heather and Etienne Turpin (eds.), *Art in the Anthropocene: Encounters among Aesthetics, Politics, Environments and Epistemologies* (London: Open Humanities Press, 2015).

Dean, Carolyn and Dana Leibsohn, 'Hybridity and its Discontents: Considering Visual Culture in Colonial Spanish America', *Colonial Latin American Review*, vol. 12/1 (2003): 5–35.

Dean, Rob and Giles Tillotson (eds.), *Modern Indian Painting: Jane and Kito de Boer Collection* (Ahmedabad: Mapin, 2019).

Dehejia, Vidya, *Discourse in Early Buddhist Art: Visual Narratives of India* (New Delhi: Munshiram Manoharlal, 2005).

Deliss, Clémentine, 'Conjuring Tricks: "Magiciens de la Terre"', *Artscribe International*, no. 77 (September–October 1989): 48–53.

– (ed.), *Object Atlas: Fieldwork in the Museum* (Berlin: Kerber Verlag, 2012).

Demos, T. J., *The Exiles of Marcel Duchamp* (Cambridge, MA: MIT Press, 2007).

– *The Migrant Image: The Art and Politics of Documentary during Global Crisis* (Durham, NC: Duke University Press, 2013).

– 'The Art and Politics of Ecology in India: A Roundtable with Ravi Agarwal and Sanjay Kak', *Third Text*, vol. 27/1 (2013): 151–61.

– *Decolonizing Nature: Contemporary Art and the Politics of Ecology* (Berlin: Sternberg Press, 2016).

– *Against the Anthropocene: Visual Culture and Environment Today* (Berlin: Sternberg Press, 2017).

Derrida, Jacques, *La verité en peinture* (Paris: Flammarion, 1978).

Dickel, Hans, *Natur in der zeitgenössischen Kunst: Konstellationen jenseits von Landschaft und Materialästhetik* (Munich: Verlag Silke Schreiber, 2016).

Dilly, Heinrich, *Kunstgeschichte als Institution: Studien zur Geschichte einer Disziplin* (Frankfurt am Main: Suhrkamp Verlag, 1979).

Dissanayake, Ellen, 'The Arts after Darwin: Does Art have an Origin and Adaptive Function?', in Zijlmans and van Damme (eds.), *World Art Studies*, 241–63.

Dogramaci, Burcu, 'Kunstgeschichte in Istanbul: Die Begründung der Disziplin durch den Wiener Kunsthistoriker Ernst Diez', in Ruth Heftrig, Olaf Peters and Barbara Schellewald (eds.), *Kunstgeschichte im 'Dritten Reich': Theorien, Methoden, Praktiken* (Berlin: Akademie Verlag, 2008), 114–33.

Dogramaci, Burcu and Birgit Mersmann (eds.), *Handbook of Art and Global Migration: Theories, Practices, and Challenges* (Berlin: De Gruyter, 2019).

Dommann, Monika, 'Alles fließt: soll die Geschichte nomadischer werden?', *Geschichte und Gesellschaft*, vol. 42/3 (2016): 516–34.

Dornhof, Sara, Nanne Buurman, Birgit Hopfener and Barbara Lutz (eds.), *Situating Global Art: Topologies – Temporalities – Trajectories* (Bielefeld: Transcript, 2018).

Doshi, Saryu (ed.), *Pageant of Indian Art: Festival of India in Great Britain* (Bombay: Marg Publications, 1983).

Draxler, Helmut (ed.), *Andrea Fraser, Christian Philipp Müller and Gerwald Rockenschaub: Österreichs Beitrag zur 45. Biennale von Venedig 1993* (Cologne: König, 1993), 185–203.

Du Crest, Sabine, *L'Art de Vivre Ensemble. Objets Frontière de la Renaissance au XXIe Siècle* (Rome: Gangemi Editore International, 2017).

Dube, Saurabh (ed.), *Handbook of Modernity in South Asia: Modern Makeovers* (New Delhi: Oxford University Press, 2011).

Duchamp, Marcel, 'Apropos of "Readymades"', in Michel Sanouillet and Elmer Peterson (eds.), *The Writings of Marcel Duchamp* (New York: Oxford University Press, 1973), 141–42.

– 'The Creative Act', in Sanouillet and Peterson (eds.), *The Writings of Marcel Duchamp*, 138–40.

Duda, Dorothea, 'Die Kaiserin und der Großmogul: Untersuchungen zu den Miniaturen des Millionenzimmers im Schloß Schönbrunn', in Karin K. Troschke (ed.), *Malerei auf Papier und Pergament in den Prunkräumen des Schlosses Schönbrunn* (Vienna: Schloss Schönbrunn, 1997), 33–55.

Dumbadze, Alexander and Suzanne Hudson (eds.), *Contemporary Art. 1989 to the Present* (Chichester: Wiley-Blackwell, 2013).

Dye III, Joseph M., 'A Bibliography of the Writings of Stella Kramrisch', in Stoler Miller (ed.), *Exploring India's Sacred Art*, 35–48.

Earle, Thomas F. and Kate J.P. Lowe (eds.), *Black Africans in Renaissance Europe* (Cambridge: Cambridge University Press, 2005).

Eather, Michael (ed.), *Dreamtime: Zeitgenössische Aboriginal Art* (Klosterneuburg: Ed. Sammlung Essl, 2001).

Eaton, Natasha, *Mimesis across Empires: Artworks and Networks in India, 1765-1860* (Durham, NC: Duke University Press, 2013).

– 'Nomadism of Colour: Painting, Technology and Waste in the Chromo-zones of Colonial India ca. 1765– ca. 1860', *Journal of Material Culture*, vol. 17/1 (2012): 61–81.

– 'Notes from the Field: Materiality', *The Art Bulletin*, vol. 95/1 (2014): 10–38.

Eaton, Richard M., *India in the Persianate Age 1000-1765* (London/New Delhi: Penguin Random House, 2019).

Eck, Diana L., *Darśan: Seeing the Divine Image in India* (New York: Columbia University Press, 1996).

Eckert, Andreas, 'Bringing the "Black Atlantic" into Global History: The Project of Pan-Africanism', in Conrad and Sachsenmaier (eds.), *Competing Visions*, 237–57.

Einstein, Carl, *Negerplastik* (Munich: Wolff, 1915).

Elias, Jamal J., *Aisha's Cushion: Religious Art, Perception and Practice in Islam* (Cambridge, MA: Harvard University Press, 2012).

Elkins, James, *The End of Diversity in Art Historical Writing: North Atlantic Art History and Its Alternatives* (Berlin: De Gruyter, 2021).

– 'Afterword', in Kaufmann, Dossin and Joyeux-Prunel (eds.), *Circulations in the Global History of Art*, 203–29.

–   'Different Horizons for a Concept of the Image', in James Elkins, *On Pictures and Words that Fail Them* (Cambridge: Cambridge University Press, 1998), 188–209.

–   Review of *Real Spaces*, *The Art Bulletin*, vol. 86/2 (2004): 373–81.

–   (ed.), *Is Art History Global?* (New York: Routledge, 2007).

Elkins, James, Zhivka Valiavicharska and Alice Kim (eds.), *Art and Globalization* (University Park: Penn State University Press, 2010).

Elliott, Mark J., 'Sculptural Biographies in an Anthropological Collection: Mrs Milward's Indian "Types"', in Kate Hill (ed.), *Museums and Biographies: Stories, Objects, Identities* (Woodbridge: Boydell Press, 2012), 215–28.

Elshahed, Mohamed, 'Egypt Builds: A Revaluation of the History of Modernism', in Georg Schöllhammer and Rubin Arevshatyan (eds.), *Sweet Sixties: Specters and Spirits of a Parallel Avant-Garde* (Berlin: Sternberg Press, 2014), 137–49.

Elsner, Jaś, 'The Birth of Late Antiquity: Riegl and Strzygowski in 1901', *Art History*, vol. 25/3 (2002): 358–79.

–   'Style', in Robert S. Nelson and Richard Shiff (eds.), *Critical Terms for Art History* (Chicago: University of Chicago Press, 2003), 98–109.

–   (ed.), *Comparativism in Art History* (London and New York: Routledge 2017).

Enwezor, Okwui, 'Modernity and Postcolonial Ambivalence', *South Atlantic Quarterly*, vol. 109/3 (2010): 595–620.

–   'The Black Box', in Enwezor (ed.), *Documenta 11: Platform 5* (Ostfildern: Hatje Cantz, 2002), 42–55.

–   'The Judgment of Art: Postwar Art and Artistic Worldliness', in Enwezor et al. (eds.), *Postwar*, 20–41.

–   (ed.), *Archive Fever: Uses of the Document in Contemporary Art* (Göttingen: Steidl, 2008).

Enwezor, Okwui and Atreyee Gupta (eds.), *Postwar – A Global History, 1945–1965* (Durham, NC: Duke University Press [forthcoming]).

Enwezor, Okwui and Chika Okeke-Agulu (eds.), *Contemporary African Art Since 1980* (Bologna: Damiani, 2009).

Enwezor, Okwui, Katy Siegel and Ulrich Wilmes (eds.), *Postwar: Art between the Pacific and the Atlantic, 1945–1965* (Prestel: Munich, 2016).

Enwezor, Okwui and Olu Oguibe, 'Introduction', in *Reading the Contemporary: African Art from Theory to the Marketplace* (Cambridge, MA: MIT Press, 2000), 9–14.

Epple, Angelika, 'Globale Mikrogeschichte: Auf dem Weg zu einer Geschichte der Relationen', in Ewald Hiebl and Ernst Langthaler (eds.), *Im Kleinen das Große suchen: Mikrogeschichte in Theorie und Praxis* (Innsbruck and Vienna: Studien Verlag, 2012), 37–47.

Ettinghausen, Richard, 'The Emperor's Choice', in Millard Meiss (ed.), *De Artibus Opuscula: Essays in Honor of Erwin Panofsky* (New York: New York University Press, 1961), 98–120.

Ettlinger, L. D., 'German Expressionism and Primitive Art', *The Burlington Magazine*, vol. 110 (1968): 191–201.

Fabian, Johannes, *Time and the Other: How Anthropology Makes its Object* (New York, Columbia University Press, 1983).

Fanon, Frantz, *The Wretched of the Earth* (London: Penguin Books, 1967).

Farago, Claire J., *Cultural Memory in an Era of Climate Crisis: Writing Borderless Histories of Art* (London: Routledge [forthcoming 2023]).

–   *Leonardo da Vinci's Paragone: A Critical Interpretation with a New Edition of the Text in the Codex Urbinas* (Leiden: Brill, 1992).

–   'The Status of the "State as a Work of Art": Re-Viewing Burckhardt's Renaissance from the Borderlines', in Gunnar Sorelius and Michael Srigley (eds.), *Cultural Exchange between European Nations during the Renaissance* (Uppsala: Almquist & Wiksell, 1994), 17–32.

–   'Artisanal Epistemologies and Artless Art of Post-Tridentine Painting', in Camilla S. Paldam and Jacob Wamberg (eds.), *Art, Technology and Nature: Renaissance to Postmodernity* (Farnham: Ashgate Publishers, 2015), 117–32.

–   'Imagining Art History Otherwise', in Jane C. Davidson and Sandra Esslinger (eds.), *Global and World Art in the Practice of the University Museum* (Routledge: London and New York, 2017), 115–30.

–   'The "Global Turn" in Art History: Why, When, and How Does it Matter?', in Savoy (ed.), *The Globalization of Renaissance Art*, 299–313.

–   '"Vision Itself Has Its History": "Race", Nation and Renaissance Art', in Farago (ed.), *Reframing the Renaissance*, 67–88.

– (ed.), *Reframing the Renaissance: Visual Culture in Europe and Latin America, 1450–1650* (New Haven: Yale University Press, 1995).

– Review of Hans Belting, *Florence and Baghdad: Renaissance Art and Arab Science, Renaissance Quarterly*, vol. 65/3 (2012): 879–81.

– 'The Future of the Past: What Comes After World Art History?', in Helen Westgeest and Kitty Zijlmans (eds.), *Mix and Stir: New Outlooks on Contemporary Art from Global Perspectives* (Valiz: Amsterdam, 2021), 395–400.

– '"The whole world in his hands": A Decolonial Approach to European Concepts of Art', in Amelia Jones and Jane C. Davidson (eds.), *A Companion to Contemporary Art in a Global Framework* (Oxford: Wiley Blackwell [forthcoming 2023]).

Fisher, Jean, 'The Syncretic Turn: Cross-Cultural Practices in the Age of Multiculturalism', in Zoya Kocur and Simon Leung (eds.), *Theory in Contemporary Art Since 1985* (Malden: Blackwell, 2008), 233–41.

– 'Fictional Histories: "Magiciens de la Terre" – The Invisible Labyrinth', *Artforum*, 28/1 (1989): 158–62.

– 'Other Cartographies', *Third Text*, vol. 3/6 (1989): 79–82.

Flam, Jack D. and Miriam Deutsch (eds.), *Primitivism and Twentieth-Century Art: A Documentary History* (Berkeley: University of California Press, 2003).

Flood, Finbarr B., *Objects of Translation: Material Culture and Medieval 'Hindu-Muslim' Encounter* (Princeton: Princeton University Press, 2009).

– 'Between Cult and Culture: Bamiyan, Islamic Iconoclasm and the Museum', *The Art Bulletin*, vol. 84/4, (2002): 641–59.

Flores, Patrick, 'Errant in Form', in Asia Art Archives, *An Expanded Questionnaire on the Contemporary*, 22–23.

– 'The Possibility of a World Art History', Round Table with John Clark, Parul D. Mukherji, Omuka Toshiharu, Patrick Flores and Woo Jung-Ah, *Australian and New Zealand Journal of Art,* vol. 9/1–2 (2008): 42–47.

Foster, Hal, 'An Archival Impulse', *October*, Issue 110 (Fall 2004): 3–22.

– 'The "Primitive" Unconscious of Modern Art', *October,* Issue 34 (Autumn 1985): 45–70.

– 'What's Neo about the Neo-Avant-Garde?', *October,* Issue 70 (Fall 1994): 5–32.

Foster, Hal, Rosalind Krauss, Yves-Alain Bois and Benjamin H. D. Buchloh, *Art Since 1900: Modernism, Antimodernism, Postmodernism* (London: Thames and Hudson, 2004).

Frankel, Lory (ed.), *Festival of India in the United States* (New York: Harry Abrams, 1985).

Frodl-Kraft, Eva, 'Eine Aporie und der Versuch ihrer Deutung: Josef Strzygowski – Julius von Schlosser', *Wiener Jahrbuch für Kunstgeschichte*, vol. 42/1 (1989): 7–52.

Fulda, Bernhard, 'Noldes Autobiografie: Das verkannte Genie im Kampf um die deutsche Kunst', in Bernhard Fulda, Christian Ring and Aya Soyika (eds.), *Emil Nolde: Eine Deutsche Legende*, 2 vols. (Munich: Prestel Verlag, 2019), vol. I, 69–75.

Gallop, Annabel T., 'The Genealogical Seal of the Mughal Emperors of India', *Journal of the Royal Asiatic Society*, vol. 9/1 (1999): 77–140.

Gänger, Stefanie, 'Circulation: Reflections on Circularity, Entity, and Liquidity in the Language of Global History', *Journal of Global History*, vol. 12/3 (2017): 303–18.

Gaonkar, Dilip P., 'On Alternative Modernities', *Public Culture*, vol. 11/1 (1999): 1–18.

Gardner, Helen, *Art through the Ages*, 2 vols. (Washington DC: Harcourt Brace, 1926; 13th edition).

Gareis, Sigrid, *Exotik in München: Museumsethnologische Konzeptionen im historischen Wandel am Beispiel des Staatlichen Museums für Völkerkunde München* (Munich: Anacon-Verlag, 1990).

Garimella, Annapurna, *Vernacular, in the Contemporary*, 2 vols. (New Delhi: Devi Art Foundation, 2010–11).

– 'Aboriginalisthan in the Gallery', in Hill et al. (eds.), *Sakahān*, 72–84.

Gell, Alfred, *Art and Agency: An Anthropological Theory* (Oxford: Clarendon Press, 1998).

Genge, Gabriele (ed.), *Art History and Fetishism Abroad: Global Shiftings in Media and Methods* (Bielefeld: Transcript Verlag, 2014).

Gerritsen, Anne and Giorgio Riello (eds.), *The Global Lives of Things: The Material Culture of Connections in the Early Modern World* (London: Routledge, 2017).

Geschiere, Peter, *The Perils of Belonging: Autochthony, Citizenship, and Exclusion in Africa and Europe* (Chicago: University of Chicago Press, 2009).

Ghose, Madhuvanti (ed.), *Jitish Kallat: Public Notice 3* (Chicago: Art Institute of Chicago, 2011).

Ghosh, Amitav, *The Great Derangement: Climate Change and the Unthinkable* (Chicago: University of Chicago Press, 2017).
- *The Nutmeg's Curse: Parables for a Planet in Crisis* (Chicago: University of Chicago Press, 2021).
Gibson, Ann, 'Avant-Garde', in Robert S. Nelson and Richard Shiff (eds.), *Critical Terms for Art History* (Chicago: University of Chicago Press, 2003, 2nd edition), 202–16.
Gikandi, Simon, 'Picasso, Africa and the Schemata of Difference', *Modernism/Modernity*, vol. 10/3 (2003): 455–80.
- 'Preface: Modernism in the World', *Modernism/Modernity*, vol. 13/3 (2006): 419–24.
Ginwala, Natasha (ed.), *My East is Your West: A Collateral Event at the 56th Venice Biennale* (New Delhi: Harper Collins, 2016).
- (ed.), *Jitish Kallat* (Ahmedabad: Mapin Publishing, 2018).
Ginzburg, Carlo, 'Clues: Roots of an Evidential Paradigm', in *Clues, Myths, and the Historical Method* (Baltimore: Johns Hopkins University Press, 1989) 96–125.
Glaser, Curt, 'Die Chinesische Kunst', in Springer, *Handbuch*, vol. VI, 3–121.
- 'Vorwort', in Springer, *Handbuch*, vol. VI, vii–ix.
Göttler, Christine and Mia Mochizuki (eds.), *The Nomadic Object: The Challenge of World for Early Modern Religious Art* (Leiden: E.J. Brill, 2018).
Gombrich, Ernst H., *The Story of Art* (London: Phaidon, 1950, 1st edition).
Gonzales, Valerie, 'Confronting Images, Confronted Images: Jahangir versus King James I in the Freer Gallery Mughal Group Portrait by Bichitr (circa 1620)', in Frank Peter, Sarah Dornhof and Elena Arigita (eds.), *Islam and the Politics of Culture in Europe: Memory, Aesthetics, Art* (Bielefeld: Transcript Verlag, 2013), 219–35.
Goodman, Nelson, *Ways of Worldmaking* (Indianapolis: Hackett, 1978).
Goswamy, B. N. and Eberhard Fischer, *Wonders of a Golden Age: Painting at the Court of the Great Mughals* (Zurich: Museum Rietberg, 1987).
Grabar, Oleg, 'The Implications of Collecting Islamic Art', in Stephen Vernoit (ed.), *Discovering Islamic Art: Scholars, Collectors and Collections 1850–1950* (London: I. B. Tauris, 2000), 194–200.
Gray, Basil, 'The Art of India and Pakistan with Special Reference to the Exhibition at the Royal Academy', *Journal of the Royal Society of Arts*, vol. 96/4758 (1947): 75–81, 69–72 (plates).
- 'The Mughal School', in Barrett and Gray (eds.), *Painting of India*, 76–114.
Greenblatt, Stephen, 'A Mobility Studies Manifesto', in Stephen Greenblatt, Ines Zupanov et al. (eds.), *Cultural Mobility: A Manifesto*, Cambridge (Cambridge University Press, 2010), 250–53.
Greenough, Paul, 'Nation, Economy, and Tradition Displayed: The Indian Crafts Museum, New Delhi', in Carol A. Breckenridge (ed.), *Consuming Modernity: Public Culture in a South Asian World* (Minneapolis: University of Minnesota Press, 1995), 216–48.
Grosse, Ernst, *Die Anfänge der Kunst* (Freiburg: J. C. B. Mohr, 1894).
- 'Ethnologie und Ästhetik', *Vierteljahrsschrift für wissenschaftliche Philosophie*, 15 (1891): 392–417.
Grossman, Wendy A., 'From Ethnographic Object to Modernist Icon: Photographs of African and Oceanic Sculpture and the Rhetoric of the Image', *Visual Resources*, vol. 23/4 (2007): 291–336.
Guha, Ramachandra, *Savaging the Civilized: Verrier Elwin, His Tribals and India* (Chicago: University of Chicago Press, 1999).
Guha-Thakurta, Tapati, *In the Name of the Goddess: The Durga Pujas of Contemporary Kolkata* (Delhi: Primus Books, 2015).
- *Monuments, Objects, Histories: Institutions of Art in Colonial and Post-Colonial India* (New Delhi: Permanent Black, 2004).
- *The Making of a New 'Indian' Art: Artists, Aesthetics and Nationalism in Bengal, c. 1850–1920* (Cambridge: Cambridge University Press, 1992; repr. 2008).
- 'Marking Independence: The Ritual of a National Art Exhibition', *Journal of Arts and Ideas*, nos. 30–31 (1997): 89–114.
Guhl, Ernst and Wilhelm Lübke, *Denkmäler der Kunst zur Übersicht ihres Entwickelungs-Ganges von den ersten künstlerischen Versuchen bis zu den Standpunkten der Gegenwart* (Stuttgart: Ebner & Seubert, 1851–56), 4 vols.
Guilbaut, Serge, *How New York Stole the Idea of Modern Art: Abstract Expressionism, Freedom and the Cold War*, trans. Arthur Goldhammer (Chicago: University of Chicago Press, 1983).

Gupta, Atreyee, 'After Bandung: Transacting the Nation in a Postcolonial World', in Enwezor et al. (eds.), *Postwar*, 632–37.
– 'Art History and the Global Challenge: A Critical Perspective', *Artl@as Bulletin*, vol. 6/1 (2017): 20–25.
– 'On Territorialty, Temporality, and the Politics of Place', in Asia Art Archives, *An Expanded Questionnaire on the Contemporary*, 73–80.
– 'The Global, the Local, the Contemporary, the Collaborative: *Ghari/Ghar Pe/At Home*, Dharavi, Mumbai, 2012', in Hutton and Brown (eds.), *Rethinking Place in South Asian and Islamic Art*, 78–93.
– 'Francis Newton Souza's Black Paintings: Postwar Transactions in Color', *The Art Bulletin*, vol. 103/4 (2021): 111–37.
Gupta, Latika, 'Pushpamala N. And Clare Arni', in Jodi Throckmorton (ed.), *Postdate: Photography and Inherited History in India* (Berkeley: University of California Press, 2015), 100–11.
Gupta, Narayani, 'The Age of Replacement', *The Indian Express*, 19 September 2019.
Guy, John and Jorrit Britschgi, *Wonder of the Age: Master Painters of India 1100–1900* (Ahmedabad: Mapin India, 2011).

Hacker, Katherine, '"A Simultaneous Validity of Co-Existing Cultures": J. Swaminathan, the Bharat Bhavan and Contemporaneity', *Archives of Asian Art*, vol. 64/2 (2014): 191–209.
Hagedorn, Annette, 'The Development of Islamic Art History in Germany in the Late Nineteenth and Early Twentieth Centuries', in Stephen Vernoit (ed.), *Discovering Islamic Art: Scholars, Collectors and Collections 1850–1950* (London: I. B. Tauris, 2000), 117–27.
Hall, Stuart, 'Creolization, Diaspora and Hybridity in the Context of Globalization', in Okwui Enwezor (ed.), *Creolité and Creolization: Documenta XI Platform 3* (Ostfildern: Hatje Cantz, 2003), 185–98.
Hannerz, Ulf, 'Notes on the Global Ecumene', *Public Culture*, vol. 1/2 (1989): 66–75.
Haraway, Donna, 'Situated Knowledges: The Science Question in Feminism and the Privilege of Partial Perspective', *Feminist Studies*, vol. 14/3 (1988): 575–99.
Hardtwig, Wolfgang, *Geschichtsschreibung zwischen Alteuropa und moderner Welt: Jacob Burckhardt in seiner Zeit* (Göttingen: Vandenhoeck & Ruprecht, 1974).
Harney, Elizabeth, *In Senghor's Shadow: Art, Politics, and the Avant-Garde in Senegal, 1960–1995* (Durham, NC: Duke University Press, 2004).
– 'Postcolonial Agitations: Avant-gardism in Dakar and London', *New Literary History*, vol. 41/4 (2010): 731–51.
– 'The Densities of Modernism', *South Atlantic Quarterly*, vol. 109/3 (2010): 475–503.
Harney, Elizabeth and Ruth B. Phillips (eds.), *Mapping Modernisms: Art, Indigeneity, Colonialism* (Durham, NC: Duke University Press, 2018).
Harris, Jonathan (ed.), *Globalization and Contemporary Art* (Malden, MA: Wiley-Blackwell, 2011).
Hartney, Eleanor, 'The Whole Earth Show', *Art in America*, vol. 77/7 (1989): 91–97.
Hassan, Salah M., *Ibrahim El-Salahi: A Visionary Modernist* (Seattle: University of Washington Press, 2012).
Havell, E. B., Review of Stella Kramrisch *Grundzüge der indischen Kunst*, *Rupam*, nos. 27–29 (July–October, 1926): 74–77.
Hayum, Andrée, 'The 1902 Exhibition, Les Primitifs flamands: Scholarly Fallout and Art Historical Reflections', *Journal of Art Historiography*, no. 11/2 (2014): 1–20.
Hergott, Fabrice, 'Réponses au Questionnaire: "Accrocher une Oeuvre d'Art"', *Cahiers du Musée nationale d'art moderne*, nos. 17/18 (1986): 204–15.
Hill, Greg A., Candice Hopkins and Christine Lalonde (ed.), *Sakahàn: International Indigenous Art* (Ottawa: National Gallery of Canada, 2013).
Hiller, Susan (ed.), *The Myth of Primitivism: Perspectives on Art* (London: Routledge, 1991).
Hlavajova, Maria and Simon Sheikh (eds.), *Former West: Art and the Contemporary after 1989* (Cambridge, MA and Utrecht: MIT Press/BAK, 2017).
Hog, Michael, *Ziele und Konzeptionen der Völkerkundemuseen in ihrer historischen Entwicklung* (Frankfurt am Main: R. G. Fischer Verlag, 1981).
Horn, Eva and Hannes Bergthaller, *Anthropozän zur Einführung* (Hamburg: Junius, 2020, 2nd, expanded edition).
Hoskote, Ranjit, 'Atul Dodiya: An Encyclopaedist's Desire for the World', in idem (ed.), *Atul Dodiya* (Munich: Prestel, 2013), 12–87.

–   'Biennials of Resistance: Reflections of the Seventh Gwangju Biennial', in Elena Filipovic, Mareike van Hal, Solvieg Øvstebø (eds.), *The Biennial Reader* (Ostfildern: Hatje Cantz, 2010), 306–21.
–   'Everyone Agrees: It's About to Explode', *Seminar*, 2014, http://www.india-seminar.com/2014/659/659_ranjit_hoskote.htm.
–   'Kaleidoscopic Propositions: The Evolving Contexts of Contemporary Indian Art', in Christian Gether et al. (eds.), *India: Art Now* (Ostfildern: Hatje Cantz, 2012), 54–62.
–   'Now that the Trees Have Spoken', *Pundoleartgallery.in*, exhibition brochure, 2009.
–   'Signposting the Indian Highway', in *Indian Highway*, 190–93.
–   'The Afterlife of the Past, the Mimesis of Climate: Jitish Kallat's Interventions in the Space and Time of the Museum', in Ginwala (ed.), *Jitish Kallat*, 234–71.
Hoskote, Ranjit and Nancy Adajania (eds.), *Atul Dodiya: The Dialogue Series* (Mumbai: Popular Prakashan, 2011).
Hulks, David, 'World Art Studies: A Radical Proposition?', *World Art*, vol. 3/2 (2013): 189–200.
Hung, Wu, *The Double Screen: Medium and Representation in Chinese Painting* (Chicago: Chicago University Press, 1996).
Hunt, Lynn A., *Writing History in a Global Era* (New York: Norton, 2014).
Hutton, Deborah S., 'Portraits of "A Noble Queen": Chand Bibi in the Historical Imaginary', in Aitken (ed.), *A Magic World*, 50–63.
Hutton, Deborah S. and Rebecca M. Brown (eds.), *Rethinking Place in South Asian and Islamic Art, 1500-present* (London and New York: Routledge, 2016).
Huyssen, Andreas, *William Kentridge and Nalini Malani: The Shadow Play as Medium of Memory* (Milan: Edizione Charta, 2013).
–   *Present Pasts: Urban Palimpsests and the Politics of Memory* (Stanford: Stanford University Press, 2003).
–   *Twilight Memories: Marking Time in a Culture of Amnesia* (London: Routledge, 1995).
–   'Geographies of Modernism in a Globalizing World', *New German Critique*, vol. 34/1 (2007): 189–207.
–   'The Search for Tradition: Avant-Garde and Postmodernism in the 1970s', *New German Critique*, vol. 22 (Winter 1981): 23–40.
–   'The Memory Works of Vivan Sundaram', in Ananth and Schneider (eds.), *Vivan Sundaram: Disjunctures*, 88–101.

Ingold, Tim, *Making: Anthropology, Archaeology, Art and Architecture* (London: Routledge 2013).
Ingold, Tim and Gisli Palsson, *Biosocial Becomings: Integrating Social and Biological Anthropology* (Cambridge: Cambridge University Press, 2013).
Iversen, Margaret, 'Readymade, Found Object, Photograph', *Art Journal*, vol. 63/2 (2004): 45–57.
Iversen, Margaret and Stephen Melville, *Writing Art History: Disciplinary Departures* (Chicago: University of Chicago Press, 2010).

Jain, Jyotindra, *Ganga Devi: Tradition and Expression in Mithila Painting* (Ahmedabad: Mapin Publishing, 1997).
–   *Jangarh Singh Shyam: A Conjuror's Archive* (Bangalore: The Museum of Art and Photography, 2018).
–   'Ganga Devi: Tradition & Expression in Mithila Painting', *Third Text*, vol. 3/6 (1989): 43–50.
Jain, Kajri, *Gods in the Bazaar: The Economies of Indian Calendar Art* (Durham, NC: Duke University Press, 2007).
–   *Gods in the Time of Democracy* (Durham, NC: Duke University Press, 2021).
–   'India's Modern Vernacular – On the Edge', in Sambrani (ed.), *Edge of Desire*, 170–83.
Jakimowicz, Marta, 'The Self Versus Self-Images and the Cliché', in *Pushpamala N: Indian Lady* (New York: Bose Pacia, 2004), n.p.
James, Rajesh and Sathyaraj Venkatesan, *India Retold: Dialogues with Independent Documentary Filmmakers in India* (London: Bloomsbury Academic, 2021).
Janson, Horst W., *History of Art* (London: Thames and Hudson, 2016, 8th edition).
Jantjes, Gavin, 'Red Rags to a Bull', in Rasheed Araeen (ed.), *The Other Story: Afro-Asian Artists in Post-War Britain* (London: Hayward Gallery, 1989), 125–127.
Jardine, Lisa and Jerry Brotton, *Global Interests: Renaissance Art between East and West* (London: Reaktion Books, 2000).

Jayakar, Pupul, *The Earthen Drum: An Introduction to the Ritual Arts of Rural India* (New Delhi: National Museum, 1980).

Johns, Karl, 'Josef Strzygowski (1862–1941)', *Journal of Art Historiography*, vol. 17 (2017): 1–46.

Jones, Owen, *The Grammar of Ornament* (London: Quarich, 1910).

Joselit, David, *Heritage and Debt: Art in Globalization* (Cambridge, MA: MIT Press, 2020).

Joyeux-Prunel, Béatrice, *Les avant-gardes artistiques 1918–1945: Une histoire transnationale* (Paris: Gallimard, 2017).

– 'Art History and the Global: Deconstructing the Latest Canonical Narrative', *Journal of Global History*, vol. 14/3 (2019): 413–35.

– 'Provincializing New York: In and Out of the Geopolitics of Art After 1945', *Artl@s Bulletin*, vol. 10/1 (2021): Article 12, https://docs.lib.purdue.edu/artlas/vol10/iss1/.

– 'Provincializing Paris: The Center-Periphery Narrative of Modern Art in Light of Quantitative and Transnational Approaches', *Artl@s Bulletin*, vol. 4/1 (2015): Article 4, https://hal.archives-ouvertes.fr/hal-01479104.

– 'The Global History of Art and the Challenge of the Grand Narrative', *Art@tlas Bulletin*, vol. 6/1 (2017): 3–5.

Jumabhoy, Zehra, 'A Progressive Revolution? The Modern and the Secular in Indian Art', in Jumabhoy and Tan (eds.), *The Progressive Revolution*, 18–19.

Jumabhoy, Zehra and Boon Hui Tan (eds.), *The Progressive Revolution: Modern Art for a New India* (New York: Asia Society, 2018).

Juneja, Monica, *Peindre le paysan: L'image rurale dans la peinture française de Millet à Van Gogh* (Paris: Editions du Makar, 1998).

– 'Alternative, Peripheral or Cosmopolitan? Modernism as a Global Process', in Allerstorfer and Leisch-Kiesl (eds.), *Global Art History: Transkulturelle Verortungen von Kunst und Kunstwissenschaft*, 79–108.

– '"A Very Civil Idea" … Art History, Transculturation, and World-Making – With and Beyond the Nation', *Zeitschrift für Kunstgeschichte*, vol. 81/4 (2018): 461–85.

– 'Braided Histories? Visuelle Praktiken des indischen Moghulreichs zwischen Mimesis und Alterität', *Historische Anthropologie*, vol. 16/2 (2008): 187–204.

– 'Das Visuelle in Sprache übersetzen? Der wissenschaftliche Diskurs und die Polyvalenz indischer Bilder', *Zeitenblicke*, vol. 7/2 (2008): http://www.zeitenblicke.de/2008/2/juneja/index_html.

– 'Global Art History and the "Burden of Representation"', in Belting et al. (eds.), *Global Studies: Mapping Contemporary Art and Culture*, 274–97.

– 'Inside/Out: Pushpamala N's Embodiment of Liberty', in Juneja and Ramaswamy (eds.), *Motherland*, 70–81.

– 'Jahangir auf der Sanduhr – Überlegungen zur Lektüre einer Visualität im Spannungsfeld zwischen Eigenem und Fremdem', in Gerhard Schneider (ed.), *Die visuelle Dimension des Historischen* (Schwalbach: Wochenschau Verlag, 2002), 142–57.

– 'Kunstgeschichte und kulturelle Differenz: eine Einleitung', Matthias Bruhn, Monica Juneja and Elke A. Werner (eds.) *Kritische Berichte. Themenheft Universalität in der Kunstgeschichte*, vol. 40/2 (2012): 5–12.

– '"Likeness" as a Migrating Concept – Artfully Portraying the Universal Ruler in Early Modern South Asia', *Histoire de l'Art*, vol. 82/1 (2018): 55–70.

– 'Migration, Dispossession, Post-Memorial Recuperations: An "Undisciplined" View of the Partition of the Indian Subcontinent', in Dogramaci and Mersmann (eds.), *Handbook of Art and Global Migration: Theories, Practices, and Challenges*, 298–314.

– '"Mikrogeschichten. Die Routen des transkulturellen Modernismus"', in Kunstsammlung Nordrhein-Westfalen (ed.), *Museum global*, 27–46.

– 'From the Religious to the Aesthetic Image – or The Struggle over Art that Offends', in Christiane Kruse, Birgit Meyer and Anne-Marie Korte (eds.), *Taking Offense. Religion, Art and Visual Culture in Plural Configurations* (Munich: Fink Verlag, 2018), 161–189.

– '"Pre-colonial" oder "Early Modern?" Das Problem der Zeitzäsuren in der indischen Geschichte', *Historische Zeitschrift*, Beiheft 47 (2009): 449–68.

– 'Reading Culture through Art – Jacob Burckhardt in the Twenty-first Century', in Beyer, Burghartz and Burkart (eds.), *Burckhardt.Renaissance*, 174–90.

– 'The Breast-Feeding Mother as Icon and Source of Affect in Visual Practice – a Transcultural Journey', in Kumkum Roy (ed.), *Looking Within, Looking Without: Exploring Households in the Subcontinent through Time* (Delhi: Primus Books, 2015), 105–33.
– 'Tracking the Routes of Vision in Early Modern Eurasia', in Karin Gludovatz, Juliane Noth and Joachim Rees (eds.), *The Itineraries of Art: Topographies of Artistic Mobility in Europe and Asia* (Paderborn: Fink Verlag, 2015), 57–85.
– 'Translating the Body into Image: The Body Politic and Visual Practice at the Mughal Court in the Sixteenth and Seventeenth Centuries', in Axel Michaels and Christoph Wulf (eds.), *The Body in South Asia – Image, Ritual, Performativity* (New Delhi: Routledge, 2009), 235–60.
– 'Universal Principles and Intransigent Contexts: Wölfflinian Aesthetics and the History of South Asian Art', in Evonne Levy and Tristan Weddigen (eds.), *The Global Reception of Heinrich Wölfflin's 'The Principles of Art History'* (Washington: National Gallery of Art and Yale University Press, 2020), 165–78.
– 'Crafts and the Spiritual' (with an excerpt from Ananda K. Coomaraswamy, *The Indian Craftsman),* in Beate Söntgen and Julia Voss (eds.), *Why Art Criticism? A Reader* (Berlin: Hatje Cantz, 2022), 52–61.
– 'Comment' in Trede, Wakita and Guth (eds.), *Japanese Art: Transcultural Perspectives*, forthcoming.
– (ed.), *Architecture in Medieval India: Form, Contexts, Histories* (New Delhi: Permanent Black, 2001).
Juneja, Monica and Anna Grasskamp, 'EurAsian Matters: An Introduction', in Anna Grasskamp and Monica Juneja (eds.), *EurAsian Matters: China, Europe, and the Transcultural Object, 1600–1800* (Heidelberg: Springer, 2018), 3–33.
Juneja, Monica and Christian Kravagna, 'Understanding Transculturalism', in Model House Research Group (ed.), *Transcultural Modernisms* (Berlin: Sternberg Press, 2013), 22–33.
Juneja, Monica and Franziska Koch (eds.), 'Multi-Centred Modernisms – Reconfiguring Asian Art of the Twentieth and Twenty-First Centuries', themed section, *Transcultural Studies*, vols. 2–3 (2010–11).
Juneja, Monica and Sumathi Ramaswamy (eds.), *Motherland: Women and Nation in Pushpamala N's Photo-Performances* (New Delhi: Roli Books, 2022).

Kalra, Vandana, 'Painting on the Wall', *Indian Express*, 13 October 2012.
Kandinsky, Wassily, *Über das Geistige in der Kunst insbesondere der Malerei* (Bern: Benteli Verlag, 2009; orig. 1911).
Kanwar, Amar and Daniela Zyman (eds.), *Amar Kanwar, The Sovereign Forest,* (Berlin: Sternberg Press, 2014).
Kapur, Geeta, *When Was Modernism? Essays in Contemporary Cultural Practice in India* (New Delhi: Tulika Books, 2007).
– 'Curating Across Agonistic Worlds', in Parul D. Mukherji, Naman P. Ahuja and Kavita Singh (eds.), *Influx: Contemporary Art in Asia* (New Delhi: Sage Publications, 2013), 158–81.
– 'Dismantled Norms: Apropos an Asian/Indian Avantgarde', in *When Was Modernism? Essays in Contemporary Cultural Practice in India*, 365–413.
– 'Gender Mobility: Through the Lens of Five Women Artists', in Maura Reilly (ed.), *Global Feminisms: New Directions in Contemporary Art* (London: Merrell, 2007), 79–96.
– *Contemporary Indian Artists* (New Delhi: Vikas Publishing, 1978).
– 'Modernist Myths and the Exile of Maqbool Fida Husain', in Ramaswamy (ed.), *Barefoot Across the Nation*, 21–53.
– 'Mortal Remains', in Charles Merewether and John Potts (eds.), *After the Event: New Perspectives on Art History* (Manchester: Manchester University Press, 2010), 132–55.
– 'Proposition Avant-Garde: A View from the South', *Art Journal*, vol. 77/1 (2018): 87–89.
Karge, Henrik, 'Projecting the Future in German Art Historiography of the Nineteenth Century: Franz Kugler, Karl Schnaase and Gottfried Semper', *Journal of Art Historiography*, vol. 9, 2013: 1–26.
– 'Die Kunst ist nicht das Maaß der Geschichte: Karl Schnaases Einfluß auf Jacob Burckhardt', *Archiv für Kulturgeschichte*, vol. 78 (1996): 393–431.
Karlholm, Dan, *Art of Illusion: The Representation of Art History in Nineteenth-Century Germany and Beyond* (Bern: Peter Lang, 2004).
– 'Reading the Virtual Museum of General Art History', *Art History*, 24/4 (2001): 552–77.
Kasfir, Sidney L., *African Art and the Colonial Encounter: Inventing a Global Commodity* (Bloomington: Indiana University Press, 2007).
Kaufmann, Doris, '"Pushing the Limits of Understanding": The Discourse on Primitivism in German *Kulturwissenschaften*, 1880–1930', *Studies in History and Philosophy of Science*, vol. 39 (2008): 434–43.

Kaufmann, Thomas DaCosta, 'Reflections on World Art History', in Kaufmann, Dossin and Joyeux-Prunel (eds.), *Circulations in the Global History of Art*, 25–45.

Kaufmann, Thomas DaCosta, Catherine Dossin and Beatrice Joyeux-Prunel (eds.), *Circulations in the Global History of Art* (Farnham: Ashgate Publishers, 2015).

Kaufmann, Thomas DaCosta and Elizabeth Pilliod (eds.), *Time and Place: The Geohistory of Art* (Aldershot: Ashgate, 2005).

Kaur, Ravinder, *Brand New Nation: Capitalist Dreams and Nationalist Designs in Twenty-First Century India* (Stanford: Stanford University Press, 2020).

Khullar, Sonal, *Worldly Affiliations: Artistic Practice, National Identity and Modernism in India 1930–1990* (Oakland: University of California Press, 2015).

Kirshenblatt-Gimblett, Barbara, 'Folklore's Crisis', *The Journal of American Folklore*, vol. 111/441 (1998): 281–327.

Kleeblatt, Norman L., 'Identity Roller Coaster: From *Magiciens de la Terre* to Documenta 11', *Art Journal*, vol. 64/1 (2005): 61–63.

Koch, Ebba, *Shah Jahan and Orpheus: The Pietre Dure Decoration and the Programme of the Throne in the Hall of Public Audiences at the Red Fort of Delhi* (Graz: Akademische Druck- und Verlagsanstalt, 1988).

– 'The Hierarchical Principles of Shah Jahani Painting', in Milo C. Beach, Ebba Koch and Wheeler M. Thackston, *King of the World: The Padshahnama, an Imperial Manuscript from the Royal Library* (London: Azimuth Editions, 1997), 130–43.

– 'The Influence of the Jesuit Missions on the Symbolic Representations of the Mughal Emperors', in Christian W. Troll (ed.), *Islam in India: Studies and Commentaries* (New Delhi: Oxford University Press, 1982) 14–29.

– 'The "Moghuleries" of the Millionenzimmer, Schönbrunn Palace, Vienna', in Rosemary Crill, Susan Stronge and Andrew Topsfield (eds.), *Arts of Mughal India: Studies in Honour of Robert Skelton* (Ahmedabad: Mapin Publishing, 2004), 152–67.

Kogoj, Cornelia and Christian Kravagna, *Das amerikanische Museum: Sklaverei, schwarze Geschichte und der Kampf um Gerechtigkeit in Museen der Südstaaten* (Berlin: Mandelbaum Verlag, 2017).

Komaroff, Linda (ed.), *Beyond the Legacy of Genghis Khan* (Leiden: E. J. Brill, 2006).

Komaroff, Linda and Stefano Carboni (eds.), *The Legacy of Genghis Khan: Courtly Art and Culture in Western Asia, 1256–1353* (New Haven: Yale University Press, 2002).

Kramrisch, Stella, *The Hindu Temple*, 2 vols. (Calcutta: University of Calcutta, 1946).

– 'An Indian Cubist', *Rupam*, no. 11 (July 1922): 107–9.

– 'Exhibition of Continental Paintings and Graphic Arts' (1922), reprinted in Bittner and Rhomberg (eds.), *The Bauhaus in Calcutta*, 2.

– 'Indian Art and Europe', *Rupam*, no. 11 (July 1922): 81–86.

– (ed.), *Unknown India: Ritual Art in Tribe and Village* (Philadelphia: Museum of Art, 1968).

– *Grundzüge der indischen Kunst* (Hellerau: Avalun-Verlag, 1924).

– 'Die indische Kunst' in Springer (ed.), *Handbuch der Kunstgeschichte*, vol. VI, 229–368.

Kravagna, Christian, *Transmoderne: Eine Kunstgeschichte des Kontakts* (Berlin: b_books, 2017). Eng. trans, *Transmodern: An Art History of Contact, 1920–1960* (Manchester: Manchester University Press, 2022).

Kreiser, Klaus, 'Clio's Poor Relation: Betrachtungen zur Osmanischen Historiographie von Hammer-Purgstall bis Stanford Shaw', in Gernot Stein and Grete Klingenstein (eds.), *Das Osmanische Reich und Europa 1683 bis 1789: Konflikt, Entspannung und Austausch* (Munich: R. Oldenbourg Verlag, 1983), 24–43.

Kugler, Franz, *Handbuch der Kunstgeschichte* (Stuttgart: Ebner & Seubert, 1842).

Kuhn, Herbert, 'Primitive Kunst', in Max Ebert (ed.), *Reallexikon der Vorgeschichte*, vol. 10 (1927–28): 264–92.

Kühnel, Ernst, 'Die Islamische Kunst', in Springer, *Handbuch*, vol. VI, 373–550.

Kühnel, Ernst and Hermann Goetz, *Indische Buchmalerei aus dem Jahangir-Album der Staatsbibliothek zu Berlin* (Berlin: Scarabaeus Verlag, 1924).

Kumar, R. Siva, *Santiniketan: The Making of a Contextual Modernism* (New Delhi: National Gallery of Modern Art, 1997).

– 'Ram Kinkar Baij and Modernism's Dual Commitments', in Anshuman Dasgupta (ed.), *Santhal Family: Positions around an Indian Sculpture* (Antwerpen: MUKHA, 2009), 14–19.

– 'Shantiniketan: A World University', in Bittner and Rhomberg (eds.), *The Bauhaus in Calcutta*, 109–16.

– 'The Black House: In the Context of the Santiniketan Murals', in Sanjoy K. Mallik (ed.), *Black House* (Calcutta: Vishva-Bharati, 2016), 29–58.

Kunstsammlung Nordrhein-Westfalen (ed.), *Museum Global: Mikrogeschichten einer ex-zentrischen Moderne* (Weyertal: Wienand Verlag, 2018).
Kurtha, Aziz, *Francis Newton Souza: Bridging Western and Indian Modern Art* (Ahmedabad: Mapin, 2006).

Lalonde, Christine, 'Introduction: At the Crossroads of Indigeneity, Globalization and Contemporary Art', in Hill, Hopkins and Lalonde (eds.), *Sakahàn: International Indigenous Art*, 13–20.
Lamoureux, Johanne, 'From Form to Platform: The Politics of Representation and the Representation of Politics', *Art Journal*, vol. 64/1 (2005): 64–73.
Lamprecht, Karl, 'Fragen moderner Kunst', *Neue Deutsche Rundschau*, vol. 12 (1901): 734–41.
LaPena, Frank, 'The Fourth World', in National Museum of the American Indian (ed.), *The Path We Travel: Celebrations of Contemporary Native American Creativity* (Washington DC: Smithsonian Institution and Fulcrum Inc., 1994), 1–22.
Latour, Bruno, *Politics of Nature: How to bring the Sciences into Democracy* (Cambridge, MA: Harvard University Press, 2004).
– *Reassembling the Social: An Introduction to Actor-Network-Theory* (Oxford and New York: Oxford University Press, 2005).
– *We Have Never Been Modern* (New York: Harvester Wheatsheaf, 1993).
Leeb, Susanne, *Die Kunst der Anderen: 'Weltkunst' und die anthropologische Konfiguration der Moderne* (Berlin: b_books, 2015).
– 'Primitivism and Humanist Teleology in Art History around 1900', *Journal of Art Historiography*, vol. 12 (2015) n.p.
– 'Weltkunstgeschichte und Universalismusbegriffe', *Kritische Berichte*, vol. 40/2 (2012): 13–25.
Le Fur, Yves (ed.), *Picasso primitif* (Paris: Flammarion, 2017).
Leibsohn, Dana, 'Introduction: Geographies of Sight', in Leibsohn and Peterson (eds.), *Seeing across Cultures in the Early Modern World*, 1–22.
Leibsohn, Dana and Jeanette F. Peterson (eds.), *Seeing Across Cultures in the Early Modern World* (Farnham: Ashgate, 2012).
Lentz, Thomas, Glenn D. Lowry and Jonathan Rabinovitz (eds.), *Timur and the Princely Vision: Persian Art and Culture in the Fifteenth Century* (Washington DC: Smithsonian Institution Press, 1989).
Levi, Giovanni, 'On Microhistory', in Peter Burke (ed.), *New Perspectives on Historical Writing* (Cambridge: Polity Press, 1991), 93–113.
Levy, Evonne and Tristan Weddigen (eds.), *The Global Reception of Heinrich Wölfflin's 'The Principles of Art History'* (Washington, DC: National Gallery of Art and Yale University Press, 2020).
Lévy-Bruhl, Lucien, *La mentalité primitive* (Paris: Alcan, 1922), published in German as *Die geistige Welt der Primitiven* (Munich: F. Bruckmann, 1927).
Lévy-Bruhl, Lucien, *L'âme primitive* (Paris: Alcan, 1927), published in German as *Die Seele der Primitiven* (Vienna: Braumüller, 1930).
Lewis, Martin W. and Kären E. Wigen, *The Myth of Continents: A Critique of Metageography* (Berkeley: University of California Press, 1997).
Lewison, Jeremy, '"Bilderstreit" and "Magiciens de la Terre": Paris and Cologne', *The Burlington Magazine*, vol. 131/1037 (1989): 585–87.
Lloyd, Jill, *German Expressionism: Primitivism and Modernity* (New Haven: Yale University Press, 1991).
Locher, Hubert, 'Das "Handbuch der Kunstgeschichte": Die Vermittlung kunsthistorischen Wissens als Anleitung zum ästhetischen Urteil', in Wessel Reinink and Jeroen Stumpel (eds.), *Memory and Oblivion: Proceedings of the XXIXth International Congress of the History of Art held in Amsterdam, 1–7 September 1996* (Dordrecht: Kluwer Academic Publishers, 1999), 69–87.
Losty, Jeremiah P., 'Towards a New Naturalism: Portraiture in Murshidabad and Avadh, 1750–1780', in Barbara Schmitz (ed.), *After the Great Mughals: Painting in Delhi and the Regional Courts in the 18th and 19th Centuries* (Mumbai: Marg Publications, 2002), 3–55.
Lübke, Wilhelm, *Grundriss der Kunstgeschichte* (Stuttgart: Ebner & Seubert, 1860).
Luis, Sandip K., 'Between Anthropology and History: The Entangled Lives of Jangarh Singh Shyam and Jagdish Swaminathan', in Sasanka Perera and Dev Nath Pathak (eds.), *Intersections of Contemporary Art, Anthropology and Art History in South Asia: Decoding Visual Worlds* (Cham: Palgrave Macmillan, 2019), 139–79.

MacDonald, Sharon, *Memorylands: Heritage and Identity in Europe Today* (London: Routledge, 2013).

Madden, Kathleen and Sam Philips (eds.), *Indian Highway – the Catalogue* (London: Koenig Books, 2008).

Maddipatti, Venugopal, 'Water in an Expanded Field: Art, Thought and Immersion in the Yamuna River: 2005–11', in Hutton and Brown (eds.), *Rethinking Place*, 60–77.

Maharaj, Sarat, 'The Congo is Flooding the Acropolis: Art in the Britain of Immigrations', *Third Text*, vol. 5/15 (1991): 77–90.

Mahmood, Saba, 'Religious Reason and Secular Affect: An Incommensurable Divide?', *Critical Inquiry*, vol. 35/4 (Summer 2009): 836–862.

Maholay-Jaradi, Priya, *Fashioning a National Art: Baroda's Royal Collection and Art Institutions* (1875–1924) (Oxford: Oxford University Press, 2016).

– (ed.), *Baroda: A Cosmopolitan Provenance in Transition* (Mumbai: Marg Publications, 2015).

Malraux, André, *Picasso's Mask* (London: Macdonald and Jane's Publishers, 1976).

Manjapra, Kris K., 'Stella Kramrisch and the Bauhaus in Calcutta', in R. Siva Kumar (ed.), *The Last Harvest: The Paintings of Rabindranath Tagore* (Ahmedabad: Mapin Publishing, 2011), 34–40.

Marchand, Suzanne L., *German Orientalism in the Age of Empire: Religion, Race and Scholarship* (Cambridge: Cambridge University Press, 2009).

– 'Leo Frobenius and the Revolt Against the West', in *Journal of Contemporary History* vol. 32/2 (1997): 153–70.

– 'The Rhetoric of Artifacts and the Decline of Classical Humanism: The Case of Josef Strzygowski', *History and Theory*, vol. 33/4 (1994): 106–30.

Marosi, Erno, 'Josef Strzygowski als Entwerfer von nationalen Kunstgeschichten', in Ruth Heftrig, Olaf Peters and Barbara Schellewald (eds.), *Kunstgeschichte im 'Dritten Reich': Theorien, Methoden, Praktiken* (Berlin: Akademie Verlag, 2008), 103–13.

Martin, Jean-Hubert, *L'Art au large* (Paris: Flammarion, 2013).

– 'Est-Ouest, Nord-Sud: nouveaux venus, nouveaux continents', in Daniel Soutif (ed.), *L'art du XXe siècle, 1939–2002: de l'art moderne á l'art contemporain*' (Paris: Citadelle & Mazenot, 2005), 459–78.

– 'The Death of Art – Long Live Art, 1986' (translation and reprint of an earlier curatorial statement of the author), in Steeds et al. (ed.), *Making Art Global (Part 2)*, 216–22.

– (ed.), *Magiciens de la Terre* (Paris: Editions du Centre Pompidou, 1989).

Martínez-Jacquet, Elena (ed.), *African Art, New York and the Avant-garde, Tribal Art Magazine*, special issue, 2012.

Mathur, Saloni, 'A Response to Kapur's "Proposition Avant-Garde"', *Art Journal*, vol. 77/1 (2018): 90–94.

– 'Ends and Means: A Conversation with Geeta Kapur', *October*, Issue 171 (Winter 2020): 115–38.

– 'Partition and the Visual Arts: Reflections on Method', *Third Text*, vol. 31/2–3 (2017): 205–12.

– 'The Edifice Complex', in *A Fragile Inheritance: Radical Stakes in Indian Contemporary Art* (Durham, NC: Duke University Press, 2019), 72–95.

– 'The Exhibition as "Re-Job": Reconstructing the Bauhaus in Bengal', in Bittner and Rhomberg (eds.), *The Bauhaus in Calcutta*, 191–99.

Mathur, Saloni and Kavita Singh, 'Reincarnations of the Museum: The Museum in an Age of Religious Revivalism', in Vishakha Desai (ed.), *Asian Art in the 21st Century* (New Haven: Yale University Press, 2007), 149–68.

Mathur, Saloni and Kavita Singh (eds.), *No Touching, No Spitting, No Praying: The Museum in South Asia* (London and New Delhi: Routledge, 2015).

Mbembe, Achille, 'Necropolitics', *Public Culture*, vol. 15/1 (2003): 11–40.

– 'Theory from the Antipodes: Notes on Jean & John Comaroffs' TFS', *Society for Cultural Anthropology*, 25 February 2012, https://culanth.org/fieldsights/theory-from-the-antipodes-notes-on-jean-john-comaroffs-tfs.

McEvilley, Thomas, 'Doctor Lawyer Indian Chief: "Primitivism" in 20th Century Art at the Museum of Modern Art in 1984', *Artforum*, vol. 23/3, 1984: 54–60, reprinted in Thomas McEvilley, *Art and Otherness: Crisis in Cultural Identity* (New York: McPherson and Co., 1992), 27–56.

– 'Marginalia: Thomas McEvilley on the Global Issue', *Artforum*, vol. 28/7 (1990): 19–21.

McMaster, Gerald, 'Towards an Aboriginal Art History', in W. Jackson Rushing (ed.), *Native American Art in the Twentieth Century: Makers, Meanings, Histories* (London: Routledge, 1999), 81–96.

Mehta, Tasneem Z., 'Why You Must Catch Asymmetrical Objects At The Dr. Bhau Daji Lad Mumbai City Museum', *Verve Magazine*, 13 March 2018, https://www.vervemagazine.in/arts-and-culture/why-you-must-catch-asymmetrical-objects-at-the-dr-bhau-daji-lad-mumbai-city-museum.

- *A Unique Partnership: The Restoration and Revitalisation of the Dr. Bhau Daji Lad Mumbai City Museum* (Mumbai: Dr. Bhau Daji Lal Museum Trust, 2009).

Meister, Michael W., 'Image Iconopraxis and Iconoplasty in South Asia', *RES: Anthropology and Aesthetics*, no. 51 (2007): 13–32.

Mercer, Kobena, *Travel and See: Black Diaspora Art Practices Since the 1980s* (Durham, NC: Duke University Press, 2016).

- (ed.), *Cosmopolitan Modernisms* (Cambridge, MA/London: Institute of International Visual Arts, 2005).
- (ed.), *Discrepant Abstraction* (Cambridge, MA: MIT Press, 2006).

Merleau-Ponty, Maurice, 'Le doute de Cézanne' (1945), repr. in *Sens et non-sens* (Paris: Gallimard, 1996), 13–33.

Meskimmon, Marsha, *Contemporary Art and the Cosmopolitan Imagination* (London: Routledge, 2010).

- 'Art Matters: Feminist-Corporeal Materialist Aesthetics', in Hilary Robinson and Maria Elena Buszek (eds.), *A Companion to Feminist Art* (Chichester: Wiley-Blackwell, 2019), 353–67.
- *Transnational Feminisms, Transversal Politics and Art: Entanglements and Intersections* (London: Routledge, 2020).

Michaud, Yves, 'Doctor Explorer Chief Curator', *Third Text*, vol. 3/6 (1989): 83–88.

Mignolo, Walter D. and Catherine Walsh (eds.), *On Decoloniality: Concepts, Analytics Praxis* (Durham, NC: Duke University Press, 2018).

Minissale, Gregory, *Images of Thought: Visuality in Islamic India 1550–1750* (Newcastle: Cambridge Scholars Publishing, 2006).

Mirzoeff, Nicholas, 'Visualizing the Anthropocene', *Public Culture*, vol. 26 /2 (2014): 213–32.

Mitchell, W. J. T., *Picture Theory* (Chicago: Chicago University Press, 1994).

Mitchell, Timothy, 'The Stage of Modernity', in Timothy Mitchell (ed.), *Questions of Modernity* (Minneapolis: University of Minnesota Press, 2000), 1–34.

Mitter, Partha, *Art and Nationalism in Colonial India 1850–1922: Occidental Orientations* (Cambridge: Cambridge University Press, 1994).

- *Much Maligned Monsters: History of European Reactions to Indian Art* (Oxford: Clarendon Press, 1977).
- *The Triumph of Modernism: India's Artists and the Avant-Garde 1922–1947* (London: Reaktion Books, 2007).
- 'Indian Artists in the Colonial Period: The Case of Bombay', in Sinha (ed.), *Art and Visual Culture*, 24–39.
- 'Interventions: Decentering Modernism: Art History and Avant-Garde Art from the Periphery', with responses by Alastair Wright, Rebecca M. Brown, Saloni Mathur and Ajay Sinha, *The Art Bulletin*, vol. 90/4 (2008): 531–74.
- 'The Artist as Charismatic Individual: Raja Ravi Varma', in Brown and Hutton (eds.), *Asian Art*, 167–76.

Moin, A. Afzar, 'Peering through the Cracks in the *Baburnama*: The Textured Lives of Mughal Sovereigns', *Indian Economic and Social History Review*, vol. 49/4 (2012): 493–526.

Moore, Jason W. (ed.), *Anthropocene or Capitalocene? Nature, History, and the Crisis of Capitalism* (Oakland: PM Press, 2016).

Mosquera, Gerardo, 'Some Problems in Transcultural Curating', in Jean Fisher (ed.), *Global Visions: Towards a New Internationalism in the Visual Arts* (London: Kala Press, 1994), 133–39.

- 'The Third Bienal de la Habana in its Global and Local Contexts', in Rachel Weiss et al. (ed.), *Making Art Global (Part 1): The Third Havana Biennial 1989* (London: Afterall Books, 2011), 70–79.

Müller-Schareck, Maria, '"Ich beabsichtige, meinen eigenen Weg auszubauen". Moderne am Beispiel des Malers Yorozu Tetsugorō', in Kunstsammlung Nordrhein-Westfalen (ed.), *Museum global*: 72–90.

Mukherji, Parul D., 'Anatomy Lessons from *Shadanga*: Abanindranath Tagore and T. Venkatappa's Shaping of a New National Self', in Achar and Pushpamala N. (eds.), *Mysore Modernity, Aesthetic Nationalism* (forthcoming 2023).

- 'Art History and its Discontents in Global Times', in Casid and D'Souza (eds.), *Art History in the Wake of the Global Turn*, 88–106.
- 'Putting the World in a Book: How Global Art Can be Today', in Jaynie Anderson (ed.), *Crossing Cultures: Conflict, Migration and Convergence* (Carlton: Miegunyah Press, 2009), 109–15.

– 'Self in Stills, Conflict Within the Frame. In Conversation with Pushpamala N.', in Gayatri Sinha (ed.), *Voices of Change: 20 Indian Artists* (Mumbai: Marg Publications, 2010), 62–75.
– 'The Possibility of a World Art History', round table with John Clark, Parul D. Mukherji, Omuka Toshiharu, Patrick Flores and Woo Jung-Ah, *Australian and New Zealand Journal of Art,* vol. 9/1–2 (2008): 42–47.
– 'Whither Art History in a Globalizing World', *The Art Bulletin*, vol. 96/2 (2014): 151–55.
– 'Who Is Afraid of Mimesis? Contesting the Common Sense of Indian Aesthetics through the Theory of "Mimesis" or Anukaraṇa Vâda', in Arindam Chakrabarty (ed.), *Indian Aesthetics and the Philosophy of Art* (London: Bloomsbury, 2016), 71–92.
Murali, Sharanya, 'An Eye for an Eye: The Hapticality of Collaborative Photo-Performance in *Native Women of India*', *Theatre Research International*, vol. 44/2 (2019): 118–34.

Naef, Silvia, *Bilder und Bilderverbot im Islam: vom Koran bis zum Karikaturstreit* (Munich: Beck Verlag, 2007).
Nagy, Peter 'Atul Dodiya: A Gargantuan Responsibility', in *Atul Dodiya: Broken Branches* (Bose Pacia Modern, New York, 2003).
Nair, Janaki, *Mysore Modern: Rethinking the Region under Princely Rule* (Minneapolis: Minnesota University Press, 2011).
– 'Drawing a Line: K. Venkatappa and his Publics', *The Indian Economic and Social History Review*, vol. 35/2 (1998): 179–210.
Necipoğlu, Gülru, 'The Scrutinizing Gaze in the Aesthetics of Islamic Visual Cultures: Sight, Insight, and Desire', *Muqarnas*, vol. 32 (2015): 23–61.
Nelson, Robert S. (ed.), *Visuality before and beyond the Renaissance: Seeing as Others Saw* (Cambridge: Cambridge University Press, 2000).
Neumayer, Erwin and Christine Schelberger (eds.), *Raja Ravi Varma: Portrait of an Artist* (New Delhi: Oxford University Press, 2005).
Nolde, Emil, *Welt und Heimat: Die Südseereise 1913–1918* (Cologne: Dumont, 1965; orig. 1936).

Okada, Amina, *Indian Miniatures of the Mughal Court* (New York: Harry N. Abrams, 1992).
Okeke-Agulu, Chika, *Postcolonial Modernism: Art and Decolonization in Twentieth Century Nigeria* (Durham, NC: Duke University Press, 2015).
– 'Globalization, Art History, and the Specter of Difference', in Dumbadze and Hudson (eds.), *Contemporary Art: 1989 to the Present*, 447–56.
Onians, John, *Art, Culture and Nature: From Art History to World Art Studies* (London: Pindar Press, 2006).
– *Neuroarthistory: From Aristotle and Pliny to Baxandall and Zeki* (New Haven: Yale University Press, 2007).
– *The Art Atlas* (London: Lawrence King, 2008).
– 'Neuroarthistory: Making More Sense of Art', in Zijlmans and van Damme (eds.), *World Art Studies*, 265–86.
– (ed.), *Compression vs. Expression: Containing and Explaining the World's Art* (New Haven: Yale University Press, 2006).
Ortiz, Fernando, *Cuban Counterpoint: Tobacco and Sugar*, trans. Harriet Onís (New York: Knopf, 1947); reprinted with an Introduction by Fernando Coronil (Durham, NC: Duke University Press, 1995).
Osten, Marion von and Sarat Maharaj, 'Der Überschuss des Globalen', *Texte zur Kunst*, vol. 23 (2013): 133–51.
Osten, Marion von and Grant Watson (eds.), *Bauhaus Imaginista: A School in the World* (London: Thames and Hudson, 2019).
Osterhammel, Jürgen, *Die Entzauberung Asiens: Europa und die asiatischen Reiche im 18. Jahrhundert* (Munich: C. H. Beck, 1998); Eng. trans. *Unfabling the East: The Enlightenment's Encounter with Asia*, trans. Robert Savage (Princeton: Princeton University Press, 2018).
– *Die Flughöhe der Adler: historische Essays zur globalen Gegenwart* (Munich: C. H. Beck, 2017).
– *Jacob Burckhardts 'Über das Studium der Geschichte' und die Weltgeschichtsschreibung der Gegenwart* (Basel: Schwabe Verlag, 2019).
– 'Global History and Historical Sociology', in James Belich, John Darwin, Margret Frenz and Chris Wickham (eds.), *The Prospect of Global History* (Oxford: Oxford University Press, 2016), 23–43.
– '"Peoples Without History" in British and German Historical Thought', in Benedikt Stuchtey and Peter Wende (eds.), *British and German Historiography 1750–1950: Traditions, Perceptions, and Transfers* (Oxford: Oxford University Press, 2000), 265–87.

Ott, Michaela, 'Die kleine ästhetische Differenz', *Texte zur Kunst*, vol. 23 (2013): 101–9.

Pall, Priya, 'The Wake', in *Atul Bhalla: You Always Step into the Same River* (New Delhi: Vadehra Art Gallery, 2014), 39–43.

Pan, David, *Primitive Renaissance: Rethinking German Expressionism* (Lincoln: University of Nebraska Press, 2001).

Pandian, Anand, 'Ripening the Earth: On Maturity and Modernity in South India', in Dube (ed.), *Handbook of Modernity*, 157–69.

– *Crooked Stalks: Cultivating Virtue in South India* (Durham, NC: Duke University Press, 2009).

Panikkar, Shivaji K., 'Reading the Regional through Internationalism and Nativism: The Case of Art in Madras, 1950 to 1970', in Shivaji K. Panikkar, Deeptha Achar and Parul D. Mukherji (eds.), *Towards a New Art History: Studies in Indian Art* (New Delhi: D.K. Printworld, 2003), 105–21.

Panofsky, Erwin, 'Die Perspektive als symbolische Form', in Fritz Saxl (ed.), *Vorträge der Warburg-Bibliothek 1924–25* (Berlin: Teubner, 1927), 258–330.

Papastergiadis, Nikos, *Cosmopolitanism and Culture* (London: Polity Press, 2012).

Parimoo, Ratan, *The Paintings of the Three Tagores: Abanindranath, Gaganendranath, Rabindranath. Chronology and Comparative Study* (Baroda: Maharaja Sayajirao University, 1973).

Parthasarathy, Shruti, 'Group 1890: The Journey of a Moment', in Kishore Singh (ed.), *Group 1890: India's Indigenous Modernism* (New Delhi: DAG Modern, 2016), 18–136.

Penny, Glenn, 'Municipal Displays: Civic Self-Promotion and the Development of German Ethnographic Museums, 1870–1914', *Social Anthropology*, vol. 6/2 (1998): 157–68.

Pernau, Margrit, *Transnationale Geschichte* (Göttingen: Vandenhoeck und Ruprecht, 2011).

Pernau, Margrit and Dominic Sachsenmaier (eds.), *Global Conceptual History: A Reader* (London: Bloomsbury, 2016).

Petersen, Anne R., *Migration into Art: Transcultural Identities and Art-Making in a Globalised World* (Manchester: Manchester University Press, 2017).

Pfisterer, Ulrich, 'Origins and Principles of World Art History: 1900 (and 2000)', in Zijlmans and van Damme (eds.), *World Art Studies: Exploring Concepts and Approaches*, 69–89.

Phillips, Ruth B., 'Aesthetic Primitivism Revisited: The Global Diaspora of "Primitive" Art and the Rise of Indigenous Modernisms', *Journal of Art Historiography*, no. 12 (June 2015): 1–25.

Pinney, Christopher, 'Creole Europe: A Reflection of a Reflection', *Journal of New Zealand Literature*, vol. 20 (2002): 125–61.

Pinney, Christopher and Nicholas Thomas (eds.), *Beyond Aesthetics: Art and the Technologies of Enchantment* (Oxford: Berg Publishers, 2001).

Piotrowski, Piotr, *In the Shadow of Yalta: Art and the Avant-Garde in Eastern Europe 1945–1989* (London: Reaktion Books, 2009).

– 'Towards a Horizontal History of the European Avant-Garde', in Sascha Bru and Peter Nicholls (eds.), *European Avant-Garde and Modernism Studies* (Berlin: De Gruyter, 2009), vol. 1, 49–58.

Poggioli, Renato, *The Theory of the Avant-Garde* (Cambridge, MA: Belknap Press, 1968).

Poinsot, Jean-Marc, 'Review of the Paradigms and Interpretative Machine, or, The Critical Development of "Magiciens de la Terre"', in Steeds et al (eds.), *Making Art Global (Part 2)*, 94–108.

Pollock, Griselda, *Avant-Garde Gambits, 1888–1893: Gender and the Colour of Art History* (London: Thames and Hudson, 1993).

– *Differencing the Canon: Feminist Desires and the Writing of Art's Histories* (London: Routledge, 1999).

Porter, David (ed.), *Comparative Early Modernities 1100–1800* (New York: Palgrave Macmillan, 2012).

Porter, Yves, 'From the "Theory of the Two Qalams" to the "Seven Principles of Painting": Theory, Terminology and Practice in Persian Classical Painting', *Muqarnas*, vol. 17 (2000): 109–18.

Poshyananda, Apinan, *Contemporary Art in Asia: Traditions – Tensions* (New York: Abrams, 1996).

Prakash, Gyan, 'Museum Matters', in Bettina M. Carbonell (ed.), *Museum Studies: An Anthology of Contexts* (Chichester: Wiley-Blackwell, 2012), 317–23.

Prange, Regine, *Die Geburt der Kunstgeschichte: Philosophische Ästhetik und empirische Wissenschaft* (Cologne: Deubner Verlag, 2004).

Pratt, Mary Louise, *Imperial Eyes: Travel Writing and Transculturation* (Routledge: London, 1992).

Preziosi, Donald, *Brain of the Earth's Body: Art, Museums and the Phantasms of Modernity* (Minneapolis: University of Minnesota Press, 2003).

– *Rethinking Art History: Meditations on a Coy Science* (New Haven: Yale University Press, 1989).
– *The Art of Art History: A Critical Anthology* (Oxford: Oxford University Press, 2009; 2nd revised edition).
Pushpamala N. and Claire Arni (eds.), *Native Women of India: Manners and Customs*, exh.cat. (Bangalore: India Foundation for the Arts, 2004).

Quijano, Annibal, 'Coloniality of Power, Knowledge and Latin America', *Nepantla: Views from the South*, vol. 1/3 (2000): 533–80.

Raffel, Suhanya, 'Ruminations on the Grammar of a Universe: Back to the Future', in Ginwala (ed.), *Jitish Kallat*, 202–33.
Rajadhyaksha, Ashish, 'The Last Decade', in Gulammohammed Sheikh (ed.), *Contemporary Art in Baroda* (New Delhi: Tulika Publications, 1996), 215.
Ramaswamy, Sumathi, *Gandhi in the Gallery: The Art of Disobedience* (New Delhi: Roli Books, 2020).
– *Terrestrial Lessons: The Conquest of the World as Globe* (Chicago: University of Chicago Press, 2017).
– 'The Wretched of the Nation', *Third Text*, vol. 31/2–3 (2017): 213–37.
– (ed.), *Barefoot across the Nation: Maqbool Fida Husain and the Idea of India* (London: Routledge, 2010).
Rampley, Matthew, *The Seductions of Darwin: Art, Evolution, Neuroscience* (University Park: Penn State University Press, 2017).
– *The Vienna School of Art History: Empire and the Politics of Scholarship, 1847–1918* (University Park: Penn State University Press, 2013).
– 'Construction of National Art Histories and "New" Europe', in Matthew Rampley, Thierry Lenain, Hubert Locher et al. (eds.), *Art and Visual Studies in Europe: Transnational Discourses and National Frameworks* (Leiden: Brill, 2012), 231–46.
Rancière, Jacques, *The Politics of Aesthetics: The Distribution of the Sensible* (London: Bloomsbury, 2013).
Raqs Media Collective, 'Nowhere and Elsewhere", in Julieta Aranda, Brian K. Wood and Anthony Vidokle (eds.), *What Is Contemporary Art? An Introduction* (Berlin: Sternberg Press, 2010), 40–57.
Raunig, Gerald and Gene Ray (eds.), *Art and Contemporary Practice: Reinventing Institutional Critique* (London: MayFly Books, 2009).
Ray, Romita, 'The "Clumsy" Lion? Disruptions and *Darshan* in Pushpamala N's Imaging of Mother India', in Juneja and Ramaswamy (eds.), *Motherland*, 44–57.
Ray, Sugata, *Climate Change and the Art of Devotion: Geoaesthetics in the Land of Krishna, 1550–1850* (Seattle: University of Washington Press, 2019).
Ray, Sugata, 'Introduction: Translation as Art History', *Ars Orientalis*, vol. 48 (2018): 1–19.
Reichle, Ingeborg, '*The Origin of Species* and the Rise of World Art History: Ernst Grosse's Encounter with the Beginnings of Art', in Trede, Wakita and Guth (eds.), *Japanese Art – Transcultural Perspectives* (Leiden: Brill, forthcoming 2023).
Revel, Jacques, *Jeux d'Échelles: La micro-analyse à l'expérience* (Paris: Gallimard et Le Seuil, 1996).
– 'Microanalysis and the Construction of the Social', in Jacques Revel and Lynn A. Hunt (eds.), *Histories: French Constructions of the Past* (New York: The New Press, 1998), 492–502.
Rice, Yael, 'Workshop as Network: A Case Study from Mughal South Asia', *Artl@s Bulletin*, vol. 6/3 (2017): 50–65.
Rickard, Jolene, 'The Emergence of Global Indigenous Art', in Hill et al. (eds.), *Sakahàn*, 54–60.
Riegl, Alois, 'Kunstgeschichte und Universalgeschichte', in *Festgaben zu Ehren Max Büdinger's von seinen Freunden und Schülern* (Innsbruck: Wagner, 1898), 449–57.
Rizvi, Kishwar (ed.), *Affect, Emotion and Subjectivity in Early Modern Muslim Empires: New Studies in Ottoman, Safavid, and Mughal Art and Culture* (Leiden and Boston: E. J. Brill, 2018).
Rockefeller, Stuart A., 'Flow', *Current Anthropology*, vol. 52/4 (2011): 557–78.
Rogers, J. M., *Mughal Miniatures* (London: British Museum, 1993).
Rogoff, Irit, 'Interview with Irit Rogoff by Hammad Nasar', in Dadi and Nasar (eds.), *Lines of Control: Partition as Productive Space*, 101–10.
– 'Hit and Run – Museums and Cultural Difference', *Art Journal*, vol. 61/3 (2002): 63–73.
Rosenthal, Stephanie (ed.), *Black Paintings: Robert Rauschenberg, Ad Reinhardt, Mark Rothhko, Frank Stella* (Ostfildern: Hatje Cantz, 2006).
Roxburgh, David J., *Prefacing the Image: The Writing of Art History in Sixteenth-Century Iran* (Leiden and Boston: E. J. Brill, 2001).

– *The Persian Album, 1400–1600: From Dispersal to Collection* (New Haven: Yale University Press, 2005).

– 'Kamal-al Din Bihzad and Authorship in Persian Painting', *Muqarnas*, vol. 17 (2000): 119–46.

– 'Two-point Perspective: On Hans Belting's Florence and Baghdad', *Artforum*, vol. 50/8 (2012): 61–64.

Rubin, William (ed.), *'Primtivism' in 20th Century Art: Affinity of the Tribal and the Modern*, 2 vols. (New York: Harry N. Abrams, 1984).

Russo, Alessandra, 'Light on the Antipodes: Francisco de Holanda and an Art History of the Universal', *The Art Bulletin*, vol. 102/4 (2020): 37–65.

Rycroft, Daniel J., *Representing Rebellion: Visual Aspects of Counter-Insurgency in Colonial India* (New Delhi: Oxford University Press, 2006).

– 'Santalism: Reconfiguring the Santal in Indian Art and Politics', *The Indian Historical Review*, vol. 33/1 (2006): 150–74.

Saint-Raymond, Léa, *Fragments d'une histoire globale de l'art* (Paris: Éditions Rue d'Ulm, 2021).

Sakai, Naoki, 'Modernity and its Critique: The Problem of Universalism and Particularism', in *Translation and Subjectivity: On 'Japan' and Cultural Nationalism* (Minneapolis: University of Minnesota Press, 1997), 153–76.

Sambrani, Chaitanya, *Edge of Desire – Recent Art from India* (London: Philip Wilson Publishers, 2005).

– 'An Experiment in Connectivity: From the "West Heavens" to the "Middle Kingdom"', in Michelle Antoinette and Caroline Turner (eds.), *Contemporary Asian Art and Exhibitions: Connectivities and World-Making* (Acton: ANU Press, 2014), 89–107.

– 'Of Bones and Salt: Jitish Kallat's *Public Notice 2*', in Art Gallery of New South Wales & Sherman Contemporary Art Foundation (ed.), *Jitish Kallat: Public Notice 2* (Sydney: Art Gallery of New South Wales, 2016), 11–17.

– 'The Progressive Artists' Group', in Gayatri Sinha (ed.), *Indian Art: An Overview* (New Delhi: Rupa & Co., 2003), 97–111.

Sanouillet, Michel and Elmer Peterson (eds.), *The Writings of Marcel Duchamp* (Oxford: Oxford University Press, 1973).

Santos, Boaventura de Sousa, 'Globalizations', *Theory, Culture & Society*, theme issue: Problematizing Global Knowledge, vol. 23/2–3 (2006): 393–99.

Sarkar, Bhaskar, *Mourning the Nation: Indian Cinema in the Wake of Partition* (Durham, NC: Duke University Press, 2009).

Sassen, Saskia, *Territory, Authority, Rights: From Medieval to Global Assemblages* (Princeton: Princeton University Press, 2006).

Savoy, Daniel (ed.), *The Globalization of Renaissance Art: A Critical Review* (Leiden: Brill, 2017).

Sawant, Shukla, 'Artist Collectives in the Age of Anxiety, 1940–1950', in Sinha (ed.), *Art and Visual Culture*, 136–49.

Schaffner, Ingrid and Matthias Winzen (eds.), *Deep Storage: Sammeln, Speichern, Archivieren in der Kunst* (Munich: Prestel, 1997).

Schapiro, Meyer, 'The Nature of Abstract Art', *Marxist Quarterly*, vol. 1/1 (1937): 77–98, reprinted in *Modern Art 19th and 20th Centuries: Selected Papers* (New York: George Braziller, 1978), 185–211.

Schmidt, Paul Ferdinand, 'Weltkunst oder Völkerkunde?', *Vorwärts: Berliner Volksblatt*, 30 July 1926.

Schmidt-Linsenhoff, Viktoria, *Ästhetik der Differenz*, 2 vols. (Marburg: Jonas Verlag, 2010).

– 'Das koloniale Unbewusste in der Kunstgeschichte', in Irene Below and Beatrice von Bismarck (eds.), *Globalisierung – Hierarchisierung. Kulturelle Dominanzen in Kunst und Kunstgeschichte* (Marburg: Jonas Verlag, 2005), 19–38.

– (ed.), *Weiße Blicke: Geschlechtermythen des Kolonialismus* (Marburg: Jonas Verlag, 2004).

Schnaase, Carl, *Geschichte der bildenden Künste*, 8 vols. (Düsseldorf: Verlag Julius Buddeus, 1843–79).

Scholz, Piotr Otto (ed.), *Von Biala nach Wien: Josef Strzygowski und die Kunstwissenschaft* (Vienna: European University Press Verlagsgesellschaft, 2015).

Schubbach, Arno, 'Das Bilden der Bilder. Zur Theorie der Welterzeugung und ihrer bildtheoretischen Verpflichtung', *Soziale Systeme*, 18/1–2 (2012): 69–93.

Schwarzer, Mitchell, 'Rethinking the Introductory Art History Survey', *Art Journal*, vol. 54/3 (1995): 24–29.

Seggerman, Alexandra D., 'Mahmoud Mukhtar: "The First Sculptor from the Land of Sculpture"', *World Art*, vol. 4/1 (2014): 27–46.

Seiberling, Dorothy, 'Jackson Pollock: Is He the Greatest Living Painter in the United States?' *Life*, 8 August 1949: 42–45.

Selz, Peter H. (ed.), *New Images of Man* (New York: Arno Press, 1959).

Semsar, Mohammad-Hasan, *Golestan Palace Library: A Portfolio of Miniature Paintings and Calligraphy* (Tehran: Zarrin and Simin Books, 2001).

Serres, Michael and Bruno Latour, *Conversations on Science, Culture and Time* (Ann Arbor: University of Michigan Press, 2008).

Seyller, John, *Pearls of the Parrot of India: The Walters Art Museum Khamsa of Amir Khusraw of Delhi* (Baltimore: Walters Art Museum, 2001).

–   'Farrukh Beg in the Deccan', *Artibus Asiae*, vol. 55/3–4 (1995): 319–41.

–   'Recycled Images: Overpainting in Early Mughal Art', in Canby (ed.), *Humayun's Garden Party*, 49–80.

–   'Scribal Notes on Mughal Manuscript Illustrations', *Artibus Asiae*, vol. 48/3–4 (1987): 247–77.

–   'The Inspection and Valuation of Manuscripts in the Imperial Mughal Library', *Artibus Asiae*, vol. 57/3–4 (1997): 243–349.

Shabout, Nada, *Modern Arab Art: Formation of Arab Aesthetics* (Gainesville: University of Florida Press, 2007).

Shalem, Avinoam, '"What a Small World": Interpreting Works of Art in the Age of Global Art History', *Getty Research Journal*, vol. 13 (2021): 121–42.

Sheikh, Gulammohammed, 'The World of Jangarh Singh Shyam', in Jyotindra Jain (ed.), *Other Masters: Five Contemporary Folk and Tribal Artists of India* (New Delhi: Crafts Museum, 1998), 17–34.

–   (ed.), *Contemporary Art in Baroda* (New Delhi: Tulika Books, 1997).

Sheriff, Mary D. (ed.), *Cultural Contact and the Making of European Art since the Age of Exploration* (Chapel Hill: University of North Carolina Press, 2012).

Shimada, Akira, 'The Use of Garden Imagery in Early Indian Buddhism', in Ali and Flatt (eds.), *Gardens and Landscape Practices*, 18–38.

Shiner, Larry E., *The Invention of Art: A Cultural History* (Chicago: University of Chicago Press, 2001).

Shulman, David, *More than Real: A History of the Imagination in South Asia* (Cambridge, MA: Harvard University Press, 2012).

Siegel, Katy, 'Art, World, History', in Enwezor et al. (eds.), *Postwar*, 42–57.

Simbao, Ruth, 'What Global Art and Current (Re)turns Fail to See: A Modest Counter-narrative of "Not-another-biennial"', *Image and Text*, 25 (2015): 261–86.

Simpson, Marianne S., 'Who's Hiding Here? Artists and their Signatures in Timurid and Safavid Manuscripts', in Rizvi (ed.), *Affect, Emotion*, 45–65.

Singh, Kavita, *Real Birds in Imagined Gardens: Mughal Painting between Persia and Europe* (Los Angeles: The Getty Research Institute, 2017).

–   'The Museum is National', in Mathur and Singh (eds.), *No Touching, No Spitting, No Praying. The Museum in South Asia*, 107–31.

–   'A History of Now', *Art India*, 15 (2010): 26–33.

–   'Jangarh Singh Shyam and the Great Machine', *Marg*, vol. 53/2 (2001): 60–64.

Singh, Mani S., 'A Journey into Pictorial Space: Poetics of Frame and Field in Maithil Painting', *Contributions to Indian Sociology*, 34/3 (2000): 409–42.

–   'What Should Happen, But Has Not Yet Happened: Painterly Tales of Justice', *Contributions to Indian Sociology*, vol. 53/1 (2019): 184–216.

Sinha, Ajay, Pushpamala N. and the "Art" of Cinephilia in India', in Christiane Brosius and Roland Wenzlhuemer (eds.), *Transcultural Turbulences: Towards a Multi-Sited Reading of Image Flows* (Heidelberg: Springer Books, 2011), 221–48.

Sinha, Gayatri, (ed.), *Art and Visual Culture in India, 1857–2007* (Mumbai: Marg Publications, 2009).

Skaria, Ajay, *Hybrid Histories: Forests, Frontiers and Wildness in Western India* (Delhi: Oxford University Press, 1999).

Skelton, Robert, 'Imperial Symbolism in Mughal Painting', in Priscilla P. Soucek (ed.), *Content and Context of Visual Arts in the Islamic World* (University Park: Penn State University Press, 1988), 177–91.

–   'The Mughal Artist Farrokh Beg', *Ars Orientalis*, vol. 2 (1957): 393–411.

Sloboda, Stacey and Michael Yonan (eds.), *Eighteenth Century Art Worlds: Global and Local Geographies of Art* (London: Bloomsbury, 2019).

Smith, Cherise, *Enacting Others: Politics of Identity in Eleanor Antin, Nikki S. Lee, Adrian Piper and Anna Deavere Smith* (Durham, NC: Duke University Press, 2011).

Smith, Woodruff D., *Politics and the Sciences of Culture in Germany* (New York: Oxford University Press, 1991).

Smith, Terry, *Art to Come: Histories of Contemporary Art* (Durham, NC: Duke University Press, 2019).

Smith, Terry, Okwui Enwezor and Nancy Condee (eds.), *Antinomies of Art and Culture: Modernity, Postmodernity, Contemporaneity* (Durham: Duke University Press, 2008).

Sorensen, Diana, 'Editor's Introduction: Alternative Geographic Mappings for the Twenty-First Century", in idem. (ed.), *Territories and Trajectories. Cultures in Circulation* (Durham, NC: Duke University Press, 2018), 13–31.

Soucek, Priscilla B., 'Nizami on Painters and Painting', in Richard Ettinghausen (ed.), *Islamic Art in the Metropolitan Museum of Art* (New York: Metropolitan Museum of Art, 1972), 9–22.

Spector, Jack J., *Surrealist Art and Writing, 1919–1939: The Gold of Time* (Cambridge: Cambridge University Press, 1997).

Spicer, Joneath A. (ed.), *Revealing the African Presence in Renaissance Europe* (Baltimore: Walters Art Museum, 2012).

Spivak, Gayatri C., 'Looking at Others', in Steeds et al. (eds.), *Making Art Global (2)*, 260–66.

Springer, Anton H., *Handbuch der Kunstgeschichte: Zum Gebrauche für Künstler und Studirende* (Stuttgart: Rieger'sche Verlagsbuchhandlung, 1855; 1st edition).

Springer, Anton, *Handbuch der Kunstgeschichte*, vol. VI (Leipzig: Alfred Kröner Verlag, 1929).

Srivastava, Sanjay, 'Urban Spaces, Disney-Divinity and Moral Middle Classes in Delhi', *Economic and Political Weekly*, vol. 44/26–27 (2009): 338–45.

Stamm, Rainer, 'Weltkunst und Moderne', in Hartwig Fischer and Uwe M. Schneede (eds.), '*Das schönste Museum der Welt': Museum Folkwang bis 1933* (Göttingen: Steidl, 2010), 27–46.

Steeds, Lucy, '"Magiciens de la Terre" and the Development of Transnational Project-Based Curating', in Steeds et al. (eds.), *Making Art Global (Part 2)*, 24–92.

Steeds, Lucy et al. (eds.), *Making Art Global (Part 2): 'Magiciens de la Terre' 1989* (London: Afterall Books, 2013).

Stemmrich, Gregor, 'C. Schnaase: Rezeption und Transformation Berlinischen Geistes in der kunsthistorischen Forschung', in Otto Pöggeler and Annemarie Gethmann-Siefert (eds.), *Kunsterfahrung und Kulturpolitik in Berlin Hegels* (Bonn: Bouvier, 1983), 263–84.

Stoichita, Victor I., *The Self-Aware Image: An Insight into Early Modern Meta-painting* (New York: Cambridge University Press, 1997).

Stokstad, Marilyn, *Art History* (New York: H. Abrams, 1995; 1st edition).

Stoler Miller, Barbara (ed.), *Exploring India's Sacred Art: Selected Writings of Stella Kramrisch* (Philadelphia: University of Pennsylvania Press, 1983).

Stronge, Susan, 'Jahangir's Itinerant Masters', in Mahesh Sharma and Padma Kaimal (eds.), *Themes, Histories, Interpretations: Indian Paintings: Essays in Honour of B. N. Goswamy* (Ahmedabad: Mapin Publishing, 2013), 125–35.

Strother, Zoë S., *Inventing Masks: Agency and History in the Art of Central Pende* (Chicago: University of Chicago Press, 1997).

– 'Gabama a Gingungu and the Secret History of Twentieth-Century Art', *African Arts*, vol. 32/1 (1999): 18–31.

Strzygowski, Josef, *Die indische Miniaturen im Schlosse Schönbrunn*, 2 vols. (Vienna: Wiener Drucke, 1923).

– *Die Krisis der Geisteswissenschaften* (Vienna: Kunstverlag Anton Schroll, 1923).

– 'Ein besonders beachtenswertes Stück ostasiatischer Frauenkunst', in Bimala C. Law (ed.), *D. R. Bhandarkar Volume* (Calcutta: India Research Institute, 1940), 205–11.

– 'India's Position in the Art of Asia', *Journal of the Indian Society of Oriental Art*, vol. 1 (1933): 7–17.

– 'Mschatta. Kunstwissenschaftliche Untersuchung', *Jahrbuch der Königlich Preussischen Kunstsammlungen*, vol. 25/4 (1904): 225–373.

– 'The Indian Room of the Empress Maria Theresia', *Rupam*, nos. 15–16 (1923): 59–66.

– 'Three Northern Currents in the Art of the Chinese People', *Journal of the Indian Society of Oriental Art*, vol. 5 (1937): 42–57.

– 'Die Miniaturenschätze der Großmoguln in Wien im Rahmen der indischen Kunst, *Belvedere*, 11/1–2 (1932): 35–42.

Strzygowski, Josef (in collaboration with Heinrich Glück, Stella Kramrisch and Egon Wellesz), *Asiatische Miniaturmalerei im Anschluß an Wesen und Werden der Mogulmalerei, Im Anschluß an die Bestände in Wien* (Klagenfurt: A. Kollitisch-Verlag, 1932).

Subramanyan, K. G., 'The Artist on Art', *Lalit Kala Contemporary*, vol. 3 (1965): 13–15.

Subrahmanyam, Sanjay, 'Connected Histories: Notes towards a Reconfiguration of Early Modern Eurasia', *Modern Asian Studies*, vol. 31/3 (1997): 735–62.

– 'Global Intellectual History Beyond Hegel and Marx', *History and Theory*, vol. 54/1 (2015): 126–37.

Summers, David, *Real Spaces: World Art History and the Rise of Western Modernism* (London: Phaidon, 2003).

Sundar, Nandini, *Subalterns and Sovereigns: An Anthropological History of Bastar, 1854–1996* (Delhi: Oxford University Press, 1997).

Sunderason, Sanjukta, *Partisan Aesthetics: Modern Art and India's Long Decolonization* (Stanford: Stanford University Press, 2020).

– 'In Search of a New Visual Culture', (in conversation with Tapati Guha-Thakurta, Regina Bittner and Kathrin Rhomberg), in Bittner and Rhomberg (eds.), *The Bauhaus in Calcutta*, 93–100.

– 'Making Art Modern, Re-visiting Artistic Modernism in India', in Dube (ed.), *Handbook of Modernity*, 245–61.

Sutton, Peter (ed.), *Dreamings: The Art of Aboriginal Australia* (New York: Asia Society, 1988).

Swaminathan, Jagdish, *The Perceiving Fingers: Catalogue of Roopankar Collection of Folk and Adivasi Art from Madhya Pradesh, India* (Bhopal: Bharat Bhavan, 1987).

Swietochowski, Marie and Sussan Babaie, *Persian Drawings in the Metropolitan Museum of Art* (New York: The Metropolitan Museum of Art, 1989).

Sydow, Eckart von, *Die Kunst der Naturvölker und der Vorzeit* (Berlin: Propylaen Verlag, 1923).

Szeemann, Harald, *Live in Your Head: When Attitudes Become Form: Works – Concepts – Processes – Information* (Bern: Stämpfli Cie, 1969).

Tan, Seng and Amitava Acharya (eds.), *Bandung Revisited: The Legacy of the 1955 Asian-African Conference for the International Order* (Singapore: NUS Press, 2008).

Tauber, Christine, '"Das Ganze der Kunstgeschichte": Franz Kuglers universalhistorische Handbücher', in Wolfgang Hardtwig and Philipp Müller (eds.), *Die Vergangenheit der Weltgeschichte: universalhistorisches Denken in Berlin 1800–1933* (Göttingen: Vandenhoek & Ruprecht, 2010), 90–121.

Taussig, Michael, *Mimesis and Alterity: A Particular History of the Senses* (London/New York: Routledge, 1993).

Tawdros, Gilane, 'Running with the Hare and Hunting with the Hounds', in Mora J. Beauchamp-Byrd and M. Franklin Sirmans (eds.), *Transforming the Crown: African, Asian and Caribbean Artists in Britain 1966–1996* (New York: Caribbean Cultural Center, 1997), 58–62.

Taylor, Nora A., 'Hunter-Gatherer or the other Ethnographer? The Artist in the Age of Historical Reproduction', *Journal of Material Culture*, vol. 27/1, 2022: 10–29.

Terracciano, Emilia, 'Disappearing Worlds', *The Caravan. A Journal of Politics and Culture,* (February 2014): 106–13.

Thackston, Wheeler M. (ed. and trans.*), The Jahangirnama: Memoirs of Jahangir, Emperor of India* (Oxford and New York: Oxford University Press, 1999).

Thausing, Moriz, 'Die Stellung der Kunstgeschichte als Wissenschaft: Aus der Antrittsvorlesung an der Wiener Universität im Oktober 1873', *Wiener Jahrbuch für Kunstgeschichte*, 36 (1983): 140–50. Eng. trans.: Karl Johns: Moritz Thausing, 'The Status of Art History as an Academic Discipline', *Journal of Art Historiography*, vol. 1 (2009): 5–22.

Thomas, Julia A., 'History and Biology in the Anthropocene: Problems of Scale, Problems of Value', *American Historical Review*, vol. 119/5 (2014): 1587–1607.

Thomas, Nicholas, '"Artist of PNG": Mathias Kauage and Melanesian Modernism', in Harney and Phillips (eds.), *Mapping Modernisms*, 163–86.

Thurnwald, Richard, 'Die eingeborenen Arbeitskräfte im Südseeschutzgebiet', *Koloniale Rundschau*, vol. 10 (1910): 607–32.

Tiampo, Ming, *Gutai: Decentering Modernism* (Chicago: University of Chicago Press, 2011).

– 'Transversal Articulations: Decolonial Modernism and the Slade School of Fine Art', in Okwui Enwezor and Atreyee Gupta (eds), *Postwar – A Global History, 1945–1965* (Durham, NC: Duke University Press [forthcoming 2023]).

Tomii, Reiko, "How to Build a World Art History on Stones: Robert Smithson, Horikawa Michio, and 1960s Art in Japan', in Trede, Wakita and Guth (eds.), *Japanese Art: Transcultural Perspectives* (forthcoming 2023).

Trede, Melanie, Mio Wakita and Christine Guth (eds.), *Japanese Art: Transcultural Perspectives* (Leiden: E.J. Brill [forthcoming 2023]).

Trivellato, Francesca, 'Is There a Future for Italian Microhistory in an Age of Global History?', *California Italian Studies*, vol. 2/1 (2011), n.p.

Troelenberg, Eva-Maria, *Mschatta in Berlin: Keystones of Islamic Art* (Dortmund: Verlag Kettler, 2017).

Trouillot, Michel-Rolf, 'The Otherwise Modern: Caribbean Lessons from the Savage Slot', in Bruce M. Knauft (ed.), *Critically Modern: Alternatives, Alterities, Anthropologies* (Bloomington: Indiana University Press, 2002), 220–37.

Truschke, Audrey, *Culture of Encounters: Sanskrit at the Mughal Court* (New York: Columbia University Press, 2016).

Tsing, Anna L., *Friction: An Ethnography of Global Connection* (Princeton: Princeton University Press, 2005).

Turner, Caroline and Michelle Antoinette (eds.), 'The World and World-Making in Art', *Humanities Research*, vol. XIX/2 (2013): 1–9.

Vajpeyi, Udayan, 'From Music to Painting: The Strange Yet Not-So-Strange Tales of Pardhaans', in Monica Narula (ed.), *Frontiers: Sarai Reader VII* (Delhi: CSDS, 2007), 212–20.

Varadinis, Mirjam and Catherine Schelbert, 'Zerbrochene Freiheit = Shattered Freedom', *Parkett*, no. 90 (2012): 204–6.

Varma, Rashmi, 'Primitive Accumulation: The Political Economy of Indigenous Art in Postcolonial India', *Third Text*, vol. 27/6 (2013): 748–61.

Vasold, Georg, 'Riegl, Strzygowski und die Entwicklung der Kunst', *Ars*, 41/1 (2008): 95–109.

– 'The Revaluation of Art History: An Unfinished Project by Josef Strzygowski and His School', in Pauline Bachmann, Melanie Klein et al. (eds.), *Art/Histories in Transcultural Dynamics: Narratives, Concepts and Practices at Work, 20th and 21st Centuries* (Paderborn: Wilhelm Fink, 2017), 119–38.

Vázquez, Rolando, *Vistas of Modernity: Decolonial Aesthesis and the End of the Contemporary* (Amsterdam: Mondriaan Fund, 2020).

Véquaud, Yves, *L'Art du Mithila* (Paris: Les Presses de la Connaissance, 1976). German trans.: *Die Kunst von Mithila* (Geneva: Weber, 1977).

Verhagen, Marcus, *Flows and Counterflows: Globalisation in Contemporary Art* (Berlin: Sternberg Press, 2017).

Vierkandt, Alfred, *Naturvölker und Kulturvölker: Ein Beitrag zur Sozialpsychologie* (Leipzig: Duncker und Humblot, 1896).

Volk, Alicia, *In Pursuit of Universalism: Yorozu Tetsugorō and Japanese Modern Art* (Berkeley: University of California Press, 2010).

Wadley, Susan S., '*Likhiyā*: Painting Women's Lives in Northern India', in Susan S. Wadley, (ed.), *South Asia in the World: An Introduction* (New York: M. E. Sharpe, 2014), 241–60.

Wagner, Monika, 'Freiheitswunsch und Frauenbild: Veränderungen der "Liberté" zwischen 1789 und 1830', in Inge Stephan and Sigrid Weigel (eds.), *Die Marseillaise der Weiber: Frauen, die Französische Revolution und ihre Rezeption* (Berlin: Argument-Verlag, 1989), 7–36.

Wainwright, Leon, *Timed Out: Art and the Transnational Caribbean* (Manchester: Manchester University Press, 2011).

Wang, Cheng-hua, 'A Global Perspective on Eighteenth-Century Chinese Art and Visual Culture', *The Art Bulletin*, vol. 96/4 (2014): 379–94.

Waurisch, Jürgen (ed.) *Bauhaus Global* (Berlin: Gebr. Mann, 2010).

Weis, Friederike, 'Blicke in die Welt indischer Malerei', in Monica Juneja and Petra Kuhlman-Hodick (eds.), *Miniatur Geschichten: Die Sammlung indischer Malerei im Dresdner Kupferstich-Kabinett* (Dresden: Sandstein Verlag, 2017), 136–37.

Weiss, Rachel, 'Some Thoughts after Kapur and Mathur', *Art Journal*, vol. 77/1 (2018): 95–101.

Welch, Klara Kemp and Cristina Freire (eds.), 'Artists' Networks in Eastern Europe and Latin America', themed section, *ARTMargins#2*, 1 (2012): 3–13.

Welch, Stuart C., *Imperial Mughal Painting* (London: Chatto & Windus, 1978).

– *India: Art and Culture 1300–1900* (New York: Metropolitan Museum of Art, 1985).
– *The Emperor's Album: Images of Mughal India* (New York: Harry N. Abrams, 1987).
Welsch, Wolfgang, 'Transkulturalität: Zur veränderten Verfassung heutiger Kulturen', in Irmela Schneider and Christian W. Thomsen (eds.), *Hybridkultur: Medien, Netze, Künste* (Cologne: Wienand, 1997), 67–90.
Wilkinson, J. V. S., 'Indian Painting', in Richard Winstedt (ed.), *Indian Art* (London: Faber & Faber, 1947), 103–50.
Wilson, Sarah, 'New Images of Man: Postwar Humanism and Its Challenges in the West', in Enwezor et al. (eds.), *Postwar*, 344–49.
With, Karl, '*Grundzüge der indischen Kunst* by Stella Kramrisch', *Artibus Asiae*, vol. 1/2, 1925: 157–158.
Woermann, Karl, *Geschichte der Kunst aller Zeiten und Völkern*, 6 vols. (Leipzig: Bibliographisches Institut, 1900–22).
Wolf, Eric R., *Europe and the People Without History* (Berkeley: University of California Press, 1982).
Wollaeger, Mark (ed.), *Oxford Handbook of Global Modernisms* (Oxford: Oxford University Press, 2013).
Wright, Elaine, *Muraqqa: Imperial Mughal Albums from the Chester Beatty Library Dublin* (Alexandria, VA: Art Services International, 2008).

Xaxa, Virginius, 'Tribes as Indigenous Peoples of India', *Economic and Political Weekly*, vol. 34/51 (1999): 3589–95.

Yonan, Michael, 'Toward a Fusion of Art History and Material Culture Studies', *West 86th*, vol. 18/2 (2011): 232–48.

Zaman, Taymiya R., 'Instructive Memory: An Analysis of Auto/Biographical Writing in Early Mughal India', *Journal of the Economic and Social History of the Orient*, vol. 54/5 (2011): 677–700.
Ziebritzki, Jo, *Stella Kramrisch: Kunsthistorikerin zwischen Europa und Indien. Ein Beitrag zur Depatriachalisierung der Kunstgeschichte* (Berlin: Reimer, 2021).
Zijlmans, Kitty and Wilfried van Damme (eds.), *World Art Studies: Exploring Concepts and Approaches* (Amsterdam: Valiz, 2008).
Zimmerman, Andrew, 'From Natural Science to Primitive Art: German New Guinea in Emil Nolde', in Cordula Grewe (ed.), *Die Schau des Fremden: Ausstellungskonzepte zwischen Kunst, Kommerz und Wissenschaft* (Stuttgart: Franz Steiner Verlag, 2006), 279–300.
Zimmerman, Andrew, 'Primitive Art, Primitive Accumulation, and the Origin of the Work of Art in German New Guinea', *History of the Present*, vol. 1/1 (2011): 5–30.
Zitzewitz, Karin, *The Art of Secularism: The Cultural Politics of Modernist Art in Contemporary India* (London: Hurst Publishers, 2014).
– 'Infrastructure as Form: Cross-Border Networks and the Materialities of "South Asia" in Contemporary Art', *Third Text*, vol. 31/2–3 (2017): 341–58.

LIST OF ILLUSTRATIONS

Plates

1.0   The Blue Marble, 1972, photograph by Apollo 17 crew taken on December 7, 1972.
Photograph: Wikimedia Commons

1.1   Kalo Bari (Black House), 1934, conceived by Nandalal Bose and Binode Behari Mukherjee,
Kala Bhawan, Visva Bharati Campus, Santiniketan, India.
Photograph: Courtesy Atreyee Gupta

1.1a   Kalo Bari (Black House), 1934, detail of 1.1. Seal from Indus Valley,
Kala Bhawan, Visva Bharati Campus, Santiniketan, India.
Photograph: Courtesy Atreyee Gupta

1.2   Millionenzimmer, Schloss Schönbrunn, Vienna, reconstruction (detail) of a cartouche containing
collaged fragments of Mughal miniature paintings.
From: Josef Strzygowski, *Die indische Miniaturen im Schlosse Schönbrunn*, 2 vols, Vienna: Wiener Drucke,
1923, Tafel 7

2.1   Jahangir Album, single folio showing artists at work, early 17th century, gouache on paper. Berlin,
Staatsbibliothek Preußischer Kulturbesitz, Fol. 21a
Image: bpk

2.2   Single folio, showing acrobats performing to the Emperor and his retinue, 17th century, Mughal.
Berlin, Museum of Asian Art, SPKB
Image: bpk

2.3   Folio from Khamsa of the poet Nizami Ganjavi, painted by Madhu Khanazad, showing Aatun (Plato)
playing music to the animals, 1595, gouache on paper.
London, British Library, f. 298a no. 40
Image: bpk/British Library Board

2.3a   Detail of 2.3

2.4   Single folio showing Saint Matthew and the Angel, painted by Kesu Das, 1588, gouache on paper.
Oxford, Bodleian Library
Image: © Bodleian Libraries, University of Oxford, Creative Commons licence CC BY-NC 4.0

2.5   Folio from Saint Petersburg Album, composed of four fragments, early 17th century.
St. Petersburg, Russian Academy of Sciences, Institute of Oriental Studies, f. 88a
Image: bpk

2.6   Page from Jahangir Album, composed of three fragments of engravings showing Adoration of the three kings (top left), Christ and Maria Magdalena (top right), and Holy Family on the way to Nazareth (below).
Fol. 7v. Staatsbibliothek zu Berlin, Stiftung Preußischer Kulturbesitz
Image: bpk

2.7   Folio from Gulshan Album, the painted margins of which represent the stages of manuscript production, c. 1600, gouache, ink and gold on paper.
Washington D.C., Freer Gallery of Art, Smithsonian Institutions, F 1954.116r
Image: Smithsonian Institutions, Washington DC

2.8   Folio from Khamsa of Amir Khusrau Dihlavi depicting Alexander visiting the cave of the sage Plato, painted by Basawan, 1597–98, gouache, ink, gold on paper.
New York, Metropolitan Museum of Art, Acc. No. 13.228.30
Image: bpk/The Metropolitan Museum of Art, New York, Thomas J. Watson Library

2.9   Folio from Akhlaq-i Nasiri by Nasir-ud-Din Tusi showing the interior of a royal kitabkhana with painters and calligraphers at work, c. 1590–95, gouache on paper.
Toronto, Aga Khan Museum, Ms. 39, f. 196a
Image: Aga Khan Museum, Toronto

2.10   Single folio mounted on album page, painting based on an engraving by Johannes Wierix, The Visitation, by a Mughal artist, c. 1600–10, gouache, gold on paper.
Zurich, Museum Rietberg
Image: Museum Rietberg, Zurich

2.11   Folio from Jahangirnama portraying the Emperor Jahangir seated on an hour-glass throne offering a book to a Sufi saint, by Bichitr, c. 1620, gouache, ink, gold on paper.
Washington D.C., Freer Gallery of Art, Smithsonian Institutions, F1942.15a
Image: Smithsonian Institutions, Washington DC

2.12   Single folio by Farrukh Beg portraying an old Sufi, c. 1615.
Qatar, Museum of Islamic Art

3.1   Godrej Soaps Calendar, oleograph after a painting by Ravi Varma, Saraswati, 1933. Jane and Kito de Boer Collection
Courtesy Partha Mitter

3.2   Gaganendranath Tagore, Untitled, 1924–25, ink and grey wash on paper.
The Savara Foundation for the Arts, New Delhi
Image: Roohi and Savara Family Collection, New Delhi

3.3   M. F. Husain, Zameen, 1954, oil on canvas.
New Delhi, National Gallery of Modern Art
Image: NGMA, New Delhi

3.4   F. N. Souza, Crucifixion, 1959, oil on board.
London, Tate Modern
Image: Tate Modern, London

3.5   Ram Kinkar Baij, Santhal Family, 1938, on-site sculpture.
Kala Bhavan, Santiniketan

4.1   Atul Dodiya, Broken Branches, installation 2002.
Courtesy Artist

4.2   Pushpamala N., Liberty (after Delacroix), Harcourt Series, photograph, 2009.
Courtesy Artist

4.3   Eugène Delacroix, Liberty Guiding the People, oil on canvas, 1830–31.
Paris, Louvre

4.4   Nanine Vallain, Liberty, oil on canvas, 1793–94.
Vizille, Musée de la Révolution Française

4.5   Liberty, coloured engraving by Carrée after a drawing by Leclerc, 1791.
Paris, Musée Carnavalet

4.6   French postage stamps commemorating Delacroix's Liberty guiding the People. Private collection.
Courtesy Stefan Rhode

4.6a   Eugène Delacroix, Liberty Guiding the People, detail of 4.3

4.6b   Pushpamala N., Liberty (after Delacroix), detail of 4.2

4.7   Danh Võ, We the People, installation 2011.
Courtesy Artist and Galerie Chantal Crousel, Paris
Photograph Nils Klinger

4.8   Atul Bhalla, Pattaya, photograph for The Wake, 2013.
Courtesy Artist

4.9   Atul Bhalla, Pattaya, photograph for The Wake, 2013.
Courtesy Artist

4.10   Atul Bhalla, Chabeel, installation, 2006.
Courtesy Artist

4.11   Atul Bhalla, Chabeel, installation, 2006.
Courtesy Artist

5.1   Neil Dawson, Globe, Sculpture and Installation. 1989
© VG Bild-Kunst, Bonn 2022
Image: bpk/CNAC-MNAM/Béatrice Hatala

5.2   Richard Long, Red Earth Circle, Wall Painting (1989). On floor: Artists of Yuendumu community –
Francis J. Kelly, Frank B.J. Nelson, Paddy J. Nelson, Neville J. Poulson, Paddy J. Sims, Paddy J. Stewart,
Towser J. Walker, Yam Dreaming, Floor Painting, 1989
With permission of the Warlukurlangu Artists of Yuendumu
Image: bpk/CNAC-MNAM/Béatrice Hatala/Konstantinos Ignatiadis

5.3   Baua Devi, Snake, Painting on Paper, 1989
Courtesy Artist
Image: bpk/Centre Pompidou, Paris

5.4   Jangarh Singh Shyam, Ladobai, Djambawa Marawili and Liyawaday Wirrpanda, Collaborative work between Indian and Australian artists, Acrylic Painting on Canvas, 1999.
Collection: Crafts Museum, New Delhi. Photo: Laxman Das Arya
Image courtesy of RMIT Gallery, Melbourne, Australia.

5.5   Sushila and Rajendra Shyam displaying their work at their home in Bhopal, Photograph, 2009.
Private Collection

6.1   Single folio Squirrels in a Plane Tree, ascribed to Abu'l Hasan, 1605–08. Johnson Album, London, Victoria and Albert Museum

Figures

Chapter One: The World in a Grain of Sand

1   Ernst Guhl and Wilhelm Lübke, Denkmäler der Kunst zur Übersicht ihres Entwickelungs-Ganges von den ersten künstlerischen Versuchen bis zu den Standpunkten der Gegenwart, Stuttgart: Ebner & Seubert, 1851. Supplement to Franz Kugler, Handbuch der Kunstgeschichte, 1851: Tafel X

2   Ernst Guhl and Wilhelm Lübke, Denkmäler der Kunst zur Übersicht ihres Entwicklungs-Ganges von den ersten künstlerischen Versuchen bis zu den Standpunkten der Gegenwart, Stuttgart: Ebner & Seubert, 1851. Supplement to Franz Kugler, Handbuch der Kunstgeschichte, 1851: Tafel XI

Chapter Two: Making and Seeing Images

1   Philips Galle after Maarten van Heemskerk, Saint Matthew and the Angel, engraving, 1562, Amsterdam Rijksmuseum (public domain)

2   Raphael Sadeler after Maerten de Vos, Dolor, engraving, 1591, New York, Metropolitan Museum of Art (public domain)

3   Johannes Wierix, The Visitation, engraving, 1602–03
Reproduced in Hollstein's *Dutch & Flemish Etchings, Engravings and Woodcuts 1450-1700*, Vol. LIX, The Wierix Family, Part I Nr. 76., Amsterdam, Van Gendt, 2003 (public domain)

4   Albrecht Dürer, Saint Jerome in his Study, engraving, 1514
New York, Metropolitan Museum of Art (public domain)

Chapter Three: Traversing Scale(s)

1   The Progressive Artists' Group, Art Centre, Bombay 1950
Photograph: Chemould Art Centre, Mumbai

2   The Santhal Rebellion, Illustrated London News, 1856 (public domain)

3   Ram Kinkar Baij, Santhal Family, sculpture, 1938, detail

Chapter Four: Beyond Backwater Arcadias

1   Pushpamala N. Toda, Photograph, 2004
Courtesy Artist

2   Maurice V. Portman, Female Andamanese, photograph, 1890s
© The Trustees of the British Museum.

3   Pushpamala N., The Slave and her Slave, Harcourt Series, photograph, 2009
Courtesy Artist

Chapter Five: When Art Embraces the Planet

1   Catalogue entry, Magiciens de la Terre

2   Jangarh Singh Shyam, Nankusia Shyam and Jagdish Swaminathan, photograph, 1987.
Image: Jyoti Bhatt, Asia Art Archive

3   Jangarh Singh Shyam, Vichhi, Portrait of a Scorpion, pen-and-ink drawing on paper 1995.
Museum of Art and Photography, Bangalore (PTG.0734)
Image: MAP, Bangalore

INDEX